The American
COCKER SPANIEL

The American
COCKER

SPANIEL

Author and
Executive Editor
Dr. Alvin Grossman

The Pure-Bred Series

Doral Publishing
San Jose, California
1988

Published by Doral Publishing, 7023 Wooded Lake Drive, San Jose, California 95120. Printed in the United States of America.

Copyedited by Beverly Black, Nancy Bridge and Robin Stark
Book Design by Tomiko Edmiston
Cover Photo by John Garrison
Typesetting by Get Set, Gilroy, California 95020

Library of Congress Card Number: 87-730-56
ISBN: 0-944875-00-9

To Marjorie . . . at last!

Ch. Hi-Boots Such Sparkle.
Bred, owned and handled by the late Marjorie Grossman.

CONTENTS

CONTENTS

CONTENTS

CONTENTS

SECTION IX—Life in the Dog Show World

SECTION X—The Breed in Other Lands

SECTION XI—Appendices

CONTENTS

SECTION XI—Appendices, *cont'd.*

SECTION XII—Bibliography & Index

ACKNOWLEDGMENTS

The author would like to thank the American Spaniel Club for its kind permission to use material from two important bodies of work. From a *Century of Spaniels—Volume I*, I have utilized the excellent work of Dr. Francis Greer in detailing the history of the Spaniel Club. The Spaniel Club has also graciously granted me permission to use the material from the new slide/tape presentation of the standard and Ralph Craig's field training manual.

The American Kennel Club has also granted permission to use the slide/tape material.

B & E Publications has given kind permission to quote extensively from Frank Sabella and Shirlee Kalstone in their book *The Art of Handling Show Dogs*.

To the editors of *Akita World* magazine, many thanks for permission to use several parts of various issues concerning kennel management.

To Michael Allen, editor of the *American Cocker Magazine* for permission to use numerous quotes both of my work and others from a variety of issues.

To Lynn Lowy, editor and publisher of the *Great Dane Reporter*, many thanks for permission to use significant material from a number of issues.

To Susan Coe, editor of *The Basenji*, for granting permission to use special material for this text.

To Joe McGinnis, of Doll/McGinnis Publications, for kind permission to use material from the "stable" of magazines they publish.

To Marie Tayton, widow of Mark Tayton, for permission to quote from his book *Successful Kennel Management*.

I would like to acknowledge the use of statistics on top producers gleaned from Irene Castle Schlintz's two volumes of *Top Producing Spaniels* as well as the contribution of Dr. Marge Saari without whose help the ranking and producing records would not be possible.

Many thanks to J.B. Lippincott Company for permission to quote from *The Human Pedigree* by Anothony Smith.

Permission has been granted by Donald Sturz, Jr. Editor/Publisher of the *Golden Retriever Review,* to use specific material from various issues.

American Sporting Dogs, edited by Eugene V. Connett and published by D. Van Nostrand Company, Inc. is the source of much of the material on scent in hunting dogs.

Finally, to my former publisher, William Denlinger and his editor-in-chief, R. Annabel Rathman—many thanks for their help and assistance over the years.

FOREWORD

It would seem that credentials for preparing the foreword to a book are based on longevity rather than suitability, else another would be filling this allotted space. With this in mind and reflecting on our long association, I cannot help but fall into reminiscing on our common interest—the Cocker Spaniel. The mind dredges up old and dusty images: One, of a stylish buff dog, whelped in 1957, much like one of today's top winners in type and outline—the buff son of the immortal Ch. Maddie's Vagabond's Return and the beautiful black and tan bitch, Ch. DeKarlos Day Dreams (bred by Al and his late wife, the dedicated breeder, Marge), named Ch. Hi-Boots Such Crust; the plush and wonderfully typey black and tan son of Such Crust whelped in 1962, Ch. Hi-Boots Such Brass whose dam was from the producing Palmwood Kennels of Bert Homan, long retired from breeding dogs, but still appearing on judging panels around the country. While not a fan of the color, I would nonetheless commit an act of piracy were it possible to bring him back into the ring today—with his beautiful head and short, hard and sloping topline so rare and so missed. As I was "specialing" a parti-color at the same time that Ray McGinnis was escorting "Digger," the foundation for a 25-year long association was formed.

Recalling Dr. Grossman's first book, *Breeding Better Cocker Spaniels*, published in '77, then the more recent *The Standard Book of Dog Breeding* and *The Great American Dog Show Game*, and now *The American Cocker Spaniel*, one observes an interest in the breed that places him squarely in the 5% of the dog fanciers who remain in "The Game" longer than 20 years. In *The Great American Dog Show Game*, the reader sees a thinly-disguised Dr. Grossman being guided through the labyrinth of the show scene by his handler, sharing his sometimes amusing—and always instructive—experiences with us, drawing from his years of successful breeding and exhibiting, in an attempt to aid us in avoiding the common pitfalls of this consuming hobby of ours.

His newest effort, *The American Cocker Spaniel*, contains a tremendous amount of informative and educational material invaluable to the Cocker fancier and places a great deal of emphasis on field work, the original purpose of this cheerful little spaniel and coincides with the revival of interest in this aspect of the breed. While the fancier should always avail himself of any and all published material relating to their breed, some treatises are more useful than others and, it is the opinion of this old wag that, Dr. Grossman's latest effort fills comfortably all aspects of husbandry including material on frozen and extended semen.

The underlying humor so entertaining in *The Great American Dog Show Game* is more subtle here as the aspect of the new book is channeled toward different goals.

Reading is learning. *The American Cocker Spaniel* fills the void of a modern and comprehensive treatise covering more than just the physical aspects of breeding, whelping and nurturing puppies . . . it is more than just pictures of dogs . . . it is a handbook, guiding the breeder and owner into a fuller understanding of the potential of their chosen breed. In addition, it is good reading.

Michael Allen, Editor
American Cocker Magazine

SECTION I
Background

- *A History*
- *The American Spaniel Club*
- *The Golden Era—*
  The First Peak of Popularity
- *The Golden Era—*
  Resurgence of the Breed
- *The First National*
  Cocker Spaniel Specialty

CHAPTER 1

A History

Anthony Smith, in his treatise *The Human Pedigree*, points out a study of ancient history. He taught us:

> All the main groups of dogs were created long before Christ had appeared. In fact, they already existed when written history was making its first appearance, and when their various canine shapes and sizes were being made readily recognizable on stone and pottery. The breeding of dogs is extremely ancient, and modern breeders (who held their first dog show—in England at Newcastle—in 1859) have added little, whatever they may think, to the work done by the end of the Neolithic period of history.
>
> There are several points of interest in dog evolution. First, although these animals are still happily able to identify one of their own kind, there has been tremendous variation in dog variety. There is curly hair, straight hair, wiry hair, silky hair, long faces, compressed faces, floppy ears, erect ears. There is a world of difference in the tail alone. As for weight, the Chihuahua can be confronted by Mastiffs forty times their size. Second, the bulk of this differentiation has been caused by man, deliberately and for different purposes. Man has controlled their random mating and has demonstrated the extraordinary variability inherent in the species (for it is just one species). Natural selection tends normally to enforce a greater uniformity among individuals, but given artificial selection or the artificial world of cohabitating with man, this variability can express itself.

We know from a reading of history that when men were banding together to form large village communities, they brought their dogs with them. Since then, both have experienced in similar fashion the cultural and environmental changes that have occurred—canned food, heated rooms, soft furnishings, urban compression, disease control, and increasing unnaturalness. At the same time, dogs with their quicker breeding cycle have passed through some 400 generations, while man has experienced a tenth of that number. It is these facts, according to Marsha A. Burns and Margaret N. Fraser in *Genetics of the Dog*, an excellent book on dog behavior, which suggest a hypothesis: "The genetic consequences of civilized living have been intensified in the dog, and therefore the dog should give us some idea of the genetic future of mankind . . . In short, the dog may be a genetic pilot experiment for the human race."

There is one further important point. Evolution, or rapid genetic change, happens fastest when a population is divided into small isolated groups that have only occasional genetic contact with each other. (In American Cockers that was precisely what was happening in pre-World War II America. Travel was very limited, so not many dogs were shipped any great distance to be bred. As a result, there grew to be a "western type" with long sloping shoulders, a steeper topline, and with finer bone which did not fully develop until about two years of age. On the opposite coast the style was different. The "eastern type" had a blockier head, was straighter and heavier through the shoulders, had a shorter back and more coat. With the advent of regular commercial air travel, the Cocker has been largely homogenized.) According to Smith, this was precisely the condition of mankind 10,000 years ago, when dogs were becoming a part of each isolated scene. The trading, or warring, or friendly association between each group permitted a degree of genetic involvement with the dogs next door. For instance, with living areas spaced well apart, American Indians each had their own breed of dog. These breeds were not greatly different from those of each neighboring tribe, but across the continent the differences became intense. So, too, in earlier times—with all the fairly isolated, semi-independent groups of people that were the ancestors of us all.

John C. McLoughlin, writing in *The Canine Clan*, agrees with Smith that during the Neolithic time in history mankind took off in its present direction. The various breeds of dog were dotted everywhere. They had been nurtured in isolation and were then ready to accompany their migrating masters, to be sold or captured along the way. It is interesting to note that practically every dog name is based upon the geographical area from which that creature had arrived. The spotted dog, for example, may not have originated in Dalmatia (in fact it was India) but it came through there, and that was good enough for its new owners; so too, with the Spaniel (allegedly Espagnol), the Greyhounds (allegedly Greek), the Saluki (thought to be Seleucid).

As the age of discovery began, man's movements became more frenetic. No longer did small groups wander along conventional lines, but boatloads leapfrogged among the continents. Everyone took dogs with them, and they brought dogs back. There was much *panmixis*, or widescale interbreeding. Sometimes this was successful, sometimes not. New breeds were formed, often at the expense of native varieties that died out, as in America and South Africa.

The American Cocker Spaniel is a perfect example of this *panmixis* in modern times. In the middle 1880's there was a degree of confusion over some of the Spaniels. The base dog was called a Field Spaniel. He tended to be a large dog. Smaller Spaniels, even ones from the same litter, were called Cockers and shown in a different class. Gradually, the

Sussex, and Field Spaniels drifted away. And the Cocker, which had been imported to America, became a big hit. He drew from the best of the base Spaniels and left them in his wake. Today, Sussex and Field Spaniels in this country struggle for survival, while the Cocker (with some 100,000 registrations per year) is the number one dog in American Kennel Club (AKC) registrations. After the turn of the century, Cockers in the United States were of English type and American type. In fact one of the pillars of the American Cocker breed has an English Cocker dam. They were shown as one breed.

Finally, in the 1950's, Mrs. Geraldine Dodge, a patron of the English Cocker conducted a thorough pedigree study which convinced the AKC to grant the English Cocker status as an independent breed.

The *Canidae* (the family of Dog) itself was derived, at least in historical terms, fairly recently. They came from more primitive and ancestral predators. They fanned out rapidly into different regions but never lost their ability to adapt. They evolved in a direction that would permit them a wider selection of food options available from the world's ecosystems. They could survive by eating various vegetable foods in addition to flesh. The wild carnivore was not rigidly tied to the condition of any one food chain position and very nearly approaches man in dietary adaptability. Among the *Canidae* were the wolves *(Canis lupus)*, a species having much in common with early man, that exhibited cooperative behavior when attacking its prey. The *Canidae* expresses in form and function an ancestral invasion of open country, wherein prey must be hunted by tireless running rather than by stalking. Reading *The Canine Clan* certainly indicates wolf and man were direct competitors, and this similarity of life style may have had much to do with their eventual union. From the study of archeology and related sciences, it is known that all modern dogs derive only from the various races of the wolf species and that the association of wolf and man leading to dog happened again and again. American Indians were frequently accustomed to taking wolf cubs, either to amend their dog stock or to start afresh. Probably this process of turning wolves into dogs was spurred on when man's extreme inability to smell out his prey, in that tangle of hiding places, became a terrible disadvantage.

The mighty sense of smell in *canids* may be illustrated by the fact, (experimentally shown) that a dog can detect, for example, the odor of fear in the urine of another which has long since passed by, and thus be on the lookout for trouble in advance. *Canids* are aided in their sense of smell by a pair of small openings, Jacobsen's organs, in the front of the roof of the mouth. Using these, a *canid* "tastes" the air as he smells it, curling his lips to do so in a motion referred to by the German word *flehmen*. In *flehmen*, the animal raises his nose, wrinkles his snout, and ceases breathing, while he bares his fore-teeth and samples the air with his Jacobsen's organs. In a later chapter on training the Cocker for the field, it should be noted that major emphasis is placed on this smelling ability.

Anyway, as Smith points out:

The dog, a remarkable social invention, was the first domestic animal. The new accomplice could be tamed, if caught early enough or reared in human company. It could hunt. It could herd animals. It could protect and give warning, although wild *Canidae* are not given to protective barking as much as the tame varieties. Each tribe must have wanted this new aid to living, and good bitches must have been tremendously in demand.

However, a good forest dog is not necessarily suitable either for the open plains, or for herding semi-domestic stock, or for guarding the encampments. Therefore, there had to be selective breeding for specific purposes. Therefore, there evolved hunting dogs, sheep dogs, and even the "toy" dogs of the Maltese type. Living with the early Egyptians there were at least five major kinds: the Basenji, the Greyhound, the Maltese, the Mastiff, and a sort of Chow.

It is important to appreciate that the changes, however striking, were not basic. They were more of degree of proportion. Of course, dogs also differ in those characteristics that were different even in the basic wolf, such as: color, temperament, and wiriness, smoothness or furriness of hair.

A large number of dog differences are the result of the retention of juvenile features. This occurs when any creature stops growing or achieves its adult state while still possessing characteristics previously associated with its more immature form. Puppies, for example, have silkier, less wavy hair. Their ears, in general, are floppier, less straight, and less erect than with the adult. Their tails are more likely to droop, less likely to stay firmly away from the legs. There is no law that states that these features must be linked with the juvenile form, but some of the dog changes have inclined toward these puppylike features. (Many of the Pekingese characteristics are an example.)

Early man lived in different environments, therefore, his dog requirements differed from place to place. These have also changed in more recent times, and the breeders have had to adapt the supply. The pet or toy breeds, suitable for living within a household, have been more favored. A 1987 study by AKC indicated that more small breeds have moved into the top 20 dogs in registration, led of course by the American Cocker with nearly 100,000 registered each year.

In the early Aztec world, dogs were bred for eating, for their hair (as wool), and for their role as beasts of burden. The whiteness of the English Terriers was a requirement for greater conspicuousness within the undergrowth. Even the arrival of breech-loading guns demanded a different animal; the steadfast and entirely patient behavior of the pointing breeds, doggedly stationary while his master fulfilled the ritual of preparing a muzzle-loader, was far too steadfast when a more capable firing piece became available. Therefore, Setters were deliberately bred from

Spaniel stock (the English primarily) to sit or "set" when the quarry was detected and then to move forward when the quicker gun was ready. As the gun became better, the Spaniel—who worked close in flushing game—became more of a favorite.

In short, different dogs have been our steady requirement. The breeders (whether putting their animals out at night to be mated by wolves, or actively preventing such an event, or trading particular animals up and down the migration routes) have always been attempting to satisfy most particular needs. Smith indicated that during the past 20,000 years these men have been outstandingly successful in unleashing the potential variation in the domestic dog—the animal that once was a wolf.

Not only have physical characteristics been selected for; behavior has always been important. The breeder has had to provide an animal's ferocity (guard dogs), or overall friendliness (Cocker Spaniels), or individual friendliness (loyalty to one person alone). There is, for example, the matter of barking. Some individual dogs bark more than others; some breeds do. It can even be proved (in *Animal Behavior*, John Paul Scott and John L. Fuller have done so) that this behavioral trait has a genetic basis.

For their experiment they took the Basenji, a poor barker, and the Cocker Spaniel, a sometimes noisy creature.

> Basenjis not only bark rarely, but make less noise when they do and stop quicker when they start. Presumably the barking facility served less purpose in the African forests, or the barker was pounced on more readily by dog-loving leopards. Whether their masters selected them for their quietness or whether leopards saved them the trouble, the modern examples of this breed howl or yowl more than they bark. Any kind of howl, with its wavering note, is harder to locate and pinpoint than the bark. The Cocker, on the other hand, named after its ability to flush out woodcock, is a standard barker. Given a form of incentive to do so, the Cockers barked, during the experiment, on 68 percent of these occasions. The Basenji not only barked less loudly and more briefly when subjected to similar stimuli, but responded on only 20 percent of the occasions.

As of now, the tendency toward diversity has gone to greater lengths in dog than in man for two reasons. First, natural selection for the dog has been relaxed for a longer time—in terms of generations—than for man. Second, artificial selection—of the dog by man—has deliberately preserved some unwelcome canine mutations merely to increase that diversity. Has the dog species therefore suffered genetically? Natural selection is impartial, favoring no species in particular, but has its lack of influence caused some kind of lack and unfitness in the dog?

> The answer is that the dog does not seem to be genetically weak. For example, the current breeds are largely more fertile than their wolf ancestors. Wolves mature at the age of two and produce four or five

cubs per litter. There may be selective reasons for this casual growth, such as the inability of the habitat to support large numbers of predators, but the wolf's infertility is still the case. The dog is, generally speaking, sexually mature before the age of one and can produce two litters a year. By this criterion, man-handling has not harmed the dog.

Nor has it in the range of capabilities. Variety is the keynote, and today's dogs have broadened all the old wolf characteristics. "Terriers," to quote Scott and Fuller again, "are more aggressive than their wolf forebears; the hound breeds less so. Greyhounds are faster than wolves; short-legged dogs, like the Dachshund, less so. The good scent dogs are better trackers than wolves, while terriers are poorer. Sheep dogs can herd more effectively; other breeds would not know where to begin. Many game dogs are, reasonably enough, more interested than wolves in game and share man's enthusiasm about birds."

American Cockers originally belonged to a large family of animals that assumed a wide variety of sizes, shapes and colors. Over time, they aligned themselves into two distinct groups, land Spaniels and water Spaniels. Members of the the land Spaniels group include the American Cocker, the English Cocker, the English Springer, the Sussex and the Welsh Springer. The water group consists of the Irish Water Spaniel and the American Water Spaniel. At one time, there was an English Water Spaniel in the water group and a Norfolk Spaniel in the land group. But these have disappeared from this country over the last fifty years. Also, at one time, Toy Spaniels were a part of the land group.

According to Ella B. Moffit in her book *The Cocker Spaniel*, "Spaniels, until the middle of the 19th century, were classified according to size of the individual dog. In England, it was not until 1883 that classes for Cockers were listed in shows, and not until 1893 that the English Kennel Club granted the Cocker Spaniel a place for himself in the Stud Book. In the last quarter of the 19th century, the Cocker lost his place in the field to the English Springer. It was evident that the long and low-set dog that Cockers had become (bred for those exaggerations, then considered beautiful), was responsible for their fall from grace as a field dog supreme. We do owe a debt of gratitude to those breeders of yore for having established a definite strain which is the foundation of our Cockers of today. However, the contrast between Champion Obo II of 1882 and the modern Cocker of 100 years later is astonishing. Obo, the sire of Obo II, bred by a Mr. Farrow, was whelped on June 14, 1879. He is recorded as being 'by Fred out of Betty.' " My, what might the AKC think if we attempted such simplicity?

Ch. Obo II, 1882.

According to Dalziell's *British Dogs*, Obo had the following measurements:

Weight .... 22 pounds
Height .... 10 inches
Length from nose to ears .... 2¼ inches
Length from nose to occiput .... 7¼ inches
Length from nose to set-on of tail .... 29 inches

Today, a typical American Cocker male would weigh nearly 30 pounds, be 14¾ to 15½ inches tall and measure 15 percent less from withers to set-on of tail than his height from the ground to the withers. This certainly shows the dramatic changes our breed has undergone.

It was in 1790 that one first finds reference in English literature to the Springing Spaniel and the Cocking Spaniel. The Cocking Spaniel was so small that today he would be put into the Toy group. His weight was estimated at between 11–16 pounds. Mrs. Moffit felt that it was inconceivable that a dog of that size should be valued for sport. In her opinion, their size could only be explained by the fact that they were used in numbers as noisy drivers. In the early 19th century, there is mention of them being used in conjunction with Greyhounds to spring the hare which the latter would course.

Ch. Tagalong's Winter Frost, a top winner of today. Owned by Frank DeVito and Jose Serrano and pictured here with his handler, Wilson Pike.

There is much in our breed history to learn. Many good books which contain historical data are to be found. I can especially recommend *The Complete Cocker Spaniel* by Milo Denlinger, published by Denlinger Publishers. This book is out of print but if you can find a copy—treasure it. Ella Moffit's book, *The Cocker Spaniel,* is also a gem.

There is also a great deal of history of the breed to learn by perusing the section to appear later in this book entitled, *Famous People and Dogs Who Influenced The Breed.*

An artist's conception of an ideal Cocker Spaniel head.

CHAPTER 2

The American Spaniel Club

One January afternoon in 1881, James Watson called at Clinton Wilmerding's office in New York City. The purpose of his visit was to suggest that they form a Spaniel Club.

Moving rapidly, the two men contacted other Spaniel lovers. In February, thirteen other charter members were present at the organizational meeting in addition to Watson and Wilmerding. Present were George McDougall (Watson's partner in Lachine Kennels); Dr. J.S. Niven, E. Tinsley, and J.F. Kirk from Canada; J. Otis Fellows, M.P. Mckoon, A.E. Goddefroy, Dr. J.S. Cattanack, Dr. J.L. Morrill, A.H. Moore, C.B. Cummings, J.H. Whitman, and A. McCollom. They named the new club the American Cocker Spaniel Club and elected Mr. Moore president.

First order of business was to draw up standards which would officially separate Cocker Spaniels and Field Spaniels. In England, small Field Spaniels were usually called "Cockers" by the breeders. But the English Kennel Club did not recognize Cockers as a separate breed until 1892, even though early dog shows frequently had classes for large Field Spaniels and small Field Spaniels.

It was difficult to draft these standards. Into them had to go a blending of opinions that would please and satisfy the majority. After all, a standard is a statement of intent and not a commandment from a higher source. Following months of compromises, disagreements, and reconciliations, the standards were completed. There was little difference between the two breeds except weight, height, and length. The Field Spaniel became proportionately heavier, lower, and longer than the Cocker. A Cocker could weigh between 18 and 28 pounds; the Field was over 28 and up to 45 pounds.

The length of a Cocker Spaniel "from tip of nose to root of tail should be twice the height at shoulder, rather more than less," according to the first standard. All colors to be acceptable, but "beauty of color and markings must be taken into consideration."

The physical characteristics that separated the two breeds were more semantic than real in the early days. For example, Ch. Compton Brahmin, a Cocker champion, sired Ch. Compton Bandit, a Field champion, out of a Cocker-sized bitch.

Not all members were happy with the standards. At the club's annual meeting in 1886, member Arthur E. Rendle made the motion that "Owing to the interbreeding of Cockers and Field Spaniels for years past, the two breeds are so mixed up that it would be advisable to call them all Field Spaniels, to be divided by weight—lightweight and heavyweight."

That motion lost, but Mr. Rendle persevered. He introduced the motion again in 1894, and again it was defeated. This was the last time in the history of the club that an effort was made to recombine the breeds.

After the American Kennel Club was formed, it accepted Field and Cocker Spaniels as separate breeds for show and championship purposes, but registered them together in the Stud Book. By 1905, the two breeds had become sufficiently divergent in type and ancestry for the AKC to separate them for registration.

After the purpose for founding the club had been accomplished, the name was changed to the American Spaniel Club and the members turned their attention to other activities. The enthusiasm of some was diminished, however, and the club came close to extinction before its fifth anniversary. Mr. Wilmerding recalled in an interview that the membership had dwindled to seven in 1885, and had a record of $35 in the treasury. In a reorganization move, Roger Hemingway was elected president and Mr. Wilmerding the secretary-treasurer. Mr. Wilmerding could account for the seven members, but as he said, "I never found the $35!"

Major activities of the club during the first 20 years included development of standards, selection of approved judges from its membership, inauguration of puppy sweepstakes, attempted organization of field trials, and struggling to keep itself financially sound. And lest one think that these early members were gentlemen without flaw or passion; they disagreed, they argued, charges and countercharges abounded. Mr. Wilmerding was the peacemaker, who soothed injured feelings and kept the club alive.

Most American Spaniel Club members bred and hunted over Sussex, Clumber, and Irish Water Spaniels in addition to their Cocker and Field Spaniels. It was decided that these other breeds were also entitled to the support and protection of the club. The Irish Water Spaniel—established in type and performance many years before the club was formed—was adopted with the same standard as published in England. The Clumber Spaniel Standard as drawn up by its committee, was not accepted until a number of revisions were made. Mr. Wilmerding and Mr. F. Kitchell on the east coast, Mr. A.L. Weston of Denver, and Mr. F.H.F. Mercer and Mr. Joseph Hill of Canada imported the blood of top

Circa 1919

Field Spaniel

Clumber Spaniel

Cocker Spaniel

English Clumbers to try to increase their numbers and quality in North America.

The Sussex Spaniel was almost orphaned a century ago. He had nearly been lost as a distinct breed in England, and was still in the process of attempted rejuvenation to his earlier magnificient stature as a sporting dog. Some Sussex were imported to North America but were entered in the Stud Book as Field and Cocker Spaniels. Three of the first Field Spaniel champions in the United States were imported animals with the purest Sussex pedigrees.

Mr. Wilmerding helped save the Sussex from extinction, although he regretted the crossbreeding of Sussex and other Spaniels. "This, however," he wrote, "may be overlooked when we realize the rarity of the breed and the difficulty and expense entailed in mating them so scattered." He made this plea to the club: "It seems better by far, that this much-neglected breed should receive the assistance of the Spaniel Club and, like the Cockers, the Springers (*viz.* Field Spaniels), and Clumbers, be brought into public notice and prominence through the effort of this club."

And so, the Sussex joined the American Spaniel Club. But it was well into the 20th century before they were registered and shown under that name. Five breeds had joined the club during its first 20 years. In the next 20 years, the English Springer Spaniel and the Welsh Springer Spaniel would follow into the ranks.

The American Spaniel Club, as a display of its eminence as a club, was justly proud of the sterling silver challenge cups awarded to each of its breed winners and best brace from each breed. Because the annual Spaniel show was far in the future; the all-breed shows at which the cups were awarded were decided a year in advance. Only some of the cups were awarded at each chosen show. The judge had to be a person duly approved and elected by the club and only ASC members were eligible to win a "leg" on the cup. For permanent possession, a cup had to be won five times by the same individual.

In those days an elegant cup cost between $25 and $35. The treasury seldom boasted a balance sufficient to buy such challenge cups. However, by soliciting the members for donations of $5 or more the necessary funds were raised. Excitement was in the air at the executive committee meeting of March 12, 1891, when a letter was read from Dr. N. Rowe of Chicago. Dr. Rowe offered the club a $100 sterling silver challenge cup to be awarded as the club saw fit provided it was offered first at Westminster in 1892.

This trophy was named the "American Field Trophy" and was the most expensive award in ASC records for many years. It was first offered at Westminster's 1892 show for Best American-Bred Spaniel.

Puppy sweepstakes for Cocker Spaniels and Field Spaniels were inaugurated in 1887. The entry fee was $3, and the money was divided as follows: 40% to winner, 30% to breeder of winner, 20% to second place, and 10% to third. The club donated an additional $20 to the winner. The sweepstakes contest continued until it gradually evolved into the annual Futurity for Cocker Spaniel puppies in 1923.

Field trials might seem to have been a natural outgrowth of the American Spaniel Club's activities, but such was not the case. In May, 1892, Mr. Wilmerding was appointed chairman of a committee to investigate sponsoring ASC field trials. No progress was made. By February, 1906, the committee was still stalemated. This inability to kindle member enthusiasm continued for another five years. In 1911, Mr. Wilmerding resigned his chairmanship and the executive committee dispensed with the field trial committee. It would be more than another decade before this facet of ASC activity would be realized.

During the time ASC was busy with its own affairs; the American Kennel Club was formed in 1884. You will note its founding was three years after the Spaniel Club's. During its first year, AKC it did not envision being a registration body. But this soon became necessary. In late 1887, the AKC issued a ruling affecting all dog breeders and exhibitors. This new rule was read at the American Spaniel Club's executive committee meeting in January, 1888. It was not well received! The following resolution was passed by the committee:

> Whereas, the American Kennel Club has altered its rules so as to compel the registration of all dogs in the Club Stud Book, and
>
> Whereas, it is the opinion of the Committee of the American Spaniel Club that such action is detrimental to the best interests of dog breeding, apart from any consideration as to the wisdom of compulsory registration, and
>
> Whereas, the Committee believes that the members of the Club should have a voice in the decision of the question, it being one outside of the routine business of the Club management, it is hereby resolved, that the members be requested to vote on the following question: (viz) "Shall the Club funds be distributed at shows where compulsory registration is enforced?"

The first mail vote recorded in the ASC history showed 44 ballots returned, 35 of which agreed that club funds should be withheld from shows requiring dogs to be registered. In this matter, the ASC was fighting a losing battle.

This slight misunderstanding with the American Kennel Club was resolved rather rapidly. When the AKC began to accept club memberships, it was moved and carried at the annual meeting of 1889, that "The Spaniel Club make application through its secretary, for admission to the American Kennel Club." In August 1889, it was moved and carried that, "Mr. James Watson be appointed as delegate to represent the American Spaniel Club at the meetings of the AKC—in case of the election of the Spaniel Club to that body." The Spaniel Club became a member later in that year.

The second 20 years of the American Spaniel Club saw dramatic increases in membership and its first specialty show in 1894. The "big name" kennels, that both bred and bought Cocker Spaniels in quantity, appeared on the scene during this period. Many more shows were held and it followed that many more Cocker Spaniels would become champions.

As the ASC matured as an organization it evolved, as many organizations of its time, as an eastern-dominated club of people with money and leisure time in control of the organization. This is not meant to be a "put down" of the influential people who controlled the ASC, but a simple statement of the way the world was in the 1920's and 30's. In fact, the ASC was looked upon as a well-run organization, putting on excellent shows which continued to grow in popularity.

As the Cocker rose to the Number One position in all of dogdom, and breeders from other parts of the country became involved in the activities of the club, the eastern domination began to be challenged. This was a period of large kennels, many with expert kennel managers in residence. These exhibitors of wealth and standing, dominated the club and were major winners in the show ring.

The executive committee, heeding the cries throughout the country for better representation within the club and for more prestigious shows in local areas, created the zone concept. For its time and place this became a stroke of genius.

The zone concept divided the country into four regions or zones (a fifth was added later). A new prestige show called, logically enough, the Zone Show was created. Clubs within a zone could make application to hold a Zone Show. Upon approval, the ASC would help to support the event financially and would assist the local club in the management of the show. Only one designated Zone Show could be held in a given zone each year. The winners of these events were featured prominently, along with the winners of the January ASC show, in the annual report.

Perhaps the wisest move by the executive committee was to have zone representatives sit as members of the newly-constituted Board of Directors. Much credit for this innovation should be given to Bart King, the editor of the *Cocker Spaniel Visitor*, the predominant breed magazine of the day. In his editorial column called "Thoughts While Shaving," Bart used to take the Spaniel Club to task for their narrow views. In turn, credit should also be given to the club for listening to its members.

Although the zone shows became popular, there was still a feeling among the fancy that it was a limited show—one that only brought out the best in that zone. Occasionally, a widely-campaigned dog from another area would be shown. But this only served to whet the appetite of local exhibitors to see more such specimens.

Throughout the first 80 some years of the club's existence, there had been only one BIG show: the New York City Show. The breeders distant from New York found it difficult and expensive to travel to New York, especially during the first week in January. The west coast was beginning to make noises about proper representation on the Board, until the mid 1960's, only Ralph Brown (a wealthy northern California lumberman) had sat on the Board.

By the early 1970's, sentiment was running deep in the west to move the annual Specialty show, or to rotate its location around the country. Capitalizing on that sentiment, Robert Walker (of California) ran as an alternate candidate and won the presidency over the nominating committee's choice. In office, he turned out to be the maverick he said he would be. He was not nominated for a second term. Once again he ran as an alternative candidate and was reelected. Although many considered his time in office disruptive, he was in part responsible for establishing the concept of the summer National which is now rotated among the five zones.

Following Walker, the office of the presidency was held by persons from Illinois, Kentucky, Texas and again California. The club also elected its first woman president, Jeannie Meister of California. The club had truly become national in outlook.

Fortunately, the leadership of the club has been in good hands since its beginnings. Faced with the drastic problem of congenital cataracts in the breed, a responsible board in the 1970's, set-up and still maintains a Health Registry for unafflicted dogs. Additional heritable problems have also been included in the Registry.

In response to the growing worldwide popularity of the Cocker, the position of Liaison to Foreign Breed Clubs was established in the 1970's.

The American Spaniel Club's history has been one of steadfast loyalty and, at times, dynamic leadership. It has grown from the original 15 members to well over 1600. It is now the largest breed club in the country. The entries at its two premier shows have continued to climb, and being selected to officiate at an ASC event is indeed an honor for a judge. There are still new paths to carve and ways to strengthen the club, however, there is good reason to be proud of the American Spaniel Club.

Ch. Carmor's Rise and Shine.
Winner of Best in Show at Westminster.

CHAPTER 3

The Golden Era
The First Peak of Popularity

The Cocker's first bid for popularity began in the early 1900's. From that time on, the golden era of America's Number One Sporting Dog flourished. In 1921, a Cocker Spaniel became the first of the breed to be named the winner of Best in Show at the Westminster Kennel Club. William T. Payne's Ch. Midkiff Seductive, a black and white Parti-Color, had this signal honor. Not until 1940 and 1941 did another Cocker hold the spotlight at the Westminster Dog Show. The winner at that time was the famous Ch. My Own Brucie owned by the legendary Herman Mellenthin. In the 43 years that followed, only one other Cocker has topped that famous event—Ch. Carmor's Rise and Shine, handled by Ted Young, Jr.

Ch. My Own Brucie

In 1922, the Cocker Spaniel Breeder's Club of New England staged its first specialty show at Boston where W.T. Payne judged an entry of 106 dogs. Eight years later—in 1930—this same club ran up an unprecedented entry of 256 Cocker Spaniels. Only the "Shamrock" show held in Houston in 1951, and the Cocker Spaniel Club of Kentucky in 1986, had a larger entry (of course, this does not count ASC events). The 1930 show was judged by Mrs. A.R. Moffit, and was won by the Black bitch, Ch. My Own To-Day owned by the Windsweep Kennels of Miss Alice Dodsworth. My Own To-Day was of good size and essentially female in all details. Years later, Henry McTavey (one of the later breeders and judges of Cockers) stated that "Ch. My Own To-Day was the greatest dog-show Cocker up to that time."

Other winners of the New England specialty show were Ch. Lucknow Creme de la Creme, owned by Mr. and Mrs. Fred Brown; Ch. The Great My Own, property of Leonard Buck; the celebrated Ch. Idahurst Belle II carrying the banner of the O.B. Gilmans of Boston; Miss Dodsworth's Ch. Windsweep Ebony Boy; Ch. My Own Brucie, three times Best in Show, 1938, 1939, 1940; and Ch. Nonquitt Nola's Candidate, owned jointly by Mrs. Mildred Brister and Mrs. R.K. Cobb of Nanuet, New York. Oddly, the name of Ch. Torohill Trader, perhaps the greatest show dog of the time, does not appear on the roster.

The American Spaniel Club held its annual specialty at the Hotel Roosevelt in New York City until the 1970's. Starting in 1920, when Ch. Dunbar was Best in Show, the parent club's annual fixture grew in popularity. The greatest Cockers of the times were shown at the Roosevelt. Such names as Ch. Princess Marie, Ch. Midkiff Miracle Man, Sand Spring Storm Cloud, Ch. Windsweep Ladysman, Ch. Torohill Trader (1936 and 1937), Ch. My Own Brucie, Ch. Found, Ch. Nonquitt Nola's Candidate (1943 and 1945), and Ch. Try-Cob's Favorite Girl are some of the immortals who, in their year, wore the ermine robes.

The American Spaniel Club introduced the futurity stake in 1923, to encourage the breeding of better Cocker Spaniels. Bitches belonging to club members and due to whelp between February 1 and July 1, were eligible for nomination in the futurity stake. This innovation was of tremendous popularity. The first futurity stake winner, and incidentally first for Mepal Kennels, was Mepal's Fortunata; second was Rees' Meteor, owned by Latimer Rees; third, was Mrs. W.M. Churchman's Jim Crow's Glow (bred by Dr. H.B. Kobler); and fourth was Sheila of Cassilis, owned by Cassilis Kennels.

Herman E. Mellenthin and his My Own Kennels, from Poughkeepsie, New York were beginning to be heard from in the 1930's. Mellenthin, a tall, soft-spoken man, took advantage of an offer of a free stud service to Robinhurst Foreglow. From this mating came the celebrated red Cocker, Red Brucie, a son of Foreglow and Ree's Dolly. Red Brucie

Ch. Idahurst Belle II

Ch. Torohill Trader

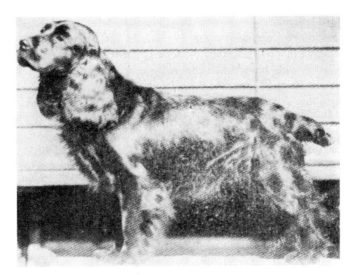

Ch. Princess Marie

Red Brucie

never completed his championship, and wrote no show ring history. None, however, was needed to perpetuate his name, for the contribution of Red Brucie and his three half-brothers (all sons of Robinhurst Foreglow) propelled the Cocker Spaniel to the top of the AKC list of registrations in 1936. This truly opened the first golden era which lasted for some 16 years at which time, the Cocker was supplanted by the Beagle as the number one dog in America.

The names of the four sons of Foreglow, one or more of whom appeared in the pedigrees of most of the winning Cockers of the day, were Ch. Midkiff Miracle Man, Ch. Sand Spring Surmise, Ch. Limestone Laddie, and Red Brucie. In Red Brucie, Mellenthin had a dog that took him and his kennel to the heights.

Often called the "Wizard of Cockers," Mellenthin's contribution to the breed is preeminent. His home kennel, small and restricted, could not house all his bitches. Because of this, Mellenthin evolved a "farming out" system. Farmers of Duchess County were given bitches on breeding terms. Mellenthin was to pick the stud and to select his choice of the litter. At one time, Mellenthin had as many as 150 bitches farmed out. Naturally, breeding on this extensive scale gave Mellenthin a free hand in experimenting with bloodlines, crossing strains and breeding back to them, a thing no small breeder could hope to do.

Out of this experimentation came many of the greatest Cockers of the day. Ch. Torohill Trader, Ch. Princess Marie, Ch. My Own Again, Ch. My Own Straight Sale, Ch. My Own Brucie, Ch. The Great My Own, Ch. Merry Monarch of Falconhurst, Ch. Found and others too numerous to mention, were all the result of Mellenthin's breeding. It was not until after World War II that the Artru Kennels of Ruth and Art Benhoff would rival Mellenthin in producing such a string of great Cockers.

In the matter of Trader, the Torohill Kennels are the breeder of record, but it was Mellenthin who arranged the mating, who owned and later sold Trader to Leonard Buck's Blackstone Kennels.

A great deal of Mellenthin's success came from breeding back and into the Red Brucie strain. In addition to being a shrewd and intelligent breeder, Mellenthin was also a clever showman.

During this period Miss Alice Dodsworth purchased the Cordova Kennels and started to breed American-type Cockers. With such dogs as Ch. Coldstream Guard of Cordova, Ch. Cordova Cordial, Ch. Cordova Coccade, and with a dose of Mellenthin's advice, Miss Dodsworth's Windsweep Kennels soon swept to the pinnacle of success. In the 1930's, she introduced Ch. Windsweep Ladysman to the show ring. Ladysman, a Black dog of great refinement, became the top sire of his day. He died in 1944 and Miss Dodsworth had this to say about Ladysman and Mr. Mellenthin:

"I like to hear good things said of my Ch. Windsweep Ladysman as I think he deserved them all. In his day he was a grand Cocker of real show and stud type, and in his old age he was game to the end.

"I miss him greatly . . . I lay my success to Red Brucie and to Ch. Coldstream Guard of Cordova and to Mr. Mellenthin's kindly advice . . ."

Ch. Windsweep Ladysman

One of the great confrontations of the day occurred in the show ring when Ch. Windsweep Ladysman met Ch. Torohill Trader at the Morris and Essex show of 1934. Judged by Harold Johnson (owner of the Midbrook Kennels of Long Island), Ladysman was in for Specials while Trader was making his debut being ably handled by Bain Cobb, manager for Leonard Buck's Blackstone Kennel. Trader came up from the classes to Best of Winners and met Ladysman for Best of Breed. Mr. Johnson decided in favor of Trader and launched his record-breaking career. It was his great movement that was in large measure responsible for his appeal and popularity. A sluggish dog and a lazy dog on the bench; the minute Bain Cobb put him down in the show ring he electrified the spectators with his unsurpassed showmanship. Up to that time, there had been no dog matching Trader in flash, in his instinct for a flawless performance, and his ability to overcome competition and win the plaudits of the crowd.

As a sire, this great Black dog gave immeasureable help to the breed. He was behind the pedigree of the immortal Ch. Stockdale Town Talk as well as many other great ones. He carried on the long, graceful necks we see today, stamped his progeny with clean shoulders, and straight short backs. He put the Cocker "up" on the leg and was responsible for the gently sloping topline, withers to tail, so necessary to the perfect outline and type.

Following Torohill Trader, My Own Brucie was the next in the cycle of famous Cockers. Mellenthin seldom introduced a dog to the public until it was three or four years old. The Poughkeepsie genius did not believe a Cocker was at his show peak until throroughly matured. Brucie, a "farmed out" product, did not do well at first. Mrs. Constance Wall, when judging one of the New Jersey shows, put Brucie down in his class. Later, Ch. Blackstone Reflector defeated Brucie several times. But in Chicago under Harry McTavey, Brucie turned the tables and from then on could not be stopped. Taking nothing away from Brucie's greatness, he was not the showman Trader was. Brucie had his off moments when even Mellenthin could not get him to move with the necessary verve and gaiety. When so disposed, My Own Brucie was a perfect show dog. He stands out as probably the most publicized Cocker Spaniel of all time. Winning Best in Show at Westminster, in 1940, was of tremendous value to the breed. No Cocker had done this since 1921, and then go back the next year and repeat the sensational win made the public truly Cocker Spaniel conscious. My Own Brucie did more to create interest in the Cocker than any other dog.

An understanding of his great popularity can be gained from the fact that when he passed away in the early 40's, the *New York Evening Sun* published his obituary on its front page, crowding out the war news to make room for it.

With the passing of Herman Mellenthin and My Own Brucie, a chapter in the book of American Cocker Spaniels was closed. Another was to begin with R. Kenneth Cobb and a dog called Ch. Try-Cob's Candidate. Ken Cobb (a brother of Bain Cobb and Trader's handler in all his triumphs), entered the dog world as manager of the Holmeric

Ch. Try-Cob's Candidate

Kennels of New York. One of the most noted dogs from that kennel which Cobb put through to his championship was Ch. Mr. Holmeric, the sire of Ch. Holmeric of Brookville, himself the sire of 19 champions.

With the closing of Holmeric Kennel, Cobb opened his own place at Huntington, Long Island, New York, where, with Candidate, he was soon to top all other Cocker breeders both from the point of winning and stud services. Candidate, one of the happiest and most fearless Cockers, established his own bloodlines on the Foreglow foundation and an English Cocker outcross. From this cross came Ch. Nonquitt Nola's Candidate, Ch. Try-Cob's Favorite Girl, and a host of other well known champions. All this stemming from Ch. Holmeric of Brookville through Try-Cob's Suzie Q. (one of the finest producing bitches in the country).

Ch. Holmeric of Brookville

On the west coast, C.B. Van Meter had established the Stockdale Kennel at Van Nuys, California. From this kennel came many sensational Cockers, among them the noted Ch. Stockdale Town Talk. Town Talk was brought east in 1944, to the Westminster show, defeated Ch. Nonquitt Nola's Candidate for Best of Variety and then won the Sporting group. Town Talk went on to sire 80 champions.

Other breeders of this era who made important names for their kennels and finished many champions were the Pinfair Kennels of Mrs. H. Terrel Van Ingen, Greenwich, Connecticut; Mr. and Mrs. Hagood Bostick, Columbia, South Carolina; the Log O'Cheer Kennels of Birmingham, Alabama; the Claythorne Kennels of Mr. and Mrs. Joseph Crabbe, Cleveland, Ohio; the Easdale Cocker Kennels, owned by George

Ch. Stockdale Town Talk

Wuchter, Akron, Ohio; the Windridge Kennel owned by Arline Swalwell, Everett, Washington; the Bob-Bets Kennel of Robert Gusman, Atlanta, Georgia; the kennels of Andrew Hodges, on Long Island, New York; the Sugartown Kennels of Dr. and Mrs. Lewis Hart Marks, Paoli, Pennsylvania; and the Maplecliff Kennels of the Dautel's at Chesterland, Ohio. All were built on the foundation of Blackstone Chief and his son Foreglow.

CHAPTER 4

The Golden Era
Resurgence of the Breed

During its heyday, from 1936 until 1952, the Cocker Spaniel captured the top spot in AKC registrations and held it firmly for 16 years. The breed went into a decline after that time and actually, after a period of years, slipped out of the top ten in AKC registrations.

As happens to almost all overly popular breeds, too many breeders (who bred soley for profit) leapt in to bring about a deterioration of the breed. Puppy mills spawned "Cockers" by the thousands. These animals, who were shipped far and wide from their homes in the mid-west, along with the other fast-buck opportunists who bred only to cash in on the breed's popularity, brought the quality and disposition of the merry Cocker to a sorry state.

Coupled with the decline in quality, the pet-buying public saw that the breed was almost rent asunder by the problem of "Juvenile Cataracts." Many famous dogs were accused of perpetuating the dreaded fault and a witch hunt ensued. Thank goodness for cooler and saner heads. Mari Doty and her *American Cocker Review* (ACR) magazine began to air the issue and supported a campaign to research the problem.

William L. Yakely, D.V.M. at Washington State University began a multi-year study into the problem. His research was supported, in part, by contributions encouraged by the ACR.

The American Spaniel Club became alarmed by the problem and began an annual Health Registry, in early 1976, to include cataract-free dogs and also dogs tested for Factor 10 (a blood clotting problem). Progressive retinal atrophy (PRA) and hip dysplasia (HD) were also included. The club formed the Hereditary and Congenital Defects Committee to deal with these problems and to publish the Registry. The compendium has been published yearly since then. While not fully eradicated, the cataract problem seems well under control today.

The drop from the lofty Number One position also brought new and very capable people onto the scene. Ruth and Art Benhoff come to mind immediately. Ruth was voted the Breeder of the Century by the

ASC at their 100th anniversary show in 1981. Having bred 71 champions and being an adviser to nearly everyone, it was an honor richly deserved. She, along with Herman Mellenthin and C.B. Van Meter, will stand on a pedestal in the Cocker Hall of Fame.

Listing everyone who made a major contribution to the breed since the close of World War II would fill two books. However, I will give my own biased views. Having lived and judged in all parts of the country, I have had the privilege of knowing many of the stalwarts of our time.

Tom O'Neal, a two-term president of the ASC, with his "Dreamridge" prefix has dominated the Parti-Color scene for well over 20 years. This would not have been possible without his teaming-up with one of the most successful of handlers, Ron Fabis. Ch. Dreamridge Dominoe, the sire of over 100 champions and Ch. Dreamridge Dinner Date headline this kennel's achievements.

Another daring duo, that preceded O'Neal and Fabis, was the one-two punch of Bea Wegusen and Norman Austin. Bea with her famous Parti-Color Honey Creek Kennel, together with Norman, one of the foremost handlers of that day, made Cocker history with their multiple champion litters.

A major success story is that of Mari and Norm Doty and their string of Nor-Mar Champions and her wonderful work with the *American Cocker Review* (now *American Cocker Magazine*).

Karen Marquez, assisted by her husband Vernon, are consistently producing top Parti-Colors. Year after year, they have been among the top producing kennels in the nation.

Bud and Ida Hamsher put their imprint on the breed with their Shiloh Dell Cockers in Ohio. Bud is a top all-rounder today and is often seen judging in show rings all across the country.

The Kraeuchi's of St. Louis, Missouri produced top winners like clockwork at their famous Silver Maple Kennel. Ruth is also an author of note, having penned two books on the Cocker.

Byron and Cameron Covey, and their outstanding dogs in all colors, were preeminent on the west coast under the Camby prefix. Their son Bob is one of the top handlers of the breed today.

Carl and Rosalie Anderson, two of our popular judges today, were quite successful under the Carro pefix. Carl was a top-notch handler and their son, Gregg, has followed in his dad's footsteps.

Kudos to Jean Petersen, a past vice president of the Spaniel Club, and her history-making Ch. Rinky Dink's Sir Lancelot, a Black/Tan dog who is now the top-producing Cocker in history. I vividly remember judging the 1977 ASC futurity and thinking how alike my Black class winners were, and later finding out that three of the four were sired by Lance.

Edna Anselmi has long been a dominant force in the breed with her

Windy Hill Kennels. Her dogs, headlined by Ch. Windy Hill's 'Tis Demi's Demon (sire of 83 champions), are among the top-producing dogs and bitches in the breed. Edna has also become a judge.

Jim and Beth Hall in Washington State, whose astute breeding created the bloodlines that produced Ch. Scioto Bluff's Sinbad (sire of 118 champions) who, in turn, sired Dominoe, are to be highlighted for their leadership in furthering the cross between buffs and partis.

During the dark days between 1952 and 1977 only one Cocker, Ch. Carmor's Rise and Shine, won Best in Show at Westminster. He was handled by one of the most noted handlers of our time, Ted Young Jr. Ted's accomplishments are legendary. He was, for many years, the president of the Professional Handlers Association and today can be found officiating in the ring from coast to coast.

A model of a small kennel that made it in a big way is the Camelot Kennels of Lou and Amy Weiss of Sacramento, California. Their Black bitches are a sight to behold. Anita Roberts of Novato, California is another small-scale breeder who has done very well. Anita has also joined the ranks of famous judges of our day.

Harriet Kamps in Maryland, with her "Kamps" prefix, produced Kaptain Kool and Kojak along with other great ones. I have always admired the way she sets up a dog.

Laura and Kap Henson and their Kaplar prefix are in the forefront of breeders today. They have been the most consistent breeders of high-quality Cockers in the last 10 years. In fact, I have learned they were the top-producing kennel in England for 1985 and 1986 as well. Laura is also a consistent winner handling in the ring.

Dee Jurkiewicz, of Palm Hill fame, has made many sit up and take notice. Dee's bitches are behind some of the top-winning dogs of the day.

Hugh and Marilyn Spacht are riding high with their top winning ASCOB dogs. These boys are producers as well as winners.

Along about 1977, the fortunes of the breed took a turn for the better and the breed began a slow but accelerating climb back into the "top ten" in registrations. The year began auspiciously when a record futurity entry of 208 puppies were entered at the ASC show. It began to be evident that the hard work of the ASC and the ACR magazine had begun to pay off. By then the puppy mills had gone on to other breeds and the fast-buck operators were avoiding Cockers.

During the hiatus from the top rungs, the breed went through a number of metamorphoses. In the 1950's, the standard was changed to limit the height to 15½ inches. A further standard change better specified the range of allowable markings on the black and tan. Still another change in the 70's more exactly specified the heighth/length ratio. And finally, in the early 80's, the black and tan was included with the Black variety; the liver and tan was recognized officially and placed in the ASCOB (**A**ny **S**olid **C**olor **O**ther Than **B**lack) variety; and tri-color markings were specified more clearly.

The Spaniel Club, with great support from the membership, developed a summer national show. Officially known as the National Cocker Spaniel Specialty, this rotating specialty is for American Cockers only. This premier event is now a fixture. How did we ever do without it?

The breed has prospered. New clubs and new fanciers are everywhere and entries at the shows are excellent. An interesting observation of what happened to our breed during 1952–1977 is that while registrations dropped, show entries and top-winning Cockers did not show any real decline.

Recent statistics show the Cocker is back on top. As those of us who rode the roller coaster from "fame to blame" and back up again know, it won't be easy to maintain high quality and keep the scourges of the Cocker at bay.

CHAPTER 5

The First National Cocker Spaniel Specialty Show

On July 16, 1977, a landmark event was held by the American Spaniel Club. After nearly 100 years of the club's existence, a rotating national specialty exclusively for Cocker Spaniels became a reality. Chapter Two describes the beginnings of the ASC and its development over the years. It was, for all practical purposes, a club for the New England and Middle Atlantic states. As the years went by the club became more national in scope. However, the club's premier event, the annual specialty show, continued to be held in New York.

I recall rather vividly, while living in Seattle, how "out of it" we felt in the Pacific Northwest. After moving to California, I found that same feeling. The Spaniel Club show was too far away for many of us. In the 1960's, there was some clamor to move the show to either a more central location or to have two shows: one in the east and one in the west. Neither of these ideas panned out.

Finally, after much soul searching by the board and the membership, a realizable compromise was reached: the Spaniel Club's annual specialty for all Flushing Spaniels would remain in New York and would be held at the same time each year, the first weekend in January. Another show, to be called the "National Cocker Spaniel Specialty," was to be held in each zone (on a rotating basis) during the month of July. This show was to be solely for Cocker Spaniels. There was to be both a Futurity and a Sweepstakes (the sweepstakes has subsequently been dropped). The concept met with overwhelming approval.

The newest zone created was to be the host. Zone V went all out to host the first show in Oklahoma City. The judges for this important event were:

Miss Sunny Dutton	Jr. & Sr. Futurity
Mrs. Ruth Kraeuchi	Puppy Sweepstakes
Mr. John H. Boyd	Blacks and Best of Breed
Mrs. Byron Covey	ASCOBs
Mr. Kenneth Miller	Parti-Colors
Mrs. Mary Wiggins	Obedience

BEST OF BREED (Black BOV)—Ch. Liz-Bar Magic Of Music (by Ch. Liz-Bar Magician ex Ch. Liz-Bar Merry Magic), bred and owned by Mary Barnes, handled by Don Johnston. Pictured left to right: Honorable James Towson, Majority Leader of the Oklahoma House of Representatives, presenting trophy offered by Mrs. Matthew Hoffmann in memory of her late husband; Breed judge, Mr. John Boyd; Mrs. Matthew Hoffmann; and Mr. Thomas O'Neal, President of the ASC.

Ch. Liz-Bar Magic of Music, owned by Mary N. Barnes of Atlanta and handled by Donny Johnston, went Best of Breed.

To paraphrase the words of Mari Doty, then the editor of the *American Cocker Review* who reported on the show:

If you had attended every Specialty Show leading up to The American Spaniel Club's First National Cocker Spaniel Specialty, you would have to admit that NONE could touch the magnitude of this ASC event held during the month of July in Oklahoma City!

Conceived in the minds of few, the show was the work of many. It is impossible to convey to you the excitement of this show and the excellence with which it was staged. Everyone there felt it. The ASC first National Cocker Spaniel Specialty was a success.

Show chairman Otto Walzel was assisted by Henry Krause and the Futurity chairperson was Bonnie Baker.

There were 22 entries in the Obedience Classes. The ring was large and well laid out and the judging moved along briskly.

Many months of planning and hard work resulted in the success of this show which will be long remembered and which made history! The entry was superb and the panel of judges was outstanding. Each judge evaluated their quality-filled classes with such expertise that the decisions were almost above reproach.

The location of the show—the state of Oklahoma—gave many fanciers from the states west of the Appalachians, who were unable in the winter to attend the ASC National Show on the eastern seaboard, a chance to see for themselves some of the outstanding dogs of the Breed, to watch the top handlers in action, and to seek and receive advice from well-known breeders. Oklahoma was indeed, a central location and the breeders, exhibitors and spectators flocked in from every point of the compass.

We certainly endorse this National Cocker Spaniel Specialty. The idea of rotating it each year is, to us, the BEST part!

Two innovations were instituted at this show, both of which met with hearty approval from the exhibitors and the spectators. A hurry-up meeting of the Bench Show Committee produced a unanimous vote to stop all class judging in other rings when a Variety was being judged. We do not know whose idea this was, but it was a good one! It was endorsed by the AKC representative before the Show Committee's vote was taken. The committee felt that the *piece de resistance* of any show, other than the breath-holding climax of Best of Breed, is watching the large and beautiful classes of Specials competing for the Varieties. This move even afforded the exhibitors in the other rings a chance to watch the Variety judging. And the handlers, who might have been tied up in a class ring, to present the Special they were hired to show. This move on the part of the Show Committee was appreciated by everyone and should be adopted at each National Show. (*Authors Note: It has been.*)

The other innovation was the drawing at the conclusion of the Variety judging between the three scheduled judges to see who would make the Best in Show decision. This was added excitement to the total activities as no one knew . . . not even the judges . . . who would have the honor until it was time for it to be done!" (*Authors Note: This practice has been discontinued*).

The Variety winners were Ch. Liz-Bar Magic of Music, Black; Ch. Russ' Winter Beauty, ASCOB; and Ch. Rexpointe Shazam, Parti-Color. The winner, of course, was the Black and BOS was Winter Beauty.

Best in Senior Futurity was Dee Dee Wood's Ch. Frandee's Celebration. The Best in Junior Futurity was Butch's Kissin' Cousin. (*Author's Note: Today there is only the one Futurity.*) Highest Scoring Obedience Dog was Kimbar Klings to Mei-Hardt.

The summer national is now an institution. It has now made the rounds of all the zones twice and is proving its great value to the breed in that more and more breeders, who have been unable or unwilling to attend the winter show, have gained knowledge from attending the event.

BEST OPPOSITE SEX TO BEST OF BREED (ASCOB BOV)—Ch. *Russ' Winter Beauty, bred and owned by Norma and Larry Russ, handled by Don Johnston. Pictured left to right: Show Chairman, Otto Walzel; Breed judge, Mr. John Boyd; and Trophy Chairman, Betty Duding.*

The whole atmosphere at the summer show is different from the formal surroundings of the annual Flushing Spaniel Specialty. Before long the total entry of Cockers alone may exceed the total entry of the January classic.

PARTI-COLOR BEST OF VARIETY—*Ch. Rexpointe Shazam, owned by Karen Marquez, handled by Ron Fabis. Judge: Mr. Ken Miller.*

BEST IN SENIOR FUTURITY (Best Parti-Color Puppy)—Ch. Frandee's
Celebration, bred and owned by Frank and Dee Dee Wood and handled by
Mrs. Wood. Pictured left to right: Futurity Judge, Miss Sunny Dutton; Henry
Krause, Asst. Show Chairman presents trophy offered by Shirley Glassi.

BEST IN JUNIOR FUTURITY (Best Black Puppy)—Butch's Kissin'
Cousin, bred and owned by Walter and Rachel Thompson, handled by
Charlotte Stacy. Pictured left to right: Trophy presenter, Marie Walzel,
Futurity Judge Miss Sunny Dutton.

SECTION II
What Makes Up
A Standard

- *Blueprint of the Cocker Spaniel*
- *Form Follows Function*
- *A Standard Needing Inspection*

CHAPTER 1

Blueprint of the Cocker Spaniel

With the kind permission of the Board of Directors of the American Spaniel Club and the American Kennel Club, the ASC Slide Show script and pictures are presented for your information and education.

The description of the standard itself is in regular text while the elaboration of the standard is italicized.

As shown in Figure II-1, the Cocker Spaniel is a small, versatile, merry sporting dog who has been a favorite companion at home and in the field for centuries. This presentation is to help you evaluate the components which determine quality in the Cocker Spaniel. These dogs are exemplary Cockers.

The Cocker Spaniel standard is a detailed description of correct conformation. The pictures in this presentation are intended to help you form an image of quality in the Cocker, and what detracts from it.

Figure II-1

General appearance. The Cocker Spaniel is the smallest member of the Sporting Group. He has a sturdy, compact body and a cleanly chiseled and refined head, with the overall dog in complete balance and of ideal size (see Figure II-2). He stands well up at the shoulder on straight forelegs with a topline sloping slightly toward strong muscular quarters. He is a dog capable of considerable speed, combined with great endurance. Above all he must be free and merry, sound, well balanced throughout, and in action show a keen inclination to work; equable in temperament with no suggestion of timidity.

Figure II-2

Balance, soundness, stability: these components make up proper Cocker type. Cocker Spaniels were bred to work cheerfully all day in the field. The dog shown in Figure II-3, is sturdy and strong and is in proper condition. The bitch shown in Figure II-4, is nicely balanced. She is well up on leg and her parts fit together harmoniously. Temperament is also an important part of type. The Cocker Spaniel is a happy, willing worker. He performs his tasks with good cheer; those who do not, should not be considered for top placements.

Head. To attain a well-proportioned head, which must be in balance with the rest of the dog, it embodies the following:

Skull. Rounded but not exaggerated with no tendency toward flatness; the eyebrows are clearly defined with a pronounced stop. The bony structure beneath the eyes is well chiseled with no prominence in the cheeks.

Figure II-3

Figure II-4

A male's head should be stronger in appearance than a female's but both have the typical, soft expression. These heads (shown in Figure II-5) have correct proportions, with proper chiseling and clean back skull. You can see the bony structure beneath the eyes. A well chiseled head is an important element of Cocker type.

Figure II-5

Figure II-6

Muzzle. Broad and deep, with square, even jaws. The upper lip is full and of sufficient depth to cover the lower jaw. To be in correct balance, the distance from the stop to the tip of the nose is one-half the distance from the stop up over the crown to the base of the skull. (As shown in Figure II-6.)

The dog shown in Figure II-7, has an excellent foreface with proper chiseling and proper proportions of muzzle and crown. The width of the muzzle should approach, as nearly as possible, the width of the crown. The muzzle should have sufficient depth with no tendency toward snipiness.

Figure II-7

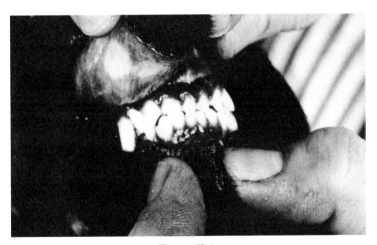

Figure II-8

Teeth. Strong and sound, not too small, and meet in a scissors bite.

Figure II-8 shows a correct bite with strong sound teeth. The mouth must be large enough to grasp and carry a bird.

Nose. Of sufficient size to balance the muzzle, with well-developed nostrils typical of a sporting dog. It is black in color in the Blacks and

Black and Tans. In other colors it may be brown, liver or black, the darker the better. The color of the nose harmonizes with the color of the eye rim.

As a bird dog, the Cocker must have sufficient nasal capacity to find game. Thus, large, open nostrils are important. Although the nose may be brown or liver in addition to black, darker is preferred. Nose color should harmonize with eye rim color. In Figure II-9, this red and white Cocker has proper pigmentation and a good big nose. A pink nose or a spotted nose is faulty.

Figure II-9

Eyes. Eyeballs are round and full and look directly forward. The shape of the eye rims gives a slightly almond-shaped appearance; the eye is not weak or goggled. The color of the iris is dark brown and, in general, the darker the better. The expression is intelligent, alert, soft and appealing.

The standard's description of the eye and expression is very explicit. The eye shape on the bitch in Figure II-10 is quite typical and the expression is soft and pleasing. In Figure II-11, the lack of pigment in these eye rims makes them appear larger than they are. In Figure II-12, the markings of the dog's face and the difference in pigment in the slightly drooping eye rims, makes it difficult to assess his expression. In Figure II-13, the eyes are correct in placement, shape and color.

Figure II-10

Figure II-11

Figure II-12

Figure II-13

Ears. Lobular, long, of fine leather, well feathered, and placed no higher than a line to the lower part of the eye.

Ear leather should reach at least to the end of the nose when brought forward, and the ears should be well set. More importance should be given to ear placement than ear length and that the ear leather be fine, not thick or heavy. The ears are correct in Figure II-14.

Figure II-14

Neck and Shoulders. The neck is sufficiently long to allow the nose to reach the ground easily, muscular and free from pendulous "throatiness." It rises strongly from the shoulders and arches slightly as it tapers to join the head. The shoulders are well laid back forming an angle with the upper arm of approximately 90 degrees which permits the dog to move his forelegs in an easy manner with considerable forward reach. Shoulders are clean cut and sloping without protrusion and so set that the upper points of the withers are at an angle which permits a wide spring of rib.

While some skin fold is necessary on a fairly long neck, there should not be pendulous folds. A good neck, fitting into well knit, sloping shoulders enables the Cocker to cover ground efficiently. A Cocker with a short neck and straight front assembly is unable to reach full extension and gait will be restricted. This is very faulty.

As seen in Figure II-15, in an effort by breeders to create a taller dog, some current Cockers have suffered loss of proper front angulation. In Figure II-16, the dog's straight front is a serious fault and should be heavily penalized.

Figure II-15

Figure II-16

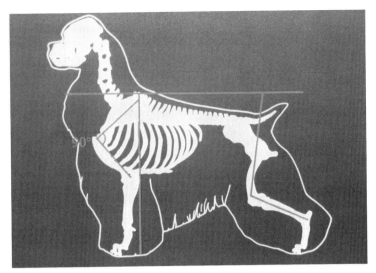

Figure II-17

Since sporting spaniels must move efficiently all day, proper and balanced angulation as seen here, is an absolute must.

Figure II-17 *indicates the ideal angulation for the Cocker Spaniel. The shoulder blade and upper arm form nearly a 90 degree angle. The space between the tips of the shoulder blades should be minimal—about a thumb's width is most desirable. A straight line can be drawn from the top of the shoulder blade and touch the back of the elbow as it falls to the ground. The upper arm is nearly equal in length to the shoulder blade. The elbows fit close to the body, are not prominent, and are set well under the dog.*

The hind legs should have sufficient angulation to balance the front assembly with strong stifle joint and powerful thighs. The hocks are well let down.

Body. The body is short, compact and firmly knit together, giving an impression of strength. The distance from the highest point of the shoulder blades to the ground is fifteen (15%) percent or approximately two inches more than the length from this point to the set-on of the tail. The back is strong and sloping evenly and slightly downward from the shoulders to the set-on of the docked tail. Hips are wide and quarters are well rounded and muscular. The chest is deep, its lowest point no higher than the elbows, its front sufficiently wide for adequate heart and lung space, yet not so wide as to interfere with the straightforward movement of the forelegs. Ribs are deep and well sprung. The Cocker Spaniel should never appear long and low.

The relative height-to-length ratio should be apparent when the dog is in motion as well as when stacked. Cockers should appear to be well up on leg. As shown in Figure II-18, excessive furnishings on a correctly proportioned dog can make it appear too low on leg. The dog shown in Figure II-19 is correctly proportioned.

Figure II-18

Figure II-19

The standard calls for a slightly sloping topline. The dog shown Figure II-20 has a level topline which is incorrect. While the standard calls for a slight slope of the back, the exaggerated slope, as shown in Figure II-21, is increasingly seen in the ring. In Figure II-22, the dog has a correct topline, tail set and carriage, even in motion. The back should be strong and hard, with no

Figure II-20

Figure II-21

tendency toward rumpiness, either standing or moving. Hip bones should never be readily apparent. There should be a good cushion of muscle.

Figure II-22

The ribs must be wide, well sprung and deep. This does not mean so wide as to force the elbows out, as seen on the dog on the right in Figure II-23. The Cocker is never barrel-chested, but the rib cage should have sufficient width and depth to provide ample room for heart and lungs.

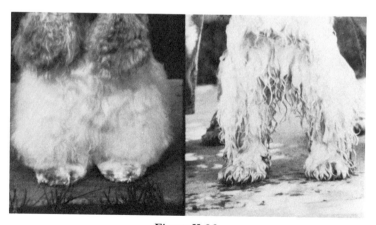

Figure II-23

Tail. The docked tail is set on and carried on a line with the topline of the back, or slightly higher; never straight up like a terrier and never so low as to indicate timidity. When the dog is in motion the tail action is merry.

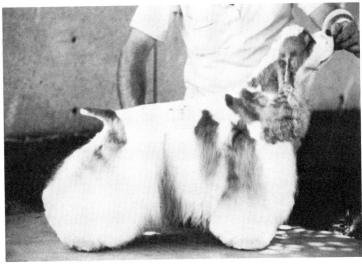

Figure II-24

The tail is the barometer of temperament. The merry Cocker should naturally hold its tail confidently as seen in Figure II-24. The length of the tail should be in balance with the size of the dog—not short and stubby like the example in Figure II-25, nor excessively long. As this is a man-made error, the penalty should be slight.

When the dog is stacked, the tail should never be spiked (pushed unnaturally out of position), although spiking is seen in the ring more frequently than a natural tail carriage.

The set of the tail will determine the tail carriage. A steep croup will cause a low tail set, and a flat one will frequently cause a high tail set. The dog in Figure II-26 has a correct tail set and is being stacked correctly. A slightly higher tail carriage is preferable to a lower one.

Legs. Forelegs are parallel, straight, strongly boned and muscular and set close to the body well under the scapulae. When viewed from the side with the forelegs vertical, the elbow is directly below the highest point of the shoulder blade. The pasterns are short and strong. The hind legs are strongly boned and muscled with good angulation at the stifle and powerful, clearly defined thighs. The stifle joint is strong and there

Figure II-25

Figure II-26

is no slippage of it in motion or when standing. The hocks are strong, well let down, and when viewed from behind, the hind legs are parallel when in motion and at rest.

Feet. Compact, large, round and firm with horny pads; they turn neither in nor out. Dewclaws on hind legs and forelegs may be removed.

Proper construction of legs and feet is crucial in a sporting dog. The dog must be balanced fore and aft with corresponding front and rear angles and sufficient bone for strength and endurance. The clipped down bitch in Figure II-27 shows good balance in angulation and proportion even though her hind

Figure II-27

Figure II-28

feet are incorrectly placed. The well-muscled thighs on the dog in Figure II-28 indicate sufficient muscle mass for propulsion, while the wet dog in Figure II-29 lacks rear angulation.

The portion of the leg from the hock joint to the ground should be short in comparison to the leg from hip to hocks. The rear pastern should be perpendicular to the ground. Trimming and the way a dog is stacked can mislead the eye. For example, in Figure II-30, Cocker Spaniel feet should be large, but

Figure II-29

Figure II-30

heavy furnishings can make the foot look larger than it is. Judges should check the actual size of the foot by examining the pads. This will also reveal the condition of the pads which should be horny, not smooth or flat.

Coat. On the head, short and fine; on the body, medium length, with enough undercoating to give protection. The ears, chest, abdomen and legs are well feathered (as shown in Figure II-31), but not so excessively as to hide the Cocker Spaniel's true lines and movement or affect his appearance and function as a sporting dog. The **texture** is most important. The coat is silky, flat or slightly wavy, and of a texture which permits easy care. Excessive or curly or cottony textured coat is to be penalized.

Figure II-31

The dog in Figure II-32 has an undesirable curly, cottony coat. The standard insists on the importance of sufficient but not excessive, coat. However, Figure II-33 shows a coat that is an example of the norm rather than the exception. The dog in Figure II-34 carries a more moderate coat that does not obscure his outline, which is more desirable.

The standard stresses the importance of correct coat texture as seen in Figure II-35. It is improper coat texture more than amount that can cause grooming problems. A coat with good texture is relatively carefree. Excessive coat is a grave problem in the breed, though the texture in Figure II-36 is very good.

Figure II-32

Figure II-33

Figure II-34

Figure II-35

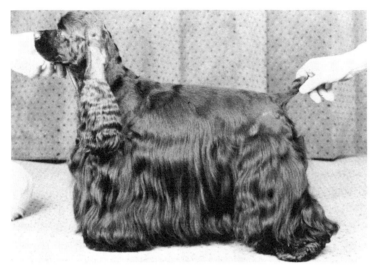

Figure II-36

Although it is not discussed in the standard, grooming is an important element in presenting the Cocker Spaniel. Proper grooming not only enhances the dog's line and elegance, but is also necessary for good hygiene.

Hair that is too long around the eyes, face, and the underside of the ear can lead to infection, so the head is neatly trimmed as seen in Figure II-37.

Figure II-37

Hair around the vent and between the pads of the feet will catch burrs and dirt and render the dog lame, so those areas are carefully trimmed. The trimmed areas should be blended neatly with the untrimmed areas for clean lines. Zealous breeders have cultivated great amounts of coat so that the Cocker Spaniel requires more artful trimming and therefore more careful examination by judges to evaluate the dog beneath the coat. Figure II-38 shows good coat texture and expert trimming.

Figure II-38

Color and Markings. Solid color black, to include black with tan points (as shown in Figure II-39). The black should be jet: shadings of brown or liver in the sheen of the coat is not desirable. A small amount of white on the chest and/or throat is allowed, white in any other location shall disqualify.

While the tan shades can vary, the standard is clear that the black must be solid and shiny. A white spot larger than the area equivalent to a half-dollar should be penalized, but not disqualified.

Any solid color other than black (as shown in Figure II-40) and any such color with tan points (as shown in Figure II-41). The color shall be of a uniform shade, but lighter coloring of the feather is permissible. A small amount of white on the chest and/or throat is allowed, white in any other location shall disqualify.

Figure II-39

Figure II-40

Color of furnishings can vary widely from the body shade. Uniform color is preferred, but texture of coat is more important. A white spot larger than the area equivalent to a half-dollar should be penalized, but not disqualified.

Parti-Color Variety. Two or more definite, well broken colors, one of which must be white, including those with tan points (as shown in Figure II-42); it is preferable that the tan markings be located in the

Figure II-41

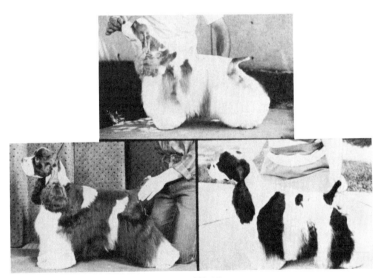

Figure II-42

same pattern as for the tan points in the Black and ASCOB varieties. Roans are classified as Parti-Colors, and may be of any of the usual roaning patterns. Primary color which is ninety percent (90%) or more shall disqualify.

At this time, roan Cockers are very rare.

Tan points. The color of the tan may be from the lightest cream to the darkest red color and should be restricted to ten percent (10%) or less of the color of the specimen. As shown in Figure II-43, tan markings in excess of that amount shall disqualify.

The tan markings shown in Figure II-44, are correct in color and placement.

Figure II-43

Figure II-44

In the case of tan points in the Black or ASCOB variety, the markings shall be located as follows:

1. A clear tan spot over each eye
2. On the sides of the muzzle and on the cheeks
3. On the undersides of the ears
4. On all feet and/or legs
5. Under the tail
6. On the chest, optional, presence or absence not penalized

Tan markings which are not readily visible or which amount only to traces, shall be penalized.

The markings in Figure II-45 are minimally acceptable. Any less tan than this should be penalized.

Figure II-45

Tan on the muzzle which extends upward, over and joins, shall be penalized. The absence of tan markings in the Black or ASCOB variety in any of the specified locations in an otherwise tan-pointed dog shall disqualify.

The specimen in Figure II-46 has correct tan markings. The standard is quite explicit on color requirements. The coloring on the ASCOB Cocker may vary from very light cream (sometimes called silver) to very dark red and liver or brown. The Cockers in Figure II-47 have good color.

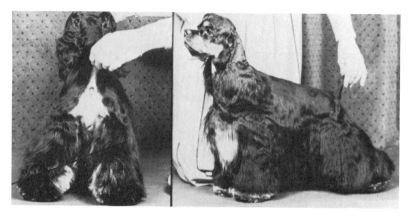

Figure II-46

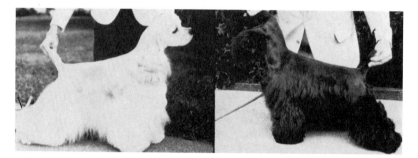

Figure II-47

Movement. The Cocker Spaniel, though the smallest of the sporting dogs, possesses a typical sporting dog gait (as in Figure II-48). Prerequisite to good movement is balance between the front and rear assemblies (as in Figure II-49). He drives with his strong, powerful rear quarters and is properly constructed in the shoulders and forelegs so that he can reach forward without constriction in a full stride to counterbalance the driving force from the rear. Above all, his gait is coordinated, smooth and effortless. The dog must cover ground with his action and excessive animation should never be mistaken for proper gait.

The dog in Figure II-50 has excellent front reach and rear drive. In Figure II-51, the dog's gait is quite restricted. The experienced eye can detect proper front and rear movement regardless of the amount of furnishings. Coming toward you, the dog must show a straight column of support, as seen in Figure II-52. The legs should converge toward a center line of gravity as speed

Figure II-48

Figure II-49

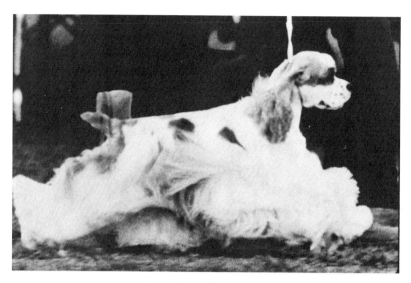

Figure II-50

Figure II-51

Figure II-52

Figure II-53

increases. Seen from the rear, the dog in Figure II-53 moves correctly. Excessive animation, excessive speed, and clever handling should never be mistaken for fluid and correct gait as seen in Figure II-54.

Height. The ideal height at the withers for an adult dog is 15 inches and for an adult bitch 14 inches. Height may vary one-half inch above or below this ideal. A dog whose height exceeds 15½ inches or a bitch whose height exceeds 14½ inches shall be disqualified. An adult dog whose height is less than 14½ inches or an adult bitch whose height is less than 13½ inches shall be penalized. Note: Height is determined by a line perpendicular to the ground from the top of the shoulder blades,

Figure II-54

the dog standing naturally with its forelegs and the lower hind legs parallel to the line of measurement.

Leeway of one-half inch is allowed, a difference hardly apparent to the eye. As a judge, if you have any doubt whatsoever about a Cocker's height, you must call for the wicket. Figure II-55 demonstrates the correct placement of the wicket.

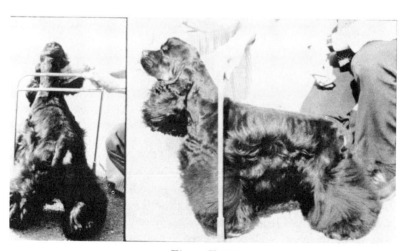

Figure II-55

Disqualifications. *Color and markings* — Black Variety—White markings except on chest and throat. Any Solid Color Other Than Black Variety—White markings except on chest and throat. Parti-Color Variety—Primary color ninety percent (90%) or more. Tan Points—(1) Tan markings in excess of ten percent (10%); (2) Absence of tan markings in Black or ASCOB variety in any of the specified locations in an otherwise tan pointed dog. Height—Males over 15½ inches; females over 14½ inches.

Above all, the Cocker must be free and merry, sound, well balanced throughout, and in action show a keen inclination to work. He must be equable in temperament with no suggestion of timidity.

Breeders and judges must always keep in mind the function of the Cocker Spaniel. He is a sturdy, compact, loving sporting dog whose winning ways in the field and at home have long made him a valued companion.

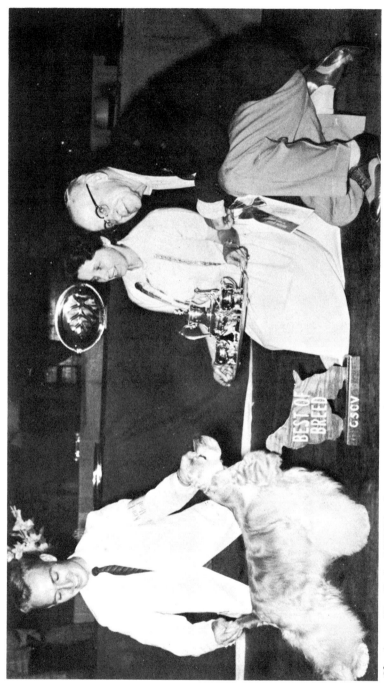

Ch. Artru Hot Rod—ASCOB—shown winning the Breed at the ASC Zone II Show, September 1958. Host Club: Cocker Spaniel Club of Virginia. Best of Breed, Ch. Artru Hot Rod, owned by Mrs. Arthur H. Benhoff, Jr. Photo shows W. Everett Dean, Jr., handler; Mrs. John H. Nugent, III, Host Club President; and judge William Wunderlich.

CHAPTER *2*

Form Follows Function

That form follows function is very important for you, as a breeder, to know. In many ways that is a way to tell the differences in many breeds. A Cocker Spaniel with its long neck—allowing the nose to be close to the ground so its long ears can help waft the scent of game is a good example. The galloping, hunting hound, because of its function, has a unique physical form (flexible spine, arched loin with somewhat sloping croup and low tailset and flat ribs) follows the function which is the speed to run down game and/or kill or hold for the hunter. Or the Dachshund, whose function is to go to ground after game (up to and including the dangerous badger), has the form to perform such work—long, low body, heavy bone and digging feet, and a long, powerful head and jaw.

If you have ever designed anything with functional parts, you know that structural design implies more than bare bones of anatomy. A good design takes into account all factors that will help the structure serve its purpose. Similarly, the structural design of a dog must provide for all the needs of its owner.

In keeping with the principles of good architectural design, body and head structure must take into account the specific properties the animal uses in his work. These materials must be able to withstand the stresses implicit in the design. Therefore, no breeder of a dog designed to herd flocks would think of placing a thin unprotected skin where a tough layer of subcutaneous muscle and bristly coat should go. Here again, the interrelationship of structure and function is obvious—the two go together. One of the most important things in designing and working with any breed is to always keep in mind the inseparability of structure and function. That is, the form of the animal must be designed for the function for which it has been originally bred. Staying with that theme, the American Cocker Spaniel has some major structural problems that must be addressed if it is to perform as its originators desired. Cocker breeders have changed their standard to provide for a dog that is two inches shorter from withers to tail than from floor to withers. This creates a pretty "stacked dog" but a badly-engineered mover. Unless the shoulders are rotated far forward, the dog cannot get out of the way of its correctly-designed rear. This causes the dog to step either inside or outside of his front legs thus forcing him to sidewind down the ring.

Mother Nature, seeing breeders tamper with the natural design of things, has pitched in to help solve the problem. She has helped to create a dog which could move correctly within the standard's measurements. She has done this by rotating the pelvis and croup (thus throwing the angle of the rear quarters further back and allowing for more time for the rear leg swing so the front has time to get out of the way).

What are the consequences of this engineering change? First, logically enough, with the changed angle of the croup, the Cocker now has a terrier tail. How some purists howl about this; not aware that they themselves caused the problem by invoking an improper standard change. The second consequence of the croup angle change is that there are fewer moving dogs who display a sloping topline. A level topline is what the croup change will produce.

The function for which dogs were originally bred is not the function for which they are utilized today. Most Cockers are kept in a house or apartment as the family pet and seldom have the opportunity to demonstrate their specific skills.

To go along with function we have established breed types. That is a physical form which allows the dog to perform its function and around which we can weave an artistic word description. The definition of breed is type. The division of animals into groups of their species, according to differences in physical type, is the basis of breeds. A definite recognizable type must be common to all members of the group. For, without BREED type there is no breed. A BREED is the highest form of a species, that over a number of generations of controlled breeding, has developed definite physical characteristics that, taken together, are the consistent type of that species.

Organic Engineering

You can get a better understanding of the functional aspects of a breed of dog if you think of them in terms of engineering. Consider, for example, the role of the early breeders in England. They had two kinds of jobs. First, they tried to design a useful product: a dog who could go after upland birds, stay close to the hunter, have a good nose, be steady and have the ability to go all day long in the field. Originally these hunting dogs had to put food on the table, only later were they hunted for sport. Then these early breeders had to find a way to manufacture these products. In bringing a new product into being, an engineer first lays out a method of operation. He might even design and build a new tool just for making this one product. With the breeder, he might bring in another breed and cross it and re-cross it and introduce others until he got the correct mixture. The breeder might have to go through dozens of developmental stages before turning out a satisfactory replica of the designed product. But no matter how many steps you must take, a good product engineer (breeder) never departs from the intent of the basic design. He recognizes that the design has a special purpose which his efforts must serve. The farmer in England, who had to protect his livestock and fowl against the incursion of foxes who holed up in dens in rocky lairs, invented a sturdy little dog to take care of that problem. This dog had to get along with the pack of hounds who were to be used to run the fox to ground. Added to the design was the necessity of having a skull and rib cage that were flat enough to allow him to squeeze into any crevice the fox could. Finally, to have punishing jaws to dispatch the fox and haul him out. This little dog was called the Lakeland Terrier. He is about the same size as the Cocker but certainly built for an expressly different function.

But whether we are talking about a dog breeder or an engineer, they both design their products or devise techniques to make use of certain basic designs. For example, an engineer must use only those geometrical figures that would yield desired structural strength. He must also use shapes that will conserve on materials and yet provide for the greatest efficiency. Futhermore, he must also concern himself with simplicity of design. Therefore, whenever possible he must construct simple machines (levers, pulleys, and inclined planes) rather than intricate combinations of these machines.

Obviously, a dog—or any living organism—is its own engineer. Throughout its life, it constantly refers to a basic design and manufactures the product it needs. In so doing, it makes use of the same principles of design that men use in building machines and other conveniences. The dog also makes use of the same mechanical principles that underline the operation of man-made devices. Consider, for example, the transmission of force. When an animal moves its movable parts, it transmits force in much the same way that machines do. In so doing, the animal uses its built-in, simple machines. You can see this quite clearly in locomotor structures and that is why judging the gait of a dog in terms of its ability to perform its function is so very important in the overall approach to judging dogs.

Movement

For many years vast majority of dog people, and even physiologists, believed that animals running at higher speeds would exact a higher "cost" in terms of energy burned—it didn't turn out that way! Recent studies have shown that animals use up energy at a uniform, predictable rate as the speed of movement increases.

As if that shattering piece of information wasn't enough—they found out that for any given animal, the amount of energy expended in getting from point A to point B was the same regardless of how fast the trip was taken. A Cheetah running 100 yards at a top speed of 60 mph, uses the same amount of energy as it would *walking* the same distance. The running is more exhausting because the calories are used up more quickly.

Size, however, does make a difference. Small dogs require much more energy per unit of weight to run at top speed than a Great Dane would. Small dogs appear to have higher "idling" speeds. The cost of maintaining muscular tension and of stretching and shortening the muscles are higher in small animals.

These same series of studies suggest that as much as 77 percent of the energy used in walking comes, not from the operation of the muscles themselves, but from a continual interplay between gravity and kinetic energy. From an engineering standpoint it seems that the body tends to rotate about a center of mass, somewhat like an egg rolling end on end or the swing of an inverted pendulum. The 30 percent of effort supplied by the muscles is imparted through the limbs to the ground to keep the animal's center of mass moving forward.

At faster speeds, four-footed animals appear to be capable of calling into use a work-saving scheme that relies upon the elastic storage of energy in muscles and tendons. Some are better at it than others. Some are capable of storing more energy per stride than others.

During running or trotting the built-in springs for propulsion are the muscles and tendons of the limbs. When the animal has need to move even faster, he has the ability to use an even bigger spring. As the dog shifts from the fast trot to a gallop they tend to use their bodies as a large spring to store more energy. They do *not* change the frequency of their strides, rather they increase the length of them.

Simple Bio-Machines

Let us now consider how the dog compares with man-made machines. The dog can be compared to combinations of simple machines and other mechanical systems you might find in any factory. A few familar examples will quickly clarify this analogy. The dog's legs for example. You could diagram them as levers. The appendages of all animals in fact, serve as levers. If laid out side by side, they would present a rather special array of "machines." As we have certainly seen dogs—from the Chihuahua to the Great Dane—present a wide variety of angles and levers.

Of course you would expect this, for their owners have widely different ways of life. Modifications in such bio-levers reflect the animal's way of life. So you would expect the Saluki's leg to be the kind of lever that gives the advantage of speed and distance. By the same token, you would expect the design of the front legs of the Basset "a burrowing animal," to provide for the multiplication of force, rather than the advantage of distance or speed.

Another simple machine that is easy to detect in nature is the pulley. You will find the living counterpart of the pulley wherever you find a muscle-tendon joint apparatus. Whenever a tendon moves over a joint, it behaves like a pulley. Such mechanisms enable the dog to change the direction of force. A notable example of an application of the pulley principle is the action of the tendons and muscles in the dog's neck. When the handler "strings the dog up" on a tight lead, the ability of the dog to use that pulley correctly is gone. What you have looks like a spastic alligator moving.

Inclined planes are prevalent in all living things, but their presence is not always obvious. They frequently appear as wedges, which are made up of two inclined planes arranged back-to-back. The incisors of the dog, for example, are wedges. The cutting action of these teeth is an application of the wedge principle in nature. The terrier-type of mouth is vastly different from that of the sporting dog. The sporting dog mouth is designed to hold a bird gently without crushing it. Therefore, its construction does not allow for great force to be generated. In contrast, the terrier jaws are punishing and can generate enough force to kill game. Another illustration is when a standard calls for a sloping topline in movement. The sloping plane from withers to tail is designed to harness the thrust or drive from the rear quarters and move the dog along a straight line with power.

Hydraulics and Life

Any person who has tried to dam up a creek, or in some other way tried to manage moving water, has had experience with hydraulics. It involves the application of energy to practical uses. Frequently, therefore, hydraulics deals with the transfer of mechanical energy of moving fluids to the powering of machinery. It also deals with the the use of pressure created by fluids (hydraulic pressure). All this, of course, finds an application in biology, wherein fluid is of paramount importance. Applications of hydraulic pressure are evident in dogs. Certainly the pumping action of the heart (as being responsible for the movement of blood through the circulatory system) is an appropriate example. A standard asking for a deep chest and the front wide enough for adequate heart and lung space is telling us we need room for a pump big enough to keep the dog going under pressure all day long. This pump exerts pressure, directly or indirectly, on all body fluids. As you know, when the heart is in need of repair or is worn out, the blood pressure of the animal varies abnormally. When this happens, the animal finds it hard to maintain a proper fluid balance of its tissues and organs. The final result is interference with the movement of the materials of life. Death can occur if the equipment designed to maintain hydraulic pressure fails in its function. As you may recall from your school studies of anatomy, it takes more than the pumping of the heart to maintain normal fluid pressure in an animal. The condition of the arteries and the veins is equally important. If these circulatory structures do not have the proper strength or elasticity, this condition could cause abnormal variation in the hydraulic pressure of the body. The arteries and veins are fluid conduits. Therefore, they must have a structural design that will enable them to withstand and adjust to sudden changes in hydraulic pressure.

From your studies, you may recall how effectively the design met the need. The walls of the arteries are designed to have heavier muscular construction than the veins. That's because the blood being pumped under great pressure from the heart goes out through the arteries and returns under less pressure through the veins. Thus, the arteries can withstand greater pressure than the veins can tolerate. The arteries tend to be more elastic than the veins so they can react more quickly to changes in pressure and so regulate the movement of fluid to compensate for the change in the situation.

Organic Architecture (Type)

The shape of a building usually reflects its function. The design of its various parts (roof, doors, ventilators) also relates to special functions. So it is with the shape of the dog. In a large dog, the design often calls for a shape that will provide the necessary strength, compactness and capability to perform certain functions. For example, dogs such as the Malamute were used to haul heavy loads. They were designed with a shoulder construction and balanced size that would enable them to perform this function. On the other hand, for example, a long and slender shape characterizes the coursing type of dog (Afghan, Greyhound, Borzoi and Saluki). This shape facilitates the faster movement of energy from place to place. The Cocker, on the other hand, is designed with a balanced shape to be neither a hauler or speed demon, but to go at a moderate pace for a sustained period of time.

In all cases we need to consider how we recognize the shape we are dealing with. First we must consider outline. Outline encompasses every aspect of the individual animal, making it immediately clear as to what breed or species it belongs.

Structure, Shape and Symmetry

As we have noted, overall body shape has a definite relationship to a dog's way of life. It relates, for example, to the use of energy. It also has to do with the animal's ability to relate to its environment and to perform the function for which it was originally bred. As you continue to study dogs, you will see more and more how the shape of things facilitates their function. Take the opportunity to see how the smooth functioning of an animal or of its parts, relates to its function.

A major identifying characteristic of a breed is its head. The head and expression is the very essence of a dog. Without proper breed type, an individual is just a dog, not a Cocker, a Springer or even a Great Dane.

Balance is also very important. No part should be longer, shorter, larger or smaller than is compatible with the whole. Everything must fit together to form a pleasing picture of "rightness."

Most breed standards call for a short back. Rightly so, for this is where the strength is. However, a short back is not synonymous with a short dog. The back is actually that small portion of the topline which lies between the the base of the withers and the loin. A dog with a long sloping shoulder and a long hip may give the impression of a longer dog. A dog which gives the impression of being taller than it is long, is a dog badly out of balance. This dog is quite likely to have such a short croup that it appears to have none at all. A short steep croup will straighten the leg bones and leads to a highly ineffective and inefficient rear movement. A dog properly angulated at one end, but not on the other, is in even worse balance.

The too-upright shoulder is probably the worst imbalance of all because it affects every other part of the body. It puts great stress on a moving dog, making it pound its front feet into the ground, or crab sidewise to avoid interference with its hind feet.

As you look at your dog in the yard at home, in the show ring or out in the field working birds, look for the features of its design that might account for its survival and popularity. Look for the relationship of structural design to vital functions. Ask yourself: "How is this shape most suitable for the function of this structure?" "How is the body shape of this animal related to the environment in which it has to live?" In searching for answers, go beyond the obvious facts and look for subtle relationships. Look for special problems. For example, in reading many of the breed magazines today, we find breeders bewailing the promiscuous breedings and the terrible things that have happened to their breed. They often point out their breed is no longer able to perform its primary function because of straight shoulders, over-angulated rears or too much coat. Their claim is the breed is no longer functional. FORM NO LONGER FOLLOWS FUNCTION! . . . What are the breeders of today going to do about it?

CHAPTER 3

A Standard Needing Inspection

The previous two chapters covered the current standard and its interpretation and opened the door on a discussion of structural engineering in dogs. This chapter discusses the standard from a different point of view.

Does it seem to you that the higher Cocker registrations climb, the fewer Cockers win Best in Show? That's a startling thought! Unfortunately, it's true.

The standard change of 1972 was probably the most significant change in breed history and might well be the root cause of the lack of Best in Show and Group awards.

Conversations with other Sporting Group judges around the country have left me with the definite impression that something is "rotten in Denmark." Among their most persistent comments are:

1. The Cocker can't get out of the way of its over-angulated rear.
2. His back is so short he hasn't got room to execute proper leg extension fore and aft.
3. I have never seen such steep shoulder placements.

If these were the kind of comments that came from a few judges I would overlook them. However, they have become too numerous to ignore and they are coming from some of the top all-breed judges.

Earlier mention was made of the standard change which, within a decade, caused a serious change in the structure of the Cocker Spaniel. The previous standard described the Cocker as being as tall (at the withers) as he was long (from the top of the withers to the set-on of the tail). The winning dogs of the day did not look like that. They tended to look shorter. The standard committee changed the description of the dog to fit the dog being shown; so that now he is supposed to measure two inches shorter from withers to set on of the tail, than he is tall. A wise change? Maybe not. What are some of the ramifications of this change fifteen years later?

Before going into the matter specifically, there are major issues that should be addressd that have a bearing on the discussion. The first is: Should a breed standard be consistent or should it be changed because the breeders of the day have produced a different kind of dog? The question is one that has faced many breeds. If you look at the Sporting Group overall you can recognize an English Setter or an Irish Setter circa 1925, or 1975, as a specimen of that breed looks the same. Perhaps somewhat fancier today, but the same dog. Looking at the American Cocker Spaniel for those same years it's a totally different story. It's almost as if a new dog had been substituted every twenty-five years. Figure II-56 illustrates these time tables in the evolution of the Cocker Spaniel.

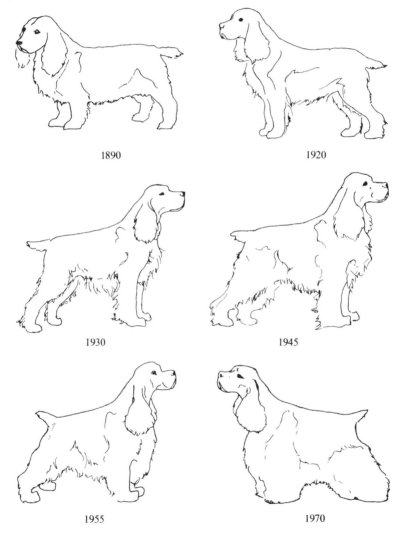

1890

1920

1930

1945

1955

1970

Figure II-56. Evolution of the Cocker

Gradual evolution has happened in most breeds. However, with the Cocker, it is still going on. When will it stop? Have breeders gone too far and created a non-sporting dog? A "non-hunter" who may not really belong in the Sporting Group?

The second issue is the one for which breeders in most breeds are famous; that is, "if some is good a lot must be better." It's as if breeders looking at the 1972 standard change said "OK, if you want a short back, I'll really give you a short back." I remember a cartoon from the time when the auto industry was being forced to acknowledge the in roads the Japanese had made with their small cars. It showed the president of Gigantic Motors shouting to his Board of Directors, "All right, if we have to build a compact car, we will build the biggest damn compact around."

Let's see what has been created by the 1972 standard change. The standard described a dog who ideally (in the pre-1972 change) was 15 inches tall and 15 inches long to the base of the tail. That was the blueprint, and the breeders built their machine tools to turn out a product that fit the blueprint. A sloping topline was called for, which breeders found a bit hard to achieve in a square dog, so we redesigned the jigs and rotated the shoulder forward to give additional height at the shoulder. Figure II-57 illustrates this change. This now gives us more topline but at what price?

A forty-five degree shoulder angle has two main advantages over any other configuration. First, it has two and a half times more ability to propel the dog forward. And second, because the blade is longer, it can rotate the leg forward and backward in a longer arc. Due to the fact that the dog can reach further back, this type of shoulder propels the dog more forward than upward, reducing fatigue. The upright shoulder causes the leg to propel the dog in too high an arc, thereby causing strain and lack of efficiency. This would be similar to our hopping as we moved—more up than straight ahead. Such dogs tend to break down quickly in the field. Dogs who bounce like this should *not* win, but they do. It seems their competition is doing the same thing.

The dog with the straight shoulder wears himself out, through the pounding his front end has to take, by having to hit the ground before his full forward motion has been expended; and he hits with a bang. It's like tripping, and in recovering our balance we come down hard on one foot. Imagine the concussion each time a pad hits the ground in this manner. Exhibitors seldom realize the wear and tear on the dogs, for they are shown only a short time in the ring. The rest of the time they are in a crate or in a run with limited room. They don't have a chance to really run hard and breakdown. It's a pity our dogs are not hunted more, for this would quickly bring home the point.

Let's now return to our inspection of the standard. While it calls for

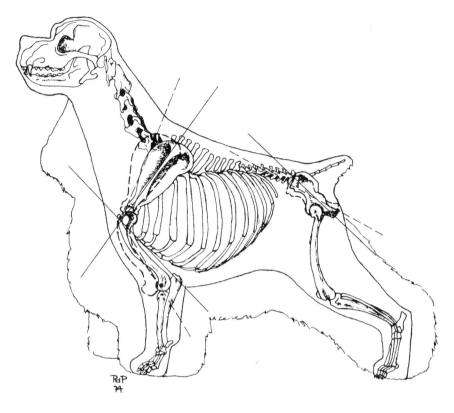

Figure II-57. Solid lines represent skeleton of ideal specimen, while broken lines represent deviations resulting from forward rotation of bones at withers and croup.

a shorter-backed and taller-at-the-shoulder dog, it continues to call for a 45 degree shoulder angle. Mother Nature thinks this is tough to do and provides her own solution; a steeper shoulder. If only the standard committee had called for a moderately angulated rear to go with such a shoulder. But, unfortunately, there is no mention made of any changes in the rear quarters. As a result, breeders continue to produce an over-angulated rear (which seems to be the curse of our breed). A moderately angulated rear would not propel the dog beyond its shoulders. When coupled with the prevalent steep front it could provide more direct usable power.

The most efficient way to transfer power from the rear pads to the dog itself is a straight line. The leg with less angulation presents a more compact, straighter line than does the well angulated leg.

Once again, Mother Nature has had to step in to save us from ourselves. She has attempted to reassert her need for balance in all living things by changing the angle of the croup on the Cocker Spaniel. By changing the angle so that it allows the rear quarters to rotate backwards slightly, she has allowed a later leg swing by the rear quarters. Thus, allowing the steep-shouldered front to clear out of the way in time for the rear legs to set down in the place just vacated by the front pad. If this had not occurred the dog would overdrive his front, and would have to place his rear quarters either inside or outside the front legs, thus causing him to sidewind down the ring.

The telltale sign that this change has been effected is the terrier tail on a dog whose standard calls for a level tail. Interestingly enough, the framers of the 1972 standard added language about the tail that states it should be "never straight up like a terrier . . ." Funny, they were trying to prohibit something that helps the unbalanced dog they created move decently.

In order for the Cocker Spaniel to conform to the wording of the standard, "The docked tail is set on and carried on a line with topline of the back or slightly high; never straight up like a terrier," much selective breeding will have to be done and a greater understanding of the dog in motion will have to be gained.

The tail cannot be considered as an appendage by itself. It is a part of the spinal column which is made up of at least 30 separate vertebrae; seven in the neck, thirteen in the thorax, seven in the loin area and three sacral. Figure II-57 illustrates the skeleton of the dog and shows the spinal column. In addition, the dog's tail as an appendage is made up of from three to twenty-three caudal (tail) vertebrae. This too, can be seen in Figure II-57.

One of the major ways of determining correct rear construction is the appearance of the croup, which is that section just before the tail. Croup contour, which influences, to a great extent, the tail set of all breeds, can add to or detract from structural balance. Because of its docked tail, the Cocker Spaniel resorts to a spread stance for static balance. One wonders if docking had not been carried out, how might the balance and moving characteristics differ? The tail set serves, almost as an x-ray, in determining the hip bone angle, which is generally 30 degrees. This short, rounded section behind the pelvic crest can be labeled as flat when the sacral and part of the coccygeal vertebrae appear above the horizontal and, as they extend rearward, often tend to rise (sometimes sharply) to achieve a high tail set. Thus, the statement "the dog is flat in the croup," simply means that in relation to the horizontal, there is a lesser downward slope to this section of the dog's rear assembly. This can be seen in Figure II-57 as well.

The "terrier tail" has become widespread throughout the breed. There must be a good structural reason for it and there is. You can read more about this in the chapter entitled "Form Follows Function."

In dogs the tail is an essential aid in the maintenance and recovery of equilibrium. Balance appears to be necessary in everything that moves. It should be noted that the tail is an integral part of a kite and the tail, or similar surfaces, are necessary for airplanes as well.

When viewing the dog from the rear, slow-motion photography shows that the tail serves well as a stabilizer in helping to control lateral motion. These shifts which are necessary for gait to occur, can cause rolling or torsion.

When a dog begins to move forward, the loin is flexed, or arched, by groups of muscles. This arch of the loin is the "starter" for the effective vertical flexing necessary for agile movement. The next step, the flattening of this arch of the loin, is accomplished by the contraction of powerful muscular tissue (which has its origin on the hip bone and has attachments along the spinal column extending into the lower neck). This straightening action (can be likened to the squeezing of an accordian), will:

1. Aid greatly in initial acceleration, as forward-weight mass gives an assist to hip rearing muscles.
2. Tend to flatten the croup and possibly elevate the tail.
3. Tend to displace forward reach of rear and minimize crabbing.

During this sequence of events, there is a tendency for the dog to lower its head, to tighten up and elevate its tail as it breaks into a fast trot. This flattening of the croup is a positive barometer of this action taking place and the shifting forward of the weight center for more effective propulsive effort.

In the Cocker Spaniel, which is minus a part of his tail, this shifting is accomplished by compensatory forces taking over. As we have all observed, the Cocker tends to have a wider and more extended rear stance than most breeds. This is needed to secure lateral stability. The Cocker Spaniel typically carries its head from about a 9:00 to 9:30 o'clock position. The Irish Setter, for example, carries its head closer to a 10:30 o'clock position. This is often why we have great cheers for the Irishman in the group, as it streams around the ring making a noble picture indeed, with its head up there in the clouds.

Alas, many at ringside are not aware that the flushing Spaniel generally is not designed to hold its head that way. But many Cockers with this type of head carriage have been winners. While this is true, it presents a real challenge to breed and train a dog with this head carriage while having the correct balance, action and style.

The moderately low head carriage of the Cocker was designed for field activity. After all, the Cocker is a flushing Spaniel and its head is carried low to pick up the scent of the bird.

Let's now look at what the ideal stance and gait characteristics should be when viewed from the side. In the unposed stance, the head and the well-arched neck should be carried at about the 9:30 o'clock position. The topline should be slightly sloping and flow into a nicely-rounded croup, with the tail carried on a line with the topline or slightly higher. As the Cocker moves into a fast trot, there is a slight initial lowering of the head to a 9:00 o'clock position, then rising again as the dog hits its stride. Its smooth, far-reaching stride is enhanced by its head carriage, which gives a desirable balance between lift and reach. The tensing or flattening of the loin gives matching tail carriage at, or just above, the backline. A quick, upward twirl of the tail is to be expected when rapid acceleration takes place.

In the early 1960s, it was apparent that the breed was changing. A 55 degree shoulder angle was beginning to become the norm, giving an up-on-leg look, and supposedly enabling the Cocker to compete more successfully in the Sporting Group. Also, over the years, the angle of rotation of the pelvis was changing from the normal 30 degrees as breeders sought to further "let down" the rear end to give a more extreme topline. This type of construction has basically altered the support along the longitudinal plane. This altered hip placement is shown in Figure II-58. The support center falls vertically from the hip joint and

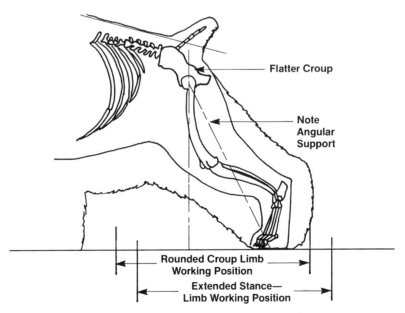

Figure II-58. In the extended stance, the hip joint lacks vertical support and the dog is usually out of longitudinal equilibrium. Note the sloping backline and flatter croup.

almost always terminates somewhat forward of the rear pad. This can be termed the "apparent working center." There is seldom any vertical support, or at least not in this kind of posed show position. How many specimens have you seen that look like they are posing with their stifles almost touching the ground?

Earlier it was mentioned that the American Cocker Spaniel standard describes a dog with a back shorter than the dog is tall and calls for a short-coupled dog. This description does not necessarily mesh with the exclusion of the "terrier tail."

A steeper-shouldered dog with shorter coupling would tend to overdrive its front with its well angulated rear. The timing of the rear action is such that the rear pad arrives forward a fraction before the straighter shoulder can snatch the front pad out of the way.

To compensate for this problem, Mother Nature has struck back to keep things in balance. Apparently she has attempted to change the rearward angular static support. To do this, she has begun a change in the well-rounded croup—to a flatter one. The dog can still have an extended rear, but its propulsion angles will be somewhat straighter and in some instances, probably more effective. Figure II-58 shows this changed stance. Since flattening of the croup and the rotation of the pelvis tends to bring limb work rearward, as is also shown in Figure II-58, the limb swinging arc of the dog with the flatter croup is a bit more rearward of the well-rounded one. This allows better timing between front and rear, allowing the front legs to get out of the way of the driving rear ones. There has now been produced a dog with a flatter croup which in turn produces a terrier-like tail, but with rear construction that allows proper gait. The outline looks a bit longer, but the dog will most likely measure properly down the back.

Once an evolutionary trend begins, it is most difficult to arrest. As a result, the flatter croup with its "terrier tail" effect is likely to continue rather than disappear. Saying "it's not right" will not make it go away. Paying proper attention to breeding a forward assembly with the proper shoulder layback is the only way to correct the problem. Once this change is accomplished, the rear assembly will begin to change also. Until, once again, breeders produce a dog with a nearly 45 degree angle of shoulder and a pelvis with a 30 degree matching angle, there will continue to be "terrier-tailed" American Cocker Spaniels.

Continuing this evaluation of the standard. With the steep shoulder to give height and the over-angulated rear to give slope, our friend the Cocker Spaniel, in a show pose, now looks like a ski jump at Lake Placid. Breeders, of course, have tried to fit these two "unbalanced" parts together with an extremely short back. Good support principles say a dog should have a "short back," but *within* reason. In the first place, breeding a dog that is higher than long is asking for trouble. It's just bad dog engineering. The rest of the breeds in the Sporting Group must think so too, for their standards emphasize balance. Their standards emphasize a square dog, or insist upon enough room between front and rear quarters so a dog can move properly. The Irish Setter standard might be of some help. It states under body length, "sufficiently long to permit a straight and free stride." Many judges would only add that adequate length of body is important to good movement. No matter how well the legs, shoulders, etc., are assembled, if the body is too short the rear legs will interfere with the front.

A correct specimen always exhibits balance whether standing or in movement. Each part of the dog flows and fits smoothly into its neighboring parts without calling attention to itself. A *well balanced* dog possesses neither glaring faults nor overdone features. The various features are in *correct* relation to one another. The Cocker Spaniel standard with its emphasis on a two-inch differential (between height and length), is out of balance.

Crabbing and sidewinding have already been discussed. The dog may also "elect" to solve his problem by other methods. He can hold his front legs off the ground longer, by extreme tensing of the front legs' muscles, causing padding. To the ringside spectators, this looks like the dog is floating along and evokes ecstatic applause from novice onlookers who think this is the ultimate. What it is, however, is a condition that would cause a dog to break down in the field because of the stress on the front-end musculature. Another solution the dog may apply is lifting the front legs up high to get them out of the way of reaching, rear legs. This also looks flashy to the inexperienced. However, it is extremely faulty and is called "hackney gaiting." A dog with this gait is going up and down with little forward progress. This gait is not correct in a sporting dog. Figure II-59 shows a well balanced dog in motion. Notice how the front foot does not interfere with the straight-ahead rear action. It gets snatched out of the way just as the rear foot lands in almost the same spot that the front foot just vacated. The other legs show full extension front and rear.

Now, what to do about all this? Cockers are a fortunate breed because there have always been capable and dedicated people serving as officers and committee chairs of the parent club. Over the years, the standard committee has come under able leadership and there have been no wild-eyed heretics attempting to revolutionize the standard. So why take aim at some portions of the standard? It's simply because of the belief that the standard change of 1972 has not turned out as intended. Mainly, the description of the body which states "the distance from the highest point of the shoulder blades to the ground is fifteen percent (15%) or approximately two inches more than the length from this point to the set-on of the tail."

Figure II-59. A well-balanced Cocker in motion.

This has been taken to mean that the dog is shorter than he is tall. This is not so! Most sporting dog standards state the body should be short from shoulders to hips, and the distance from the forechest to the back of the thigh should approximately equal the height from the ground to the top of the withers.

With this kind of guideline, breeders could truly understand what the pre-1972 standard wanted to say but didn't: There should be a square dog.

The current steep-shouldered specimen has to lack forechest since by rotating the shoulder forward it would have to take away from the forechest and brisket. Therefore, the dog lacking forechest will not measure shorter in length *overall* than his height. A dog with a well laid back shoulder (45 degrees) will have forechest and should measure the same in both horizontal and vertical planes. It is generally believed the framers of the 1972 standard change meant to keep our dogs as sporting dogs—in balance—but also wanted to emphasize that *the Cocker Spaniel is never long and low.* What was intended and what happened are two different things.

Somehow breeders seem to have lost sight of the part of the standard that states "he is a dog capable of great speed, combined with great endurance—*well balanced throughout.*" A dog with steep shoulders may be able to move fast, but there can be *no endurance* without a forechest (room for heart and lungs). Add the over-angulated rear to this configuration and you have a dog that wouldn't last long in the field.

Look closely at the Labrador Retriever standard which states "a dog well balanced in all points is preferable to one with outstanding good qualities and defects." Such a statement at the outset of the Cocker standard might go a long way in getting rid of the steep shouldered, over-angulated rear specimens who are also coat factories. Ann Rogers Clark, the "noted all-arounder," insists that the judge always keep in mind what the dog was bred for—and for the Cocker that was to hunt upland game. Breeders can keep a pretty dog who can work birds if they clarify the standard a bit. No radical change is needed or even wanted.

Breed standards are retrospective. They can only describe the most desirable features in relation to dogs who have previously existed. They cannot anticipate the development of features which may occur and may be valued as improvements because dogs possessing them win. A great many knowledgeable people contend that the more extreme hindquarter angulation coupled with the steeper shoulder are *not* improvements.

These changes could not have come about without the approval of judges and breeders. Judges, by themselves, cannot change the standard. Someone had to produce these specimens. Breeders will continue to produce dogs the public wants and judges place. Therefore, the judge and his interpretation of the standard is the key to putting the Cocker back into the Sporting Group.

Adding some clarifying language to the standard might help the judges. Suggested new portions are italicized.

Under the General Section

The Cocker Spaniel is the smallest member of the Sporting Group. He has a short, compact body and a clean chiseled and refined head, with the overall dog in complete balance and of ideal size. *A dog well balanced in all parts is preferable to one with outstanding good qualities and defects.* He stands well up at the shoulder on straight forelegs with a topline sloping slightly toward strong, muscular quarters. It is a dog capable of considerable speed, combined with great endurance, *and in order to achieve this, his fore and rear quarters must work in harmony.*

Under the Section on Body

The body is short, compact and firmly knit together, giving an impression of strength. The distance from the highest point of the shoulder blades to the ground *is approximately equal to a measurement from the forechest to the back of the thigh, presenting a square appearance.* Ribs are deep and well sprung. While a Cocker Spaniel never appears long and low, *the body must be sufficiently long to permit a straight and free stride.*

This kind of clarification would go a long way toward helping judges and breeders understand the standard so it could be properly used as the "official yardstick."

One last gasp! Why not ask the standard committee to modify that part of the standard on coat so that it states that—excessive coat is to be *severely* penalized?

The way today's judges interpret the standard reminds me of a story. At the intermission of a play, an elderly gentleman—puffing on a big cigar—was standing in the theater lobby under a big sign that said "no smoking." An usher came along, pointed at the sign, and asked him to put out the cigar. The elderly gentlemen continued to smoke. When the agitated usher again pointed to the sign, the elderly gent replied, "It doesn't say positively."

SECTION III
The Basis of Heredity

- *Basic Genetics*
- *They Come in Coats of Many Hues*
- *Analyzing a Pedigree*

CHAPTER 1

Basic Genetics

Consistent breeding of show-quality dogs should be considered an art. To some breeders it comes naturally, others have to learn this art. Still others will never achieve success in this vital and important facet of pure bred dogs.

To some breeders "having an eye for a dog" is second nature. Breeders lacking this natural talent can become self-taught provided they have the intelligence and motivation to discern between the good and poor examples set before them.

Consistent breeding of show-quality specimens depends on important factors besides the natural or acquired talents of the breeder. The breeding stock itself is of prime importance and should be the very best the breeder can obtain. Many breeders still operate under the illusion that second best will produce as well as the choice specimen, pedigrees being equal. This will hold true in isolated instances, of course, but it will not hold true consistently.

Another important element contributing to the success or failure of any given breeding program is that of chance. Everything else being equal, sex distribution, puppy mortality, timing, transmission of the best factors (or the poorest), etc., all depends to a great extent on chance.

There is no shortcut to breed improvement—no miraculous or secret formula which can put Mother Nature out of business and place the breeder in full control. There are, however, many do's and don'ts which can be used as a formula of sorts to minimize the chances of failure and to encourage the chances of success. These do's and don'ts are axioms of our breed, yet there are breeders who ignore and bypass them.

The first step in your breeding program is to decide what is ideal. Until a breeder knows what kind of specimen he wants, he is stopped cold and can neither select the best nor discard the worst. This is where the breeder's capabilities and talents come into play. For this is the basis of selective breeding, and the backbone of any breeding program.

Characteristics such as height and coat color are known as inherited traits. They are traits which an offspring "inherits" or receives from his parents. Every living thing has an inheritance, or "heredity." Inherited traits are passed along from generation to generation. As a result of heredity, each generation is linked to older generations and to past generations. For example, a dog may resemble his parents with respect to height, head shape, and coat color. His grandsire or great grandsire may have also possessed the same identifying features.

A whole science known as genetics has grown up around the study of heredity. Specifically, the science of genetics is the study of how the reproduction process determines the characteristics of an offspring and how these characteristics are distributed.

According to Anthony Smith, writing in *The Human Pedigree*:

> Gregor Mendel, a 19th-century monk living in Czechoslovakia, is credited as the founder of genetics. Basically, Mendel's work had proved that traits can be passed from one generation to the next, both with mathematical precision and in separate packets. Before this time, it had been assumed that inheritance was always the result of being colored water of a weaker hue. Mendel foresaw genes, the differing units of inheritance (that are named, incidentally, after the Greek for race). Genes remain distinct entities. They do not blend, like that of colored water. They produce, to continue the analogy, either plain water, or colored water or a mixture between the two. Moreover, assuming no other genes are involved to complicate the story, they continue to create three kinds of product in generation after generation. The packets remained distinct.
>
> The mathematics also has a pleasing simplicity at least in the early stages. The human blue-eye/brown-eye situation is a good elementary example. There are genes for brown and genes for blue, everybody receives one of each from each parent. To receive two browns is to be brown-eyed. To receive two blues is to be blue-eyed. To receive one of each is also to be brown-eyed because the brown has the effect of masking the relative transparency of the blue.

This also signifies that brown is dominant over blue and will always cover over the recessive blue color. Blue will only be expressed when it, as a recessive, is inherited from both parents.

The clarity of Mendel's vision certainly helped science. It was assumed that all of inheritance was equally clear cut, with a ratio of 3:1, or his equally famous ratio of 9:3:1 (involving two characteristics) explaining all of our genetic fortunes. So they do (in a sense) but the real situation is *much* more complex. Only a *few* aspects of inheritance are controlled by a single pair of genes. Only a few more are controlled by two pairs. A feature like height, for example, or coat color may be organized by twenty or so pair of genes. Each pair is working in a Mendelian manner, but the cumulative effect of all of them working together is a bewilderment. The mathematics still have the same precision, but it is only for mathematicians, not for the rest of us. As for a feature like intelligence, with the brain differentiated to fill a tremendous range of different tasks, its inheritance cannot be thought of in a simple ratio of any kind.

There are literally thousands and thousands of paired genes within each animal. There are enough of them, and enough possible variations, to ensure that each specimen is unique. Never in history has there been a duplicate of any specimen. Never in all of future history will there be another one just like it again. Each dog is a combination that is entirely individual and yet his/her genes are common to the population they live in. There is nothing unique about them.

Piggybacking now upon Mendel's work and that of later scientists, let us look at how breeders can use this knowledge and breed better dogs.

Each dog contains a pair of genes in each of its cells for each trait (characteristic) that it inherits. One of the genes is contributed by the sire and the other by the dam. When a black dog is bred to a buff one, all the first-generation offspring will be black. Each parent contributed one gene for color to each offspring. Since they were different colors, the offspring were hybrid. One parent, contributed a "factor" for black color while the other parent passed along a "factor" for buff coat color. Why, then, were all the hybrid offspring black? Because black is *dominant* over buff.

The recessive characteristic (buff) was the hidden or masked one that did not appear in the hybrid offspring. A dog can show a recessive trait such as a buff coat, only when both factors (genes) are recessive in one individual (remember the blue-eye/brown-eye example?). The dominant trait will appear when one or both genes are present.

When a dog is dominant for a trait it is called homozygous for that trait. When it carries recessive genes for that trait *i.e.*, "plush head," it is called heterozygous.

To clarify the matter a bit, let's see what happens when an all black hybrid specimen is crossed with another just like it. Every hybrid can pass on to each of its offspring either the black or buff characteristics. Therefore, buff and black has a 50/50 chance of being transmitted to the offspring. These hybrids have a black (dominant) gene and a buff (recessive) gene. Let's symbolize them B-Dominant, b-Recessive. Since the combination is random, the ways in which these can be combined in a hybrid × hybrid cross are shown in Figure III-1. As shown, it is possible to predict not only the possible combinations of factors, but also the probability for each of the combinations.

Chance plays a part in both the biological and physical worlds. By "chance," it is meant events that happen at random. Mendel was aware of this and knew something of the laws of probability. He used these in explaining his results. These laws say: "Be wary of interpreting the occurrence of a single random event." However, it goes on to postulate that if large numbers of occurrences of the same event take place at random, there is a kind of order in the result, in spite of the uncertainty

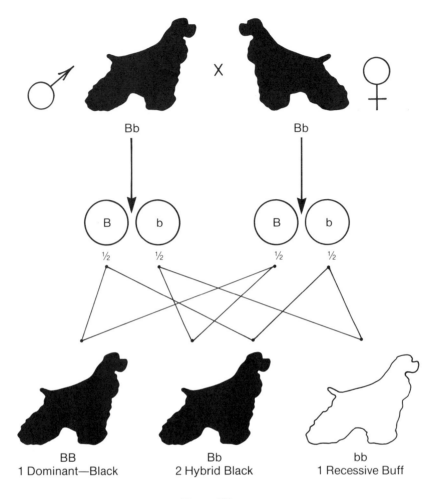

Bb × Bb

B ½   b ½   B ½   b ½

BB
1 Dominant—Black

Bb
2 Hybrid Black

bb
1 Recessive Buff

Figure III-1

of the occurrence of a single event.

By moving from the inheritance of a single trait to the inheritance of two traits simultaneously, life gets a bit more complex. Start by breeding a homozygous (pure) black dog that is tall (also homozygous) to a short buff specimen that is also homozygous for its traits. Naturally enough, the breeding produces tall black offspring, since those traits are dominant. They look exactly like the black parent. Take these hybrid (heterozygous) offspring which are hybrid-tall, hybrid-black and mate them with like specimens. The resultant types can be quite interesting. There might be four different types produced. There could be a small black type and a tall buff one. These types are new combinations of the two traits.

Continuing in this vein, and for all other traits as well, the distribution ratio turns out to be just about 9:3:3:1. This means for every nine tall, black dogs in a hybrid × hybrid mating there should be three tall dogs with buff coats, three small dogs with black coats and one short, buff specimen.

A quick glance at the above will show twelve tall dogs to four short ones and twelve blacks to four buffs. Both demonstrate the 3:1 ratio already established for the inheritance of a single trait in which segregation occurs.

For example, Mendel and later researchers also uncovered the fact that tallness is independent of color. This is called the "law of independent assortment" and is supported by numerous experiments. The probability of two or more related events is calculated by multiplying the individual probabilities. Thus, if the probability of one event occurring is $\frac{1}{4}$ and the probability of a simultaneous event is also $\frac{1}{4}$, then the probability of the two occuring together is $\frac{1}{4} \times \frac{1}{4}$, or $\frac{1}{16}$. That is, one in every sixteen.

In breeding for color in dogs, we find that the majority of factors which determine coat color appear to be "single factors," inherited according to Mendel's laws. However, many of these color factors are influenced by other genes which have the ability to modify the expression of the "key" gene in numerous ways and thus account for considerable variation in the finished product. As an example, while a dog may possess the "key" genes which have the ability to create the black and tan pattern, independent modifying genes may alter its appearance by restricting or allowing full expression to the tan pigment in its coat, so that it looks like a black dog or a tan dog.

Though the color of a dog's coat may be determined by a single gene or by a pair of genes, the skeletal structure of a dog is determined by the interaction of a large number of genes. It should be easy to understand why something as highly complex as the structure of a dog's head or body is controlled by the actions of multiple hereditary factors.

Movement is a good example. No one gene labeled "gait" has the ability to determine whether an individual puppy will move properly or improperly. Rather, there are countless genes, working in concert which determine these facts.

What factors enable an individual dog to move in a way which has been designated as correct for its particular breed? Every breed has a characteristic gait, which is determined by its structure; not the structure of the legs, or the feet, or the hips, or the shoulders, but the structure of all the parts working in concert for this breed. Thus, the Chow Chow moves with short steps and stilted action, the Pekingese and Bulldog "roll" along, the Miniature Pinscher has its hackney gait and the German Shepherd Dog covers ground rapidly with far-reaching steps and a smooth action. These differences in gait are the result of differences in structure—the manner in which all the body parts are assembled in an individual.

Whether a stifle is straight or short, or whether a foreface is deeply chiseled or built up is not determined, in all probability, by hereditary factors alone. When breeders seek to determine the manner in which any part of an animal's skeletal structure is inherited, they are not dealing with single-factor inheritance, but with multiple-factor inheritance.

Any attempt to explain multiple-factor inheritance fully would prove to be a real puzzle, for most dog breeders have no formal training in advanced genetics. However, the following facts may serve to give a better understanding of this complex subject:

1. What is seen and described as a single character (a leg, a foot, a tail, etc.) is often affected and influenced in its development by a large number of different and unrelated genes which are capable of independent assortment.

2. It is extremely difficult to sort out the various genes which influence a particular characteristic and to determine the specific effect each has on that characteristic. In other words, just how important is a given gene in the development of a particular characteristic?

3. Some genes have a direct, complete influence on the development of a character (dominant genes). Some have only a partial effect, being neutralized to some extent by the action of the opposing member of the pair of which it is one (incompletely dominant genes). Some genes are completely masked and have no effect unless such genes comprise both members of a given pair (recessive genes).

4. The combination of multiple gene effects together with environmental influences, is the rule rather than the exception in such characteristics as body length, height, weight, head and muzzle development, tooth characteristics, foot size and shape, muscle and bone development, and such recognized faults as loose shoulders, flat ribs, cowhocks, weak pasterns and splay feet. As an example, body size depends upon some genes that affect all the tissue and upon others that influence only certain regions, such as the legs, neck, head or tail. In addition, diet, exercise and other environmental influences determine the degree to which genes are able to stimulate and produce growth of the different tissues, organs and body parts.

There are some 130 breeds eligible for registration with the American Kennel Club. None of the breeds is "pure bred" in the true genetic sense of the word. All of them are subject to variations of form and type which may account for considerable differences in appearance between specimens of the same breed. Unlike certain strains of laboratory mice, which have been standardized by inbreeding and selection, and which are like peas in a pod, no breed of dog exists which duplicates its own kind without variation.

Major differences between breeds are probably due to independent genes which may be found in one breed and not in another. Therefore, the manner in which the multiple hereditary factors responsible for the construction of a Greyhound's body are inherited, may differ from the manner in which countless genes which build a Chihuahua's body are inherited. To understand the manner in which complex parts such as the body, legs, head, and other structural parts are inherited, the following will be necessary:

1. Observations of a large number of animals, resulting in careful and accurate records of the differences in structure which exist within the breed.
2. Accurately recording breeding tests between the animals of contrasting structural types, and recording observations of their resultant offspring. This may well require the crossing of breeds at one or more genetic research laboratories (as was done in the controlled experiments done by Dr. C.C. Little at the Jackson Memorial Laboratory of Bar Harbor, Maine). In this way, extreme types can be compared and the inheritance of marked differences in structure can be studied.
3. The making available of these records to scientists who are qualified to analyze them. The task of breeding and raising a large enough number of animals representing different breeds, the recording of observations of their structural types and the types of their offspring is beyond the finances and ability of any one person or any one institution. However, such data could be collected by breeders at no additional expense and a small amount of additional work. Each breeder's records could be sent to a central laboratory for analysis and any resulting conclusions could, in turn, be made available to breeders.

What kind of questions pertaining to inheritance in dogs can geneticists answer right now? Information pertaining to a great variety of subjects is available, including: color differences found in the coat, eyes, and skin of most breeds of dog; differences in the length, quantity, texture and distribution of hair; various reproductive problems such as fertility, fecundity, the production of stillborn or non-viable young, and such conditions as monorchidism; various abnormalities of the eye; malformations resulting from arrested development such as harelip, cleft palate, cleft abdomen, etc.; such diseases as hemophilia and night blindness; differences in ear, eye, nose, jaw, foot and tail characteristics; differences in head size and shape; and numerous physiological differences resulting in characteristic patterns of behavior.

Many of the characteristics in the above list are influenced by multiple genes and/or are affected in varying degrees by environmental factors. Therefore, the available information pertaining to most of these subjects is incomplete; though in some breeds and for some characteristics it is surprisingly extensive. New information is being added daily, as geneticists all over the world make their contributions available.

Many breeders have practiced linebreeding (grandfather to granddaughter, etc.) but have only skirted around the edges of inbreeding (brother to sister, father to daughter, and mother to son matings) shying away from carrying it to its full potential. As a means of finding out which animals have the best genes, inbreeding deserves more use than it has received. Not only does it uncover recessives more surely than any other method, but also, it increases the relationship between the inbred animal and its parents and other relatives so that the animal's pedigree and the merits of the family to which it belongs become more dependable as indicators of its own genes.

Considerable inbreeding is necessary if family selection is to be very effective. The gene is the unit of inheritance, but, for our purposes, the animal is the smallest unit which can be chosen or rejected for breeding purposes. To breed exclusively to one or two of the best specimens available would tend to fix their qualities, both good and bad. In fact, that is the essence of what happens under extreme inbreeding. Moreover, the breeder will make at least a few mistakes in estimating which animals have the very best inheritance. Hence, in a practical program, the breeder will hesitate to use even a very good stud too extensively.

The breeder also is far from having final authority, to decide how many offspring each of his bitches will produce. Some of his basic stock may die or prove to be sterile or will be prevented by a wide variety of factors from having as many get as the breeder wants. Bitches from which he wants a top stud dog may persist in producing only females for several litters. Consequently, he must work with what he has because he did not get what he wanted from more desirable specimens.

The ideal plan for the most rapid improvement of the breed may differ from the plan of the individual breeder chiefly in that he dare not risk quite so much inbreeding deterioration. If the object were to improve the breed with little regard for immediate show prospects, then it would be a different story. This is an important point and deserves more attention.

Inbreeding refers to the mating of two closely-related individuals. Most breeders practice inbreeding to a limited extent, even though they may call it "close line breeding." Actually, the breeding of half brother × half sister, as well as niece × uncle or nephew × aunt is a limited form of inbreeding. For purposes of this discussion, however, inbreeding will refer to the mating of full brother × full sister, father × daughter, and son × mother. Most breeders probably consider these three categories as representative of true inbreeding.

It is not the purpose of this chapter to advocate or condemn the practice of inbreeding, but rather to ascertain what it can and cannot accomplish. It will also be the objective to present known facts and dispel some common fallacies.

It would certainly be interesting to know exactly what percentage of inbreeding takes place in various breeds and what results are obtained. Speaking in generalities, it would probably be safe to say that only one or two percent of all champions finishing within the past ten years were the products of inbreeding. On this basis, it would be reasonable to conclude that the practice of close inbreeding on these terms is relatively rare.

In the breeding of domestic animals, such as cattle, chickens, etc., as well as plant breeding, inbreeding is regarded as a most valuable tool to fix a desired type and purify a strain. This raises the question as to why inbreeding has not gained more widespread acceptance among dog breeders. By combining inbreeding with the selection of those individuals most nearly ideal in appearance and temperament, the desired stability of the stock is quickly obtained.

Breeding the offspring of the father × daughter or son × mother mating back to a parent is called "backcrossing." To illustrate this, suppose an outstanding male specimen is produced and the breeder's thought is to obtain more of the same type: the male is bred back to his dam, and the breeder retains the best bitch puppies in the resulting litter. By breeding these back to the excellent male (backcrossing), there is a good chance that some of the puppies produced as a result of this backcross will greatly resemble the outstanding sire. In backcrossing to a superior male, one may find some inbreeding degeneration in the offspring, but this is improbable according to Dr. Ojvind Winge in his book, *Inheritance in Dogs*.

The mating of brothers × sisters is far more likely to produce inbreeding degeneration. This is because a brother × sister mating is the most intense form of inbreeding. Studies show that those breeders who have attempted to cross full brothers and sisters, for the purpose of fixing good characteristics in their stock, give very contradictory reports of their results. It has been found that the mating of brother × sister results in somewhat decreased vitality and robustness in the offspring.

It may happen that abnormal or stillborn individuals are segregated out in the litter if special genes are carried in the stock. Everything depends upon the hereditary nature of the animals concerned. Inbreeding degeneration is of such a peculiar nature that it may be totally abolished by a single crossing with unrelated or distantly related animals. However, if it had made its appearance, the breeder should know it was present in the hereditary make-up of his stock.

Most of the studies on inbreeding are in agreement with one another. The decline in vigor, including the extinction of certain lines, follows largely the regrouping and fixing (making alike) of *recessive* genes which are, on the whole, injurious to the breed. However, along with the fixing of such recessives, there is also a fixing of gene pairs which are beneficial and desirable. It is a matter of chance as to what combination gene pairs a family finally comes to possess, except that selection is always at work weeding out combinations that are not well adapted to the conditions of life. There is a common belief that inbreeding causes the production of monstrosities and defects. Seemingly reliable evidence indicates that inbreeding itself has no specific connection with the production of monstrosities. Inbreeding seems merely to have brought to light genetic traits in the original stock. Inbreeding does not *create* problems or virtues, it *uncovers* them.

One of the most interesting and extensive investigations of inbreeding in animals was done by the U.S. Department of Agriculture. Thirty-five healthy and vigorous females were selected from general breeding stock and mated with a like number of similarly selected males. The matings were numbered and the offspring of each mating were kept separate and mated exclusively brother × sister. Only the best two of each generation were selected to carry on the succeeding generations.

Two striking results followed this close inbreeding. First, each family became more like itself. While this was going on, there was a gradual elimination of sub-branches. Second, there was a decline in vigor during the first nine years, covering about 12 generations. This decline applied to weight, fertility and vitality in the young.

During the second nine years of inbreeding, there was no further decline in vigor of the inbred animals as a group. This stability was taken to mean that after 12 generations, the families had become essentially pure-bred—that is, no longer different with respect to many genes.

What does all this mean in relation to breeding good dogs? From the foregoing data, several conclusions come to mind. Inbreeding coupled with selection can be utilized to "fix" traits in breeding stock at a rapid rate. These traits may be good or they may be undesirable, depending entirely upon the individual's hereditary nature. Inbreeding creates nothing new—it merely intensifies what is already present. If the hereditary nature of an individual already contains undesirable traits, these will naturally be manifested when the recessive genes become grouped and fixed. This applies to the desirable traits as well.

The term "genotype" refers to the complete genetic make-up of an individual, in contrast to the outward appearance of the individual, which is called "phenotype." In selecting puppies to retain for breeding stock, breeders must rely on phenotype because they have no way of

---

knowing an unproven individual's genotype. Inbreeding can reduce genotype and phenotype to one common denominator.

Suppose that an outstanding specimen appears as the product of inbreeding. What would this mean in terms of breeding? It would mean that this specimen has a greater chance of passing on his visible traits rather than possible hidden ones. Prepotent dogs and bitches are usually those that are pure for many of their outstanding characteristics. Since such a limited amount of inbreeding has been carried on in most breeds, prepotent specimens have become pure for certain traits more or less by chance, for they have appeared in most breeds as products of outcrossing, as well as by line breeding. Since line breeding, and especially close line breeding, is a limited form of inbreeding, the same good and bad points apply to line breeding, but in a much more modified degree. The practice of inbreeding appears to be extremely limited in dogs, so one must assume that breeders are willing to trade slower progress for a lower element of risk with respect to degeneration.

Now to review present conclusions insofar as a breeding program is concerned. Assume that you have selected a given bitch to be either line bred or outcrossed and the proper stud dog which compliments her has been chosen. The breeding has been made, the puppies are tenderly watched over, and have begun to grow up. Hopefully, it will be a good breeding and the results will yield several good prospects, all carrying the dam's good traits but showing great improvement in the areas where she needed help. But what if it doesn't turn out this way? What if the breeding results in general disappointment with none of the puppies showing much improvement? You might well ask how this can possibly happen when all the proper aspects were taken into consideration in planning this breeding.

Remember the concept of "dominance"? Test breeding is the only true way of determining whether a dog or bitch is especially dominant. Here again, line breeding comes into play, for the closely line-bred dog or bitch has a *much* better chance of being dominant by virtue of a concentrated bloodline than the dog or bitch that is not line bred. When selecting a stud to compliment your bitch, it is important to take into consideration the qualities of his parents as well. For example, suppose a stud is sought to improve the bitch in head. Obviously, a dog with a beautiful head is chosen, but it is also important that his parents had beautiful heads. Then the stud can be considered "homozygous" for this trait. If the dog selected does not have parents with beautiful heads, or only one parent has a beautiful head, he is said to be "heterozygous" for this characteristic and his chances of reproducing it are diminished. Dominant dogs and bitches are homozygous for more of their traits, while less dominant dogs and bitches are primarily heterozygous in their genetic make-up.

The great majority of dogs and bitches are probably dominant for some of their traits and not especially dominant for others. It is up to the breeder to attempt to match the proper combination of dominant traits, which is why the dog and bitch should compliment each other— that being the best practical way of attempting to come up with the right combinations. There are some dogs and bitches that are completely non-dominant in their genetic make-up when bred to a dominant partner, so good things result provided that their partner is of top quality. In this fashion, a number of dogs and bitches in a breed have "produced" top-quality offspring when they themselves were of lesser quality. When a non-dominant bitch is bred to a non-dominant stud, the resulting litter is bound to be a disappointment. When a dominant bitch is bred to a dominant stud it is possible that the resulting litter will be a failure. This explains why some "dream breedings" result in puppies which do not approach the quality of either parent.

There are some dominant sires which pass on their ability to produce to their sons which, in turn, pass on their producing ability to their sons, etc. Likewise, there are dominant bitches which pass on their producing ability to their daughters, granddaughters, great grandaughters, etc. Thus, some lines are noted for their outstanding producing sires and/or bitches. Such a line is a true "producing bloodline." A producing bitch, usually with a heritage of producing bitches behind her, bred to a proven stud dog will usually come through with those sought-after champions. To this, only one additional qualification need be added— that the breeder exercise some degree of intelligence.

Much discussion between breeders has centered on the subject of which parent contributes the most, the sire or the dam. As we have seen, each contribute 50% of their genetic heritage; but by so doing, their respective factors of dominance and recessiveness are brought into play. Thus, in reality, there is not an equal contribution. If there were, there would be no outstanding producers.

The producing bitch is a very special entity unto herself. Those fortunate enough to own or to have owned one will surely attest to this. When a bitch has produced champion offspring she is singled out for recognition, and well she should be. Depending upon his popularity, the stud dog's production is unlimited; this is not true in the case of the bitch. Many stud dogs, in achieving a producing record, have sired hundreds and hundreds of puppies. The average bitch will produce between 20 and 30 offspring in her lifetime, which drastically limits her chances of producing champions in any great numbers. Taking this limitation into account, it becomes quite obvious that those bitches which produce quality in any amount must possess an attribute different from the average. That attribute is dominance.

The producing bitch may or may not contribute the qualities she herself possesses. Her puppies will, however, bear a resemblence to one another and to subsequent puppies she will produce, regardless of the sire. Whether closely line bred or outcrossed, whether bred to a sire of note or to a comparative unknown, the consistency of quality and type will be apparent in the offspring.

There is no foolproof way to determine in advance those bitches destined to become "producers." The odds will have it, though, that their dams were producers and their granddams and even their great-granddams. Chances are, they will come from a line noted for the producing ability of its bitches.

Occasionally a bitch will come along with little or no producing heritage close behind her, yet she will be a standout in producing ability. It can only be assumed that such a specimen inherited a genetic make-up "different" from that of her immediate ancestors, or else the potential was always there, but remained untapped until some enterprising breeder parlayed it to advantage. There are known instances when specific bitches will produce only with one particular dog and not with others. In such cases, the desired results are achieved through an ideal "blending" rather than by virtue of dominance. It might be well to mention the fact that some bitches are extremely negative. Such a bitch bred to a prepotent sire will necessarily produce only as a result of the stud's dominance.

The availability of a true producing bitch is necessarily limited. Whereas all are free to breed to the outstanding sires of the breed, few have access to the producing bitches. Their offspring can and should command top prices; demand always exceeds supply. Their bitch puppies especially are highly valued, for it is primarily through them that continuity is achieved.

The producing bitch imparts something extra special to her offspring. Though all but impossible to define, this "something extra" is determined genetically, as well as the more obvious physical traits which are handed down. She is also a good mother, conscientious but not fanatical, calm, and possessing an even temperament.

In summary a basic knowledge of genetics will allow the breeding of better specimens and thus improve the breed. It is not possible to be a successful breeder by hit and miss breedings. Hoping that Dame Fortune will smile on you is trusting to chance; not scientific principles. Utilizing the contents of this chapter and other parts of this section will enable a conscientious breeder to score and score well in the winners circle.

Ch. Pinetop's Fancy Parade—ASCOB—shown winning the Breed at the January 1961 National Specialty of the ASC. Owned by William J. Laffoon, Jr. and Rose Robbins. L to R: Dr. John Eash, President; Norman Austin, handler; Clyde S. Heck, judge.

CHAPTER 2

They Come
In Coats of Many Hues

Because of the great variety of colors allowable under the Cocker Spaniel standard, color genetics have always held a fascination for the breeder. No sooner is a breeding made than the breeder begins to wonder what colors the litter will contain. Unfortunately, many breed on a "hit or miss" basis and are completely surprised by the results.

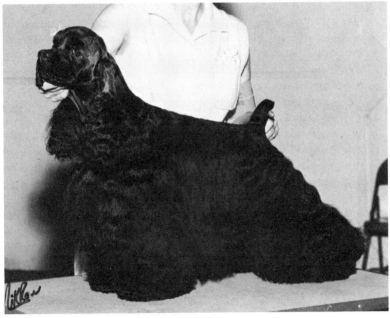

Ch. Bobwin's Sir Ashley—A Black Cocker Spaniel.

Blacks

"A good dog is a good color" is a statement that is often quoted and one with which most breeders seem to agree.

As noted in the chapter on Genetics, certain physical traits can be associated or linked with certain colors. This is much less the case today because of the use of the dilute type breeding in all three varieties. This has caused a "homogenization" process of the varieties.

Thirty years ago the blacks were generally acknowledged as being superior to all other colors. Viewing a show from ringside, an impartial observer of the time would have been forced to concede that the blacks, and parti-colors were two separate breeds.

One of the major differences between the blacks and the Cockers of other colors was coat. Only a few of the black and tans carried good coat. A buff or parti-color with a heavy coat was rarely seen. Therefore, the most obvious physical trait associated with the blacks was coat.

There were also other superior traits with the blacks. Among these traits were flatter and heavier bone, better top line, shorter backs, smoother muscles (and different muscular placement), better chiseling, etc. This all pointed to the fact that a color linkage (a tendency of certain characteristics to appear together because the genes for those characteristics are located on the same chromosome) exists between the black color and desirable features of conformation.

This was proven time and again when black puppies born of parents that were other than black tended to be of "black type" while litter mates of other colors were not.

Many sparsely coated buffs and parti-colors were bred to blacks in the hope of attaining coat. However, in the resulting litters only the black offspring carried "black type" coats. This highlights a key factor in color breeding and one focused on throughout this chapter, namely with the infusion of the dilution gene, certain blacks can pass on "black type" characteristics to their recessive colored offspring.

With blacks, as with Cockers of all colors, there are multiple geno-types (genotype is the sum of a dog's contribution to its offspring—phenotype, on the other hand is surface color or other characteristics). The surface color does not tell the full story. It is necessary to do test-matings or have pedigrees that are truly informative as to what the dogs in the preceding generations produced. (See Analyzing a Pedigree chapter for more information on the meaning behind pedigrees.)

As breeders, most have long believed that there was a dominant black and a recessive black, and only one kind of liver; the same was thought to be true for the buff color. These assumptions are not entirely true. The following pages delve into the various color combinations that are possible within the breed. Certainly a wide variety of colors is possible, but not always accepted by the breeders. The sable and sable/white colors are an example. Many people bred them and some finished their championships, but their adherents were unable to muster the 2/3 vote necessary to allow them a place in the standard. Today we are seeing

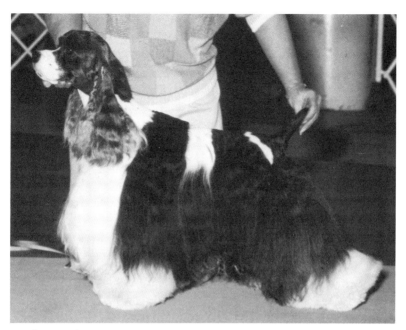

Ch. Paradise's Blue Rebel Rouser—A Blue and White Cocker Spaniel.

some breeders beginning to push a "bluish" color dog. Its fate remains to be seen. Figure III-2 illustrates the nine levels of dominance in the breed. As you will note, there are four distinct types of blacks. The Class Number 2 black explains how the dilute blacks came about. The dilute black is, in reality, a buff dog who is black in all his characteristics—the same genotype but different phenotype—he lacks the ability to extend his black factor into his coat color.

There is no way to differentiate these four types of black just by appearance. Knowledge of specific pedigrees can point out differences in some cases but the true test comes in breeding.

All mating ratios given here are based on the laws of averages. The larger the litter, the better the chance of coming up with the specified ratios. The smaller the litter, the poorer the chance. However, should the smaller litter be repeated once or twice more, the breeder would then find the specified ratios would probably hold true. Today the vast majority of blacks are of the Class Number 2, Class Number 3, and Class Number 4 hybrids. Alas, the dominant black is seldom found, for breeders—in their desire to get a variety of colors—have not sought to perpetuate this characteristic. Naturally, when a dominant black is bred to any other color only blacks will result. The section on mismarks spells this out further.

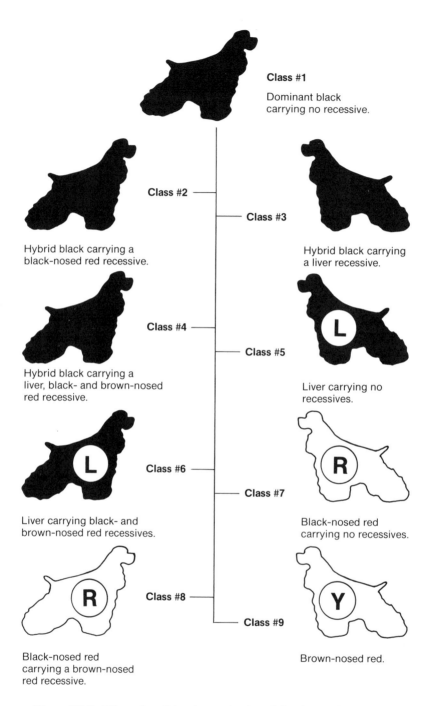

Class #1

Dominant black carrying no recessive.

Class #2

Hybrid black carrying a black-nosed red recessive.

Class #3

Hybrid black carrying a liver recessive.

Class #4

Hybrid black carrying a liver, black- and brown-nosed red recessive.

Class #5

Liver carrying no recessives.

Class #6

Liver carrying black- and brown-nosed red recessives.

Class #7

Black-nosed red carrying no recessives.

Class #8

Black-nosed red carrying a brown-nosed red recessive.

Class #9

Brown-nosed red.

Figure III-2. Hierarchy of dominance in the solid-color Cocker Spaniel.

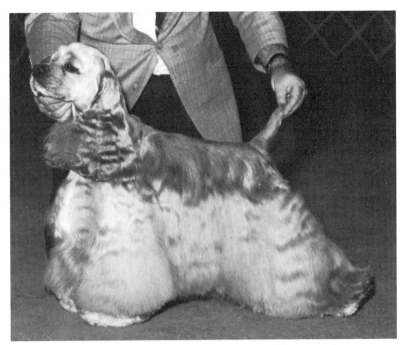

Ch. Tompark's Little Rock—A Buff Cocker Spaniel.

Buffs

Many years around the show ring have impressed me with the fact that there are more hues of buff coloration in Cockers than in any other breed. What makes "buff" so difficult to describe is the ambiguity of terminology—not only among breeders but also among geneticists. Such terms as "blond," "golden," "red," "dark buff," "silver," etc., all describe the buff-colored Cocker Spaniel. That same latitude is found in the black and tan Cocker whose description states the color may be from the lightest of cream to the darkest of red. Those same spectrum ranges are to be found in the buffs.

All of the variations in color describe phenotypes, but genotypically there are only three types of buffs. Two are described as "black-nosed reds" and one is called a "brown-nosed red."

The black-nosed reds can be differentiated only by test matings, for they produce quite differently from other buffs. One, the Class Number 7 black-nosed red, will not throw liver color regardless of the color of dog to which he is bred. This dog does not carry liver genes. He is further described under the section on chocolates (see Figures III-3a and III-3b). This Class Number 7 black has been called a "dilute black." In fact, he is a black who lacks the extension factor (the ability to extend

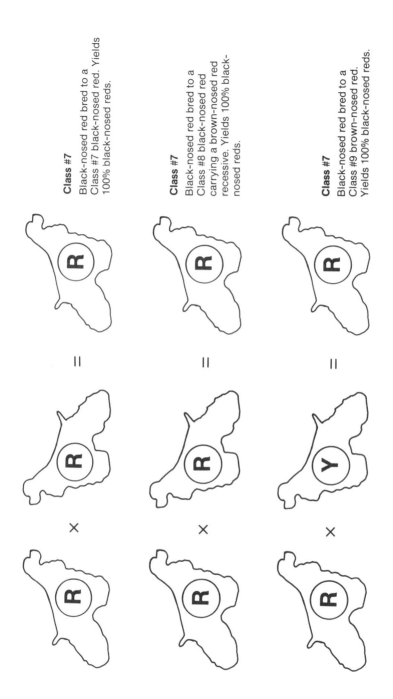

Class #7

Black-nosed red bred to a Class #7 black-nosed red. Yields 100% black-nosed reds.

Class #7

Black-nosed red bred to a Class #8 black-nosed red carrying a brown-nosed red recessive. Yields 100% black-nosed reds.

Class #7

Black-nosed red bred to a Class #9 brown-nosed red. Yields 100% black-nosed reds.

Figure III-3a. Buffs.

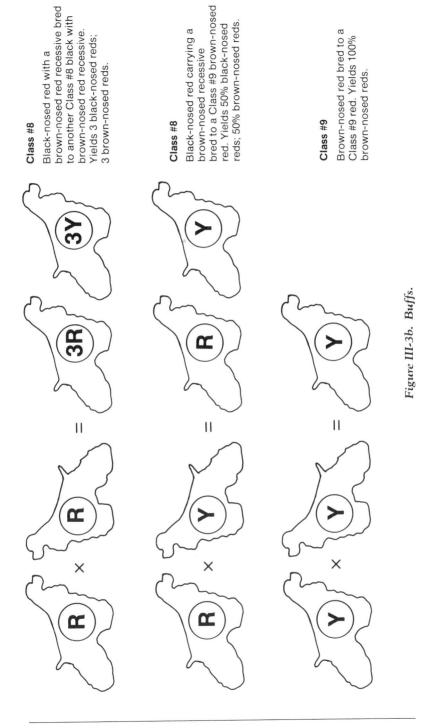

Class #8

Black-nosed red with a brown-nosed red recessive bred to another Class #8 black with brown-nosed red recessive. Yields 3 black-nosed reds; 3 brown-nosed reds.

Class #8

Black-nosed red carrying a brown-nosed recessive bred to a Class #9 brown-nosed red. Yields 50% black-nosed reds; 50% brown-nosed reds.

Class #9

Brown-nosed red bred to a Class #9 red. Yields 100% brown-nosed reds.

Figure III-3b. Buffs.

black color throughout his coat). His nose, paws, and skin are usually blue/black or blue/black spotted. This dilute black has revolutionized the buff Cocker. Due to a genetic crossover (as explained in the next paragraph), it can pass black characteristics to all other colors. Before a "crossover" occurred, this was not possible. The Class Number 7 black-nosed red which has often been called a "black-nosed yellow, lacking the extension factor for black coat color," is genetically black in type and conformation but lacks the coat color. Now this is important! Because of the dilution factor, it is impossible to obtain dark reds and chocolates from breeding to a Class Number 7 black-nosed red.

Certain structural changes are commonly associated together. This is due to a phenomenon known as "linkage." Any body characteristic which is located in one pair of chromosomes—and in no other—will be inherited in accordance with Mendelian laws. Characteristics which have determiners (or genes located in different chromosomes) will be independent of one another in transmission. All possible combinations of them will occur just as various combinations of numbers appear when dice are cast . . . according to the laws of chance.

When two characteristics have genes located on the same chromosome, they will stay together so long as the chromosome remains intact. Such characteristics are said to be "linked."

It is known that chromosomes are, at times, in close contact with their mates. At such a stage, breaks sometimes occur—usually at the same level in each chromosome of the pair. If the breaks are repaired in such a way as to cause the upper part of one chromosome to become attached to the lower part of its mate and vice versa, a regrouping of the genes occurs in the new cell. Such a phenomenon occurring in a germ cell is called "crossing over." This is illustrated in Figure III-4.

Where it has been possible to study crossing over by statistical methods, it has been found that the phenomenon occurs in definite percentages for the same characteristics. A single characteristic can have more than one gene, each of which may be located on a different chromosome. These act together in a cumulative manner. Research indicates that a crossover probably occurred in the buffs in the immediate ancestry of Ch. Maddie's Vagabond's Return. Literature of the day described dogs that are strikingly similar to the dilute blacks as we know them today.

The second type of black-nosed red is known as a Class Number 8 dog. While the Class Number 7 specimen appears to be yellow, lemon, or cream-colored, the Class Number 8 dog ranges the spectrum from light buff to dark red. The Class Number 8 dog can be used to produce both chocolates and dark reds.

Last, there is the brown-nosed red, or the Class Number 9 dog. Like the Class Number 7 buff, he is not really a buff at all. He is a chocolate

1

The two chromosomes are lying
side by side.

2

They are twisted.

3

They break and recombine.

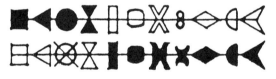

4

The new alignment of genes in
the two chromosomes.

Figure III-4. Crossing over. Each geometric figure represents a gene. Alle-lomorphic genes occupy the same level on the two chromosomes. Identical shapes represent homozygotes; slightly different shapes represent heterozy-gotes. It will be noted that the linkage between the two adjacent heterozy-gotes below the break is unaffected, whereas the linkage between either of these and the heterozygote above the break is reversed. Where the characters on the two chromosomes were homozygous in the first place, the recombina-tion has no effect on linkage.

lacking the ability to extend color throughout his coat. Instead of black markings on the skin and pads, this type of buff has chocolate markings. When bred to one type of chocolate, the Class Number 9 dog will produce only chocolates. When bred to a Class Number 6 chocolate, he will produce 50% chocolates. These three buffs—whose phenotypes look basically alike—are genetically different.

Ch. Pineshadows Coco Cub—A Chocolate Cocker Spaniel.

Chocolates

Liver or chocolate Cockers have been known in the breed since early times. Early breeders, unable to get dark eyes and noses and an acceptable coat, gave up on chocolates, for it was impossible to predict how they would reproduce.

Today, largely through the efforts of Arline Swalwell of Windridge Kennels, and the late Bill Ernst of Be Gay Kennels, handsome chocolates compete successfully within the ASCOB (Any Solid Color Other than Black) variety.

As in the buffs, there is more than one type of chocolate. Figure III-5, shows that there is a Class Number 5 chocolate as well as a Class Number 6. The only way to determine *which* type chocolate is by test-

Class #5

Liver carrying no recessives bred to each other. Yields 100% liver.

Class #5

Liver carrying no recessives bred to a Class #6 liver carrying black- and brown-nosed red recessives. Yields 100% livers.

Class #5

Liver carrying no recessives bred to a Class #7 black-nosed red. Yields 100% blacks.

Figure III-5a. Livers (Chocolates).

Class #5   Liver carrying no recessives bred to a Class #8 black-nosed red carry brown-nosed red as recessive. Yields 50% black and 50% liver.

Class #5   Liver bred to a Class #9 brown-nosed red. Yields 100% liver.

Figure III-5b. Livers (Chocolates), cont'd.

Class #6 Liver bred to a Class #6 liver each carrying a brown-nosed red recessive. Yields 75% liver and 25% brown-nosed red.

Class #6 Liver carrying a brown-nosed recessive bred to a Class #8 black-nosed red carrying a brown-nosed recessive. Yields 25% black, 25% black-nosed red, 25% liver, 25% brown-nosed red.

Figure III-5c. Livers (Chocolates), cont'd.

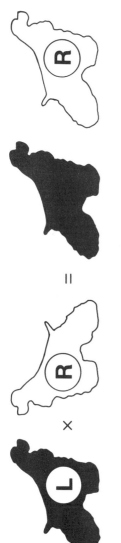

Class #6 Liver carrying a brown-nosed red recessive bred to a Class #7 black-nosed red. Yields 50% black, 50% black-nosed reds.

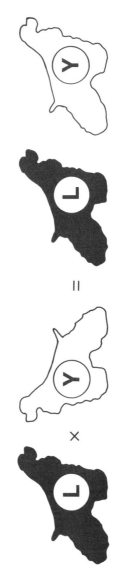

Class #6 Liver carrying brown-nosed red recessive bred to a Class #9 brown-nosed red. Yields 50% liver, 50% brown-nosed red.

Figure III-5d. Livers (Chocolates), cont'd.

matings. The Class Number 5 dog, when bred to another Class Number 5 specimen, produces only chocolates. When the Number 5 dog is bred to a Class Number 6 type, again only chocolates are produced. However, when two Class Number 6 types are bred together, the predicted ratio is three chocolates to one brown-nosed red.

When buff dogs are bred to each other, no matter what their genotype, they cannot produce chocolates. Even the brown-nosed reds of Class Number 9 (which was described as a chocolate without the extension factor for chocolate color in its coat), when bred to another brown-nosed red, will produce only brown-nosed reds. It is evident, then, that in the hierarchy of dominance, solid black is first, followed by chocolate and then the buff/reds.

In the chocolates, hair grows as long, or nearly as long, as in the blacks but tends to have a softer, more wooly texture. From this, it can be concluded that wooly hair in chocolates is probably dominant. It is also important to know that in chocolates light noses and light eyes are dominant over dark.

In further discussions, this chapter will deal with hybrid-blacks, buff/reds, and chocolates. Figure III-6a–b shows that a specimen cannot carry as a recessive, *the color of one above it in dominance.* Chocolate can be carried by a hybrid-black and can be reproduced at any time. The hybrid-black may also be carrying a recessive for buff/red, as well as black and tan and parti-color. A treasure chest this one!

The illustrations in Figures III-6c–k give a good picture of what possible combinations can be realized in a solid-color breeding program. For more detailed information, I refer you to *Breeding Better Cocker Spaniels* by the author and published by Denlinger Publisher's, Ltd.

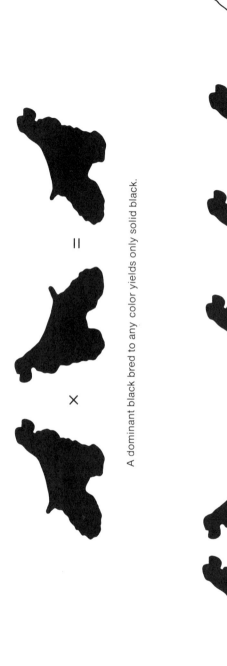

A dominant black bred to any color yields only solid black.

Two hybrid blacks (Class #2), each with a buff parent, yields 75% black and 25% buff (black-nosed red).

Figure III-6a. Blacks.

A hybrid black (Class #2) with one buff (black-nosed red) parent bred to a hybrid black (Class #3) with one liver parent and not carrying the recessive buff gene. Yields 100% blacks.

A hybrid black (Class #2) with one buff (black-nosed red) parent bred to a hybrid black (Class #3) with one buff (brown-nosed red) parent. Yields 75% black, 25% buff (black-nosed red).

Figure III-6b. Blacks, cont'd.

A hybrid black (Class #2) with a black-nosed red recessive bred to a liver (Class #5) not carrying the buff factor. Yields 100% blacks.

A hybrid black (Class #2) with a black-nosed red recessive bred to a liver (Class #6) carrying the buff factor (brown-nosed red). Yields 75% black and 25% buff (black-nosed red).

Figure III-6c. Blacks, cont'd.

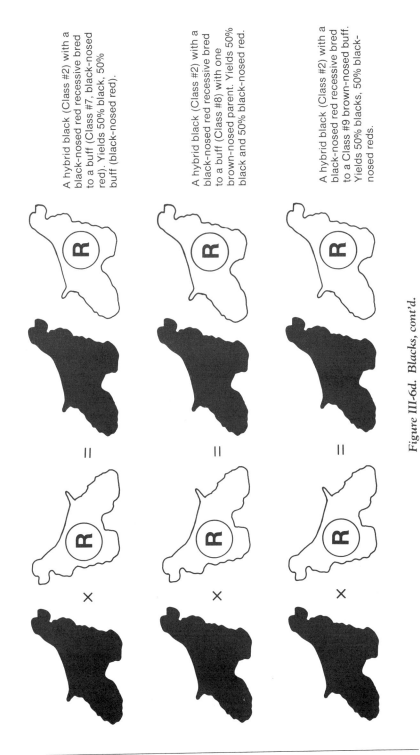

A hybrid black (Class #2) with a black-nosed red recessive bred to a buff (Class #7, black-nosed red). Yields 50% black, 50% buff (black-nosed red).

A hybrid black (Class #2) with a black-nosed red recessive bred to a buff (Class #8) with one brown-nosed parent. Yields 50% black and 50% black-nosed red.

A hybrid black (Class #2) with a black-nosed red recessive bred to a Class #9 brown-nosed buff. Yields 50% blacks, 50% black-nosed reds.

Figure III-6d. Blacks, cont'd.

A hybrid black (Class #2) with a black-nosed red parent bred to a Class #9 brown-nosed red. Yields 50% blacks and 50% black-nosed reds.

A hybrid black (Class #3) having a liver recessive bred to another hybrid black with the same factors. Yields 75% blacks and 25% livers (chocolates).

Figure III-6e. Blacks, cont'd.

A hybrid black (Class #3) having a liver recessive bred to a Class #4 black having liver and brown-nosed recessives. Yields 75% black and 25% liver (chocolate).

A hybrid black (Class #3) having a liver recessive bred to a Class #5 liver with no buff recessive. Yields 50% black and 50% liver (chocolate).

Figure III-6f. Blacks, cont'd.

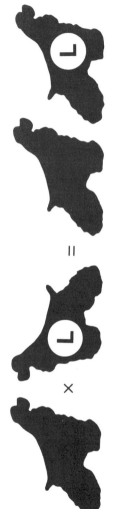

A hybrid black (Class #3) carrying a liver recessive bred to a Class #6 liver carrying a brown-nosed red recessive. Yields 50% black and 50% liver (chocolate).

A hybrid black (Class #3) carrying a liver recessive bred to a Class #7 black-nosed red not carrying the brown-nosed red factor. Yields 100% black.

Figure III-6g. Blacks, cont'd.

A hybrid black (Class #3) carrying a liver recessive bred to a Class #8 black-nosed red carrying a brown-nosed red recessive. Yields 75% black and 25% liver (chocolate).

A hybrid black (Class #3) carrying a liver recessive bred to a brown-nosed red Class #9. Yields 50% black and 50% liver (chocolate).

Figure III-6h. Blacks, cont'd.

Two hybrid blacks (Class #4) carrying liver, black-nosed and brown-nosed reds bred to each other. Yields the perfect Mendelian ratio of 9:3:3:1.

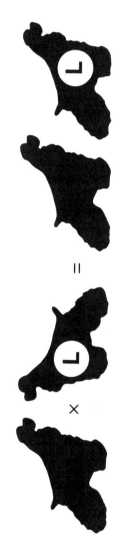

A hybrid black (Class #4) carrying recessives for liver, black-and brown-nosed reds bred to a Class #5 liver with no black-nosed red recessive. Yields 50% black and 50% liver (chocolate).

Figure III-6i. Blacks, cont'd.

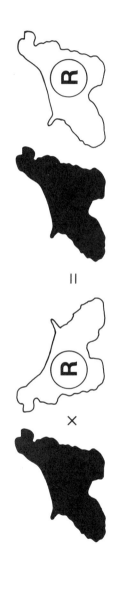

A hybrid black (Class #4) carrying liver, black-, and brown-nosed red recessives bred to a Class #7 black-nosed red. Yields 50% black and 50% black-nosed red.

A hybrid black (Class #4) carrying recessives for liver, black-, and brown-nosed reds bred to a Class #6 liver with black- and brown-nosed red recessives. Yields 3 blacks, 3 livers, 1 black-nosed red and 1 brown-nosed red.

Figure III-6j. Blacks, cont'd.

A hybrid black (Class #4) carrying recessives for liver, black- and brown-nosed reds bred to a Class #8 black-nosed red carrying a brown-nosed red recessive. Yields 3 blacks, 3 black-nosed reds, 1 liver, 1 brown-nosed red.

A hybrid black (Class #4) carrying recessives for liver, black- and brown-nosed reds bred to Class #9 brown-nosed red. Yields 25% black, 25% black-nosed red, 25% liver and 25% brown-nosed red.

Figure III-6k. Blacks, cont'd.

Ch. Hi-Boots Such Brass—A Black and Tan Cocker Spaniel

Bi-Colors

This coloration includes the black and tans, chocolate and tans, blue and tans, and red and tans. For most, the mention of the blue and tan and red and tans may seem puzzling for these colors are rarely seen. Well, rest assured, they are valid colors (see Figure III-7 for full description).

In breeding bi-colors, one is dealing with a whole series of multiple recessives, something which is not present in any other color category in Cockers. These multiple recessives apply not only to coat color but also to characteristics that come to bi-colors through the colors of black, buff/red, chocolate, and white on some. The other colors in Cockers are a matter of single recessives or dominants in color inheritance. The sable color also uses multiple recessives to produce its pattern. In a bi-color, the solid color is not a dominant color but, rather is an "imperfect dominant."

The remarks and theories presented in the buff section apply equally to the bi-colors. Just because a dog is bi-color does not ensure that he will have the conformation or "type" of that color.

Bi-color is recessive to all solid colors. Solid colors can produce bi-color offspring only if both parents carry the recessive bi-color genes.

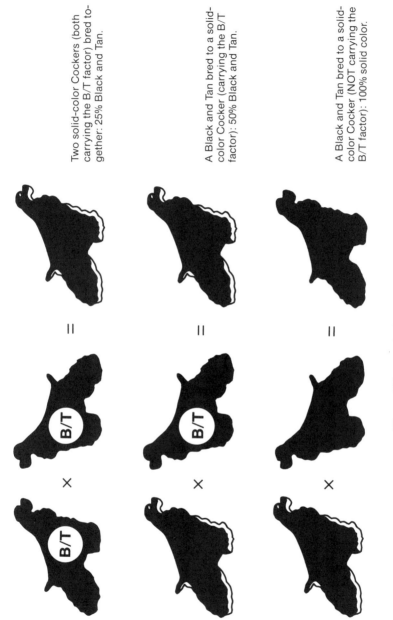

Two solid-color Cockers (both carrying the B/T factor) bred together: 25% Black and Tan.

A Black and Tan bred to a solid-color Cocker (carrying the B/T factor): 50% Black and Tan.

A Black and Tan bred to a solid-color Cocker (NOT carrying the B/T factor): 100% solid color.

Figure III-7a. Black and Tans.

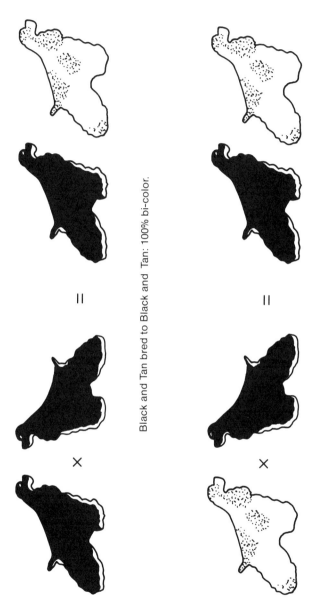

Black and Tan bred to Black and Tan: 100% bi-color.

Buff and Tan bred to Black and Tan: 100% bi-color.

Figure III-7b. Black and Tans, cont'd.

Since solid color is dominant, the recessive bi-color gene is denied expression when it is paired with a solid-color gene. The bi-color gene may be covered up by the solid-colored gene and handed down for many generations. It is only when the bi-color gene becomes paired with another bi-colored gene that bi-color offspring result.

An example of this pattern being handed down for five generations without being seen was Ch. Bigg's Believe It Or Not, a black and tan who was Best in Show at the 1952 Annual Flushing Spaniel Specialty. His breeders, successful buff breeders, didn't dream the gene was there. Whether the bi-color offspring are black and tan, blue and tan, chocolate and tan, or buff/red and tan depends on what color the parents are and what colors they carry. Two buff/red parents cannot be expected to produce bi-color offspring. However, some of the buff/red puppies produced by these parents may be buff/red and tan with the contrast between the buff and tan being so slight as to make recognition of the pattern impossible. These puppies will, however, reproduce like bi-colors.

Matings of bi-color to bi-color can result in a small percentage of buff/red puppies. From the chocolate and tan, the expectation would be that they would be brown-nosed reds. All the buff/red puppies resulting from the breedings of bi-color parents are genotypically buff and tan. They look like solid buff/reds. The bi-color pattern is recessive to solid color, so therefore, two bi-color dogs cannot produce the dominant solid color. Buff and tan Cockers breed true insofar as the bi-color pattern is concerned. For example, if a buff/red and tan is bred to a black and tan who does not carry buff/red as a recessive, all the puppies will be black and tan in color. A black and tan not carrying buff/red as a recessive, bred to a solid buff/red or a buff/red carrying the black and tan factor, would produce all blacks in the first case and a combination of blacks and black and tans in the second instance. The same would hold true when the other bi-colors are bred this way. Thus, bi-color bred to bi-color produces 100 percent bi-color offspring.

Chocolate and tans mated to black-nosed reds which carry the pattern will produce black and tan puppies in true Mendelian ratio according to the genetic makeup of their parents.

Introduction of the dilution factor can cause the black to become blue, and chocolate to turn silver-fawn. This would explain the appearance of the blues that have been seen.

Bi-color has long been recognized as a *pattern* and this fact has been emphasized in the most recent standard change which now has a dog with tan markings in all three varieties. As a result, it now becomes important—in the breeding of bi-colors—to obtain a clear, easily recognizable pattern. Because the breeding of bi-colors is genetically a series of multiple factors, double matings are necessary to preserve the correct pattern. However, the constant breeding of bi-color to bi-color will tend to destroy the pattern. The sharpness and clarity will disappear and the pattern will become "fuzzy" and indistinct. Constant breeding of bi-color to bi-color may also result in less and less coat. If well-marked bi-colors are constantly bred together, the chances of getting overly marked dogs also increases. Breeding to solids with the bi-color factor can help to control this spread. Breeding to buff/reds with the bi-color factor can assist in increasing markings. A stage that falls in between is the brindling often seen on bi-colors.

Now is a good time to differentiate between brindling and pencilling. All bi-color dogs have some amount of pencilling. It looks like pencil marks on top of, but not intermixed with, the tan hairs. Brindling is different in that not all bi-colors are brindled. This is a condition in which black or chocolate hairs are intermixed throughout the tan pattern, resulting in a smudged, dirty, or gray look. Some say this is related to the sable pattern but I cannot vouch for that as fact.

Genetically, the clear copper-red color is dominant over all other colors in the bi-color pattern. Recessive to the clear copper color, yet dominant over the cream color, is brindling. Brindling is the first step in dilution from red. Recessive to both is the clear cream color.

Parti-Colors

The parti-color variety has made enormous strides over the past 30 years. At one time, the parti-colors seemed almost a separate breed, rather than a separate variety. What happened within recent memory to change this? First, Honey Creek Kennels revolutionized the parti-color by making them pretty and adding some coat. Then the same factors which changed the buff/reds caused a change in the partis. Better bone, toplines and coat became identified with partis as much as the other colors. The funny thing is that the early parti-colors coming from the dilute breedings were really not from the basic parti-color stock. Instead, the buff hairs were gradually diluted to a light lemon color which served as the "white" background upon which a red/tan color was superimposed. These dogs, when seen next to a white-background looked different than the normal parti-color.

When the genes which produce white spotting are combined with the genes which produce a black Cocker, a black and white is created. When the genes representing white spotting are combined with the genes which represent red, a red and white is created. The genes which produce white spotting are recessive to the genes which produce a completely solid-colored dog. Thus, white spotting is recessive to solid black, chocolate, buff/red and bi-color. As a result, when two dogs carrying the genes representing white spotting (or two parti-colors) are bred

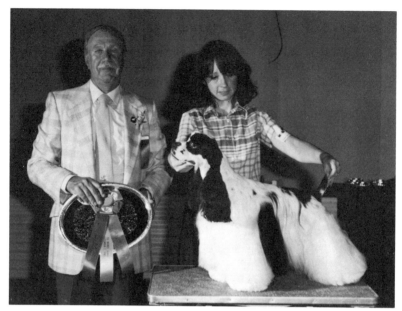

Ch. Yerly's Hot Off The Press—A Black and White Cocker Spaniel.

together, they can be expected to produce only parti-color offspring.

In parti-colors, ticking is dominant over plain white backgrounds but is also recessive to solid color. Roan, which is rare in the American Cocker but popular in the English Cocker, is usually superimposed upon ordinary ticking so that a mottled color results. Thus, roan is dominant over plain ticking, and ticking is dominant over pure white in the splashed areas.

In his book, *How to Breed Dogs*, Dr. Leon Whitney makes an interesting, general observation about black and white parti-colors. His observations led him to believe that black and white puppies usually have larger pigmented areas than do those of any other shade of red and white. This was subsequently borne out by Dr. C.C. Little at the Jackson Memorial Laboratory. Earlier investigations by Dr. Phillips (who did the pioneering work on color in Cockers), led him to conclude that red and whites usually have smaller areas of color than do black and whites in the same litter.

Therefore, the constant, promiscuous breeding of black and white to black and white results in more heavily-marked offspring in each succeeding generation. Continuous non-selective breeding of red and white to red and white usually shows a tendency for the white to increase in each succeeding generation. Today, it is evident that there are more and more puppies that show one-sided head markings and too much white

Ch. Kamps' Kaptain Kool—A Red and White Cocker Spaniel.

on the body. In fact, there are ever increasing numbers of red and whites that barely have enough color to qualify as a parti-color.

In red and whites, both colors are recessive, while in black and whites, the black is dominant and the white recessive. Therefore, it is more difficult to breed consistently good black and whites. The dominant black in a black and white will have to be reduced to a state of "imperfect dominance" (as in the bi-colors) to allow consistently good black and whites to be bred. This seems to be happening. Carried to the extreme, black and whites can be produced rivaling their red and white brethren when it comes to lack of color. Parti-color breeders should be aware of losing the correct color pattern.

The percentage of black and white and/or red and white puppies expected in any given litter will depend upon the color of both the sire and dam and their backgrounds, and will follow the same inheritance pattern as the solid colors. For example, there are black and whites which, like dominant blacks, can produce nothing but black and whites when bred to a parti-color. These, when bred to a red and white, will produce 100% black and whites. In turn, however, the puppies will be hybrid and be able to produce both black and white and red and white.

There are very few dominant black and white Cockers around, although they can, and do, exist.

Red and white when bred to red and white will usually produce only red and whites.

Applicable to the red and whites as well as to the buff/reds and bi-colors, are the different shades from Setter red to pale lemon. Variation in depth of shade within a continuous series of a single hereditary color variety is usually considered to be the result of so-called "modifying factors." These influence the degree of development or expression of the main genes which produce the color in question. Deep reds would be described as having "plus" modifiers which encourage the formation of more red pigment, while the lighter shades would be considered to be the result of "minus" modifiers which allow a lesser degree of red pigment to develop. Thinking of it in another way, hair follicles baked in the oven at 350° for 30 minutes would be lighter in color than ones that baked for an hour. Figure III-8a–b illustrates the genetic combinations and results.

Ch. Carronade Trigger—A Tri-Color Cocker Spaniel.

Tri-Colors

In the American Cocker Spaniel, a good deal of mystery has surrounded the breeding of tri-colors. True, tri-colors are not as common as their brethren the black and white and the red and white. However,

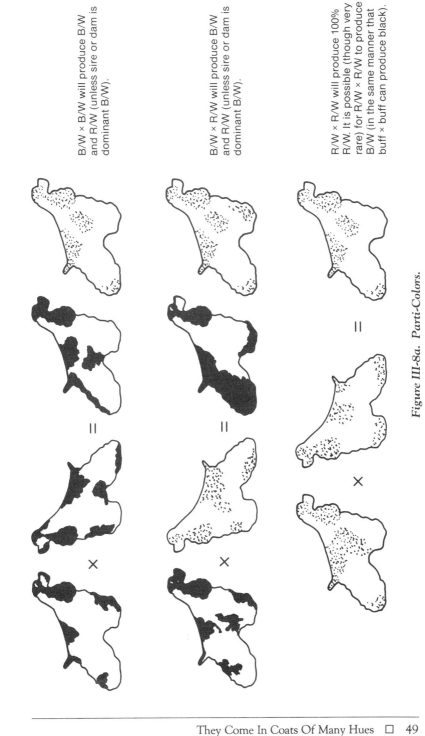

B/W × B/W will produce B/W and R/W (unless sire or dam is dominant B/W).

B/W × R/W will produce B/W and R/W (unless sire or dam is dominant B/W).

R/W × R/W will produce 100% R/W. It is possible (though very rare) for R/W × R/W to produce B/W (in the same manner that buff × buff can produce black).

Figure III-8a. Parti-Colors.

Parti-Color × solid (carrying Parti-Color factor) will produce both solids and Parti-Colors.

Parti-Color × solid (NOT carrying Parti-Color factor) will produce all solids and/or mismarks.

The percentage of B/W and/or R/W to be expected in any given litter will follow the same inheritance pattern as the solid colors.

Figure III-8b. Parti-Colors, cont'd.

the breeding of tri-colors should not be any more difficult than the breeding of any other color. The major difficulties seem to be the ability to obtain desired markings (but lack of desirable comformation and type), or desired conformation and type (but lack of desirable markings). The purpose here will be to explain just what tri-colors are and to show how they can be obtained. Along these lines, perhaps some inferences can be drawn, showing how desired markings can be obtained along with desired conformation.

All of the remarks pertaining to the description of the bi-colored pattern and its variations apply equally to the tri-color pattern. Tri-color obviously means "three color," and, in dogs, one of these colors is always white. The other colors may be any one of the color combinations found in bi-color dogs, such as black and tan, chocolate and tan, blue and tan, or red and tan.

The foundation of the tri-color pattern is the bi-color pattern, the only difference being that tri-colors have inherited an independent set of genes which are capable of covering up a part of the bi-color pattern with white.

The amount of white found on tri-color dogs may vary from a great deal to very little. In Cockers, the genes for white spotting cover up most of the bi-color pattern. Of course, not all tri-colors are marked alike, any more than all parti-colors or all bi-colors are marked alike. The same variations in color and pattern which occur in bi-color and parti-color dogs may be expected to occur in tri-colors.

The average black, tan, and white Cocker has an easily recognizable bi-color pattern with the two tan spots over the eyes and tan on the cheeks, inside the ears, and under the tail. The muzzle, legs and feet are usually well ticked with tan. The latest standard change in 1981 has been more specific about the markings.

Since tri-colors are basically bi-color dogs, they have the same ability as bi-color dogs to reproduce the bi-color pattern. Whether or not their offspring will have white spotting in addition to the bi-color pattern depends on whether the chosen mate has or carries the independent spotting factor as well as the bi-color pattern factors.

Remember, white spotting is recessive to bi-color. Tri-colors, therefore, represent a combination of two sets of independent genes, both of which are recessive in their manner of inheritance. When a recessive characteristic is visible in an individual, that individual is always homozygous (pure for that trait) and that individual can contribute only one kind of gene to its offspring. Therefore, it must breed true. Thus, when two tri's are bred together, they can be expected to produce only tri-color puppies. Whether the pups are black and tan and white, chocolate and tan and white, etc., depends entirely on what the parents are and what colors they carry recessively.

If tri-colors are desired, the bi-color pattern must be present in the pedigree and the white spotting factor as well. The only way to be certain that a particular animal has the ability to hand down to its offspring a particular recessive characteristic is by knowing that (1) the animal itself shows the characteristic; (2) the animal has one parent which shows the characteristic; or, (3) the animal has been test mated and has proven by its offspring that it has the ability to reproduce the characteristic.

The majority of breeders consider the combination of black (chocolate), tan, and white to be a bona fide tri-color. If the breeder wishes to produce this combination, he must make certain that the mating prospects have the black or chocolate pigment in their coat, for black and chocolate are dominant and must be shown by one parent before it can be expressed in the offspring. Any combination of colors known in Cockers may produce tri-colors provided both parents either show or carry the two patterns which are needed to produce the tri-color effect.

Figure III-9 illustrates some of the many ways in which tri-colors can be produced, and gives expectancy percentages.

A word to the wise: By all means, use the black and tan and the chocolate and tan to produce your tri's. You may cross back and forth between the bi- and tri-colors at will. The bi-colors can help strengthen the pattern. Probably the most successful at this is the Trojan Kennels of Alice and Sheldon Kaplan of Texas.

Another method open to the breeder of tris would be to use buffs/reds which carry both the bi-color factor and the parti-color factor. There are many such dogs available. And while tri's coming from these dogs may be slower to appear, they can appear. By using this color combination the risk of too much black (chocolate) from breeding to the bi-colors will be reduced appreciably. For example, if a black and white (carrying the bi-color or tri factor) is bred to a buff/red (carrying the bi-color and parti factor), theoretically one out of eight puppies will be a tri-color. However, the other seven puppies will not be all mismarks and some of the parti-colors coming from such a breeding will possess the ability to produce tri-colors. Figure III-9 illustrates the possible genetic combinations and results.

Mismarks

No discussion of color breeding would be complete without discussing the mismarked dog. All of us could empathize with the heartbreak of breeding a beautiful specimen and having it be disqualifiable because of improper markings. The standard is strict on this. It allows a small amount of white on the chest and throat without penalty but disqualifies a dog with white in any other area. Light-colored buffs where white

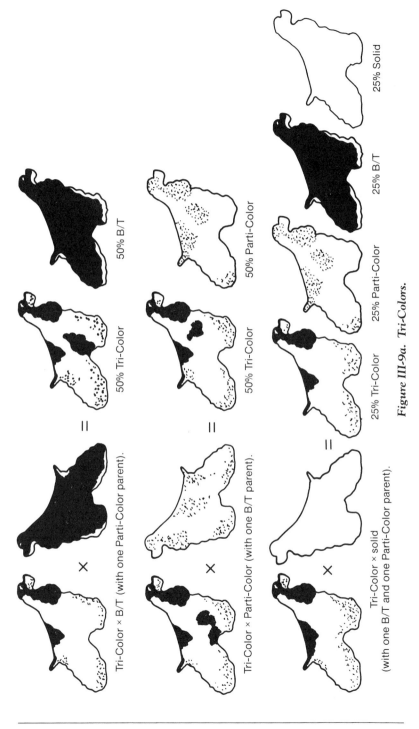

Figure III-9a. Tri-Colors.

75% Parti-Color

25% Tri-Color

=

Parti-Color × Parti-Color
(each having one B/T and one Parti-Color parent).

75% Bi-Color

25% Tri-Color

=

B/T × B/T (each having one Parti- or Tri- parent).

Figure III-9b. Tri-Colors, cont'd.

hairs are seen from chest to chin intermingled with the buff are a problem. Their markings are *wrong*, and under the standard, they should be disqualified.

Just as it is possible to determine the relative amount of pigment formed by red or black parti-colors, it is also possible to compare the effects of these two coat colors in mismarked animals. Mismarking in Cockers occurs when white appears in certain areas which are usually well defined and predictable. The feet, chest, and tail tip are the areas which usually show white. In addition, one frequently finds a white blaze or star on the forehead and a white muzzle in red animals.

Mismarked individuals may occur in the progeny of matings between two entirely solid colored dogs. In such cases they may, and usually do, represent modifications of the solid color type rather than true parti-color animals.

Mismarked Cockers can be produced in any of three ways (see Figure III-10):

1. They may be solid-color animals with a weakening of the ability to form or extend pigment over the whole body. This loss of the ability to form or extend pigment shows up by the formation of white (unpigmented) areas in those parts of the body which develop shortly before birth. This is why the feet, chest, muzzle, forehead, and tip of the tail are the areas affected. Animals which are mismarked for this reason usually, if not always, will pass on to their descendants the decreased pigment-forming ability which they themselves possess.

   In some cases, however, the decrease in power to form or extend pigment may produce so little white that ordinary examination fails to reveal it. The animal, therefore, appears to be solid-color and can be so classified. Thus, a few white hairs on the chest may be surrounded and covered by pigmented hairs and will not be visible by a surface examination. However, these animals are *genetically* mismarked and will transmit that characteristic to their offspring just as if they had more white.

2. A solid-color carrying a parti-color recessive may, or may not, be able to disguise the fact completely. If it can do so, it will appear just as a solid-color—as though it had no ability to produce parti-colors. Sometimes however, the parti-color pattern is not covered completely. In these cases, white appears. Interestingly enough, it is again located in the "vulnerable" spots: the feet, chest, forehead, muzzle, or tail tip.

3. In some breeds, such as a Basenji or Boxer, a condition that would be considered a definite mismarking for a Cocker has become the common and established pattern for the breed. Such animals often "breed true" and give only offspring like themselves with few, if any,

solid-color animals and few, if any, with large or irregular white areas. It may well be that some mismarked Cockers are of this type.

A breeder may wish to use a highly desirable mismarked specimen for breeding and that can be all right. However, the breeder *must* appreciate the consequences of such actions on future generations and proceed cautiously.

Cockers come in literally any color combination. A breeder may—if they wish—breed esoteric colors. Many people have tried. Sometimes these esoteric colors can be sold for a good price because they can be described as "rare." However, the trick is to breed good Cockers which conform to the current standard. "Rare" seldom means "correct."

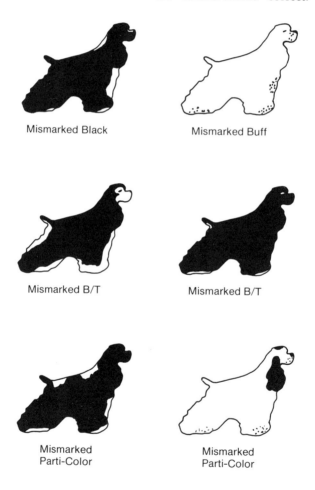

Mismarked Black   Mismarked Buff

Mismarked B/T   Mismarked B/T

Mismarked
Parti-Color

Mismarked
Parti-Color

Figure III-10. Mismarking in the three varieties.

CHAPTER 3

Analyzing A Pedigree

Anyone who has ever purchased a purebred dog has received a pedigree which, when used correctly, can be a real skill tool in breeding better specimens. It contains a list of names that usually go back to the fifth generation. Most newcomers have pored over their first pedigrees with great intensity, trying to sort out the infrequent "Ch." preceding a dog's name. In addition, most pedigrees list the breeder's name, the date of birth, and the American Kennel Club registration number.

Unfortunately, most pedigrees, even those with many champions listed, have little meaning. A more meaningful pedigree would list the color of each dog (perhaps his/her measurements) and the number of champions it has produced. A picture of each dog in the first three generations would add frosting to the cake. To most owners the list of names has little significance other than to highlight the champions of renown scattered here and there through an otherwise nondescript pedigree.

As a list of the dog's forebearers, the pedigree can be used by the wise breeder as a predictor of what kind of offspring the dog/bitch will throw. In effect, pedigree analysis is supposed to be able to help predict the next generation based upon previous generations.

That this is possible is true only in part. A good pedigree confirms what a dog's type and his proven ability to produce good stock have already proclaimed. The proof of the dog/bitch is in the puppies. The role of the ancestors is but a prelude to what is contained in the puppy's chromosomes.

It is a proven fact that an offspring of two parents who are themselves of high quality and are recognized producers of stock of consistent excellence, is likely to produce well.

Remember at all times, quality begets quality. A good example of the breeders' art is illustrated in the black bitch, Ch. Feinlyne Fetch and Go. Bred by Annette Davies from excellent stock, she was sold to Karen and Vernon Marquez of Marquis Kennels. For them she produced seven champions. That in itself is quite an accomplishment. However, the quality of her get and her grandchildren are nothing short of spectacular. For example at the August 1985 Houston Kennel Club, Fetch and Go's grandchildren won all three Varieties with good competition. The winners were:

Black: Ch. Glen Arden's Real McCoy
ASCOB: Ch. Marquis Just Baggot
Parti: Ch. Marquis It's The One

Fetch and Go was bred to Blacks twice and produced Black champions in one litter and B/T champions in the other. When bred to B/T she produced Black champions. Bred to a B/W Parti-Color, her offspring were non-champions but were producers. Her grandchildren are champions in all three varieties. Her pedigree is shown in Figure III-16.

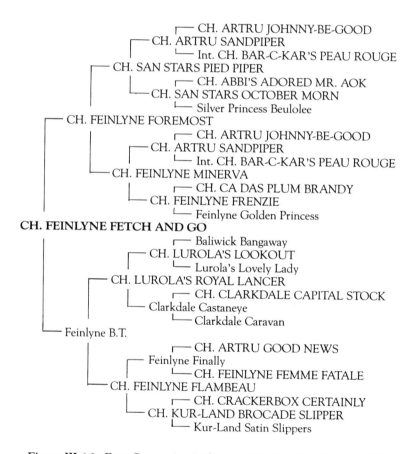

Figure III-16. Four-Generation Pedigree of Ch. Feinlyne Fetch and Go.

Ch. Feinlyne Fetch and Go.

A look at her producing record reveals the following:

Bred to Alorah's Engarde (B/T), she produced:

1. Ch. Marquis Black Is Beautiful   (Bitch)   Black
   BOS to Best of Breed, Summer National—1980
   Specialty Best of Breed winner

2. Ch. Marquis Flick Your Bic   (Dog)   Black

Bred to Ch. Frandee's Federal Agent (Black), she produced:

3. Ch. Frandee's Forgery   (Dog)   Black
   Best in Show, Annual Flushing Spaniel Specialty—1987
   Multiple Group winner
   Multiple Specialty Best of Breed winner

   Sire of:
      Ch. Glen Arden's Real McCoy—Black/Tan
         Top Specialty Best of Breed winner—1985–1986
         Multiple Group and Best in Show winner
         Top 10 Black winner—1986

Ch. Riviera's O'Riley—Black
  Multiple all-breed Best in Show winner—1987
  Mutliple Specialty Best of Breed winner—1986
Ch. Camelot's Counterfeit—Black/Tan
  Multiple Best of Breed winner—1986-1987

4. Ch. Marquis Revered Night Watch (Dog) Black
5. Ch. Marquis Luv and Kisses (Bitch) Black

Bred to Ch. Frandee's Federal Agent (Black), she produced:

6. Ch. Marquis Sergio (Dog) Black/Tan
7. Ch. Marquis Sex Pot (Bitch) Black/Tan

Bred to Ch. Rexpointe Shazam (B/W), she produced:

8. Marquis Black Shazam (Dog) Black
  Sire of:
    Ch. Marquis It's The One—Black/White
      #1 Parti-Color—1984, 1985 & 1986
      #1 Cocker Spaniel—1985
      ASC Variety winner at 11 months of age, January 1984
      10 Specialty Best of Breeds
      Multiple all-breed Best in Show winner
    Ch. Danzata's Mr. Ed—Black/White
      #3 Parti-Color—1985
      #4 Parti-Color—1986
      Specialty Best of Breed winner—1985-1986
    Ch. Marquis Tug of War—Black/White
      Sire of Parti-Color WB at 1985 Summer National
    Ch. Marquis Spend A Buck—Black/White
      Sire of BOS to BOV, Parti-Color Sweepstakes—
        1987 Annual Flushing Spaniel Specialty
    Ch. Marquis Just Baggot*—Buff
      Top 10 ASCOB—1985-1986
      Variety winner, Purina Invitational—1986
      Specialty Best of Breed winner

9. Marquis The Brat (Bitch) Mismarked

On the male side, the most dramatic example of linebreeding is to be found in the pedigree of Ch. Artru Skyjack (Figure III-17) from the Artru Kennels. Skyjack is one of the breed's all-time top producers with 87 champion get.

Ch. Marquis Just Baggot's dam is a litter sister to Ch. Danzata's Mr. Ed.

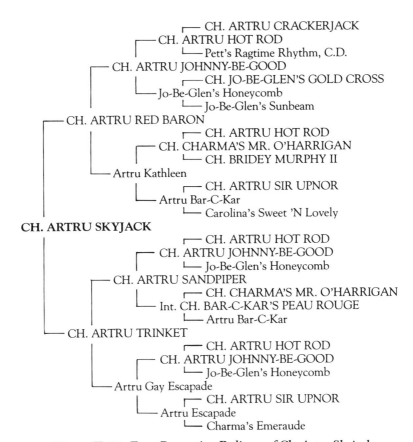

```
                              ┌── CH. ARTRU CRACKERJACK
                   ┌── CH. ARTRU HOT ROD
                   │          └── Pett's Ragtime Rhythm, C.D.
          ┌── CH. ARTRU JOHNNY-BE-GOOD
          │        │          ┌── CH. JO-BE-GLEN'S GOLD CROSS
          │        └── Jo-Be-Glen's Honeycomb
          │                   └── Jo-Be-Glen's Sunbeam
     ┌── CH. ARTRU RED BARON
     │    │                   ┌── CH. ARTRU HOT ROD
     │    │         ┌── CH. CHARMA'S MR. O'HARRIGAN
     │    │         │         └── CH. BRIDEY MURPHY II
     │    └── Artru Kathleen
     │              │         ┌── CH. ARTRU SIR UPNOR
     │              └── Artru Bar-C-Kar
     │                        └── Carolina's Sweet 'N Lovely
CH. ARTRU SKYJACK
     │                        ┌── CH. ARTRU HOT ROD
     │              ┌── CH. ARTRU JOHNNY-BE-GOOD
     │              │         └── Jo-Be-Glen's Honeycomb
     │    ┌── CH. ARTRU SANDPIPER
     │    │         │         ┌── CH. CHARMA'S MR. O'HARRIGAN
     │    │         └── Int. CH. BAR-C-KAR'S PEAU ROUGE
     │    │                   └── Artru Bar-C-Kar
     └── CH. ARTRU TRINKET
          │                   ┌── CH. ARTRU HOT ROD
          │         ┌── CH. ARTRU JOHNNY-BE-GOOD
          │         │         └── Jo-Be-Glen's Honeycomb
          └── Artru Gay Escapade
                    │         ┌── CH. ARTRU SIR UPNOR
                    └── Artru Escapade
                              └── Charma's Emeraude
```

Figure III-17. Four-Generation Pedigree of Ch. Artru Skyjack.

Ch. Artru Skyjack.

Skyjack is an excellent example of close linebreeding. Note that he is founded on Ch. Artru Johnny-Be-Good, himself the sire of 52 champion offspring. Johnny-Be-Good is the sire of Ch. Artru Sandpiper (the sire of 68 champions) and Ch. Artru Red Baron (the sire of 49 champions). Red Baron, bred to a Sandpiper daughter, produced Skyjack.

Another example of successful linebreeding is the pedigree of one of the great producing Parti-Colors of recent years: Ch. Dreamridge Dominoe, bred and owned by Tom O'Neal of Dreamridge Kennels. His pedigree is shown in Figure II-18. Dominoe is the sire of 109 champions. Breeding the great bitch, Dinner Date (9 champions) to the great producer Sinbad (118 champions) produced Dominoe who proved to be a *prepotent* sire almost from the beginning. Note the line breeding through Hoot Mon and Sinbad. This triumvirate, Hoot Mon with 43 champions, Sinbad with 118, and Dominoe with 109, is producing one of the most potent lines in any breed. Hoot Mon was a black/white but traced his ancestry

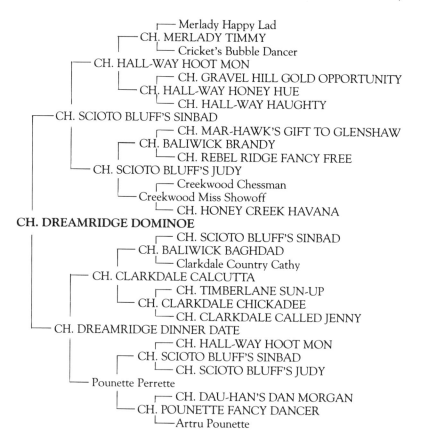

Figure III-16. Four-Generation Pedigree of Ch. Dreamridge Dominoe.

Ch. Dreamridge Dominoe.

two generations back to Ch. Maddie's Vagabond's Return, an outstanding buff producer. Sinbad was red/white and Dominoe, of course, black/white.

In 1977, Ron Fabis—Dominoe's handler—wrote this about him and these bloodlines:

> We have found that granddaughters and great granddaughters bred back to him, but on an individual basis, produce better overall progeny. Take a well-bred bitch with no outstanding faults but with one or two virtues and breed her to a proven sire *in her own line* to come up with improvement; in other words, the essence of line-breeding.

> Even the greatest sire may have a tendency to produce a fault . . . this is where the breeder is called upon to display and exercise the breeding art. He has to decide how to secure the desirable features and lose the undesirable things that may crop up. Step-by-step building up a strain possessed of every desirable characteristic is like fashioning a mosaic.

Genetic research done by Francis Galton led to his so-called "Law of Filial Regression," which states, in effect, the tendency of races to revert to mediocrity. This is what dog breeders refer to when they use the term "drag of the race."

Galton reached his conclusions from statistical studies. He found that the adult children of very tall parents tended to be, while taller than the average of the population, not so tall as the mean height of the parents; and that the children of short parents tended to be shorter than the average but of greater height than the mean height of the parents. His statistics reveal the tendency of exaggeration of type in the parents to grow smaller or to disappear in the progeny.

In order to be a good breeder, one must use the pedigree as a basic record. A good breeder uses records to identify outstanding bloodlines possessing the ability to pass its traits on to its progeny. Such bloodlines, coupled with descriptive data (for example, superior head, deep stop, and pronounced eyebrows) should constitute the information to be considered in planning a mating. In Europe, many breeders ask for the critiques done in the show ring on the dogs they plan to use for breeding. This gives them added objective information on which to make their breeding judgements.

Experienced breeders are able to prepare an intelligible pedigree, and as a result they can read meaning into a similarly prepared pedigree. Basically, however, most pedigrees are totally useless because they are incomplete and too often are only a jumble of names arranged in chronological order, linking one generation to the next. For most breeders, the pedigree could be written in Greek for all the good it does them.

The record of Feinlyne Fetch and Go accompanying her pedigree is more in the model of what is needed. Many breedings are well conceived and lead to the production of suitable specimens to carry on into succeeding generations. However, breedings of some famous dogs were made on a catch-as-catch-can basis.

A true story tells of a breeder (in another breed) who sent his nice bitch to a heavily campaigned and advertised stud dog. Now this dog was a sometimes breeder. If he didn't like the bitch, too bad. On this occasion he didn't take to the bitch and so ignored her. When the handler called the owner of the bitch to inform him, the owner said to breed her to any available stud since she would be out of season by the time he got her home and bred to another dog. This was done. From this chance mating came the top winning and producing dog in that breed's history. That such matings produce top specimens is more a tribute to Lady Luck than to the breeder's art.

There are wide differences existing in the gene structure of dogs, even from the same litters, and only a few of any breeding can be outstanding as producers. Thus, the existence of famous names in a pedigree is not enough. It is no assurance whatever that the pedigree is a good one.

Good breeders follow the maxim of "Every generation a good one." This means that each individual in a pedigree was a producer (check Dominoe's pedigree as an example) and that the line came down in a fixed series of progressions. It is not enough to have famous sires or dams spotted throughout the pedigree. It is necessary that their offspring were also producers so the qualities of those famous dogs can be brought down to succeeding generations.

Each ancestor contributes to the heredity pool in its own unique way. Some improve upon the genes they receive while others degrade those qualities. A good bloodline is one in which each individual specimen has contributed to the "goodness" of the gene pool. Certain individual animals dramatically improve upon those characteristics and it is these animals that should be perpetuated.

An outstanding pedigree shows an unbroken line of production in a form that a breeder can recognize immediately. Unfortunately, many a good pedigree has been turned into a poor one when one of the animals involved turns out to be an inferior producer (especially one close up) or a producer of serious faults. Unless each specimen is in turn followed by superior producers, it may reach a dead end for that line.

To have only a few good individuals in a pedigree is not enough. One has to appreciate that these individuals moved the breed toward the ideal. However, the ones to which they were bred may have carried genes detrimental to the breed, and, as a result, the influence of the noted producer may have been nullified.

While it is difficult for a modern breeder to assess the capability of any given dog or bitch in a pedigree to produce specific characteristics; he can be assured by an unbroken string of top producers that the gene pool is tending toward the overall ideal of the breed.

Livestock breeders have for many years recognized the necessity of maintaining an unbroken record of each line of ancestry. Voluminous computerized records are kept by the dairy cattle industry. Painstaking care is shown in selecting herd sires and keeping track of the milk and butterfat production of their offspring. The industry's ability to select proper specimens through computer analysis puts dog breeding to shame. Of course the payoff in dollars is so great that this type of record keeping can be justified.

A great producing sire or dam produces a much higher average of good dogs among its progeny than does its less outstanding sons or daughters. When the great producing sire and the great producing dam are mated together, the average quality of the progeny is brought to its highest level. Even in this extremely favorable mating, however, the sampling nature of Mendelian inheritance and the range of natural variations would ensure that some of the offspring would be above and some below the average of the parents. In this case, "the drag of the race" would provide an entirely practical guarantee that the great majority of the offspring would be inferior to their great producing parents, as producers. Only the occasional one would be superior or even their equal. (See Dominoe's pedigree, a great bitch bred to a great dog produced the occasional great producer who nearly equalled his sire's producing record.)

With a pedigree that contains little but names, the older, more experienced breeder has an advantage, for he has undoubtedly seen many of the specimens listed. To the novice, pedigrees are to a large extent a mystery—a genealogical puzzle. The experienced breeder fills in, from his own knowledge, whatever he knows of the weighted averages of individuality and producing powers of each of the parents, the direct ancestors, and many collateral relatives. This is truly reading a pedigree, a gift of knowledge and insight which few breeders of any breed ever obtain.

The case of the newcomer is not so hopeless as it may seem, however. Before the usual pedigree can ever begin to become a reliable part of the basis of breeding, it is necessary to find out how superior or inferior each of the different ancestors was as a producer.

As pointed out earlier, progeny from superior sires and dams are more likely to be superior producers than the progeny of animals selected on the basis of individual merit and pedigree. However, it is sad to report that vast numbers breed to the winner of the day without regard for the genetic make-up of the dog. Perhaps that's why the average staying power of a breeder is only five years. It's like the Las Vegas syndrome—hit it big now or forget it.

Progeny testing is invaluable, for it reveals the true genetic make-up of the sires and dams. It is the heredity concealed in the genes of an individual which determines its value as a producer. All methods of arriving at the true nature of this heredity are merely estimates or approximations, except the actual testing in which this true nature definitely is revealed in the progeny itself.

The most accurate index of the breeding worth of sires and dams is the average quality of their offspring as a whole. In the absence of an ability to gauge this average accurately, the index lies in a random sample of the offspring rather than in the production of one super individual with the qualities of the other offspring unknown. As a consequence, a bloodline or a single mating which is known to produce a high average of good individuals must be considered a better bet. It offers more substantial assurances that a champion will be forthcoming in the next litter, than one which has produced one champion but a lower average quality in all of the other offspring.

Experience has shown that the great mass of every breed fails to produce the required degree of excellence and is lost insofar as the perpetuation of the breed is concerned. The same principle applies to each line of ancestry and to the offspring of even the greatest sires and dams, no matter how carefully the selections are made. It is common knowledge that the most *prepotent* sires of every breed have sired puppies which were inferior producers or even carried serious genetic faults. Thus it may be said that the purity of the line, even in the best appearing pedigrees, is no purity at all unless the progeny test can definitely be applied to each of the ancestors.

It is equally apparent that the mere appearance of famous individuals in a pedigree is not a sufficient guarantee that the line now retains any of those individual's good qualities, which may have been dissipated in their own or any succeeding generation by one or more inferior producers. To provide a reliable tool for the breeder bent on producing winners, the pedigree must show only lines of ancestors which are known to have a strong degree of purity for the sought after qualities.

Decidedly more data is needed in most pedigrees. Until such data can be supplied, the short pedigree going directly to the superior producers is the best pedigree. Genetic research has shown that by far the greatest hereditary influence is exerted by the parents themselves, and that hereditary influence decreases rapidly in each more remote generation. Until tested, the most desirable breeding animal is one directly descended from known superior producers. Each intermediate generation of ancestors of undetermined or unknown breeding powers greatly lessens the probabilities of producing superior puppies.

The following are the Executive Editor's *Cardinal Principles of Breeding:*

1. Breed only to a dog that is old enough to have a history of producing top-flight stock.
2. Stay close within your own bloodline.
3. Be sure the breeding stock you use has an unbroken producing line.
4. Do not breed to the current winner unless it meets the above stated standards.

Ch. BeGay's Tan Man—Parti-Color—shown winning the Breed at the January 1970 National Specialty of the ASC. Bred and owned by Bill and Gay Ernst. L to R: Walter Tuddenham, 2nd Vice-President; Bill Ernst, owner/handler; Mrs. Mildred T. Imrie, judge.

SECTION IV
Becoming a Breeder

- *The Stud Dog*
- *The Bitch and Her Puppies*
- *Nutrition for Puppies and Adults*
- *Problems of Early Puppyhood*
- *Choosing the Best Puppies*
- *Frozen and Extended Semen*
- *Building and Running a Breeding Kennel*

CHAPTER 1

The Stud Dog

The dog you select to stand at stud should have certain things going for him. First, he should be masculine in appearance and, to at least your appraisal, conform closely to the breed standard. A major mistake made by breeders is to keep a dog that is overdone in some features in the hope he can overcome a bitch with deficiencies in these areas. It doesn't work that way! Breeding an oversize dog to a small bitch in the hope of getting average size puppies is a futile effort. The hallmark of a good breeder, one who understands basic genetics, is breeding to dogs who conform to the standard. Extremes should be avoided like the plague. They only add complications to a breeding program down the road.

Second, it is extremely important that the stud dog come from an unbroken line of producers on both his sire's and dam's side. By unbroken it is meant that at least his sire, grandfather and great grandfather should have produced ten or more champions each. If his sire is still young he may not have hit that mark, but from reading the magazines and seeing his offspring an intelligent breeder can tell if he is going to make it. This unbroken line helps to ensure that he is likely to be homozygous for his good traits. An unbroken producing bitch line is frosting on the cake. It's usually more difficult to find because bitches have fewer offspring. So, when a dog is found that has unbroken producing lines for three generations on his sire's and dam's side, there is an excellent chance of having a prepotent stud.

Third, is appearance. Let's face it, if the male is not constructed right or if his color is not quite right, he is not going to be a great show dog. While the dog doesn't have to be a great show winner to attract the bitches, it helps. Believe me, it helps. Of course there are outstanding examples of non-titled dogs being excellent studs. However, they are few and far between.

There is more to breeding than just dropping a bitch in season into the stud dog's pen and hoping for the best.

First off, let's talk about a subject that never seems to be addressed in the literature about stud dogs, the psyche of the dog. Young stud dogs need to be brought along slowly. If he is a show dog to begin with, he is most likely outgoing and the "gung ho" type. If he is not, please do not think about using him at stud. Behavior traits such as shyness and lack of aggressiveness are transmitted to the next generation just as beautiful necks or slipped stifles are.

He should be taught to get along with other male dogs. Do *not* put him in with an older male too early on. If you do, there is a good likelihood that he will be intimidated and it may harm his prospects of being a good stud. Good stud dogs have to be aggressive in the breeding box. Dogs who have been intimidated early seldom shape up. However, running, playing and even puppy fighting with littermates or slightly older puppies doesn't seem to have a detrimental effect.

The young male, until he is old enough to stand up for himself, should be quartered first with puppies his own age and then introduced to older bitches as kennel mates. It's not a good idea to keep him in a pen by himself. Socialization is extremely important. Time for play as a puppy and a companion to keep him from boredom helps his growth and development.

His quarters and food should present no special problems. Serious breeders all feed their dogs a nourishing and balanced diet. Study after study in colleges of veterinary medicine and by nutritionists at major dog food companies, have shown that the major brands of dry dog food come as close to meeting the total needs of the dog as any elaborately concocted breeder's formula. Each of you has probably learned to add three drops of this and two teaspoons of that, but honestly, a good dry food does the trick. Many breeders spice up the basic diet with their own version of goodies, including table scraps, to break up the monotony or to stimulate a finicky eater. However, for the most part, this is more cosmetic than nutritional. If it makes you feel better, feed him those extra goodies. Supplements will be discussed in the chapter on Nutrition For Puppies and Adults. Do not get him fat and out of condition. That could do terrible things to his libido.

A very important aspect of being the owner of a stud dog is to make sure he can produce puppies. Therefore, at around 11–12 months of age it's a good idea to trundle him off to the vet's for a check on his sperm count. This will tell you if he is producing enough viable sperm cells to make sure he can fertilize eggs in the ovum of a bitch. Sometimes it is found that while a stud produces spermatozoa, they are not active. The chances of this dog being able to fertilize an egg is markedly reduced. While this problem is usually found in older dogs, it happens often enough in young animals to be of concern. Thus the sperm count exam is important, and should be done yearly.

Since we are dealing with the breeding of a warm-blooded mammal, there is need to be concerned with his general health. Sexual contact with a variety of bitches exposes the dog to a wide variety of minor infections and some major ones. Some, if not promptly identified and treated, can lead to sterility—and there goes the farm! Other non-sexual infections and illnesses, such as urinary infections, stones, etc., can also reduce a dog's ability to sire puppies. Since it is not desirable for any of these things to happen stud dog owners need to watch their young Romeos like a hawk.

It's a good idea to have your vet check all incoming bitches. While checking them for obvious signs of infection, especially brucellosis, he can also run a smear to see when they are ready to breed. The dog should also be checked frequently to see if there is any type of discharge from his penis. A dog at regular stud should not have a discharge. Usually he will lick himself frequently to keep the area clean. After breeding it is also a good idea to rinse off the area with a clean saline solution. Your vet may also advise flushing out the penile area after breeding using a special solution.

The testicles and penis are the male organs of reproduction. Testicles are housed in a sac called the scrotum. The AKC will not allow dogs who are cryptorchids (neither testicle descended) nor monorchids (a dog that has only one testicle descended) to be shown.

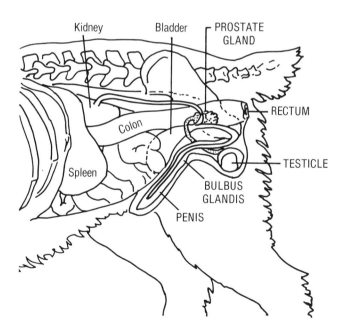

Figure IV-1. Left side of dog showing genital organs and related parts.

The male's testicles are outside the body because the internal heat of the body would curtail the production of sperm. There is a special muscle that keeps them close to the body for warmth in cold weather and relaxes and lets them down to get air cooled in hot weather.

In the male fetus the gonads, or sex organs, develop in the abdominal cavity—migrating during gestation toward their eventual position. Shortly before birth they hover over an opening in the muscular structure of the pubic area through which they will descend to reach the scrotal sac. This external position is vital to the fertility of the animal, for production of live sperm can only proceed at a temperature several degrees cooler than normal body temperature. The glandular tissue of the testes are nourished and supported by arteries, veins, nerves, connective tissue and duct work, collectively known as the spermatic cord. The scrotum acts as a thermostat. As noted above, there are many involuntary muscle fibers within it that are stimulated to contract with the environmental temperature pulling the testes closer to the body for warmth. Contraction also occurs as a result of any stimulus which might be interpreted by the dog as a threat of physical harm—sight of a strange dog, being picked up, etc. This contraction does not force the testicles back up into the abdominal cavity of the adult dog because the inguinal rings have tightened and will not allow them to be drawn back up. The tightening of the rings usually occurs at about ten months of age.

There are a number of reasons why a dog may be a monorchid or cryptorchid. For example the size of the opening through the muscles may be too small to allow for easy passage of the testes, or the spermatic cord may not be long enough for the testes to remain in the scrotum most of the time, and as the proportions of the inguinal ring and testes change in the growing puppy, the time comes when the testes may be trapped above the ring as they grow at different rates. Also, there exists a fibrous muscular band which attaches both to the testes and scrotal wall, gradually shortening and actually guiding the testes in their descent. Possibly this structure could be at fault.

The important thing about all of this is to help the prospective stud dog owner learn about the anatomy of the reproduction organs of the dog. From the foregoing, is it any wonder that many puppies are described as being down one day and up the next?

Next time you place that favorite male puppy up on the grooming table be wary when probing for all of his standard equipment. The scrotal muscles may contract and the still generous inguinal rings may allow the disappearance of the parts sought.

Great luck, a youngster has been found that has "IT" and it is decided to let the world share in the good fortune of owning him. It's a good idea to get him started on the right foot with a cooperative, experienced bitch, one of your own preferably. By introducing the young and inexperienced stud to a "woman of the world," his first experience will result in an easy and successful breeding. Like all males, his ego will soar as a result. This is important. He needs to have the feeling of accomplishment and success. A feisty, difficult bitch the first time around could very well frustrate the youngster and, as a result, he may not be too enthusiastic about future breedings. Remember, we want a confident and aggressive stud dog in the breeding box. There will be difficult bitches to come so it's best to bring him along slow and easy until he will be a match for these fearsome females.

When the bitch is ready to breed (as your stud gains experience he will not pay too much attention to her until she is really ready) both animals should be allowed to exercise and relieve themselves just before being brought together. It's also a good idea not to feed them before mating. Bring the bitch in first. The place should be quiet and away from noise and other dogs. Spend a few minutes petting her and telling her how wonderful she is. Then bring the dog in on a lead. Do not allow him to come lunging in and make a frustrated leap at her. This can cause her to panic and bite him out of fear.

After a few minutes of pirouetting around together—she throwing her vulva in his face and he, with his ears curled on top of his head, trying to lick fore and aft—take off the lead. Allow them to court for a few minutes. She should tell you she is ready by being coquettish and continually backing into the dog.

Now comes the important time for the future success of the young stud. The dog needs to learn the owner is there to help and should not back away from breeding the bitch just because someone is holding her.

Having planned ahead, there will be a large non-skid rug on the floor. Place the bitch on the rug, add a little vaseline around the vulva and face her rump toward the dog. Pat her on the fanny to encourage the dog to come ahead. Generally speaking, he will. As a rule he will lick her again around the vulva. Some dogs are truly considerate lovers, they will go around to the front and gently lick at the bitches eyes and ears. These are true gentlemen. However, this will get him nowhere, so again encourage him to come around to where the action is. If he is unsure of himself, lift the bitch's rear and dangle it in front of the dog's nose.

By now, encouraged and emboldened, the male will mount the bitch from the rear and begin to slowly probe for the opening to the vagina. Once he discovers it, he will begin to move more rapidly. This is a critical time. Some young dogs are so far off the target they never get near the right opening. It's time to gently reposition the bitch so he can have a better angle. This may occur any number of times. He may get frustrated and back off. Don't get excited, this is normal in a young dog. He may even get so excited and confused that he swings around and tries to breed her from the front. This approach never ends successfully.

If he is getting all hot and bothered and not having much success; take a break. Put the dog back by himself for a couple of hours. Don't let him wear himself out. This lack of success can make him lose interest. Pet him and tell him how great he is. At the end of that time, try again. The approach should be the same. If it happens a second time the bitch may not be ready. And if after 20 minutes of fruitless endeavor you do not have a tie, there is always tomorrow. Do not work the young dog to the point of exhaustion. When the next day rolls around you can begin again, giving him maximum encouragement. Don't let him fool around again or he will learn bad habits and think that he has to perform these antics before breeding the bitch.

Get him back on track. Show him the business end again, and encourage him to proceed. By now you have noticed a red, bone-like protuberance sticking out from the penis sheath. This, of course, is the penis itself. When, as a dog continues to probe and finds the opening, he will begin to move frenetically. As he moves in this fashion, a section just behind the pointed penis bone begins to swell. It is capable of great enlargement. This enlargement of the bulbous takes place due to its filling with blood, and it becomes some three times larger than the rest of the penis. In this way the dog, once having made penetrance, is "tied" to the bitch; it is entirely due to the male, the bitch having no part in the initial tying.

When a tie has occurred the semen is pumped in spurts into the vagina. The bitch then helps to keep the penis enlarged as she begins to have a series of pulsating waves which cause a slight tightening and relaxing of the vagina. Some males will stay tied for up to sixty minutes and others as little as five. A five minute successful tie is just as satisfactory as a longer one, because the semen has moved up through the uterus and fallopian tubes to the ovarian capsules by the end of five minutes.

Once the dog and bitch are successfully tied, the male characteristically tries to lift his rear leg over the bitch to keep the tie in a back-to-back position. Some dogs merely slide off the back of a bitch and maintain a tie facing in the same direction. One thing you can count on, they will not stay in one position for any length of time. If someone were to chart the moves of a dog and a bitch during a thirty minute tie, it would look like break dancing at its best. Because of this it's a good idea to have two people involved at this point. One at the bitch's head and one at the male's.

Every now and then a fractious bitch will be sent for breeding. She can be frightened about being shipped, or just plain spooked by a variety of things. Certainly one doesn't want the dog to be bitten by a frightened bitch, nor to have one's fingers lacerated. The easiest solution to this problem is to tie her jaws loosely with wide gauze. This muzzle should tie behind her ears to make sure it doesn't slide off. Pet her, reassure her, but hold her firmly during the breeding so she doesn't lunge at the dog.

After the tie has been broken, there sometimes will be a rush of fluid from the bitch. Don't worry about it, the sperm is well on its way up the fallopian tubes. Gently move the bitch to a quiet pen, apart from other dogs, and give her fresh water and an opportunity to relieve herself. The dog should be petted and told how well he has done. This is also a good time to flush out his sheath, and if your vet has recommended any medication, apply it now. Then, he too should be put in a separate quiet pen with fresh water. It is not a good idea to put him back with a group of male dogs. The opportunity for a serious fight is greatest at this time. The other dogs smell him and get quite upset that it wasn't their turn.

How often can the dog be used at stud? If the dog is in good condition he should be able to be used every day for a week. Some serious breeders who, when faced with many bitches to be bred to a popular stud, have used the dog in the morning and the evening for at least three days. If a dog is used regularly he can be used from day-to-day for a long time. However, if a dog is seldom used, he should not be expected to be able to service day-after-day for any great length of time.

Nature is most generous with sperm. In one good mating a dog may discharge millions, and by and large, a copious amount of sperm is produced in dogs who are used regularly. Dr. Leon Whitney in his book, *This is the Cocker Spaniel*, describes a stud left with a bitch who copulated five times with her, and remained tied at least 18 minutes each time.

All this Olympian activity may be possible for a short time, but for good health and good management, three times a week in normal use seems about right. Of course most breeders would give their eye teeth for such a popular stud. An individual bitch should be serviced twice— once every other day—for the best chance of conception.

For some breeders to breed to a stud of their choice is often difficult, especially in countries that have quarantine restrictions. In the U.S., the basic cost of shipping, the possibility of the dog being booked, the chance of making connections with a popular stud who is out on a circuit being campaigned, etc., are some of the problems that can produce a great deal of frustration. The use of frozen sperm opens up many new possibilities. Owners of popular stud dogs should definitely look into it. At the time of this writing, there are five AKC-sanctioned collection stations. There should be many more in the near future.

Collecting sperm from dogs is not like collecting from cattle. One collection from the latter produces enough to inseminate over 100 cows. The largest amount collected, at one time, over the many years of research in dogs was 22 vials. Usually two to three vials are used to breed a bitch on two to three occasions while she is in season.

The estimated time to store enough semen to inseminate 30 bitches differs by age, health, and sperm quantity and quality. Estimate approximately a month for a young dog, approximately three months for a dog of eight or nine years of age or older. Collection is still time consuming.

It doesn't take one long to recognize that, in the early stages, those males of outstanding quality will make up the main reservoir of the sperm bank. It is suggested by the collection centers that collection be done at a young age—three to five years.

Limitations in quality and quantity due to old age lengthen the period necessary to store enough sperm for even a few bitches. In addition, the daily routine of a dog's life may limit freezability: The settling down in a new environment, changes in diet/water, minor health problems, etc. It is also not uncommon to get poor freeze results from a stud dog that has not been used for a month or longer. For the dog, once he settles down, the process of collection is a pleasant experience. The chapter on Frozen and Extended Semen goes into greater depth on the subject.

Up to now the discussion has touched only on the "easy" part of being a stud dog owner. Next is a look into the day-by-day tasks of the business. Trying to plan a schedule is virtually impossible. Even though some bitch owners say they plan to breed to your dog at the bitch's next season, that can be three to seven months away. Certainly knowing the exact week, let alone the day, is clearly impossible. The bitch's owner will call and say the bitch is on the way. (My God, I've got three unanticipated bitches here now!) Mother Nature does not keep an exact schedule. Unless the bitch's owner has actually sent a deposit to hold a stud service for June of 19__ (this is so rare it would come as a shock), a breeder can only approximate the arrival of his dog's fan club. That's why it is important to keep the stud in top condition . . . he may need to perform yeoman service on short notice.

Okay, now it's known the bitch will be arriving on Tiddlewink Airlines, flight #111, at 1:05 a.m., and has to be picked up at the airport. Those living in a metropolis where there are dog delivery services available that provide for both pickup and delivery are most fortunate. However, these services are expensive. Therefore, being a typical small breeder, it means trudging off to the airport giving up a good night's sleep in the process. When a bitch is shipped air freight or air express, the airlines seem to have a conspiracy as to how long to make you wait to pick up live cargo.

The plane arrives and gets unloaded. No dog! It seems they wait until all the baggage is unloaded to take off the livestock and then they transport them to the air freight building at the other end of the field. This means that 1:05 a.m. has now stretched to close to 3:00 a.m.

before they release the bitch. After letting her relieve herself, putting her back in the crate, driving home and then putting her safely in an isolation pen (hopefully you have planned ahead and provided a special quiet run) we're talking 5:00 a.m. before you get to sleep. Now that's fun!

A good stud dog owner will have found out that various dog food companies, and others, print standard stud contracts. These usually provide for payment in advance and a guaranteed return service if the bitch misses. Both of these stipulations are well advised. As well meaning as most breeders are, many stud fees are either late or not paid at all. Some breeders even wait until they are sure the bitch is pregnant before taking pen in hand. Be firm, no check, no service. This is an expensive hobby, you deserve to be paid for breeding, feeding, picking up and delivering the bitch to and from the airport. By the way, it is a good idea to call the owner collect when the bitch has arrived and also when the bitch is being returned.

What if the dog is either standing at stud at his handler's or being actively campaigned? This can get tricky. If the handler is taking care of the breeding, he expects to be paid for his services. So . . . expect very little from the stud fee unless the dog is so famous as a *prepotent* stud that the stud fees allow you to drive a Mercedes. Expect the handler to ask for 50% or more of the stud fee. Don't complain, they work hard for their money. When the dog is at home, all of the fee can go into the piggy bank. Of course, someone has to perform 100% of the work connected with it.

A real problem can occur when you try to get the in-season bitch together with an actively campaigned dog. Airline schedules and the phone become your steady companion. You arrange for the bitch to be shipped to Toonerville and to arrive at 3:30 in the afternoon. This looks like good planning, because there is a show in Slyville the same day and your handler has to drive through Toonerville on his way to Lizard Butte where the third show on the circuit is being held the following day.

Lucky you, your dog goes Best in Show at Slyville! After the pictures and the congratulations, your handler feeds his string of dogs, cleans up, packs his motorhome and looks at his watch, it's 6:45 p.m. He needs to get going for he has to be in Lizard Butte by 10:00 p.m. to hold his reserved overnight parking at the show grounds. He also needs to pick up that bitch at the Toonerville airport and then find a decent place to eat. He also must call and tell you that your dog went "all the way" that day, before you plow a furrow in the rug pacing around waiting for the news.

Now, are you ready for this? When he arrives at the airport he finds the air freight office is closed—not to open until 7:00 a.m. Don't laugh, it happens! Small airports don't stay open all night. So, what does the handler do? He's showing his client's Beagles at 8:00 a.m. the next morning! The purpose of this commentary is not to try to solve this particular problem, but to allow some insight into the problems of breeding to a dog being actively campaigned.

Now, for a most important item: How much should be charged for the dog's services? A good rule of thumb says that for a young unproven stud, charge 65%-75% of the average being charged. Don't include the Mr. Big's who have already sired 20 or more champions in your calculations. Their fees are elevated based upon accomplishment. You are charging a fee based upon hope and good bloodlines. After the dog has sired at least five champions boost his fee to the average being charged. If he should prove to be a *prepotent* stud and sires some 115 champion offspring, a price more commensurate with his siring abilities should be set. Don't be afraid to ask a price above the average. The average breeder, like the average buyer of goods, equates a good price with a good product.

There are four major things to consider when you decide to promote a stud dog: How often to advertise? How big should the advertisement be? How to use words and pictures to get people to do what you want them to do? And, where to place the advertising to get the best results?

A cardinal rule of advertising is repetition. It has been found that no matter how good the advertisement is, it won't sell unless it is repeated often. The more often an ad is seen, the more likely it will be remembered.

On average, both readership and responses increase as the size of the advertisement increases. However, a full page will not get twice as much attention as a half page. A half-page advertisement will usually be noticed by such a high percentage of readers that it would be impossible to double the readership. On the other hand, a single column ad—a couple of inches deep—will attract the attention of such a small percentage of readers that doubling its size is likely to double its readership. Advertising experts say that nearly everyone involved with print advertising would like their ad to be larger than it should be.

Get their attention. Try to prove that you have a better stud dog for their bitch than anyone else. The more physical the better. Push—better puppies, better puppy sales, etc., and you need to back it up with logic and proof. Cite examples. The magic formula could be stated, "to get what you *want*, do what I want." By citing all the famous and near famous breeders who have bred to your dog, you get them to identify— "if I do the same thing as those famous people did, I will be right in line with those big shots and get champions to boot." This type of identification advertising is highly successful, because it appeals to the need to belong to a group and it unifies people.

First promote his winning look to all-breed magazines and newspapers to catch the eye of both the all-rounders and specialty judges and to help his career along. Then, after his winning record is established, turn greater emphasis to the breed magazines to promote his offspring.

When promoting the dog both as a show dog and as a stud, you have a chicken-and-egg situation. The early advertisements should emphasize his winning record and his winning (producing) ancestors. Later, as the bitches come in, is the time to stress the numbers of bitches being bred to him. Finally, as he produces, trumpet the achievements of his offspring and the history of the producers behind him.

Ch. Caroling's Mohamed Aly shown winning Best of Variety under Mrs. Peggy Adamson; Gregg Anderson handling.

CHAPTER 2

The Bitch and Her Puppies

It has been said that a good bitch is worth her weight in gold. I don't know what gold is selling for today but it's a good bet a really good bitch is worth it. "Really good" doesn't necessarily mean one who will win Westminster. However, she should be a solid bitch who is good enough to finish—or come mighty close—and who comes from a top-producing bloodline. In the chapter, The Stud Dog, emphasis was placed on the continuous, unbroken line of champion ancestors. This holds true in bitches as well, although it is somewhat harder to obtain because of the limited number of puppies they produce when compared to the male.

To begin, assume you have been fortunate and have procured the best bitch that is affordable and she comes from producing bloodlines. Now all that has to be done is sit back and count the champions in each litter. Right? Wrong! There are many extraneous factors to deal with before that can even be a possibility.

It's best to start at the beginning. When thinking about breeding that good bitch, first make sure she is in good condition. Take her to the veterinarian to have her thoroughly checked out. This should include checking for heartworm and other parasites and to make sure she is not carrying a sexually-transmitted disease like brucellosis, which can cause sterility and abortions. All this should be done at least a couple of months before she is due in season.

If there are any problems they can be taken care of early. It is important that she be parasite free. Check for this once again just before she is to be bred. Parasites can be quite debilitating to the puppies. The bitch needs to be in tip-top shape.

Her diet should continue along normal lines with plenty of exercise and fresh water. Be sure she is lean and hard. A fat bitch spells trouble in the whelping box.

Once she has been bred, there is nothing special to do for the first few weeks. She should have good nourishment, fresh water and normal exercise. Be sure her diet is well balanced. Most of the good commercial dry foods provide this. After the third week increase her intake to twice what she has been eating. Feed her twice a day to make digestion easier.

After week seven has gone by, feed at the same level but spread it over three feedings. All this time she should be getting regular exercise. In the last three weeks cut out any hard-to-digest foods and walk her briskly on lead, but don't let her overextend herself physically. The week before she is due to whelp, modify her diet by making it more liquid—to assist her to eliminate easily. Within three days of whelping give her a teaspoon full of milk of magnesia daily.

The average whelping time is 63 days after conception. No two bitches are alike, and whelping can occur from the 59th day to the 65th day just as easily. Remember the Boy Scout motto—"Be Prepared!"

There are a number of things that can be done to prepare for the arrival of the puppies. First, prepare a comfortable, quiet place for the bitch to whelp. This is not time for a block party, so set-up to keep vistors out. Either make or buy a whelping box. This box should sit above the floor (a minimum of 2") to be out of drafts. It should have enough room for the dam to lie just outside an area where the puppies will snuggle but allow her some respite from them when she needs it. Of course, the bigger the bitch, the larger the box. It should have a lip to keep the puppies in. It should also have enough room for her to whelp the puppies without feeling crowded and allow you room to assist her if you need to. The whelping area should have a good supply of newspaper for sterilization reasons (newsprint is antiseptic) and to allow the bitch in labor to dig as she tries to nest. The floor itself should be covered with a rough surface like indoor/outdoor carpeting, to allow the puppies to gain traction while they are nursing. After a couple of weeks, cover this over with newspaper since the mother will probably no longer clean up after them and it can get messy.

It's also a good idea to have a "pig rail" (a protective barrier) around the inside flooring. This rail can be constructed from large broom handles. Its purpose is to protect the puppy that may crawl behind his mother and be trapped or crushed before she can see, smell or hear him. This is more prone to happen when there is a large litter. There should be an outside heating source (either under the flooring or just above) to make sure the puppies don't get chilled. Newborn puppies are unable to generate enough body heat to insulate themselves. It's imperative to supply that warmth externally. Listen for crying, this indicates something is wrong and it's often lack of warmth. Puppies will pile on one another to help keep warm. After about ten days their internal "furnace" can stoke up enough body heat to protect themselves. If the puppies are scattered around the box and not heaped together, the heat is too high.

There are some other supplies that are needed. Since the puppies usually don't come all at once, a place is needed to keep the puppies that have arrived in sight of the mother but out of the way as she whelps the next one. Most people use a small cardboard box with high sides. (Get a

Table IV-1. Sixty-Three Day Whelping Table

Date Bred	Puppies Due	Date Bred	Puppies Due	Date Bred	Puppies Due	Date Bred	Puppies Due	Date Bred	Puppies Due	Date Bred	Puppies Due	Date Bred	Puppies Due	Date Bred	Puppies Due	Date Bred	Puppies Due	Date Bred	Puppies Due	Date Bred	Puppies Due	Date Bred	Puppies Due
JANUARY	MARCH	FEBRUARY	APRIL	MARCH	MAY	APRIL	JUNE	MAY	JULY	JUNE	AUGUST	JULY	SEPTEMBER	AUGUST	OCTOBER	SEPTEMBER	NOVEMBER	OCTOBER	DECEMBER	NOVEMBER	JANUARY	DECEMBER	FEBRUARY
1	5	1	5	1	3	1	3	1	3	1	3	1	2	1	3	1	3	1	3	1	3	1	2
2	6	2	6	2	4	2	4	2	4	2	4	2	3	2	4	2	4	2	4	2	4	2	3
3	7	3	7	3	5	3	5	3	5	3	5	3	4	3	5	3	5	3	5	3	5	3	4
4	8	4	8	4	6	4	6	4	6	4	6	4	5	4	6	4	6	4	6	4	6	4	5
5	9	5	9	5	7	5	7	5	7	5	7	5	6	5	7	5	7	5	7	5	7	5	6
6	10	6	10	6	8	6	8	6	8	6	8	6	7	6	8	6	8	6	8	6	8	6	7
7	11	7	11	7	9	7	9	7	9	7	9	7	8	7	9	7	9	7	9	7	9	7	8
8	12	8	12	8	10	8	10	8	10	8	10	8	9	8	10	8	10	8	10	8	10	8	9
9	13	9	13	9	11	9	11	9	11	9	11	9	10	9	11	9	11	9	11	9	11	9	10
10	14	10	14	10	12	10	12	10	12	10	12	10	11	10	12	10	12	10	12	10	12	10	11
11	15	11	15	11	13	11	13	11	13	11	13	11	12	11	13	11	13	11	13	11	13	11	12
12	16	12	16	12	14	12	14	12	14	12	14	12	13	12	14	12	14	12	14	12	14	12	13
13	17	13	17	13	15	13	15	13	15	13	15	13	14	13	15	13	15	13	15	13	15	13	14
14	18	14	18	14	16	14	16	14	16	14	16	14	15	14	16	14	16	14	16	14	16	14	15
15	19	15	19	15	17	15	17	15	17	15	17	15	16	15	17	15	17	15	17	15	17	15	16
16	20	16	20	16	18	16	18	16	18	16	18	16	17	16	18	16	18	16	18	16	18	16	17
17	21	17	21	17	19	17	19	17	19	17	19	17	18	17	19	17	19	17	19	17	19	17	18
18	22	18	22	18	20	18	20	18	20	18	20	18	19	18	20	18	20	18	20	18	20	18	19
19	23	19	23	19	21	19	21	19	21	19	21	19	20	19	21	19	21	19	21	19	21	19	20
20	24	20	24	20	22	20	22	20	22	20	22	20	21	20	22	20	22	20	22	20	22	20	21
21	25	21	25	21	23	21	23	21	23	21	23	21	22	21	23	21	23	21	23	21	23	21	22
22	26	22	26	22	24	22	24	22	24	22	24	22	23	22	24	22	24	22	24	22	24	22	23
23	27	23	27	23	25	23	25	23	25	23	25	23	24	23	25	23	25	23	25	23	25	23	24
24	28	24	28	24	26	24	26	24	26	24	26	24	25	24	26	24	26	24	26	24	26	24	25
25	29	25	29	25	27	25	27	25	27	25	27	25	26	25	27	25	27	25	27	25	27	25	26
26	30	26	30	26	28	26	28	26	28	26	28	26	27	26	28	26	28	26	28	26	28	26	27
27	31	27	May 1	27	29	27	29	27	29	27	29	27	28	27	29	27	29	27	29	27	29	27	28
28	Apr 1	28	2	28	30	28	30	28	30	28	30	28	29	28	30	28	30	28	30	28	30	28	Mar 1
29	2			29	31	29	Jul 1	29	31	29	31	29	30	29	31	29	Dec 1	29	31	29	31	29	2
30	3			30	Jun 1	30	2	30	Aug 1	30	Sep 1	30	Oct 1	30	Nov 1	30	2	30	Jan 1	30	Feb 1	30	3
31	4			31	2			31	2			31	2	31	2			31	2			31	4

clean one from your supermarket.) At the bottom of this box put a heating pad or a hot water bottle. Cover it with a rough towel. Make sure it doesn't get too warm. After the dam has cleaned up each puppy, roughly licking it with her tongue and drying it off, she may wish to nurse it. Let her try. But most of the time Mother Nature is telling her to prepare for the next whelp. If the bitch starts to dig at the papers on the floor of the box, remove the puppy and place it in the cardboard box. You may wish to leave the box in the corner of the whelping box. However, if the bitch starts to whirl around while whelping, get the box out of there and up on some surface where it won't be knocked down. Be sure the bitch can see it at all times.

Clean, sharp scissors, alcohol and string should also be present. The scissors—which along with the string—should be sitting in the alcohol, are to cut the umbilical cord if necessary. Cut it at least 2″ from the puppy. Later, when the puppy is in the cardboard box, tie off the cord with the string. Disposable towels, washcloths, cotton swabs, toenail clipper, garbage pail and pans for warm and cold water are among the other supplies that you should have on hand.

Harking back to the "Be Prepared" motto, there should also be on hand a small syringe with a rubber bulb on it. These can be found in most drug stores and are called "aspirators." They are like the kind used for basting, only smaller. If you can't find the proper tool, use your basting syringe. The purpose of this device is to clear the puppies nostrils and lungs of excess fluid. Some puppies are born sputtering because fluid has accumulated in their nostrils or lungs during their trip through the birth canal. Try to suck the fluid from the nostrils first. Listen for a wheezing sound, this means there is still fluid. The puppy will also cough or choke. If all the fluid is still not out and the puppy is still sputtering, take the next step. Wrap the pup in the rough washcloth and—grasping it under the chest and hindquarters—raise it above head level and then swing it down between your legs to try and give centrifugal force a chance to expel the fluid. Hold the puppy face down during this maneuver. Be firm but gentle—never do this violently. Repeat two or three times. This should do the trick. The heat in the bottom of the cardboard box should dry out any excess fluid.

As the time of whelping approaches, the bitch will have been giving all sorts of signs. In the last ten days her shape begins to change as the puppies drop down lower. She now begins to look like a stuffed sausage. As the fateful day approaches, she will seem restless and be unable to settle down for any length of time. She acts as though she can't get comfortable. She will also want to keep you in her sight. She may or may not show an interest in the whelping box. Some bitches go to it, sniff around and walk away, while others lie in it and occasionally dig it up. Take her temperature on a regular basis as she grows more restless.

A reading of 101.5 is normal for a dog. Just before whelping she can take a sudden drop to about 98 degrees. Unless the temperature drops, it's pretty sure there will be no immediate action. Oh yes, just so there is no misunderstanding, this may not be a piece of cake. Most bitches whelp at night. There are exceptions to these rules—but, "Be Prepared." It's a good idea for someone to stay close by the whelping box to keep an eye on things. You can take turns as the time draws near.

The most important sign to look for after her temperature starts to drop is the breaking of the water sac. There will suddenly be a small pool of water around her. This is often referred to as "the water breaking." This means that real action is close at hand, at least in a matter of hours.

When her temperature goes down, alert the vet that a whelping is imminent and request that he stand by if any problems come up. Of course, being a well-prepared person, the vet was alerted at least a month ago that you might need his help. He was alerted, wasn't he?

If this is the bitch's first litter she may be a bit confused and frightened by all this. Pet her and tell her how wonderful she is. Get her over to the whelping box and make her comfortable. She may pace, she may dig or she may settle down. But, rest assured, she will probably do all three. She will also make everyone nervous. Allow things to proceed on their own. Don't panic! Let her go four or five hours *if she seems in no distress.* HOWEVER, if she goes into hard labor and has not delivered a puppy in a few hour's time, check with your vet. "Hard labor" means digging up papers, heavy panting, obvious straining followed by short rest periods. She may also issue large groans as she bears down. All this is normal if it is followed by the birth of a puppy.

As she bears down, sometimes standing in a defecating position, sometimes lying on her side, a blob will appear issuing from her vagina and with one big push, she will force it out. Usually she will reach back and break the sac, cut the umbilical cord with her teeth, and start to lick the puppy to stimulate a cry. If she does not do so immediately or if she seems confused you need to step in, cut the cord, and take the puppy out of the sac. Then clear its lungs and nose and give it back to its dam to stimulate.

Many dams will eat the afterbirth (the blueish/black blob attached to the sac the puppy came in). Let her eat a couple. It stimulates delivery of the next puppies. If she makes no move to do so, remove it and put it into a garbage pail. *Keep track of the afterbirths*—make sure they are all accounted for. A retained afterbirth can cause great harm to the bitch. In fact, once she has finished whelping, be sure to take her to the vet—to check her over and to make sure no afterbirths have been retained. The vet may give her a shot of pituitrin or a similar drug to induce the uterus to force out anything that's been retained.

Puppies may come one right after the other or there can be hours between deliveries. Remember, as long as she does not seem in distress, any pattern can be considered normal. If labor persists for a prolonged time and no puppies are forthcoming, call the vet even though she has already whelped one or more puppies. You *may* have a problem. (For more detailed information on whelping, read *The Great American Dog Show Game*, by Alvin Grossman, published by Denlinger Publishers, Ltd.)

The vet will probably advise bringing her to the clinic where he can examine her to determine her problem. In most cases, it is usually only a sluggish uterus and he will give her a shot to speed things along and send her home to whelp the rest of the puppies. On occasion, there is a problem and he might opt to do a Caesarean section—that is, to take the rest of the puppies surgically. Usually he will perform this surgery immediately. Some bitches have a problem and cannot even push the puppies down into the birthing canal. The vet may take these puppies by C-section without having her try to go into serious labor. It's a good idea to have another small box, with a hot-water bottle in it, when you go to the vet so any puppies delivered there can be taken care of.

Mary Donnelly, writing in the March 1987 issue of The *Min Pin Monthly* also says to take a crate along to bring the bitch home if she has to have a Caesarean.

If you feel the trip from the vet will take an hour or more, you may consider giving the puppies the opportunity to nurse before you leave the office. This will also help you see if you will have any problems introducing them to nursing. You can take a supply of formula with you in the event you have to feed or supplement them.

Once home, the dam should be your first concern. Position her on her side with her back flush against the side of the whelping box. Don't worry, she won't be going anywhere for several hours. With the pan of warm cleaning water, dip your disposable towel and clean any blood from her incision or vaginal area. Because she has had a C-section, she will bleed a bit more than she would from a normal birth. (In a normal birth, the bitch will have a blackish discharge at first turning to bright red shortly thereafter.) Those little pups won't take long learning to explore the dam so you must keep her clean until she can take over. If you will notice, her tongue is probably hanging from the side of her mouth. Take a bowl of clean water and dip a cloth in, squeeze most of the excess water back into the bowl and just moisten her tongue and mouth. Never put water into her mouth at this point. She could choke because her natural reflexes are on vacation because of the anesthetic.

Don't leave the puppies alone for too long a period. They will get cold and hungry. There are a number of things that need to be done promptly. Begin with the smallest ones. Use a toenail clipper and take the tips off their nails to preclude their causing problems with the stitches. Eliminate as much discomfort for the dam as possible. Once this is done, introduce the puppy to his dam. Let it sniff and try on its own to fit a teat to nurse. If the pup needs help, gently open its mouth and squeeze a bit of milk on the pup's tongue. (Even without a C-section some pups have to be shown how to nurse and others just dig right in.) If the puppy won't cooperate, go ahead and give it a bit of formula. Continue this process until all the puppies have had their toenails cut and have been fed.

It is important to remember *you* must do everything for the puppies. The bitch may be "out of it" anywhere from 6 to 12 hours . . . or more. This is normal. During the time she is helpless, someone must carefully watch her and care for the puppies at the same time. Hopefully there will be help and shifts can be rotated. If not, roll up your sleeves.

As soon as the puppies are fed and the bitch has been cleaned up again, help the pups to eliminate their waste. Dip a cotton ball in warm water, squeeze out most of the excess and gently rub it on their genitalia. This should produce urination. Do the same around the anal area for a bowel movement. (This doesn't always work for there is a "plug" in there that is a bit hard to intially dislodge.) If there is not initial success in getting a bowel movement, be patient and try tickling the anal area with a swab. If that doesn't work, don't be too alarmed for the dam will soon be awake and will take care of this.

Generally, most puppies are worn out by now and ready to curl up next to their dam and go to sleep . . . but you can count on one or two little brats to be obnoxious and climb on her or try to see what's on the other side of the box. Let them explore but try to convince them to stay in the heated area. The dam is not going to grab them and cuddle them, so you want to keep them warm. They expected life to be different and are finding out that their mother isn't doing her job. Go ahead and clean the bitch again while they explore and you cast longing eyes at the bed nearby. NO!! you can't go to sleep yet!

Try and moisten the bitch's mouth again. While taking care of business, be aware if the bitch feels cold to the touch. Once all the puppies have settled down for a nap, you can drape a light sheet over the dam and the puppies. (Do not attempt to do this with a dam who has not had a C-section.) Now it's possible to lay down. There is a specific way to lay down. (Why should this be easy?) Stretch out, but be sure you are close enough to the box so a hand can rest against the bitch. It is not advisable to fall asleep but since you are exhausted, it will happen anyway. The bitch will undoubtedly wait until you have just fallen asleep to wake up. (Just like she had her emergency C-section at 3:00 a.m.) Hopefully, you will feel her stir and awaken.

Just because she starts to stir does not mean she is anywhere close to being left alone. Do not not let her stand on her own right away. She is not in control. She may think she is but she could fall and injure herself and/or her puppies.

Usually the first time she stirs she will not need to relieve herself. She may, or may not, be interested in her litter. In most cases, she is going to be convinced to go back to sleep. Offer her a bit of water but not too much. Too much water at this time can cause nausea. Just about five good laps is all she needs. Be assured she needs cleaning again and the pups have been awakened and want to eat. So take care of this all over again.

Some dams will shake as they come awake. More often than not, this is caused by the anesthetic. This shaking can be slight or strong. In the event she shakes to the extent it could cause injury to the puppies, calm her by petting and covering the puppies a bit away from her. If at any time the shaking is too much, or there is a concern for any reason, call the veterinarian.

When the bitch really becomes restless she won't be talked into going back to sleep. Try to judge by the control she exhibits as to how stable she is. Take her outside when she becomes too restless. On her first trip, carry her. Place her in a safe area and be ready to assist her should she fall.

The rest of the recovery consists of your attention to the dam and the safety of her and her litter. If you are patient and see her through her "time of need," she will eventually ease you right out of a job.

Now, whether the puppies have arrived normally or by C-section, they are pursuing normal puppy behavior. Their primary concerns are keeping warm and being fed. A healthy dam will be able to take care of those needs. Be sure to keep a keen eye on both the dam and the puppies; watch for signs of distress . . . crying, being unable to settle down, and/or looking bloated—all portend trouble for the puppies. Call the vet. Watch the bitch to see if her discharge turns from a blackish color to bright red. See if she has milk and if the puppies can nurse from her. It is *extremely* important to stay vigilant for the next three weeks. It's a critical time.

There are times, however, when you may be faced with either losing the dam through complications from whelping or she cannot nurse her puppies due to a variety of reasons. YOU are now the mother and must deal with these orphaned puppies. Times like these test the mettle of any dog breeder. R.K. Mohrman, Director of the Pet Nutrition and Care Center at the Ralston Purina Company has some sage advice when you find yourself in this predicament.

Several critical problems must be addressed in caring for orphan puppies. Among these are chilling, dehydration and hypoglycemia. These problems are interrelated and may exist concurrently. Close observation and prompt attention if any of these problems develop are essential to survival. Of course, proper feeding of the orphan puppies is extremely important. A veterinarian should examine the puppies to determine if special therapy is needed.

Chilling

Chilling in newborn puppies (as described in the chapter Problems of Early Puppyhood) can lead to significant mortality. A puppy will dissipate far more body heat per pound of body weight than an adult dog. The normal newborn puppy depends on radiant heat from the bitch to help maintain its body temperature. In the absence of the bitch, various methods of providing heat can be used, such as: incubators, heating pads, heat lamps or hot water bottles.

Rectal temperatures in a newborn puppy range from 95 to 99°F (Fahrenheit) for the first week, 97 to 100°F for the second and third weeks, and reach the normal temperature of an adult dog (100.5 to

102.5°F) by the fourth week.

When the rectal temperature drops below 94°F, the accompanying metabolic alterations are life-threatning. Therefore, immediate action is necessary to provide the warmth the puppy needs to survive. A healthy newborn can survive chilling if warmed slowly.

During the first four days of its life, the orphan puppy should be maintained in an environmental temperature of 85 to 90°F. The temperature may gradually be decreased to 80°F by the seventh to tenth day and to 72°F by the end of the fourth week. If the litter is large, the temperature need not be as high. As puppies huddle together, their body heat provides additional warmth.

CAUTION: *Too rapid warming of a chilled puppy may result in its death.*

Dehydration

The lack of regular liquid intake or the exposure of the puppy to a low humidity environment can easily result in dehydration. The inefficiency of the digestion and metabolism of a chilled puppy may also lead to dehydration and other serious changes.

Experienced breeders can detect dehydration by the sense of touch. Two signs of dehydration are the loss of elasticity in the skin and dry and sticky mucous membranes in the mouth. If dehydration is severe or persistent, a veterinarian should be contacted immediately

An environmental relative humidity of 55 to 65 percent is adequate to prevent drying of the skin in a normal newborn puppy. However, a relative humidity of 85 to 90 percent is more effective in maintaining puppies if they are small and weak.

CAUTION: *The environmental temperature should not exceed 90°F when high humidity is provided. A temperature of 95°F coupled with relative humidity of 95 percent can lead to repiratory distress.*

Feeding

Total nutrition for the newborn orphans must be supplied by a bitch-milk replacer until the pups are about three weeks of age. At this age, the pups are ready to start nibbling moistened solid food.

Bitch-milk replacers are:
1. Commercial bitch-milk replacers, *e.g.* Esbilac, Vetalac, etc.
2. Emergency home-formulated bitch-milk replacer:
   1 cup milk
   1 tablespoon corn oil
   Salt (a pinch)
   1 drop high-quality oral multiple vitamins for dogs
   3 egg yolks (albumin)
   Blend mixture uniformly
3. Purina Puppy Chow brand dog food: 20 grams (2/3 oz. by weight) or 1/4-cup (8 oz. measure). Water: 80 grams (2-2/3 ounces by weight) or 1/4-cup (8 ounce measure). Blend into a soft gruel. Other formulas are to be found in the chapter Nutrition for Puppies and Adults.

Food Temperature

Since the newborn may have trouble generating enough heat to maintain its body temperature, the milk replacer should be warmed to 95-100°F for the best results. As the puppies grow older, the replacer can be fed at room temperature.

Feeding Methods

Spoon-feeding is slow and requires great patience. Each spoonful must be slowly "poured" into the puppy's mouth to prevent liquid from entering the lungs. The pup's head must not be elevated, or the lungs may fill with fluids. Newborn pups usually do not have a "gag" reflex to signal this.

Dropper-feeding accomplishes the same result as spoon-feeding but it is somewhat cleaner and generally speedier.

Baby bottles with premature infant-size nipples can be used for some puppies. Some doll-size bottles with high-quality rubber nipples are even better. Bottle-feeding is preferable to spoon or dropper-feeding but is less satisfactory than tube-feeding. Tube-feeding is the easiest, cleanest and most efficient way of hand-feeding.

The following equipment is needed for tube-feeding:

Syringe: 10 to 50 ml., preferably plastic

Tubing: No. 10 catheter or small, semi-rigid tube that can easily be passed into the puppy's stomach. (Consult your veterinarian.)

Adhesive tape: To mark the depth of the tube in the puppy's stomach.

Disinfectant: To flush tube and syringe after each feeding. (Be sure to rinse thoroughly after disinfecting.)

1. Mark the tube. The feeding tube should extend into the puppy's stomach but not far enough to cause either pressure or perforation. Measure the tube alongside the puppy's body on the outside. (Tube should extend almost to the far end of the ribcage.) Place tape on the tube to mark the correct distance of the insertion. As the puppy grows, the tape can be moved so the tube can be inserted further.
2. Fill the syringe and expel all the air.
3. Hold the puppy horizontally, with the head extended but not raised, so the tube will slide into the esophagus. This helps keep fluids from entering the lungs.
4. Moisten the tube with a few drops of milk replacer for lubrication. Insert the tube gently through the mouth, throat and esophagus into the stomach. If the puppy struggles, withdraw the tube and try again. Do not force it.
5. Gently inject syringe contents into the stomach. If a slight resistance is met, the stomach is probably full. Withdraw the tube.
6. Massage the genital and anal area with a moist cotton cloth to stimulate excretion. Stimulating the pups following each feeding teaches the pup to defecate.

Amount To Feed

Puppies being fed by spoon, dropper or bottle reject food when they are full. When tube-feeding, care must be taken not to overfeed, since fluid can be drawn into the pup's lungs. When adequate liquid has been injected into the pup the syringe plunger will become more difficult to push as resistance to flow increases.

In establishing the amount to feed a newborn puppy check the recommendations in the chapter on Nutrition in Puppies and Adults. Basically, a one pound puppy (when fed four times a day) should consume 21 cc per feeding.

Some puppies, during their first feedings, cannot handle the determined amount per feeding. More than the scheduled four feedings may be necessary for the appropriate caloric intake.

Monitor the pup's weight and continue to adjust the pup's intake proportionally throughout the use of milk replacer formula.

CAUTION: *Diarrhea is a common digestive disorder in very young puppies. Consult your veterinarian if diarrhea develops, as alterations in the feeding program may be necessary.*

Feeding Schedule

Three meals, equally spaced during a 24-hour period are ample for feeding puppies when adequate nutrients are provided. Four or more daily feedings may be necessary if the puppies are small. Tube- and hand-feeding can generally be ended by the third week and certainly by the fourth. By this time, the puppy can consume food, free-choice, from a dish.

Cleaning Puppies

As has been stated earlier in this chapter and elsewhere, the puppy's genital and anal areas must be stimulated after feeding to effect urination. Use a moist cloth or a piece of cotton to do this. This cleaning should continue for the first two weeks. If you do not do this, the puppy may suffer from constipation.

Bowl Feeding

By two-and-one-half to three weeks, the puppies can start to eat food from the dish along with the bitch-milk replacer.

A gruel can be made by thoroughly moistening dry puppy food with water to reach the consistency of a thick milkshake. The mixture must *not* be sloppy, or the puppies will not consume very much. As the consumption of supplemental food increases, the amount of water can be decreased.

By four weeks, orphaned puppies can consume enough moistened solid food to meet their needs.

It is better to avoid starting puppies on a meat-milk-baby food regimen. This creates extra work and can also create finicky eaters. Many times such foods will not meet the nutritional needs of growing puppies.

Size and Sex of a Litter

It is helpful to understand how the size and sex of a litter is determined. One of the most informative and entertaining articles I have read on the subject was written by Patricia Gail Burnham, a Greyhound breeder from Sacramento, California. Her article "Breeding, Litter Size and Gender" appeared in an issue of the *American Cocker Review* and I will attempt to paraphrase the information so that it is most applicable.

The number of puppies in a litter at whelping time is determined by several different factors. The order in which they occur, are:
1. The number of ova (gametes) produced by the dam;
2. The number of ova that are successfully fertilized and implanted in the uterus;
3. The prenatal mortality rate among the embryos while they are developing.

It is not possible to end up with more puppies than the number of ova that the bitch produces. As a bitch ages, the number of ova will often decrease. Bitches don't manufacture ova on demand the way a male dog can manufacture sperm. All the ova a bitch will ever have are stored in her ovaries.

In each season some of them will be shed (ovulated) into her uterus for a chance at fertilization. Elderly bitches quite commonly produce two or three puppy litters. Sometimes, just living hard can have the same effect on a bitch as old age.

If a bitch does produce a large number of ova, what happens next? The ova need to be fertilized. If they are not fertilized, or if they are fertilized and not implanted, they will perish. If a bitch ovulates over an extended period of time and she is bred late in her season, then the ova which were produced early may have died unfertilized before the sperm could reach them, and the result can be a small litter.

Sometimes there is a noticeable difference in birth weight. It is a good idea not to consider the small ones runts. They may have been conceived a few days later than their larger litter mates and may grow up to be average-sized adults.

All the puppies in a litter are never conceived simultaneously, since all the ova are not released at once. Ovulation takes place over an extended period, so at birth some of the puppies may be 59 days old while others may be 64 days old. A few days' difference in puppies of this age can create noticeable differences in size.

The mature size of a dog is determined by its heredity and its nutrition. Its size at birth is determined by the size of its dam, the number of puppies in the litter, and their individual dates of conception. The small puppies could just be more refined than the others and could always be smaller. Only time will tell.

The sire is always responsible for the sex of the offspring. The rule applies equally to people and dogs. While dams are often blamed for not producing males, they have nothing to do with the sex of their offspring. If the bitch determined the sex of the offspring, then all the puppies would be bitches, because the only chromosomes that a bitch can contribute to her offspring are those that she and every female has, homozygous (XX) sex chromosomes.

What's the difference between boys and girls? It's not sugar and spice and puppy dog's tails. It's the makeup of their sex chromosomes. All of the chromosome pairs are matched to each other with the exception of one pair. Dogs (and people) each have one pair of chromosomes that may or may not match. This is the chromosome pair that determines sex. Sex chromosomes may be either X chromosomes (which are named for their shape) or X chromosomes that are missing one leg, which makes them Y chromosomes (again named for their shape).

All females have two homozygous X chromosomes. They are XX genetically. All males are heterozygous (unmatched). They have one X and one Y chromosome to be XY genetically.

In each breeding, all ova contain an X chromosome, which is all a female can donate, while the sperm can contain either an X or a Y chromosome. If the X-carrying ovum is fertilized by an X-carrying sperm, then the result is female (XX). If the X-carrying ovum is fertilized by a Y-carrying sperm, then the result is a male (XY).

What influences whether an X- or a Y-carrying sperm reaches the ovum to fertilize it? The Y chromosome is smaller and lighter weight than the X chromosome. This enables the Y chromosome-carrying (male) sperm to swim faster than the heavier X-carrying (female) sperm. This gives the males an edge in the upstream sprint to reach the ovum that is waiting to be fertilized.

As a result, slightly more than 50% of the fertilized ova are male. More males are conceived than females. However, things even up, because males have a higher mortality rate than females, both in the womb and later.

What if ova are not ready and waiting when the sperm arrive? If sperm have to wait in the uterus or fallopian tubes for an ovum to arrive, then the odds change. Female sperm live longer than male ones. As the wait increases, the males die off and leave the female sperm waiting when the ovum arrives.

This is the reason that some breeders advise breeding as early as the bitch will stand to maximize the chance for female puppies. The idea is to breed—if she will allow it—before the bitch ovulates. This allows the male sperm time to die off and leaves the female sperm waiting when the ova arrive. Whether this has a basis in fact is not known.

What can influence the number of males and females in a litter other than the time of the breeding? The age of the sire can influence the gender of the puppies. As a stud dog ages, all his sperm slow down. Instead of a sprint, the race to fertilize the ova becomes an endurance race in which the female sperm's greater lifespan and hardiness can offset the male sperm's early speed advantage. When they are both slowed down, then the male sperm's higher mortality rate gives the female sperm the advantage.

With the information gleaned from this section on Becoming A Breeder, you should have the knowledge to breed good ones and to be a successful exhibitor. Now it's up to you to put into practice what you have learned. Good luck!

Ch. Frandee's Celebration, a red and white bitch illustrated beautifully by Michael Allen.

CHAPTER **3**

Nutrition for Puppies and Adults

Nutrition of dogs can be maintained at a high level through the use of good commercial diets. It is not necessary for the owner to be an expert in nutrition, but some background in this science is helpful in understanding the problems that may be encountered in the normal care of your dog.

Dog food is generally prepared in one of two ways; dry and canned. Dry food is usually cooked cereal and meat blended together. The cereal grains need to be cooked or heated to improve digestibility. Fats are added to increase calories; vitamins and minerals are added as needed. Dry foods contain about 10% moisture.

A subject frequently discussed among "dog people" is the addition of supplements to commercially prepared dog foods. But supplements are usually unneccessary because major dog food manufacturers incorporate into their products all the protein, vitamins, minerals, and other nutrients dogs are known to need. The diet may be specific for a particular life stage such as adult maintenance or growth, or it may be shown as complete and balanced for all stages of life. When it is fed to normal dogs of any breed, no additional supplementation in the forms of vitamins, minerals, meats or other additives is needed.

Dry meals are usually pelleted, sprayed with oil and crumbled. Biscuit and kibbled foods are baked on sheets and then kibbled or broken into small bits. Expanded foods are mixed, cooked and forced through a die to make nuggets which are then expanded with steam, dried and coated with oil. Food to be expanded must be at least 40% carbohydrates or the expansion process will not work.

Soft-moist foods, which are considered dry foods, contain about 25% moisture. They can be stored in cellophane without refrigeration due to the added preservatives.

Canned foods come in four types:
1. "Ration" types are usually the cheapest and are a mix of cereals, meat products, fats, etc. to make a complete diet containing 50–70% water.
2. All animal tissue may be beef, chicken, horsemeat, etc. Generally this type is not balanced although some may add supplements. These are

sometimes used to improve palatability of dry foods.

3. "Chunk" style has meat by-products ground and extruded into pellets or chunks. Some of the cheaper ones have vegetable matter mixed in. A gravy or juice is added.

4. "Stews" are meat or chunks mixed with vegetables.

Nutritional Requirements

The exact nutritional requirements of any dog are complicated by the wide variation in size, hair coat, activity, etc. Diets can be suggested based on body weight, but the final determination must be based on how the individual responds to the diet. Gain or loss in weight, change in activity, etc. must be observed and some adjustments made.

WHEN TO SUPPLEMENT. There are generally two exceptions to the rule that supplementation is not necessary when dogs receive a complete and balanced commercial diet. These instances are: (1) to correct a specific deficiency due to the dog's inability to utilize the normal level of a particular nutrient, and (2) to stimulate food intake, particularly during periods of hard work or heavy lactation. This includes hard-working dogs such as bird dogs or sled dogs and bitches with large litters that require a high level of milk production. The addition of 10% to 20% meat or meat by-products to the diet will normally increase food acceptance and as a result will increase food intake. At this level of supplementation, the nutritional balance of the commercial product would not be affected.

WATER. Fresh and clean water should be available at all times. The amount of water needed is dependent upon the type of food provided (dry, canned, semi-soft, etc.), but generally a dog gets 25% of its total water requirements from drinking.

PROTEIN. Ten of the approximately twenty amino acids that make up protein are essential for the dog. The dog must receive adequate amounts of these ten proteins for good nutrition. The natural sources containing these ten are milk, eggs, meat and soybeans. Sources such as gelatin, flour and wheat are incomplete.

Also important is the ratio of nitrogen retained to the amount of nitrogen taken into the body. In this respect, eggs, muscle meat and organ meat are all good. Some legumes such as soybeans are only fair. Most other vegetative proteins are poor. As dogs get older, this vegetative type of food tends to overwork the kidneys. This is especially important with chronic kidney disease in old dogs. More dog food companies produce products for each stage in a dogs life—from puppyhood to old age and including special diets for lactating bitches.

Another important aspect of protein is digestibility. A good quality dry ration has about 75% digestibility, while canned foods are up to

95%. Some typical figures for digestibility are:

Horsemeat	91%	Meat scraps	75–86%
Fishmeal	99%	Soybean meal	86%
Liver meal	88%	Linseed meal	81%

The dog's utilization of protein is dependent upon both the biological value and the digestibility. The digestibility of protein in the dog is related to the temperature to which the protein is subjected during processing. Some dog foods that seem to have proper ingredients at the time they are mixed, can give disappointing results. This may well be due to the processing at high temperatures or heating for long periods of time.

It is generally recommended that the dietary crude protein for adult dogs be 18 to 25% on a dry basis. For example, if a canned food is 12% protein and has a 50% moisture content then it is really 24% protein on a "dry basis." If the protein is of high quality, such as from milk, eggs, and meat, the total needed would be less than if it contains substantial amounts of the vegetative proteins.

FAT. Fats and oils have an important effect on palatability. A small increase in fat in a diet may greatly increase its acceptability to the dog. Fats supply essential fatty acids, particularly linolenic and arachidonic acids. Pork fat is an excellent source of these essential fatty acids. Other sources are animal fats, corn oil, olive oil, and raw linseed oil. A dietary deficiency of the essential fatty acids leads to defective growth, dry hair, scaly skin, and susceptibility to skin infections.

The absorption of vitamins A, D, E, and K is associated with the absorption of fats. Rancid fat destroys vitamins A and E. Extended use of rancid fats can cause hair loss, rash, loss of appetite, constipation progressing to diarrhea and even death. Commercial dog foods must therefore use an antioxidant to retard rancidity.

The principal danger of excess fat in the diet is that it contains more energy than is needed and leads to storage of fat and obesity.

CARBOHYDRATES. Requirements for carbohydrates in the dog are not known. The dog can utilize as much as 65 to 70% in his diet. Since this is the cheapest source of energy, it composes the major part of commercial foods. Carbohydrates are well utilized if properly prepared. Potatoes, oats and corn are poorly utilized unless cooked. High levels of uncooked starch can cause diarrhea. Milk can upset some dogs as some do not have the lactase enzyme needed to digest lactose, the milk sugar. Fresh cow's milk is 50% lactose. In some dogs, a ration with as much as 10% dried skim milk may cause diarrhea.

FIBER. Fiber is also a part of the carbohydrate portion of the ration. It is only slightly digested. Some fibers absorb water and produce a more voluminous stool. This can help stimulate intestinal action, especially in old or inactive animals. Fiber aids in the prevention of constipation and other intestinal problems. Most foods have 1 to 8% fiber. Reducing diets may have as much as 32% fiber. Sources of fiber are cellulose, bran, beet pulp, and string beans.

GROSS ENERGY. Dogs expend energy in every form of body activity. This energy comes from food or from destruction of body sources. Carbohydrates and fats provide the main source of energy for dogs. Caloric requirements are greater per pound of body weight for small dogs than for large dogs. From Table IV-3, determine the number of calories per pound of body weight a puppy requires for his age. For example, a ten-week old puppy weighing 10 lbs. would require 650 calories per day. At twelve weeks and weighing 15 lbs. he would need 840 calories daily. Divide the number of calories contained in one pound of feed into the number of calories required by the puppy on a daily basis to determine how much to offer the puppy initially. Using the example: At ten weeks, he requires 650 calories per day. Divide this by 690 (the number of calories in one pound of a popular dry puppy food) and the answer is approximately 1.0 lbs.

There are various theories on how often to feed a dog. The *Gaines Basic Guide To Canine Nutrition* establishes this schedule: Up to 5 months feed 3 times daily; from 5 to 12 months feed twice daily; over 12 months feed twice daily for the rest of the dog's life.

Divide the amount of food needed each day into the appropriate number of feedings to determine the amount of food to give the puppy at each feeding. For example: For a twelve-week old pup, the appropriate number of feedings per day is three. Divide the puppy's 1 lb of food into 3 servings of 1/3 lb. each.

Russel V. Brown writing in the February 1987 issue of *The Basenji*, points out "While caloric needs vary with age and activity, a rule of thumb is that for dogs of 5 to 65 lbs. the need is $S(33\text{-}1/4\ X) = kcal/day$. In this case "X" is the body weight in pounds. A 20-lb. dog would work out as $20(33\text{-}20/4) = 20(28) = 560$ kcals per day. For dogs over 65 lbs., the formula is $18X = kcal/day$. The following adjustments are recommended:

a. Age adjustments
   1. add 10% for dogs 1 year of age
   2. add 30% for dogs 6 months of age
   3. add 60% for dogs 3 months of age
b. Activity variable
   1. add 25% for moderate activity
   2. add 60% for heavy activity (hunting or coursing)

Daily Caloric Needs of Puppies

Weeks	1	2	3	4	5	10	15	20	25	30	40	50	60	70
5	100	200	300	400	500	1000	1500							
6	90	180	270	360	450	900	1350							
7	80	160	240	320	400	800	1200							
8	75	150	225	300	375	750	1125	1500						
9	70	140	210	280	350	700	1050	1400						
10		130	195	260	325	650	975	1300	1625					
11			180	240	300	600	900	1200	1500					
12				224	280	560	840	1128	1400	1680				
13				208	260	520	780	1040	1300	1560				
14					240	480	720	960	1200	1440	1920			
15						450	675	900	1125	1350	1800			
16						420	630	840	1050	1260	1680	2100		
17							585	780	975	1170	1560	1950		
18								720	900	1080	1440	1800	2160	
19									825	990	1320	1650	1980	2100

To determine the number of calories needed by a particular puppy, find the dog's weight in the top row of numbers and move downward until you come to the line corresponding to the dog's age. The figure in the spot where the two lines intersect is the number of calories that puppy needs during a 24-hour period.

Table IV-2. Daily Caloric Needs of Puppies

c. Pregnancy and lactation
  1. from conception to whelping—increase 20%
  2. at whelping—increase 25%
  3. 2nd week of lactation—increase 50%
  4. 3rd week of lactation—increase 75%
  5. 4th week of lactation—increase 100%

Authors Note: "Kcal" is the scientific term for what laymen call calorie."

Some find that the portion-control methods such as the feeding schedule listed above is inconvenient. They opt for the self-feeding method which is also called the free-choice method. Free choice ensures that the puppy's food consumption correlates with his rate of growth. The idea behind free-choice feeding is that it provides reasonable assurance that the puppy is obtaining all he needs for growth, even though these needs are essentially changing.

Free-choice advocates believe that dogs generally know quite accurately what their needs are and eat accordingly. (This is generally true.) Free-choice works especially well for the pup who dawdles over his food for hours. A slight variation on the free-choice scheme is to feed the pup all he can eat in a specified time period, usually 20 minutes. The pup would be fed for those time periods a certain number of times a day. This timed method may not be suitable for the slow or picky eater (or the glutton) for that matter. Studies have indicated that free-choice eaters tend to turn out heavier by some 23% and that these weight differences were principally in body fat.

Other controlled studies have proven that overfeeding can cause skelatal problems. When overfed, puppies may develop hip dysplasia (a disintegration of the ball and socket joint) more often, earlier, and more severely, than littermates who were fed less. Breeds larger in size are particularly vulnerable to these skeletal defects.

If in doubt on how much to feed, slight underfeeding is preferable to overfeeding. Studies have shown no serious effects from slight underfeeding. On the contrary, when obesity develops through overfeeding, the number of fat cells increase in the puppy. Facts prove that the chance of a dog being obese as an adult has its roots in overfeeding as a puppy.

Regardless of the feeding method used, food should be served lukewarm or at room temperature. If the food is prepared with an ingredient that can spoil quickly, such as meat or milk, be sure to serve fresh food only.

Estimating Caloric Content

In determining how much to feed a dog, use the following:

a. Dry food usually contains about 1360 calories per pound.
b. Canned food can be estimated at 475 calories per pound.

MINERALS. Calcium and phosphorus are needed in a ratio of 1.2 parts calcium to 1 part phosphorous. A deficiency causes rickets and other less serious diseases. Young and old dogs need additional calcium. Common sources are bone meal, skim milk, and alfalfa leaf meal. Sources of phosphorous are bone meal and meat scraps. Vitamin D is necessary for proper utilization of the calcium and phosphorous.

Magnesium is needed for bones and teeth—bone meal is a good source. Sodium chloride should be in the diet as 1% salt. Sulphur and potassium are needed, and are usually in the foods dogs eat. Iron's best sources are liver and eggs. A strict vegetarian diet will cause iron deficiency. Trace minerals (copper, cobalt, manganese, zinc, and iodine) are contained in milk, liver and egg yolks for copper, in fish scraps for iodine and most other foods contain the rest.

VITAMINS. Vitamin A is important to vision, bone growth and skin health. Deficiency may cause lack of appetite, poor growth, excessive shedding, lowered resistance to disease and infection etc. Severe deficiency can cause deafness in dogs. On the other hand, too much is harmful and can cause birth defects, anorexia, weight loss and bone problems.

Vitamin D deficiencies are most often found in large breeds. Deficiencies cause rickets in the young and softening of the bones in adults, and irregular teeth development or eruption. Sources of vitamin D are sunlight, irradiated yeast, fish liver oils and egg yolks. Too much vitamin D can cause anorexia, calcification, and other problems.

Vitamin E deficiency may involve reproductive and lactation problems. It may be involved in muscular dystrophy. Natural sources are corn oil, wheat germ oil, fish and egg yolk. It seems to be of some value topically in wound healing.

Vitamin K is involved in blood clotting. It is found in egg yolk, liver and alfalfa. Most dogs can synthesize enough in the intestines.

Thiamine deficiency causes anorexia, weight loss, dehydration, paralysis, and convulsions. Over-heating during the processing of dog food destroys thiamine. It is also commonly destroyed if dry food is stored in a hot location, such as a feed store without adequate cooling facilities. Best natural sources are raw liver, wheat germ and brewer's yeast. High-carbohydrate diets (particularly bread and potatoes) increase the need for thiamine. Fats may decrease the need.

Riboflavin, niacin and pyridoxine are all B vitamins found in liver, wheat germ, leafy vegatables, yeast and milk. Riboflavin deficiency can cause dry scaly skin, muscular weakness, abnormal redness of hindlegs and chest due to capillary congestion, anemia, and sudden death. Niacin deficiency can lead to pellagia or black tongue disease with oral ulcers. Pyridoxine deficiency can also cause anemia.

Choline deficiency causes fatty liver. Best sources are liver, yeast and soybean oil.

Biotin deficiency causes posterior paralysis and seborrhea. Raw egg whites contain a substance that ties up biotin. A diet of all raw egg whites should not be fed. Natural sources are liver and yeast.

B-12 is important in blood formation. Dogs used in heavy work need a good supply. Dogs produce B-12 in their intestines and when given foods that have enough B-12, can function adequately. Large doses of antibiotics may stop this synthesis. Best sources are liver, milk, cheese, eggs and meat.

Vitamin C (ascorbic acid) deficiency may cause delayed wound healing and scurvy-type lesions of the mouth and gums, loose teeth, bloody diarrhea, and tender joints. Generally the bacteria in the gut produce sufficient C. However, intestinal problems can effect the amount produced.

Table IV-3. Milk from the Lactating Bitch

	Bitch	Evaporated Milk	Cow
Fat	8.3%	6.6%	4.0%
Protein	7.5%	5.8%	3.5%
Lactose	3.7%	8.2%	4.9%
Calories	1.2	1.15	0.68

The 7.5% protein in bitches milk is equivalent to 30% dry dog food, but is probably all digestible. Dry dog food protein is only about 80% digestible unless it comes from a meat or fish source. A pup must consume twice as much cow's milk to get the protein of bitches' milk, but would then get three times as much lactose sugar which it has difficulty digesting. As a result, pups frequently have diarrhea on cow's milk. Non-fat dry milk is even worse for without the fat the percentage of lactose is even greater. (For more information on feeding the bitch, see chapter on The Bitch and Her Puppies.)

Weaning Puppies

It's a good idea to feed puppies a diet of 115 calories for each pound of their body weight three to four times a day. Begin to wean them at four to seven weeks of age. Seven to ten days should see the puppies no longer dependent on their mother. Often the dam will begin to wean the puppies on her own. During the weaning process, take the dam away during the day for gradually longer periods of time. Feed them three times a day. Puppies often gulp a lot of air when learning to eat solid foods. Slow them down by spreading out the food in a large pan. Chopped meat and small kibble may be better than finely ground meal because it passes through the intestines more slowly, causing fewer digestive problems.

Feeding Older Puppies

The first step in any puppy's feeding program is to weigh him. From birth through six months the breeder should weigh and record each pup's growth weekly.

The next step is to determine the diet to be fed. This depends, in a large measure, on the stage of growth the puppy has reached. Young puppies require twice as much energy per unit of body weight as an adult dog. But feeding the rapidly-growing puppy twice as much food of the adult variety is not the answer. The diet must include a protein with high net protein utilization value. This is because the puppy's digestive tract is immature and cannot fully digest and utilize the energy and nutrients which adult foods include. The total need for all nutrients is double for a puppy, and the nutrients must be in an easily digestible form.

When acquiring a puppy from a breeder be sure to find out the details of his feeding program. The breeder should provide you with the type of food the pup is used to, the feeding times and the amount of food to be fed. Whether you agree with the program or not, duplicate it for several days until the pup is accustomed to his new surroundings.

After the puppy is settled, don't hesitate to change food or feeding methods if there is a need to do so. Using the information above, use good judgment in selecting the commercial dog food best suited to his size and needs. Make the change in his diet gradual so as not to cause diarrhea. Dry food is the most popular because it is normally most convenient, feed efficient, and economical.

Be sure to choose a high quality dog food. Not only will it be better for the dog's health but it will also require less food to meet his nutritional needs. Don't be misled by how much the puppy eats, it's the performance of the food that counts. A lower quality food is also less digestible and will result in the puppy eating more to compensate; the increased food eaten will further reduce the digestibility of the food.

Don't try to save money by feeding maintenance, or low-quality foods. The pup can't possibly eat all he would need to meet his requirements for growth. The puppy will end up with a pot-bellied appearance, slower growth, poor muscle and bone development and less resistance to disease and parasites.

Regardless of the form of commercial dog food used, Donald R.

Collins, DVM, author of *The Collins Guide To Dog Nutrition*, believes every growing puppy should have liver in his diet. Liver is a good source of most of the good things an animal needs. It can be fed chopped, raw, or slightly braised. To avoid giving the puppy diarrhea, feed small amounts at first and gradually increase to no more than 10% of his total diet.

Catering to a dog's nutritional needs is one thing; catering to his nutritional desires is yet another. Do not permit a puppy to dictate his food preferences. This reverses the positions of authority and can cause training problems as well. It could also create nutritional deficiencies.

The goal should be that by the time a pup has reached maturity, his digestive system should be capable of handling all the foods he will eat during his adult life. This programs should help him to reach the average (as stipulated in the breed standard) height and weight. A great deal of time, effort, and money will—no doubt—be invested in this young prospective puppy. Many hopes and dreams may be fulfilled through him; help him to fulfill those aspirations by providing him with the best possible feeding program.

And when he reaches adulthood, continue feeding him a well-balanced nutritious diet. The payback is a healthy, handsome dog.

Material for the content of this chapter is drawn from three main sources: (1) "Nutrition and Feeding of Basenjis," by Russel V. Brown which appeared in the February 1987 issue of *The Basenji*; (2) "Feeding Your Puppy," by Ann Bierman which appeared in the March 1987 issue of *Golden Retriever Review*; and, (3) "Supplementation—May Be Hazardous to Your Pet's Health" by R.K. Mohrman published in the March/April 1980 issue of the *Great Dane Reporter*.

CHAPTER 4

Problems of Early Puppyhood

Breeding and raising puppies is a complex process. There are many factors that decide how puppies will turn out. Will they survive the embryonic stage only to fall victim to the myriad diseases of puppyhood? Often a puppy has no control over its own destiny. The health of the dam, the presence of parasites, the cleanliness of the environment and the quality of care his dam and breeders give to him, are all controlling factors in whether he survives. Whether or not a puppy develops along normal lines either before or after birth depends entirely on its environment and the hereditary characteristics and tendencies which have been handed down by its parents. Puppies which are fed inadequate, unbalanced diets not only fail to grow properly but also develop nutritional diseases and structural distortions such as anemia, rickets, etc. The diet provided his dam and that provided for the growing puppy constitutes part of his environment. If the diet is unsuitable, the puppy's environment is unfavorable for proper development.

Nursing

Bruce R. Wittels, DVM, writing in the January/February 1985 issue of the *Great Dane Reporter* states:

> The ability to nurse is the most important factor in determining whether a newborn pup will survive the first few hours and days of life. Nursing ability depends upon the maturity of the litter, body temperature and adequate lung function. If a bitch is underfed or improperly nourished before and during pregnancy, the likelihood of premature whelping is greatly increased. This leads to underdevelopment of the lungs and therefore failure of the lungs to fully oxygenate the blood. This limited respiratory capacity causes a decreased nursing time due to more time needed for breathing. With a premature whelping there is a lack of subcutaneous fat on the newborn and as a result a decreased body temperature and chilling. Because of this, energy is expended to keep the body as warm as possible and less energy is available for nursing. Diminished nursing ability is directly caused by chilling with lack of energy secondary. Therefore, it is important not to let the litter become chilled no matter what the cause.

There are other diseases, cited later in this chapter, other than malnutrition of the bitch, that affect the nursing ability of the newly born.

It is very important that the pups suckle within the first few hours. The ingestion of nutrients gives them energy and strength since they are no longer being nourished by the placenta. Colostrum is only present in the mammary glands for four to six hours and nursing during this time provides maternal immunity to many viral and bacterial diseases. The puppy acquires some maternal immunity via the placenta during pregnancy, but the most important acquistion is by the ingestion of colostrum. If a pup isn't nursing, it must be placed on a nipple and encouraged to do so. It may be necessary to milk the bitch and force feed the pup. If all efforts are unsuccessful, put the pup on antibiotics, watch it closely, and keep it confined until it can be started on a series of adult vaccines.

Most people know that at six weeks of age their dogs need to be vaccinated, but apparently what isn't known is which vaccines are given. Almost all puppies seen in my practice that have previously been vaccinated have been given an adult vaccine at six weeks of age; i.e. distemper, hepatitis, leptospirosis, and parvovirus combination—this is not proper. If the bitch had previously been vaccinated, this vaccine has no beneficial effect and can do possible harm.

Colostrum contains many antibodies called immunoglobulins which function to destroy bacteria and viral infections to which a pup is exposed. These immunoglobulins last for approximately eight to ten weeks. If an adult vaccine is used at six weeks of age they act as foreign viruses and are destroyed by the antibodies of maternal immunity. This vaccine can be injurious to the animal if it is simultaneously being infected with the real disease entity. The specific immunoglobulins are then divided between destroying the real infection and the vaccine. If the viral strength is more than that of the antibodies, the body will succumb to the disease.

Many immunologists believe that six-week old dogs should be vaccinated with a human measles vaccine and a killed parvovirus vaccine. Human measles vaccine boosts the maternal immunity against canine distemper and does not challenge it. A killed parvovirus vaccine is used due to the lack of transmission of adequate antibodies from the bitch to properly protect the pups for more than six weeks. This vaccination will often help to stimulate the pups own immune system to produce antibodies against this potentially deadly virus.

Puppies should nurse for three to four weeks. During this nursing period the major emphasis is on nutrition of the mother, as well as all of the dietary needs of the litter which are derived from her. With a very large litter or if the dam is not producing enough milk, the diet should be supplemented with such milk replacements as Esbilac or Unilac. Generally, a pup should be gaining weight daily, at the rate of approximately one gram for each pound of body weight expected at maturity. However, attempts to over-supplement in order to reach this goal are highly inadvisable. The following table, abstracted from Lab Report 2, #4 Neonatal Puppy Mortality was prepared by the Cornell Research Laboratory, Veterinary Virus Research Institute, New York.

Weight Gain

Two-fold increase at 8–10 days
(1 gm. of expected adult weight/day)

Body Temperature

Week 1–2; 94–99°F
Week 2–4; 97–100°F

Water Requirements

2–3 oz./lb./day (newborn puppies)

Caloric Requirements

60–100 kcal/lb./day
(newborn puppies can become hypoglycemic if not fed every day)

Parasites

An unfavorable environment may seriously hinder normal development before birth as well as afterward. The prenatal environment provided for the growing embryo may be unsuitable because the mother has been improperly fed and cared for during pregnancy or because she is infested with worms. Even though nature will rob the mother to feed the unformed young, the puppies may be so lacking in vitality as the result of malnutrition that they are either born dead or die shortly after birth. Newborn puppies which are suffering from malnutrition are not necessarily skinny puppies. They may be well formed and appear to be healthy, but like adult dogs that have waxed fat from an unbalanced diet and lack of exercise, they may be anemic and so weak that they are unable to cope with the difficulties encountered during birth and unable to adjust themselves successfully to the new environment. Puppies which are born with worms acquired from their dam, may not show signs of illness until they are three or four weeks of age, when they may sicken and die very quickly. There are a number of worm infestations that a breeder needs to be concerned about. Table IV-4 illustrates the wide variety of internal parasites and the probability of infestation at any age by percent. People have misconceptions about internal parasites. Some think you can immunize dogs against them. Others apparently think that when parasites are removed that is the end of them. Yet others have the idea that when a dog reaches a year of age he is no longer susceptible to them. By studying the table you will see that there is no time in a dog's life when he is immune to parasites, but in certain cases—such as coccidiosis—he is more likely to be infected when he is quite young. Because information concerning the proper care of the bitch (see chapter on The Bitch and Her Puppies) during pregnancy and

Table IV-4. *Estimated Probability of Intestinal Parasite Infestation at Any Age by Percent**

Age	Roundworms	Hookworms	Whipworms	Tapeworms Flea-Host	Tapeworms Rabbit-Host	Rivolta	Coccidiosis Bigemina	Felis
0–3 weeks	40	20	0	3	0	0	0	8
4–11 weeks	50	20	5	9	1	9	1	7
12–23 weeks	42	20	10	10	1	6	1	5
24–51 weeks	27	20	25	14	1	3	2	3
1 year	17	20	28	14	3	2	3	3
2 years	16	20	30	14	5	2	1	2
3 years	15	20	30	14	4	2	1	1
4 years	14	20	30	14	4	2	1	1
5 years	13	20	30	14	3	2	0	1
6 years	12	20	30	14	2	2	0	1
7 years	11	20	30	14	1	1	0	0
8 years	10	20	30	14	0	1	0	0
9 years	9	20	30	14	0	1	0	0
10–15 years	8	20	30	14	0	1	0	0

*Based on a study of 4,000 fecal examinations of Connecticut dogs.

From The Cocker Spaniel, by Leon F. Whitney, DVM, *Practical Science Publishing Co.*

the prevention of worm infestations is readily available today, malnutrition and parasites need not be major causes of puppy losses.

Injuries

Injuries recieved either before or after birth may result in the death of one or more puppies in a litter, in spite of the fact that every precaution may have been taken to prevent such injuries. In the case of a large litter (but even in a small or average size litter), the embryos may be crowded together too closely to allow for proper development, resulting in distortions or in the premature birth of small, weak puppies.

Carelessness on the part of a nervous or inexperienced bitch undoubtedly accounts for the loss of many puppies which are born alive and which appear to be strong and healthy at birth. Even the best of mothers may occasionaly sit or lie on a puppy, crushing or smothering it.

Pre-Natal Problems

The bitch's endocrine system—which is responsible for the secretions of such important glands as the thyroid, pituitary, adrenal and reproductive glands—may fail to work properly during pregnancy because of disease or hereditary factors, resulting in the arrested development or malformation of the embryos or in the premature birth of the litter. Abnormal functioning of the endocrine system may also cause various mating and whelping difficulties, such as dystocia (painful or delayed delivery), and lack of an adequate milk supply, which may account for puppy losses. If an inadequate amount of endocrine secretions (hormones) is produced within the unborn puppy itself, its development may be temporarily or permanently stopped at any stage. If development is arrested in the early stages, the partly-formed embryo or embyros affected may be aborted or reabsorbed by the bitch, or they may lie dormant in a "petrified" state awaiting the termination of gestation. If development is arrested in latter stages, the embryo may be born alive but malformed.

Many so-called "freaks" are the result of arrested development during the embryonic stage, resulting in such malformations as harelip, cleft palate, cleft abdomen, cleft skull, etc. All of the malformations are the result of the parts of the embryo failing to unite properly during development. If this failure is complete, any part of the embryo may be disunited by a deep cleft which may affect one side of the body more than the other, or it may affect both sides equally. If the growth of the embryo is retarded in a very late stage of development, only a slight cleft or other malformation may mar its perfection.

An analysis of litter records done by the Roscoe B. Jackson Memorial Laboratory indicates a higher percentage of puppies are stillborn or die shortly before birth in the first litter than in the second, third, fourth, and fifth litters. In a study of 337 litters, the percentage of dead puppies in the first litter was 5.7 percent, while in the fourth litter the percentage was 2.0 percent and in the fifth litter 2.8 percent. Because the cause of death could not be determined accurately in most cases, it is assumed that inexperience on the part of the bitch in whelping and caring for her first litter is partly responsible for the higher death rate. After the fifth litter, however, the death rate increased considerably, the percentage of dead puppies in the sixth litter averaging 18.7 percent. However, the steady decrease in incidence of death until the fourth or fifth litters indicates intra-uterine conditions in older bitches are more likely to be unfavorable for the production of normal young.

Fading Puppies

Fading puppy syndrome is often confused with toxic milk syndrome. It is estimated that 28% of all puppies die in the first week after birth. Some of these puppies suffer from lethal congenital defects, maternal neglect or accidents, such as being crushed in a whelping box. A large proportion of them, however, die from what is defined as the "fading puppy syndrome." The syndrome is part of a specific disease entity but perhaps the true "fading puppy" is the individual who: (1) was born malnourished because its dam did not receive adequate nutrition during gestation; (2) is too weak to nurse effectively; (3) is not receiving an adequate supply of milk; (4) is in an environment that is not sufficiently warm; or, (5) a combination of these factors. Unless supplementary feeding is started within a few hours of birth, with frequent weight checks to monitor progress, and unless adequate heat is provided, these puppies become chilled, weak, and ultimately "fade" and die.

Newborn puppies differ physiologically from adult dogs in several important ways. It is necessary to understand these differences to realize why puppies succumb rapidly to stress and to appreciate the importance of proper environment and care. They have body temperatures of 94 to 97°F for the first two weeks of life as compared to the adult dog's normal temperature of 100 to 101.5°F. They do not have a shivering reflex until about six days of age and thus cannot maintain body heat. Their heart beats and respiratory rates are faster than the adult dog. Newborns must be kept in an environmental temperature of 85 to 90°F for the first week of life; the temperature is gradually decreased to 70°F by the time the puppies are weaning age. They should gain 1 to 1½ grams daily for each pound of anticipated adult weight and should double birth rate in eight to ten days.

Neonatal Septicemia

Neonatal septicemia affects puppies from one to four days of age. It is caused by a staphylococcus infection in the vaginal tract of the bitch, transmitted to the puppy at birth. An unclean environment should not be overlooked as a precipitating factor in the disease.

Infected puppies have swollen abdomens with bluish discoloration on the flanks. They cry, are hypothermic, dehydrated and refuse to nurse. Death occurs 12 to 18 hours after bloating and crying unless antibiotic treatment is started immediately. Supportive therapy (heat, glucose and water) as described under Puppy Septicemia also must be administered.

Prevention involves a pre-breeding veterinary examination with antibiotic therapy if necessary to counteract infection. Since an unsanitary environment is frequently involved in neonatal (and puppy) septicemia, kenneling should be clean and so should everything to which the newborn puppies are exposed. This includes your hands and the scissors used to cut the umbilical cords. The cords should be dipped in or swabbed with iodine.

Puppy Septicemia

Puppy septicemia is the leading cause of death by disease in infant puppies, occurring from four to forty days of age. It happens typically in vigorous puppies that were born normally and are efficient nursers. Illness is sudden. First one puppy starts to cry. It has abdominal distension, diarrhea and may have rapid respiration. Then it refuses to nurse, becomes dehydrated and loses weight rapidly. Death usually follows 18 hours after onset of symptoms. Another puppy becomes sick, then another and another. Septicemia can demolish most or all of a litter within five to six days.

It is caused by bacteria of the streptococcus, staphylococcus, escherichia or pseudomonas types and frequently is associated with a metritis or mastitis (inflamation of the womb or of the breasts) infection in the bitch. Metritis is a uterine infection that may be acute or chronic. In the acute phase, the bitch becomes ill soon after the litter is whelped; depressed with an abnormal vaginal discharge and a temperature which may rise to 104°F. Chronic metritis may not cause overt symptoms in the bitch and, in fact, may not be evidenced until she whelps stillborn puppies or puppies that succumb to infection shortly after birth. Mastitis is painful and fever producing for the bitch. It can transmit bacterial infection to the litter.

Sick puppies are chilled, have low blood sugar, and are dehydrated. Immediate concerns are to counteract these conditions. Otherwise, the puppies will die too quickly for further therapy to be effective. They must be taken from the bitch and the following actions taken:

For Chilling: Slow warming. The sick puppy's body temperature has usually fallen to 78 to 94°F. It must be placed in an environmental temperature—incubator, heat lamp or heat pad—of 85 to 90°F until the body temperature has risen to normal for the infant puppy. Circulation must be stimulated by frequently turning and massaging the puppy during the slow warming process. Only the surfaces of the puppy's body will be warmed if this is not done. Temperature of the newborn puppy can be taken with an infant's rectal thermometer. Hold the puppy up by the base of the tail and insert the thermometer one-half inch into the rectum. Enviromental temperature can be monitored with an inside thermometer on the floor of the whelping box or incubator. Relative humidity should be 55 to 60 percent; this can be accomplished by using a home humidifier in the room in which the whelping box is placed.

For Low Blood Sugar (Hypoglycemia): Glucose therapy. The sick puppy's blood sugar must be increased rapidly and the administration of glucose solution, which is absorbed directly into the stomach, is the best way of doing this. Give the puppy 5 to 15% glucose in water, orally, 1 to 2 cc. (milliliters) every half hour. As the puppy's condition improves, gradually increase the dosage to 4 to 6 cc. These puppies should not be given formula; it may not be absorbed and thus may cause intestinal blockage.

For Dehydration: Water, given orally. The glucose and water therapy described above should be sufficient. If the puppy's condition is extremely serious, the veterinarian may think it advisable to administer subcutaneous hydrating solutions.

Other therapy, recommended by the veterinarian, may be to give antibiotics in some cases. Gamma globulin serum is considered effective. The owner may also be asked to give the puppies commercial formula or a few drops of *very fresh* liver juice every few hours after they have started to rally; this is strength enhancing.

As was learned in a preceding chapter, prevention starts with a pre-breeding veterinary examination of the bitch. Bacterial culture and sensitivity testing should be performed on specimens removed from the vagina. These tests should be mandatory when a bitch has a history of uterine infection, stillborn puppies or puppies that die soon after birth from bacterial infection. Appropriate antibiotic therapy should take place before breeding if the bitch tests positive. It may be advisable to have another course of antibiotics 48 hours before whelping and immediately after whelping. In no case should this be done haphazardly; antibiotics should be given only when necessary and under veterinary supervision.

Every effort should be made to have all the puppies take colostrum, the "first milk" produced by the bitch for 24 hours after whelping. This protects the puppy from disease for the first weeks of its life. Lack of colostrom seems to be among the precipitating factors of puppy septicemia.

The bitch should be in a state of nutritional good health, fed ample quantities of good-quality commercial dog food product recommended complete for gestation and lactation. A feeding alternative is a complete and balanced puppy food product. Its high caloric density and protein content are advantageous for the gestating or lactating bitch. Liver, one-half ounce per thirty pounds, is considered an excellent food supplement for the gestating bitch, contributing to the strength and vigor of the newborn litter.

Kenneling should be clean and well ventilated with appropriate temperature and humidity. Unsanitary quarters will predispose the litter to disease.

Canine Herpes Virus (Puppy Viremia)

This is another leading cause of death in young puppies, transmitted at whelping as puppies pass through the vagina of a recently infected bitch. Puppies can also be infected by littermates or infected adult dogs. The disease is usually fatal if contracted by puppies during the first three weeks of life. Older puppies with herpes virus usually have mild upper respiratory infections from which recovery is uneventful. Susceptibility of infant puppies is thought to be caused by their low body temperature. The canine herpes virus has been shown to multiply optimally at temperatures of 94 to 97°F, that of the neonatal puppy. It grows poorly at the body temperature of the adult dog.

Affected puppies have soft, green odorless bowel movements; this is the first symptom. They may vomit or retch, have shallow respiration which becomes gasping as the disease progresses, and they refuse to nurse. They cry pitifully and continuously.

Keeping puppies in a high environmental temperature for 24 hours is the only effective treatment; but even this is problematical. For three hours the temperature must be 100 degrees. The puppies need fluid to be given orally every 15 minutes, to prevent dehydration. Then the temperature can be reduced to 90° for the remainder of the 24-hour period. If the puppies survive, the chances are better than average that they will live. Treatment is not advised if a puppy already has started to cry; this indicates that hemorrhaging has started and survival is doubtful. If it should live, chronic kidney disease may develop during the first year of life.

In kennels where herpes virus is a recurrent problem, a preventive method is giving gamma globulin serum as an immunizing agent to neonatal puppies from dogs recovered from the disease. Since canine herpes virus is spread by direct contact with infected dogs, urine and other body secretions, overcrowding in kennels is a factor in disease transmission.

Toxic Milk Syndrome

Bacterial toxins in the bitch's milk, caused by incomplete emptying of the uterus, produce toxic effects in very young puppies, (up to two weeks of age). Sick puppies cry, bloat, have diarrhea and red swollen protruding rectums.

They must be taken from the bitch, placed in a warm environment and given 5 to 15% glucose in water orally until the bloating has subsided. The bitch should be treated with appropriate medication to cleanse the uterus and antibiotics to prevent infection. The puppies can be put back with her as soon as treatment has started. They should be given a simulated bitch's milk product during the interval between glucose and water therapy and being returned to the bitch.

Hemorrhagic Syndrome

Puppies have minimal production of a plasma protein called prothrombin during their first two or three days of life. Prothrombin is produced in the liver and, in conjunction with vitamin K_1, controls the clotting function of the blood. Without sufficient prothrombin, a hemorrhagic tendency can develop.

Affected puppies die within the first two or three days. They are lethargic, weak and decline rapidly in condition. Signs of hemorrhage may be lesions on the lips or tongue. Surviving puppies in the litter should receive vitamin K_1. Most complete and balanced dog foods have sufficient vitamin K for growth and maintenance of normal dogs.

Canine Parvovirus

Canine parvovirus has been recognized only since 1978 when epidemics were reported throughout the world. In 1979, the virus became a formidable disease in the United States. At this time, random studies revealed that between 20 and 50% of dogs tested had significantly high antibody titers suggestive of previous parvovirus infection. By the summer of 1980, new cases seemed to occur primarily among puppies under six months of age and in family pets that had not encountered the virus previously. Recent information indicates that while the over-all mortality of those dogs infected with canine parvovirus is less than 1%, the mortality among clinically-ill dogs may be as great as 10-50%. These figures vary greatly among certain populations, since the severity of the disease appears to be influenced by such factors as crowding, age, and coinciding parasitic, protozoan infections. The incidence of the disease can be expected to decline as more dogs become resistant to the virus following infection or vaccination.

Canine parvovirus manifests itself in two distinct forms: enteritis and myocarditis. This chapter will concern itself only with the myocarditis form since it principally attacks puppies.

The myocarditis form occurs only in puppies born to a female that has no antibodies to parvovirus (one that has not had either the infection or current vaccination) and becomes infected with the virus during the first few days after giving birth. Lesions develop slowly in the puppies' heart muscle and heart failure is apparent several weeks later. The mortality rates in affected litters usually exceed 50%. Fortunately, the prevalence of the myocardial form already seems to be decreasing. The disease is due to the fact that many breeding bitches have been infected previously and thus have circulating antibodies which are transferred to the puppies through the placenta and in the colostrum. This maternal antibody protects the newborns during their first five weeks when they are the most susceptible to the myocardial form of parvovirus.

Parvoviruses are especially hard to inactivate because they are resistant to heat, detergents, and alcohol. They have been known to remain active in dog feces, the primary source of infection, for more than three months at room temperature. A dilute (1:30) bleach solution is recommended for disinfection, because it will inactivate the virus. Since sanitation alone is not adequate to completely halt the spread of parvovirus, vaccination is the most effective method for control.

Brucellosis

Brucella Canis is relatively newly found and just recently recognized. Infections frequently become chronic. It occurs explosively and spreads rapidly among dog populations. The all-prevailing nature of this disease under kennel conditions has been documented. One study found 86% of adult dogs became infected and 41 of 118 females aborted.

Although all breeds of dogs are susceptible and the disease is widespread in the U.S., reported incidence rates vary from one through six percent, depending upon the area samples (there seems to be a higher concentration in the south) and the type of diagnostic test employed.

Manifestations of B. Canis are similar to each of the other species of Brucella.

In the bitches:
1. Infected females may abort their litter without previous illness (typically in the final two weeks of gestation).
2. Pups born to infected mothers may be extremely weak; all or part of the litter may be still born.

3. Following an abortion there is usually a discharge from the vagina lasting for several weeks.
4. Early embryonic deaths with termination of the pregnancy may occur, suggesting to the owner that the bitch failed to conceive.

Once the disease has been established in the male, the organisms are primarily transmitted venerally.

Other Causes

When confronted with neonatal puppy deaths, the breeder also should consider the possibility of other infectious canine diseases: distemper, leptospirosis, canine infectious hepatitis and the "newest" disease coronavirus.

Most puppy deaths are preventible. With: (1) selection of sound breeding stock; (2) a healthy, well-nourished bitch; (3) clean kenneling; (4) adequate heat for the bitch and the litter; (5) careful supervision of puppies' early weight gains; and, (6) prompt veterinary assistance should puppies start to "fade," cry, or have any of the early symptoms of puppy diseases.

CHAPTER 5

Choosing the Best Puppies

Heredity and environment both play a major role in the development of a puppy. Understanding how a particular bloodline "works" can help a breeder immeasurably. By keeping careful records of each litter, a breeder should be able to more or less predict the outcome of each puppy in a given litter. And optimizing the puppies' environment should allow the puppies to reach their maximum growth potential.

Of course, no system is foolproof. Puppies which start off looking like real winners may end up as pet quality. Also, a puppy could seem like pet quality, be sold at a pet price, and end up succeeding in the show ring. It's impossible to be 100 percent absolute each and every time. But the information in this chapter should help reduce the number of bad judgment calls, and should help you—the breeder—develop puppies to their maximum potential and select the best show quality puppies in each litter.

Keeping Records

Keeping records of each litter provides the breeder with an invaluable tool. It allows the breeder to learn from the past, to predict the development of each puppy with a measure of confidence, and to relax a little during the "plaining out" and awkward phases (more about this later).

The more information available on past litters, the better. More information allows the breeder to predict more accurately the outcome of a particular puppy. It also makes apparent patterns of development peculiar to a given bloodline. For instance, the "plaining out" phase for bloodline X may start at three months and end at eight months. So if a puppy still looks "iffy" at seven months, the breeder need not worry too much. However, if he still has a case of the "uglies" at ten months, he's got to go.

Development is always easier to predict if the breeder is dealing within one family. When new bloodlines are added to the genetic maze, development and outcome will probably be different from earlier results. Even experienced breeders can expect unpredictable results and a few trying times when outcrossing.

This is not to say that results are always completely predictable even if the bloodline has not changed. Individual differences will always play a major role in the genetic makeup of puppies. No system, no matter how extensive and accurate, can guarantee results every time. But by keeping good records, a breeder should be able to stack the deck in his or her favor.

What kind of records? The measurements that are most useful are weight, height (floor to withers, floor to elbow, elbow to withers), and length (withers to tailset, point of shoulder to tailset.) The measurements should be taken at birth, two weeks, four weeks, and then every four weeks until maturity is reached. Notes on head development, heaviness of bone, and personality should also be recorded.

With enough "statistical" information the breeder should be able to answer the following types of questions with some accuracy:

1. At what age will this puppy attain ultimate size?
2. At what age will this puppy attain ultimate development?
3. Will ultimate size and development be reached at the same time?
4. Can ultimate size be predicted by size at birth?
5. Do puppies in bloodline X develop at a uniform rate or do they go through growth spurts?
6. When will the growth spurts most likely occur?
7. When is the "plaining out" period for this bloodline?
8. Will one part of the body develop sooner than another part?
9. If more than one bloodline is bred at the kennel, what are the differences between them?

Being able to answer questions such as these can help the breeder predict the development of each puppy and to select the best show quality puppies from the litter. **Caution**—*just because a puppy is the best in his litter does not automatically make him a showdog.*

Puppy Development

Puppies are so cute and cuddly when they are born, each one is a winner in his own way. One may have a promising head, another may have great markings and a wonderful disposition. Your personal favorite may be the shy, gentle one in the corner. One thing is certain; most of these puppies will go through the awkward "plaining out" stage. Slowly, their promising heads will turn into ski slopes which could rival Sun Valley. Their bodies will lose all signs of cuddliness as they take on an adolescent appearance becoming gangly "teenagers." But have patience! Most puppies emerge unscathed from this stage, and redisplay most of their original promise. **Caution**—*a poor puppy going into this phase will most likely emerge still a poor puppy.*

Not all puppies go through this phase. Some puppies are born beautiful and maintain beauty, balance, and proportion throughout their first year. These puppies, called "flyers," outshine their gangly siblings. These puppies are few and far between. In some cases their litter mates also become outstanding dogs. However, when one of these comes along, treasure it.

A good rule of thumb for beginning breeders is to pick the show quality puppies at eight weeks of age, before the onset of the "plaining out" phase. At this time they usually will reflect their adult potential more accurately than later during the awkward phase. More sophisticated breeders can draw from past experience to determine the appropriate timing for selecting show quality puppies from their bloodlines.

It is impossible to predict the exact timing of a puppy's awkward stage. It can start as early as eight weeks, but may not start until the puppy is three or four months old. Most puppies are out of the awkward stage by the time they are eight months old. Or, a puppy could come out of it at six or seven months. Generally, the timing is similar within the same bloodline. From past litters, a breeder could determine that progeny of bloodline X usually enter the awkward stage between three and seven months of age. Then, when the next litter is born, the breeder can expect the same general timing. This helps reduce the amount of anxiety felt by the breeder. He or she may mentally "lock the puppy away" until it is seven months old and then pull it out for reevaluation.

Dentition (the loss of baby teeth and subsequent replacement with adult teeth) and rapid growth rate are the two main causes of the awkward stage(s) in puppies. During this period, the head can "plain out," losing all previous chiseling and embellishment. Even the deepest stop can turn into a sloping muzzle.

Generally, the head will improve with maturity, regaining its former promise. If the head remains in balance during the "plaining out" period, if the muzzle retains its squareness, the puppy's head will probably turn out nicely. If, however, the skull becomes broader than the muzzle, or the head loses its original balance, the puppy may not grow into a top-quality show dog.

The rapid rate of growth during this time can cause many puppies to develop an awkward, uncoordinated body. To make matters worse, different parts of the body can develop at different times. One puppy's legs may develop before its chest, giving it an "up-on-leg," pipestem look. It may walk around on stilts for months before finally filling in. Another pup may develop his forechest early. This may cause him to look low-to-the-ground and "dumpy" until his legs catch up.

Usually the body parts even out by the time maturity is reached, but not always. Many dreams of best-in-shows have been shattered by a puppy whose forelegs just never caught up with his hindlegs. Try to take it all in stride; learn from experience which dogs to pin your hopes on. Depend on overall balance rather than a few great parts.

An extremely enlightening article appeared in the September 1987 *AKC Gazette* by Patricia Gail Burnham (whom we have quoted before) titled "Understanding Flexibility and Soundness." She points out:

> . . . dogs with lots of front reach have long, flexible tendons and ligaments which allow the leg to reach forward freely. The problem is that you cannot just have flexible tendons and ligaments in the shoulder. If a dog has them there, then he has them all over. And if they are excessively flexible, then the topline may get a little slack, and there may not be enough support in the rear quarters to prevent cow hocks. On the other hand, if a dog has very tight, inflexible tendons, he will indeed have a strong rear, but if the tendons are too short and inflexible then the dog may have a restricted or hackney front, and can also have an inflexible back.
>
> Since breeders want considerable front reach on dogs that also have strong, sound rears, it may help them if they realize that those qualities are opposed. If one breeds for unlimited front reach and the flexibility that allows it, then that quality is likely to be accompanied by a tendency toward cow hocks and slack toplines. If the choice is to breed for super strong rears and the short, tight tendons that support them, then the breeder is likely to have to excuse some very restricted fronts and inflexible backs. What is actually desired, of course, is a dog with enough flexibility to give it considerable front reach, while he still has enough inflexibility to support a strong rear. And while that is a lovely dog when it does appear, breeding for it is like breeding for a razor's edge between the two extremes.

Moderation and balance should be your choice at all times when picking the best puppies. Burnham goes on to say:

> So, how much flexibility and reach is desirable and how much is dangerous [leading to hip dysplasia]? . . . When, if a little is good then more is considered better, and soundness and even the dog's health can be sacrificed in pursuit of an extreme. The key is to know when enough is enough. If a moderate extended trot is attractive, then a more extreme one with even more reach and the feet flying out in front like they are only loosely connected to the body is not better. It is worse both genetically and orthopedically . . . The only solution that seems promising is to breed for the middle ground, between the extremes of excessive restriction and excessive flexibility.

That advice is sound when followed in considering the total dog you breed. In balance with the whole, each part appearing to be more than the sum of its parts.

Environment

A puppy's genetic potential is determined at conception. But beneficial environmental factors help the puppy reach that potential. Having a doting mother, avoiding illness, eating nutritious food in the right amount, and proper grooming and handling all help the puppy develop into a healthy, happy dog.

Not all good bitches make good mothers. If a bitch is lacking in maternal instinct, a lot of tender loving care may be required on the part of the breeder. You will need to pick the puppy up, fondle it gently in your lap and stroke and speak to it. This needs to be done at least twice a day. Nothing is as cute as a baby pup who needs to nuzzle up to a warm, comforting body. Do not handle the puppy roughly. Use two hands when picking it up and putting it back with its littermates. Gentleness is most important.

If a puppy gets off to a poor start, either through poor eating habits or illness, it will probably catch up with the rest of the pack eventually. It may continue growing after its littermates have reached maturity in order to make up for earlier lost time. Similarly, an older puppy which may have been set back through illness will usually end up being about the same size as its littermates. Sometimes a breeder will write these puppies off before they reach their full size. This can be a heart-breaking mistake.

Another mistake commonly made is to discard the too thin or too chubby puppy. If a puppy doesn't have enough meat on him, the breeder should seek to determine the reason for his lack of appetite. There may be something in his genetic makeup which does not allow him to properly utilize all his nutrients. On the other hand, sometimes a puppy will simply be a poor eater. If it's an ingrained part of his personality there may be nothing the breeder can do to help him fill out. Read the chapters on "The Bitch and Her Puppies" and "Nutrition for Puppies and Adults" for more information on this vexing matter.

Chubby puppies tend to look the most awkward during the "plaining out" phase. Their extra weight exaggerates faults. Before the breeder's final evaluation, this type of puppy should be put on a diet. Watch their weight closely, for extreme and prolonged obesity can lead to permanent structural defects.

The normal, healthy puppy will display a glossy coat. Proper grooming is necessary for good coat development. Left dirty and matted, the coat will never obtain its potential.

Even if all the above guidelines are followed, even if the puppy has the benefit of the most experienced breeder, it still needs that magic spark to be a winner. This elusive spark of personality adds life and spunk to an otherwise empty, albeit lovely, animal. Without it, the dog may never be able to handle itself with confidence in the ring. A winning dog is flashy and knows it. He prances into the ring and says "look at me, aren't I something!" And sure enough, he IS something. A duplicate of that dog, minus the personality, could become the all time reserve winner.

Personality can be developed to a degree. Gently—and I do mean gently—playing with a puppy can help the puppy see that human beings are okay. Never lunge at a puppy or hold it in an improper manner. Both hands supporting the puppy underneath at the chest and at the rear legs is the proper way. Never frighten it or be rough. Puppies, like human babies, thrive on love and tenderness. Providing that emotional food will help the puppy gain confidence, and hopefully that "spark" of personality.

When grading out the puppies at eight weeks, do not judge them only in a posed manner. First of all, it's possible to crank a puppy around to get it to look the way you think it should look. All you achieve when you do this is deceive yourself. Look for a neck blending correctly into the shoulder. Check for balance—balance—and balance! Check for strong rears without evidence of hocking in or out. Look at the distance between the withers and set-on of the tail. Being a trifle long here isn't too bad. On the other hand do not exult because the puppy is shorter than the standard requires. How will he get his front legs out of the way of his driving rear quarters? Do not seek extremes. Put them down on the ground. It's important to see how they handle their feet and the shifting of weight as they move about. Any puppy that appears well coordinated, is up on his toes and cuts and turns easily—that's the one to seriously consider. A posed dog does not give you the view that you need to fully evaluate the puppy. Down on the ground, on his own, the puppy that acts like he is king and goes all out, plus handling himself well, is the one to mark and keep an eye out for his future development.

CHAPTER **6**

Frozen and Extended Semen

American Dogs have made their presence known throughout the world. Breeders in such far-away countries as Australia, Sweden, New Zealand, etc. have made remarkable strides in successfully introducing the breed to their countries. There is, however, a major problem in importation of high-quality breeding stock. Stringent quarantine rules make it extremely difficult and financially prohibitive to import quality stock. Now, at long last, there may be a solution to this problem. Artificial insemination has been approved by the AKC under certain controlled conditions for use in this country. However, shipping semen over long distances has proven to be a formidable task.

In October and November of 1986, Howard H. Furumoto, D.V.M., Ph.D. writing in *Ilio*, Hawaii's dog magazine, cast a new light on the problem. Dr. Furumoto writes:

Recent research on canine semen preservation and storage offers Hawaiian dog breeders a promising future *[as well as foreign countries and continents that maintain strict quarantine regulations such as the state of Hawaii requires]*. The technology and expertise are available today to overcome the hitherto insurmountable barriers of time, logistics, and statutory requirements when considering the importation of new bloodlines.

To properly understand and appreciate the significance of these advancements, a short review of the evolution of the two methods of semen preservation are in order.

When approval was granted by the American Kennel Club to legitimize registration of litters conceived by stored semen and artificial insemination, the way was opened for Hawaii's breeders *[and breeders of other countries]* to take advantage of the golden opportunity presented by the new technology. Here, at last, was an AKC-accredited program which provided the means to circumvent the quarantine requirements and to eliminate the expense, inconvenience, and stress shipping animals to and from destination points. An added attraction for many breeders was the preservation of valuable bloodlines for posterity by the establishment of frozen semen banks.

The original work on frozen semen was done by Dr. Stephen Seager and co-workers at the University of Oregon under the auspices of the American Kennel Club. The widespread interest he created led to *[a collaboration with the University of Hawaii]*. The objective was to determine whether or not we could duplicate the results obtained by Dr.

Seager and his co-workers with the additional variables of air shipping frozen semen and bitches in estrus cycle. Much to our disappointment the four bitches shipped to Hawaii and inseminated with frozen semen shipped from Oregon failed to become impregnated. Subsequently, other investigators have reported similar negative results.

Because of the unreliable results obtained from the insemination of stored semen, canine theriogenologists began searching for more productive methodologies. Two such programs came to my attention. [One effort was led by] Dr. Frances Smith who had obtained her Ph.D. from the University of Minnesota. Her dissertation was based on the successful development of a semen extender which prolongs the viability of spermatazoa for up to seven days after collection without freezing.

Dr. Smith is widely recognized by dog breeders throughout the continental United States for her work with top line-breeding stock of various breeds. In her experience she has been just as successful in obtaining pregnancies with the use of the newly formulated extended semen as with natural breeding.

The second source of information [led me to] Mr. George Govette of the Cryogenics Laboratories in Chester Spring, Pennsylvania. Mr. Gavotte has earned the reputation of being the foremost frozen semen specialist in the country, having successfully registered 44 litters out of the approximately 50 now-recognized by the AKC by this method. In addition, he has reported successful frozen semen usage in Japan.

Gleaning germane information from both sources, Dr. Furumoto wrote a second article in which he briefly described the methods employed in semen collection, extension, preservation, storage, and preparation for artificial insemination.

He then projected the long-term benefits and potential hazards of these new technologies as they relate to breed improvement.

Semen Collection

Semen is collected for a number of overlapping reasons—for qualitative and quantitative evaluation, for immediate insemination when natural breeding fails or cannot be used due to physical and psychological inhibitions, for extending the volume of semen, for semen preservation and storage and for legal reasons (quarantine restrictions).

To collect semen, it is generally helpful to excite the dog with the scent of a bitch in estrus. Ejaculation is usually performed by digital manipulation and the semen is collected in a graduated sterile collecting tube fitted to a funnel-shaped latex sleeve which is held around the penis.

Three distinct fractions are observed from the ejaculate. The scant first fraction is clear and is secreted by the glands of the urethral mucosa; the opaque second fraction is secreted by the testicles and contains spermatozoa; the third and most voluminous fraction is clear and is secreted by the prostate glands.

Qualitative and quantitative evaluations are made after the semen is collected. The volume and turbidity of the semen are noted. Microscopically, the sperm concentration, motility, ratio of live to dead sperm cells and the shape and size are evaluated. Fresh undiluted semen is used for immediate artificial insemination.

Semen Extenders and Semen Preservation

After semen evaluation, semen of good to excellent quality is selected for preservation by one of two basic methods: chilling or chilling and freezing. In both methods, a vehicle—or media for dilution and maintenance called "semen extenders"—is used.

A great deal of research has been done to determine which media serves as the best semen extender. Various combinations of sterlized skim milk, homogenized milk, egg yolk, glucose, sodium citrate, sodium bicarbonate, potassium chloride and other substances have been used. The tremendous success in conception rate obtained by Dr. Frances Smith is the direct result of her newly-developed and tested semen extender.

Fresh, undiluted semen maintains its viability for 24 to 48 hours. Beyond this period, the viability of the semen may be prolonged for approximately 4 more days by suspending it in special media known as semen extenders and chilling. The viability of spermatozoa may be continued over an indefinite period of years by freezing the semen after it is suspended in a suitable vehicle (semen extender). By a gradual chilling process spermatozoa are conditioned for freezing at –70°C. The extended semen suspension is then shaped into pellets by placing single drops into super-cooled styrofoam wells. Enough frozen pellets are placed in each vial to yield about 50 million spermatozoa. Each vial is properly identified and stored at –70°C in a liquid nitrogen tank.

An alternative method of preservation is to pipette the extended semen into straws, one end of which is presealed. When the straw is filled, the top end is sealed and the semen is conditioned for freezing as with the pelletized semen, frozen, and stored.

Preparation for Insemination

The reverse of cooling and freezing is carried out to prepare frozen semen for artificial insemination. A suitable number of pellets or straws are selected to yield 100 to 300 million spermatozoa and gradually thawed to ambient temperature. At this point, an evaluation of the thawed semen quality is made. If viability and motility are satisfactory the semen is introduced in the anterior vagina or cervix of the bitch. At least two inseminations usually 24 to 48 hours apart is recommended.

Long-Term Benefits of Extended and Frozen Semen

In the context of *[foreign countries with]* quarantine restrictions, the greatest advantage to be derived from the use of extended and frozen semen is the by-passing of the trans-oceanic shipment of stud dogs and their confinement in *[government]* quarantine facilities for a specified period of time (10 days beyond the last insemination date). Extended or frozen semen *[on the other hand]* may be shipped in special compact containers over long distances.

Another attraction of extended and frozen semen is the flexibility and convenience of synchronizing semen shipment with the optimal breeding period in the estrus cycle of a prospective bitch. This advantage is particularly applicable when long distance shipment of stud dogs and bitches is involved in conventional breeding programs.

Venereal diseases, particularly canine brucellosis and transmissible venereal tumor may be circumvented, simply by the process of screening out potential carriers in the collection process.

By far the most significant benefit to accrue from extended and frozen semen is the concentration of proven or select gene pools for the improvement of the breed to more rapidly attain that elusive goal known as the ideal breed standard. By extending and freezing semen many more bitches can be inseminated with "matching" semen which would complement the desirable qualities of the sire and dam.

Disadvantages of Extended and Frozen Semen

In addition to the purely technical difficulties of implementing an artificial insemination program which *[uses]* extended and frozen semen, the success rate among breeders *[so far]* has been very limited.

The greatest concern regarding frozen and extended semen is the potential for intensifying or replicating undesirable genetic traits. Just as much as the potential for breed improvement over a shorter period exists, there is also the danger of perpetuating undesirable heritable traits, *i.e.,* juvenile cataracts, subvalvular aortic stenosis, hip dysplasia, etc. within an abbreviated time frame. Therefore, a great deal of selectivity and objectivity must be exercised in the utilization of preserved semen. Any abnormal offspring must be dealt with objectively and decisively and either euthanized or neutered so that the genetic defect will not become established within a given line or breed.

Another area of concern is the requirement for meticulous attention to details of proper identification and documentation. One only needs to refer to the AKC regulations on "Registration of Litters Produced Through Artificial Insemination Using Frozen Semen" to appreciate the complexity of the stringent requirements.

Conclusion

Notwithstanding the objectionable features of semen preservation and storage, the technical and scientific feasibility of their application to canine reproduction have been amply demonstrated. The acceptance of the program depends—to a large extent—on the interest and support of dog breeders and the professsional and technical competence of veterinarians to deliver the "goods" when the chips are down. Ultimately, the success of the program depends on the development of special interest and expertise in the handling of extended and frozen semen from collection to insemination.

Success breeds success. Nowhere is this truism more important than in the pioneering *[use of these techniques.]*

Building and Running
A Breeding Kennel

Most of the people showing dogs today are hobby breeders and seldom have what might be termed a large kennel. A kennel of six to ten dogs seems to be the norm. Sometimes the puppy population can raise that to fifteen. The days of the 1920's and 30's, where there might be as many as 75 dogs and a full-time kennel manager and handler are long gone. Today the world of purebred dogs is peopled largely by middle-class families. Large kennels which covered more than an acre of ground have given way to the converted garage or small kennel building.

Because most of us are "small time" breeders and usually have to do all the kennel work ourselves, a good idea is to seek the easiest type of maintenance arrangements possible. One of the best setups I've seen was located in a residential neighborhood. The home had a utility room that led out to a two-car garage. The utility room had been converted to a combination crating, bathing, and trimming area. Visiting bitches were also bred there. The whole room was probably 14 × 4. Cabinets which held grooming and whelping gear had been installed at shoulder height. There were whimsical pictures of dogs painted on the shocking-pink exterior of the cabinets. The garage had been converted into a kennel by putting acoustical tile on the wall and ceiling. The light was supplied by fluorescent fixtures and a heat pump supplied cool air in the summer and heat in the winter. The floors were leveled with concrete and covered with indoor/outdoor carpeting. Finally, there were chain link runs both inside and out with trap doors controlling who could come and go.

Most stalls are built as box stalls with dimensions from as small as 2 × 2 to as large as 4 × 8. This depends on the size and number of dogs assigned to each one. Since chain link fencing tends to be a bit expensive, many people construct stalls out of a combination of plywood and masonite. Frame the stall with wood and lay in a rough cut of plywood for the floor and walls. Then cover with smooth exterior masonite for the walls and floor. Be sure to get as tight a fit as possible at the corners of the floor. Then put in rounded moulding to help seal the corners.

All this should be built at least 4″ off the ground to help keep the dogs out of ground-level drafts and to facilitate sweeping and hosing out underneath the runs. Unfortunately, dogs are messy. If chain link is selected you can still build the floors out of masonite and wood and add the chain link as sides and gate area. The gate into the kennel area should allow someone to easily reach in and work with a dog but should not be so low that the dog can easily clamber out.

Getting the dogs in and out of their runs can sometimes be a challenge. If there is a small number of dogs and an equal number of runs, the problem is straightforward and easy to solve. Either buy or make the type of trap door that allows the dog to make his own egress. The center part can be made of plastic or hard rubber. Either way, it closes behind the dog. This type of arrangement has many advantages. The dog can come and go at will and the door retains either the warm or cool air inside. Its main disadvantage is in shutting the dogs in at night. This usually entails manually sliding a piece of metal into a groove that covers the center section. This task has to be performed each evening and morning.

If there are a limited number of runs to use and the dogs have to be rotated, another type of door may be desirable. This involves a guillotine type door that slides up and down in a slot. This door is located just above the exit and can be controlled by a pulley arrangement. Put a hook and eye in the wood door and attach a rope to a pulley above.

Kennel run with guillotine-type door.

Enough rope should be provided so that the rope can be pulled from the gate area and it will lift the door. By using a simple hook above the gate, it can hold only those runs open that need to be used. Of course this also entails frequent opening and closing of those runs.

Still another technique is to keep the dogs in crates (which can be stacked within a kennel building) and exercise groups of compatible dogs during the day. This way each dog can be handled on a daily basis and a weather eye can be kept on any problems which may be developing. Ray McGinnis, formerly one of the country's foremost handlers swears by this method. A drawback to this approach, it's difficult to make sure that all dogs get enough exercise time. This can be especially hard to do when you are ill or away. Be sure you have a way to funnel the dogs into their run when they are released from their crates. They are full of vim and vigor at this time and may want to romp and play and not go into the exercise area.

Example of stacked six-cage unit. *Courtesy of Moses Fence Co., Inc.*

Example of seven-cage unit. *Courtesy of Moses Fence Co., Inc.*

How much room should the dogs have to exercise and what should be the composition of the run? There is room for wide divergence on this point. The amount of room depends on the size and number of dogs you decide to install in each run. There should be a jumping platform that can be used to either play "king of the hill" or to snooze in the sun. It should also be high enough for the dog to wiggle underneath to partake of some shade. The surface should also depend on the type of drainage and the amount of sun that will hit it during the day. Be sure your dogs have access to shade and clean water at all times. The shade-giving structure will also protect them from rain and snow. Advocates of concrete swear by it and claim it builds great foot pads. It also will not harbor fleas or other vermin. It, like asphalt, must be built with a slight slope so that urine and other matter can be washed off daily. There must be a trough at the end of each run so that water and other matter can drain into some type of sewer or cesspool arrangement. The runs and troughs should be thoroughly flushed so there is no residual odor. If you are not in an area where the sun shines all the time, the runs are going to be wet a great deal of the day. Unless you want to go to the expense of installing radiant heat, these damp runs could cause problems.

Asphalt runs have the advantage of being cheaper to install but seem

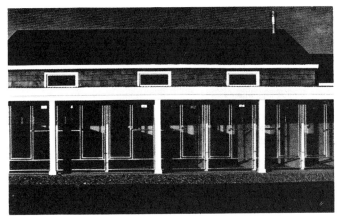

Courtesy of Moses Fence Co., Inc.

Courtesy of Moses Fence Co., Inc.

Richy Boarding Kennel—Northeast, Pennsylvania

Example of "portable, rolling" runs with wire-screened bottoms for coated breeds such as Cocker Spaniels. Courtesy of Townehouse Kennels.

to have few other advantages. In the heat of the summer, asphalt can get mighty hot and almost unbearable for the dogs. It doesn't drain as well as concrete and has a tendency to form little depressions in which urine and feces can gather. It also has a tendency to begin to break up after four or five years.

The third choice, and perhaps the best one overall, is pea gravel. Pea gravel is the smallest size gravel and is available from most lawn and garden centers. To have a good gravel run you need to prepare the soil correctly. First dig out the area to be used to a depth of 10″. Then, add a 2″ layer of crushed limestone. Cover that with 4″ of sand, then 2″ of soil. On top of that mixture place the pea gravel to the level of the surrounding ground. The fencing material should be attached to a 6″ baseboard all the way around the run so that the gravel won't be easily kicked out.

The major advantages of pea gravel are: (1) urine drains easily through the soil; (2) there is no odor from the urine; (3) feces are easily picked up with no residual to attract flies; (4) this type of surface makes it difficult for the flea larvae in the feces to burrow into the soil to complete the adult cycle. Frequent watering and exposure to sunlight make this a virtually foolproof system. Depending upon the number of dogs occupying each run, replacement gravel will probably not be

Same "portable" runs rolled back into garage with sawdust for absorbency. Courtesy of Townehouse Kennels.

Outdoor pea-gravel paddock runs. Courtesy of Guileann Kennels, June & Geoffrey Maudlen—Adelaide, Australia.

needed more than every other year. A disadvantage is that some dogs get the gravel stuck between their pads. Plan to vary the size of the gravel depending on the size of your stock.

The back of the kennel should be heated just enough in winter so you can work out there comfortably and cool enough in the summer for the same purpose. The floors should have drains so hosing can be done easily. Proper disinfectants should be used weekly. Check with your vet on this and also clear with him or her on the proper use of insecticides. Vacuuming and mopping are the main ingredients of a clean and healthy environment for your dogs.

If newspapers are used in the stalls they should be picked up both in the morning and evening, especially after feeding time. Leftover food attracts insects and rodents. The runs should also be picked up at least twice a day to keep down the flies and odor and to ensure that flea larvae can't make its way down through the ground to emerge later as fleas and continue a vicious cycle.

From the back end of the kennel, let's move to the the part the public gets to see. When selling puppies, or boarding dogs, there needs to be some kind of facility set off from the kennel proper. A small combination office and display area is ideal. Seal it off from the kennel by a door, preferably one that can keep down the noise. It is a good idea to use a good grade of indoor/outdoor carpeting in the office area. It lends a degree of "class." Keep this area clean. This is where the desk and files should be kept.

A shelf about 3' high divided into a few compartments is a wonderful way of showing puppies. Puppies can be brought out individually for inspection and then placed in a compartment while another is being brought out. After the customer has looked at each puppy individually he can then look down on the puppies as a group and have their good points explained and let the puppies sell themselves.

It's also a good idea to have a grooming stand in the room for stacking the puppies and for showing off stud dogs.

Inside the kennel building proper, hang pesticide strips and tacky fly traps. Some people go to the expense of adding an electrical fly zapper which electrocutes flies on contact. Outside, a fly trap such as "Big Stinky" does wonders.

The office/"show room" should be attractive. Paneling on the walls adds the right touch. In strategic spots around the room place major ribbon awards and trophies. Additionally, AKC championship certificates are very impressive to the buying public.

There are a number of kennel designs and illustrations shown in this chapter. The breeder would do well to investigate his current, as well as expected, needs before deciding to break ground.

Mark Tayton had great words of wisdom about kennel construction and running a kennel as a business, in the 1982 edition of his book *Successful Kennel Management*. Much of the balance of this chapter is based upon his writings.

In the matter of the type of construction, there are also many ways to build a building. Unfortunately, the cost of comfort, convenience and efficiency in a building has little to do with the fact that it is built for a kennel. Heating, cooling, lighting, ventilation and plumbing are expensive, even more so, in fact, sometimes for kennels than for residences. Just as in a home, there are certain principles to bear in mind which may have a material effect on the success or failure of your efforts. The colder the climate, the higher the temperature requirements needed in a kennel in the winter (and vice versa in the summer), the more valuable insulation, weatherstripping and storm protection becomes.

In ordinary building construction, two-thirds of the heat lost in winter is through doors, walls and glass. Only about a third goes out with ventilation. Anything that can be done therefore to stop heat losses through walls and glass results in great dollar savings.

In an ideal kennel layout, walking should be minimized and the food may be distributed from a handy nearby kitchen; or, if you have many dogs, from a handy truck or wagon. A kennel should be a single structure if possible. There should be separate rooms for dogs, bitches, bitches in season, whelping matrons and for puppies. Unfortunately this arrangement for most of us is not possible but some natural separation along these lines is encouraged.

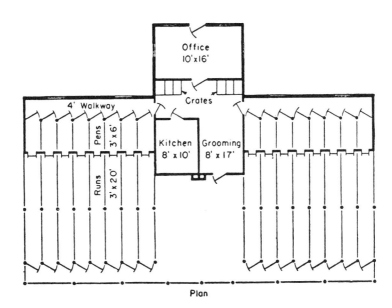

An ideal kennel layout.

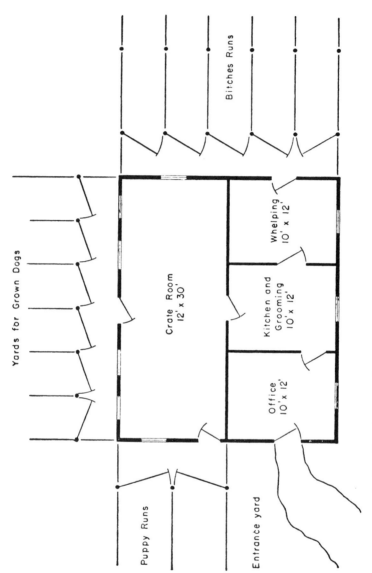

A nice plan for a small breeding kennel under one roof for operation with crates and exercise runs.

Bitches Runs

Yards for Grown Dogs

Crate Room
12' x 30'

Whelping
10' x 12'

Kitchen and
Grooming
10' x 12'

Office
10' x 12'

Puppy Runs

Entrance yard

In a kennel, as in a house, the major part of the work is done in the kitchen. A good sink with plenty of hot water for washing pans is absolutely necessary; and so is a refrigerator, or preferably a freezer. Don't panic if this seems beyond you now. Many of us are used to working from our own kitchen and carrying the food out to the kennel. We are looking toward the ideal. Storage drums or bins are also a good idea for different kinds of dry dog food.

Ideally, there should be a place where dogs can be bathed and groomed, medicines administered and other kennel work performed.

Make this area as nice and as workable as possible. You will be spending a great deal of time there.

How To Sell Your Puppies

To be a successful breeder you must be a student of bloodlines and genetics. To raise healthy puppies [you] should be a lover of dogs. To show them [you] must have patience, and to win public recognition [you] need to have the ability to advertise and publicize them. For financial success, however, [you] must learn to sell.

You don't have to be a "born" salesman to learn how to promote and sell your dogs. Practically anyone, with a little study of the principles involved, and with a bit of effort, can learn to sell.

Selling dogs is probably a bit harder than selling Fuller brushes, but the fact that you are dealing with humanity in both instances gives a common basis to the selling problems and their solutions. To illustrate: It is common knowledge that it tends to make anyone angry to contradict his statements and argue with him. Hence, one of the cardinal principles of selling is to avoid arguments at any cost. It is suggested that anyone who wants to do a good job selling should read some of the better available books on salesmanship.

You *don't* have to be a high-pressure salesman! Good selling sometimes consists simply of knowing what *not* to say. Many a would be salesperson in their zeal to praise their own dogs by comparison has so belittled his rival's dogs that his prospect may mentally rally to his rival's defense.

Have you ever heard a statement such as: "You wouldn't want a puppy from Ch. Whooziz. He has slipped stifles and his offspring often go blind before the age of two."? Of course you have—or at least variations on that theme. Any statements about the evils of the other fellow's dogs may lead to an investigation by the prospect, to see if they are as bad as he heard they were and may eventually result in selling a rival's dog instead of your own; plus the fact he may tell him what you said about his dogs. There goes goodwill down the drain!

Mark Tayton believes:

Ordinary people are more than half sold before they ever come to your kennel, the greatest proportion of the job having already been done by the dog show, the pictures they have seen, and the magazines they have read. Most kennel visitors have decided they want a dog and further, that they might want one of your dogs, so if your percentage of sales to visitors is not fairly high, you should investigate to find out where your trouble lies. Some kennels succeed in selling puppies to as high as a third to a half of those who visit them.

People desire things that appeal to them through their five senses: sight, touch, smell, hearing, and taste. Dogs appeal to us principally through our eyes. Therefore, you should make every effort to have your dogs look their best at all times and the surroundings should tend to heighten rather than detract from this effort. Salesmen call this a "front." If selling is to take place at your kennel or home, it means your place of business must be attractive.

Most of us, when we arrive at the stage of having prime prospects for sale, turn to breed magazines to advertise our products. However, be prepared. You will need to be able to answer correspondence and answer phone calls intelligently. Remember, you don't have the trappings of your succesful kennel about you and you must now sell through another medium. Lets discuss correspondence first.

Although, as a general rule, all inquiries should be answered, some kennel owners ignore post cards unless they appear to be written by someone knowledgable. Writing a letter in answer to an inquiry can be laborious and time consuming. Assuming you have an inquiry that is definite enough to lead you to undertake an answer, what is the best way to frame a reply?

Mark Tayton discussed a women he knew who, when asked how she sold so many puppies through the mail, stated, "I just sit down and try to imagine what kind of dog would suit the prospect, and then I describe it to him just as though he were sitting in front of me and I was talking to him."

One way of answering the varied, and often general questions about your dogs and your kennel is to make up a brochure telling about your kennel, the success you have had and an insert telling about the specific dog(s) you have for sale at the present time. Append a personal note so that it will not seem to be a cut-and-dried commercial operation. This often leads to follow up correspondence that is more focussed and sells many a dog.

If the inquiry is specific, I would suggest you write out as definitive a description as possible of any one, or at most, two dogs that seem to fit his wants, and offer them in your reply.

The prime characteristic of good selling is enthusiasim. Karl Schwartz, a famous breeder (DeKarlos Kennels) of the 1950's, was so enthusiastic in his letters that you literally could see all the champions dancing off the pages. Fortunately for Karl, many of the dogs he sold did turn out that way. It is certainly a good idea not to misrepresent. It causes ill will and your name will be bandied about in that owner's locale until you will probably never be able to sell a dog to that area again. However, there is no reason why one cannot tell the truth in glowing terms if the dog has virtues. The woman Mark Tayton referred to used to sprinkle liberally through her correspondence, like raisins in a pudding, such words as "gorgeous," "handsome," and "showy" . . . and, her letters did sell dogs.

Another principle to follow is to answer correspondence immediately. This is vital in selling by mail. Presumably your prospect made similar inquires of other advertisers in the same magazine in which he found your ad. If so, the first person who gets an answer back may make the sale. If the inquiry is for a dog that you think you can supply, and the distance isn't that great, it may be wise to answer by a long-distance telephone call.

A phone conversation should roughly follow the form of a conventional sales approach: An "opening," in which the name of the party is verified, so that they can be properly addressed by name; a "sales message" revolving around more than two or three points, and in which the customer is encouraged to speak at least enough to show their thinking; and, if possible, a "closing," where a positive agreement to buy is asked for or sought. Also, and most important in the case of a sale, get the customer's correct address and phone number and the closest airport for shipping. A desk check list before you at this point is helpful, to make sure you will not forget some important detail.

If any information has been included in previous correspondence, you should get the facts clearly in mind before attempting to talk. Thus the pedigree of the specific dog (and any other alternatives) should be handy as a reference so you can be specific instead of making only general statements. The way to present your facts should be organized, even to the extent of writing them out, or at least outlining your proposed sales talk.

Careful thought should be given to the words you will be using. Don't forget the customer cannot see your facial expression and gestures over the phone. Your words, your tone of voice, your enthusiasm will have to do the selling for you. Use positive and powerful adjectives. "Gorgeous," "fantastic coat," etc. Don't be bashful if the dog is deserving. Further, in trying to give a clear and colorful description, care should be taken not to omit faults, though there is no necessity to stress them.

Again, do not misrepresent! This is the way to handle faults: Frankly admit them, and then go on to discuss virtues.

Selling over the phone is a disadvantage in that the puppy cannot be handed over to the prospect in order that he may sell himself as puppies often do. But the phone has certain advantages too. There are no distractions. It is fast and "relatively" cheap, the reply is known immediately, and the call can be timely. Having the phone number of your kennels emphasized in advertising and on your stationery will encourage the prospect to call you rather than write, thus giving you the first chance at the customer and an opportunity for a good sales talk when the customer is in the mood to buy.

Good Accounting Practices

Few people in the dog game care to keep sufficient records to make studies of costs or to analyze where their profits lie. The interest for most dog breeders is in breeding and showing and they feel that it is immaterial where they come out at the end of the year. With the new tax laws, that casual attitude will not suffice.

Today practically all businesses of any size use double-entry book-keeping. However, with a small entity like a hobby kennel, the single-entry system, which consists of noting every expenditure or receipt of money and what it was paid or received for, is sufficient.

It must be realized, of course, that if the books are kept in this way and the costs of acquiring dogs are written off as expense when the purchases are made, no deductions should be allowed for losses when the dogs die, are lost, or otherwise disposed of.

Although the capitalizing of costs of raising dogs for breeding, or even an occasional purchase of a dog or bitch for that purpose, is not contemplated in the single-entry system of bookkeeping suggested here, there may be some circumstances in the kennel business when it might be desirable to do so. There are also some occasions when gains from the sales of animals that have been retained as part of the breeding kennel for a period of longer than six months may be reported as capital gains for tax purposes. It is suggested that a consultation with a financial adviser on the subject of applicable tax-law provisions is called for if the kennel operations result in a sufficient yearly net income to make it necessary.

It may seem rather meaningless to talk about cost accounting with respect to keeping dogs and raising puppies. It has often been demonstrated that if a man likes a dog, money is no object to him. Price is a minor item in such a case, and therefore it is often argued that being precise in determining how much it costs to raise a dog is superfluous. There is certainly merit in the contention that instead of worrying about how much it costs to raise dogs, the time might better be spent in finding customers for them. Presumably, price would take care of itself if the demand for dogs were sufficient; that is, if a good enough job of selling them is done.

This argument, however, loses sight of the fact that the question of whether or not a profit remains after all costs have been met depends not on individual sales, but on the *average* of all sales made. The kennel owner should, therefore, know fairly well what it costs on the average to raise puppies, and what it costs to keep them and to sell them. Many kennel owners have only the vaguest idea of costs and live in a fool's paradise. Thinking of sales in terms of pure profit, when only simple arithmetic would show them that after allowing a reasonable amount for overhead, their sales would be *losses* rather than profits. Putting it another way, they are actually paying out money for the dubious pleasure of providing other people with puppies. Does the fun of showing compensate for all of that?

One reason why people sometimes fail to realize what it costs to raise puppies is because they do not include any charges for items that are necessary to maintain a kennel but are also used for other purposes, such as the telephone, the car, buildings, fuel and sometimes even food bought for the household, but fed to the puppies.

Difficult as it may be to evaluate such overhead expenses, there are many direct expenses that can be appraised rather easily. Such items as food, some of the major labor costs, particularly kennel help, and veterinary bills chargeable to litters can be estimated on a per dog basis. It should be fairly easy to estimate how much it costs, on the average, to keep a grown dog in any kennel. Similarly, a fair estimate could be made for puppies.

One fruitful field for study would be the cost of raising puppies from weaning age to the average date when they are sold. One of the greatest problems all breeders have is to pick the best ones, classify them as show prospects, and sell the rest quickly. But how is it possible to judge the difference in the kennel cost of a puppy eight-weeks old and one three- or four-months old? Many breeders make little or no price differential between pups at these ages although there is probably a very material difference in costs and resulting profits.

How much more money could be spent for gainful advertising if the average holding period for pet puppies between weaning and selling could be reduced by, say, a month? It may be that such a question is too complex for the average breeder. But even though a definite answer might not be obtainable, every breeder would do well to think along these lines, with his accounting records, of course, to help him.

There are other major records that need to be kept in an on-going kennel. Some kennels keep them on cards or sheets of paper, with a card or sheet for each animal. The most important record is the Inventory of Stock. Figure IV-2 illustrates such a record. Figure IV-3 is that of Kennel Bitches Bred and Figure IV-4 is that of Outside Bitches Bred. The amount of the stud fee should be entered here also.

It is important to know what your veterinary bills are and Figure IV-5 shows the record for each dog. The cost for the treatment should also be recorded. All of us like to keep a record of the show careers of our winning dogs and so Figure IV-6 can be used for this purpose.

If you maintain boarding facilities, use a form like that shown in Figure IV-7. As breeders we should keep very accurate records of each litter and what became of each puppy. Figure IV-8 illustrates a workable form for this purpose.

Figure IV-2. Inventory of Dogs: _____ 19 ___

AKC No.	Sex	Name	Date Whelped	Sire	Dam	Disposal	Value

Figure IV-3. Kennel Bitches Bred

Name	Date		Stud	Date		Puppies	
	In	Bred		Wormed	Whelped	Alive	Dead

Figure IV-4. Outside Bitches Bred

Name	Owner's Name & Address	Date Rec'd.	Dates Bred	Stud Used	Remarks

Figure IV-5. Treatment Record

Date	Name	Remarks

Figure IV-6. Show Record

Show	Date	Dog(s) Entered	Wins	Judge

Figure IV-7. Boarding Record

Dog's Name	Breed	Rate	Owner's Name Address & Phone	Date: In	To Go	Remarks*

Remarks should contain feeding and other special instructions, grooming to be done, addresses of friends, etc. (use two or more lines per dog if necessary).

Figure IV-8. Litter Record

Bitch _____ Sire _____ Bred To: _____

AKC No. _____

Dam _____ Dates: _____

Litter Reg. No. _____ Date Whelped: _____

Pup No.	1	2	3	4	5	6	7
Name							
Reg. No.							
Sex							
Color, Markings							
Disposed of							
Remarks							

Contracts and Guarantees

Akita World Magazine has a feature called "The Breeders Forum." The January/February 1985 issue addressed the topic of contracts and guarantees. One particular segment written by T.K. Arndt was of great interest and with the permission of the magazine I have paraphrased its contents.

Everyone has heard the phrase "get it in writing" when conducting business dealings. Even when dealing with family and friends it is a good rule to put an agreement down on paper. For one thing, memory is weaker than people like to admit . . . no matter what your age. After one, three or five years, who can recall explicit details with 100% accuracy? There can be little doubt however, when a written contract is available for reference.

The preservation of friendships can often rely on the written word, without needless strains through misunderstandings. Most of all, the presence of a written agreement provides protection for the interest of *both* parties . . . for the present or any time in the future. Who can forsee at some future date, when personal business affairs, or those of the persons with whom there is a binding agreement, may have to be handled by an agent or executor? The executor may be unable to act properly if only one party's memory is the sole available recourse in handling business transactions.

Contracts should be used primarily for puppy sales, purchases of adult stock, leases and stud services. The agreement should contain a minimum of legal language and spell out in clear English what both parties agree to.

The title of a document for the sale of stock should read *Conditional Sales Contract,* and in the body of the contract list the conditions. It should state that both parents are registered and give their AKC registration number and a description of the dog(s) involved.

Depending upon whether the animal is sold as show/breeding quality or soley as a pet, it should be stated what basic requirements the dog (owner) must fulfill prior to showing or breeding (*i.e.,* be free from major genetic faults, be in good health and bred only to the dog of the breeder's choosing).

A good breeder will require that the dog be well cared for and provide a book on care and training to the new novice owner. To make sure the purchaser stays on the right track, the breeder should offer future consultation.

On some specific bitch sales the breeder might wish to sign the AKC registration papers as co-owner to ensure the terms are kept (co-ownership requires the signatures of both parties for puppy registrations), and sign off the papers when all terms are fulfilled. A form used for such purposes is shown in Figure IV-9.

Figure IV-9. Sample of Sales Agreement and Guarantee

PUPPY SALES AGREEMENT AND GUARANTEE
(May be used for Pet Sales/Show Sales/Co-Ownerships)

THIS AGREEMENT is made and entered into this _____ day of _____ 19____, by and between _____ of _____, (City, State), hereinafter called SELLER/BREEDER, and _____ of _____ , hereinafter called BUYER.

WITNESSETH:

WHEREAS, Seller agrees to sell and hereby does sell the following described dog, delivered to Buyer on the _____ day of _____, 19____:

Breed _____ AKC No. _____ Sex _____ Born _____

Color _____

Sire _____

Dam _____

Name _____ Tattoo _____

WHEREAS, Seller guarantees the above dog to be in good health and free of disease for 48 hours after date of delivery,

NOW THEREFORE, in consideration of the covenants and promises as hereinafter set forth, and other good and valuable consideration, the parties do hereby agree as follows:

1. BUYER has paid SELLER the sum of _____, and receipt thereof is hereby acknowledged; BUYER AGREES to pay to Seller the additional sum of _____ by the _____ day of _____.

2. ADDITIONAL TERMS: _____
_____
_____
_____
_____
_____
_____

3. Said dog may be shown on the following terms: _____
_____

4. Breeding expenses to be paid as follows: _____
_____

5. Buyer agrees and binds himself to take good and reasonable care of said dog; feed and house him properly, control him when off his premises and to avoid loss by theft, running away, damage by other dogs or otherwise, and to promptly secure the best of veterinary attention to the physical welfare of said dog for the duration of the term of this agreement. Buyer is responsible for all medical expenses that may be incurred on behalf of said dog. Buyer agrees to hold Seller harmless from any damages to property, other dogs or

persons that may be caused by said dog. Buyer further agrees that if he does not desire to keep said dog for any reason at any time prior to completion of conditions herein, Seller shall have first priority to claim said dog as follows: _____

_____

Buyer further states that he has a fenced yard and agrees that he will not chain, tie or otherwise mistreat the said dog. Buyer agrees if said dog is returned to Seller, Buyer will execute AKC registration to sole ownership of Seller; and that said dog will be up-to-date on all vaccinations and in as good health as when dog was sold to Buyer.

    6. Buyer understands that this dog is sold as _____ and guaranteed as stated herein.

    7. Buyer agrees and understands that if any conditions herein are not completed as set forth: Seller has the right to repossess said dog forthwith and Buyer shall not be entitled to any refund of any monies paid to Seller pursuant to the agreement contained herein. Under such circumstances, Buyer agrees to relinquish his interest in said dog and to execute the AKC registration certificate to the sole ownership of Seller. Buyer agrees that in the event litigation in a court of law becomes necessary, Seller may request damages in addition to the value of dog, attorney's fees and costs incurred.

Buyer's initials _____
Seller's initials _____

    8. When all conditions set forth herein have been completed, Seller shall execute the AKC registration certificate to sole ownership of Buyer.

    9. Seller states the said dog has received the following: (Health)

_____
_____
_____
_____

GUARANTEE:

    10. Seller guarantees that the above dog will x-ray normal or better, at age of two (2) years, or dog will be replaced with another dog of similar quality and breeding when available, upon the following terms and conditions:

    (a) That said dog has not been used for breeding without the consent and knowledge of Seller; and

    (b) That a copy of the OFA certification or other radiologist report (qualified radiologist ONLY) shall be provided to Seller; and

    (c) Provided said dog has received proper exercise, vitamins, proper diet as prescribed by Seller, and has been properly maintained for his size and weight; and

    (d) No hip X-ray prior to two (2) years of age shall be considered pertinent to this guarantee; and

    (e) that notice of neutering executed in writing by a vet, is sent to Seller within thirty (30) days of the date of (b) above; and

    (f) that Seller is given the opportunity to reclaim said dog if desired and/or make arrangements mutually agreed upon by Buyer and Seller as circumstances warrant.

11. Seller guarantees that if said dog is being sold to Buyer as "show quality," then said dog is guaranteed to be a proper representative of the breed in accordance with the AKC breed standard, provided the said dog has been properly maintained for his size and weight, fed the diet and vitamins as prescribed by Seller, so that he may reach his full potential as set forth in the breed standard. If said dog does not fulfill the requirements in this paragraph by 18 months of age, said dog shall be replaced with another dog of similar quality and breeding when available. This guarantee shall be null and void if said dog has been used for breeding. Buyer and Seller shall further mutually agree whether said dog shall be returned to Seller, neutered, or other terms mutually agreed upon between the parties hereto.

Other known hereditary problems (eyes, testicles, bites, etc.) detected in said dog will be handled in the same manner as hip problems.

_____
_____
_____
_____

12. The sum of _____ ($_____)
DOLLARS will be refunded to Buyer upon written proof of neutering by a qualified veterinarian if said dog is neutered within _____ months hereof. This clause is null and void if said dog is used for breeding without consent of Seller.

BY AFFIXING HIS SIGNATURE BELOW, BUYER(S) UNDERSTAND AND APPROVE THE PROVISIONS AND TERMS STATED HEREINABOVE, CLAUSES #1-12, AND AGREES THERETO.

_____   _____
Buyer   Buyer

Address: _____

_____   Phone: _____

_____   Your Kennel Name
Seller/Breeder   Name
                                        Address & Phone

A conscientious breeder should stipulate that the dog being sold is, at this time, free from any of the genetic faults prevalent in the breed. Should any of the faults manifest themselves, a replacement puppy or agreed upon compensation for a pet puppy price may be agreed upon. The contract should state that a second veterinary opinion on the state of a major genetic fault may be requested in case of controversy.

Since most dogs are sold as pets it should also be stated in writing that they are not guaranteed to be show or breeding stock.

On lease agreements the terms should be decided pretty much as a mutual agreement by both parties. The co-ownership concept can be used here as well. AKC provides a formal lease certificate which can be used for these purposes.

Withholding of the AKC registration papers is a good way of making sure a less than desirable puppy is not bred and create more poor specimens. A registration witholding agreement is shown in Figure IV-10.

Figure IV-10. Sample of AKC Withholding Agreement

A.K.C. REGISTRATION WITHHOLDING AGREEMENT

Date: _____

    The undersigned fully understands and agrees that the purchase of the within described dog is for the purposes of a family pet ONLY and the dog is not to be used for breeding or show, other than obedience. The undersigned further agrees that they are not to receive the American Kennel Club registration papers on the said dog and said papers are being withheld by the Seller of said dog until such time as a certificate from a veterinarian is presented to the Seller within _____ of the date of this agreement, as proof that the said dog has been neutered, at which time the A.K.C. registration papers will then be delivered to the undersigned Buyer AFTER SAID DATE, registration papers will be returned to the A.K.C. with a copy of this agreement.

    The Seller hereby certifies that the within described dog is healthy and free from disease, and guarantees said health for a period of forty-eight (48) hours from the date of this agreement.

    It is further understood and agreed if the Buyer(s) do not desire to keep the said dog, it shall be returned to the Seller in a good and healthy condition and the purchase price will be applied toward the purchase of another dog, of the same type and value, when available, unless other arrangements are made. UNDER NO CIRCUMSTANCES, shall the said dog be offered for sale or given away to anyone, until the Seller has been contacted.

    As it is understood by the Buyer that said dog is being sold as "pet quality," no further guarantees other than immediate health status are offered.

    The Seller of the said dog shall have the prerogative of re-evaluating the said dog, if requested by the Buyer. In the event said dog is considered breeding quality or conformation quality, this agreement shall become null and void and a new agreement shall be effected. IT IS AGREED THAT ONLY THE SELLER SHALL HAVE THE AUTHORITY TO RE-EVALUATE SAID DOG.

Breed _____ AKC No. _____ Sex ____ Born _____
Color _____

Sire _____
Dam _____
Name _____ Tattoo _____
Other Identifying Marks: _____
_____

Other Comments: _____
_____
_____

WE HAVE READ AND UNDERSTAND AND AGREE TO THE ABOVE
AGREEMENT, AND SIGNED SAME THIS ____ day of _____,
19____.

SELLER: BUYER:

Name   _____

Address   _____

Phone   Phone: _____

_____   _____
(Signature)   (Signature)

For stud services there are a number of basic forms. *Dog World Magazine* sells its version and the Professional Handlers Association has a recommended form for use by its members. You should modify either of these forms to suit your own needs. A typical form is shown in Figure IV-11.

Figure IV-11. Sample of Stud Service Contract

STUD SERVICE CONTRACT/CERTIFICATION

THIS IS TO CERTIFY THAT my stud dog _____

(_____) ex (_____)

Reg. No. _____ was mated to the bitch _____

(_____) ex (_____)

Reg. No. _____ on this date _____, 19____.

CONDITIONS OF CONTRACT

1. Payment for the stud service shall be made as follows:

2. If the Bitch fails to whelp, the Owner of the Bitch must give written notice to the Owner of the Stud Dog delivered at (ADDRESS),

not later than thirty (30) days after the "anticipated date of whelp-ing." A return service will be given to the same Stud Dog without an additional fee ONLY at the next heat to the same Bitch. If the Bitch does not conceive and proper notice is not given by the Owner of the Bitch, the right to a return stud service is forfeited.

3. All expenses of shipping (both ways) will be paid by the Owner of the Bitch. Bitches being shipped to (CITY) by air freight will be met and brought back to the respective airport at no extra charge.

4. One week's board is included in the stud service fee. If the Bitch is to be maintained at Stud Owner's property longer than one week (7 days), Owner of Bitch agrees to pay $____/day board.

5. The Owner of the Bitch is responsible for the health of the Bitch. The Owner of the Stud Dog may request a veterinary certificate of health of the Bitch before breeding, at the expense of the Owner of the Bitch.

6. Should "artificial insemination" be required to accomplish this breeding, it will NOT be attempted without permission of Owner of Bitch. Any extra charges for artificially inseminating the Bitch will be borne by the Owner of the Stud. Owner of Bitch agrees to pay for these charges should the Bitch be physically impossible to breed naturally and ONLY after thoroughly discussing possible health implications with a veterinarian.

7. The Owner of the Bitch agrees that any and all puppies produced from the litter resulting from the breeding to the above two ani-mals will not be sold directly or indirectly to or through a pet shop, specialty shop, or a wholesaler of purebred dogs.

8. The Owner of the Stud Dog is not obligated to sign the application for registration with the American Kennel Club of the subject litter until and unless the conditions of payment as well as all other conditions of this contract are fulfilled.

9. The laws of (STATE) shall govern this contract.

Signature of Owner of Bitch

Signature of Owner of Stud or
Authorized Agent for Owner of Stud

Bitch Owner's Full Address

Stud Owner's Address (Place of Mating)

Phone

Phone

Date

Date

ONE COPY OF THIS EXECUTED CONTRACT AND CERTIFICATION WILL BE PROVIDED BITCH OWNER AND STUD OWNER.

ANTICIPATED WHELPING DUE DATE: _____

The piece of paper in the end is only as good as the honesty of the people who have signed it. No matter how scrupulously the screening technique is applied, there are always some irresponsible people or even well-intentioned buyers who fall by the wayside and do not fulfill their end of the bargain. More often than not, it's the breeding arrangement which is broken. When the dog has been sold to out-of-town buyers, it is difficult to ensure that the terms of the agreement are fulfilled. It is easier to monitor a contract and form relationships with people whom you can see on occasion.

The alternative to legal action for breach of contract is pressure brought to bear by organizations related to the dog game. The national, local breed or all-breed clubs can sometimes be helpful in these matters. Peer pressure, threats of spoiling their reputations, or as a last resort, Small Claims Court are all possible solutions. Generally, action in a court of law results in cutting off all lines of communication and seldom works to the best interest of the dog. However, if it is your intention to recover monetary damages, the courtroom may be the best bet.

There have been cases of overzealous breeders who have resorted to breaking and entering to retrieve dogs that were used for unauthorized purposes. Mistreated dogs have been known to have been rescued in this manner. While philanthropic in nature, these acts are illegal and can boomerang on the perpetrator.

Most states have laws that protect the buyer against deceit and fraud. How can the seller also be protected? To protect against cases of a mis-used or poorly-used dog, the terms of an agreement should state "Breech of terms of the contract entitles the seller to repossession." The legalities of breaking and entering should be discussed with a lawyer, but a repossession clause in a contract at least cautions the buyer you mean business.

There should be some flexibility in the clause offering full replace-ment should the breeder prefer to refund the sales price instead. This may occur when the buyers did not represent themselves honestly or did not treat the animal well. The last thing a conscientious breeder would want to do is provide them with another animal to potentially ruin.

Serious thought should be given to whether to sign as co-owner with buyers who appear to have questionable stability or have been irrespon-sible in any previous dealings. There is always the chance that legal prob-lems and liability questions may come up.

Stud service agreements usually guarantee a repeat service should the first attempt not result in puppies. The stud fee should be non-refundable because of the time, board and breeding involved in the ser-vice. The stud fee should also be payable at the time of the service.

Many stud service agreements stipulate one surviving puppy as con-stituting a litter. A certain amount of fairness should be involved in interpreting this clause. If such a circumstance came about it might be best to offer a repeat service or other considerations. A lot is dependent on the situation and the attitude of the people involved. It may be best to include strict terms in the contract and then interpret them more loosely in favor of a cooperative party.

Some interesting points seen in other agreements include: A stipulation that should a bitch not live to fulfill the agreed upon breeding terms, the buyer would be responsible for payment of an additional sum of money (this surely would not encourage good will). Some sellers charge pet prices on sale, then require additional payments if the animal develops into a show/breeding prospect. This is known as having your cake and eating it too.

Examine any contract that you are offered with an eye to whether it's possible to live up to the terms described. The bottom line for all contracts is . . . morality cannot be legislated. A person's written signature is only as good as that persons integrity.

SECTION V
The Versatile Cocker Spaniel

- *As a Show Dog*
- *As an Obedience Dog*
- *As a Hunting Dog*
- *Elementary Spaniel Field Training*
- *It's Written On The Wind*

CHAPTER 1

As A Show Dog

The show ring is where the Cocker has always excelled. The ringside crowds at all-breed shows are always larger when the Cockers are being shown. The breed with its variety mixture of colors and outgoing disposition has always been a crowd pleaser.

Developers of the breed wanted a small energetic dog who would be a willing worker with great stamina. He would need to have an outgoing disposition that could take anything thrown at him and still come back for more. The modern Cocker, the Number 1 breed in America, is all that and more.

The Cocker's head has always been his showpiece. Those large soulful eyes, the affectionate expression, and the long ears are the Cocker's trademark. So much so, that many a judge has gotten hung up on the head to the neglect of the rest of the dog. This type of judge is often called a "headhunter."

But there is far more to the Cocker than his beautiful head. He is a sporting dog par excellence. He still has the natural hunting instincts he was originally bred for. He is built to cover ground, to move up and through heavy cover and to flush, mark, and retrieve whatever game the hunter has chosen for sport. To accomplish these tasks the Cocker has to be built right. Previous chapters discussed the breed standard and how form should follow function. His function is to hunt upland birds and he has been designed to do that very well.

The Cocker competes in the Sporting Group at dog shows in America. In many other countries this group is called the Gun Dog Group. In still other countries he competes in a group exclusively for Spaniels. He is placed in this competitive setting because he, like all others in this group, was bred for sport—to hunt/retrieve birds. Literally all members of this group have the same general demands made on their conformation.

If one were to take the Cocker standard—written to make a Cocker a good field dog—into the show ring, there is an excellent fit in what makes a Cocker a good hunter and what makes for a good show dog. The standard asks for the dog to be merry; that is, his tail should be going incessantly. That's easy for any Cocker. That outgoing disposition serves him in good stead. He wants to please at all times. The standard asks for a slightly sloping topline while moving. A Cocker built to go all day in the field comes with that built in. All in all, the standard describes a willing little worker who would just as soon work in the show ring as in the field or obedience ring—no phlegmatic dog he. The Cocker calls attention to himself by his willingness to show—to be *up*—to *ask* for the win. Properly trained, properly set down, a good Cocker is hard to beat.

The Cocker is one of the most versatile dogs of any breed. We have seen him in the obedience ring, we have seen him in the field, and of course around home as a loving family dog. Now let's look at him as one of the leaders in the show ring.

Even though Cocker registrations fell markedly during the 1950's and 60's, show entries indicated little decline. The earnest and sincere breeders hung in there while the fly-by-nights fled the breed. These dedicated breeders continued to breed top-flight show stock and the Cocker continued to get his due in the show ring.

The Cocker can be a true showman. With his coat of different hues and long ears sailing in the wind he is an impressive dog going around the ring. Cockers have been rewarded with some of the premier wins the dog show game has to give. While the Cocker is anxious to please and can become a fine showman, it does not happen without proper training and grooming and both take time and patience. Training your dog properly can make the difference between a winner and an also-ran. To insure you get words of wisdom about training I am going to quote one of the greatest handler/trainers of modern show dogs, Frank Sabella. Frank is now an AKC licensed judge. In his book (written with Shirlee Kalstone) *The Art of Handling Show Dogs*, published by B & E Publications, he covers all the bases in the early training of a show dog.

Introduction

Show training is so important that it becomes a part of the puppy's life. Training for the show ring should begin as soon as you purchase your puppy or from the time it is weaned, if you were its breeder. Especially with a baby puppy, your main objective is to begin establishing a pleasant, loving relationship which will become the basis of more formal training in the future.

Dogs are required to do two things in the conformation ring: to be set up or posed (and to hold that pose for an indefinite length of time during the judge's examination) and to gait (individually and in a group). While show training is not difficult, it does require time, patience, sensitivity and consistency on the part of the trainer.

Many people make the mistake of waiting for a puppy to grow up and then begin to train it. We don't mean to imply that some successful dogs did not start this way but, without a doubt, dogs that have the right kind of basic training as puppies are always the ones that stand in the ring with head and tail up, full of assurance. Just the repetition of correctly posing and leading the puppy will teach it to walk confidently on lead and to feel comfortable while being handled—and that's really what early training is for—to ensure that your puppy will grow into an adult that is confident and self assured in the show ring!

At what age should you begin training your puppy? Each dog is an individual and should be treated as such, so there are no "set" age limits as to when to begin basic or advanced show training. Generally, when you start basic training depends not only on your patience, sensitivity and consistency, but also on the puppy's capabilities and desire to accept being posed and lead trained.

Very young puppies are highly motivated by and responsive to their owners but, like babies, they have short concentration periods. Even though intelligence develops rapidly in a puppy, early training should always be started on a "fun" basis. Don't be in a hurry to start formal training too early; the first part of a puppy's life should be fun time and every dog should be allowed to enjoy its puppyhood.

Early Socialization Important

As the owner or breeder of a young puppy, you alone are responsible for its early socialization and training. Socialization can be described as the way in which a dog develops a relationship with its dam, littermates, other animals and man. Just as a youngster must receive a formal education and also learn to become a responsible member of society, so must you provide the best environment for your dog's potential to be brought out and developed completely. A young puppy is very impressionable and the socialization and training it receives at an early age sets the tone for its lifetime characteristics. If a puppy receives the proper socialization, is treated with sensitivity, patience and consistency, if it learns to be loved and respected, then it will always be happiest when pleasing you.

Earlier in this chapter, we mentioned that with a young puppy you want to begin basic training by establishing a happy and loving rapport between you and the dog. Pat and handle the puppy frequently, speaking reassuringly and using praise often. Let the puppy become accustomed to being petted and handled by strangers. A well-socialized puppy loves to make new friends and this kind of interaction between puppy and humans or other animals will be a prerequiste for the basic show training to follow. Hopefully, by the time the puppy is about 7 to 8 weeks old, it has learned a little about life. If it has been properly socialized, it is light-hearted and untroubled, because it has learned that it is loved and respected. Now it must be taught certain basics which lead eventually to more formal training for the show ring.

Here are some suggestions to consider before you begin basic training:

1. First training sessions should be given in familiar surroundings, preferably at home, and without noises or other distractions.
2. Make the first training periods short, not more than 10 minutes in length. As the sessions progress successfully, gradually lengthen each training period, but never more than 30 minutes in any single session.

3. If the puppy is restless or won't concentrate, postpone the lesson and try again the following day. Be sure, too, that you are not tired or impatient for the training sessions should always be relaxed and enjoyable for both of you.

4. Be consistent during the lessons. Use a firm tone of voice when giving commands. Some of the first words your puppy will learn in posing and lead training are "Come," "Stand," "Stay," and "No." Be sure you use the same word for the same command each time.

5. Remember that a young puppy is inexperienced, so be gentle and patient. Don't rush your puppy; give it time to understand what you expect and to learn how to respond.

6. Don't be too insistent at first. Puppies learn by repetition, correction and praise. Don't punish a puppy if it seems confused; instead, correct it until it does what you want, then offer plenty of praise. It is important that your puppy understand each training step thoroughly before going on to the next.

7. Always end each training session on a pleasant note and once again, give plenty of praise and perhaps reward the puppy with its favorite treat. A puppy can learn almost anything if given love and understanding.

Table Training

A grooming table should be one of your first investments, for it will be an indispensable help in establishing habit patterns. Most professional handlers, experienced exhibitors and breeders table train puppies at an early age because, aside from the convenience of having the animal at their working height, there is also an invaluable psychological advantage to table training (Figure V-1). Even though the puppy is off the ground and experiencing a new situation, it is given confidence by the presence of its owner and submits to any handling or grooming, thereby establishing a rapport between the puppy and trainer.

It is easier to control a young puppy by teaching it to pose on a table . . . and recently, it is common to see judges using tables in the ring to examine other small breeds. On larger breeds, even though adult dogs are posed on the ground, early table training will be invaluable for teaching ground posing later on.

The majority of coated breeds require some type of regular grooming in addition to preparation at the show before going into the ring. Even smooth-coated breeds need regular care. Early grooming training on the table will teach the dog to learn to relax. Later on, when the coat grows longer or the dog needs special attention, it will not object if it has to spend longer periods on the table and will rest and feel totally secure while being worked on. As a part of the training you should practice posing the dog at the end of each grooming session.

The table you select should be sturdy and covered with a non-slip rubber top. There are many different types of grooming tables: portable (which fold up and are easy to carry along to matches and shows), adjustable (which move up or down) or a combination crate with grooming table top (these often have drawers between the crate and top to hold equipment). Some tables are equipped with a post and loop collar, which can be slipped around a dog's neck to hold the head up

Figure V-1. A grooming table is of indispensable help in training young puppies. The portable type illustrated here is covered with a non-slip surface and has an adjustable post and loop which can be removed when not in use. Portable tables are easy to fold up, making them convenient to transport to and from matches and shows.

and keep it from moving or jumping off the table. If you do use a loop to give the puppy more confidence, never use one with any type of choking action. Never leave a young puppy alone with its head in a loop or standing by itself on a table unless you are sure it will stay.

Posing

You can start posing your puppy on a table as early as 6 weeks. In the beginning just stand the puppy on the table and get it used to being off the ground. Once this has been accomplished, then start positioning the legs in a show pose. Next, begin training it to be handled—feel its body, look at its teeth and let other people do the same. Experiencing all this at an early age will give the puppy confidence and make it used to being handled by strangers, which will be invaluable later on for the puppy's show career. If you persevere in the beginning you will discover that your puppy will never forget this basic training and later it will be much easier to work with.

When lifting the puppy for the first time, care should be taken not to frighten it. Don't come down too quickly on the puppy or attempt to lift it by grasping the back of the neck or picking it up by the front legs. Instead, kneel down to the puppy's level and let it come to you. Speak assuringly and pat the puppy if you can. Then using both hands to lift the puppy's front and rear, pick it up and place it on the table. Do be aware that a puppy might try to wiggle out of your arms so make sure you have a secure grip on the dog as you lift it and after you set it down on the table.

Be sure the table surface is not slippery and use the following method to pose the puppy:

Figure V-2—Grasp the puppy with your left hand between the back legs and your right hand under the chest, at the same time giving the command 'stand' or 'stay'. When you pose the dog in the ring, in the majority of times this is the way it will be facing the judge. If the puppy fusses and does not want to stand, keep your hands in the same position and slightly lift the front feet off the table and put them down, then lift the rear legs off the table and put them down, doing both movements in a slight rocking motion. Repeat this several times to distract the puppy and get it to settle down.

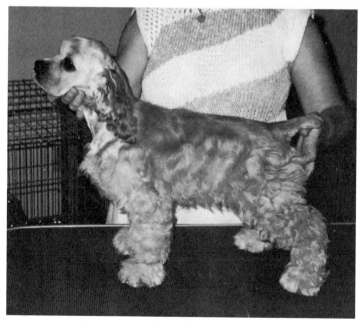

Figure V-2.

Figure V-3—Move your right hand from under the chest and place it on the neck as shown, with the weight of the head resting on the top part of your hand. Don't grasp the neck too heavily; use a light touch, just enough so that you can control the puppy from moving to either side or out of your hand.

Figure V-3.

Figure V-4—Move your left hand from under the legs to support the tail and hold it in position as shown, so that the puppy learns to support its own weight on the table.

Figure V-4.

Figure V-5—shows the puppy posed.

These are the basic procedures for setting up the the puppy. If you can accomplish all this in one session, excellent! Otherwise, work on the first position until the puppy assumes that pose without fussing, then go to the next position and so on. Each time the puppy assumes a correct pose, praise it lavishly. At all times when you are moving your hands to the various positions, be aware that the puppy might squirm and pull away, therefore you must be ready to recover it immediately by using the first position.

Figure V-5.

Figure V-6—To adjust the puppy's right front foot, control the dog by holding its head in your right hand. Release the hold on the tail with your left hand and allow it to grasp the right leg below the elbow and while pushing the puppy's head away from that foot, place the right leg down, then swing the the puppy's head back into position to distribute its weight evenly again.

Figure V-6.

Figure V-7—To adjust his left front foot, with the puppy's head still in your right hand, reach over the dog with your left hand, grasp the left front leg at the same point you did on the right. Twist the puppy's head toward you (putting the weight on the right leg) and correctly position the left leg, then return the head to its normal position.

Figure V-7.

Figure V-8—If you have a small dog with an excellent front, simply grasp the puppy under the neck, raise it off its front legs, then drop it back onto the table.

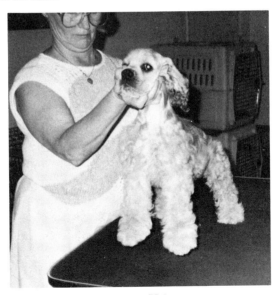

Figure V-8.

Figure V-9—To position each back leg, grasp the leg between the hock joint and foot and place it in the correct position. This procedure for positioning the back legs is used when you have the dog on lead or with your hand under the neck.

Figure V-9.

Figure V-10—The procedure for posing a puppy on a lead begins by following the same steps as shown in Figs. V-6–9. Pick up the dog and place it on the table.

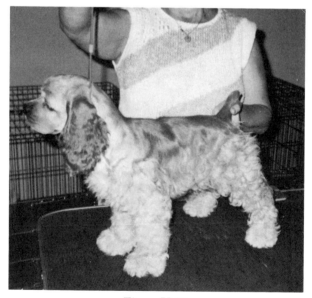

Figure V-10.

Figure V-11—Holding the lead in your right hand with the head in an upright position, move your left hand between the dog's back legs. If the dog moves its left or right front leg, position them as described before. Corrections to the rear are done the same as instructed in Fig. V-9.

Figure V-11. ➤

◄ **Figure V-12.**

Figure V-12—Shows the dog posed in profile by lead and tail.

Figure V-13—If the puppy has a tendency to lean back when being posed, grasp the puppy under the throat with the right hand and place your left hand between the hind legs. Draw the puppy slowly backwards off the table, and then place it back on the table so that its weight is distributed evenly on all four legs.

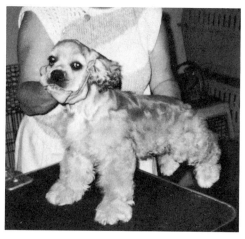

Figure V-13.

Figure V-14—If a large puppy has a tendency to lean back when posed on the table, take hold of the tail and apply a pulling back pressure which will make the dog lean into its front. Later on, when the dog is posed on the ground, this method also may be used to correct leaning back.

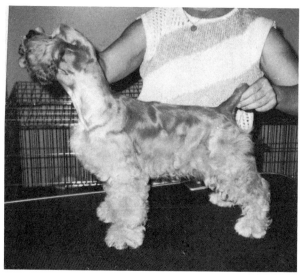

Figure V-14.

After your puppy learns how to stand properly, start posing it for longer periods of time. When the puppy can pose without fussing, the next step is to enlist the help of friends by having them go through the motions of lightly examining the dog—checking its bite and feeling the body—doing the things a judge will do in the ring. If you are training a male, in the ring the judge will check to see if both testicles are in place, so do remember to train your puppy to accept this procedure at an early age.

As the posing sessions progress, you can begin practicing the more subtle aspects of show posing, *i.e.*, setting up the puppy in a variety of situations and on different ground surfaces, especially grass.

Author's Note: Special thanks to Wanda Towne of Townehouse Cockers for posing her puppies for these illustrations.

Lead Training

Of all the steps necessary to prepare a puppy for the show ring, probably lead training is the most important because there have been many potentially fine show dogs ruined by improper lead training. So many exhibitors wait until the last minute to lead break a dog then expect it all to happen in one try. Then they become impatient and treat the dog roughly and the puppy's reaction to all this is fear. Do remember that extreme patience is necessary because introduction to a collar and a lead can be a frightening experience for a young puppy.

Most canine behavior experts agree that at 6 weeks, a dog can have a small soft collar put around its neck. The younger the puppy becomes accustomed to wearing a collar around its neck, the easier it will be to lead train it later on. Begin by placing the collar around the puppy's neck for short periods of time and only while someone is in attendance. The first few times the puppy wears the collar, it may roll on the ground or try several other things to get the collar off, so never allow a baby puppy to be unsupervised. Make the first lesson short, not more than 5 to 10 minutes, then remove the collar, play with the puppy and praise it for being such a good dog.

After a period of about a week (or when the puppy is relaxed about wearing the collar) snap a lightweight lead onto the collar and let the puppy drag the lead freely about the floor. Allow the puppy to walk wherever it wants to go. If it starts to follow you, fine; but the first time the lead is attached, don't pick it up and jerk and pull the puppy in any way. After a few times of allowing the puppy to drag the lead around the floor, pick up the lead in your hand and let the puppy take you for a walk. Speak gently and walk wherever the puppy wants to go. Once again, don't pull or tug on the lead in an attempt to make the puppy follow you until it is completely accustomed to wearing the collar and lead.

When this has been accomplished, the next lesson is to try to walk the puppy on lead. The first time you try this, don't be surprised if your puppy pulls back or rolls over on the floor. Don't panic, just learn to be patient and speak gently. Put the snap adjustment under the puppy's neck at first so it won't be tempted to look over its shoulder or try to bite the lead. Squat down and call the puppy's name and the word "come" in your most inviting voice, to get the dog to move forward to you. If it balks or sits, try coaxing it to come forward for its favorite tidbit. You may have to give a slight forward pull to the lead to start the puppy toward you but remember, a slight pull does not mean a neck-breaking jolt for you can injure the neck and the puppy will associate the resulting pain with an unpleasant experience. If this is done several times without thinking, it can develop into a deep seated fear of the lead.

When the puppy comes to you, pat and praise it; then walk ahead with the lead in your hand and repeat this action to make the puppy move forward again. It should only take a short while until the puppy follows you. Eventually, the puppy will learn that if it obeys and follows you, there will be no pulling or jerking of the lead and that it will receive plenty of praise.

Once again, we caution that because a puppy's attention span is short, try to make each session brief, 10 minutes at most, then remove the lead, praise and play with the puppy. The main idea at this stage of training is to make the first lessons a "train and play" time that the puppy looks forward to and not something it dreads. After a few lessons, you'll find your puppy can be lead trained rather quickly and what is more important, that it enjoys the experience.

At this point, we want to offer some advice about early training. Always try to train the puppy to move on a loose lead to help develop its natural carriage. In the show ring you will be asked by many judges to move your dog on a loose lead and you will be prepared if you accustom your puppy to do it at an early age. When a puppy is taught to gait only on a tight lead, it gets used to leaning into the lead and without that pressure, feels completely lost. There is nothing harder to break than a dog that is used to leaning into the lead for support. Dogs that are trained on a tight lead also lose their natural head carriage and they often learn many other bad habits including sidewinding. In the ring, it is not uncommon to see exhibitors string up their dogs so tightly that the front feet hardly touch the ground. There is a trend to show certain breeds on a tight lead to make a more positive topline.

However, if a knowledgeable judge wants to discover whether the dog's topline is natural or man-made, he will ask that the dog be moved on a loose lead and, if that fault is present, it will be exposed.

While the puppy is being lead trained, don't train it to be hand posed at the same time. At first, these should be two seperate procedures. Animals learn by repetition and, if each time you stop leading the dog and then get down and set it up, the dog will anticipate this action and will become discouraged from learning to stand naturally and pose itself without being set up by hand. So many exhibitors hand pose their puppies after each gaiting session and when this happens, a puppy soon gets the idea that every time it stops on lead, someone will bend down to hold its head and tail. In the ring, after you have individually gaited your dog, many judges will ask you to let the dog stand on its own. If your puppy hasn't learned to stand naturally at the end of its lead, it won't be able to do so in the ring.

As the gaiting sessions progress, teach the puppy to move on your left side (eventually the dog should learn to move on your right side as well as your left). Encourage the puppy to stand naturally at the end of the lead each time it stops. To help get the puppy to stand alert, try

---

attracting its attention with a squeaky toy, a ball or by offering its favorite tidbit. Doing this will start to teach the puppy the fundamentals of baiting.

After a while you will be ready to begin more advanced training. Replace the training collar with a one-piece show lead or, on large breeds, switch from the training collar to a choke chain or a more substantial type of collar for better control. (As the dog grows older, remember that any collar or chain should be worn only during practice sessions and then removed to prevent the hair from wearing away around the neck.) Before starting advanced training, be sure that the lead is correctly positioned around the dog's neck. It should be high under the chin and behind the ears to keep the dog under control at all times. This position will also help to train the puppy to keep its head up because for the first few weeks, a puppy may need a gentle reminder under its chin to learn to keep its head up.

Next you should begin advanced training by teaching the dog to move down and back in a straight line. Once the dog does this well, then try moving it in a circle. As a prerequisite to executing the individual patterns, practice doing figure-eights because this will teach the dog how to turn smoothly. Then you can begin the other movement patterns that will be used in the show ring—the "L," the "T," and the "Triangle." Vary the movement patterns in each session and remember not to overtrain. Always end each session on a pleasant note and give the dog lots of praise.

As your puppy matures, it should learn to gait on grass, concrete floors and other surfaces including rubber mats (these are used at indoor shows). Once the lessons go well at home, take the puppy out and get it used to walking on a lead and being posed in new and different surroundings. Parking lots of supermarkets and department stores are excellent for this as there are usually lots of people and all kinds of distractions. For the first few outings, be patient and give the puppy plenty of time to adjust and respond to strange surrondings. Occasionally, because of a pup's insecurities, it may revert back to not being well trained for the first few outings.

The greatest pitfall for most young dogs seems to be going to indoor shows because the lighting is strange and the echoes inside a building can sometimes distract a young dog. The inside of a department store or shopping mall can help you to overcome this problem. Always try to anticipate experiences that might distract and frighten a puppy at a show and try to solve them while the puppy is young. If you live in a rural area and none of these suggestions apply to you, take the puppy to matches as often as you can for this is the best place to gain experience with the least amount of tension.

You must work with your dog to determine its best speed in gaiting. Each dog is an individual and looks best when moving at a certain speed and if you want to show your dog to its best advantage, you should determine that correct speed. Have a friend move your dog at varying speeds in front of a knowledgeable person to learn the right speed for your puppy. Then practice the movement patterns at that speed until the dog can do them smoothly. No dog can move at its best speed if the handler moves improperly, so you should take long strides when gaiting the dog. A common error of the novice is to move the dog too slowly.

Short, stilted steps look clumsy and prevent the dog from moving smoothly. If you do not move fast enough yourself or with free and easy strides, you will prevent your dog from executing its most efficient movement. If you are showing a small breed take normal walking steps. For the medium or large breeds, move at a fast walk or run.

We should end the puppy lead training section with some advice about two common problems: sitting and sidling.

Sitting

When stopping, if you find that your puppy constantly sits, keep moving forward a few steps while attracting its attention at the same time with a piece of food or a toy, until the puppy understands that it must stand when it stops. If that does not work, bring the puppy forward a few steps, stop, then put your toe under its stomach to prevent it from sitting.

Another solution is to ask a friend to stand holding a long piece of rope or a show lead which encircles the dog's stomach. When you bring your puppy forward and it starts to sit, have your friend brace up its rear, but do not make this correction with a jerking motion. Breeds that sit when stopped are difficult to train to stand at the end of the leash with tail up (if that is desired in the breed). To remedy this, after you have trained the dog to stand when it has stopped, reach gently from a standing position and put up the tail, stroking underneath the tail until the puppy gets the idea of what you want it to do.

Sidewinding

A common characteristic during lead training is when a dog has a tendency to sidle. This can be caused by:

A. *The dog pulling away from you.* Solution: When the dog starts this habit on the lead or shows indications of doing so when moving individually, train the dog to move on your opposite side. In other words, if you are going away or coming back with the dog on your left side and it sidles, switch to going and coming with the dog on your right.

B. *A dog that has a tendency to look up at its handler while being gaited.* Solution: Never show a dog a toy or food while you are gaiting it as this can cause the dog to look up which may cause sidling. You can also try the alternate side method mentioned in (A) above.

C. *A dog is too short in back.* Solution: If you move at a faster speed, it will go sideways to be able to move at a faster speed. The best way to deal with this problem is to get someone to move the dog at different speeds so you are able to decide at what speed the dog levels off. Another solution to sidling is to put two show leads on a dog and have one person walk on either side of the puppy so that the puppy walks straight in the center. If after a few tries you feel this method is working, the best way to keep the problem from recurring is by constantly alternating the sides each time you take the dog up and back. Gaiting next to a fence or a wall so that the dog can only move straight ahead is another solution to sidling.

Temperament

Temperament plays a major role in puppy training. While most dogs need consistent training to learn what is required of them in the show ring, some dogs are "naturals" at showing. They are outgoing and love being the center of attention and always seem to show themselves off to the best advantage. While these extroverted dogs are exceptions, they always train quickly and easily.

If you experience a temperament problem ("sound" shyness or hand shyness for instance), try to determine what is causing the problem and especially whether you might be the cause of it, as poor temperament can be the result of environment as well as from breeding. In the event you have purchased an older puppy that exhibits temperament problems, consider obedience training for that is a good way for an animal to learn regimentation and to get out among people. Obedience training has been used successfully on dogs that were kennel raised without adequate human socialization at the proper time.

Another part of training your puppy for the show ring has nothing to do with the ring itself, but a means of making going to the show a lot easier on you and the dog. This part of the training has to do with getting the puppy "crate trained." At an early age the puppy should be introduced to the crate that will be his home away from home. One of the best approaches is to put the crate down on the floor near where the puppy has his water bowl. Leave the door open. Put a favorite tidbit inside and let the puppy size it up. Most puppies will be somewhat leery of this new object. However, the puppy—by its very nature—is a curious animal and so will begin to approach it, at first giving it a wide berth. Now this process may take hours as the puppy, often unsure of what this thing is will leave the room for awhile before screwing up its courage and coming back. Gradually, it will approach closer and closer until finally it will be within inches of the crate. Typically, this is when the puppy stops short and reaches out its neck and head while keeping the body ready for flight if this "thing" should prove to be unfriendly. If nothing jumps out of the crate the puppy will feel safe to try to go further and eventually get the tidbit. However, staying inside, oh no, not me!

With this first success you know you have him hooked. Leave the crate down and pay no attention to it or the puppy. A couple of times during the day, place a tidbit in the crate. You will find it gone sometime later. After a few days of this game and you are sure the puppy (and not the cat!) is eating the tidbits, place a favorite toy in the crate. Let this game go on for a couple of days as well. Your next step is to gently pick up the puppy and place it in the crate with a tidbit inside and gently close the door. Be sure the puppy can see you as you go about your daily chores. He will most likely fuss about being confined. Talk to him, tell him what a great fellow he is and—if necessary—give him another tidbit. He should be confined for only about 10 minutes the first time. When you let him out, praise him lavishly for being a good dog. Over the next weeks you can extend the time slowly until the puppy comes to accept a few hours confinement as natural.

Once you have gotten to this point you can begin to let him sleep in the crate. Be sure you get up early enough so he will be let out of the crate before he soils himself. It's a good idea to put in some rough toweling or carpeting. Later on you might want to use a wire bottom or papering.

Next, you want to take him for a car/van ride to accustom him to motion. One of the trips to a shopping center referred to above would be ideal. Don't make his first voyage out into the world too long, however. Many puppies get car sick rather easily so keep the trip short and talk reassuringly to the puppy the whole time you are on the road. If people pull up along side of you at stop lights and see you talking to yourself, don't be worried, just put your hand up to your ear and they will think you have a car phone.

Grooming

Last, but not least in the preparation of a Cocker for the show ring, is proper trimming. In our family, my late wife Marjorie did the show trimming. I was shunted off to groom only the old dogs who would not be seen by the general public. This gives you an idea of my dog grooming skills. So, I turned to a real pro on Cocker grooming. Susan Kelley is a member of the Mission Valley Cocker Spaniel Club and the owner of the West Valley Grooming Salon in San Jose, California. Susan has groomed, shown and, of course, finished many of her own Cockers.

The most important thing to bear in mind when undertaking to trim a Cocker is time; be sure to have lots of it. Do not attempt to do your trimming at the last minute, or when you are tired or irritated. Patience is a prime factor. Be sure the dog is dry, thoroughly combed out, free of snarls, mats and body parasites before starting to trim.

The proper equipment will help to make the task easier. Most groomers use an Oster electric clipper with a #10 and #15 blade. Scissors are also quite important and a straight regular shears complemented by a thinning scissors. The kind with the blades on one side only, work the best. Be sure you keep your clippers oiled and the scissors sharp. A dryer with enough power to get through the profuse Cocker coat is also a necessity. Figure V-15 shows a Cocker Spaniel before grooming.

Use the clipper cautiously and only on head, ears, neck and shoulders; never on the body. Experience will teach you the proper method of operating the clipper. Use firm but not heavy strokes. Do not attempt to cover too large an area with any one stroke. Clipper burns most often result from working too rapidly thus pulling out hair, rather than allowing the clipper to cut it. A dull clipper will also cause burns. Keep your clipper in good working order; clean hair from the teeth after each trim job. Do the clipper work first and then bathe the dog and continue with the scissors.

It's a good idea to begin with the ears and clean out the underside and along the edges using a #10 blade, as shown in Figure V-16. Experience will help you to select the appropriate time when to use the #15

Figure V-15.

Figure V-16.

and when the #10. For example, depending upon the way the hair grows and the thickness of the hair on the face, you may wish to interchange the blades to give the best effect. Use the #15 to clear out the stop coming down from the top.

Once you have done the skull with clippers, as pictured in Figure V-17, you should next work with thinning shears to "clean it up" and give a soft, rounded appearance. As shown in Figure V-18, DO NOT get

Figure V-17.

Figure V-18.

so close as to give the dog a scalped look. Be sure to leave enough hair on the sides of the muzzle to give whatever help the dog needs to give a square appearance. Figure V-19 shows the desired appearance.

The neck and shoulders are extremely important in a Cocker. After the rough work has been completed (as shown in Figure V-20), you need to carefully look at how you will finish blending the neck into the

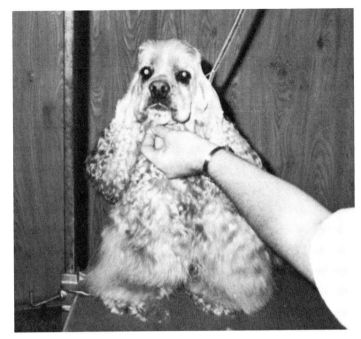

Figure V-19.

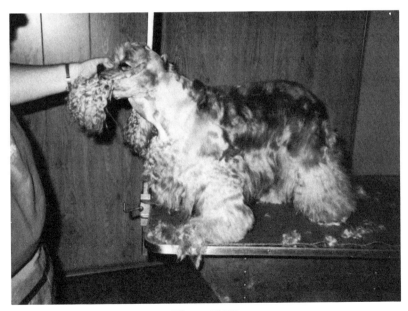

Figure V-20.

shoulders. Lift and feather the hair along the juncture of the neck and shoulders as you cut it so it will lie flat and give a smooth look, as shown in Figure V-21.

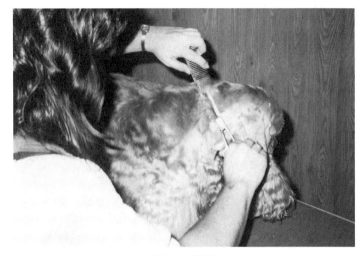

Figure V-21.

The back should never be clippered. Flat-coated dogs present few problems—simply trim under the guard hairs so the coat lies flat and make sure it does not give the appearance of over-barbering. This is particularly true when you are attempting to thin out the hairs over the rump of a dog who is too high there, as is illustrated in Figure V-22.

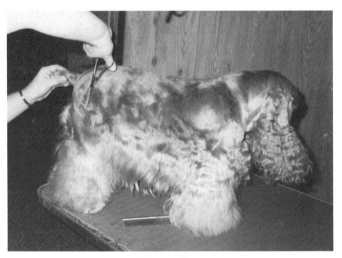

Figure V-22.

Dogs with the rougher or curlier coats present a different kind of a challenge. Try using the teeth side of your thinning shears to smooth out the coat. Be careful not to gouge—you are taking out all the guard hairs and poor workmanship will be quite apparent.

Think of yourself as a sculptor and try to imagine carving out the outline of the dog you want . . . it will go easier that way. Always remember that you want to take away excess hair and leave smooth lines. Get to know your dog so you can plan your work like an artist. There are certain areas that it's best to leave hair to cover up faults—i.e., a small dip just behind the shoulders. Other areas you may wish to take off as much hair as possible—i.e., the high-in-rump problem. In all cases, think in terms of balance. Don't trim to over-emphasize one area over the other. Remember, the dog "in proportion" is what the judge is looking for.

With that in mind, we move to the flanks. They should be well rounded and the hair should not fly in all directions when the dog is moving. This applies to the front legs and body coat just behind them. This calls for astute work with the thinning shears. Check your work as you go along. It's most helpful to have a mirror to check your progress. Don't try to thin it all at once. Take a little at a time and then check your work.

Thinning shears should also be used around the vent and down as low as the hocks. Watch that you do not cut in too deeply going down from the tail to the hocks. This can give the appearance of lacking muscle and depth in the dog's thighs.

Next, it's on to the feet. Clean out the hair between the pads (as shown in Figure V-23) and cut the nails. Nails should never "clack" on

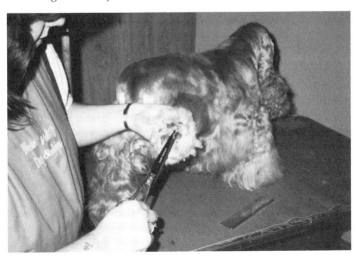

Figure V-23.

the floor. It's a good idea to wrap a 3″ × 5″ card around the leg, securing it with a rubber band just above the foot, so you can see the area you are working on. Trim the foot neatly (as shown in Figure V-24), emphasizing a "cat's" paw look; round and firm. Once you have finished the four feet, take off the card and brush the hair down over the feet. Then, using the regular scissors, you should "neaten up" your work so the leg coat does not distract from the foot. Do not cut off the leg coat too far above the foot or the dog will look like he is wearing knickers.

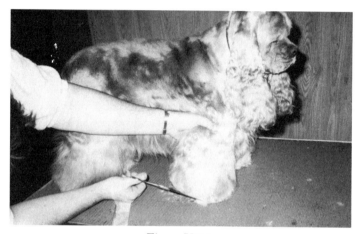

Figure V-24.

It's a good idea to have someone gait the dog so you can tell if it will be necessary to stop or remove more hair to minimize his faults. For example, if a dog is out at the elbows, leaving a great deal of coat there will only emphasize the problem; if the dog has a tendency to being cow-hocked, leaving more feathering on the outside of the leg will accentuate this fault.

Our finished product is shown in Figures V-25 and V-26.

Beware of self-appointed experts; seek advice and constructive criticism from those with the knowledge and experience which qualifies them to help you. Do not subject your dog to the well-meaning, but often disfiguring, ministrations of another novice. The real professional who devotes his full time to the conditioning and showing of dogs is best qualified to render assistance in this respect. There are few handlers who will refuse to help the novice. Remember, however, that the handler has no way of knowing you seek advice and help, unless you ask him.

The photos on these pages are illustrative of the proper grooming techniques. For a more in-depth treatment of grooming read Mari

Doty's "Trimming Guide." This can be obtained from the author at 202 So. Clovis Avenue, Fresno, California 93727.

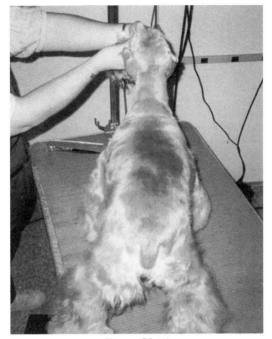

Figure V-25.

Figure V-26.

Ch. Caroling's Comet shown winning Best of Variety under breeder/judge Marilyn Spacht. Handled by Gregg Anderson for breeder/owner Carolyn A. Calkins.

CHAPTER 2

As An Obedience Dog
by Amy Weiss

Figure V-27. Amy Weiss, pictured with Ch. Camelot's Confetti (Black and Tan), Ch. Camelot's Court Jester (Black), and two 7-week old puppies.

Photo courtesy of Sacramento Bee.

It is with much enthusiasm that I urge you to enter the wonderful world of obedience with your Cocker Spaniel. Lucky you . . . you have perhaps one of the most responsive, intelligent and loyal breeds and, as you enter into a training program with him, you will make him a joy to own and a pleasure to live with.

Whether your aim is to pursue an active obedience show career, or simply to have a more controllable and livable companion, obedience training can, and should, be a most positive experience for both of you. In this chapter, I am going to discuss the formal part of obedience training, going for obedience show awards and training your dog to be the best type of companion.

The first step will be to locate the best training classes you can possibly find. While I don't usually recommend serious training for a puppy under six months of age, I've seen great results with younger puppies entered in a so-called "kindergarten class." Here, the puppies are deliberately exposed to other puppies, sounds, smells, noises, etc., while learning gentle control from their owner. With the proper training methods and a good instructor, these early experiences can be invaluable. On the other end of the scale, it's just not true that "you can't teach an old dog new tricks." My Ch. Camelot's Cupcake, CD had a very successful obedience show career at 7 years of age!

Shop around for a good training class no matter what age your dog is. You might inquire of other breeders, contact the local kennel club or the local obedience club. Once you learn of a class, attend the first few times without your dog and observe the training methods used. A Cocker Spaniel is a sensitive, willing worker and you want your training done with kindness, love and respect. Most of all you want to use lots of praise. If you pursue a training program in this manner your dog will respond to you and be a happy, tail-wagging worker.

Many trainers have found that using food as a reward *only* for an exercise done perfectly can be a great training incentive. While this method may be somewhat controversial, I have found it to be of the greatest incentive in training my Cockers. Try to exercise thought and reasoning in your training. A Cocker thrives on gentleness and praise. Keep in mind what our standard preaches—"Above all he must be merry." Remember, his attitude toward this whole endeavor is learned only from you. A happy working, obedience-trained Cocker is a tribute to your training efforts and a wonderful advertisement for our breed. For those of you interested in showing your dog in obedience trials, the AKC Obedience Degrees are:

CD — Companion Dog
CDX — Companion Dog Excellent
UD — Utility Dog

TD — Tracking Dog
UDT — Utility Dog Tracker
UDTX — Utility Dog Tracker Excellent

To earn each of these degrees, your dog must score more than 50% of the available points in each exercise with a final score of 170 or more points (out of a possible 200) under three different judges, in at least three different shows. Obedience classes are divided into A and B classes. Let me break down the scoring for you.

The exercises and available points are as follows:

NOVICE *(To qualify for the CD Degree):*

Heel on Leash .... 40 points
Stand for Examination .... 30 points
Heel Free .... 40 points
Recall .... 30 points
Long Sit .... 30 points
Long Down .... 30 points

Novice A Class — The AKC Obedience Regulations state that the "A" Class shall be for dogs that have not won the title of CD and that a person who has previously handled or trained a dog that has won a CD may not be entered in this class. It's a true class for novices. No person may handle more than one dog in Novice A Class.

Figure V-28. Shirley Isola with Shirl's Donnie-Mite, CD. Shown winning First Place in Novice A at the Redwood Empire Kennel Club. "Donnie" scored 196½, earning his final "leg" on his CD and defeating 26 dogs in the process.

Novice B Class — This class is also for dogs that have not won their CD. However, dogs in this class may be handled by their owner or any other person. An exhibitor may handle more than one dog in this class. After you obtain your first CD on a dog, you must show all future entrants in this class. No dog may be entered in both Novice A and Novice B classes at any single trial.

OPEN *(To qualify for CDX Degree)*. All exercises are done off the leash.

Heel Free . . . . 40 points
Drop on Recall . . . . 30 points
Retrieve on Flat . . . . 20 points
Retrieve over High Jump . . . . 30 points
Broad Jump . . . . 20 points
Long Sit *(handler out of sight)* . . . . 30 points
Long Down *(handler out of sight)* . . . . . 30 points

Open A Class — This class is for dogs that have won the CD title but have not as yet won their CDX Degree. Each dog must be handled by its owner or by a member of the immediate family.

Figure V-29. Ch. Charmary Consomme, CDX, TD and Ch. Dabar Agitator, UDT on the "Long Down." Owned, trained and handled by Liz Doyle. Consomme was High Scoring Dog at the ASC Summer National in 1978.

Figure V-30. Ch. Melodie Lane Mystique, UDT, Can. CD, TD shown retrieving over the high jump in the Open class. Owned, trained and handled by Billie Robbins.

Open B Class — This class is for dogs that have won the title CD or CDX. A dog may continue to compete in this class even after it has won the UD title. Dogs in this class may be handled by the owner or any other person. No dog may be entered in both Open A and Open B classes at any one trial.

Figure V-31. Deidree Shannon Dodge, CDX, WD going over the broad jump in the Open class. Owned, trained and handled by Debbie Dodge.

Figure V-32. Deidree Shannon Dodge, CDX, WD shown presenting the dumbbell to owner/trainer/handler Debbie Dodge.

Figure V-33. Chidal's Something Special, CDX going over the broad jump. Owned, trained and handled by Joy Rosenbauer.

UTILITY *(To qualify for Utility Degree)*

Signal Exercise . . . . 40 points
Scent Discrimination *(Article 1)* . . . . . . 30 points
Scent Discrimination *(Article 2)* . . . . . . 30 points
Directed Retrieve . . . . 30 points
Directed Jumping . . . . 40 points
Group Examination . . . . 30 points

Utility A and B Classes — A club may chose to divide the Utility class into "A" and "B" classes. When this is done the "A" class shall be for dogs which have won the title CDX and have not as yet won their UD title. The "B" class shall be for dogs that have won the title CDX and also UD (the latter may continue to compete in the Open B).

Figure V-34. Ch. Dabar Agitator, UDT. Winner of the Dog World Award in Novice and earned her TD at 1½ years of age. "Aggie" has ten High Scoring Dog in Trails (eight at Cocker Specialties and two at all-breed shows). Her children are now being trained by their capable breeder/owner/handler, Liz Doyle.

TRACKING *(To qualify for TD Degree)*

The purpose of the Tracking Test (as set forth in the *AKC Obedience Regulations Book*) is to demonstrate the dog's ability to recognize and follow human scent and to use this skill in the service of mankind. Tracking, by its nature, is a vigorous noncompetitive outdoor sport. Tracking Tests should demonstrate willingness and enjoyment by the dog in his work, and should always represent the best in sportsmanship and camaraderie by the people involved. The regulations require that each track be designed to test dog and handler with a variety of terrain and scenting conditions. The dog is not asked to find the tracklayer, but he must overcome a series of typical scenting problems and locate objects dropped by the person whose track is being followed.

Figure V-35. Ch. Melodie Lane Mystique, UDT, Can. CD, TD shown working the scent discrimination articles in the Utility class. "Jennie" is owned, trained and handled by Billie Robbins.

The Tracking Test must be performed with the dog wearing a harness to which is attached a leash between 30 and 40 feet long. The length of the track is to be not less than 440 yards nor more than 500 yards. The scent to be not less than one-half hour nor more than two hours old and that of a stranger who will leave an inconspicuous glove or wallet, dark in color, at the end of the track where it must be found and picked up by the dog. Tracking Tests require two judges for their conduct.

With each entry form for a dog that has not passed an AKC Tracking Test, there must be filed an original written statement, dated within six months of the date of the Test, signed by an AKC-approved tracking judge certifying that the dog is considered by him or her to be ready for such a test.

Figure V-36. Camelot's Second Hand Rose, Am. & Can. TD shown surveying her tracking field. "Rosie" is owned by Lou and Amy Weiss and was trained and handled by Billie Robbins.

TRACKING DOG EXCELLENT *(to qualify for the TDX Degree)*

The TDX Track shall not be less than 800 yards nor more than 1000 yards. The scent shall be not less than 3 hours nor more than 5 hours old and must be that of a stranger. Double cross tracks shall intersect the actual track at two widely separated points at right angles. The dog shall be challenged at several points on the track by changes in scent conditions. All types of terrain and cover, including gullies, woods and vegetation of any density may be used. Four personal articles shall be dropped on the track. Only the last article may be a glove or a wallet. The first article should be placed at the starting flag and be clearly visible to the handler. The 2nd, 3rd, and 4th articles should be dropped on the track at intervals and should not be visible to the handler from a distance of 20 feet.

The first Cocker Spaniel to earn a Tracking Dog Excellent Degree is Ch. Sandor's Coming Attraction, UDTX. She is a red/white Parti-Color who is owned, trained and handled by Judy Iby of Ohio.

It is said that "tracking is sport in the truest sense." The animal works for the sheer love of scenting. No dog can be forced to track. The tracking fraternity is known for its friendliness, its hospitality, and its encouragement to all participants. The thrill for the handler when the dog completes the test and locates the articles may be unsurpassed in any other AKC event.

It is possible for obedience dogs to attain championship status after they have achieved a Utility Degree. Obedience Trial Championship

Figure V-37. Ch. Melodie Lane Mystique, UDT, Can. CD, TD and See-nar's Seraphin Sheaint, CDX, TDX, Can. TD. These two black bitches are shown with their "tracking gloves" and are owned, trained and handled by Billie Robbins.

titles were approved by the AKC in 1977. Championship points will be recorded and any dog that has been awarded the title of Obedience Trial Champion may preface their name with O.T. Ch.

Requirements for the Obedience Trial Champion are as follows:

1. Must have won 100 points.
2. Must have a first place in Utility (at least 3 dogs competing).
3. Must have won a first place in Open B (at least 6 dogs).
4. Must have won a third first place under conditions 2 & 3 above.
5. Must have won these three first places under 3 different judges.

The points available are determined by the number of dogs competing both in Open B and Utility classes.

The first Cocker Spaniel to earn an Obedience Trial Championship was Ch. Mar Lee's Folly O'Blarney. He is also a red/white Parti-Color and was owned, trained and handled by Mary Whiting of Minnesota.

There are several non-regular classes offered for competition at some shows and trials. They include:

Graduate Novice	Versatility
Brace	Team
Veterans	

Figure V-38. Ch. Tabaka's T. Tissue Tucki, CDX and Ch. Tabaka's Tidbit O'Wynden, CDX shown winning Best Obedience Brace in Show at the American Spaniel Club National Specialty. Owned, trained and handled by Ruth Tabaka.

There are no degrees to be earned from competition in these classes. Scent Hurdle Demonstrations may be offered by any show-giving club, but they are not an AKC-recognized event. Obedience show classes are offered by dog training clubs, many all-breed clubs, and an increasing number of specialty breed clubs. It is interesting to note that many Cocker breeders compete successfully in both the breed and obedience rings. (Note that the previously cited O.T. Ch. Cockers were *both* conformation champions!) At the 1984 Mission Valley CSC Specialty there were 18 Cockers competing in obedience classes of which 11 were champions!

For more information, and in-depth explanations of each of the levels of obedience training and appropriate exercises, write to the American Kennel Club (51 Madison Avenue, New York, New York 10010) and ask for the *Obedience Regulations Book.* Single copies are free.

Now let's look at another reason for training your dog. There are many of you who won't want the formal competition of the obedience ring but want your dog to behave and be a good companion. For those of you who are interested in this aspect I would like to quote Curtis B. Hane writing in the March/April 1987 issue of the *Great Dane Reporter.*

Americans have always placed a high value on education. With students lining up for admission to colleges and graduate programs, schooling is again becoming big business. When it comes to their dogs, Americans are equally keen on education. Thus, the fields of obedience training, animal behavior modification, and counseling are also quickly becoming big business, offering countless services as complex as any university curriculum.

Figure V-39. Merlyn's Jasper of Camelot, CDX shown winning First Place for her first "leg" in Novice A at the Mission Valley Cocker Spaniel Club Specialty in 1983. Owned, trained and handled by Kim Steiner.

If you yourself are considering instruction for you and your dog, your choice must be an educated one. While some people harbor delusions of transforming the family pet into "Rex the Wonder Dog," your goals should be more realistic—teaching Spot not to pull your arms off when walked on a leash or competing in a local obedience trial. Perhaps you are part of a smaller number who have a serious problem—a dog that bites, barks incessantly, or has the family in such a state of upheaval that permanent separation from the dog looms as the only solution (witness the need for many dog rescue organizations).

Whatever the problem, you may consider seeking the help of professionals in solving it. With some basic knowledge and a bit of consumer investigation, most people can find a program that suits the needs of both dog and owner.

Most dog training methods can be roughly divided into two groups: (1) obedience drills and exercises; and (2) behavioral counseling and training (to correct such problem behaviors as chewing, biting, and jumping up). This is an informal categorization, however, as many programs do not fit neatly into either group, offering aspects of both types of training. Therefore, choosing the right training program for your dog must be done carefully. You'll want to consider your own goals and financial resources and your dog's needs if you want the best chance for effective humane training.

There are four methods of dog training most commonly considered by dog owners: (1) the do-it-yourself method using one or more training manuals; (2) kennels or schools that board dogs for a predetermined length of time for training by in-house handlers; (3) the private trainer or counselor who provides individualized instruction (often in the pet owner's home); and (4) group classes for both dog and owner. Each method has its benefits and drawbacks.

Dog Training Manuals. It is possible with the aid of books to train your dog yourself. While this method can prove effective and economical, it also requires a little more care both in planning and in execution.

First, carefully read, cover to cover, at least two books before you begin the actual training. Many books cover only basic obedience exercises. With a bit of bookstore or library searching, however, you should be able to find at least one book that deals directly with the problem behavior(s) you are experiencing with your dog.

Second, keep in mind that a group class outside the home method has the advantage of introducing your dog to strange sounds and odors and especially, other dogs. Should you decide to train your dog yourself, avoid practicing soley in the familiar and isolated backyard. Once you have your dog under control, it is usually best to move training sessions to a public park or an isolated corner of a parking lot. This is the environment the two of you will ultimately face, so accustom your dog to its surroundings early.

Three good training books are *Playtraining Your Dog* by Patricia Gail Burnham (New York: St. Martin's Press, 1980); *The Dog Training Manual* by Kathryn Braund (Virginia: Denlinger Publishers, Ltd., 1984); *A Training Manual for Dog Owners* by the Monks of New Skete (Boston: Little, Brown and Company, 1978). These books deal with both obedience exercises and specific behavioral problems.

Kennels and Schools. Dog boarding facilities that house your dog for a period of time and promise to return to you an "obedient" dog are often merely profiting from an owner's laziness or insecurity. The handlers may employ inhumane methods and return dogs to untrained owners who dishearteningly watch their animals quickly revert to their previous poor behavior within a matter of days.

While not a recommended method, if you do intend—for whatever reason—to leave your dog in any facility for training by a professional handler, be certain to investigate carefully. These operations make a great many promises. Don't be innocently drawn in by a free school bus service, recorded telephone tips, elaborate graduation ceremonies, and other costly frills.

First, visit several kennels and evaluate what you see, smell, and hear.

Is there a noticeable odor? A well-run facility will be clean and neat. Do all fences and runs look and feel secure? Many dogs have escaped from poorly-designed runs. Listen for any sounds of shouting or confusion from the staff or tell tale signs of abuse or abusive equipment. Phyliss Wright, a former dog trainer, suggests a dog owner visit a facility at least twice before leaving a dog for training; three visits are not too many. Also, keep in mind that the "five-day quick train" method offered by many handlers is a myth. No reputable professional should offer or recommend such a program.

Second, it is essential that you insist upon follow-up sessions for you and your dog with the trainer. Any lessons the dog has learned will be wasted if the still uneducated owner returns to unsuccessful methods at home.

The Private Trainer. This method is perhaps the most effective means of correcting a dog's problem behavior. It is, for obvious reasons, also the most expensive, at $20 or more an hour. On the positive side, many private trainers are behaviorists who specialize in individualized programs emphasizing counseling for the owner and in-the-home instruction for dog and owner.

While most private trainers are reluctant to divulge their professional secrets, Mr. Bob Maida who operates a pet counseling and training facility in northern Virginia offers some tips he uses to stop destructive behavior:

1. Tie balloons on any area that your dog is chewing. When you see your dog near the area, walk over and casually pop the balloon.
2. Leave your radio on when you go out (no rock music—rock may make him aggressive) and turn on a light if it is or will be dark before you return.
3. When giving your dog verbal commands, change the inflection of your voice to a more powerful, no-nonsense tone.

Private instruction may be a worthwhile choice for all dogs but may be *essential* for some. Some dogs do not do well in a group setting, for example, aggressive dogs with meek owners. The disadvantage of a group setting, which often involves 15 or more dogs and owners is the amount of individual time that can be spent with each dog. Group classes sometimes cannot zero in on the person whose dog is having specific problems at home. By the very nature of such a class, instructors must come up with a universal method, a choreographed routine.

This individualized attention can be costly. Approximate prices can range anywhere from $50 for a two-hour session to over $350 for a complete program of behavioral counseling, in-the-home training, individualized lesson plans, and homework plans for the owner.

Two helpful books that explain dog counseling are *The Evans Guide for Counseling Dog Owners* by Job Michael Evans (New York: Howell

Book House, Inc., 1985) and *Understanding Your Dog* by Dr. Michael W. Fox (New York: Coward, McCann & Geoghegan, 1972).

The Group Obedience Class. With the exception of books and manuals, the group class is certainly the most common method of dog training. However, when approached with the idea of training his dog in a group obedience class, the novice's first words may be: "But I want my Cocker Spaniel to stop jumping on visitors, not win a blue ribbon in a show!" True, most dog owners want to solve behavior problems and equally true, very few group instructors are behaviorists who have the time and expertise to address your specific needs. However, many dog trainers believe that obedience training in a group setting can both aid in the dog's socialization and establish a positive dog/owner relationship that carries over into behavior problem solving. When the dog misbehaves (for example, jumps up on a visitor) the dog can be told to "sit." If the classroom training has been successful, the dog will sit; thus the owner now has a means of communication through which he can make corrections.

"Whatever a dog learns in class should be transferable to the home. The goal is for the dog and family to live in harmony," says Phyliss Wright. She emphasizes the importance of dog and owner simply spending time together: "Obedience training gives the dog an interaction with you, and the more interaction you have the closer you become as companions. Training sessions should be quality time between you and your dog." By taking an active role in your dog's training, the bond between owner and pet is strengthened.

As mentioned earlier, when looking for an obedience class, be sure you observe at least one session before enrolling. An instructor who welcomes visitors is more likely to employ humane methods and enjoy working with both dogs and people. Carefully observe how the instructor handles dogs. Is a reward system used? Do not assume that all dog training instructors are, because of their daily involvement with animals, great lovers of dogs. As unfortunate as it may seem, some are in the business only for profit.

If you have decided to enroll yourself and your dog in an obedience class, seek the recommendations of any acquaintances who have attended classes previously. If you have difficulty obtaining first-hand information, don't head for the Yellow Pages yet! Check first with one or more of the following resources: (1) your humane society; (2) your veterinarian; (3) the Better Business Bureau; and (4) your local consumer-protection agency.

Group classes designed specifically for beginners usually emphasize the rudimentary obedience skills: heel on the leash, down, down-stay, heel-sit, sit-stay, and come when called. The knowledgeable instructor, however, will attempt to deal, whenever possible, with specific behavior

Figure V-40. A group of obedience-trained Cocker Spaniels in the Phoenix, Arizona area.

problems. Don't expect individual attention at every turn, but don't be afraid to ask questions and get involved. You will get out of the program only what you put into it.

The class will normally last from eight to ten weeks, one meeting per week. A knowledgeable instructor will stress at-home practice; set aside at least one-half hour (an hour if possible) for you and your dog to review the previous week's lesson. Also keep in mind that preliminary veterinary attention, particularly up-to-date vaccinations, is essential before exposing your dog to other animals.

Most good trainers endorse a training method with foundations in sound humane principles. They work to build a team . . . so the dog and owner have to work together, and they have to enjoy their work. Instruction should emphasize the practical benefits of training, always making a connection between class exercises and the home, yard and sidewalk. It's an excellent idea to explain to the class the purpose of the exercise.

As for the use of painful punishment devices, just about all the good teachers feel that anything that connects pain in the dog's mind with the owner should not be used. Positive reinforcement should be used. You don't punish your dog for getting on the sofa; you praise him for getting down. Praise and reprimand must be immediate: "Two seconds is too late. The dog will have forgotten already."

Let's look in on an advanced beginners program for adult dogs. This class is offered by a private training facility and held in the multi-purpose room of a suburban YMCA.

Twenty dog/owner teams attend the Friday night class, the mid point in an eight-week series. Most arrive early to walk their dogs, to socialize, and to practice a few lessons before class. Terry, the instructor, stresses punctuality by closing the doors at the stroke of nine.

The class includes a wide variety of purebred and mixed-breed dogs and an equally diverse selection of owners, young and old, male and female. The owners attach training collars and long leads to their charges and take advantage of a short practice period, vying for space to put the finishing touches on that perfect heel. Terry, in a booming, no-nonsense voice, sets the class in motion, ordering the pairs to one side of the large and suddenly hushed room. Both dogs and owners are well trained in obeying verbal commands; the two-legged pupils obediently line up like happy recruits, their four-legged partners heeling at their sides.

The first lesson is "heel on a leash with turnaround," in which the dog must follow closely at its owners side while he walks several steps, quickly turns 180°, and then continues for several more steps. Most of the teams perform this exercise with relative ease, with two exceptions. Terry helps one team by simply correcting the attachment of the leather lead and collar and encouraging those having difficulty to intensify practice sessions at home.

Terry then moves quickly to the next exercise: the dog must stand for examination while the owner stands three feet in front holding the leash. Next, as an added temptation, the leash is dropped. The dog must stand perfectly still; any foot movement is corrected immediately. When this exercise is completed, Terry gives the signal to praise, and an echoing chorus of "Gooooooood Dog!" fills the room.

As a final drill for the evening, the dogs practice their "sit-stay," their passive poses belying their eagerness to run to their masters for some well-earned praise.

As the class winds down, Terry explains the homework for the week. Teams are to practice the "go to place" lesson, which teaches the dog to go on command to a physically defined place, such as a rug or dog bed and lie down. After a few student questions, the class ends.

A final word . . . as was said in the beginning of this chapter, the dog is first and foremost a companion animal. As such, its training should make dog and owner better companions through close interaction. Achieving this simple goal need not be a painful or inhumane process. Finding the training program that meets your needs requires some legwork, knowledge, and a large dose of common sense. With the right program, dedicated effort, and respect for your animal companion, the rewards for both of you can be impressive. Your bonds of companionship, respect, and understanding will be strengthened, and most importantly, the home you share will be more comfortable for both of you. □

The Southern California Dog Obedience Council holds a Top Dog Exhibition every year. The purpose of Top Dog is to provide an opportunity for the handlers and dogs who have earned the privilege to represent their clubs in competition for Top Dog honors. The success of this event relies on the integrity and good sportsmanship of the clubs, their members and the exhibitors. The winners of this competition go on to the California State Obedience Competition, and perhaps, eventually, to compete for the honor of the Top Dogs in the nation.

All member clubs of the Southern California Dog Obedience Council may enter a team in Top Dog. Most are all-breed obedience clubs with a few specialty clubs, including the West Coast Cocker Spaniel Club. A team is made up of two Novice, two Open and two Utility dogs. In addition, teams may also have three alternates, one for each class. The team is picked with the goal in mind of the consistently best working dogs, rather than the occasional high-scoring dog, as only the team score counts.

The West Coast Cocker Spaniel Club has been proud to have had a team in this exhibition since the Sixties. The 1984 team proved to be the best placing team to date and the club members have the drive to continue to improve in years to come, as more Cocker exhibitors become involved in obedience.

Figure V-41. The 1984 West Coast Cocker Spaniel Club Top Dog Team. Pictured from left to right: Elaine Hansen and Ch. Kederdon's Derby, CDX; Todd Shuey and Sir Blake The Gentleman, CD; Roy Rosenbauer with Chidal's Licorice Kiss, CD and Chidal's Something Special, CDX; Marnie Wood and Ch. Glenmurray's Tally Ho, CDX; Lori J. R. Huff and Ch. Chidal's Licorice Prince, CDX; Col. William Mellen and Jet Job's Jolly Rajah, CDX; Liz Doyle and Ch. Dabar Agitator, UD, TD.

CHAPTER 3

As A Hunting Dog

by Kenna Griffin
(formerly Chairperson, ASC Committee on Field Trials/Field Tests)

Cockers have been hunting dogs since the first hairy pads hit solid ground on the east coast. They hunted in England, and they were often among several breeds kept in American kennels for hunting.

Figure V-42. Charlie's Ebony Angel, UD holds one of her birds that earned her a WDX at the English Cocker Spaniel Fanciers of Dallas field test on May 12, 1984. She is owned by Heather Bartelme; Charles Palacheck was the judge.

With that kind of consistent use, it seems strange that the first attempt at instituting a field work committee within the American Spaniel Club would melt away from lack of interest, but it did just that. Frances Greer, writing in the ASC publication *A Century of Spaniels* reported that a committee chaired by A. Clinton Wilmerding was appointed in May of 1892 to study the sponsoring of field trials. No progress had been made by February 1906, and when Wilmerding resigned as committee chairman in 1911, the committee was dissolved. Yet he, and many other ASC founders, kept Cockers and other sporting spaniels and hunted them frequently.

The first field trial for Cockers and other flushing spaniels was finally held in 1924. Thus started a heyday for Cockers in the field, and it lasted until the next decade. Interest then waned, but picked up again in the 1950's, when most of the field-titled Cockers earned their field trial championships (FTChs).

An early promoter of Cocker field trials was Ella B. Moffit. In her 1941 edition of *The Cocker Spaniel, Companion, Shoot Dog and Show Dog,* she noted that "The first field trials for Spaniels were held on January third and fourth, 1899, sponsored by the Sporting Spaniel Club in England. It is noteworthy that both stakes were won by Stylish Pride, a 25 pound Cocker."

She dedicated her book, first written in 1935, to the memory of Rowcliffe War Dance, who contributed physical and hunting attributes to his offspring in the effort to re-establish Cockers as hunting dogs in the mid-1920's.

In her book, Moffit included in the chapter on "The Shooting Dog" some history of field trialing as well as training advice. She noted that it was 1903 before the first Cocker events were included in an English spaniel field trial. Two trials were held for Cockers in England in 1904; six in 1913; and eighteen in 1918. Two chief problems held back the sporting Cocker, she suggested: "First, the fancier's obsession for breeding for physical points without regard for brains, stamina and hunting instinct—the Cocker in short, had become an animal bred for exhibition purposes and a pet for the house. Second, the tremendous task of persuading the sportsmen of the desirability of the Spaniel in his pursuit of game."

Moffit included in the book a report of the first field trial for Cockers held, in 1924, in Verbank, New York. There were three stakes, with practically the same dogs in each. A. Clinton Wilmerding and William Hutchinson judged. Moffit's Rowcliffe Diana, acquired from Canada only two weeks before the trial, won the puppy stake.

"Only seven months old, she was so small that she provoked merriment from the gallery and I came in for my share of teasing," Moffit wrote. "Her only experience till she came to me was 'a few chases in the woods with her dam' in the words of her former owner. The masterful way in which she retrieved a full grown cock pheasant bigger than herself, turned the ridicule to respect and thus began a new era for the Cocker Spaniel in America."

Moffit admitted she was waging the war for field Cockers by herself. Others, she said, had wanted to change the breed's type which resulted in antagonizing many breeders. Her goal was to put the Cocker in the field as the breed existed, while trying to avoid dividing the breed into bench, field trial, and shooting factions, as the pointers had developed.

She described the hunting capabilities of a number of her dogs and others descended from them. She also noted, "The irony in the fact that, although we all admit that our ideal working dog should be a bit larger and a bit rangier than the typical show-type Cocker, we so often find the 'huntingest,' fastest and most intelligent to be on the small side. If someone has an explanation for that one, I would like to hear it."

Reports from ASC field committee chairmen reveal an overall view of Cocker Spaniel field trial history from the 1940's to the 1960's.

ASC Field Committee Chairman Ralph Craig, in the 1948 annual report, gives an indication of the trials and tribulations of establishing field activities for Cockers—something that never seems to change much.

> The Field Trial Committee is happy to report that 1947 presented a more favorable picture of Cocker Spaniel field work and that continued improvement is expected in 1948.

Figure V-43. Ch. Carcyn's Chula Vista, WDX retrieving in water. This impressive dog is owned by Carlos and Cynthia Dominguez.

Field trials were held in zones 1, 3, and 4. Zone 2 is the only zone where the interest has not yet developed to the point of actually running at least sanctioned trials, where members can match their training skills in the competition of their dogs. However, in this zone several clubs have appointed field committees and it is hoped these committees will soon be able to start active work.

During the year the American Spaniel Club published an *Elementary Spaniel Field Training* booklet which was distributed to members, to secretaries of member clubs and to owners of registered Cocker Spaniels wishing to train them. Requests for this booklet have been received from every state in the Union and from England, China and Germany. Its effect in stimulating interest has already been noticed." (*Author's note:* An updated version of this booklet is included as the next chapter.)

In the next two years progress continued, as is evident in this report in the 1950 Annual Report of 1949 activities, again by Ralph Craig.

Your field trial committee is happy to report the amount of progress which has been made in Cocker Spaniel field trials in zone 1 during the past year. Cocker entries have frequently exceeded Springer entries both in total entries and also in the important all-age stakes. In quality, there have been some outstanding performances and there are enough young dogs and puppies in training to ensure a steadily improving average quality for the future.

Two items in that report are especially interesting. 1) The comment about combined Cocker entries portends the Springer take-over in the field trial arena; and 2) a mention of the lack of interest in the midwest reveals no indication that it would become the most active area for Springer field trialing by the 1980's.

A 1952 report by field committee chairman Henry Berol made some interesting proposals:

. . . a National Championship for Cockers;
. . . encouraging the idea of running a Field Dog Stake which we hope will lead to more interest in hunting Cockers in the field;
. . . and finally, but by no means least, I think the greatest accomplishment of this Field Trial Committee is the fact that the second oldest field trial club in the country, namely the Cocker Spaniel Field Trial Club of America, was taken over by a group of Cocker enthusiasts who, I am sure will do a real job for this club and keep its name before the public as one of the great field trial clubs of the country.

1953 holds out great prospects for the Cocker Spaniel to become really famous in the field. It is the first time in history that there is a likelihood that a championship stake will be held this coming fall.

This is the first mention, in an annual report, of a championship stake or trial. Berol proposed that holding such an official event, even though it might not be warranted considering the quality of the dogs' performances, would encourage more "cockerites" into participating in the field work. Over the years, this strategy has seemed to work but it has always been flawed because interest has never been sustained. Remember, the Cocker winning the National Championship earned the title of National Field Trial Champion as well as earning the FTCh.

The Field Trial or Field Dog stakes, by the way, must have been held by various clubs at their field trials and supported by the American Spaniel Club to encourage novices' interest in Cocker field work. The Field Dog Certificate probably was similar to today's Working Dog title.

The year 1957 seemed to hint more strongly than usual of the lessening of interest. However much the ASC morally supported field activities, the limited number of participants had been the problem. It seemed no matter what incentives were offered, relatively few Cocker fanciers became involved in field work. For example, Berol in his 1957 report described ASC's next incentive plan:

> The Field Dog Stake has rapidly disappeared, and I regret this extremely. Under the new ruling of the American Spaniel Club, a prize of $500 is being donated to the first dual champion, and a prize of $1,000 to the first triple champion. This should therefore interest a great number of newcomers to the field. I believe the ideal dogs trying for this dual or triple championship would come from the obedience class, rather than the bench class... They have a golden opportunity not only for enjoying their work with their dogs in the field, but also to obtain this large cash prize, which I am sure should tempt a great many people.

The $1,000 prize was never won. Probably it was dropped when the FTCh died. The $500 award was won by Ch. Minnopa's Mardi Gras UDT, a black and white dog owned and trained by Adelaide Arnisen of Jarretsville, Maryland. He finished his UD on August 20, 1961. His owner said she and his breeder, Ellen Waldner, took a cruise to Bermuda with the money. She didn't say whether Mardi Gras went, too.

"A nebulous dream until a few years ago, this first national event for Cockers, sponsored by the Spaniel Club, might be said to have been in the making since 1924," Berol wrote, and went on to describe that first trial much the same as did Moffit in her book.

> Six years later when the first annual trial of the American Spaniel Club was held at Clinton, New Jersey, the ranks of Cocker enthusiasts had grown considerably. This trial included stakes for Cocker Spaniels, for English Springer Spaniels and a special class for any sporting spaniel in which there was one entry, in this case a Field Spaniel. The winner of the Cocker Open All Age was Howard Stout Neilson's F.T. Ch. Rowcliffe Gallant.
>
> For the three years—1931, '32 and '33—annual trials sponsored by the Spaniel Club, were held on the Dix Hills estate at Huntington, Long Island. In the 1933 event, the Cocker All-Age winner was a bench show champion (later becoming a field champion as well), Herman E. Mellenthin's Ch. My Own High Time.
>
> There was a long period when field trial interest in Cockers lagged,

Figure V-44. Dual Ch. My Own High Time.

but it came back with a great rebound of enthusiasm during the middle 1940's and in recent years. It has risen so remarkably that it is not now uncommon to have 30 or 40 Cockers entered in a trial.

In the national trial held December 6–7, 1954, the catalog carried this description, again probably written by Berol:

It is with considerable pride that we greet the Second National Field Trial Championship for Cocker Spaniels.

The first National, also held at Herrin, Illinois in December of 1953, marked the first trial of national scope to be sponsored by the American Spaniel Club in its 73 year history. The running of that inaugural event, with 20 qualified starters, left no doubt that the Cocker had well earned the national fixture granted by the American Kennel Club. The stake was highlighted by keen and exciting competition through four land and two water series at the end of which the title was awarded to Camino's Cheetah, owned by H.C. McGrew of Fortuna, California, handled by J. Stanley Head. California also produced the runner-up in F.T.Ch. Wildacre Harum Scarum, owner handled by Dr. J. Eugene Dodson of San Francisco.

In 1953 at the English Springer Spaniel F.T. Association trial, the trophy for "Best Dog in the Meeting" went to a Cocker, F.T. Ch. Berol Lodge Glen Garry. This was the first time a Cocker had won the award in the 30-year history of the parent organization of the Springer Spaniel breed.

During the nearly two decades when the Cocker was forgotten as a gun dog, through the magic of his personality he survived as America's No.1 pet and companion dog. Today his qualities as a gun dog are becoming even more widely recognized. In the early hunting days in America, the flushing spaniel lost place to the wider-ranging dogs needed for the broad shooting grounds of the midwest and the south, and for market hunting. Now that America's hunting is confined more and more to restricted areas, the "comeback" of the flushing Cocker seems well assured.

A third national trial was run in 1955 but this was hampered by severe winter conditions which cut down the number of spectators and the entry. The fourth trial was run in November of 1956 and W. Chalmers Burns, the ASC president, wrote at that time "The American Spaniel Club through its executive committee is fully cognizant of the incalculable value of the field trials and this national championship in establishing and maintaining the Cocker as a gun dog. To this end we have initiated and underwritten the financing of these national championships; we have a field trial specialist serving as our first vice-president; we have given every consideration and cooperation to the requests of the field trial committee; and we have given our name and prestige to these great National Championship Field Trials."

Figure V-45. F.T. Ch. Camino's Red Rocket, winner of the Sixth National Cocker Championship Trial held at Lumberton, N.J., December 6-7, 1958. Owned by Clark Gable. Handler, Ivan Brower, who was also best amateur handler.

Even though the ASC lent their support, the years, from 1955 to 1962 saw a seesaw of interest. The field trials became a financial burden to the ASC and in 1962 they ceased to support the trials and they were abandoned. As has seemed to be the pattern throughout the history of Cocker field work, a small group of people were providing almost all the time, energy, money, dogs and entries it took to continue a field trial effort. In a 1983 analysis, Evelyn Monte Van Horn said, "It wasn't chance that brought the Cocker back to an eminent place in field trials. It was the result of diligent effort on the part of a few stalwarts who firmly believed that the Cocker's ability as a gun dog could and would survive."

"Today there are people who use Cockers as their favorite gun dog but whether there is enough interest to promote Cocker field trials, it is hard to say."

Cocker field trials ". . . faded for various reasons; among them, the limited number of breeders of field Cockers, lack of field Cockers to breed to, scarcity of interest," she noted.

On the positive side, when the ASC named Frank Wood of Norco, California, national field trial committee chairman in 1976, Cocker field activity increased. The Working Dog/Working Dog Excellent (WD/WDX) test was adopted and coordinated with similar tests given by English Cocker and English Springer Spaniel clubs. Though the requirements for passing a working test aren't as stringent as those for a trial, the dogs still must show ability and willingness to hunt.

Since the first working test was given by an ASC-approved club in October of 1977 in Connecticut, at least 36 WDX and 36 WD certificates—35 and 34 to Cockers, respectively—have been issued through 1984.

The Cocker Spaniel Club of Orange County, California held field training classes beginning in 1974, and has continued holding some classes and working tests since then. This club along with the Washington State Cocker Spaniel Club are among the very few clubs to actively participate and hold field events.

Many American Cockers have earned field titles participating in tests held by English Springer or English Cocker field tests. Other multi-breed groups, such as the Maryland Sporting Dog Club, also hold spaniel field tests in which American Cockers are welcomed. The Welsh Springer Spaniel Club of America has opened its sanctioned field trials to other spaniel breeds as well.

The ASC began holding working tests in conjunction with its national Cocker Spaniel specialties in 1978 in Huntington Beach, California, with the CSC of Orange County as the host club. Nine Cockers, four English Cockers and one Springer entered. Seven Cockers earned WDs and two earned WDXs.

Figure V-46. Lady Rebecca D'La Swanson and Lady Melissa D'La Swanson pose with the trophies they earned at the American Spaniel Club Sanctioned B Field Trial, January 1984. They are owned and were handled by Pat Swanson of Tukwila, Washington.

In his ASC annual report that year, Field Trial Chairman Wood noted the number of certificates awarded and the 14 entries in the national attest to the fact that "our drop in the bucket of a few years ago has grown into a small puddle. Let's hope by 1979 we can grow into a pond . . . with another year or two under our belts, we could be ready to hold Cocker Spaniel Field Trials again. Wouldn't that be nice. After all, they WERE bred for the field."

He reported progress again in 1979. The second working test was held in July in Cincinnati, six dogs participated. One WDX and three WD's were awarded.

Wood related a typical experience of Cockers entering field tests for the first time, that of:

. . . Q-Bush Happy Leroy, CDX. This fine fellow, a mere 10 years young, astonished the gallery, not to mention his owner, Marjorie L. Quackenbush of South Weymouth, Massachusetts. You see, Leroy had never seen a bird up close before. He had never heard a gun shot, at least at close range, and I don't think he or his handler ever had so much fun together before.

Leroy charged out into the field on command and beautifully quartered on command. His CDX training really helped him here. When he found the bird he put it in the air like a veteran of many a hunt. The gunner downed the bird with one shot and Leroy didn't flinch but looked for another bird. Here came the advantage of his CDX training again. His handler stopped him with hand signals and sent him for his retrieve. He obeyed and went directly for the bird. But this time it was a downed bird. Leroy just wasn't sure.

Our judge, Mr. Dennis Blake of Orange, California, gave Leroy every opportunity to pick up the bird but Leroy wasn't sure he was supposed to, so he didn't qualify. After some exposure to downed birds, Leroy made one of the best water retrieves of the day.

The third national test was held, July 13, 1980, near Tampa, Florida. Charles Rowe of San Diego, California judged and awarded one WD and one WDX.

In her report for 1983, ASC Field Committee Chairman Kenna Giffin announced the major accomplishment for the year:

"The most exciting news is that we've taken the first step toward reviving the field trial championship. The ASC is now approved to hold AKC sanction B field trials—the equivalent of B-OB matches. We had no trouble getting that approval."

Figure V-47. Diamond's Jacobus Jonker, CD makes his water retrieve to finish his WDX at the English Cocker Spaniel Fanciers of Dallas field test on May 12, 1984. He is owned by Sherry Creighton of Dallas. Charles Palachek was the judge.

Other achievements for 1983 included the first breed column featuring Cocker field activities to be in the AKC *Gazette*; allowing dogs earning field titles to receive ASC plaques and plates; and drastically increased communication with other Spaniel club field directors.

The next year's accomplishments included holding the first sanctioned match in January and the first trial in conjunction with a national specialty in July. Field dog and bitch classes were approved for the ASC Annual Flushing Spaniel Specialty. The ASC working dog program rules were clarified, and sections on philosophy and reporting procedures were added. Again, one of the AKC *Gazette* columns featured Cocker field news.

Late in 1984, the American Kennel Club Field Trial Department announced proposed rules for a master hunting spaniel title to be used after the dog's name on AKC pedigrees. Patterned after the master hunting retriever tests worked out the preceding two years, the tests focus on evaluating dogs as companion hunters rather than field trial perfectionists. They are similar to the working tests most sporting breed parent clubs have.

As the working test program grew so did the desire to return to some form of competition in field work. This was aided somewhat by the inclusion of special Cocker stakes at two English Springer Spaniel field trials in 1983 and 1984.

In 1983, the Washington State Cocker Spaniel Club's dedicated group of field fanciers, under the leadership of Ruth Tabaka, applied and received approval to hold a sanctioned field trial. The first one was in October of 1983, the second in April of 1984, and the third in September of 1984.

About the same time, it seemed only natural for the ASC to apply for sanctioned field trial status as well, considering the parent club's experience and resources. Again, AKC granted permission, and the first ASC sanctioned field trial in more than 20 years was held in January of 1984 in Houston, Texas.

Figure V-48. The following photographs were taken at the January 1984 American Spaniel Club Sanctioned B Field Trial in Houston, Texas. They depict Pam Cullum Pena of Houston directing her sable and white dog, Lancer's Chardonnay, WDX in quartering and in following through with the retrieve.

Figure V-49. Lance—making a retrieve.

Figure V-50. Lance—fetching the bird.

Figure V-51. Lance—returning to handler.

Figure V-52. Lance—releasing the bird.

The Washington State CSC opened two new chapters in ASC field history at two of their working tests by having the first Clumber Spaniel and American Water Spaniel earn their Working Dog titles.

In theory, it's possible for Cockers to earn a FTCh. Cocker stakes are allowed in conjunction with English Springer Spaniel field trials. However, only one open stake (for all dogs six months of age and older) is allowed at any trial, and it is doubtful a Springer club would give up its open stake to Cockers.

According to current AKC regulations, American and English Cockers are allowed to compete together to make up the six dogs needed for a Cocker stake. All pointers and retrievers, however, can run together in their respective trials. A number of spaniel field trial enthusiasts are working toward changing the rule to allow all spaniels except English Springers to compete in the same trials for FTCh wins.

Only the English Springers have licensed field trials now, and should other spaniels reach licensed trial status there is no desire to compete with the long-established English Springer trial system. Hence the move to establish an all-other-spaniel trial system.

English Cocker field fanciers are increasing in number and activity. The English Cocker Spaniel Club of America (ECSCA) working test rules differ somewhat from those of the ASC, as do those of the Welsh Springer Spaniel Club of America (WSSCA), and the English Springer Spaniel Field Trial Association (ESSFTA).

All spaniels usually are invited to participate in working tests and sanctioned trials sponsored by another breed's club. However, the working test score sheets must be sent to the secretary or field chairman of the appropriate breed club for a dog to receive a WD or WDX. English Cockers must be on the ECSCA score sheets and the ECSCA guidelines must be signed and returned. The other clubs accept each other's score sheets.

The first dog of any breed to win titles in three areas—about as close to a triple champion as it was possible to get at the time—was Dual Ch. Miller's Esquire CDX, a black and white American Cocker owned by Lauren Miller of Elgin, Illinois. He was whelped in 1938. He earned his field title in the spring of 1941, after having earned more field trial points than any other Cocker in 1940.

Another famous field Cocker was Dual Ch. My Own High Time, one of Herman Mellenthin's dogs. Mellenthin gave a memorial trophy in the dog's name for the annual Flushing Spaniel Specialty, with the stipulation that it go to the top Cocker being shown in the field and bench shows. Ted Young, Sr., renowned for his training, handling, and judging of field Cockers, retired the trophy at the 1955 show after winning three times, once with Ch. Tedwin's Lady Petite and twice with Ch. Tedwin Tommy Tucker.

Figure V-53. Dual Ch. Miller's Esquire, CDX. Whelped 1/3/38 by Ch. My Own Peter The Great ex Ch. Miller's Peachie. Breeder/owner: Lauren T. Miller.

Once again in 1986, due to lagging entries the Board of the ASC specified that the host club for the summer National Cocker Spaniel Specialty may choose, at its discretion, whether or not to hold a field event.

As frustrating as the attempts at keeping field work alive, it is worth the effort. The Cocker is a natural in the field and only needs an opportunity to prove himself. The next two chapters are designed to help those of you who are interested and willing to train and work your dogs in the field. As this book goes to press, the 1988 summer National Cocker Spaniel Specialty plans to hold a field event along with the regular classes.

CHAPTER 4

Elementary Spaniel Field Training

In the interest of furthering the cause of field work for Cocker Spaniels, and with the club's permission, the American Spaniel Club's booklet on Elementary Spaniel Field Training is being reproduced with minor editorial changes.

The booklet was written by Ralph C. Craig of Albany, New York. Ralph was a former President of the Spaniel Club serving from 1947–1949. He was also its Field Trial Chairman for a number of years. He was a protege of Ella Moffit and was a mainstay of the Albany Spaniel Field Trial Club.

Correspondence with Cocker fanciers all over the country continually emphasizes the wide field of usefulness of this, the smallest member of the gundog family. So many owners value him for his merry, winning, companionable ways that his value in the field has been overshadowed by his bench show popularity.

However, the Cocker Spaniel gives a good account of himself in the field. He is used in all parts of the country and on all kinds of game. He is the "handyman" who is the family pet the year round, then becomes the capable assistant to the sportsmen of the family when they go afield. The Cocker is an all-rounder, he will do an adequate job on fur or feathers. A conveniently-sized family dog, he is right at home where you can train him yourself. Many sportsmen have trained their own Cocker Spaniels and from the experiences of some the following elements of training essentials have been developed.

Group Training

Experience has shown that much more rapid progress can be made where a number of people interested in a common purpose pool their efforts. If a coach can be obtained who has had experience in training spaniels, so much the better. Where such a person is not available, however, an exchange of ideas and the common observance of the work of various trainee Cockers makes for the more rapid progress of all.

Getting Your Puppy

The puppy should be strong and active—one which shows clearly by his actions that he is outgoing and fearless. You do not want a shy dog. If he is still with his littermates, have them all put out on the lawn. Stand and study them a long time. Look for a puppy which continually uses his nose—one which comes out of its yard promptly. Then, after the first friendly once over, leaves you to explore the scents which have been left by passing animals. If you can find a puppy from proven field stock, so much the better. If you can't, don't worry; many excellent field dogs come from strains which have not had an opportunity to hunt for generations.

Brains are an important part of a field Cocker's equipment. This cannot be readily measured in a small puppy but you are looking for a puppy which has brains and has the temperament which will take training.

Paul Brown

Chasing during early field walks.

There is no choice between a dog or bitch puppies for field work. The puppy's sex makes no difference in hunting ability.

You can train dogs relatively easily to do things which are based on control. You cannot give a dog a nose and it is almost impossible to train a timid dog to become a bold one. As an old saying puts it, "You can always keep a dog in but it is hard to get him out." Avoid a shy, nervous puppy.

Don't put any stock in claims that only certain colored Cockers will hunt. There is no genetic correlation between coat color and nose, stamina and common sense. Some prefer parti-colors in the belief that the dog is easier to see in the field. In really thick cover, however, you can only see the weeds moving anyway. So look for the bold puppy that shows a talent for using his nose, rather than place primary importance on his coat color.

When To Start Training

Professional trainers advise you not to start serious training until a puppy is from seven to eighteen months old. That is good advice if reasonably prompt results are the major objective. If you are training your own puppy for the fun there is in it and you have him at home, you can start much earlier than the age recommended by the professionals. But don't overdo it with a young puppy. You can spoil him by trying to cram too much into a young head, too quickly.

Know Your Dog Thoroughly

Live with your puppy. Study his character and temperament. They vary as much as humans. Gain his confidence. Make him want to please you. Above all have him look forward to going out for walks with you. These walks should be planned frequently—every day if possible. They must be in open spaces where the puppy can run without traffic hazards. He must be encouraged to get out away from you and not to hang around your heels. Do not attempt any field training initially; plan those walks for his enjoyment. If you can find a place where he may stumble on game, so much the better. If he chases do not try to stop him. These walks are to get him to love to hunt. Let your puppy chase butterflies or flying birds. You can steady him down later.

Hints On Trainer's Manner

Make training as pleasant as possible, not boring. Be gentle in voice and action. When you give a command, however, speak positively. Persist in your efforts. Never lose your temper. When you are through with a lesson review your own behavior. Did you measure up as well as a trainer as your puppy did as a trainee? Never continue a lesson when a puppy obviously is tired of it all. Come to a reasonably satisfactory conclusion and end the lesson.

HOME TRAINING

Home training or yard work as most professional trainers call it, covers a variety of training which can literally be done at home. The most important single phase of training of any kind is general obedience. The puppy is taught that he must obey commands given him by his handler. It is a long, slow, repetitious process with a young puppy. Each step in the training, however, forges another link in the chain. The length of time required depends upon the character of the puppy and also the character of the trainer. Puppies vary widely in temperament, in intelligence, and in aptitude. So do we would-be trainers.

The basic factor in all training is to have the puppy realize that when he receives a command he must *obey*. Essentially this requires patience, firmness, a great deal of persistence, and self control on the part of the trainer. This factor applies to all contacts with the puppy, not merely during a training session. If a puppy is supposed to stay out of the dining room during meals, he must stay out every meal, not merely when you feel like making him.

Commands

Avoid unnecessary commands. Do not give a command, with which your dog is familiar, unless you are prepared to see that it is carried out. Once a command is given insist upon a reasonable facsimile of obedience. This applies to all contacts with the puppy whether it is in the living room after a comfortable dinner or whether it's during a training session.

A puppy can be readily taught to respond to the following commands before field training is started:

HUP — to sit.
BACK — to return to handler.
ON — to leave handler in direction indicated.
HEEL — to walk at handler's heel.
FETCH — to retrieve.

The same command must be used each time. That command must mean one thing and one thing only. Do not say "back" one time and "come here" the next when you want the dog to come. This merely confuses the puppy.

Rewards And Penalties

Rewards and penalties must be developed to fit the individual dog. Some recognition of a satisfactory training performance and some penalty for an unsatisfactory one are fundamental. Not that a dog should be given food every time he does well, or that he should be switched every time he does badly. A word of praise or a pat is sufficient recognition as a rule. A sharply spoken word of condemnation is usually enough punishment. However, a trainer must study the reaction of the dog and then fit the rewards and penalties according to the dog's temperament.

Teaching A New Command

The keynote of successful training is to plan situations so that the movements of a puppy can be controlled while the new command is repeated or so that he can be induced naturally to perform the desired action as the command is given.

For example: A lead and hand pressure downward on the puppy's hind quarters will cause the puppy to sit as the command "hup" is repeated. Then it is simply a matter of repetition until the command and resulting action are associated in the puppy's mind.

A method which will produce satisfactory results with most dogs may not be the best one for the dog you are training. The bibliography found in the back of this book gives you access to methods used by some of the best trainers in the world. If a more common method fails after a thorough trial—and I mean very thorough trial—try another training method to establish the relationship between command and performance.

Voice And Hand Commands

Where possible, both vocal commands and hand signals should be given simultaneously. For example, when you say "hup" hold your hand up, palm facing the puppy.

During the early stages give your commands both ways; later use either. It is a good idea to keep both voice commands and hand signals fresh in the puppy's mind. You never know where you may need to use one method and not be able to use the other. Later in field work you will rely a great deal on hand signals and a whistle.

Commands In Home Training

"Hup" means to sit. Either of the two words may be used. If your dog has had obedience training, continue with "sit." "Hup" is more generally used in field work. It is hard to keep little puppies quiet so do not start this training too young.

Attach a lead. Face the puppy. Give the command and at the same time gently press the puppy's hindquarters down so that he sits. Hold him in this position while repeating the command.

After about ten seconds remove your hand and let the puppy move around. Repeat until you believe the puppy begins to understand the command. Then remove your hand and stand quietly with hand upraised, palm facing the puppy. The command "hup" should be repeated at frequent intervals during the early lessons.

When the puppy remains hupped without hand pressure and without repetition of the command, back away from him repeating the command with hand upraised, palm to puppy.

If the puppy rises, return immediately and press him downward into a sitting position repeating the command. Then back away again. Call the puppy after keeping him hupped for a short time.

"Back" means to return to the handler. Experts differ on whether you should use this command for very young puppies or wait to introduce it when they are three to five months of age. In most cases, puppies which were brought up at home come naturally as they are eager to play with the boss.

If you have any trouble, this matter is covered in books on field and obedience training.

The accompanying hand signal is to raise the arm to nearly a horizontal position at the side and drop it to the thigh.

"On," sometimes given as "hie on," means to start hunting in the direction given. This requires little training but the command should be given every time you unleash the puppy when you take him for a walk. In this way he associates the command with the action in a perfectly natural way. It is not a necessary command in taking your puppy for a walk but it will help later in his field training.

For the same reason, you should accompany the vocal command with a hand signal, an upward sweeping motion of the arm in the direction you are starting to walk.

"Heel" means to walk at the trainer's heel. This is not one of the most important commands and many people do not start it with too young a puppy.

Obedience training books give several good methods of teaching this command but here is an old field method:

Cut a piece of brush three- or four-feet long. Remove all the leaves except a bunch at the end. Hold the branch in your right hand while taking the shortest possible hold of the lead in your left hand so the puppy has little play. Start walking with the left hand held slightly to the rear. Repeat the command "heel" at intervals. If the puppy cannot be held in a heel position with the lead but insists on forging ahead, brush the leaves across his nose repeating the command.

If the leaves do not keep him in a heeled position try pulling sharply backward on the leash. If this is not effective try both leaves and jerking on the leash. Do not expect immediate results as, here again, continued repetition is the secret of success.

If the puppy continues to tug at the leash after a reasonable amount of time has been spent, substitute a choke collar (chain with one end passing through a ring attached to the other end) for a regular collar. Be careful that you set this collar up correctly so that the pressure of the chain is relaxed as you release the pressure, otherwise you can harm the dog. If the puppy insists on disobedience after a good many training sessions when you are sure he knows what the command means, he is probably a pretty bold puppy. Then try removing the leaves and use a switch *lightly* across his shoulder.

"Fetch" means to retrieve. This command can be taught to even the youngest puppy. It should be given, however, by the trainer as a basic part of field training. It must never degenerate into a period of fooling with the puppy, of exercising him by throwing a ball, or of tugging the thrown object away from him.

Many professional handlers "force break" spaniels to retrieve. This is done by applying pressure to force the dog to do what is required. It should never be attempted with a young puppy. Methods for force breaking may be found in the bibliography.

Some handlers claim that a natural retriever will let you down in a crucial series. I differ with this opinion and definitely prefer a natural retriever. However, there is a great difference between training a spaniel which comes to you as an adult—and is only one of a group of dogs to be trained—and training your own dog at home.

For the very young puppy, start with a soft object such as an old glove. Tie it into a small knot so there will be no dragging fingers. Have your puppy in surroundings to which he is accustomed. Precede your training with a period of playing so that the puppy is relaxed. Get the puppy's attention fixed on the glove and throw it about three feet, repeating the command "fetch." Practically always the puppy will run after the glove and bring it back for more play.

Take the glove gently from the puppy's mouth. If he resists, hold the glove in your right hand and gently press the upper lips against his teeth with your left hand. This will cause his jaws to separate and so release the glove.

Then play with the puppy some more before throwing the glove again.

Do not throw more than two or three times on the first lesson and only gradually increase the distance.

When the puppy is three months of age, make a dummy out of 5″ of broom handle wrapped with cloth and your old glove. A little later, tie game bird's wings around the dummy. If no game bird wings are

The dog used to demonstrate field training is Ginger Kansas Summer Sunglow, U.D., W.D., owned and trained by Kenna Giffin of Houston, Texas. Photos by Kenna Giffin. Assisting with training is Brent Aronson. Ginger is shown being encouraged to develop an interest in birds, by using a wing to tease her. Training to retrieve becomes a quick progression to throwing the wing and then introducing a dead bird the same way.

available use pigeon wings instead. Wings should be thoroughly wrapped around with string so that loose ends do not provide a temptation to drag the dummy.

Don't continue any training session past the point where the puppy loses interest. Be sure to praise him each time he does well. Make him look forward to his training sessions.

Once wings are added to the dummy it should only be thrown out occasionally. Then, it is preferable to hide the dummy and send the puppy out to "fetch." This can be done in your back yard.

Practice the retrieve and start to steady the dog to wing and shot; hold the dog in place and throw the bird. Shoot off a cap pistol or blanks. Restrain the dog until the retrieve command is given.

Whenever you send him out to make a retrieve where he has not marked the fall, give your puppy the direction. This is usually done with an upward sweeping motion of the hand beginning near the puppy's nose and ending up pointing in the direction of the hidden dummy.

Should he look back at you again, give him the direction with your arm. This time with either a side pointing motion if required or an overhead pointing motion if he is on the line but hasn't gone far enough.

Don't repeat the hidden dummy lesson the first day. Then be careful not to let your puppy become bored by too much repetition in subsequent lessons.

In all retrieving lessons, encourage your puppy to return quickly and directly to you. He should deliver the dummy cleanly and gently to your hand.

FIELD TRAINING

Introduction

Field training gives a Cocker Spaniel an opportunity to exercise a talent which comes down to him through many generations. When given the opportunity, it is frequently his greatest pleasure.

Naturally a location for field training will be chosen which provides suitable cover and in which there is a possibility of finding game scent. The easiest way for a young puppy to learn to hunt is to work with an older dog. This is not a must, however, as many dogs learn to hunt without any human training whatever.

In starting field training accustom your dog to being on a leash. In getting out of the car always make him walk at least a short way on a leash. In group training it is necessary, of course, to have the dogs not actually working on a leash. In any event walking a way on a leash will make him realize that is part of the program. It is also much easier to get the dog in the habit of starting off quickly at a vigorous pace when you cast him loose. First impressions are important and field trial judges are no exceptions. So follow the methods outlined under "on" in home training when turning your dog loose in the field.

The only basic equipment needed is a shrill whistle which should be fastened on a string or lanyard around the trainer's neck. It should be noted that field training is the most important part of the entire training program.

Quartering

A well-trained spaniel should thoroughly cover a beat extending approximately 30 yards on either side of his handler. To do this he quarters the ground or follows a zig-zag course which, by using both body and foot scent, allows him to put up any fur or feathers which may be on the beat. On a hunting trip he will naturally work birdy places more painstakingly and follow hot-foot scent till he flushes the game.

To teach quartering, place the dog on lead, walk in a zig-zag pattern until the dog finds and flushes the bird. With each change of direction, give the dog a vocal or whistle command to indicate the directional change. Directing Windsor in his quartering is Susan Dean of Houston; judge George Keiller, Jr. of Houston watches closely. Windsor earned a WDX in this performance at the 1982 National Flushing Spaniel Field Test near Conroe, Texas.

In a field trial (because of planted birds and the limitations of time), he must even more completely cover all of the designated beat and, on command, he should leave foot scent which goes off the beat.

In either event, quartering his ground is a basic must in spaniel field training. Many spaniels do it naturally. However, it is a good idea for the handler to walk on a zig-zag course with a young dog until he gets the hang of it. When a turn is made give one short blast on the training whistle. This will attract the dog's attention. A pointing motion with the full arm should be given. This with the trainer's change of direction is usually enough and the dog follows suit. Be careful to discontinue your quartering promptly as soon as the dog gets the idea. In a trial, a handler should always walk in a straight line.

Whistle Commands

Different handlers use a wide variety of whistle signals—combining blasts and trills in different combinations. Let's stick to two simple ones.

One blast means to change direction when a dog is quartering.

Two blasts means to stop and look for a hand signal which should always be given immediately. The hand signal may be "back", or it may be direction if a dog is being sent to an unmarked fall. This later signal can best be taught with an assistant having the dog on a leash. The assistant stops on the whistle signal and releases the dog when the hand signal is given.

When the dog quarters on his or her own, hand signals can be used with voice or whistle commands to indicate the directional change.

Introduction To A Gun

In many kennels of gun dogs, puppies are called to the feeding pan by discharging a cap pistol. This is an excellent way to have them relate pleasurable experiences with a report of a gun.

If your puppy has not been accustomed to a cap pistol, introduce him to gunfire very gradually. There is no need to start until field training has begun. The first shot should be from a small caliber gun such as a .22. It should be fired when the dog is at a distance and is showing interest in something that his nostrils bring in. The long odds are that he will do little more than look around. Speak reassuringly and direct him on if necessary by a command and hand signal.

Gradually decrease the distance between the dog and the shot until he shows no sign of nervousness at a distance of 15 feet.

When he has become accustomed to the light report of a .22, gradually increase the size of the firearm until the dog shows no nervousness when a 12-gauge shotgun is fired.

Be sure you approach this gradually. The speed with which you increase the noise and reduce the distance depends entirely upon the dog's reaction. Remember that the muzzle blast of a shotgun is something. If you have ever had a gun fired over your head on a swinging shot you will realize why sometimes good gun dogs are ruined by a careless introduction to gun fire.

Retrieving An Unmarked Fall

This is merely an extension of the training outlined under retrieving in the Home Training Section. Out in the field you have more range and a greater choice of direction. By this time it is important that your retrieving dummy is wrapped with game bird wings.

Retrieving Very Long Unmarked Fall

Unless a dog has had competent preliminary training, it is often difficult to get him far enough out on an extremely long unmarked fall. He is very apt to start circling before he has gone out far enough on the line.

One aid in this training is to choose your location so that the dummy (or dead bird) is hidden in thick cover which lies beyond a strip which has no cover to hide a downed bird. The ideal location is one which has normal rough cover for approximately 40 yards followed by a cleared strip such as a golf fairway or plowed land, of maybe 30 yards wide.

The dog will probably start circling when he reaches the end of the rough cover. You are then probably in for a long tedious wait before he is convinced that no bird is to be found on this side of the strip.

When you get his attention, point in the direction of the bird and say "on." Occasionally bring him back to you and start him out fresh on the line to the fall.

Do not continue any one session when the dog has obviously lost interest. In any event, be certain that the dog retrieves the bird. You may have to walk to the edge of the cleared strip to give him a new direction, or even walk up to within a few yards of the bird but have him retrieve it before you stop.

Making the retrieve.

Marking A Fall

Marking a fall is an attribute of a good field spaniel. This is developed best by plenty of bird work. However, it can be improved in a training field.

Place an assistant with a retrieving dummy wrapped in game bird wings some distance ahead of you and your dog. The assistant should be hidden from the dog.

The dummy is thrown high in the air away from the dog. At the height of the dummy's flight, fire a training pistol. Release your dog promptly and say "fetch."

Aid your dog with vocal and hand signals. If he starts to leave the line to the fall before he is far enough out, say "on." After he has left the line, give one blast of your whistle with a hand signal in the direction of the dummy.

Retrieving From Water

After your dog has completely learned to retrieve on land, he should be given some water work. This is not only a requirement in all age stakes in field trials but in many sections of the country it is a necessary part of field work in ordinary hunting.

The chances are that a little urging will be all that's necessary to get your dog into the water after a thrown dummy. Start him when the water is warm. If you have trouble, one good way is to take the dog swimming with you or to let him play in the water with other puppies.

Sunny shown making a water retrieve.

If he won't follow you into the water, carry him out so that he has to swim a short distance to the shore. Praise him for swimming and play with him on shore for a few minutes before you call him into the water. It may be necessary to again carry him in before he becomes accustomed to the water. If so, carry him in and upon releasing him, wade further out into the water calling the dog as you go.

If you have to carry your dog into the water during training, lower him carefully into the water so that his head does not bob under. Hold him until he is in a natural swim position before you release him.

Introduction To Freshly Killed Bird

A hazard exists if you try to carry your dog over from a dummy to a freshly *shot* bird. The sense of newness and the unaccustomed smell of blood may present a hurdle that some dogs find difficult to overcome. This can be avoided by killing a pigeon by thumb pressure on the top of the skull and substituting the freshly killed bird for the dummy in a retrieving lesson.

Prior to this lesson, the dog should have been allowed to flush a pigeon or two to become accustomed to the scent. This technique of planting pigeons is described under "Steady to Flush."

Hard Mouth

This means damaging the game brought in. It will not be covered here. It does not usually happen if you are careful to teach the puppy to deliver the retrieving dummy gently. If the dummy is wrestled away from him, you may be in for trouble later. Books listed in the bibliography on field training suggest various methods to overcome this fault which is a serious one.

Steadiness

"Hupping" to flush or shot is a matter frequently underrated by Cocker owners who are not familiar with training methods and field trial procedures. This may be due to the fact that in such cases the dog may be mostly self trained. The owner justifies his dog's lack of training by saying, "I like to have him under the bird when it falls."

Actually, steadiness is not an artificial requirement of field trials. It is based on sound common sense. Frequently, game is found in the same general feeding locality, not in a tight covey like quail, but spread out so that only one bird at a time is put up by the dog.

If the untrained dog chases the first bird, he is apt to put up others while his master's gun is empty.

If the dog drops to flush, the owner has a chance to reload before sending the dog to retrieve or to resume hunting as the case may be. He is then ready if another bird is flushed.

Actually, the pause of a few seconds makes little difference in the dog's chance of making a retrieve. The dog finds the bird with his nose. He does not run him down by sight.

In an all-age stake in a field trial, steadiness is a must.

Steady To Shot

This phrase, seen repeatedly in spaniel literature, means that the dog "hups" when a gun is fired. He is taught to do this so that he will not interfere with a brace-mate's retrieve or if he is out alone, to give his handler time to reload if a bird flushes wild and is shot.

Your dog now "hups" on command or on hand signal. With a training pistol behind your back, give both the command and hand signal to "hup." At the same time, fire the pistol. The dog "hups" as he has been trained to do. Repeat until he associates the gunfire with the other two commands to "hup." Then omit the vocal command but give the hand signal when firing the pistol. Finally, omit the hand signal. If the dog has not learned, begin again with all three signals.

Steady To Flush

Your dog has been trained to be steady to shot and to command. Your next problem is to correlate this with steadiness to flush.

Heretofore, your dog has been allowed to chase birds which he has flushed in order to increase his love of hunting. Now you must train him to be steady to flush.

If possible, make an arrangement with a breeder of homing pigeons (it is less expensive). As you will work your dog on a check cord the pigeons should not be injured. They will fly home so the expense should not be too great. If you can't make such an arrangement, buy your pigeons. By attaching a light fish line to the bird's leg, his flight can gently be "braked" by playing out the reel.

Plant the pigeon by placing its head under its wing. Place it on the ground and hold it there with a gentle but noticeable pressure of your hand for four or five seconds. This will give you an opportunity to walk away before the bird stands up. Planting should be done out of sight of your dog.

Attach a check cord—a 30 foot piece of hard clothesline with a snap on the end—to your dog's collar. Start at a little distance and work your dog up to the planted bird. When he flushes the bird he will attempt to chase—as in the past. However, he should be stopped with the check cord and a loud and authoritative "hup."

Here again, it will be necessary to patiently repeat the process a good many times to get the idea across.

Ability To Take Cover

No cover is too tough for a good spaniel. Frequently, a Cocker will get under heavy cover that a larger spaniel cannot break through.

Briars which keep out pointers and short-haired hunting dogs have no terrors for a spaniel. In training, you should take your dog where he has experience in briars as they are found in many hunting locations and on many field trial courses.

Facing briars is a must in a hunting spaniel. If your puppy tends to be briar-shy, spend plenty of time on working him in briars after he has learned to love to hunt.

Introduction To Hunting Conditions

By this time, the dog has received all of his fundamental training. The stage should now be set for a full dress rehearsal.

A pigeon should be planted as described above and the dog unleashed at a distance (do not use a check cord). The handler should walk on a line to the planted bird. He should be accompanied by a friend with a gun who can be counted on to kill the bird when flushed. This is important. The handler should not carry a gun in this initial training. Very few people—even after long experience—can keep their attention on the dog when a bird flushes, and now you want to be ready with an instantaneous "hup" if your dog needs it.

When the bird flushes, the gun should let it get pretty well out. The handler should be prepared to let out an authoritative "hup," if necessary, and keep his fingers crossed hoping for the best. The dog should be kept in a hupped position very briefly before he is sent out to retrieve.

This should all go through without a hitch. If it does, be enthusiastic in your praise of your dog, and incidentally, you can give yourself a little pat on the back, too. If your dog retrieves even though he breaks (is unsteady) you are well on your way. You can steady him down later.

Introduction To Varying Game Birds

This does not usually present too much difficulty, although your first woodcock will probably cause some trouble. They apparently smell differently than other game birds. However, you should try to give your dog some experience with pheasants before the open season or the first field trial. In many states there are licensed game farms which, for a fee, provide shooting during a longer season than the regular open season. In other states, pheasants raised on game farms may be purchased and used in the same manner as training pigeons.

Care of Your Spaniel

Only a dog in good health and condition can respond to training or perform well in the field. Don't take chances on exposing your puppy to infectious diseases. Consult your veterinarian early about vaccinating your puppy against distemper, canine infectious hepatitis and leptospirosis. Follow up with booster shots, according to his advice. When the puppy is old enough, have him vaccinated against rabies. Rabies exists in wildlife of all kinds and hunting dogs should have protection from any chance encounter.

It's wise practice to have your dog checked regularly for intestinal parasites. Worm infestation can weaken and debilitate a dog rapidly. It's especially important for puppies to be checked often. Your dog should have a test for heartworm which, today, exists in all parts of the country.

A puppy should be brushed and combed regularly. This will make him more agreeable to having burrs and snarls combed out later.

Keep your dog's ears clean. Ear mites thrive in dirt, wax and moisture. A piece of cotton moistened with peroxide followed by a dusting with BFI powder will help in keeping the outer ear canal clean and dry. Indiscriminate probing into the ear or your own "doctoring" can make the condition worse. Ears that are sore or painful when touched should be treated by your veterinarian.

Every week or so, part his coat and inspect his skin. At the first sign of skin trouble, have it treated. Look for signs of fleas, too. After each time afield, inspect the coat for ticks and remove them. Ticks not only sap the dog's strength by living on his blood but they can drop off and multiply. Regular use of dips, sprays or powders will discourage ticks and fleas.

Inspect your dog's feet for small stones or grass bristles after being in the field. They may be imbedded between his toes and cause infection and lameness if not removed. Wood seeds in the eyes should be washed out with cotton dipped in an eye solution.

Keep a couple of turkish towels in your car. If your dog is wet from rain, snow or water work, rub him dry before putting him in the car or his crate. It will help a lot in preventing chill and rheumatic conditions.

Whether it is the hunting season or not, keep your dog fit by regular exercise. He can't be expected to work for hours in the field if he has been lying in the kennel for weeks.

Good nutrition is a large part of keeping your dog in top condition. He must be well nourished to be a good and willing worker. Your dog uses up a lot of energy pushing through fields and woods all day and a mid-day snack carried along is a good idea.

If you're going to be in an area where there are no brooks or streams, carry a flask of water with you. Water is vital for a dog that is working hard and greatly increases his efficiency and endurance.

Your dog should have a comfortable kennel; dry and off the ground with solid flooring to prevent dampness and with protection from wind and rain.

A Finished Field Cocker

The following brief description will give you a thumbnail sketch of the final product you have been trying to develop.

A gay-moving Cocker with a nose that will find any fur or feathers on his beat, which he covers thoroughly, moving at a good pace; under control at all times; never flushing beyond gunshot, yet showing the drive and eagerness of a keen desire to hunt.

Steady to flush, shot or command, marking even the most distant fall, out instantly when ordered to fetch, with a quick pick-up, retrieving at a good pace to gently deliver the game to hand.

Training a spaniel means hours of pleasant work in the field and the final result is worth it. You will find that your dog is as eager for a hunting trip as you are and it will work out so that you are a fine team in the field, each complementing the other.

GOOD HUNTING!

CHAPTER 5

It's Written On The Wind

A finely trained bird dog, quartering a field, shows clearly the superiority of his nose over our own. In observing the performance of a hound following the most meager of trails, the contrast becomes even more evident. But the sense involved is the same as ours; it depends on the same type of sensory and nervous system. The dog's sense of smell and our own differ only in functional capacity. In the dog it is a superior sense while in man it is not.

Almost all materials give off minute amounts of their substance into the air, thereby producing a scent. A living animal is no exception. It is a teeming factory of chemical processes. An animal's breath, its secretions and waste products, and the incidental fragrances from the surface of its skin all produce powerful scents. As animals move about they leave trails on the ground and nearby objects. This is the key to the use of the dog as a hunting companion. Because of their superior sense of smell, dogs can detect the whereabouts of animals in the general area.

Differences in the field performance of dogs may result from a multitude of factors, including genetic variation. The processes of heredity are so dependable that a good pedigree is likely to guarantee a good nose. But not even a superior bloodline provides for a foolproof guarantee for every dog. Only trial can help determine if a particular specimen has an acute sense of smell.

A dog's performance usually depends on his interest in tracking and in his training. Even a potentially good bird dog can be diverted by the scent of a rabbit unless he has been trained properly.

Another variable in a dog's performance is the effect of physical conditions on the identity of the scent. The potency of a scent increases as the air becomes warmer; therefore, when the temperature is low, dogs have a harder time picking up a scent. Humidity may also have a negative effect. A heavy dew, by dissolving the minute traces of material on a trail, may render some odors more volatile and therefore may improve the scent. But too much water may wash away and disperse their traces and obliterate the trail. (The effect of water on a scent can be understood by the following example: A dry dog emits a distinct, but not overwhelming, odor. A wet dog smells rather pungent. But a dog who has just been given a bath—and thereby has had most of his scent removed—is temporarily odor free.)

With these conditions in mind, think of the situation confronting the dog in the field. There is never an ideal situation for seeking any one kind of game. Small rodents, rabbits, and other small game, as well as small game predators compound the scent problem. Some of the sparrows, meadowlarks and other song birds spend much of their time on the ground and leave evidence of their passing to complicate the wide range of scents the dog encounters. As he ranges over a field, his keen nose picks up the traces of all these animals, including old scents and new, cold trails and hot ones. It is quite natural that more recent odors should arouse the strongest reaction in the dog.

How, then, can a dog sort out from this mixture of stimuli those which are significant for his task? If he crosses the hot trail of a rabbit that has fled from his approach, what keeps him from bolting after the rabbit? And what force can keep his attention on the faint scent of a bird that passed this way hours before? The fact that he stays on the proper scent is a tribute to the thoroughness of his training; it is not necessarily an expression of the fundamental instincts that come from his heritage. He detects and presumably recognizes the subtle gradations in the complexity of scents that reach his nose, but he has learned through rigorous training that the object of the day's hunt is to find birds, not to chase rabbits, and so he disregards the lure of other trails.

Probably no one fact is a greater tribute to the relationship between dog and hunter than the apparent offensiveness of the smell of woodcocks to bird dogs. As was pointed out in the preceding chapter, evidently these birds are actually repugnant to them. Yet a well-trained dog will hunt and retrieve woodcocks when his owner bids him to do so.

When a dog is free to range over a field, he is aware of the different kinds of animals that have been over the ground before him. Whether he can follow any given scent in this maze of strange trails is doubtful. There is every reason to believe, however, that he can follow a strong scent with some accuracy and may then reach the vicinity of the animal which has left it.

The difference between scents of an animal which has already passed and one which is presently nearby is of prime importance. Foot scents are strong enough to reveal the passing of game and may lead the dog to areas where the game has recently passed. But body scent, when the dog comes near enough to detect it, is much stronger and is, therefore, a better guide to the game's location.

The high body temperature of birds favors the giving off of scent. When lessened distance, or the direction of the wind, enables the dog to pick up a bird's scent, the dog has only to follow the course of increasing scent in order to approach the bird. A bird in action gives off even more scent than an immobile bird and may also emit sounds that the dog's acute hearing can pick up. Movement of the bird, coupled with its smell, helps the dog locate quarry.

In following a trail, it is probable that the dog receives an increasing stimulus as he proceeds toward the animal and a decreasing stimulus if he back-tracks; something like the childhood game where a person is told whether he is hot or cold as he seeks an object. It seems that such discrimination must depend on a fairly fresh trail, but presumably any scent strong enough for him to follow would show such gradation in potency.

Once a dog has approached the game, only experience can tell him how far he may safely go without running the risk of flushing it. Any trained pointer or setter who actually sees a bird would halt at once and point it out. But if the dog is depending on scent alone, his ability to approach closely, but not too closely, is one of the finest demonstrations of the exquisite sensitivity of his nose and the nicety of his judgment.

The spaniel is both a game finder and a retriever. These two functions are carried out as a part of the ordinary day's hunting. He is a hunting dog covering all the ground in front of the hunter and on either flank. The bigger spaniels range further to the sides. All spaniels flush the bird instead of pointing it. And either upon the report of the gun or the flush, he sits until ordered to retrieve.

The pointer and setter breeds approach the game by quartering a much wider swath and at a faster pace. As they become more certain of the game, they slow down sometimes to almost a pantomime-like movement, lifting their paws delicately as not to disturb the quarry and then lock into a point. They only flush the game on command. The English and German pointers range widely, as does the Irish Setter. The Irishman probably is the most uninhibited in gait. The English Setter has some spaniel in him and he "hunkers down" on a point by dropping his neck down between his shoulder blades, a unique type of point. The Gordon Setter is a more massive dog and moves at a slower, but sure, pace.

The retriever breeds work in the field and out of a duck blind or boat. Their task is to retrieve what is shot and to be a sure marker of game. They sometimes act as flushing dogs when sent in front of a hunter in the field. Notice the ears on these breeds are set well above the eye so they will be clear of the water while swimming after game.

All of these sporting dogs in the act of retrieving must concentrate on the job of finding the fall, following a wounded bird if necessary, and retrieving it to hand promptly. The should ignore all other sights and sounds. The spaniel is equally adept in water and on land in retrieving game.

The function of the retriever breeds is essentially to seek and retrieve fallen game. They are adept at marking multiple falls and retrieving, especially in water.

When a game dog nears a bird, training must again check his natural impulses. Instinct would lead him to pounce on his prey and kill it, while hunting procedure demands that he leave the kill to the hunter. When the dog finally retrieves a dead bird he must not yield to his normal appetite for flesh but must mouth it gently and bring it in unbitten. The standards for all the sporting breeds specify characteristics which ensure a soft mouth. Punishing jaws are not called for in this group of dogs.

A good nose, combined with a pedigree which shows the field experience of his ancestors, bodes well for a given dog's success in the field. These features, together with careful training and mutual affection between dog and hunter, remain the most dependable guarantee of good hunting.

SECTION VI

Famous People and Dogs Who Influenced The Breed

- *Outstanding Breeders and Kennels*
- *Dogs Who Influenced the Breed*

CHAPTER 1

Outstanding Breeders and Kennels

HERMAN MELLENTHIN—"My Own Kennels"

Many have called him "the father of the modern American Cocker." His forethought and planning produced Red Brucie, who marked the beginning of a new era in Cocker type and to whom the vast majority of today's outstanding dogs trace their ancestry.

It was no accident that produced Brucie, for Herman's experience in dogs dates back to his childhood. His program of breeding was started as early as 1912 when he maintained the Nihtnellem Kennels in Wisconsin. His kennel had begun to win with Cockers, but he also showed Collies and Airedales.

In 1915, he came east to live with Thomas McCarr and his wife, where he developed a love for trotting horses and began breaking and training them for Mr. McCarr.

He later went to Poughkeepsie where for four years he trained harness horses for Tommy Murphy, one of America's greatest trainers of the day. He often stated that it was his experience with horses that enabled him to be successful in dogs.

In 1926, he registered the kennel name "My Own" for his kennels at Poughkeepsie, New York and discontinued the prefix "Nihtnellem." As he was living in an increasingly crowded apartment, Mellenthin first came up with the idea of of "farming out" dogs. It was that or have no room for living quarters for himself.

He set as his goal the breeding of a stud dog which would be the foundation of the modern Cocker. The Cocker Spaniel needed help badly when he began to seriously breed Cockers. He wanted to breed a merry, sporting type that was sturdy, yet small. He wanted spirit, cobbiness, ample bone, and substance. He envisioned a straight front, a dark eye. He wanted a bold dog, yet one readily amenable to discipline. He was very concerned that the Cocker Spaniels should be able to go in the field and do the work for which they were intended. He was one of the first to work toward establishing field trials for the breed, and he strove to produce specimens that could make their mark both in the field and on the bench.

In 1921, Mr. Mellenthin made a legendary trade whereby he secured

Ree's Dolly, whom he bred to Robinhurst Foreglow, owned by Judge Townsend Scudder. It was this mating that produced Red Brucie and from the first, Mellenthin recognized in him the type that was needed to produce the modern Cocker. A further description of Red Brucie is to be found in the chapter on "Dogs Who Influenced The Breed." This chapter also describes the "Big 4" litter out of Princess Marie which catapulted him to fame.

Herman Mellenthin's plan for a "new" Cocker had its roots in his long-range plans. As Ella Moffit said, "If it were luck, he would have a host of detractors; but even his greatest rivals in the sport of breeding of dogs admitted—even if grudgingly—that he was able to find combinations that were overlooked by others."

The next goal he set out for himself was to breed the "perfect" Cocker and he was certain he had achieved this in a black son of Brucie. He named this one "My Own Brucie." He had been holding this name in reserve until such a specimen came along. Ch. My Own Brucie, as we all know, is the the *only* Cocker to have taken back to back Best in Show awards at Westminster. *(In point of fact, only one other Cocker, Ch. Carmor's Rise and Shine, has ever won Best in Show there.)*

Ch. My Own Brucie

Mellenthin always said that he got the greatest satisfaction in interesting others in the breed, in seeing them win, in helping them through pitfalls of breeding, more than in winning himself. He was satisfied in producing the good ones and letting others have the fun of carrying off the trophies.

Another of his major goals was to judge Best in Show at Westminster. He was able to realize that goal.

C.B. VAN METER—"Stockdale Kennels"

"Van" established the Stockdale kennels in California in 1927. However, he had a number of Cockers before moving to California from his home in Kansas City, Missouri. Prior to becoming interested in Cockers, Van bred Boston Terriers and a few other breeds. Both his schooling and breeding plans were interrupted by World War I but he resumed them both with a vengeance when he returned to Kansas City following the cessation of hostilities in Europe.

His first breeding specimen in Cockers was a red bitch but her career as a brood bitch was less than a rousing success. He had better luck with others.

Business brought him to the Central Valley of California where he first settled in Bakersfield. He played golf at that time at the Stockdale Country Club and it was an easy choice to make when naming his kennel. Van reportedly loved the layout and beauty of the club. It was in Bakersfield that he met Myrtle Smith who was to be his lifelong companion. She owned many of the great Stockdale dogs.

From Stockdale Dinah, one of Van's very nice original bitches, he obtained Ch. Bubble Up of Stockdale. She was sired by Ch. Sand Spring Follow Through. This breeding set him off on the path to becoming one of the top breeders of all time. Coincidentally, as was Herman Mellenthin, Van was also a lover of flowers. Orchids were his specialty.

Stockdale's greatest success came in the Black variety. He spent many a long hour planning his breedings and laid out in detail the next two to three generations of his breeding program. He was a perfectionist when it came to the dogs. Capitalizing on some good western breeding, Van Meter concentrated on breeding beautiful heads and long sloping shoulders. He also wanted to breed that elusive "perfect" dog.

Van purchased Ch. Sand Spring Stormalong from the east coast and he became Stockdale's first true stud dog. He, in turn, produced Ch. Stockdale Startler who was famous for his bitch-producing ability. It was Startler's daughters that put Stockdale on the map. Fully 20% of Ch. Stockdale Town Talk's 81 champions were out of Startler daughters. Ch. Gaming Acres Maid of War, a Startler daughter, produced the first Cocker five-champion litter. A Startler daughter, Audacious Lady, was Town Talk's dam.

Names like Ch. Adams Black Perfection, Ch. Stockdale Red Rocket, Stockdale the Great and a host of others, came from the Town Talk and Startler crosses. Van believed that Startler had as much to do with Stockdale's success as did Town Talk.

Van was another who loved to help the novice. There is many a breeder in southern California who owes his or her success to the help

Ch. Stockdale Town Talk

of Van and Myrtle. His gentle guidance and encouragement make him and Stockdale a name to long be remembered.

BEA WEGUSEN—"Honey Creek Kennels"

The story of Ada, Michigan's Honey Creek Kennels, is the story of a very determined woman who set out to revolutionize the Parti-Color Cocker Spaniel. About the time Bea began her planning and showing, in the late forties and early fifties, Parti-Colors were the "step children of the breed." They had little coat, less substance and lacked the pretty features that first the Black and later the Buff color varieties enjoyed.

Honey Creek is the tale of the remaking of a variety. Before Bea was done, some 50 Honey Creek dogs had gained their championships. But, more than that, they won from coast to coast and in many other countries as well. Their producing ability is a matter of record, with literally all of today's Parti winners sharing a Honey Creek heritage.

Early on, Bea had purchased from her handler, Clint Callahan, Ch. Sogo Showoff, (then unshown) for the then princely sum of $1500. Eager to have offspring of her newly acquired prize, she bred him to Ch. Honey Creek Cricket (the dam of 10 champions). The breathlessly awaited litter proved to be a shock as they were all undershot. Some months later Bea returned home from a dog show and her kennel man informed her that Showoff had climbed the fence and had bred Cricket again. In due time the litter arrived and this time all had perfect bites and one became the immortal Ch. Honey Creek Vivacious, the top winning bitch of her day. Not only did Vivacious win in the ring, she made

Am./Can./Cub./Mex. Ch. Honey Creek Vivacious,
Ch. Honey Creek Heirloom and
Ch. Honey Creek Hero

her mark in the whelping box as well. With 14 confirmed champions she led the list of bitch producers for many years.

"Teddy," as she was called, made her debut as a puppy under judge Mrs. Shiras Blair to win the variety. She finished her championship under judge C.B. Van Meter. She made her debut as a special at the 1949 ASC show. Her record is history. She was shown by Ted Young Jr. at the start of his handling career, and was his first special.

Her first litter by Ch. Honey Creek Harmonizer consisted of six puppies . . . and six champions. Her second litter by her grandson Ch. Honey Creek Heir, also produced six champions. Her third litter by her son, Ch. Honey Creek Heirloom added two more champions to the list. A daughter, Honey Creek Halo, made her debut at the ASC in 1952 and won a five point major and went on to finish with all major wins.

At two weeks over one year of age, Halo became the first Honey Creek champion to go Best in Show at an all-breed event.

The foundation of Honey Creek was a birthday gift, Honey Creek Freckles, the product of a half-brother/sister mating. When bred to a son of Ch. Hadley's Trumpeter she produced nine males and two

Ch. Honey Creek Halo with Bea Wegusen.

bitches. The two bitches were "Pennie" and "Flicka" and both produced champions for Honey Creek. Flicka became the matriarch of the
kennel and every dog and bitch carrying the Honey Creek bloodlines
descended from this grand red and white.

Close line breeding and inbreeding was practiced at Honey Creek
with much success. Judges raved over the quality and Bea's kennel prefix
ruled the day. In 1950, Ch. Honey Creek Harmonizer became the top
sire and Teddy's dam, Cricket, the top-producing bitch.

In 1952, Teddy returned to the ASC Specialty and again won the
Parti-Color variety for the fourth time, a record unequalled. Of the 45
Partis entered, 30 were of Honey Creek stock. Of these 30, Teddy was
either the dam or granddam of 21. The entire specials class was of
Honey Creek breeding.

No mention of Honey Creek is complete without mentioning
Norman Austin who campaigned many of the Honey Creek dogs to
their championships and, in partnership with Bea, made Honey Creek a
potent force in the Parti-Color variety for all time.

RUTH and ART BENHOFF—"Artru Kennels"

When asked to name the most successful kennel prefix in all varieties, the first name to pop up in the minds of most is "Artru." The Cockers of Ruth and Art Benhoff have achieved unprecedented success in all three varieties with not only myriad champions but also with Best in Show winners in each variety. They have established and perpetuated noted strains in both ASCOBs, and Parti-Colors and many winners throughout the country trace their lineage to Artru dogs. In Partis, "Available" and "Remarkable" are still prominent in pedigrees today and the Black and White Ch. Artru Ambassador went to Texas and created a very nice winning and siring record in that region.

It is from their efforts in ASCOBs, however, that the greatest achievements of all time for Buffs have been accomplished. Not only have their own breedings finished with such ease that it makes it look like child's play to make up a champion, but the numbers of titled offspring sired by Artru dogs for others is overwhelming.

The ASCOB Buff strain began with Ch. Artru Crackerjack. He sired but one litter before his tragic and untimely death . . . a loss not only to the Benhoff's but most certainly to the breed. A grandson of Ch. Stobie's Service Charge and Ch. Gravel Hill Gold Opportunity, he managed—in this one litter—to leave behind a legend in the form of Ch. Artru Hot Rod. Twice a Best in Show winner at the ASC (1958–1959), Speedy also sired 25 champions including the influential Ch. Artru Johnny-Be-Good and his brother Ch. Jo-Be-Glen's Bronze Falcon. These two brothers provided a key for many of the winning Buffs of their time

Ch. Artru Hot Rod and Ch. Artru Slick Chick

as the Johnny children, when crossed with Falcon daughters, produced champions for not only the Benhoffs but numerous others as well. With this combination, the Ted Klaiss' of Sagamore, produced winning bitches including the all-time top-winning Buff bitch, Ch. Sagamore Toccoa. Many other Cocker breeders benefitted from this combination as well.

Some years ago, Ch. Artru Sandpiper was the Cocker Spaniel sire of the year and he continued to produce phenomenally to earn his place in history. He currently stands #9 on the all-time list with 68 champion offspring. Ch. Artru Adventure, another Best in Show winner, sired over a dozen champions while Ch. Artru Red Baron, again a Johnny son, has continued to build on the Artru foundation and has added an imposing shrine of his own in the annals of breed history. He is currently #15 on the all-time list with 49 champion get. The leading producer for Artru is Ch. Artru Skyjack with 87 champion get and the number is climbing. He rates at #5 on the all-time list.

Ch. LaMars London, also by Johnny, has himself made history of his own by consistently producing a distinctive kind of Buff that, in turn, seems to reproduce themselves with regularity. His descendents are noted for being well up on leg.

Ruth Benhoff has felt that Baron was the most beautiful of the Artru dogs for his wonderful red coat and his very short back. But her favorite is Skyjack who carries three crosses to Johnny in three generations and six to Hot Rod. Incidentally, the Benhoffs had no bitches of their own to breed to Hot Rod and they had to start their own Buff line by taking puppies from his and other Artru studs to incorporate into the pedigree. The dominance of this kennel has always lain with the prepotency of the sires. However, let us not forget a little lady with the Artru prefix who is also listed among the breed's top producers: Artru Delightful II, the dam of 14 champions.

There is a further word on this success story. Actually four words: "hard work and sincerity." These are the keys with which they have opened the doors to their goals. From the planning of the matings, through the careful hand-raising of the puppies, the care and attention given them when not in the ring, the presentation of the dogs to the judges and spectators—and most of all—their willingness to help other breeders have earned them the respect of the dedicated dog fancy wherever the name "Artru" has appeared.

MARI DOTY—"Nor-Mar Kennels"

Mari and her husband, Norm, played a significant role in the evolution of the Cocker Spaniel. Their kennel, Nor-Mar, is well known throughout the land for its numerous champions. However, it is not the dogs alone that have made Mari famous. It was her role as Editor of the

American Cocker Review that earned for her the niche in this particular hall of fame.

ACR was a voice to be reckoned with from the late 1950's until the early 1980's. Only recently has Mari given up her writing chores for *The American Cocker Magazine* which is the successor to ACR. On the pages of her magazine paraded the Cocker greats and novices alike. Her editorials and strong support of the research into cataracts in the breed was a major reason the work of Dr. Yakely, at Washington State University, was successful.

ACR, due to Mari's artistic talents and her ability to write lucidly, set a longevity record that previous magazines like *The Cocker Spaniel Visitor, The Wagging Tail, Cockers Calling,* and *The Cocker Southern* could not emulate. Being an active breeder kept Mari highly involved in the day-to-day happenings of the breed. With strong support from her husband, Norm, the Nor-Mar prefix was a tough one to beat.

Mari's talent as an artist always appealed to me. She did a number of the sketches for my first Cocker book and has helped many an advertiser lay out their copy properly.

Though Nor-Mar is synonymous with Black and Tans and has gained recognition in Blacks, they have not done too shabbily in Parti-Colors, either—having bred 10 Parti champions. They have also exported dogs to England, Sweden, France, Portugal, Venezuela, Colombia, Mexico, and Canada.

Today the Dotys run a large boarding kennel capable of housing over 100 dogs. They have seven full-time employees and do commercial grooming, averaging some 35 dogs per day. At last count some 58 champions carry the Nor-Mar name and the list continues to grow.

Ch. Nor-Mar's Nujac

EDNA ANSELMI—"Windy Hill Cockers"

I first met Edna in 1974, when I moved my consulting practice to New York City. Before leaving the west coast, I had asked Mari Doty about the people in the area where we had purchased a home, Westport, Connecticut. Mari told me to look up Edna and she would take me in tow. That she did. Edna and Ed Anselmi turned out to be two very warm and vibrant people who are very family oriented. Over the next few years we got to meet all the Anselmi children and to partake of Edna's bountiful hospitality. What a cook!

By the time we got to know Edna she was already a breeder of some repute. Ch. Windy Hill's 'Tis Demi's Demon was already well into establishing a name for himself and Windy Hill Cockers. I first met the next famous Windy Hill show dog and producer when this simply overwhelming Buff puppy came bounding into the room and took over. He was Windy Hill's Eagle Scout. Scout is now the sire of nearly 30 champions. I knew his sire, Ch. Bobwin's Boy Eagle quite well as I had judged him and given him Best of Breed on more than one occassion.

Ch. Windy Hill's Makes-Its-Point, winner of 1977 ASC Futurity.

Even successful breeders have learned a lot from Edna about pairing up dogs to produce the best results. As Anita Roberts said "Edna has an 'eye' as to what looks just right. She follows a discriminate breeding program but has often said rather than to match the pedigree, she prefers to match dogs."

As is consistent with outstanding people in any endeavor, to be successful takes hard work. Edna began by working for a veterinarian to help pay for her hobby. She also learned to be an expert groomer. Many newcomers to the fancy have been the recipients of her knowledge and expertise.

Probably one of her great moments came—at the 1977 ASC Futurity —when a beautiful young Black and Tan, Windy Hill's Makes-Its-Point not only walked off with the Best in Futurity rosette but also scored for a big five point major. Makes Its Point went on to become the sire of 20 champions before he died at a young age. He proved to be an especially valuable dog since he could produce tri colors. He has a number of champion tri-color grandchildren as well.

Today Edna is a well-known and popular judge. She has judged all over the United States and across Europe and Scandanavia. I have had the honor of being on judging panels with her and have also observed her from ringside. I am pleased to be able to include this astute women as one of the "famous people" who have made a significant contribution to the Cocker Spaniel Breed.

KAREN & VERNON MARQUEZ—"Marquis Kennels"

The Marquez's first litter was born in February of 1972. From that litter came their first champion. Ch. Tondee's Special Valentine. He was shown and finished by Dee Dee Wood. An auspicious beginning for a kennel which, as of date of publication, has produced 100 champions.

Vernon and Karen have specialized in black/white Parti-Colors although they have bred a number of Blacks, including the 1987 BIS winner of the Annual Flushing Spaniel Specialty, Ch. Frandee's Forgery. The Marquez's give much credit to Dee Dee Wood and Bob Covey for being their early mentors in the dog game. They also feel that Annette Davies, Dottie McCoy, Norman Austin, Mari Doty and the late Bill Ernst were instrumental in their success.

Their greatest triumphs were Ch. Denzil's Super Daddy, who won the 1981 National Cocker Spaniel Specialty and the 1987 Best in Show win of Forgery at the Annual Flushing Spaniel Specialty. They are justifiably proud of Ch. Marquis It's The One, who with 3 Best in Shows, earned the #1 Cocker award—all systems—in 1985.

Vernon and Karen's Marquis Kennel has also laid claim to an award that most breeders aspire to win just once—Top Breeder of the Year.

Ch. Marquis It's The One with handler, Ron Buxton.

Marquis has won this coveted award in 1979, 1981, 1983, 1984 and 1985. That one is going to be hard to top. In the history of the breed only the Benhoff's Artru Kennel rivals that achievement.

Vernon and Karen have been in the dog game for *only* 15 years. They have differing responsibilities when it comes to the dogs. Both of them are involved with the whelping of puppies. If the puppies need additional nursing help, Karen takes over the supplementary feeding chores. Karen also does the trimming. Vernon, in addition to his road show duties, does the bathing and training for the show ring. Most of the Marquis dogs have been shown by handlers but now and again Vernon makes an appearance in the ring.

In their opinion, Marquis It's The One is the best dog they have produced. This is not to take anything away from such outstanding dogs as Ch. Marquis Black is Beautiful, Ch. Marquis I'm Smokin, Ch. Marquis Market Tip and their producers Marquis Mistletoe, (dam of 12 champions), Ch. Frandee's Do Declare (litter sister to Celebration), and Chs. Feinlyne Fetch and Go and Friezee. They also have many other bitches who have produced 6–8 champions each. However, their best bitch was Ch. Marquis Sensational. She was sired by Super Daddy and shown by both Greg Anderson and Donny Johnson. She was then sold to Europe where she is a Best in Show winner.

Another remarkable feat accomplished by these two winners is the record of having 13 major winners in American Spaniel Club shows. Vernon and Karen attribute much of their on-going success to two things. First, they were able to obtain good quality dogs from the beginning (mainly Feinlyne, Frandee and Rexpointe lines) even though they were relatively new. And second, the "teachers" who helped them along the way, "without whose help they could not have accomplished what they did." They got top advice and listened.

LAURA and KAP HENSON—"Kaplar Kennels"

Laura and Kap Henson, along with Vernon and Karen Marquez, are probably the leading "young" breeders in Cockers today. Their success in Buffs, Black and Tans and Blacks makes them the kennel to challenge.

Kaplar got its serious start in California when they met Donna and Jim Pfrommer who had Ch. Essanar East Side. They bred their red Ch. Van-Dor Vermillion daughter to him. From that litter came two champions and their top-producing bitch, Sandrex Sangarita. Sangarita is the dam of the ASC Best in Show winner, Ch. Kaplar's Royal Kavalier.

While still in California, they bred Sangrita to Royal Lancer and that litter also produced some top ones, including Ch. Kaplar's Koka Kola.

My first introduction to the Kaplar "force" came when I judged a specialty in New Jersey. On that day, I put two puppies from the 6 to 9 Months Puppy Dog and Bitch classes to Reserve Winners in ASCOBs. They were Royal Kavalier and Kopi Kat. Both went on to great show careers.

Today Laura does most of the handling while Kap scoots around the world or tinkers in his antique shop. Kap is a great fan of the Blacks while Laura leans toward the Black and Tans. Three Kaplar dogs are to be found in the current top sires list. Kavalier, now deceased, is the sire of 25 champions while Kon-Man has sired 38 champions and Kassanova 40 champions. Both of the dogs will break into the top-twenty all-time producers and, I predict, will become among the top producing sires of the breed.

A current special is Ch. Kaplar's Jiminey Kricket who is co-owned with Deryck and Christine Boutilier. Jiminey has done very well with his handler Greg Anderson. Jiminey is another Buff in a long line of Kaplar top winners.

The Kaplar Kennels are located in Frederick, Maryland—not too far from the Artru Kennels of the Benhoff's in Baltimore. There are many similarities in the success stories of these two kennels. The Kaplar Kennel is located on seven acres, four of which are in pasture for their Appaloosa horses. There is also an 85 year-old barn on the grounds.

Their kennel set-up is small but workable with an intercom which pipes in music and keeps Laura in touch with the house. The runs are covered, and in the winter, heavy plastic runners are added for additional shelter.

The Kaplar name has been kept in the forefront not only by their great stud dogs but also by their great Black show girls. Kelly Girl and Kopi Kat are both Best of Breed winners and a host of others too numerous to mention have won top honors. To cap it off, Kaplar is well represented on the all-time top-producing bitches list with Ch. Kaplar's Kolleen, the dam of 18 champions (which places her #2 on the list) and Ch. Kaplar's Quicksilver with 10 champions (placing her #9 on the list).

Ch. Kaplar's Kelly Girl

BETTY DURLAND—"Dur-Bet Kennels"

Baldwinsville New York, a suburb of Syracuse is the setting of the famous Dur-Bet kennels. Betty, a graduate of Syracuse University with a degree in Zoology and a minor in Genetics, has put her knowledge to work to produce a line of dogs that is as well known in England and Australia as they are here in the United States.

Early on, her husband, Bob (an engineer with the telephone company) had been transferred to Syracuse. Betty, with her two children in school, faced a career decision. She had been a research assistant in Internal Medicine at New York Hospital and now searched for the beginnings of a new career. She had no intention of remaining "only a housewife," but also disliked the idea of pursuing a career that would take her away from her home and family every day. The idea of establishing a small kennel and grooming business seemed an ideal compromise.

People are constantly amazed to discover that Dur-Bet is by no means a large operation. The emphasis has always been, first and foremost, to produce a quality dog of good temperament and health that can fill the role of an ideal family companion. The camaraderie that has been developed with pet owners serves a very useful purpose. "We get to see the development and eventual outcome of these dogs brought back for grooming and this is a very valuable experience in evaluating future litters."

A surprising fact, in a kennel known for its blacks and black and tans, is that the early Dur-Bet dogs were buff. A bitch, Tedwin's Tale had been purchased when the family lived in Albany. She was sired by Norbill's High and Mighty and was out of Little Buff Specially Me. In 1961, she was bred to Ch. Hollyrock Harvester. From this breeding came the top-producing bitch, Dur-Bet's Scandal Sheet. From her two litters by Ch. Jo-Be-Glen's Bronze Falcon, came Ch. Dur-Bet's Kristmas Knight, and in the second, Ch. Dur-Bet's Leading Lady. Leading Lady became the dam of nine Dur-Bet champions, including her first important black and tan bitch and another top producer, Ch. Dur-Bet's Tantalizer. This succession of top producers from Scandal Sheet to Leading Lady, to Tantalizer, and finally to Flirtation Walk was to prove to be one of the strongest bitch lines in modern history.

Kristmas Knight was Dur-Bet's first Best in Show dog but a liver ailment (that rendered him sterile) curtailed his possible long-term influence on the breed. As it was, in the four litters he was able to sire, he produced top quality. His most famous and influential offspring was Ch. Dur-Bet's Nightie Night. Nightie deserves credit for transforming Dur-Bet from a buff kennel into one that excelled in blacks and black and tans. Nightie bred to Ch. Valli-Lo's Jupiter, produced three champions but her two breedings to another top winner and producer of the day, Ch. Hob-Nob-Hill's Tribute secured her permanent claim to fame. The first produced Ch. Dur-Bet's Knight To Remember, and the second, Am. & Can. Ch. Dur-Bet's Pick The Tiger, CD. These two boys and their closely-linebred girl friends account for almost 100% of the "look" of the Dur-Bet dogs of today.

Knight To Remember had a limited, but spectacular, specials career, winning the American Spaniel Club Show in 1969 and 1971. He became the sire of 33 champions including the well-known top producer, Ch. Shiloh Dell's Salute. He is also the sire of numerous English, Australian and Canadian champions.

Knight To Remember's kid brother, Pick The Tiger, became a top producer in his own right siring 27 champions including Ch. Windy Hill's 'Tis Demi's Demon, Am. & Eng. Ch. Windy Hill 'N Dur-Bet 'Tis Patti, one of the top winning American Cockers in English history, and Dur-Bet's own, Ch. Dur-Bet's Tantalizer, dam of eight champions. Tiger is also the sire of Am. & Can. Ch. Dur-Bet's Tiger Paws who has stamped his mark on present day Dur-Bet Cockers.

It is interesting to note that among the top producers in breed history are Demon, Salute, and Demon's son, Ch. Bobwin's Sir Ashley. Dur-Bet has, in many ways, moved alongside Artru, Stockdale and the other great kennels of the past in its influence on the breed.

As much as the Dur-Bet offspring have influenced the American scene, it may well have more far-reaching effects on the Cocker scene in Australia and England.

Dur-Bet kennels have produced well over 70 champions and the drum beat still goes on with new winners every year.

Ch. Dur-Bet's Knight To Remember

Dogs Who Influenced The Breed

Every breed has had its famous sons and daughters. Some go streaking across the sky making sure that everyone knows about them only to disappear and not leave a trace of their moment in the sun. Others, perhaps not so famous, leave a lasting impression on the breed through their sons and daughters. These dogs stamp a breed with their greatness. They found a bloodline and thrust a kennel into the spotlight with their ability as a prepotent sire.

Siring ability can be passed down through generations. The most famous producing bloodlines in *any* breed is in the Cocker Spaniel. The lineage began with Ch. Hall-Way Hoot Mon, a black/white, the sire of 43 champions, to his red/white son, Ch. Scioto Bluff's Sinbad, the sire of 118 champions, and to his black/white son, Ch. Dreamridge Dominoe, the sire of 109 champions. There are already indications that Dominoe progeny will carry on this great producing strain.

There are many famous producers in our breed and it would be impossible to list them all here. Their producing records are to be found in the Top Producing Dogs and Bitches section of this book. This particular chapter will focus on key dogs whose influence made the breed what it is today.

Red Brucie

Mrs. Ella B. Moffit, in her 1935 book titled *The Cocker Spaniel,* wrote this about a pillar of the breed:

In 1921, Mr. H.E. Mellenthin rang me up on the telephone and asked if I would like to see a dog. I did not have to be bidden twice, knowing that this must be something very special. At first glance I was somewhat disappointed when he produced a three month old red puppy which he proceeded to set up on a projection alongside of his porch steps. To my dying day I will have a vivid mental picture of this "atom of Cockerdom." Not just a lovely puppy, as most of the best of them are at that age, but the impersonation of masculinity, Cocker Spaniel quality and substance from the tip of his nose to the end of his tail. Strong-headed, heavy-boned, short-backed, an exaggeration of every single thing that a Cocker should be. Perfectly delighted and thinking I had found what I needed to "found" the Rowcliffe Kennels, I asked him the price. "That is going to be the greatest stud dog the breed has

RED BRUCIE—"Brucie"

Whelped: June 8, 1921
Sire: Robinhurst Foreglow — Dam: Ree's Dolly
Breeder/Owner: Herman E. Mellenthin

ever known and he is not for sale," he answered me. And from this position, he could not be moved, hard as I tried. Little did we think, however, that those words would be so justified as they have been by the records. Sire of 38 champions, still a producer when 13 years old. Red Brucie will be in the pedigrees of the "right" American Cockers probably two or three times over and his influence is largely responsible for the "modern Cocker."

At maturity, he was not quite so impressive as a show dog, and for that reason did not make his championship. He was a little ahead of his time. He always was a strong headed dog (some might call it a little coarse) with enormous bone for his size and unprecedented short in back. His greatest gift to Cockers was long neck and lean, sloping shoulders with higher station and short backs. There is an amusing incident connected with his name. Mr. Mellenthin was still young in the breed and had not yet acquired a kennel prefix. He applied for the name of Red Bruce to the American Kennel Club, but failed to send a second or third choice. The name of Red Bruce being for some reason unavailable, the AKC exercised its privilege and changed the ending as it now stands. I remember the owner's disgust when the certificate arrived.

Probably Red Brucie's first outstanding accomplishment as a sire was the production of the "Big Four Litter." Ch. My Own Straight Sale, Ch. Rowcliffe Princess, Ch. My Own Peter Manning and Ch. My Own Desire whelped in 1922. The dam of these, Ch. Princess Marie, a very beautiful black bitch, of course merits a very large share of the credit for this wonderful black quartette. Straight Sale, acquired by the Windsweep Kennels, founded blacks for Miss Dodsworth. Princess, as the dam of Ringleader, founded solids in the Rowcliffe Kennels. Desire was a great force in the Sand Spring Kennels. Peter Manning remained with his breeder. To properly trace this degree of ability to produce, I think a study of Red Brucie's pedigree is important. Robinhurst Foreglow was a remarkable sire. Though naturally of the most importance in solid colors, he also had great influence in parti-colors, largely through his son Ch. Rowcliffe Red Man. All Spaniel fanciers should thoroughly appreciate the service that this great dog has done for the breed.

A favorite expression with some breeders trying to promote their own stud dog is that a certain dog is a "second Red Brucie." How stupid such a statement is. There will never be another Red Brucie, any more than there will be a second George Washington, or a second Abraham Lincoln. The times and conditions created circumstances which developed both of these great men as specifics. Likewise, the demand for a Cocker of a more sporting type gave Red Brucie his chance and he proved to be the specific for the need. People making such extravagant claims for their favorite only make themselves ridiculous by showing their ignorance. True, there will be other great stud dogs, but they can carry sufficient credit of their own if the facts make them so, without trying to borrow from the greatness of another—whose records stand where all who look and read may see.

Undoubtedly, to achieve greatness, a dog—like a person—must have the necessary opportunity. I am very sure that many potentially good producers, of either sex, have gone unproven to their graves. Such an opportunity unquestionably Red Brucie had. He first came prominently into public notice with the famous Princess Marie litter. He was just past a year old when this litter was whelped and, of course, it gave him a great send off. He was tremendously bred to. I do not believe that any dog was ever in such public demand as a stud. His popularity was enhanced, in 1927, by the birth of a litter out of Sweet Georgia Brown (breeder Thomas Carleton), which turned out five champions, a marvelous record for any bitch and showing the importance of giving the necessary credit to the dam as a producer. Thus out of 38 champions, nine came out of two litters!

Ch. Torohill Trader

Bain Cobb, of the famous Cobb brothers, reported in 1952 about his experiences with Ch. Torohill Trader.

It was back in 1933 when I drove over to the Torohill Kennels with Herman Mellenthin, with whom I was staying. Mellenthin had purchased a young black dog for me to take back to the Blackstone Kennels of Leonard Buck (where I was to take over the management of the place).

As I recall, my first impression of the new young black dog, known to posterity as Torohill Trader, was of perfect balance; he was well up-on-leg, and he had a head such as one dreams of. One of the first Cockers with large, very dark eyes, his expression was unusually soft and beautiful.

As he was immature and I felt he should be given a chance for body development, I waited a year before showing him and gave him plenty of road work with a German Sheperd Dog for a lead. What a thrill to see him move. Little did I know that this same movement was to leave

CH. TOROHILL TRADER—"Trader"

Whelped: 1932
Sire: Torohill Trouper — Dam: Torohill Tidy
Breeder/Owner: Leonard Buck

an everlasting imprint on the breed. Even today the comment, "he moves like Trader" means that a dog has near perfect rhythm of movement combined with the old Trader gaiety and spirit.

Trader's first show was Morris & Essex where he defeated Ch. Windsweep Ladysman plus a huge class of current winners. This was the first of a series of wins which built for Trader a great career, more than a dozen Best in Shows, many, many Sporting Groups—and remember this—the groups at that time in the east were the strongest ever.

Trader lived with me all of his life and, as I enjoyed hunting and a good dog, it was only natural that Trader accompanied me on many a hunt. He was a natural retriever; his natural instincts for hunting were strong; he had a good nose. Fortunately he passed on those qualities and also became well known for his field get.

Until he died at the age of 14, he enjoyed life to the fullest extent. He enjoyed the show ring. Even his last appearance on exhibition at a Boston specialty when he was 11, he moved with such a proud and gay spirit that the ringside ovation was spontaneous with a tremendous admiration for the old fellow who could still give the young ones plenty of competition. Trader was a great producer and his many, many champions of truly outstanding quality built for him a monument. He will never be forgotten by Cocker breeders.

Ch. Try-Cob's Candidate

Arthur Totton, a former president of the American Spaniel Club

---

CH. TRY-COB'S CANDIDATE—"Candidate"

Whelped: 1940
Sire: Glidmere Buzz — Dam: Ch. Brightfield Delight
Breeder/Owner: Mr. and Mrs. R. Kenneth Cobb

wrote in the September 1952 special edition of *Popular Dogs*, the follow-ing enlightening information about Try-Cob's Candidate and about the state of the breed in general:

In my opinion, the greatest progress was evidenced in the show ring and breeding of Cocker Spaniels just slightly more than a decade ago, and I am sure most of my readers will immediately think that I am referring to the popular reign of "My Own Brucie." I hate to disappoint and dislike to make comparisons, which are sometimes odious, but looking back to Brucie and what he did for the breed, I am forced to the conclusion that he was not the great dog we all thought him. In the days of his show ring triumphs he was outstanding, but sad to relate, it was not a very difficult task to be outstanding in a Cocker ring at that time.

I don't think I take away from Brucie's glory by saying that he had a string of very easy triumphs. I don't get any kick out of pointing this out but I think it is necessary to prove that our progress as a breed actually began shortly after Brucie's heyday and that he had little or no part in it.

Most of our progress I attribute to two dogs. Let me take you back to the American Cocker Spaniel show of 1941, which was held at the Roosevelt Hotel in New York City. I had a good seat, so I was present at the debut of "Try-Cob's Candidate." I am not going to say another word about conformation. I am simply going to say that we were electri-fied with the gaiety, the abandon of spirit; the gaiety fused with move-ment which seemed so absolutely effortless that it was like watching a perfectly-trained athlete limbering up for some momentous event. I can remember so vividly, when Brucie and Candidate came into the ring for the judging—Brucie suffered so much by comparison when being gaited that I felt sorry for the old chap (mind you, up to this time, I had been a firm and staunch Brucie man). It was like seeing an old champ being knocked out by a cocky youngster. Very soon, sorrow gave way to elation in the realization that here was my fondest hope for the breed come true. After watching Cockers crawl around the ring on their stomachs, with their tails firmly clamped between their legs, shivering as if in the grip of some disease like palsy while being posed; let me tell you it was more than a breath of cool air on an arid desert. It was proof positive that we were afforded an opportunity of at last owning and exhibiting something in which we could have some modicum of pleasure.

I got a great kick out of the furor created at that time in the ranks and amongst the brass with regard to the merits or demerits of Candidate. I was a believer in what my eyes conveyed to my grey matter and was the first to bring a bitch over to the little house on Jericho Turnpike, but I was not the last; notwithstanding the calumny heaped upon the head of the dog and his owners by the experts. Bitches were shipped from all parts of the country and we were on the threshold of a new era. The Cocker began his triumphal march to the top spot in public favor. Exhibitors began to relax in the rings because they no longer had to be forever anxious about the gaiting or showing of their dogs. If they had Candidate breeding, they knew they had disposition aplenty and this does add to the pleasure of showing.

In my humble opinion, a dog to deserve acclaim must not only be a good animal himself, but he must be able to produce and so we have the evidence of Candidate's greatness written in the pedigrees of most, if not all, of the good ones today.

Ch. Nonquitt Nola's Candidate

Quoting Arthur Totton again:

I would like to select one dog to which, I believe, I should pay particular tribute because of his influence on the breed and the joy he gave all of us during his show career. I first saw Nonquitt Nola's Candidate at a New Jersey specialty. He was in the puppy sweepstakes and, as far as I can remember, did not place in the money. Ken Cobb had the lead on a young dog belonging to Lawrason Riggs and as he was preparing him for the show ring he asked my opinion of his dog. I very truthfully answered; he was the best colt out of that stable that I had seen, but he left much to be desired when compared with the dog Tom Godfrey was showing. Very strangely, for a long time I thought I was the only man in the ranks who was in step, because I don't think the dog did any winning until the fall of that year. Thereby hangs a tale, which I cannot refrain from telling.

At that time, probably more than at any other in our day and age, there was a very strong little clique which exercised a considerable amount of influence in Cocker circles, and to say they resented the advent of this distortion or abortion (they called him much worse names than that) was putting it mildly. They persuaded Mrs. Ross of Nonquitt kennels that she really was doing a disservice to the breed by retaining in her kennels a dog which was so foreign in type and disposi-

CH. NONQUITT NOLA'S CANDIDATE

Whelped: 1941
Sire: Ch. Try-Cob's Candidate — Dam: Ch. Nonquitt Nola
Breeder: Mrs. Henry A. Ross
Owner: Ken Cobb and Florence Brister

tion. Mrs. Ross was influenced to the extent that she sold the dog to Ken Cobb without consulting Tom Godfrey. It does not require too vivid an imagination to picture the chagrin with which Tom received the news. As a matter of historical fact, he was trimming the dog in preparation for two New England shows when Ken arrived to take possession. Mrs. Ross was residing at her summer home but when telephoned, she confirmed the sale and Nonquitt Nola's Candidate was entered at both shows but under new ownership. He went Best in Show at one and won the Sporting Group at the other. Thus began a great show-winning career and another proof of his sire, Candidate's, greatness and influence on the breed.

Ch. Argyll's Archer

The story of Archer really begins with his mother, Sand Spring Smile Awhile.

Mrs. Constance W. Bayne bought Smile, bred and due to whelp in a week, from Mrs. L'Hommedieu. Smile whelped five lovely buff puppies. This was the start of Argyll Kennels.

When Mrs. Bayne looked for another stud for Smile, she came across a young black dog—Noble Sir, or Punch as he was called. Punch was the pride and joy of the George Kirtlands. He was a magnificently built dog and had all of the features that complimented her bitch. This breeding produced Ch. Argyll's Archer and Ch. Argyll's Enchantress.

CH. ARGYLL'S ARCHER—"Archer" or "Little Punch"

Whelped: 1936
Sire: Noble Sir — Dam: Sand Spring Smile Awhile
Breeder: Mrs. Robert W. Wall
Owner: Mrs. Constance W. Bayne who sold to C. B. Van Meter

Archer became the foundation of Stockdale Kennels and Enchantress became the foundation bitch for Nonquitt Kennels. Stockdale Kennels in California used Archer to sire Ch. Stockdale Town Talk. Not only a great show dog, Town Talk was for many, many years—until unseated by Sinbad—the top-producing Cocker of all time, with 81 champion off-spring. The Nonquitt Kennels of upstate New York produced the great Cockers: Nowanda, Ch. Nonquitt Notable's Candidate, Ch. Nonquitt Notable plus a host of others. This breeding to Noble Sir started two of the most potent bloodlines in all of America.

From the time Archer was old enough to walk he was a perfect miniature of Noble Sir and hence acquired the name of Little Punch.

Archer's first show was the great Morris and Essex spectacular where he went first in a class of 15 puppies.

He was sold several times, first to Mr. Kirtland. He developed a chronic colitis and was very hard to keep in show condition. Mr. Kirtland sold him to Mrs. Suplee who sent him out on the show circuit. Because of his condition he did not win as much as he could have. He was a home dog and did not like the circuit.

The circuit ended up on the west coast, and there he came under the watchful eye of C.B. Van Meter. Van bought him from Mrs. Suplee. At that time he weighed only about 18 pounds, but with Van's expert care and devotion he very soon blossomed into a great show specimen. His show career with Van Meter was meteoric.

Van bred his Stockdale Startler bitches to him. This proved to be a perfect nick, his first champion being Town Talk; the rest of his career is a matter of record.

Ch. Stockdale Town Talk

Town Talk was the dog that put California in the forefront of the Cocker Spaniel breed. Until that time, all the action had been on the east coast. Town Talk was a showman and a producer. He was one of the first west coast dogs to journey east and take on the best. His Sporting Group win at Westminster over the "best" the east had to offer was a turning point in western Cocker fortunes.

Town Talk was the creation of the clever mind of C.B. Van Meter.

Startler seldom sired an outstanding male but many good bitches. It was his daughters that gave Stockdale many of their top Cockers. A red Startler daughter, Audacious Lady, was Town Talk's dam. In fact approximately one-fifth of Town Talk's 81 champions were from Startler daughters. That's quite a nick.

CH. STOCKDALE TOWN TALK—"Town Talk"

Whelped: 1939
Sire: Ch. Argyll's Archer — Dam: Audacious Lady
Breeder: Mr. and Mrs. S. T. Adams
Owner: C. B. Van Meter

Town Talk, like Red Brucie, changed the breed. The typical Cocker of the 40's and 50's was the so called "eastern" type. This dog was blocky in appearance with an average length of neck and a beautiful head. The shoulders were fairly laid-back. Many of these dogs matured young. On the other hand, Town Talk offspring were more up-on-leg and streamlined looking. This was accomplished by having the shoulder rotated in a more upright position, thus giving a more sloping topline. His offspring also matured more slowly, being at their best at about 2½ years of age.

While Red Brucie was famous for his great litter of four champions, Town Talk sired an equally famous litter of five. Out of a Startler daughter, of course.

Ch. Maddie's Vagabond's Return

This remarkable dog came along in the 1950's to have a major impact on the inheritance of coat color in the breed. Until the 1940's, the breeders of buff and parti-color Cockers accepted the fact that they were breeding dogs that could not compete with the black Cocker Spaniel. All of the "good" traits such as flat bones, full coats, good rears, etc., seemed linked to the black color. In an effort to get these "good" features, the early breeders bred their stock to the blacks. They were

CH. MADDIE'S VAGABOND'S RETURN—"Maddie"

Whelped: October 1949
Sire: Poling's Royal Splendor — Dam: Lee-ebs Sweetie Pie
Breeder/Owner: Madeline E. Peuquet

able to get these features in their stock but unfortunately only in the black offspring. The buff and parti-color offspring still looked like the original stock. The advent of Maddie's Vagabond's Return heralded a new age in buff and parti-color breeding. Maddie came from a line where, a few generations earlier, a successful mutation had come about. According to Louis Schmidt, one of the best amateur geneticists of his day, a mutation which produced a dog which could sire like a black but in buff color had been produced. This dog bred true. Mr. Schmidt dubbed it a "dilute black." The dog they were referring to was buff in color but had black skin. He was black in type and in the ability to produce like a black. However, he could not extend his black skin pigment into his coat.

Maddie, as one of the top winning Cockers of his day, and with a fabulous coat, attracted the notice of many. With his ability to produce the light cream-colored buffs with coat and Black type, he was an instant hit as a sire. In his career he produced 60 champions. Perhaps his greatest contribution was to Parti-Colors. His Partis had dark blue spots all over their skin, which indicated they were dilute breeding and not straight Parti-Colors. The actual source of parti-colors in this line is not a Parti-Color dog back in the pedigree, nor a combination of Parti-Color dogs. In the dilution breeding, the color is so completely washed out that it is almost white. In the process, it is a normal and simple matter for the intense white color (recessive) to take over in spots, producing a parti-color with the colored area remaining a cream tan or light buff.

Ch. St. Andrea's Medicine Man

With the possible exception of my own Ch. Hi-Boots Such Brass, I think Medicine Man (Teddy) has to be my favorite dog. I first saw Teddy, in 1951, at a specialty show in Baton Rouge, Louisiana. He was handled by Ken Cobb and that day, under judge Bill Wunderlich, he went Best of Breed. He took the rosette in his mouth as he and his handler made an extra victory lap around the ring. I have never been so impressed with a young dog. We, at Hi-Boots, bred three champions from him and he is the grandsire of Ch. Hi-Boots Such Brass by one of Medicine Man's great daughters, Ch. DeKarlos Day Dreams.

Norman Austin, in the *American Cocker Review* in June of 1978, wrote the following about Medicine Man.

> With the possible exception of Ch. Carmor's Rise and Shine, I do not believe there has been a Cocker Spaniel with which so many people have been emotionally involved as with Ch. St. Andrea's Medicine Man! His story and his influence have become legend. (Teddy died tragically at four years of age but sired 41 champions in his short lifespan.)
>
> The first time I saw Medicine Man was as a puppy with his litter brother and sister, St. Andrea's Rain Maker and St. Andrea's Ragtime Gal. I was particularly interested in this litter because it was one of the

CH. ST. ANDREA'S MEDICINE MAN—"Teddy"

Whelped: April 1950
Sire: Ch. Lancaster Landmark — Dam: Jubilo Madcap
Breeder: Ivan M. and Paula E. Wise
Owner: Major Ivan and Dr. Paula Wise

first sired by Ch. Lancaster Landmark, a young black and tan dog I finished shortly after his sire, Ch. Lancaster Great Day. Great day was a son of that incomparable black and tan bitch, Ch. Nonquitt Nowanda.

Nowanda came from an outstanding background and has become the matriarch of black and tan Cockers through linebreeding of her descendents, particularly in the Medicine Man family. Nowanda was an outstanding bitch and was the epitome of type. She carried a tremendous amount of body for her size but most importantly, she had style. These attributes she passed on to her children.

Medicine Man's story begins in Detroit, Michigan. Myrtle Haywood owned Jubilo Kennels and bred several colors, although dark red remained her favorite. When she decided to concentrate on reds only, she offered for sale the black and tan bitch named Jubilo Madcap. She was a Nowanda granddaughter and Dick Funk (Lancaster Kennels), who had always liked her, talked Myrtle into offering her for sale bred to Ch. Lancaster Landmark. Passage of time has proven this choice to have been very wise.

Madcap was sold to Major Ivan Wise and his wife Dr. Paula Wise in Vienna, Virginia. Dr. Wise, because of her European background, sentimentally chose the St. Andrea prefix for her puppies and did a beautiful job raising that litter. Soon they began to appear at puppy matches and in point shows, causing comment wherever they were shown.

It was not until I saw him with professional handler, Ken Cobb, at the New Orleans specialty show (*Editors note: As I was also there that day I can attest to the fact that he went Best of Winners and narrowly lost to the great Ch. Benbow's Tanbark for the Variety)* that the full impact of Medicine Man hit me. When this marvelous dog walked into the ring, there was no doubt in my mind that here was true greatness with beauty, power and a driving movement beyond belief! Not until I saw the same qualities in Ch. Pinetop's Fancy Parade did I fully realize what a great asset and influence Medicine Man had been.

A few telephone calls were made to people closely associated with Lancaster and bitches began to arrive for Medicine Man. William A. (Tubby) Laffoon, of Pinetop fame, was the first to have a litter by him because he had seen him prior to New Orleans and was quick to take advantage of what he saw!

The following year at the greatest of all eastern outdoor shows, the now extinct Morris and Essex Kennel Club event, the good fortune of those who bred to Medicine Man became apparent. In Cockers, judged by Mrs. Myrtle Twelvetrees, the Winners Dog, Reserve Winners Dog, Winners Bitch and Reserve Winners Bitch were all sired by Medicine Man.

Buff and Red breeders were almost thrown into a state of shock after the first winning by Medicine Man children. At that time the Varieties were separated, the Black and Tans were included in the ASCOB Variety, where they were most welcome as they helped to make points in a Variety dominated by Buffs. Occasionally, a young Black and Tan would come along with great promise but, for the most part, the Black and Tan's were plainer and lacking type compared with the Buffs. The Medicine Man children completely changed the Black and Tan image and Buff breeders scurried to reconnoiter. It was worth the effort as it pulled the ASCOB breeders together, resulting in a much better Cocker Spaniel.

The combination of Landmark and Madcap produced a composite of good traits. St. Andrea's Ragtime Gal was a good bitch and finished but the real quality was that belonging to the two brothers, Medicine Man and Rain Maker. The latter was a shade smaller than Medicine Man and perhaps a little more refined but he was a smoothly blended and beautifully balanced dog who did great winning on the west coast under the guidance of Roy Nelson. He left his imprint on the breed but with less impact than his brother.

Ch. St. Andrea's Medicine Man and Ch. St. Andrea's Rainmaker were the most influential litter brothers of the past two, nearly three decades (only Ch. Artru Johnny-Be-Good and Ch. Jo-Be-Glen's Bronze Falcon rivaled them). They contributed to stabilizing consistency of type and balance throughout the country.

Ch. Elderwood Bangaway

Norman Austin, Bangaway's handler wrote this about him in the October 1956 issue of *Cockers Calling:*

Bangaway's children have established him not only as a great sire but a real contributor to our breed. Many a sire's champion children just fade away but Bang has been most fortunate in having his sons and daughters carry on with top wins across the country. It is almost unbelievable the number of Best in Show, Sporting Group and specialty show wins that his various sons have amassed. More important than the

CH. ELDERWOOD BANGAWAY—"Bang" or "Bangaway"

Whelped: June 1950
Sire: Ch. Myroy Night Rocket — Dam: Ch. Elder's So Lovely
Breeder: H. Stewart Elder
Owner: Vivian and Bob Levy

individual show wins, there lies the knowledge that his sons are carrying on his producing powers. (*Author's note: His son Ch. DeKarlos Dashaway sired the great winning and producing dog, Ch. Clarkdale Capital Stock, the sire of 76 champions.*) Shows today are represented by his winning children, grandchildren and even more recent, by his grandchildren who are the products of half-brother/sister matings. All of these, wherever they appear, bear a distinct resemblence to Bangaway—thus paying him the greatest tribute that I think can be paid to a stud dog.

I know I am not alone in feeling great love and admiration for this wonderful dog. Retired at the height of his career, he went on to sire 45 champions. Those who renew acquaintances with him at Lazy Bend Kennels in Houston, Texas or are seeing him for the first time, all leave feeling it has been a great privilege to have shared a part, regardless of how small, in the life of this wonderful little dog that comes as close to fitting the standard of our Cocker, in my humble opinion, as any dog I have ever seen.

Bang's admiration society started at a tender age, first by his breeders, Mary and Stewart Elder, later myself as his handler and a host of others as his career grew. Ranking foremost are his owners, Vivian and Bob Levy. Vivian who keeps him in such bloom that he could step into the show ring at a moment's notice. Those who know Bob Levy cannot help but admire him, not only as a fine man, but also respect his love and unique eye for animal flesh. It was Bob who found Bang and bought him the day he went reserve and not winners. I shall never forget, that very same day, when he handed him to me with these words, "He is your's, treat him kindly." These simple words became the entree to one of the greatest experiences that will probably never be duplicated. Interesting too, it was more than a business arrangement . . . we became a family unit, united under the house of Bang.

Many people have asked me what made Bang stand out in particular. I admire his great heart, but I guess it was the overall balance and style that made him a champion among champions.

Many times I have suggested to those who have never seen him that they head down Texas way to see this remarkable dog. They would probably find Bob and Bang playing ball with a half-dozen of his champion children on the spacious lawns of Lazy Bend. He might even become to them, as he has to many, an inspiration or even a challenge to help perpetuate the shining name of Ch. Elderwood Bangaway.

Bang was a perfect example of the success of linebreeding. He was tripled up on Ch. Stockdale Town Talk through his great sons and grandsons, Ch. Stockdale Red Rocket, Ch. Myroy Masterpiece and Ch. Myroy Night Rocket.

Ch. Scioto Bluff's Sinbad

Sinbad, the dog that broke Town Talk's record by siring 118 champions, was descended, in part from the Honey Creek Kennels of Bea Wegusen and the famous cross (engineered by Jim and Beth Hall of

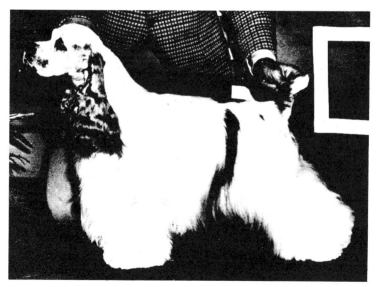

CH. SCIOTO BLUFF'S SINBAD—"Sinbad"

Whelped: August 1959
Sire: Ch. Hall-Way Hoot Mon — Dam: Ch. Scioto Bluff's Judy
Breeder/Owner: Charles D. and Veda L. Winders

Hall-Way Cockers) of Maddie's Vagabond's Return and Fraclin blood-lines. The Hall's Vagabond's Return breeding also produced Orient's It's A Pleasure, the sire of 104 champions.

Ch. Hall-Way Hoot Mon, the black/white sire of Sinbad, was a bit on the small side but was a born showman. Hoot Mon sired 43 champions, coming from a producing bitch line that was line bred to Ch. Maddie's Vagabond's Return, the sire of 60 champions.

Sinbad's dam, Ch. Scioto Bluff's Judy, was a great-great granddaughter of the fantastic producing and showing Ch. Honey Creek Vivacious. Vivacious, when bred to Ch. Honey Creek Harmonizer, produced a litter of six champions, one of which (Ch. Honey Creek Havana) was Sinbad's great grandmother. With this producing heritage it is easy to understand why Sinbad turned out so well.

I was fortunate enough to have seen Sinbad at the end of his show career. Ron Fabis brought him out to California where he went Best of Breed at the San Joaquin Valley Specialty, at that time the largest specialty show held in California.

The Artru Dogs

I know this is an unusual designation, but the Artru Kennels of Ruth and Art Benhoff have produced so many sensational producing dogs that I am hard put to single out one that can be identified as "unique." I

CH. ARTRU SKYJACK

Whelped: June 1971
Sire: Ch. Artru Red Baron — Dam: Ch. Artru Trinket
Breeder: Mrs. Arthur H. Benhoff

know Ruth prefers Ch. Artru Skyjack, now the sire of 87 champions, but when you have bred six of the top twenty producing dogs in breed history, how can you say one is best? Therefore I am exercising an author's prerogative in honoring all six of the dogs. they are:

Ch. Artru Skyjack . . . . 87 champions
Ch. Artru Sandpiper . . . . 68 champions
Ch. Artru Action . . . . 56 champions
Ch. Artru Johnny-Be-Good . . . . . 52 champions
Ch. Artru Red Baron . . . . 49 champions
Ch. Jo-Be-Glen's Bronze Falcon . . 43 champions

When you add Ch. LaMar's London, a Johnny son with 54 champions to this list, you can see what an awe-inspiring producing power was concentrated in this kennel. No wonder Ruth was chosen Breeder of the Century by the ASC. There is more about the Benhoffs and their dogs in the sections of this book about famous people and top-producing dogs.

CH. ARTRU SANDPIPER

Whelped: July 1965
Sire: Ch. Artru Johnny-Be-Good — Dam: Ch. Bar-C-Kar's Peau Rouge
Breeder: Mrs. Corinne C. Karcher

CH. ARTRU ACTION

Whelped: August 1968
Sire: Ch. Artru Sandpiper — Dam: Van-Dor Fancy Triane
Breeder: Dorothy Vanderveer

CH. ARTRU JOHNNY-BE-GOOD

Whelped: January 1961
Sire: Ch. Artru Hot Rod — Dam: Jo-Be-Glen's Honeycomb
Breeder: E.B. and J. Muller

CH. ARTRU RED BARON

Whelped: June 1967
Sire: Ch. Artru Johnny-Be-Good — Dam: Artru Kathleen
Breeder: Mrs. Arthur H. Benhoff, Jr.

CH. JO-BE-GLEN'S BRONZE FALCON

Whelped: January 1961
Sire: Ch. Artru Hot Rod — Dam: Jo-Be-Glen's Honeycomb
Breeder: E.B. and J.F. Muller

Ch. Dreamridge Dominoe

Ch. Dreamridge Dominoe was whelped in March of 1968. He is the sire of 109 champions being surpassed as a producer only by his sire Ch. Scioto Bluff's Sinbad and also by Ch. Rinky Dink's Sir Lancelot.

As Ron Fabis wrote in the June 1977 edition of *The American Cocker Review*:

> Dominoe has a "classic" pedigree. Sired by Sinbad, he is out of Ch. Dreamridge Dinner Date, a top winner and producer of nine champions out of nine pups raised.
>
> Dominoe finished his championship easily but was never specialed.
>
> A breeder once told us "Dominoe is like salt . . . most lines need a pinch of his blood for seasoning!"
>
> Actually, the Dominoe story begins with his sire, Ch. Scioto Bluff's Sinbad. Sinner was a cross between the old Honey Creek line through his granddam, Creekwood Miss Showoff (the dam of five champions), and the best of the Ch. Maddie's Vagabond's Return, and Merlady lines. Honey Creek was famous for beautiful plush red and whites with large, expressive eyes and abundant coats. His sire, Ch. Hall-Way Hoot Mon, was a very stable, showy black and white—small, sound and typey. Moving back a few years, Ch. Dau-Han Dan Morgan (the sire of 29 champions) was noted for producing proper expressions, skulls and beautiful muzzles. His daughter, Ch. Pounette Fancy Dancer was one of the most beautiful bitches of her day. Bred to Sinbad, she produced Pounette Perrette (the dam of 10 champions), the foundation bitch of Dreamridge. When bred to Ch. Clarkdale Calcutta, the sire of 33 champions and a strong stallion-type of a male, she produced Dinner Date. Dinner Date still personifies the standard for Tom O'Neal and

CH. DREAMRIDGE DOMINOE—"Dominoe"

Whelped: March 1968
Sire: Ch. Scioto Bluff's Sinbad — Dam: Ch. Dreamridge Dinner Date
Breeder/Owner: Thomas F. O'Neal

Ron Fabis, the one-two punch of Dreamridge. Dinner Date was a great bitch with proper muzzle, dome and eyes. She had long, well laid-back shoulders, was short coupled with a strong rear and showmanship to burn. I saw her years ago when Ron brought her out to the San Joaquin Valley CSC, and was much impressed.

She was bred back to Sinbad, her grandsire, to intensify the blood-lines. This mating produced Dominoe, the rest is history.

Ch. Windy Hill's 'Tis Demi's Demon

I asked Anita Roberts of Memoirs' fame, a close friend of Edna Anselmi the mistress of Windy Hill, to give me her recollections of Demon. Windy Hill is a name that has become synonymous with quality Cockers in black and tan, black and buff.

The foundation for the Windy Hill line was laid when Edna purchased a red bitch named Tracey from Liz Gorr of Stonehedge Kennels.

CH. WINDY HILL'S 'TIS DEMI'S DEMON—"Demon"

Whelped: May 1972
Sire: Ch. Dur-Bet's Pick The Tiger, CD
Dam: Ch. Windy Hill's 'Tis Demi-Tasse
Breeder: Edna T. Anselmi

Tracey was a beautifully headed and sound bodied bitch who helped to found the Windy Hill line. Quoting from Marcus Aurelius, "That which comes after, ever conforms to that which has gone before," was a perfect expression for Tracey who lived a long and healthy life.

Of the many fine dogs who have sported the Windy Hill prefix, Ch. Windy Hill's 'Tis Demi's Demon (or "Demon" as he was known to all), has exerted the most influence. He is known for his multiple-champion litters and, to date, his record stands at 83 champions—placing him sixth on the all-time producing list. Amazingly enough, his black son, Ch. Bobwin's Sir Ashley is the sire of 65 champions. Ashley is one of the six champions of Ashley's Cherry Jubilee.

Demon was sired by Ch. Dur-Bets Pick the Tiger, CD—the sire of 26 champions himself. In turn, Pick the Tiger's sire is Ch. Hob-Nob Hill's Tribute, the sire of 54 champions. Tribute's grandsire, Ch. Merry-haven Strutaway, produced 28 champion offspring.

Demon's dam, Ch. Windy Hill's 'Tis Demi Tasse was also the dam of the famous Ch. Windy Hill Makes-Its-Point, the winner of the 1977 ASC Futurity. Makes-Its-Point was the sire of 20 champions when he met an early and untimely death.

Carol Hilder of Carlens Cockers fell in love with Demon as a youngster and took him home for a few months. While in her charge, he was brought to California to try his luck at the famous San Joaquin Valley CSC Specialty. It was there he earned his first blue ribbon. After returning east, he won the Sweepstakes at the Maryland Specialty. He then returned home to Windy Hill and quickly finished his championship.

The first litters sired by Demon demonstrated his dominance in passing on substance, conformation, and lovely heads to his offspring when bred to almost any bloodline. But most of all, Demon was a gentleman with an unsurpassed disposition. When standing at stud at Memoirs, he jumped from a grooming table and suffered a nasty break in his leg and shoulder. Only the availability of the finest veterinary surgeons at the University of California at Davis saved Demon. The comments from the doctors attending him was that this boy was a lover, not a Demon.

Ch. Rinky Dink's Sir Lancelot

Lance is a dog every current breeder knows about. The sire of 135 champions at this writing he bids to become the top sire of any breed. I first "came across" Lance one very hot day in 1975, at the Cocker Spaniel Club of New Jersey. Lance, as always, was being ably handled by Terry Stacy. Lance did not especially appreciate the heat and decided that this was not what he wanted to do. Needless to say he was not the variety winner that day. Two years later I judged the Futurity at the 1977 ASC show. I found among my Black winners the 9–12 male, Main-Dales Marathon Man, the 6–9 bitch, Rinky Dink's Smooth as Silk and the 9–12 bitch, Butch's Impish Delight—all sired by Lance. That was my first inkling of his potential as a sire. He certainly has realized that potential.

CH. RINKY DINK'S SIR LANCELOT—"Lance"

Whelped: July 1972
Sire: Ch. Har-Dee's High Spirit — Dam: Ch. Rinky Dink's Robin
Breeder: Jean A. and William Petersen

Lance was whelped in 1972, out of Ch. Rinky Dink's Robin and sired by Ch. Har-Dee's High Spirit. High Spirit is the sire of 17 champions while his sire, Ch. Lurola's Lookout, is the sire of 16 champions.

A beautiful black and tan dog with all-over balance and type and the merriest disposition ever, with his tail in constant motion, Lance finished his championship in short order, winning several sweepstakes. His first Best of Breed win was owner-handled by Jean Petersen at the Cocker Spaniel Club of the Midwest. Lance went on to Charlotte and Terry Stacy where, in limited showing, he won ten specialty Best of Breeds, several Group placements, and began his stud career in earnest.

His offspring are themselves beginning to be top producers. The Kaplar dogs and the winning records of such dogs as Peeping Tom will ensure a permanent place in history for this greatest producer of our time.

SECTION VII

Representative Winning Dogs and Bitches

- *Great Winning Dogs of the Recent Past*
- *Great Winning Bitches of the Recent Past*

Great Winning Dogs
of the Recent Past

The forty-five Cocker Spaniels pictured in this chapter are some of America's top-winning male champions in the recent past.

Though unable to depict *every* top-winning male Cocker, this representative sampling of winning Cockers in all three Varieties portrays an image of some of the best that America had to offer during the last decade or so.

A top-winning dog of the 60's—Ch. Hi-Boots Such Brass.

Ch. Avondale Major Majestic

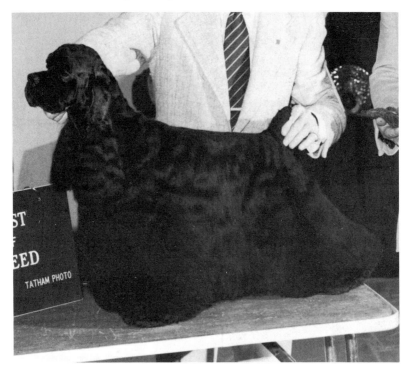

```
                              ┌──── CH. CHAMPAGNE'S DYNAMIC
                 ┌──── CH. DUR-BET'S TARTAN
                 │            └──── CH. DUR-BET'S TANTALIZER
CH. AVONDALE MAJOR MAJESTIC
                 │            ┌──── CH. DOLLY'S GOOD TIME BOY
                 └──── Dolly's Sugar and Spice
                              └──── Dolly's What A Pleasure
```

Whelped: March 24, 1978
Breeder: Stanley P. Pazden, Jr. and Marilyn A. Fink
Owner: Mrs. Edmond T. Reidy
Handler: Ted Young, Jr.

When this dog was Winners Dog from the puppy class at the January '79 ASC National Specialty, it was evident that other great wins were in the wings including: Best in Show at Holyoke KC in February '83, Best of Breed at Cocker Spaniel Breeders' Club of New England, Best of Breed in September '83 at the Zone I Show hosted by CSC of Long Island as well as Best of Breed in November '83 at the Cocker Spaniel Breeders' Club of New England.

He is the sire of champions though used sparingly.

Ch. Bara Hill's Black Diamond

```
                      ┌──── CH. ARTRU SKYJACK
        ┌──── CH. ASHLEY'S GOLDEN RULE
        │             └──── Ashley's Ramblin' Rose
CH. BARA HILL'S BLACK DIAMOND
        │             ┌──── CH. WINDY HILL'S 'TIS DEMI'S DEMON
        └──── CH. BARA HILL'S MIDNIGHT SONG
                      └──── CH. PINESHADOW'S MIDNIGHT LACE
```

Whelped: February 27, 1981
Breeder/Owner/Handler: Nina F. Biesecker

"Shaun" was always breeder/owner/handled to all his wins, including Best of Breed at specialties and Group wins.

Shaun has an outstanding temperament. He makes a pretty picture whether stacked or in motion and moves with a good topline. Shaun has a very good Cocker head with a nice, square muzzle, good shoulders, a short back with a good tail set. He has been a pleasure to own.

Ch. Brownwood Percussion

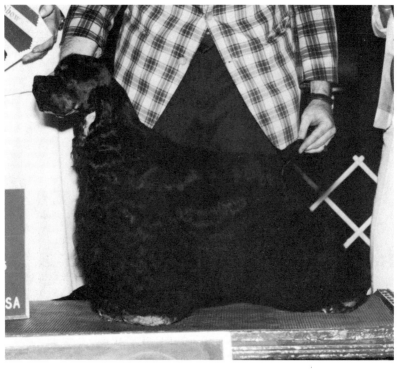

```
                              ┌──────── CH. LIZ-BAR'S DOWNBEAT
              ┌──────── CH. LIZ-BAR THE BEAT GOES ON
              │               └──────── LIZ-BAR WINDSONG
CH. BROWNWOOD PERCUSSION
              │               ┌──────── CH. BURSON'S STYLEMASTER
              └──────── Burson's Elvera
                              └──────── CH. JUBAN'S JORGEY GIRL
```

Whelped: October 17, 1983
Breeder: William H. Burson — Owner: Pat and Betty Peck
Handlers: Donnie Johnston and Charles Self

"Percy's" greatest wins include 5 Bests in Show and 30 Group Firsts. His puppies are outstanding in conformation and showmanship. Their attitudes are tremendous. One bitch finished with five majors, two from the puppy classes under Cocker breeder/judges as well as winning a Sweepstakes—breeder/owner/handled. Most all of his puppies have at least one major from the puppy class. One daughter of his accrued five majors en route to her championship as well as winning a Sweepstakes—breeder/owner/handled.

Can./Am. Ch. Buckingham's Action-Packed

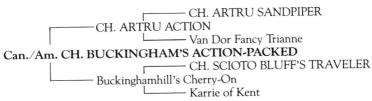

```
                              ┌────── CH. ARTRU SANDPIPER
                ┌──── CH. ARTRU ACTION
        ┌───────         └────── Van Dor Fancy Trianne
Can./Am. CH. BUCKINGHAM'S ACTION-PACKED
        │                 ┌────── CH. SCIOTO BLUFF'S TRAVELER
        └──── Buckinghamhill's Cherry-On
                          └────── Karrie of Kent
```

Whelped: August, 17, 1974
Breeder/Owner/Handler: Mary-Jeane and Susan E. Smoller

"Ethan" began his career with a Best in Sweepstakes win at the Hiawatha CSC in June of '75. He finished his American title with three majors, three Varieties and a Group Second. His Canadian title was garnered undefeated in four straight shows with four Varieties, four Bests of Breed, and four Group placements to put him among the Top Ten Cockers for that year in the Provinces. His specials career ran for two and a half years. He was owner/handled to 77 Varieties (seven of those at specialties) and 33 Group placements, including five Firsts. He has champion get in both the U.S. and Canada and two Group-winning Red sons—Ch. Dartons Buckinghamhill and Ch. Buckingham Natural Reaction. Ethan is his sire's top-winning son.

Ch. Buckingham Natural Reaction

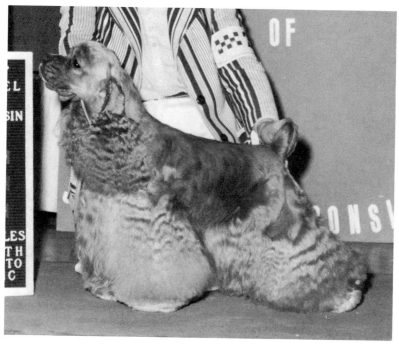

```
                          ┌──────── CH. ARTRU ACTION
             ┌──────── Can./Am. CH. BUCKINGHAM'S ACTION-PACKED
             │            └──────── Buckinghamhill's Cherry-On
CH. BUCKINGHAM NATURAL REACTION
             │            ┌──────── CH. VALLI-LO'S VENTURER
             └──────── Lady Tawny of Old Farm
                          └──────── Valli-Lo's Freedom Belle
```

Whelped: July 27, 1980
Breeder: Kurt and Ellen Karnthaler
Owner/Handler: Mary-Jeane and Susan E. Smoller

Finishing very young with four majors, three Varieties, and two Best Opposite Sex wins over specials, his first two years as a special found him among the Top-Ten ASCOBs in '82 and '83. The first half of '84 had him rated #5 ASCOB and #9 all Varieties through June. By mid-'84 he had won over 72 Bests of Variety and 19 Group placements (including two Firsts). He has two specialty Best of Breed wins and five Bests of Opposite Sex. First offered at public stud at age three, his first puppies are coming of age. His first champion, Ch. Northyork Mia's Delight, is a multiple Sweepstakes winner and completed her title with a Best of Breed at 10 months of age at the Fanciers CSC of Southern Wisconsin; her sire, "Natural Reaction," was Best Opposite to her!

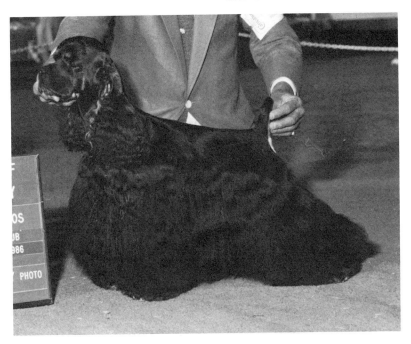

```
                                    ┌──────CH. FRANDEE'S FEDERAL AGENT
                    ┌──────CH. FRANDEE'S FORGERY
          ┌         └──────CH. FEINLYNE'S FETCH AND GO
CH. CAMELOT'S COUNTERFEIT
          │                         ┌──────CH. MEMOIR'S MARC IN THE DARK
          └──────CH. CAMELOT'S CONFETTI
                                    └──────Pryority's Holiday Hi-Lite
```

Whelped: June 20, 1984
Breeder: Louis M. and Amy Weiss — Owner: Susan Burke and Amy Weiss
Handlers: Bob and Jan Covey

"Smash's" show career started with a Reserve Winners Dog win from the 6–9 Puppy Dog class under a breeder/judge. He finished from the 9–12 Puppy Dog class with four majors, three large west coast Best in Sweepstakes, numerous Best Opposites to Best in Sweepstakes and numerous Sweepstakes Variety wins. He was nationally ranked in 1986 and in 1987.

Smash is a true "breeder's Cocker" with true breed type, elegance and the proper temperament so sought after.

Ch. Charmin's Choice of Evenstar

```
                              ┌──────── CH. WOODLANE DAN PATCH
          ┌──────── Intl./Neth./Am. CH. CHARMIN CHARADE
          │                   └──────── CH. CHARMIN MISS CAROLYN
CH. CHARMIN'S CHOICE OF EVENSTAR
          │                   ┌──────── CH. KAMP'S KAPTAIN KOOL
          └──────── Evenstar's Spot Light
                              └──────── Charmin Sugar Plum, WD
```

Whelped: April 28, 1980
Breeder: Penny Hussey — Owner: Edna B. Peirce
Handlers: Ted Young, Jr. and David W. Roberts

Though "Skipper" has many group placements and specialty show wins, winning the Parti-Color Variety at the '83 American Spaniel Club Summer Specialty was his most meaningful win.

He is a very outgoing fellow as well as being a sound dog with excellent movement. He possesses a lovely coat of correct texture with deep red markings which help create a handsome picture. He has produced quality get in all of his litters though used on a limited basis.

Ch. Chess King's Board Boss

```
                          ┌──── CH. LUROLA'S LOOKOUT
            ┌──── CH. LUROLA'S ROYAL LANCER
            │             └──── Clarkdale Castaneye
CH. CHESS KING'S BOARD BOSS
            │             ┌──── CH. HAR-DEE'S HIGH SPIRIT
            └──── CH. RINKY DINK'S SERENDIPITY
                          └──── CH. RINKY DINK'S ROBIN
```

Whelped: October 13, 1975
Breeder: Billie and Chuck Ballantine — Owner: Billie Ballantine-Hayes
Handlers: Owner and Bob Covey

His greatest wins are numerous Best of Breeds including CSC of Arizona, Las Vegas, Orange County and Mission Valley.

Through his career, "Brogue" never failed to display his "show dog" attitude in the ring. He was retired early and finished his career with handler Bob Covey as the #1 Black and Tan in the nation and #3 all colors in 1978. Brogue has continued to give his all from the veterans class (shown by his owner) and has collected numerous BOV wins over top competition. His retirement from the veterans class ended with a Best Opposite Sex to Best of Variety win at the National Cocker Spaniel Specialty in Lincoln, Nebraska at 8½ years of age—and still flying around the ring!

Ch. Cottonwood's Congressman

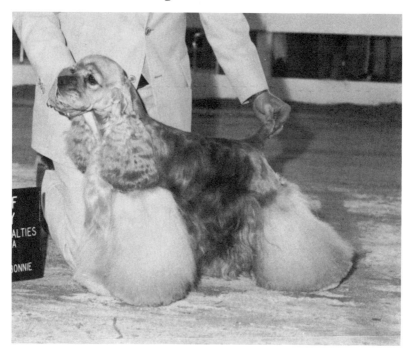

```
                        ┌──────── CH. LAMAR'S LONDON
           ┌──── CH. FORJAY'S WINTERWOOD
           │            └──────── Forjay's Buffie
CH. COTTONWOOD'S CONGRESSMAN
           │            ┌──────── CH. ATRU SANDPIPER
           └──── Lorli Gigi
                        └──────── Lorli's Matoaka
```

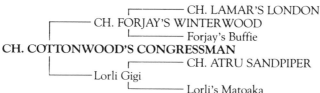

Whelped: January 2, 1976
Breeder/Owner: Calvin E. Ward
Handler: Charles Self

His greatest wins include 3 Group Firsts and numerous other placements. He won several Varieties at specialty shows.

However, his greatest fame came, not as a show dog, but as a producer of top show dogs. His get were top ASCOBs in '81, '82, '83 and '84. His daughter, Ch. Cottonwood's Colleen O'Brien was Best in Show at the January '82 ASC show, BOB at the July '82 ASC show and BOB at the January '83 ASC show. Another daughter, Ch. Makkell's Ziegfeld Girl was Best in Show at the January '84 ASC show.

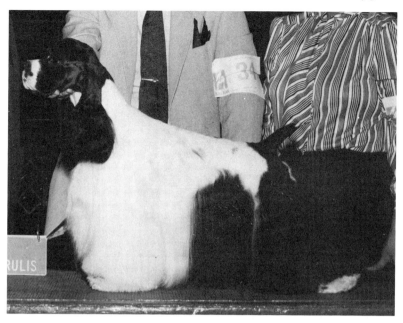

```
                              ┌──── Margon's Heads or Tails
          ┌──── CH. DAL-MAR'S DOUBLE DEALER
   ┌──                        └──── Kane Venture Meadowlark
CH. DAL-MAR'S BILLY JACK
   │                          ┌──── CH. REXPOINTE SHAZAM
   └──── Bancu Faith and Begorrah
                              └──── CH. SKYP-MITZ SNOW PRINCESS, CD
```

Whelped: May 19, 1982
Breeder: Donna Martin and Elaine McDonald
Owner: Donna Martin and Johnny J. Downing
Handlers: Donna Martin and Jeff Wright

"Billy" finished quickly and easily with four majors including two Bests of Variety over specials. Among his greatest wins include Best of Breed at the Heart of America Cocker Spaniel Club and Best of Opposite Sex to Best of Breed at the Zone 5 Specialty Show. Billy has accumulated over 20 BOVs and group placings in very limited showing.

Some of Billy's outstanding attributes include wonderful breed type with a gorgeous head, neck and shoulders. He has a short, hard back and a strong rear. He excels in showmanship and is passing these qualities on to his get.

Ch. Debonaire Dom Perignon

```
                           ┌──────── CH. DREAMRIDGE DIPLOMAT
            ┌──────── CH. DREAMRIDGE DOWNTOWN
    ┌───────┘              └──────── Candylane Cassandra
CH. DEBONAIRE DOM PERIGNON
    │                      ┌──────── CH. MAR JAC'S MISTER MANN
    └─────── Whisperwoods Sugar N Spice
                           └──────── Davis' Holiday Snowflake
```

Whelped: March 30, 1978
Breeder/Owner: Mrs. Deborah K. Bowman
Handler: Ron Fabis

Among "Perry's" most memorable wins were winning the Sporting Group three days in a row; Best of Breed at the CSC of the Midwest, Ohio Valley CSC, and The CSC of Eastern Missouri. Perhaps the most thrilling was Best in Show at the Sandemac Kennel Club.

Perry was the top-winning Parti-Color for '82. He is an upstanding, tall at the shoulder, compact dog with a sloping topline—standing and moving. He is a natural showman with spirit and an outgoing personality. His well-balanced head, correct angulation, and tremendous coat of proper texture completes the picture. Always a stable, well-rounded dog, Perry began his obedience career at six years of age and is enjoying it as much as he did the conformation ring. Perry is the sire of champions.

Can./Am. Ch. Denzil's Super Daddy

```
                          ┌──── CH. REXPOINTE FLYING DUTCHMAN
          ┌──── CH. EN MASSE LAST FLING
          │               └──── CH. MARCIE'S SCARLET O'HARA
Can./Am. CH. DENZIL'S SUPER DADDY
          │               ┌──── CH. BIRCHWOOD BANDITO
          └──── Nambut's Nun
                          └──── CH. BIRCHWOOD BANSHEE FLYNN
```

Whelped: February 10, 1977
Breeder: Denzilo W. E. Thorpe — Owner: Karen L. Marquez
Handlers: Bob Covey, Greg Anderson, Terry Stacy, Norman Austin

In his career he defeated more Parti-Colors in breed competition than any other in breed history. The record still stands. He was the second Tri-Color to win an all-breed Best in Show and among his greatest wins were Best of Breed at the American Spaniel Club at Boston, Best of Variety at the American Spaniel Club at Tampa. He is the top-winning Tri-Color in the history of the breed in both breed and group systems—having defeated over 15,000 sporting dogs.

Ch. Downy's Instigator

```
                                    ┌───── CH. RINKY DINK'S SIR LANCELOT
                     ┌───── CH. HARRISON'S PEEPING TOM
                     │              └───── Pineshadows Picturesque
CH. DOWNY'S INSTIGATOR
                     │              ┌───── CH. RINKY DINK'S SIR LANCELOT
                     └───── CH. RINKY DINK'S DOWNY'S VELVET
                                    └───── CH. ARTRU I'M A RINKY DINK
```

Whelped: September 17, 1980
Breeder/Owner: Mrs. Ronnie Muschal
Handler: Charles Self

In 1983, "Instigator" was the #1 Cocker Spaniel and the nation's #3 Sporting Dog. He won 11 Bests in Show, 5 Specialty Bests of Breed, 71 Group Firsts and 53 other Sporting Group placements.

Used at stud on a limited basis, he has sired a Best in Show and Best of Breed winners.

```
                          ┌──────── CH. REXPOINTE SNOW JOB
              ┌──────── CH. FEINLYNE FOOLISH PLEASURE
              │           └──────── CH. WOODSTOCK MAXI FEINLYNE
CH. FEINLYNE BY GEORGE
              │           ┌──────── CH. REXPOINTE SNOW JOB
              └──────── CH. FEINLYNE FONDUE
                          └──────── CH. FEINLYNE FLIRTATION
```

Whelped: August 15, 1976
Breeder/Owner: Al and Annette Davies
Handlers: Al Davies and Mike Kinschsular

"George" attained his championship from the Bred By Exhibitor class. He is a multiple Best in Show, Group and Best of Breed winner.

George excels in Cocker type and poise. Nothing rattles him. He has become one of the leading sires of the breed. He has won Best of Varieties over the age of seven years. He has been a source of pride and joy to his breeder/owners.

Ch. Frandee's Forgery

```
                          ┌─────── CH. CHESS KINGS BOARD BOSS
              ┌───── CH. FRANDEE'S FEDERAL AGENT
          ┌───┤            └─────── CH. FRANDEE'S PRIM N' PROPER
CH. FRANDEE'S FORGERY
          └───┤            ┌─────── CH. CH. FEINLYNE'S FOREMOST
              └───── CH. FEINLYNE FETCH AND GO
                           └─────── Feinlyne's B.J.
```

Whelped: December 7, 1981
Breeder: Karen Marquez — Owner: John and Dawn Zolezzi
Handler: Diana Kane

"Forgery's" greatest wins include Best in Show at the '87 ASC Annual Flushing Spaniel Specialty as well as numerous Bests of Breed and Group placements.

He has a short, hard back and shoulders that are well laid back. He has a strong rear with good length of leg. His coat is dense with proper texture. He has a very plush head with wide-set eyes and good expression. His showmanship is outstanding and he and Diana Kane make a superb team.

```
                              ┌────── CH. LUROLA'S ROYAL LANCER
              ┌────── CH. CHESS KING'S BOARD BOSS
              │               └────── CH. RINKY DINK'S SERENDIPITY
CH. FRANDEE'S TOP BRASS
              │               ┌────── CH. LUROLA'S SIR LAWRENCE
              └────── CH. FRANDEE'S PRIM 'N PROPER
                              └────── CH. MAR-JAC'S FRANDEE FOLLY
```

Whelped: December 7, 1978
Breeder: Mr. and Mrs. Frank Wood
Owner/Handler: Bob and Jan Covey

One of the top-winning dogs in American Spaniel Club history, "Brass" piled up numerous Best in Show and 17 Specialty Best of Breed wins. He won over 100 group placements including 38 Group Firsts. Brass' most memorable win was Best of Breed at the Cocker Spaniel Club of Las Vegas over 310 Cockers in competition.

He is balanced and sound with a lovely, refined head. He has clean shoulders with tremendous depth of forechest. His driving rear certainly calls attention to his sloping, firm topline. He moves as he stacks—well-balanced and with a hard back. Best of all, he has a happy, typical Cocker temperament. He has sired dozens of champions.

Ch. Glen Arden's Real McCoy

```
                        ┌───── CH. FRANDEE'S FEDERAL AGENT
        ┌───── CH. FRANDEE'S FORGERY
        │               └───── CH. FEINLYNE FETCH AND GO
CH. GLEN ARDEN'S REAL McCOY
        │               ┌───── CH. MEMOIR'S MARC IN THE DARK
        └───── Glen Arden's Molly McGee
                        └───── CH. GLEN ARDEN'S GINGER SNAPP
```

Whelped: July 23, 1983
Breeder: Dorothy M. McCoy and Arch T. McCoy
Owner: Dorothy McCoy
Handlers: Greg Anderson, Bob Covey and Mike & Linda Pitts

"Mac" won his first major from the 6–9 Puppy Dog class and was Best in Sweepstakes that same day as well. He won another major from the 9–12 Puppy Dog class. He won numerous sweepstakes and was finished at 13 months of age. All of his wins will be cherished by his breeder/owner but she has a special soft spot for his all-breed Bests in Show. He was ranked #1 Cocker for 1986 finals—Routledge System.

His get are making their presence known at recent specialties. He is truly a great dog with excellent temperament, type, balance and soundness. His breeder/owner is very proud of his accomplishments.

```
                          ┌──────── Am./Can. CH. HAR-DEE'S HIGH SPIRIT
            ┌──── CH. RINKY DINK'S SIR LANCELOT
    ┌               └──────── CH. RINKY DINK'S ROBIN
CH. HARRISON'S PEEPING TOM
    │               ┌──────── CH. MY CYN HEY RUBE
    └──────── Pineshadows Picturesque
                    └──────── CH. PINESHADOWS POKRASTANATOR
```

Whelped: February 1978
Breeder: Pauline Harrison — Owner: Mrs. Ronnie Muschal
Handler: Ted Young, Jr.

"Peeping Tom" had a sensational career which included 14 all-breed Bests in Show, 2 Specialty Bests of Breed, 54 Group Firsts and 58 other Sporting Group placements. In 1981, he was ranked the #1 Cocker Spaniel, was the nation's #1 Sporting Dog, was *Kennel Review's* Top Sporting Dog and was the winner of the Quaker Oats Award for most groups won in a year's time.

Though used at stud on a limited basis, he has sired a Best in Show and Best of Breed winners.

Ch. Homestead's McKiernan Shelby

```
                            ┌────── CH. FRANDEE'S DECLARATION
            ┌────── CH. FRANDEE'S BILL OF RIGHTS
            │               └────── Am./Mex. CH. FRANDEE'S SUSAN
CH. HOMESTEAD'S McKIERNAN SHELBY
            │               ┌────── CH. REXPOINTE SNOW JOB
            └────── Homestead's Snowbound
                            └────── Femme Fatale's Flirtatious
```

Whelped: January 29, 1981
Breeder: Bryan C. & Marleen Rickertsen and Paulette A. Swanson
Owner/Handler: Tim Kernan

"Shelby" was always owner/handled and among his many great wins were three Group Firsts and an all-breed Best in Show.

He is producing well with both specialty and group winners among his get.

Ch. Homestead's Ragtime Cowboy

```
                          ┌──────── CH. REXPOINTE FROSTEE DUTCHMAN
              ┌───── CH. REXPOINTE FLYING DUTCHMAN
    ┌──────┤            └────── Rexpointe Muriel
CH. HOMESTEAD'S RAGTIME COWBOY
    │                     ┌──────── CH. DREAMRIDGE DANDIMAN
    └───── Femme Fatale's Flirtatious
                          └─────── CH. FI-FO'S FEMME FATALE
```

Whelped: September 24, 1978
Breeder/Owner: Bryan C. and Marleen Rickertsen
Handlers: Owners, Charles Self and Charles Nash

"Joe" has won multiple Bests in Sweepstakes, Bests of Breed, Bests in Show and was ranked #1 Parti-Color in '81 after having been shown only six months that year. He won Best in Futurity at the '79 Summer National and sired the '80 BOS to Best in Futurity and Best Parti-Color in Futurity at the '84 specialty.

Joe is well known for his true Cocker temperament, his style and showmanship in the ring. These characteristics are evident in his offspring.

Ch. Homestead's Windjammer

```
                        ┌──────── CH. PINER'S POINT OF VIEW
            ┌──────── CH. WINDY HILL'S MAKES-ITS-POINT
            │           └──────── CH. WINDY HILL'S 'TIS DEMI-TASSE
CH. HOMESTEAD'S WINDJAMMER
            │           ┌──────── CH. REXPOINTE SNOW JOB
            └──────── Homestead's Snowbound
                        └──────── Femme Fatale's Flirtatious
```

Whelped: June 10, 1979
Breeder/Owner/Handler: Bryan C. and Marleen Rickertsen

"JR" finished at nine months of age with four majors and a Best in Sweepstakes. He was the #2 Parti-Color in '82 and was a multiple Group winner. He is the sire of the '83 Parti-Color Best and Best of Opposite Sex in Futurity.

JR is the product of a Parti and black and tan breeding. He is noted for his smooth, effortless sporting gait. His sound, well-angulated front and rear account for this long, easy stride. He produces these sporting qualities in all three varieties.

Ch. Hu-Mar's Good As Gold

```
                              ┌──────CH. COTTONWOOD'S CONGRESSMAN
              ┌──────CH. PALM HILL CARO-BU'S SOLID GOLD
              │               └──────CH. PALM HILL TIGER LILY, C.D.
CH. HU-MAR'S GOOD AS GOLD
              │               ┌──────CH. PINER'S POINT OF VIEW
              └──────CH. PALM HILL HU-MAR'S WILDFIRE
                              └──────CH. PALM HILL TIGER LILY, C.D.
```

Whelped: August 9, 1984
Breeder/Owner: Marilyn C. & Hugh B. Spacht
Handler: Kyle Robinson

"Floyd's" greatest win was his first Best in Show under Ted Young, Jr. . . . the first Cocker Spaniel he had given the Best in Show award to. Floyd finished 1987 as the #2 Cocker in the nation.

Floyd is an outstanding showman gifted with an even temperament. He shows all out. He knows he's on display and makes the most of it. He is another in the line of great Hu-Mar champions.

Ch. Hu-Mar's Regal Cottonwood

```
                              ┌─────── CH. FORJAY'S WINTERWOOD
                 ┌─────── CH. COTTONWOOD'S CONGRESSMAN
                 │            └─────── Lorli Gigi
CH. HU-MAR'S REGAL COTTONWOOD
                 │            ┌─────── CH. PINER'S POINT OF VIEW
                 └─────── CH. PALM HILL HU-MAR'S WILDFIRE
                              └─────── CH. PALM HILL'S TIGER LILY, CD
```

Whelped: August 14, 1982
Breeder: Hugh and Marilyn Spacht — Owner: Pat and Betty Peck
Handler: Charles Self

"Bo" was the #1 ASCOB during his year of campaigning. In all, he won eight all-breed Bests in Show, 22 Group Firsts, over 20 Group placements, and two specialty Bests of Breed. Among his greatest wins was Best of Variety at Westminster Kennel Club and his first Best in Show his third time out as a special.

He is of correct type, has a beautiful head and proper coat texture. He moves with a hard, sloping topline. He held the record for the most Best in Shows for a Congressman get.

Can./Am. Ch. Jaywyck's The One 'N Only

```
                          ┌──── CH. BUCKLODGE QUALPOINT BYLINE
          ┌──── Can./Am. CH. BAR MAR'S GIN RICKY
          │               └──── Bar Mar's Brandy
Can./Am. CH. JAYWYCK'S THE ONE 'N ONLY
          │               ┌──── Can./Am. CH. ISLE VIEW'S HO HUM
          └────Can./Am. CH. ISLE VIEW'S TRI MY FANCY, Can./Am. CDX
                          └──── Isle View's Krackers
```

Whelped: April 15, 1980
Breeder/Owner: Judith Wick Klepp
Handler: David L. Kittredge

"Jarrett" is a multiple-group and specialty Best of Breed winner in both the United States and Canada.

His masculine head, smooth shoulders, short, hard back and driving rear are assets he passes on to his offspring. His children and grandchildren are out winning groups, Best of Breeds and even Best in Shows in the United States, Canada and South Africa. In 1982, Jarrett made the Top Ten Parti-Color as rated by *American Cocker Magazine* and #8 Parti-Color according to *Kennel Review's* system. Jarrett takes his place at Jaywycks as the #1 stud dog and dabbles in obedience when time allows.

Ch. Juban's Georgia Jazz

```
                          ┌──────── CH. REXPOINTE KOJAK
            ┌──── CH. KAMPS' KAPTAIN KOOL
            │             └──────── CH. MIRWIN'S MERRY MISS
CH. JUBAN'S GEORGIA JAZZ
            │             ┌──────── CH. CANDYLANE CADET
            └──── Norrisim's No Choice
                          └──────── Norrisim's Georgian Ginger
```

Whelped: March 21, 1979
Breeder: Julian and Ann Smith — Owner: Charles and Jackie Rowe
Handler: Charles Rowe

"Jazz" completed his championship in four consecutive shows with four majors including the Summer National CSC Specialty, in July 1980. He has won numerous Bests of Variety at specialty shows and is a multiple Best of Breed winner at many large specialty shows. He has well over 20 Group placements. His greatest win was Best of Breed at the CSC of Southern California in '83. He was the #1 Parti-Color in '83.

Jazz has probably one of the most elegant heads ever seen on a Cocker. He is well-balanced and moves effortlessly using his powerful rear correctly. Jazz was the model used by the artist who designed the AKC 100th Anniversary postage stamp. He is a joy to own and looks like he will be a top producer. To top it all off, he has a great disposition.

```
                            ┌──────── CH. BURSON'S STYLEMASTER
             ┌──── CH. BURSON'S DESPERADO
             │              └──────── CH. JUBAN'S JORGEY GIRL
Can./Am. CH. JUBAN'S JOVAN
             │              ┌──────── CH. KAMP'S KAPTAIN KOOL
             └──── CH. JUBAN'S JOY IN THE MORNING
                            └──────── Norrisim's No Choice
```

Whelped: April 18, 1983
Breeder: Ann M. Smith — Owner: Mrs. Ronnie Muschal
Handler: Marty Flugel

"Joey" was a Group winner as well as a specialty Best in Show winner. In 1985, he was Best in Show at the American Spaniel Club National Specialty over the largest Cocker Spaniel entry in history. This same year he also earned his Canadian championship.

Ch. Judi-Jer's Winter's Black Touch

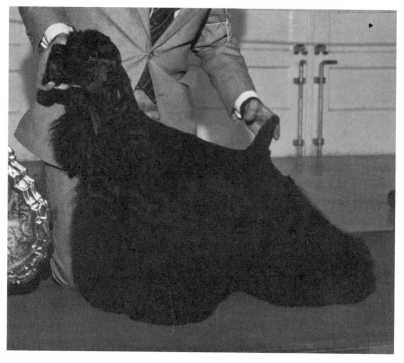

```
                            ┌───────── CH. LAMAR'S LONDON
              ┌──────── CH. FORJAY'S WINTERWOOD
              │             └──────── Forjay's Buffie
CH. JUDI-JER'S WINTER'S BLACK TOUCH
              │             ┌───────── CH. SILVER MAPLE TOUCH O'TIGER
              └──────── Judi-Jer's Roxxy of Rockdale
                            └──────── Twyneff Small Talk
```

Whelped: July 28, 1980
Breeder/Owner: Gerald and Judith Roesel
Handler: Donald Johnston

His greatest win was Best in Show at Goldcoast KC at 14 months of age. He finished at 11 months of age, undefeated. At the same age he was Best Opposite Sex to Best of Breed. A number of top bitches were bred to him. He is a tribute to his pedigree. His name will live in his numerous champion offspring. His head was his glory . . . a true Cocker head in every way.

Intl./Mex./Am. Ch. Kapewood Prince Matchabelli

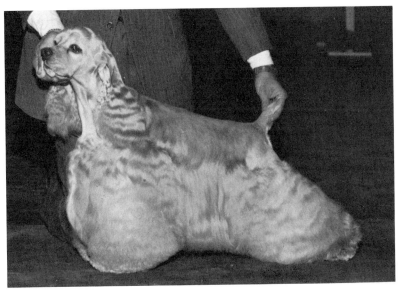

```
                          ┌──────── CH. ARTRU JOHNNY-BE-GOOD
              ┌──────── CH. ARTRU RED BARON
      ┌       │          └──────── Artru Kathleen
Intl./Mex./Am. CH. KAPEWOOD PRINCE MATCHABELLI
      │                  ┌──────── CH. ARTRU JAN-MYR'S JUPITER
      └──────────Kapewood Emeraude's Escapade
                         └──────── CH. ARTRU EMERAUDE
```

Whelped: September 30, 1976
Breeder: Kathryn Brian — Owner: Rune and Robin Enos Nilsson
Handlers: Charles Nash and Owners

"Matches" won 23 all-breed Bests in Show and 77 Sporting Group Firsts. Two of his greatest wins were Best of Variety at American Spaniel Club's '78 Summer National and Best of Opposite Sex to Best of Variety at the '84 ASC Summer National from the veterans class.

He obtained his International and Mexican championships in four shows by winning four Groups and a Best in Show as a class dog.

He was stolen at a show in November of '79 and was stripped of his coat. Luckily, he was recovered and returned to the ring a year later to win seven of his Bests in Show and 17 Groups including one Best in Show and eight Groups owner/handled. He is truly a great dog with a fascinating story of successes and triumphs!

Ch. Kaplar's Jiminey Kricket

```
                              ┌──────── CH. KAPLAR'S KON MAN
              ┌──── CH. KAPLAR'S MUSIC MAN
       ┌──────┤                └──────── CH. KAPLAR'S KOLLEEN
CH. KAPLAR'S JIMINEY KRICKET
       └──────┤                ┌──────── CH. KAPLAR'S KASSANOVA
              └──── CH. ROANN'S RUFFLES 'N FLOURISHES
                               └──────── CH. ROANN'S ROSY GLO
```

Whelped: September 9, 1984
Breeder: Robert & Ann Clement
Owner: Deryck & Christine Boutlier and Laura Henson
Handler: Greg Anderson

"Jimmy" has many all-breed Bests in Show and Group placings as well as Bests of Breed at specialty shows. His greatest win to date was Best in Show at the American Spaniel Club in 1985.

Jimmy is well-balanced, beautifully headed and is a strong moving dog with substance. He has a beautiful, correct coat.

Ch. Laurim's Tri Performance

```
                        ┌─────── CH. WINDY HILL'S MAKES-ITS-POINT
             ┌─────── CH. HOMESTEAD'S WINDJAMMER
    ┌──────  │        └─────── Homestead's Snowbound
CH. LAURIM'S TRI PERFORMANCE
    │                   ┌─────── CH. FRANDEE'S DECLARATION
    └──────── CH. LAURIM'S STARFLIGHT
                        └─────── CH. LAURIM'S STAR PERFORMANCE
```

Whelped: January 1, 1982
Breeder/Owner/Handler: Dr. James R. and Laurabeth Duncan

"Beau" was ranked #4 Parti-Color in 1984. Among his most exciting wins was Best of Variety at the American Spaniel Club Futurity in 1983 and a Group First at the Richland County Kennel Club.

Beau's extreme type is the culmination of over 40 years of breeding Cocker Spaniels for the Duncans who feel he has much to offer as a stud dog. Many of his get are doing extremely well.

Ch. Lyndale's Artru Skypilot

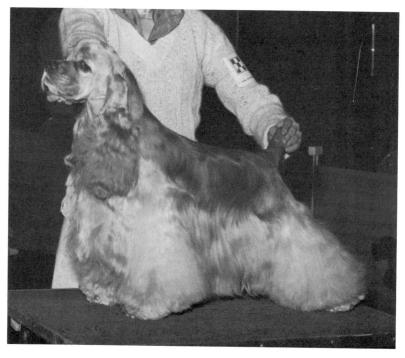

```
                              ┌──────── CH. ATRU RED BARON
              ┌───── CH. ARTRU SKYJACK
              │               └──────── CH. ARTRU TRINKET
CH. LYNDALE'S ARTRU SKYPILOT
              │               ┌──────── CH. ARTRU LA TOKA MASTERPIECE
              └───── CH. ARTRU TIFFANY OF LYNDALE
                              └──────── Gina's Powder Mist
```

Whelped: December 10, 1979
Breeder/Owner: Lynne Mahrle
Handlers: Barbara Gamache, Kyle Robinson, Marty Flugel, Mike Kinschsular

"Sonny's" greatest wins include Best of Breed at Meadowbrook CSC and many Group placements.

He is a multiple Group and Variety winner himself but, more important, he is also an outstanding producer. He is a credit to his outstanding pedigree and has been a joy to own and show. He has a constant and "sunny" disposition.

Ch. Marquis It's The One

```
                            ┌──────── CH. REXPOINTE SHAZAM
            ┌──────── Marquis Black Shazam
            │                └──────── CH. FEINLYNE FETCH AND GO
CH. MARQUIS IT'S THE ONE
            │                ┌──────── CH. MARQUIS HERE COMES TROUBLE
            └──────── Designer's French Lace
                             └──────── Marquis Mistletoe
```

Whelped: January 14, 1984
Breeder: Stella and Steve Honeycutt — Owner: Karen L. Marquez
Handlers: Kyle Robinson, Tom Campbell, Wilson Pike,
Charles Nash, Ron Buxton

"Laz's" greatest wins include Best of Breed at three Cocker specialties; Best of Variety at the '84 January Spaniel Club at 11 months of age and five Bests in Sweepstakes. He was the #1 Parti-Color (all systems) in '84.

He became a champion at nine months of age by virtue of being a very tall, short-backed dog that is long necked with tremendous stride.

Ch. Milru's Arabian Knight

```
                          ┌────── CH. KORY'S KLEIGHLIGHT
           ┌───── CH. MILRU'S KISMET TOO
           │              └────── CH. MILRU'S CANDY KISS
CH. MILRU'S ARABIAN KNIGHT
           │              ┌────── CH. WHITE DEER'S SCOTCH GUARD
           └───── Am./Bda. CH. MILRU'S TANANDORABLE
                          └────── Am./Bda. CH. MILRU'S HONEY O'GINA
```

Whelped: March 2, 1981
Breeder/Owner: Ruth C. Muller
Handler: David Roberts

"Topper's" greatest win was Best of Breed at the New York Western Cocker Spaniel Specialty. He had many group placements including four Group Firsts.

His breeder/owner is justifiably proud of him as she had bred most of the dogs in his background and he's a joy to own. She was thrilled to watch him in motion . . . flawlessly moving on a loose lead with his head held high. He lends his natural showmanship and beauty to his get.

Ch. Palm Hill's Mountain Ashe

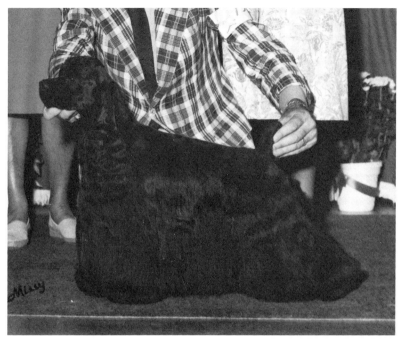

```
                             ┌────── CH. WINDY HILL'S 'TIS DEMI'S DEMON
                ┌──────CH. BOBWIN'S SIR ASHLEY
                │            └────── Ashley's Cherry Jubilee
CH. PALM HILL'S MOUNTAIN ASHE
                │            ┌────── CH. SHANNONDALE SAFARI
                └──────CH. PALM HILL'S CONVIVIALITY
                             └────── Palm Hill's Heartbreaker
```

Whelped: December 14, 1981
Breeder: deForest F. Jurkiewicz — Owner: Estate of Gladys W. Hoffman
Handler: Jerry Moon

In "Ashe's" first year out as a special he won Best in Show at three all-breed shows. Other great wins include: Best Opposite Sex to Best of Breed at '83 ASC Summer Show, Best of Breed at Washington State CSC, Best Opposite Sex to Best of Breed at the Lincoln-Council Bluff Specialty. He also had numerous Group wins and Best of Variety wins.

Truly a "true" Sporting Dog.

Ch. Palm Hill Caro-Bu's Solid Gold

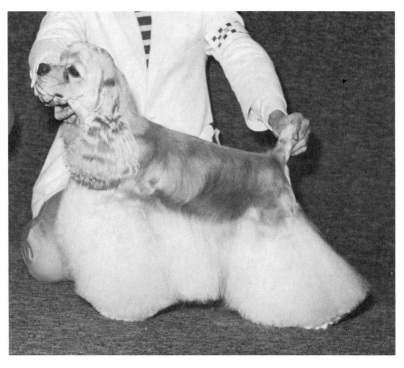

```
                              ┌───── CH. FORJAY'S WINTERWOOD
                  ┌───── CH. COTTONWOOD'S CONGRESSMAN
                  │           └───── Lorli's Gigi
CH. PALM HILL CARO-BU'S SOLID GOLD
                  │           ┌───── CH. KAMP'S SILVERSMITH
                  └───── CH. PALM HILL TIGER LILY, CD
                              └───── CH. HU-MAR'S HANKY PANKY, CD
```

Whelped: October 25, 1981
Breeder: deForest Jurkiewicz and Carolyn Emmerke
Owner: Hugh and Marilyn Spacht
Handlers: Charles Self and Greg Anderson

"Dreamer" had an exceptional show record in the short time he was campaigned. His happy-go-lucky spirit was passed on to his get as is evidenced by the fact that they, too, have had Group placings.

Dreamer has that "show ring" personality which made him very attractive to both the judges and the ringside. He has a great deal to offer to the Cocker fancy such as a beautiful head, correct topline and hard back. His puppies are exhibiting these same good features.

Ch. Rinky Dink's Bit Of Action

```
                        ┌─────── CH. ARTRU ACTION
          ┌────── CH. PINER'S PREMEDITATED
          │             └─────── CH. RINKY DINK'S PINERS EVERLOVIN'
CH. RINKY DINK'S BIT OF ACTION
          │             ┌─────── CH. ARTRU SKYJACK
          └────── CH. LANEL'S RINKY DINK'S M AND M
                        └─────── CH. RINKY DINK'S LANEL'S CINNAMON
```

Whelped: May 21, 1980
Breeder: William and Jean Petersen
Owner: Jeam Petersen and Darlene Matas
Handlers: Ron Fabis, Charles Self and Don Johnston

Among this dog's greatest wins was Best in Show at Mason City, Iowa and being a finalist in the Kennel Review Tournament of Champions. He was the #5 ASCOB in '83. As a puppy he had a number of big Sweepstakes wins.

He has a lot of showmanship and movement provided by an excellent front and rear, long neck and smooth shoulders. He is passing these attributes on to his get. He is a nice sporting dog.

Ch. Riviera's Oh Riley

```
                                  ┌────── CH. FRANDEE'S FEDERAL AGENT
                  ┌─── CH. FRANDEE'S FORGERY
                  │               └────── CH. FEINLYNE FETCH AND GO
CH. RIVIERA'S OH RILEY
                  │               ┌────── CH. KAPLAR'S KASSANOVA
                  └─── CH. JOYWALK'S CRESTWOOD CAMEO
                                  └────── CH. JOYWALK'S MOONBEAM
```

Whelped: May 23, 1985
Breeder: Faron & Nancee Long — Owner: Cheryl & Daryl Forker
Handlers: Mike and Linda Pitts

"Riley" won Best in Show at the 1988 Flushing Spaniel Specialty and was one of 1987's top winners. He has won two all-breed Bests in Show, three specialty Bests of Breed, eight Group Firsts, 24 group placements and over 42 Bests of Variety . . . all this and he's only just begun! Riley is a very handsome black dog with a bright future.

Ch. Rowingdale's Excalibur

```
                              ┌──────── CH. KAMPS' KAPTAIN KOOL
                 ┌──────── CH. JUBAN'S GEORGIA JAZZ
                 ┌          └──────── Norrisim's No Choice
CH. ROWINGDALE'S EXCALIBUR
                 │              ┌──────── CH. JIMNAN KID TARRAGON
                 └──────── CH. LOW DESERT THANKS A MILLION
                                └──────── Jimnan's Bit-O-Honey
```

Whelped: January 7, 1983
Breeders: Charles and Jackie Rowe — Owner: Gini Goetz
Handler: Charles Rowe

"Cal" did not start his show career until he was almost three years old. However, once started, his career took off like a rocket. He is a Best in Show winner, took Best of Opposite Sex to Best of Breed at the '86 Summer National Cocker Spaniel Specialty and then Best of Breed at the Cocker Spaniel Club of Arizona. His numerous Best of Variety wins were all in terrific competition.

Cal has a loyal army of people who have named him "Mr. Showman." He loves the bigger group ring and shows his best in an open area. He is a consistent showman. He has a great heart and is an intelligent, loving Cocker. This is a dog who will make his mark on the breed through his winning offspring.

Ch. Satinwood Synchronicity

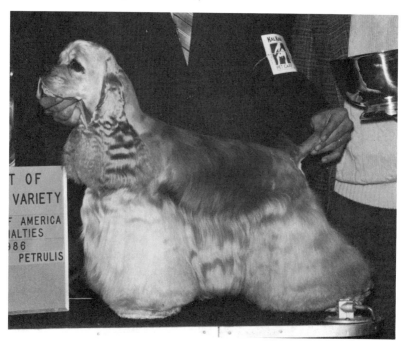

```
                              ┌──────CH. ATRU EPISODE
              ┌──────Am./Can. CH. ARTRU ATTENTION
              │               └──────Artru Sans Pure Sterling
CH. SATINWOOD SYNCHRONICITY
              │               ┌────── CH. ALORAHS ARTFUL DODGER
              └──────Alorah's Aglow
                              └────── Butch's You'll Like It
```

Whelped: March 4, 1984
Breeder: Deborah Truscott — Owner: Bob Werrbach
Handler: Bob Roundtree

"Slick" had numerous wins of import but among his greatest were Best in Show at Clearwater Kennel Club; Best in Show at Central Florida Kennel Club; Best of Breed at Heart of America Cocker Spaniel Club's '86 and '87 Specialty; Best of Breed at the Cocker Spaniel Club of Southeast Florida; Best of Breed at the Cocker Spaniel Club of San Antonio; and Best of Breed at the Houston Combined Specialty.

Slick is producing Canadian and American champion get.

Ch. Shenanigans O'Balderdash

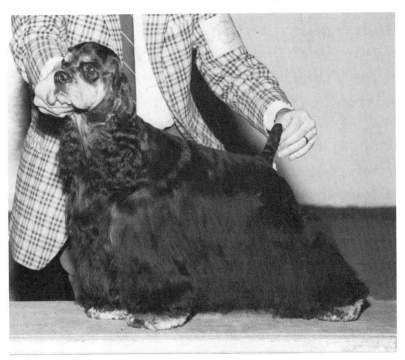

```
                            ┌────── CH. SHANNONDALE SAFARI
              ┌────── CH. BUTCH'S KOUNTRY BOY
              │             └────── CH. HEYDAY DUCAT
CH. SHENANIGANS O'BALDERDASH
              │             ┌────── CH. LUROLA'S ROYAL LANCER
              └────── CH. SHENANIGANS OF A RAGAMUFFIN
                            └────── CH. SHENANIGANS OF A REDHEAD
```

Whelped: February 24, 1979
Breeder/Owner: Gyn Gerhardt
Handlers: Ted Young, Jr., David Roberts and Bryan Rickertsen

"Balderdash" had a very limited specials career of one year at four years of age. In that year, he won one all-breed Best in Show, and was twice Best of Breed at the Omaha-Council Bluffs Cocker Spaniel Club.

He is siring multiple champion litters and his offspring are also sweepstakes and group winners. His first-born pup was the winner of the American Spaniel Club's National Futurity held in Boston.

Although a dedicated constant companion, he was able to make the transition from show ring to house dog to specials competition and back to house dog an easy adjustment. Home to stay, Balderdash finished #7 top-winning Cocker in 1983.

Ch. Tamburlaine Cirkle C Nugget

```
                          ┌────── CH. BOBWIN'S SIR ASHLEY
              ┌────── CH. SIR DUFFINGTON OF FLAIRHAVEN
              │           └────── CH. SPRINGTIME I'M A RHYME
CH. TAMBURLAINE CIRKLE C NUGGET
              │           ┌────── CH. KAMP'S SILVERSMITH
              └────── Tamburlaine's Tickled Silver
                          └────── Tamburlaine's Tickled Pink
```

Whelped: December 10, 1980
Breeder: Paula J. Rambo — Owner: Mary E. Ford & William A. Ford, Jr.
Handlers: Carolyn Phelps, Susie Stiles, Kyle Robinson and Ann Marshall

"Ben's" greatest wins include Best of Variety, '83 Westminster and more than 20 Group placements. His most outstanding attribute is his merry disposition. He never meets a stranger—greeting everyone as a long, lost friend. He delights in showing in the group. The bigger the ring, the better he shows. His patience with other dogs is seldom taxed . . . he remains cool and collected at all times.

```
                           ┌──────── CH. DAL MAR'S DOUBLE DEALER
              ┌──────── CH. DAL MAR'S BILLY JACK
      ┌                   └──────── Bancu Faith And Begorrah
CH. TERJE'S THUNDERBOLT
      └                   ┌──────── CH. SHADON SUGAR BEAR OF SWANK
              └──────── CH. SWANK'S SHORT 'N SWEET
                          └──────── Swank's September Song
```

Whelped: October 3, 1983
Breeder: Jeff Wright — Owner: Carol and Larry Dixon
Handler: Linda Pitts

"Jack's" greatest wins include a Best in Show at Marion, Ohio; Bests of Breed at the Cocker Spaniel Club of Dallas and Cocker Spaniel Club of Chattanooga as well as numerous Group Firsts and placements throughout his year and a half specials career.

Jack culminates a lengthy search for a Parti-Color dog to special. Not only does he possess correct conformation and breed type, he is sound, open-marked, of stable temperament, has "attitude" galore and (above all) presents himself with true, correct, sporting dog movement.

Ch. Victoria's Irish Dandy

```
                          ┌──────── CH. CHESS KING'S BOARD BOSS
            ┌──────── CH. FRANDEE'S TOP BRASS
            │             └──────── CH. FRANDEE'S PRIM 'N PROPER
CH. VICTORIA'S IRISH DANDY
            │             ┌──────── CH. SIR DUFFINGTON OF FLAIRHAVEN
            └──────── CH. BACHTEL'S CRATER CRITTER
                          └──────── Bobwin's Lady Petite
```

Whelped: December 12, 1982
Breeder: Lois Livingston — Owner: Ron and Anne Weinstock
Handlers: Bryan and Marleen Rickertsen

"Irish" was #1 Cocker and #5 Sporting Dog in the 1986 *Kennel Review* and Routledge Systems. Some of his greatest wins were 10 all-breed Bests in Show.

His outstanding attributes are his elegance combined with substance. He has a gorgeous head and eye appeal along with the easy movement of a true sporting dog. He was equally appealing to both breeder judges and all-around sporting judges. His temperament is superb and is the finest companion dog ever to be owned by the Weinstocks.

Ch. Windchimes Gold 'N Bold

```
                          ┌────── CH. ARTRU RED BARON
            ┌────── CH. ARTRU JAN-MYR ROCKY
            │             └────── CH. JAN-MYR'S MELODY OF LOVE
CH. WINDCHIMES GOLD 'N BOLD
            │             ┌────── CH. ARTRU SKYJACK
            └────── CH. ARTRU GOOD AS GOLD
                          └────── Gina's Powder Mist
```

Whelped: February 8, 1980
Breeder: Paul Hadfield
Owner/Handlers: Paul Hadfield and Lyn Rickertsen

"Chipper" finished with four majors and a Best in Sweepstakes. He was the #2 ASCOB in 1982 handled by 14-year old co-owner, Lyn. In 1983, the team of Lyn and Chipper were ranked as #2 Jr. Handler in the Nation. He had multiple Best of Breed and Group wins and placements as well as one all-breed Best in Show.

Chipper is well known as a small dog with a lot of heart. He is the epitome of the showy Cocker when he flies around the ring with the ideal Cocker topline. His puppies exhibit his temperament and movement as is evidenced by his get winning both Best and Best Opposite Sex in Futurity at the 1983 Futurity as well as Best in Futurity in 1984.

Ch. Woodlane Dan Patch

```
                              ┌─────── CH. DREAMRIDGE DOMINOE
                 ┌─────── CH. PETT'S YACHTSMAN
                 │             └─────── Pett's Lady Laurel
CH. WOODLANE DAN PATCH
                 │             ┌─────── CH. BE GAY'S SUPERMAN
                 └─────── Woodlane Tangerine
                               └─────── Indian Rock's English Muffin
```

Whelped: July 14, 1974
Breeder/Owner: Kenneth E. Keach
Handler: Ted Young, Jr.

"Dan Patch" retired the Cocker Spaniel Club of Rhode Island's Best Parti-Color Challenge Bowl in three consecutive years—1976, 1977 and 1978. He also was Best of Breed at the American Spaniel Club's Zone I show in 1976.

He is dominant for correct neck and shoulder placement, short hard backs and powerful driving rear ends. He moved effortlessly as a sporting dog should.

CHAPTER *2*

Great Winning Bitches
of the Recent Past

The twenty-four Cocker Spaniels pictured in this chapter are some of America's top-winning female champions in the recent past.

Though unable to depict *every* top-winning female Cocker, this representative sampling of winning Cockers in all three Varieties portrays an image of some of the best that America had to offer during the last decade or so.

A top-winning bitch of the 60's—Ch. Sagamore Toccoa.

Ch. Birchwood Bric-A-Brac

```
                                    ┌──────── CH. DREAMRIDGE DOMINOE
                    ┌──────── CH. BIRCHWOOD BACHARACH
                    │              └──────── CH. LUCK'S TRI TO REMEMBER
CH. BIRCHWOOD BRIC-A-BRAC
                    │              ┌──────── CH. DREAMRIDGE DOMINOE
                    └──────── Birchwood Butterscotch
                                   └──────── Rexpointe Tina Maria
```

Whelped: February 21, 1972
Breeder: D. S. Harrison — Owner: Cindy Mueller
Handler: Bill Ernst

"Fanci" was the top-winning Parti-Color bitch in 1974. In nine months of showing, she won 42 Bests of Variety and two Bests of Opposite Sex to Best of Breed.

Fanci became famous as the "no hands girl" . . . she turned herself into a statue when Bill set her up. She had the ability to stand free on a loose lead for judging, arranging herself in a perfect show pose when Bill said "fix yourself." Her greatest wins include BOS to BV at the American Spaniel Club's '75 National and BOV at Westminster—both wins to resounding applause. She was, indeed, "special."

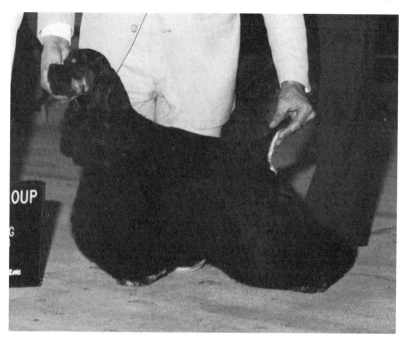

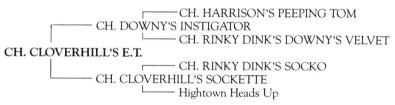

```
                               ┌──── CH. HARRISON'S PEEPING TOM
                  ┌───── CH. DOWNY'S INSTIGATOR
      ┌─────      │         └──── CH. RINKY DINK'S DOWNY'S VELVET
CH. CLOVERHILL'S E.T.
      │                  ┌──── CH. RINKY DINK'S SOCKO
      └───── CH. CLOVERHILL'S SOCKETTE
                         └──── Hightown Heads Up
```

Whelped: April 16, 1982
Breeder/Owner: Robert S. Roundtree — Owner: Breeder and Michael Pitts
Handler: Michael Pitts

"E.T.," started an eleven month limited career by winning back-to-back Group Firsts and then went on to win Best in Show at the Memphis Cocker Spaniel Club. But it was on September 1, 1984 that E.T. made breed history . . . she became the first Black and Tan Cocker in the history of the breed to win an all-breed Best in Show.

She is an extremely typey and feminine bitch. She is truly a short-backed bitch with a beautiful head and expression. Overall, she is a well-balanced bitch—enabling her to be a very powerful mover with excellent front and rear extension.

Ch. Cottonwood's Colleen O'Brien

```
                                ┌─────── CH. FORJAY'S WINTERWOOD
                  ┌─────── CH. COTTONWOOD'S CONGRESSMAN
       ┌          └─────── Lorli Gigi
CH. COTTONWOOD'S COLLEEN O'BRIEN
       │                  ┌─────── CH. LA MAR'S IVORY HAZE
       └────── CH. O'BRIEN'S ERIN GO BRAUGH
                          └─────── Our Sassy Irish Girl
```

Whelped: October 8, 1978
Breeder: Mary Ann and George F. O'Brien — Owner: Judith Case
Handler: Don Johnston

"Annie" won a host of shows, including four Bests of Breed and one Best in Show at the American Spaniel Club. She also won an all-breed Best in Show, 18 Group Firsts and multiple Group placements.

With her faultless movement, beautiful conformation, showmanship plus, and big, dark eyes (designed to melt the hardest hearts), Annie won under the best of them. She is equally as special as a daily friend and companion. She is proving herself as a producer as well.

Ch. Dal-Mar's Sevelle

```
                              ┌──────── CH. DAL-MAR'S DOUBLE DEALER
              ┌──────── CH. DAL-MAR'S BILLY JACK
              │               └──────── Bancu Faith and Begorrah
CH. DAL-MAR'S SEVELLE
              │               ┌──────── CH. DANANN'S HARD TIMES BANKER
              └──────── CH. FRAN DAL-MAR HARD TIMES AMANDA
                              └──────── Dal-Mar's Candylane Keepsake
```

Whelped: March 29, 1984
Breeder: Donna Martin and Jim Francis
Owner: Charles & Donna Harrington and Johnny J. Downing
Handler: Donna Martin-Harrington

Among "Sevelle's" greatest wins was in October 1985 when she won an all-breed Best in Show at the Wichita Kennel Club. She also was Best of Breed at the Austin Cocker Spaniel Club and the Lone Star Cocker Spaniel Club in 1986. To win Best Opposite Sex to BOV at the American Spaniel Club in January of '86 was also a thrill for her breeder/owner/handler.

Sevelle has outstanding movement, a short back, terrific attitude and a straight, hard coat. She is a fifth-generation Dal-Mar champion.

Ch. Eli Fran's Durspen Delight

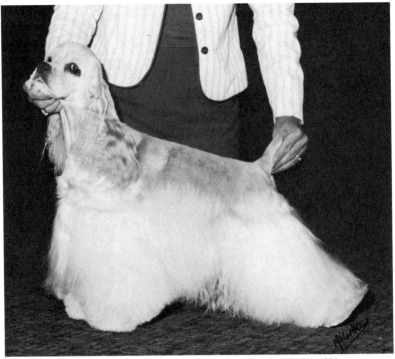

```
                                    ┌───── CH. MOJO MIGHTY MACK
                    ┌───── CH. HARLANHAVEN'S HIGH AND MIGHTY
                    │                └───── CH. TRI L TIARA
CH. ELI FRAN'S DURSPEN DELIGHT
                    │                ┌───── CH. KAPEWOOD'S COTY
                    └───── CH. ELI-FRAN'S DIANE
                                     └───── CH. PETT'S SILVERDREAM
```

Whelped: November 28, 1981
Breeder: Frank O. Pouder and Terry Seaton
Owner: Durla C. Spencer and Terry Seaton
Handlers: Kyle Robinson and Marleen Rickertsen

"Delight's" biggest win was at the Las Vegas Cocker Spaniel Club on the Summer National weekend in 1983 where she was Best Opposite Sex to Best of Breed. With only six months of showing, Delight ended up as #3 ASCOB bitch in the nation.

She was truly a "delight" for everyone of her many friends and supporters. She moved correctly and with true show spirit. In July of 1984, Delight died of heartworm infestation. She left behind many wonderful memories and three puppies.

Ch. Frandee's Celebration

```
                          ┌──── CH. PETT'S HANDSOME HARRY
            ┌──── CH. FRANDEE'S DECLARATION
   ┌        └──── CH. FRANDEE'S MISS INDEPENDENCE
CH. FRANDEE'S CELEBRATION
   │                      ┌──── Sonata's Holiday Caper
   └──── CH. FRANDEE'S SUSAN
                          └──── CH. CORWIN DIAMOND LIL'
```

Whelped: March 26, 1976
Breeder/Owner: Frank and Dee Dee Wood
Handler: Dee Dee Wood

"Celebration's" first big show win was a Best of Variety from the Open Class for a major over 5 specials. She went on to win a Group Fourth. She won the only Senior Futurity ever sponsored by the American Spaniel Club in July of '77. She was the top-winning Parti-Color in the nation in 1978.

She had four litters with a total of 14 puppies. Ten of her pups have become champions, with one son (Ch. Frandee's Footprint) becoming a Best in Show winner. She was a joy to own and to show! She was beautifully balanced and maintained condition easily. She was a terrific mother and a delightful house dog. What more could anyone ask or want? She died in 1983 of kidney failure. She was greatly loved and is greatly missed!

Ch. Junebug Southern Lace

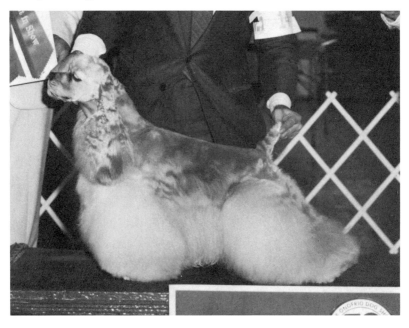

```
                      ┌─────── CH. FORJAY'S WINTERWOOD
          ┌────── CH. COTTONWOOD'S CONGRESSMAN
          │           └─────── Lorli Gigi
CH. JUNEBUG SOUTHERN LACE
          │           ┌─────── CH. SAGAMORE JUNEBUG
          └────── CH. JUNEBUG BRENDA STAR
                      └─────── CH. SAGAMORE JUNEBUG SENSATION
```

Whelped: April 20, 1982
Breeder: Mrs. Mike Biddle — Owner: Nan M. Warren and Mrs. Mike Biddle
Handler: Donald Johnston

"Lacey" has won three all-breed Bests in Show, two specialty Bests of Breed and 52 Bests of Variety—one of which was at the American Spaniel Club Summer National in 1984. Her first Best in Show at Faith City Kennel Club was a particular thrill for her owners.

She is a magnificent reflection of her outstanding pedigree. Careful planning and much love resulted in a super showgirl who enjoyed each and every show. She will be carefully bred to further the Cocker Spaniel breed.

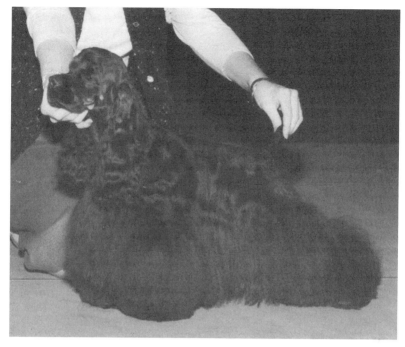

```
                        ┌───── CH. RINKY DINK'S SIR LANCELOT
         ┌───── CH. KAPLAR'S BLACK KNIGHT
         │              └───── CH. KAPLAR'S KUSTOM KUT
CH. KAPLAR'S KELLY GIRL
         │              ┌───── CH. DUR-BET'S TARTAN
         └───── CH. KAPLAR'S SENDS IN THE KLOWN
                        └───── CH. KAPLAR'S KOLLEEN
```

Whelped: May 16, 1982
Breeder: L. Henson and C. Yates — Owner: Laura and Harold Henson
Handler: Lindy Henson

"Wendy" had her career highlighted by winning Best of Variety at the American Spaniel Club in January of 1984.

She is an elegant bitch, short-backed and well up on leg. She is overall sound and has a love of the ring. Her handler, Lindy, finished her with three specialty majors from the puppy class.

Ch. Kaplar's Kwik-Kopi

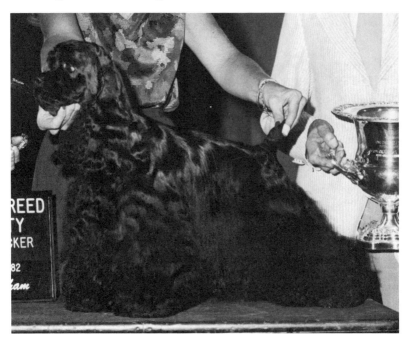

```
                         ┌─────── CH. ARTRU SKYJACK
              ┌──── CH. KAPLAR'S KASSANOVA
              │          └─────── CH. KAPLAR'S KOLLEEN
CH. KAPLAR'S KWIK-KOPI
              │          ┌─────── CH. LUROLA'S ROYAL LANCER
              └──── CH. KAPLAR'S KARBON KOPI
                         └─────── Sandrex Sangarita
```

Whelped: April 8, 1981
Breeder/Owner: Harold & Laura Hensen
Handlers: Laura Henson and Greg Anderson

"Tracy" has had many impressive wins but among her most memorable was Best of Variety at the American Spaniel Club National in 1983 and Best of Breed at the Council Bluffs-National week-end in 1984.

Tracy is the result of blending the Kaplar's two foundation lines of Artru and Royal Lancer stock. She's a compact bitch with a gorgeous front and rear, hard back, moving with tremendous reach and drive. She has a lovely coat, correct back coat, and a pretty head with a dark eye.

Ch. Kimokes Buttons N' Bows

```
                          ┌────────CH. MY-CYN HEY RUBE
              ┌────── CH. PINESHADOWS LINE MAN
  ┌─────                  └──────── CH. PINESHADOWS PARTI-LINE
CH. KIMOKES BUTTONS N' BOWS
  │                       ┌─────── CH. REXPOINTE KOJAK
  └────── Kamps Kimono
                          └─────── CH. MIRWIN'S MERRY MISS
```

Whelped: December 25, 1981
Breeder: Phillip and Charisse Krauth
Owner: Thomas W. and Lynn E. Strawson
Handler: David Roberts

"Buttons" was only campaigned for six short months. She finished her championship within her first seven shows. Since finishing, she has had numerous Group placements, including a Group First. Some of her most memorable wins include Best of Variety at Westminster Kennel Club, the Rhode Island Spaniel Club, and the Cocker Spaniel Club of Long Island; Best of Opposite Sex to Best of Variety at the Zone 1 Long Island Spaniel Club, Las Vegas Spaniel Club and American Spaniel Club.

Buttons is a personality kid—she knows she is on stage all the time.

Ch. Lipton's Made For The Shade

```
                              ┌─ CH. STONEHEDGE PROOF 'O THE PUDDIN
                  ┌─ CH. WINDY HILL'S ROYAL PUDDIN
                  │           └─ CH. WINDY HILL'S 'TIS-A-WENCH
CH. LIPTON'S MADE FOR THE SHADE
                  │           ┌─ CH. HARDEES BLACK BENJI
                  └─ Patlyn November Mahogany Kis
                              └─ CH. THURLYN ACRE TANZANIA
```

Whelped: December 20, 1981
Breeder/Owner: Susan M. Carter
Handler: Kyle Robinson

"Shady" is the first homebred champion out of the first litter for Lipton. What a wonderful start! Shady started her career by winning four Bests in Sweepstakes with two additional Bests of Variety in Sweepstakes, and finished her championship in high style with three consecutive 5-point majors at specialty shows. Since finishing she has been a dynamic force in the variety, breed and group rings.

Shady is a very typey, pretty headed, short backed bitch. She loves to show at the end of the lead—showing off her excellent topline, reach and drive.

```
                              ┌──── Baliwick Bangaway
                  ┌──── CH. LUROLA'S LOOKOUT
                  │           └──── Lurola's Lady Luck
CH. LUROLA'S SKIP TO M'LOU
                  │           ┌──── CH. JO-BE-GLEN'S BRONZE FALCON
                  └──── Lurola's Leilanni
                              └──── CH. LUROLA'S LOLETTE
```

Whelped: October 1967
Breeder: Robert G. and Lucia Lake — Owner: Louise and Russ Milner
Handler: Mike Kinschsular

"Luce," with her great style, tremendous animation and verve, was a consistent top winner. She was a top-winning black bitch and second top-winning bitch (all varieties) while being campaigned. She was the top-winning Cocker in the midwest and among the top ten nationally. Her career totals include 66 Varieties, 20 Group placements, 9 Bests of Breed and 15 Bests of Opposite Sex.

Ch. Makkell's Ziegfeld Girl

```
                          ┌──────── CH. FORJAY'S WINTERWOOD
          ┌──────── CH. COTTONWOOD'S CONGRESSMAN
          │               └──────── Lorli Gigi
CH. MAKKELL'S ZIEGFELD GIRL
          │               ┌──────── CH. MI'WAY BRASS BUTTON
          └──────── CH. PRIME-TIME PISTOL PACKIN' MAMA
                          └──────── Donn Carm's Running Bear
```

Whelped: August 24, 1980
Breeder: Marilyn A. Fink — Owner: Muriel and Ken Kellerhouse
Handler: Ted Young, Jr.

"Flo's" first big win was Best of Breed at the Connecticut-Westchester Cocker Spaniel Club in 1982. She went on to become the #1 ASCOB Cocker in 1983, was the #1 Cocker bitch (all varieties) the same year. She won seven all-breed Bests in Show, seven specialty Bests of Breed (including Best in Show at the '84 Flushing Spaniel Show), 20 Group Firsts and 52 other Group placements.

Flo is a beautiful bitch as well as a true sporting dog. She has a hard back, smooth neck and shoulders and correct reach. She and Ted were "poetry in motion." Flo combined energy, grace and stamina when she moved. Weather was no deterrent to her willingness to put on a good show—she moved well in extreme heat or in rain.

```
                         ┌──────CH. BIZZMAR'S SUPERCOOL OF KEWE
              ┌──────CH. MOZELLE'S MY BUDDY
              │           └──────Presswood's Poppin Fresh
CH. MOZELLE'S REGAL BEGINNING
              │           ┌──────CH. KAMPS' KAPTAIN KOOL
              └──────CH. JUBAN'S JEWEL BOX
                          └──────Norrisim's No Choice
```

Whelped: January 24, 1981
Breeder: Mozelle Craft and Ann Smith — Owner: Pat and Betty Peck
Handler: Charles Self

"Haley" was retired as the #1 Parti-Color Bitch in 1982. One of her greatest wins was to be Winners Bitch and Best of Winners from the 9–12 Puppy Bitch class at the January American Spaniel Club National. She was also Best Opposite Sex to Best of Breed at the Memphis Specialty and won a Group First at the Pensacola Kennel Club.

She has one of the prettiest heads ever seen on a Parti-Color and pretty, straight and silky hair.

Ch. Regal's Send In The Clown

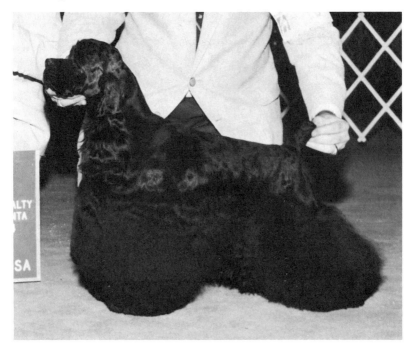

```
                         ┌──────── CH. HAR-DEE'S HIGH SPIRIT
          ┌──────── CH. RINKY DINK'S SIR LANCELOT
          │              └──────── CH. RINKY DINK'S ROBIN
CH. REGAL'S SEND IN THE CLOWN
          │              ┌──────── CH. COTTONWOOD'S CONGRESSMAN
          └──────── CH. HARRAN'S APRIL MISTY MORNIN
                         └──────── CH. HARRAN'S SILVER MIST
```

Whelped: November 24, 1982
Breeder/Owner: Pat & Betty Peck
Handlers: Pat Peck and Charles Self

"Carley's" greatest wins were Best of Variety at the Atlanta Cocker Specialty, Best of Opposite Sex at Westminster Kennel Club, and Best of Opposite Sex to Best of Breed at the Jacksonville Cocker Specialty. She was ranked as a Top Ten Bitch two years in a row.

She is always a true show dog. She has tremendous attitude and loves to show. Very typey, she moves correctly with a sloping topline and is short backed. She has pretty, pretty hair.

Ch. Rowingdale Low Desert Blosom

```
                          ┌──────CH. KAMPS' KAPTAIN KOOL
            ┌──────CH. JUBAN'S GEORGIA JAZZ
            │             └──────Norrisim's No Choice
CH. ROWINGDALE LOW DESERT BLOSOM
            │             ┌────── CH. JIMNAN KID TARRAGON
            └──────CH. LOW DESERT THANKS A MILLION
                          └────── Jimnan's Bit-O-Honey
```

Whelped: January 7, 1983
Breeder/Owner/Handlers: Charles and Jacquelyn Rowe

"Mona's" first big win was Best in Sweepstakes at the Cocker Spaniel Club of Southern California from the 6–9 Puppy Bitch class. She was Reserve Winners Bitch at the same show. She won her first Variety at ten months of age.

She's a flashy, elegant, excellent moving red and white bitch.

Ch. Russ' Winter Beauty

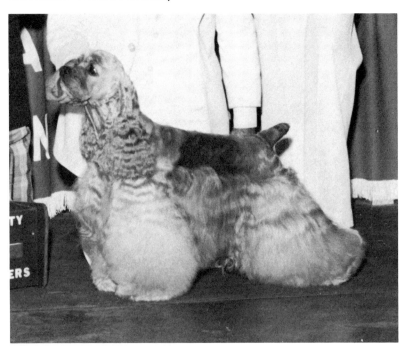

```
                                    ┌──── CH. LA MAR'S LONDON
                   ┌──── CH. FORJAY'S WINTERWOOD
                   │                └──── Forjay's Buffie
CH. RUSS' WINTER BEAUTY
                   │                ┌──── CH. LA MAR'S LONDON MARC
                   └──── CH. RUSS' BEAUTY MARC
                                    └──── Gini-J's Scarlet O'Hara
```

Whelped: October 1974
Breeder/Owner: Larry and Norma Russ
Handler: Don Johnston

"Missy's" show career was spectacular. Her first "big" win as a special was to go Best of Breed at the Cocker Spaniel Club of Kentucky. For the next three years she accrued 81 Bests of Variety, 12 Group Firsts and three Bests in Show as well as many Group placements.

She thrived on the show ring and the applause. She was a once-in-a-lifetime thrill that breeders hope and pray for but seldom see. She was the Russ' bitch on paper but she belonged to all the Cocker fancy in their hearts.

Ch. Seacliffe's Sophistication

```
                                ┌──────── CH. PINER'S PREMEDITATED
            ┌──────── CH. RINKY DINK'S BIT OF ACTION
            │                   └──────── CH. LANEL'S RINKY DINK'S M AND M
CH. SEACLIFFE'S SOPHISTICATION
            │                   ┌──────── Sarchell's Big Daddy
            └──────── Carlen's Love Me Deerly
                                └──────── Prime Times Skys The Limit
```

Whelped: September 16, 1982
Breeder/Owner: Herbert K. Kozuma
Handler: Diana Kane

This lovely buff bitch had her first big win her first time out as a special: She was Best of Opposite Sex to Best of Variety at the Mission Valley Cocker Spaniel Club. She was specialed for a brief four-month period and did very well against top competition.

She has the wonderful, soft expression that Cocker Spaniels have become so famous for.

Ch. Shardeloe's Selena

```
                              ┌────── CH. HOB-NOB-HILL'S TRIBUTE
              ┌──────CH. SHOESTRING SHOOTIN MATCH
              │               └────── Shoestring Sabrina
CH. SHARDELOE'S SELENA
              │               ┌────── CH. MAGICOURS MONOGRAM
              └────── CH. SHARDELOE'S SIGNETTE
                              └────── CH. SMYTHOLM'S GOOD GRIEF
```

Whelped: July 1970
Breeer: Mrs. Fred Hicks-Beach
Owner: Dr. & Mrs. Clarence Smith—Heyday Kennels, Reg.
Handlers: Terry and Charlotte Stacy

"Selena's" show record included 17 Bests in Show, 86 Group Firsts, 166 other Group placings, 18 Bests of Breed at specialty shows. She was Best of Breed at the '73 and '74 American Spaniel Club's shows and Best of Variety from '72 through '75 at the ASC. She was the top-winning Cocker for '73 and '74 and one of the nation's top Sporting Dogs.

Although her first litters were not whelped until she was five, her qualities as a producer were reflected in nine champions and she is the granddam of 51 champions. She was one in a million.

Ch. Showtime Classy Cheerleader

```
                            ┌───── CH. FORJAY'S WINTERWOOD
              ┌───── CH. COTTONWOOD'S CONGRESSMAN
      ┌       └───── Lorli Gigi
CH. SHOWTIME CLASSY CHEERLEADER
      │               ┌───── CH. KAMPS' SILVERSMITH
      └───── Can./Am. CH. COMAC CLASSY COED
                      └───── CH. LA TOKA ARTRU TREASURE
```

Whelped: January 1, 1985
Breeder/Owner: Donald B. and Carol Ann Harris
Handlers: Bob & Jan Covey

"Cheer" finished at 9 months and 26 days of age. She won the '86 American Spaniel Club National Futurity. She was ranked #2 overall top-winning bitch for '86, and she was the #5 ASCOB overall.

Some of her greatest wins include winning the Variety Sweepstakes at five different specialties and winning Best in Sweepstakes at three specialties.

Can./Am. Ch. Tabaka's Tidbit O'Wynden, CDX

```
                              ┌──────── CH. ARTRU SANDPIPER
                ┌──────── CH. ARTRU ACTION
                │              └──────── Van-Dor Fancy Triane
Can./Am. CH. TABAKA'S TIDBIT O'WYNDEN, CDX
                │              ┌──────── CH. SEENAR'S TALK TALK
                └──────── CH. TIMOTHY'S GOSSIP OF WYNDEN
                               └──────── Whitehall's Leading Lady
```

Whelped: July 24, 1973
Breeder: Dennis J. and Wynn N. Bloch — Owner: Ruth N. Tabaka
Handlers: Jim Hall, Bill Ernst, Ted Young, Jr.

"Termite" is the only obedience-titled dog to win a Best in Show at the American Spaniel Club! In all, she won 16 all-breed Bests in Show, 19 Bests of Breed, 50 Group Firsts, 63 other Group placements, and 173 Bests of Variety. In 1981, she came out of retirement to win Best of Breed at the Washington State Cocker Spaniel Club specialty at almost eight years of age!

"Termite" excelled in everything she attempted—as a conformation dog, as an obedience dog and as a brood bitch. One of her sons is a Best in Show dog and two of her daughters are High in Trial winners.

Can./Am. Ch. Timothy's Sparkle Plenty

```
                        ┌──────── CH. BOBWIN'S SIR ASHLEY
            ┌────── Timothy's Winterwind
            │                └────── Can./Am. CH. TIMOTHY'S SHADY LADY
Can./Am. CH. TIMOTHY'S SPARKLE PLENTY
            │           ┌─────── Can./Am. CH. TIMOTHY'S HOLY MOSES
            └────── Timothy's Lucille
                        └──────Timothy's O'Susanna
```

Whelped: July 1, 1981
Breeder/Owner: Mr. & Mrs. Charles Lilley
Handler: Diane Lilley

"Sparkle" is a multiple Group winner and specialty Best of Breed winner in Canada. She was the #4 Cocker Spaniel in Canada in 1983 and the top-winning bitch with very limited showing. Shown sparingly to her U.S. title, she was Best of Breed at two specialties.

Sparkle is a *bona fide* "show dog." Watching her fly around the ring on a loose lead . . . her beautiful head held high . . . is breathtaking!

Ch. Waltann's Lady Jane

```
                           ┌──────── CH. ARTRU SKYJACK
            ┌───────── CH. COBB'S CHANCE FOR WALTANN'S
            │              └─────── CH. COBB'S KATHLEEN
CH. WALTANN'S LADY JANE
            │              ┌─────── CH. BOBWIN'S SIR ASHLEY
            └───────── Bobwin's Lady Victoria
                           └─────── CH. BOBWIN'S STAY PUT OF FASMAR
```

Whelped: August 9, 1983
Breeder: Shirlee Lewis — Owner: Stephen Calvert, M.D.
Handler: David Roberts

"Jane" finished her title just two weeks before being chosen Best of Variety at the January American Spaniel Club in '85. Over the next two years she would go on to defeat over 25,000 dogs in specialty and all-breed competition, including four all-breed Best in Shows. This made her the third top-winning bitch in breed history.

Retired in March '87, she whelped a single puppy which embodies her beautiful type, electric personality and movement.

Ch. Whoos Summer Blossom

```
                            ┌──────── CH. DREAMRIDGE DON JUAN
            ┌──────── CH. FEINLYNE RUMBO
            │                └──────── CH. FEINLYNE FORTUNE
CH. WHOOS SUMMER BLOSSOM
            │                ┌──────── CH. DAVIS' COLA OF FREEWINDS
            └──────── CH. WHOOS HELRO'S MOONDROPS
                             └──────── Helros' Mystique
```

Whelped: July 22, 1982
Breeder: Theresa and Joe Hicks — Owner: Theresa Hicks and Jayne Kennedy
Handler: Michael Kinschsular

"Shasta" finished from the puppy classes with four majors. As a sweepstakes contender, she won two Bests of Variety Sweepstakes.

She was Best of Opposite Sex to Best of Breed at the Austin Cocker Spaniel Specialty and the Dallas Cocker Spaniel Specialty, and Best of Opposite Sex to Best of Variety at the American Spaniel Club National in 1984. She has numerous BOV's and Group placements.

SECTION VIII

Top Producing
Dogs and Bitches

- *Top Producing Dogs*
- *Top Producing Bitches*

Top Producing Dogs

(Statistics complete through the February 1987 AKC *Gazette*)

1. Ch. Rinky Dink's Sir Lancelot . . . . B/T 135
2. Ch. Scioto Bluff's Sinbad . . . . R/W 118
3. Ch. Dreamridge Dominoe . . . . B/W 109
4. Orient's It's A Pleasure . . . . R/W 104
5. Ch. Artru Skyjack . . . . Buff 87
6. Ch. Windy Hill's 'Tis Demi's Demon . . . . B/T 83
7. Ch. Stockdale Town Talk . . . . Black 81
8. Ch. Clarkdale Capital Stock . . . . Black 76
9. Ch. Crackerbox Certainly . . . . B/T 73
10. Ch. Artru Sandpiper . . . . Buff 68
11. Ch. Bobwin's Sir Ashley . . . . Black 65
12. Int. Ch. Maddie's Vagabond's Return . . . . Buff 60
13. Ch. Cottonwood's Congressman . . . . Buff 58
14. Ch. Artru Action . . . . Buff 56
15. Ch. La Mar's London . . . . Buff 54
15. Ch. Hob Nob Hill's Tribute . . . . Black 54
16. Ch. Artru Johnny-Be-Good . . . . Buff 52
17. Ch. Lurola's Royal Lancer . . . . B/T 51
18. Ch. Artru Red Baron . . . . Buff 49
19. Ch. Forjay's Winterwood . . . . Buff 47
20. Ch. Main-Dale's Mr. Success . . . . Black 46
21. Ch. Elderwood Bangaway . . . . Black 45

An analysis of the top producers certainly confirms the overwhelming dominance of the Artru bloodlines. Not only are five (5) Artru dogs listed among the top producers but the line continues through Ch. La Mar's London, Ch. Forjay's Winterwood down through Ch. Cottonwood's Congressman. A producing line that seems hard to ever beat.

In Parti-Colors, the influence of the Hall-Way Kennels of Jim and Beth Hall is seen throughout the top producers list. They began the bloodline which is behind Ch. Scioto Bluff's Sinbad, Ch. Dreamridge Dominoe and Orient's It's A Pleasure.

In Blacks, the Town Talk influence is still felt. Ch. Elderwood Bangaway and Ch. Clarkdale Capital Stock—both descended closely from Town Talk—have also perpetuated their lines.

In Black & Tans, the top producer is, of course, Ch. Rinky Dink's Sir Lancelot who set a new high for Cocker Spaniels. Lance's son, Ch. Kaplar's Kon-Man, with nearly 40 champion get, is already knocking on the door to the top-twenty producers list. Ch. Windy Hill's 'Tis Demi's Demon is the next highest Black & Tan and is followed on the list by his outstanding son, Ch. Bobwin's Sir Ashley, a Black with 65 confirmed champions.

Ch. Rinky Dink's Sir Lancelot

```
                               ┌────── Can./Am. CH. LUROLA'S LOOKOUT
                    ┌───── CH. HAR-DEE'S HIGH SPIRIT
                    │          └────── CH. HAR-DEE'S HIGH STYLE
CH. RINKY DINK'S SIR LANCELOT
                    │          ┌────── Robin Knoll's Suppose
                    └───── CH. RINKY DINK'S ROBIN
                               └────── Dawn's Harem Queen
```

Whelped: July 22, 1972
Breeder/Owner: Jean and William Petersen

The sire of 135 Champions

Ch. Artru Darling Black Magic	Ch. Butch's Evil Knievel
Ch. Artru Jericho	Ch. Butch's Impish Delight
Ch. Artru Jezebel	Ch. Butch's Irresistible Imp
Ch. Bara Hill's Midnight Date	Ch. Cal-Ore's Mystic Time
Ch. Birchwood Bluebeard	Ch. Camelot's Capri
Ch. Bonnie Jay's Nite Cantata	Ch. Camelot's Court Jester
Ch. Bonnie Jay's Nite Minstrel	Ch. Candlewick's Clockwork
Ch. Bonnie Jay's Nite Moves	Ch. Candlewick's Cosair
Ch. Brynwood's Burglar of Shire	Ch. Canterbury's Archbishop
Ch. Butch's Eightball	Ch. Caralot's Harry O
Ch. Butch's Eights N' Aces	Ch. Caribee's Night Light

Ch. Castletop's Coat of Arms
Ch. Castletop's National Velvet
Ch. Clarkdale Cachet
Ch. Clarkdale Clever Candidate
Ch. Claymore's Carefree Cora
Ch. Cobblestone Terri of Ty-Roy
Ch. Comac Royal Conqueror
Ch. Commissioner Junior Lane
Ch. Cottonwood's Smokey The Bear
Ch. Davis' Winterhawk
Ch. De-Sir-Cay's Sir Ebony
Ch. De-Sir-Cay's True Love
Ch. Dur-Bet's Black Magic
Ch. Estell's What's Your Pleasure
Ch. Faron's Baron Lancer
Ch. Frontier Cowboy Special
Ch. Frontier Million Dollar Baby
Ch. Gleanmeadow's Golduster
Ch. Gleanmeadow's Grasshopper
Ch. Gold Coast Pipe Dream
Ch. Harbinger's Happy Warrior
Ch. Harran's Black Jack
Ch. Harran's Custom Design
Ch. Harran's Shady Lady
Ch. Harrison's Peeping Tom
Ch. Harrison's Shoeshine Boy
Ch. Harrison's Tarnished Angel
Ch. Hazelwood's Fashion Focus
Ch. Hazelwood's Latest Fashion
Ch. Heyday Ducat
Ch. Heyday Helena
Ch. Heyday Herald
Ch. Heyday Highbrow
Ch. Heyday Hohum
Ch. Heyday Hotspur
Ch. Hollycrest Peppermint Patti
Ch. Hollycrest Precious Mink
Ch. Hollycrest Something Special
Ch. Horizon's Dark Intruder
Ch. I-Just-B Rinky Dink's Shadow
Ch. Jernan's Jesse James
Ch. Jersey Hill's Night Edition
Ch. Jersey Hill's Page One Gal
Ch. Kaplar's Black Knight
Ch. Kaplar's Karlings Black Label
Ch. Kaplar's Kon-Man
Ch. Kaplar's Kut Up
Ch. Kaplar's Wa-Maur Kustom Design
Ch. Karizama's Aramis
Ch. Lee Dee's Black Book
Ch. Leelon Johnar
Ch. Leelon's Niatross
Ch. Leelon Squire of Dannen
Ch. Lorli's Medicine Man
Ch. Main-Dale's Marathon Man
Ch. Main-Dale's Mr. M-Bassador
Ch. Marpet Magnolia

Ch. Mojo's Macho Man
Ch. Mojo's Mighty Mack
Ch. Oakmont Could It Be Magic
Ch. O'Nine's Life of Riley
Ch. Paddington's Poetic Justice
Ch. Paddington's Poetic License
Ch. Paddington's Poet Laureate
Ch. Paddington's Poetry N' Motion
Ch. Parksway Hale Kai Seasprite
Ch. Parksway Joy In The Morning
Ch. Parksway Kiss Me Kate
Ch. Parksway Peg O My Heart
Ch. Piner's Elvira
Ch. Pineshadow's Persuader
Ch. Pryority Promise Me
Ch. Pryority Promise To Mer-Knol
Ch. Quinstar's Rinky Dink's Abbi
Ch. Regal's Hidden Treasure
Ch. Regal's Sand Dollar
Ch. Regal's Send In The Clown
Ch. Rinky Dink's Bebe Zapata
Ch. Rinky Dink's Black Jack
Ch. Rinky Dink's Cricket Hill Gem
Ch. Rinky Dink's Delta Lance
Ch. Rinky Dink's Downey Velvet
Ch. Rinky Dink's Foreshadow
Ch. Rinky Dink's Galewind
Ch. Rinky Dink's Jus-Us Supreme
Ch. Rinky Dink's Kiss and Tell
Ch. Rinky Dink's Melissa
Ch. Rinky Dink's Rockefeller
Ch. Rinky Dink's Smooth As Silk
Ch. Rinky Dink's Socko
Ch. Rinky Dink's Sunkist Dawn
Ch. Rinky Dink's Tis Kismet
Ch. Ro-Jac's Prince Charming
Ch. Sarchell's Castletop Caper
Ch. Seesau's Sir Gallahad
Ch. Sham-O-Jet's Takes A Chance
Ch. Shardeloes Blythe Spirit
Ch. Shardeloes Coppershot Carita
Ch. Shardeloes Heaven Sent
Ch. Shardeloes Smart Trotter
Ch. Shardeloes Summer Dawn
Ch. Shenanigans of Don Juan
Ch. Sher-Ron's Delegate
Ch. Sher-Ron's Desiree
Ch. Sher-Ron's Double Take
Ch. Shoshoni's Windsong
Ch. Strack's Sportsman
Ch. Suropen's Chisom
Ch. Sweetbriar's Revolution
Ch. Val-Lee's Liberty Belle
Ch. Westwind's Black Kewpie Doll
Ch. Wood-Duff's Pick Up The Banner
Ch. Wynspun Dennis Black Duke

Ch. Scioto Bluff's Sinbad

```
                                  ┌──── CH. MERLADY TIMMY
                    ┌──── CH. HALL-WAY HOOT MON
                    │             └──── CH. HALL-WAY HONEY HUE
CH. SCIOTO BLUFF'S SINBAD
                    │             ┌──── CH. BALIWICK BRANDY
                    └──── CH. SCIOTO BLUFF'S JUDY
                                  └──── Creekwood Miss Showoff
```

Whelped: August 30, 1959
Breeder/Owner: Mr. and Mrs. Charles Winders

The sire of 118 Champions

Ch. Alsan's Autumn Blaze
Ch. Amor's Kristin
Ch. Ashdale Appraiser
Ch. Baliwick's Baghdad
Ch. Bard's Daydream
Ch. Bard's Dusky Babe
Ch. Bard's Pride-N-Joy
Ch. Be Gay's Hell's A-Poppin
Ch. Belden's Sharif
Ch. Bizzmar Boucle
Ch. Blue Bay's Bell Ringer
Ch. Bobwin's Sin-Dee
Ch. Bobwin's Touch of Illig
Ch. Boyd's Bethbaku
Ch. Boyd's Bonus
Ch. Boyd's Bosun

Ch. Boyd's Branded
Ch. Boyd's Ditan Cotton Sox
Ch. Camby's Candle Light
Ch. Camby's Cloud Nine
Ch. Campbell's Color Me Cutest
Ch. Candylane Congressman
Ch. Candylane Coronation
Ch. Carolton's Great Scott
Ch. Cia-Dee Bold Venture
Ch. Cia-Dee Carry On
Ch. Clarkdale Corvette Too
Ch. Commotion Lane's Mickey Who Me
Ch. Corwin Calico
Ch. Corwin's Davy Crockett
Ch. Corwin's Hellzapoppin
Ch. Corwin My Cheri

Ch. Corwin Triumph
Ch. Crackerbox Chenille
Ch. Cumlaude's Dot-N-Dash
Ch. Cumlaude's Knock-M-Dead
Ch. Cumlaude's Marie Elena
Ch. Cumlaude's San Souciana
Ch. Daisy Hill's Saint 'N Sinner
Ch. Dau-Han's Danigan
Ch. Dofran's Prince of Brooklawn
Ch. Dreamridge Daiquiri, CDX
Ch. Dreamridge Damsel
Ch. Dreamridge Dance Step
Ch. Dreamridge Decor
Ch. Dreamridge Decorator
Ch. Dreamridge Delegate
Ch. Dreamridge Design
Ch. Dreamridge Destry
Ch. Dreamridge Dickery Dock
Ch. Dreamridge Dominoe
Ch. Dreamridge Don Juan
Ch. Dreamridge Moenkopi Sunset
Ch. Dreamridge Peter Pan
Ch. Dreamridge Rosie O'Day
Ch. Ess's Del
Ch. Fi-Fo's Madame Spook
Ch. Flintcrest's Sin-Fan Smudge
Ch. Frandee's Tiger Lil'
Ch. Frandee's White Tornado
Ch. Gerri-Mar Sherry
Ch. Hall-Way Hard Tri
Ch. Heatherway Hillbilly
Ch. Heatherway Peppermint Twist
Ch. Heatherway Sincere
Ch. Hi-Ho's Top Billing
Ch. Hugomar Headpiece
Ch. Ideal's M and M
Ch. Illig's Double Trouble
Ch. Loafalot's Bonanza
Ch. Loafalot's Candy Spots
Ch. Mar-Geo's Star Bright
Ch. Mar-Geo's Tri-King
Ch. Mark's Favorite Captain
Ch. Marlyn's Marching Saint

Ch. Marlyn's Mister Spreckles
Ch. Matador's Mascot
Ch. Matador's Music Man
Ch. Melissa's Nosowea Navigator
Ch. Merikay's Baby Jane
Ch. Mobley's Holiday Sin
Ch. My-Ida-Ho Paddy Waggin
Ch. My-Ida-Ho Patticake
Ch. Mylislee's Suzy of Sandy Hill
Ch. Nor-Mar's Navy Blue
Ch. Nosowea's Namesake
Ch. Nosowea's Secret Sin
Ch. Par-Fra's Sunday Dinner
Ch. Pett's Broker's Tip
Ch. Pounette Pirouette
Ch. Pounette Sailing Sam
Ch. Pounette Scioto Bluff's Sybil
Ch. Rejeancy's Priscilla
Ch. Rexpointe Dutchmaster
Ch. Rexpointe Radiance
Ch. Rexpointe Rampage
Ch. Rexpointe Regalia
Ch. Rexpointe Trinidad
Ch. Scioto Bluff's High Hope
Ch. Scioto Bluff's Noso-Way'n
Ch. Scioto Bluff's Sabrina
Ch. Scioto Bluff's Sally Forth
Ch. Scioto Bluff's Sin-Bahr
Ch. Scioto Bluff's Sineron
Ch. Scioto Bluff's Smooth Sailing
Ch. Scioto Bluff's Spice
Ch. Sea-Quin Certain Smile
Ch. Sea-Quin Somebody Special
Ch. Shadowridge Saturday Sinner
Ch. Silver Maple Safari
Ch. Spindrift's Spot of Sin
Ch. Stonewalk Sharpshooter
Ch. Stonewalk Squareshooter
Ch. Susan's Dandy Brandy
Ch. Trotter's Johnny Reb
Ch. Trotter's Tammy O'Shanter
Ch. Twyneff Peter Whimsey, CD
Ch. Winsome Way's Toby

Ch. Dreamridge Dominoe

```
                                    ┌──────── CH. HALL-WAY HOOT MON
                  ┌──────── CH. SCIOTO BLUFF'S SINBAD
                  │                 └──────── CH. SCIOTO BLUFF'S JUDY
CH. DREAMRIDGE DOMINOE
                  │                 ┌──────── CH. CLARKDALE CALCUTTA
                  └──────── CH. DREAMRIDGE DINNER DATE
                                    └──────── Pounette Perrette
```

Whelped: March 12, 1968
Breeder/Owner: Thomas O'Neal

The sire of 109 Champions

Ch. Azad Shoon
Ch. Azalea Hill's Cup Runs Over
Ch. Bard's Ballyhoo
Ch. Barjohn's Soolia Mon
Ch. Birchwood Bacharach
Ch. Birchwood Bardot
Ch. Bob-Lyn's Red Button
Ch. Bob-Lyn's Bachelor Buttons
Ch. Boyd's Bite The Bullet
Ch. Boyd's Blockbuster
Ch. Brooklawn's Anchor Man
Ch. Burson's Bonanza Again
Ch. Burson's Bravo
Ch. Burson's Burdick
Ch. Campbells Color Me Current
Ch. Campbells Color Me Cuter
Ch. Carver's Candidate
Ch. Cedar Hill's Topsy Turvy
Ch. Cher Ami Cameo of Cedar Hill

Ch. Clarkdale Checkpoint
Ch. Cobb's Trail of Tears
Ch. Comfort Lane Dominoe
Ch. Corwin's Countdown
Ch. Corwin's Gandy Dancer
Ch. Co-Sett's Zephyr Lynn
Ch. Debonaire Darcy
Ch. Deep River Dazzle
Ch. Deep River Decision
Ch. Dreamridge Darn-Tootin'
Ch. Dreamridge Dear Abby
Ch. Dreamridge Dear Bobbi
Ch. Dreamridge Debut
Ch. Dreamridge Declaration
Ch. Dreamridge Delilah
Ch. Dreamridge Delta Dawn
Ch. Dreamridge Democrat
Ch. Dreamridge Desmond
Ch. Dreamridge Dexter

Ch. Dreamridge Dixie Peach
Ch. Dreamridge Domineer
Ch. Dreamridge Dory
Ch. Dreamridge Do Tell
Ch. Dreamridge Desden Doll
Ch. Dreamridge Drum Beat
Ch. Dreamridge Drum Major
Ch. Dreamridge Dustin
Ch. Dreamridge Dynamo
Ch. Flair-Rill Favorite Son
Ch. Flair-Rill Firebrand
Ch. Flair-Rill Fireside Chat
Ch. Gordon's Travelin' Man
Ch. Halltops Happy Hellion
Ch. Hi-D-Ho's Ace In The Hole
Ch. Jezabelle
Ch. Karavan's Traveling Man, CD
Ch. Lorolet's Captain Dominic
Ch. Marimaque's Jontue
Ch. Mari-Will Capo Ditutti Capi
Ch. Marlou's Laredo
Ch. Merlady Bright Banner
Ch. Merlady Maid Marion II
Ch. Merlady Mountaineer
Ch. Moderna's Snow Job
Ch. Monte Verde Innkeeper
Ch. Moody's D'Artagnan of Osage
Ch. Moody's Magic Tri
Ch. Moody's Majestic Nugget
Ch. Moody's Mr. Tr
Ch. Moody's Ms. PJ
Ch. Nambut's Manilow
Ch. Nosowea's Buttons 'N Bows
Ch. Nosowea's No Strings
Ch. Nosowea's No Trump
Ch. Nosowea's Spring Notion

Ch. Pett's Daddy's Mink
Ch. Pett's Fire and Ice
Ch. Pett's Handsome Harry
Ch. Pett's Press Agent
Ch. Pett's Twinkling Valerie
Ch. Pett's Yachtsman
Ch. Pine Bluff's Tri-Agent
Ch. Pin Oak's Loco Motion
Ch. Pounette Passe-Partout
Ch. Pounette Sans-Pareille
Ch. Rexpointe Regent
Ch. Rexpointe Roulette
Ch. Scott River's Dog Trey
Ch. Silver Maple Tri Mr. Moody
Ch. Society's Socialite
Ch. Stetson's Deborah Abigail Ann
Ch. Stu-Art's Love Spot
Ch. Stu-Art's Rusty Ragan
Ch. Stu-Art's Tanbark
Ch. Swank's Ginny-Girl
Ch. The Sundance Kid
Ch. Triple Dip's Hot 'N Smokey
Ch. Triple Dip's Tan Titan
Ch. Trotter's Lil' Miss Cutie
Ch. Waggin' Master's Jennie
Ch. Waggin' Master's Masked Bandit
Ch. Ward's Easy To Remember
Ch. Ward's High Hopes
Ch. Ward's Martinet
Ch. Ward's Winterset
Ch. Ward's Wishing Pebble
Ch. Ward's Witchcraft
Ch. Westlin Winsom Gal
Ch. Wil-Co's What Class
Ch. Wil-Co's Windsong

Orient's It's A Pleasure

```
                              ┌──── CH. POLING'S IMURGUY
              ┌──── CH. POLING'S GAY BLADE
              │               └──── CH. POLING'S SO LOVELY
Orient's It's A Pleasure
              │               ┌──── CH. DAU-HAN'S DAN MORGAN
              └──── CH. ORIENT'S TRULY YOURS
                              └──── Norbill's Novelty
```

Whelped: April 12, 1960
Breeder/Owner: Al and Dorothy Orient

The sire of 104 Champions

Ch. Alsan's Oriental
Ch. Amor's Pinch of Seasoning, CD
Ch. Black Butte's Better Moment
Ch. Black Butte's Embraceable You
Ch. Brooklawn Cinderella
Ch. Brooklawn's Parris Le Jeune
Ch. Cindy's Party Socs
Ch. Clearwater Pure Pleasure
Ch. Colleen's Cosmopolitan
Ch. Colleen's Esprit De Corps
Ch. Colleen's Hallowe'en Parti
Ch. Dassin's Dream Whip
Ch. Deer Walk Mary Quite Contrary
Ch. Dinabab's Dancer
Ch. Dinabab's Dresden Doll
Ch. Flintcrest My Pleasure
Ch. Gremora's Cream and Sugar
Ch. Gremora's Fantasia
Ch. Gremora's Pleasure Host, CD
Ch. Gremora's Tri To Love
Ch. Isle-View's Ho Hum
Ch. Jay-Re's Frostee Pleasure
Ch. Jay-Re's I'm A Doll
Ch. Jay-Re's What A Doll
Ch. Kentwood's Pak-A-Pleasure, CD
Ch. Lee's Keeper's Choice
Ch. Ma-Mar's Midnight Masquerader
Ch. Ma-Mar's Morning Miracle
Ch. McCarter's Twice Around
Ch. Merry-Len's Piacero Dinamico
Ch. Merry-Len's Poca Piacera
Ch. Merry-Len's Tri My Pleasure
Ch. Mestler's Holiday Memory
Ch. Mestler's Masquerade Parti
Ch. Mestler's Personality Plus
Ch. Orient's Adorable
Ch. Orient's Always A Pleasure
Ch. Orient's Born To Please
Ch. Orient's Choice Pleasure
Ch. Orient's Doctor Pleasure
Ch. Orient's Double Your Pleasure
Ch. Orient's Full of Pleasure
Ch. Orient's Happy Go Pleasure
Ch. Orient's Irish Pleasure
Ch. Orient's Isn't It A Pleasure
Ch. Orient's Lovable Pleasure
Ch. Orient's Love and Pleasure
Ch. Orient's Lovely Lady
Ch. Orient's Loving Pleasure
Ch. Orient's More Pleasure
Ch. Orient's Pleasing You

Ch. Orient's Pleasurama
Ch. Orient's Pleasure Alibi
Ch. Orient's Pleasure and Palaces
Ch. Orient's Pleasure Bird
Ch. Orient's Pleasure Bouquet
Ch. Orient's Pleasure Deluxe
Ch. Orient's Pleasure Lore
Ch. Orient's Pleasure Lover
Ch. Orient's Pleasure Magic
Ch. Orient's Pleasure Maker
Ch. Orient's Pleasure Perfecta
Ch. Orient's Pleasure Playboy
Ch. Orient's Pleasure Prefix
Ch. Orient's Pleasure Progress
Ch. Orient's Pleasure Rich and Rare
Ch. Orient's Pleasure Show Me
Ch. Orient's Pleasure's Treasure
Ch. Orient's Pleasure Theme Song
Ch. Orient's Pleasure Tone
Ch. Orient's Pleasure Unlimited
Ch. Orient's Pleasure Wheel
Ch. Orient's Pleasure Year Round, CD
Ch. Orient's Pride and Pleasure
Ch. Orient's Real Pleasure
Ch. Orient's Secret Pleasure
Ch. Orient's Southern Pleasure
Ch. Orient's Sparkling Pleasure
Ch. Orient's Special Pleasure
Ch. Orient's Sweetest Pleasure
Ch. Orient's Temptress
Ch. Orient's Think Pleasure
Ch. Orient's Tomorrow
Ch. Orient's Triple Your Pleasure
Ch. Orient's Truly A Pleasure
Ch. Orient's V.I. Pleasure
Ch. Orient's What A Pleasure
Ch. Parkwood Touch of Pleasure
Ch. Penthouse Personality
Ch. Penthouse Pro-Motion
Ch. Sendos Pepper 'N Salt
Ch. Sendos Shadow of Pleasure
Ch. Sendos Tribute To Pleasure
Ch. Shades of Dixie
Ch. Smarti-Parti She's A Pleasure
Ch. Smarti-Parti Triple Pleasure
Ch. Smartset's Platinum Pleasure
Ch. Towanka's Toma-Hawk
Ch. Val-Har's Venture
Ch. Val-Har's Voyager
Ch. V's Colleen's A Pleasure Kid
Ch. Waggin Master's My Buddy
Ch. Waggin Master's Sugar N' Spice

Ch. Artru Skyjack

```
                                    ┌─────── CH. ARTRU JOHNNY-BE-GOOD
                    ┌───── CH. ARTRU RED BARON
                    │               └─────── Artru Kathleen
CH. ARTRU SKYJACK
                    │               ┌─────── CH. ARTRU SANDPIPER
                    └───── CH. ARTRU TRINKET
                                    └─────── Artru Gay Escapade
```

Whelped: June 25, 1971
Breeder/Owner: Mrs. Arthur Benoff, Artru Kennels

The sire of 87 Champions

Ch. Artru All Fancy	Ch. Artru Sundance Blaze
Ch. Artru Berry Bounce	Ch. Artru Sundance Pacemaker
Ch. Artru Episode	Ch. Ashley's Golden Rule
Ch. Artru Golden Boy	Ch. Ashley's Rasberry Sherbert
Ch. Artru Good As Gold	Ch. Black Brook Crackerjack
Ch. Artru Jack-Q-Lyn	Ch. Black Brook Oscar
Ch. Artru K K Kandyman	Ch. Black Brook Red Carpet
Ch. Artru Larkspur	Ch. Butch's Anthony
Ch. Artru La Toka Ringleader	Ch. Butch's Archibald
Ch. Artru La Toka Tradewind	Ch. Cajun's W A Chabert
Ch. Artru Nelsen Midnite Sassy	Ch. Citadel's Skylark

Ch. Cobb's Allison
Ch. Cobb's Billy Jack
Ch. Cobb's Cajun Touch of Honey
Ch. Cobb's Chances For Waltan's
Ch. Cobb's Cherokee Fire
Ch. Cobb's Country Breeze
Ch. Cobb's Honey Jam
Ch. Cobb's Jessie James
Ch. Cobb's Keepsake
Ch. Cobb's Pale Moon
Ch. Cobb's Red Blazer
Ch. Cobb's String of Hearts
Ch. Conemara Tiffany
Ch. Cottonwood's Cornerstone
Ch. Debalarr Top Beige
Ch. Donnybrook Curtain Call
Ch. Dur-Bet's Walkin' On Air
Ch. Easdale's Return Performance
Ch. Feinlyne Firebird
Ch. Forjay's Skyhawk
Ch. Gina Makkell's Comedian
Ch. Gina's Bizzy Me
Ch. Gina's Cream Puff Maker
Ch. Gina's M and M
Ch. Grogan's Hit of Smacker
Ch. Heatherway Hillbilly
Ch. Janado K K Krackerjack
Ch. Jan-Myr It's A Miracle
Ch. Jawat's Talisman of Tallylyn
Ch. Kamps' Kandlelite
Ch. Kamps' Koppertone
Ch. Kaplar's Kassanova
Ch. Kaplar's Kolt Forty-Five

Ch. Kaplar's Konspirator
Ch. Kaplar's Kopper Key
Ch. Kaplar's Kopyrighted My Way
Ch. Kaplar's Skyhigh Dream
Ch. Kaplar's Quicksilver
Ch. Lanel's Cinner-Man
Ch. Lanel's Rinky Dink's M and M
Ch. Lanel's Winter Wheat
Ch. La Toka Artru Treasure
Ch. La Toka's Amberina
Ch. Libertyville Black Velvet
Ch. Libertyville Clementina
Ch. Libertyville Mr. Cleveland
Ch. Lorli's Ideya
Ch. Lorli's Miss Buttermilk Sky
Ch. Lyndale's Artru Sky Pilot
Ch. Lyndale's A Taste of Honey
Ch. Lyndale's Bronson
Ch. Lyndale's Great Gatsby
Ch. Memoir's John Silver
Ch. Mi'Way's Wayfarer
Ch. Mi'Way's Wild Escapade
Ch. Pitty Patty's Laudy Laudy Lady
Ch. Sugarbrook Most Happy Fellow
Ch. Sunshine's Shalimar
Ch. Tamburlaine's Artru Avenger
Ch. Tamburlaine's Evil Kneivel
Ch. Tamburlaine's Skyrocket
Ch. Tamburlaine's Tornado of Artru
Ch. Teragold's Miss Holy
Ch. Twin Oaks Twilight
Ch. Young's Comanche Road

Ch. Windy Hill's 'Tis Demi's Demon

```
                              ┌───── CH. HOB-NOB-HILL'S TRIBUTE
              ┌───── CH. DUR-BET'S PICK THE TIGER, CD
              │               └───── CH. DUR-BET'S NIGHTIE NIGHT
CH. WINDY HILL'S 'TIS DEMI'S DEMON
              │               ┌───── Windy Hill's Activat'd Charkol
              └───── CH. WINDY HILL'S 'TIS DEMI-TASSE
                              └───── Windy Hill's 'Tis Bit-O-Tan-Man
```

Whelped: May 7, 1972
Breeder/Owner: Edna T. Anselmi

The sire of 83 Champions

Ch. Arikaras Sweet Talker
Ch. Artru McBeth's Tokay
Ch. Ashley's Cadence
Ch. Ashley's Maid Marian
Ch. Ashley's Manor Minute Man
Ch. Ashley's Mica Minuet
Ch. Ashley's Motiff of Little Star
Ch. Bara Hill's Midnight Raider
Ch. Bara Hill's Midnight Song
Ch. Barcrest Misty Morning

Ch. Bobwin's Sir Ashley
Ch. Boney Mountain Bump At Night
Ch. Calypso's Pina Colada
Ch. Camelot's Cover Girl
Ch. Canterbury's Pygmalion
Ch. Caralot's Hells Apoppin
Ch. Caralot's Poppin' Pluto
Ch. Carbert's Citation
Ch. Carbert's Magic Merlin
Ch. Carbert's Sassy Cassy

Ch. Chaps of Stonehedge
Ch. Chess Kings Hugs 'N Kisses
Ch. Chess Kings Kiss 'N Tell
Ch. Cloverhill's Bet and Fret
Ch. Cloverhill's Contessa
Ch. Da-Dar's Imperial Image
Ch. Easdale's Jeremiah Jazz
Ch. Glenmurray's Highland Fling
Ch. Glenmurray's Royal Stewart
Ch. Glenmurray's Tam O'Shanter
Ch. Heyday Honora
Ch. Homestead's Festus
Ch. Homestead's Marshall Dillon
Ch. Kory's 'N Milru's Karryon
Ch. Lakeland's I'm Sunny
Ch. Lakeland's Total Eclipse
Ch. Libra's To Sir With Love
Ch. Lipton's Crepe-De-Chine
Ch. Lipton's Minuette
Ch. Mal-Ann's Kopy Kat In Ebony
Ch. Mal-Ann's Sally Snowshoes
Ch. Mal-Ann's Tiger Paws
Ch. Markota's Merry Maker
Ch. Memoir's Licorice Lady
Ch. Memoir's Marc In The Dark
Ch. Mine Hills Partners Choice
Ch. Moonlight Serenade of Black Magic
Ch. Must-Do's Matador
Ch. Overoak 'Tis Demon's Warlock
Ch. Phi-Tau's Coppersmith
Ch. Porter's Black Lace
Ch. Roann's Rally

Ch. Rob-Mar's A Little Nite Music
Ch. Sandcastles Tasmanian Devil
Ch. Sealane's Amphrite
Ch. Sealane's Black Bart
Ch. Sealane's Loreli
Ch. Senrab's Sinner
Ch. So-Ho's Babe In Toyland
Ch. Stonehedge Fanny Barr
Ch. Stonehedge Rhett Butler
Ch. Stonehedge Sophia
Ch. Suropen's Stop The Music
Ch. Suropen's Wright Choice
Ch. Symphony Serenade
Ch. Tanorama's Taxicab
Ch. T-Boy's Le Vie En Rose
Ch. Thurlyn Acre Tanzania
Ch. Trojan Maxie Tan
Ch. Wayfarer's Golden Memories
Ch. Wildfires Sin-D-Cated
Ch. Wildrose's Sterling Magic
Ch. Windy Hill's Delight O'Calypso
Ch. Windy Hill's Demon's Hobgoblin
Ch. Windy Hill's Great Expectations
Ch. Windy Hill's Incantation
Ch. Windy Hill's Inherit-The-Wind
Ch. Windy Hill's 'Tis Snackin-Good
Ch. Windy Hill's 'Tis-A-Wench
Ch. Windy Hill's 'Tis Witch Hazel
Ch. Windy Hill's Without-A-Doubt
Ch. Woodlane Beau Brummel
Ch. Woodlane Miss Goldisocks

Ch. Stockdale Town Talk

```
                          ┌──────── Noble Sir
          ┌────── CH. ARGYLL'S ARCHER
          │               └──────── Sand Spring Smile Awhile
CH. STOCKDALE TOWN TALK
          │               ┌──────── CH. STOCKDALE STARTLER
          └────── Audacious Lady
                          └──────── Black Winnie
```

Whelped: 1939
Breeder: Mr. and Mrs. S. T. Adams
Owner: Mr. C. B. Van Meter

The sire of 81 Champions

Ch. Adams' Black Charm	Ch. Cainewood Cadet
Ch. Adams' Black Perfection	Ch. Cainewood Scandal
Ch. Aldoran's Desert Sandra	Ch. Camby's Jack Frost
Ch. Alfmar's Town Stepper	Ch. Camby's Lamplighter
Ch. Arcadia's Typey Girl	Ch. Camby's Stardust
Ch. Bar-Kay's Sweet Talk	Ch. Cha Ra Chitter Chatter
Ch. Belden Town Blaze	Ch. Cha Ra's Corky
Ch. Belden Town Sister	Ch. Charson's Golden Whirlwind
Ch. Belden Town Talk	Ch. Co-Lo Swan-ee Sportsman
Ch. Belden Vogue Girl	Ch. Country Gossip
Ch. Black Sequin of Lodestar	Ch. Dantom's Ballyhoo
Ch. Blue Gate's Mr. Town Talk	Ch. Echo Ridge Chief Topic
Ch. Buvens' Town Talk Angus	Ch. Forest-Glen Dark Town Strutter

Ch. Gadabout Volcano
Ch. Greene-Lea Town Debutante
Ch. Hauck's Desert Runner
Ch. Hauck's Loma
Ch. Hickory Hill High Barbaree
Ch. Hickory Hill High Holiday
Ch. Hi-Tone Townsman
Ch. Hi-Tone Town Token
Ch. Ivor's Boy
Ch. Jauneta of Crestwood
Ch. Lancaster Nowanda's Pride
Ch. Lewis' Town Tattler
Ch. Maplecliffe Gossip
Ch. Marmilos Golden Lady
Ch. Marmilos Lucky Penny
Ch. Marmilos Maid O'War
Ch. Marmilos Prince Royal
Ch. Marmilos Queen's Choice
Ch. Marmilos Red Lady
Ch. Maunalani Chief Bingo
Ch. Maunalani Kandy
Ch. Myroy Masterpiece
Ch. Myroy Miss Muffet
Ch. Myroy Sandra of Edgewood Park
Ch. Nelson's Topper
Ch. Newcrest Victorian Lady
Ch. Norbill's Back Talk
Ch. Norbill's Golden Fancy

Ch. Paglen Propaganda
Ch. Ramizzou's Head Man
Ch. Ramizzou's Missy
Ch. Reichert's Golden Charm
Ch. Sem Tex Town Talk
Ch. Silver Maple Lone Ranger
Ch. Silver Prince
Ch. Smithwood Arch Apollo
Ch. Southerndown Calico Print
Ch. Southerndown Full O'Glamour
Ch. Southerndown Newsboy
Ch. Stockdale Diplomat
Ch. Stockdale James
Ch. Stockdale Red Rocket
Ch. Stockdale Sunny Sue
Ch. Stockdale Town Talk Special
Ch. Swan-ee Ace Skipper
Ch. Swan-ee Cinnamon Sue
Ch. Swan-ee Sir Don
Ch. Swan-ee Slick Chick
Ch. Swan-ee Town Showman
Ch. Talked About
Ch. Town Talk's Clipper
Ch. Town Talk's Hope
Ch. Windridge Chief Wenatchee
Ch. Wings of Fame
Ch. Zada's Queen Victoria

Ch. Clarkdale Capital Stock

```
                                  ┌──────── CH. ELDERWOOD BANGAWAY
                  ┌──────── CH. DEKARLOS DASHAWAY
                  │               └──────── CH. DEKARLOS MISS DOROTHY
CH. CLARKDALE CAPITAL STOCK
                  │               ┌──────── CH. ELDERWOOD BANGAWAY
                  └──────── CH. CLARKDALE CLOSING QUOTATION
                                  └──────── CH. CLARKDALE COPPER VALENTINE
```

Whelped: March 21, 1957
Breeder/Owner: Mr. and Mrs. Leslie E. Clarke

The sire of 76 Champions

Ch. Baliwick Behulie
Ch. Bardabra's Capital Asset
Ch. Bar-Do-Ca Bit-By-Bit
Ch. Breeze Hill Breeze Along
Ch. Champagne's Bewitched
Ch. Chandler's Charley Chan
Ch. Chandler's Lady Caprice
Ch. Chuck O'Luck's Calliope
Ch. Clarkdale Capital Bonanza
Ch. Clarkdale Capital Recap
Ch. Clarkdale Collector's Item
Ch. Clarkdale Constant Conflict
Ch. Clarkdale Corporation
Ch. Crackerbox Caption
Ch. Crackerbox Captivating

Ch. Crackerbox Quail Trail
Ch. Danzata Commodore Cappy
Ch. DeKarlos Dancin' Doll
Ch. DeKarlos Dash-O-Tan
Ch. Desert Sands Scheherazade
Ch. Ellen's Black Jabeau
Ch. Ermhaven's Derby Classic
Ch. Evdon's Royal Prince Michael
Ch. Flo-Bob's Lil Marlaine
Ch. Flo-Bob's Preferred Stock
Ch. Gaynor's Dow Jones
Ch. Har-Dee's Hell Bender II
Ch. Hardee's Hell Raiser
Ch. Hickory Hill High Caper
Ch. Hickory Hill High Caption

Ch. Hi-Jac's Hey Dere
Ch. Jackaloo's Chickasaw Squaw
Ch. Jackaloo's Wildcat
Ch. Jacwyn Jenny Lind
Ch. Juniper's Jamboree
Ch. Juniper's Jigsaw
Ch. Lanebrook's Bondsman
Ch. Lanebrook's Dividend
Ch. Lanebrook's Mr. Holden
Ch. Lazy Bend's Go Girl Go
Ch. Lazy Bend's Legacy
Ch. Leelon Homecoming
Ch. Leelon Journey's End
Ch. Loucliff's Esperance, UD
Ch. Lucho Maria
Ch. Lulu's Black Magic
Ch. Lurola's Leading Issue
Ch. Lynmark's Sweet 'N' Lovely
Ch. Mar-Wall Miss Tru-Cap Heartache
Ch. Matador's Marionette
Ch. Matador's Marquis
Ch. Meri-Glad's Meetmenow
Ch. Merry-Wag's Happy Cappy

Ch. Morrow's Melissa
Ch. Nelson's Royal Rancher
Ch. Nelson's Royal Reverie
Ch. Nelson's Royal Ripper
Ch. O'Sage Talisman
Ch. PauPat's Playboy
Ch. Pinefair Plus
Ch. Quailtrail Instant
Ch. Robiano's Mister Charlie
Ch. Rozal's Restock
Ch. Sham-O-Jet's Black Jack
Ch. Sham-O-Jet's Picked To Click
Ch. Shiloh Dell's Sunburst
Ch. Shiner's Investment
Ch. Shunga's Capital Heir
Ch. Squier's Captain Midnight
Ch. Tillary Madcap
Ch. Tillary Nightcap
Ch. Toss Up Town-N-Country Topic
Ch. Valli-Lo's Velours
Ch. Valli-Lo's Viceroy
Ch. Van-Dor Valiant
Ch. Wenmark Watussi

Ch. Crackerbox Certainly

```
                              ┌─── CH. ELDERWOOD BANGAWAY
                ┌─── CH. BALIWICK BANTER
                │             └─── CH. GENESEE GREAT DAISY
CH. CRACKERBOX CERTAINLY
                │             ┌─── CH. ST. ANDREA'S MEDICINE MAN
                └─── CH. CRACKERBOX COLLAR AND CUFFS
                              └─── CH. LANCASTER NOWANDA'S PRIDE
```

Whelped: June 1956
Breeder/Owner: Crackerbox Kennels, Reg.

The sire of 73 Champions

Ch. ABJ's Ben Tune II
Ch. Baliwick Be-Bop
Ch. Benwood Hanna
Ch. Bo-Art's Sugarfoot
Ch. Ca-Da's Velvet Swan
Ch. Charan's Tam-O-Shanty
Ch. Chuck O'Luck's Tim Tan
Ch. Clarkdale Carriage Trade
Ch. Clarkdale Certainly
Ch. Coronet Certain Hit
Ch. Coronet Certain Ways
Ch. Coronet Certainly True
Ch. Coronet Certified
Ch. Coronet Flair
Ch. Crackerbox Camouflage
Ch. Crackerbox Certified
Ch. Crackerbox Compact II
Ch. Crackerbox Confidential
Ch. Crackerbox Crepe Soles
Ch. Crackerbox Crepe Suzette
Ch. Croyden Cross Clockwork
Ch. Dellwood's Definitely
Ch. Four Palms Silver Satin
Ch. Hall-Way Hark
Ch. Hall-Way Heretic
Ch. Hall-Way Humoresque
Ch. Hazelwood's Jimmie Valentine
Ch. Hazelwood's Valencia
Ch. Hickory Hill High Note
Ch. Hickory Hill High Key
Ch. Hickory Hill High Treble
Ch. Hillcrest Ball of Fire
Ch. Holly Tree Certainly A Lady
Ch. Kur-Land Brocade Slipper
Ch. Kuykendall's Kathy-O
Ch. Leister's Certainly Fancy
Ch. Leister's Certainly Rockette

Ch. Loucliff's Autumn Breeze
Ch. Loucliff's Bridge Jett
Ch. Lurola's Certain Lad
Ch. Lurola's Lolette
Ch. Meri-Glad's Certain Bonus
Ch. Meri-Glad's Magnificence
Ch. Meri-Glad's My Fair Lady
Ch. Mijo's Moccasins
Ch. Mijo's Momentum
Ch. Milru's Tantaliza
Ch. Palmwood Pacemaker
Ch. Palmwood Pepper Pot
Ch. Palmwood Picture Pretty
Ch. Palmwood Pollyanna
Ch. Palmwood Princess Papita
Ch. Palmwood Promenader
Ch. Pinetop's Certainly Bubbling
Ch. Pinetop's Certainly Fancy
Ch. Pinetop's Fancy Patches
Ch. Pinetop's Perchance
Ch. Pinetop's Sho'Nough
Ch. R-Fun's Fun Loving
Ch. Rockcrest Stormy Weather
Ch. Rozal's Ramona
Ch. Ru-Dan's Rusty Ruffles
Ch. Sea Swing So Sure
Ch. Shady Hill's Mr. Personality
Ch. Sky Dance Topgallant
Ch. Snead's Trademark
Ch. Storyland's Jack O Lantern
Ch. Wally's Certainly Special
Ch. Wally's Top-Valued Victor
Ch. Whitfield's War Whoop
Ch. Whitfield's Why Certainly
Ch. Woodlane Sheer Delight
Ch. Woodlane Weatherly

Ch. Artru Sandpiper

```
                              ┌──────CH. ARTRU HOT ROD
                  ┌── CH. ARTRU JOHNNY-BE-GOOD
                  │           └──── Jo-Be-Glen's Honeycomb
CH. ARTRU SANDPIPER
                  │           ┌────── CH. CHARMA'S MR. O'HARRIGAN
                  └── CH. BAR-C-KAR'S PEAU ROUGE
                              └──── Artru Bar-C-Kar
```

Whelped: July 18, 1965
Breeder: Corine Karcher
Owner: Mrs. Arthur Benhoff

The sire of 68 Champions

Ch. Andra Artru Sundance
Ch. Artru Action
Ch. Artru Andra
Ch. Artru Cricket
Ch. Artru Honora's Harmony
Ch. Artru Jan-Myr's Jupiter
Ch. Artru Jan-Myr's Robin
Ch. Artru Manor Ebony
Ch. Artru Red Devil
Ch. Artru Sanderling
Ch. Artru Sundance Sandstorm
Ch. Artru Sundance Sonata
Ch. Artru Trinket
Ch. Bar-C-Kar's Julie
Ch. Bar-C-Kar's Strawberry Sundae
Ch. Beau's Fireball
Ch. Charmel's Mr. Big Stuff
Ch. Chip-A-Ru Rosy Sunbeam
Ch. Clara's Pipe Music
Ch. Clara's Swan Song
Ch. Davis' Apple Blossom Pink
Ch. Ditan's Van-Dor Val
Ch. Dorji's Copper Doll
Ch. Dorji's Sandman
Ch. Echo Valley's Gold-N-Dust Storm
Ch. Feinlyne's Minerva
Ch. Feinlyne's Toast of Highpoint
Ch. Gina's Li'l Bit O'Missy
Ch. Gina's Sassy Molassey
Ch. Honora's Fay Ray
Ch. Jan Myr's Artru Chiribiribin
Ch. Jim Joy's Light 'N' Lively
Ch. Kamps' Kopper Kettle
Ch. Lanebrook's Bittersweet

Ch. Lanebrook's Sir Charles
Ch. Lord's Scot Royal
Ch. Mal-Ann's High Wind
Ch. Mal-Ann's Vandal
Ch. Mar-Jac's Marking Time
Ch. Milru's Oh By Jingles
Ch. Mi'Way Look My Way
Ch. Mi'Way's Little Sambo
Ch. Neff's Country Lad
Ch. Neff's Sparkle
Ch. Pama's Cinderella
Ch. Pett's Soft Beige
Ch. Pett's Yum Yum Beige
Ch. Pleasant Valley Swing Dance
Ch. Roann's Rakish Barfli
Ch. Sagamore Apache
Ch. Sagamore Cascade
Ch. Sagamore Colleen
Ch. Sagamore Flirt
Ch. Sagamore Frivolity
Ch. Sagamore Silhouette
Ch. Sagamore Sprite
Ch. Sagamore Toccoa
Ch. Sanstar's Heidi
Ch. Sanstar's Pied Piper
Ch. Sarbonah Queen of Hearts
Ch. Seven's Sandpebbles
Ch. Three Crown's Torch Ginger
Ch. Three Crown's Trader
Ch. Trevleigh's Astronaut
Ch. Upson Downs Miss Artru
Ch. Valleydale Vision
Ch. Will-Mar's Gold Chip
Ch. Wistful's Would You Believe

Ch. Bobwin's Sir Ashley

```
                          ┌─────── CH. DUR-BET'S PICK THE TIGER, CD
              ┌─────── CH. WINDY HILL'S 'TIS DEMI'S DEMON
              │           └─────── CH. WINDY HILL'S 'TIS DEMI-TASSE
CH. BOBWIN'S SIR ASHLEY
              │           ┌─────── CH. ARTRU SKYJACK
              └─────Ashleys Cherry Jubilee
                          └─────── Ashley's Ramblin' Rose
```

Whelped: September 27, 1976
Breeder: Catherine Ashley
Owner: Mrs. Winnie Vick, Bobwin Kennels

The sire of 65 Champions

Ch. Arow's Allstar
Ch. Arow's Ambition
Ch. Arow's Argonaut
Ch. Baicrest's Flashy Ashley
Ch. Bobwin's Bachtel of Tamara
Ch. Bobwin's Lady Cynthia
Ch. Bobwin's Lady Harriet
Ch. Bobwin's Lady Hope
Ch. Bobwin's Lady Jus-Us
Ch. Bobwin's My Fair Lady
Ch. Bobwin's Napoleon
Ch. Bobwin's N' Cobb's Love Token
Ch. Bobwin's No Sir
Ch. Bobwin's Silver Nitrate
Ch. Bobwin's Sir Black Ash
Ch. Bobwin's Sir Bottanley
Ch. Bobwin's Sir Buffington
Ch. Bobwin's Sir Charles
Ch. Bobwin's Sir Thomas
Ch. Bobwin's Springtime Jubilee
Ch. Bobwin's To Heck With Sir
Ch. Bobwin's Yes Sir
Ch. Camelot's Commander
Ch. Camelot's Craftsman
Ch. Carmaby's Quarterback
Ch. Cobb's Mayne Man
Ch. Cobb's Soul Connection
Ch. De-Sir-Cay's Something Special
Ch. De-Sir-Cay's The Great Caruso
Ch. Doug's Spectacular Bid
Ch. Dur-Bet's Mommy's Dearest
Ch. Durspen's Bribery
Ch. Estell's Sir Michael

Ch. Flairhaven's Anna Ba Nana
Ch. Flairhaven's Fasmar Screamer
Ch. Flairhaven's Licorice Whip
Ch. Flairhaven's Miss Coray
Ch. Flairhaven's Springtime Doll
Ch. Gamblers Solitaire
Ch. Gaylyn's Parlour Maid
Ch. Glenmurray's Midnight Blue
Ch. Jus-Us Commander Kane
Ch. Kabal's Sir Rodney
Ch. Kapnera's Miss Melanie
Ch. Kapnera's Rhett Butler
Ch. Legacy's Runnin Wi' The Wind
Ch. Newton's Cream Sachet
Ch. Oceanflight's Fancy Dresser
Ch. Palm Hill's Mountain Ashe
Ch. Palm Hill's That's Mine
Ch. Piperhill's Always A Lady
Ch. Piperhill's Man In Black
Ch. Raintree's Repetition
Ch. Raintree's Roustabout
Ch. Shenanigans of the Hood
Ch. Shenanigans of the Madam
Ch. Sir Duffington of Flairhaven
Ch. Springtime Flairhaven's Brat
Ch. Springtime Flairhaven's Pryd
Ch. Starfire's Sweet Lady Ashley
Ch. Sunshine's Happy Go Lucky
Ch. Sunshine's Revilo Seneca
Ch. Sunshine's Revilo Stetson
Ch. T-Rose's Shot In The Dark
Ch. Ursa's Latratus Canis

Int. Ch. Maddie's Vagabond's Return

```
                              ┌──── CH. ARNO'S STATESMAN
                ┌── Poling's Royal Splendor
                │             └──── Poling's Misty Girl
INT. CH. MADDIE'S VAGABOND'S RETURN
                │             ┌──── CH. LEE-EB'S ROYAL CAVALIER
                └── Lee-Eb's Sweetie Pie
                              └──── Lee-Eb's Golden Jewel
```

Whelped: October 1949
Breeder/Owner: Mrs. Madeline Peuquet

The sire of 60 Champions

Ch. Anscot Sylvia
Ch. Arlington's Mary Jane
Ch. Balport's Mister Mischief
Ch. Bangor's Modest John
Ch. Bilpat's Country Bumpkin
Ch. Bilpat's Dait Bait
Ch. Bilpat's Punkins
Ch. Carolina Yankee Doodle Dandy
Ch. Coray Vagabond King
Ch. Cottonwood Miss Liz
Ch. Country Place Just Toots
Ch. Creedaire Classic
Ch. Dover Hill's Chief of Staff
Ch. Eufaula's Contender
Ch. Flo-Bob's Return Dividend

Ch. Gravel Hill Gold Opportunity
Ch. Hall-Way Haughty
Ch. Hall-Way Havoc
Ch. Hall-Way Hooligan
Ch. Hall-Way King Sirus
Ch. Hi-Boots Such Crust
Ch. Hillgarden Amy
Ch. Hilltop High Return
Ch. Hilltop Mr. Kelly
Ch. Kirklane's Miss Dusty
Ch. Lil-Yan's Honey Bea
Ch. Lil-Yan's Lanekai
Ch. Maddie's Jet Black
Ch. Maddie's Vagabond's Glory
Ch. Maddie's Vagabond's Repeat

Ch. Maddie's Vagabond's Special
Ch. Mar-Hawk's Tomahawk
Ch. McClain's Silver Queen
Ch. Merry-Mount's Man About Town
Ch. Merry-Wag's Silver Dollar
Ch. Noetown's Red Star Mars
Ch. Norbill's Fancy Vagabond
Ch. Oak Manor Hope
Ch. O'Dell's Silver Chips II
Ch. Our Pride Gay Blade
Ch. Our Pride Jewel
Ch. Our Pride Parti Girl
Ch. Our Star Bonita
Ch. Our Star Carrollita
Ch. Penny Brook Charmer

Ch. Pett's Best Regards To Nor-Mar
Ch. Plantation Lil' Lou
Ch. Richelle's Five Star Jeneral
Ch. Rural Town's Model Man
Ch. Sohio's Sequin
Ch. Stockdale Criterion
Ch. Sun Shadows of Sherristar
Ch. Timber Lane Topaz
Ch. Tradewind Vagabond Glo
Ch. Tradewind Vagabond Thrill
Ch. Tradewind Vagabond Zephyr
Ch. Whistle Stop High Note
Ch. Winsome Way's Gold Rush
Ch. Winsome Way's Orange Blossom
Ch. Yorktown's Vagabond Relief

Ch. Cottonwood's Congressman

```
                            ┌───── CH. LA MAR'S LONDON
             ┌───── CH. FORJAY'S WINTERWOOD
             │             └───── Forjay's Buffie
CH. COTTONWOOD'S CONGRESSMAN
             │             ┌───── CH. ARTRU SANDPIPER
             └───── Lorli Gigi
                           └───── Lorli's Matoaka
```

Whelped: January 1976
Breeder/Owner: Calvin E. Ward

The sire of 58 Champions

Ch. Barcrest Indian Cloud
Ch. Barcrest Misty Morning
Ch. Cloverhill's Citation
Ch. Cloverhill's Sunburst
Ch. Cottonwood's Colleen O'Brien
Ch. Cottonwood's Give 'Em Billy L
Ch. Darling Nice And Easy
Ch. Hannahs Amere Kindred Spirit
Ch. Harran's April Misty Mornin
Ch. Harran's Flying Butterfly
Ch. Ho-Win's Golden Jubilee
Ch. Hu-Mar's Helzapoppin
Ch. Hu-Mar's Regal Cottonwood
Ch. Jawat's Celebrity
Ch. Junebug Sountern Lace
Ch. Lorli Tigerwood
Ch. Magic Mountain's Tiffany
Ch. Makkell's Comedian
Ch. Makkell's Heady Scarlet O'Hara
Ch. Makkell's Leading Man
Ch. Makkell's Zeigfeld Girl
Ch. Mei-Hardt's Amber Glow
Ch. Mei-Hardt's Mlle Bernadette
Ch. Mei-Hardt's Mlle Danielle
Ch. Mei-Hardt's T.O.D.
Ch. Northyork Sly N' Family Stone
Ch. Palm Hill Caro-Bu's Solid Gold
Ch. Palm Hill Hu-Mar's Supertramp
Ch. Palm Hill's Effervescent

Ch. Palm Hill's Jelly Bean
Ch. Phi-Tau's Tall Tales
Ch. Piper Hill's Speaker of the House
Ch. Piper Hill's Go Man Go
Ch. Piper Hill's Me Special Too
Ch. Regal's Geisha Girl
Ch. Rhondo's Rembrandt
Ch. Rhondo's Rona Lisa
Ch. Richmond's Magnificent Doll
Ch. Rinky Dink's Candy Cane II
Ch. Rinky Dink's Copper Top
Ch. Rinky Dink's Top of the Mark
Ch. Sedgecreek's Elegance
Ch. Sedgecreek's Rambling Rose
Ch. Sho Gem's Southern Belle
Ch. Showtime Classy Cheerleader
Ch. Showtime Fancy Dan
Ch. Showtime Show Stopper
Ch. Sta-Mar's Member of Congress
Ch. Timothy's Gold Seeker
Ch. Toccata's Just Whisper
Ch. Toccata's Silver Sun
Ch. Valliant's She's A Foo Bear
Ch. Weatherfield Irish Mist
Ch. Weatherfield's Easter Bunny
Ch. Windy Hill's The Senator
Ch. Windy Hill's 'Tis Link's Charmer
Ch. Windy Hill's 'Tis Lipton's Rebuff
Ch. Windy Hill's 'Tis Sum-Thin-More

Ch. Artru Action

```
                                ┌───── CH. ARTRU JOHNNY-BE-GOOD
                  ┌──── CH. ARTRU SANDPIPER
                  │             └───── CH. BAR-C-KAR'S PEAU ROUGE
CH. ARTRU ACTION
                  │             ┌───── CH. HOLLYROCK HARVESTER
                  └──── Van-Dor Fancy Triane
                                └───── Mione Red Amber
```

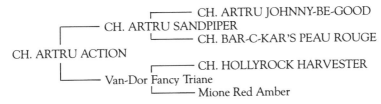

Whelped: August 1968
Breeder: Dorothy Vanderveer
Owner: Bill and Gay Ernst

The sire of 56 Champions

Ch. Al-Cyn-Don's Shur Shot
Ch. Artru Tsarevich Alexis
Ch. Begay's Ben Gay
Ch. Begay's Cleo Patti
Ch. Bigg's Sky Lark
Ch. Bigg's Snow Drift of Jemar
Ch. Brooklands Buff Action
Ch. Buckingham's Action-Packed
Ch. Candylane Carolina Classic
Ch. Castletop's High Octane
Ch. Castletop's Likety-Split
Ch. Castletop's Police Action
Ch. Castletop's Underdog
Ch. Castletop's Youthful O'Fender
Ch. Champel's Lollipop
Ch. Deer Walk Lady In Red
Ch. Deer Walk Lady of Action
Ch. Fair Acres Farm's Finesse

Ch. Fair Acres Farm's Jet Action
Ch. Girl's Delayed Action
Ch. Hob-Nob-Hill Cherry Jubilee
Ch. Manor's Born Free
Ch. Mar-Jac's Automation
Ch. Mar-Jac's Mister Mann
O.T. Ch. Mar-Lee's Folly O'Blarney, UD
Ch. McEnroe's Mystic
Ch. Milru's Charmel Number Five
Ch. Milru's Drummer Boy
Ch. Milru's Good Time Gentleman
Ch. Milru's Kismet
Ch. Milru's Sunfire
Ch. Pandora Pastel
Ch. Pandora Pirourette
Ch. Pandora Positive Action
Ch. Piner's Candor Concept
Ch. Piner's Premeditated

Ch. Rejoices Ginger Snap
Ch. Roann's Reaction To Action
Ch. Russ' Ruffian
Ch. Sarchell's Planned Action
Ch. Sarchell's Prime-Time Preview
Ch. Shenanigans of a Redhead
Ch. Stonehedge Auctioneer
Ch. Stonehedge Mr. Benfield
Ch. Tabaka's Fat Albert
Ch. Tabaka's Tidbit O'Wynden

Ch. Timothy's Wynden
Ch. Van-Dor Catch The Action
Ch. Windridge Stop The Music
Ch. Windy Hill's Delayed Action
Ch. Windy Hill's 'Tis-Fanci Action
Ch. Windy Hill's 'Tis Fanci Tam
Ch. Windy Hill's 'Tis Hope O'Carlen
Ch. Windy Hill's 'Tis Rose O'Memoir
Ch. Wynden's Fat Albert
Ch. Wynden's Weird Harold

Ch. La Mar's London

```
                            ┌───── CH. ARTRU HOT ROD
                ┌──── CH. ARTRU JOHNNY-BE-GOOD
                │           └───── Jo-Be-Glen's Honeycomb
CH. LA MAR'S LONDON
                │           ┌───── CH. NORBILL'S GOLDEN HARVEST II
                └──── CH. LA MAR'S IVORY SUMMER
                            └───── La Mar's Thumbellina
```

Whelped: September 23, 1967
Breeder/Owner: Mr. and Mrs. La Mar Mathis

The sire of 54 Champions

Ch. Blue's London Graham
Ch. Bouley's London Jewel
Ch. Bouley's London Lover
Ch. Butch's Ginny
Ch. Butch's Gringo
Ch. Candylane Chantilly

Ch. Caralot's Olympiad
Ch. Carlen's Charm of Memoir
Ch. Cheglomars Enola Gay
Ch. Cheglomars Hatter Fox
Ch. Cotillion Country Magic
Ch. Cotillion Irish Spring

Ch. Crig-Mar's Clever Countess
Ch. Crig-Mar's Sebastian
Ch. Davis' Don Jose
Ch. Davis' Dulcinea
Ch. Daymar's In The Red
Ch. Daymar's Mystic Illusion
Ch. Donnybrook Shenanigans
Ch. Forjay's Winterwood
Ch. Glen Hollow's Daisy A Day
Ch. Glen Hollow's Flying Machine
Ch. Glen Hollow's Silver Dollar
Ch. Glen Hollow's Starshine
Ch. Harlanhaven's Ivory Hunter
Ch. Heatherlane Hyperion
Ch. Joy N Tobaccoland's Tom Jones
Ch. Kekko's Daikoku of Willowood
Ch. Kuhn's Hot Wheels
Ch. La Mar's La Flee
Ch. La Mar's London Bridge
Ch. La Mar's London Lime
Ch. La Mar's London Marc

Ch. La Mar's London Mist
Ch. La Mar's Willowood
Ch. Laurie's Lady Flash
Ch. Laurie's La Lainia
Ch. Laurie's London Heir
Ch. Lewishaven Happy Talk
Ch. Lewishaven Love and Kisses
Ch. Orient's Public Defender
Ch. Pelham's Michigan Sportsman
Ch. Sagamore Counterpoint
Ch. Sagamore Nosegay
Ch. Sagamore Sophisticate
Ch. Sagamore Strutter
Ch. Shirmitch Sintenial
Ch. Shirmitch Style
Ch. Shirmitch Swiss Miss
Ch. Sho-Gem's Crown Jewel
Ch. Tallylyn My Liza Love
Ch. Willowood Wash-N-Wear II
Ch. Willowood Wicked Woman
Ch. Zizza's Katy O'Malley

Ch. Hob-Nob-Hill's Tribute

```
                               ┌──── CH. MERRYHAVEN STRUTAWAY
              ┌──── CH. HOB-NOB-HILL'S HOB-NOBBER
              │                └──── CH. HOB-NOB-HILL'S YUMBERRY
CH. HOB-NOB-HILL'S TRIBUTE
              │                ┌──── CH. KAY'S HOB-NOB-HILL HIFALUTIN'
              └──── Hob-Nob-Hill's Look Me Over
                               └──── Pett's Imp of White Satin
```

Whelped: March 1964
Breeder: Kay Hardy
Owner: Dr. and Mrs. Larry Smith

The sire of 54 Champions

Ch. Bleuaire's Loving Lady
Ch. Bleuaire's Mint Julep
Ch. Bleuaire's Pernickety
Ch. Bleuaire's Pollyanna
Ch. Bleuaire's Woodsman
Ch. Bucklodge Haymaker
Ch. Caudle's Whistle Stop
Ch. Dankrist I'm A Tiger
Ch. Dankrist Torchlight Parade
Ch. De-Sir-Cay's Tribute to Whit
Ch. Dur-Bet's Knight To Remember
Ch. Dur-Bet's Pick The Tiger
Ch. Earnscliffe Excalibur
Ch. Elm Hill's Enlightened One
Ch. Elm Hill's Pancho Villa
Ch. Hazelwood's Black Beauty
Ch. Hazelwood's Hildegarde
Ch. Hazelwood's Nick-O-Tan
Ch. Hazelwood's Sparkling Gem, CD
Ch. Heyday Happy Choice
Ch. Heyday Happy Solution
Ch. Heyday Happy Talk
Ch. Heyday Hennrietta
Ch. Heyday His Honor
Ch. Heyday Hollyhock
Ch. Jewell's Juliet, CDX
Ch. Leister's Hello Dolly

Ch. Liz-Bar Black Magic
Ch. Liz-Bar Legacy
Ch. Many Mink's Fantastic
Ch. Maplewood's Dina Mite
Ch. Memoir's Mannix
Ch. Memoir's Merry Monarch
Ch. Memoir's Merrywiggles
Ch. Merryhaven Heritage
Ch. Merryhaven Medallion
Ch. Palmwood Pattern
Ch. P'Gell's Pagan Princess
Ch. Phi-Tau's Applause
Ch. Plantation's Top Brass
Ch. Seligson's Scene Stealer
Ch. Shardeloes Samantha
Ch. Shiloh Dell's Napoleon Solo
Ch. Shiloh Dell's Sho-Man
Ch. Shiloh Dell's Sho-Tan
Ch. Shiloh Dell's Soloist of Evdon
Ch. Shoestring School Marm
Ch. Shoestring Shootin' Match
Ch. Shoestring Sugar Plum
Ch. Tobaccoland's Tribute
Ch. Trembly's Mask-O-Tan
Ch. Trotter's Dixie Hi-Light
Ch. Trotter's Lil Dainty Doll
Ch. Wagland Wear and Tear

Ch. Artru Johnny-Be-Good

```
                    ┌──────── CH. ARTRU CRACKERJACK
         ┌──── CH. ARTRU HOT ROD
         │          └──────── Pett's Ragtime Rhythm, CD
CH. ARTRU JOHNNY-BE-GOOD
         │          ┌──────── CH. JO-BE-GLEN'S GOLD CROSS
         └──── Jo-Be-Glen's Honeycomb
                    └──────── Jo-Be-Glen's Sunbeam
```

Whelped: January 17, 1961
Breeder: Bernice and John Muller
Owner: Ruth and Art Benoff, Jr.

The sire of 52 Champions

Ch. Abbi's Catch You
Ch. Ardee's Debutante
Ch. Artru Adonis
Ch. Artru Adventure
Ch. Artru Arpege
Ch. Artru Auditor
Ch. Artru Dutchess of Columbia
Ch. Artru Flirtation
Ch. Artru Globetrotter
Ch. Artru Good News
Ch. Artru Irresistable
Ch. Artru Jet Smooth
Ch. Artru Johnny Rebel
Ch. Artru Katy Did
Ch. Artru Miss Meri-Glad
Ch. Artru My-Pick
Ch. Artru Red Baron
Ch. Artru Rum Bisque
Ch. Artru Sandpiper
Ch. Artru Special Delivery
Ch. Artru Topknotch
Ch. Bar-C-Kar's Jeanne Soit Bonne
Ch. Bar-C-Kar's Mr. Chips
Ch. Bar-C-Kar's Mr. Sandman
Ch. Bar-C-Kar's Mr. Toy Town
Ch. Bar-C-Kar's Red Sherrie

Ch. Bar-C-Kar's Sweet Kream
Ch. Bar-C-Kar's Tampa Lea
Ch. Breeze Hill Skipjack, CD
Ch. Caroden's Johnny Crack Corn
Ch. Cloverlane's Happy Go Lucky
Ch. Comac's Injun Chief
Ch. Doherty's Sportsman
Ch. Feinlyne Femme Fatal
Ch. Harmony's Top Flight
Ch. In-A-Wood Chickadee
Ch. Just Plain Big Bad John
Ch. La Mar's Ivory Genie
Ch. La Mar's London
Ch. Marty's Martini Mist
Ch. Merry-Wag's Johnny Artru
Ch. Milru's Lady Be Good
Ch. Peanut Butter V
Ch. Pen Del Behave
Ch. Pen Del Be Smart
Ch. Pinetop's Dashing Hilarity
Ch. Sugarbrook Gay Lady
Ch. Twinsand's Talisman
Ch. Upsan Downs Classy Lassy
Ch. Valleydale Fascination
Ch. Valleydale Mistletoe
Ch. Van-Dor Verynice

Ch. Lurola's Royal Lancer

```
                              ┌───── Baliwick Bangaway
                 ┌───── CH. LUROLA'S LOOKOUT
                 │            └───── Lurola's Lady Luck
CH. LUROLA'S ROYAL LANCER
                 │            ┌───── CH. CLARKDALE CAPITAL STOCK
                 └───── Clarkdale Castaneye
                              └───── Clarkdale Caravan
```

Whelped: July 1969
Breeder/Owner: Lucia and Bob Lake

The sire of 51 Champions

Ch. Alorah's En Garde
Ch. Alorah's Royale
Ch. Birchwood Blackjac O'Darembi
Ch. Birchwood Bright Star
Ch. Bluechip's Stockbroker
Ch. Buckinghamhill Am Erica
Ch. Buckinghamhill Freedom Ring
Ch. Carlyn's Where It's At
Ch. Chess King's Board Boss
Ch. Chess King's Predator
Ch. Chess King's Renegade
Ch. Dorobin Duck Soup
Ch. Gina's Magic Moment
Ch. Gina's Molasses Candy
Ch. Juniper's Jam A Dai
Ch. Juniper's Just A Texan
Ch. Kaplar's Butch Kassidy

Ch. Kaplar's Kant-B-Leve It
Ch. Kaplar's Karbon-Kopi
Ch. Kaplar's Keystone Kop
Ch. Kaplar's Koko Kola
Ch. Kaplar's Kopi-Kat
Ch. Kaplar's Kouldn't Be
Ch. Kaplar's Krackshot
Ch. Kaplar's Royal Kavalier
Ch. Kaplar's Royal Keepsake
Ch. Libertyville Belinda
Ch. Libertyville Mr. Willie D
Ch. Libertyville Twinkling Star
Ch. Lurola's Lanette
Ch. Lurola's Midnight Lace
Ch. Lurola's Royal Heir
Ch. Lurola's Sir Lawrence
Ch. Penthouse Royal Rook

Ch. Piner's Point of View
Ch. Ram-Wal's Royal Lookout
Ch. Senrab's Lady Of The Lake
Ch. Senrab's Sir Lancerlot
Ch. Serenade's Lamplighter
Ch. Shannondale Sachet
Ch. Shannondale Safari
Ch. Shannondale Saphire
Ch. Shardeloes Serenata

Ch. Shelbyshire's Bold Ruler
Ch. Shelbyshire's Citation
Ch. Shelbyshire's Lurola Legend
Ch. Shelbyshire's Something Royal
Ch. Shelbyshire's Squire
Ch. Shelbyshire's Storm Warning
Ch. Shenanigans Of A Ragamuffin
Ch. Signature's Summer and Smoke

Ch. Artru Red Baron

```
                               ┌──── CH. ARTRU HOT ROD
                 ┌──── CH. ARTRU JOHNNY-BE-GOOD
                 │             └──── Jo-Be-Glen's Honeycomb
CH. ARTRU RED BARON
                 │             ┌──── CH. CHARMA'S MR. O'HARRIGAN
                 └──── Artru Kathleen
                               └──── Artru Bar-C-Kar
```

Whelped: June 1, 1967
Breeder/Owner: Mr. and Mrs. Arthur Benhoff, Jr.

The sire of 49 Champions

Ch. Abbi's Bit O'Gold
Ch. Abbi's Fancy Little Nancy
Ch. Alorah's Alamo
Ch. Alorah's Artful Dodger
Ch. Alorah's Foxfire
Ch. Alorah's Silver Baron
Ch. Alorah's Wanderlust
Ch. Artru Big Shot
Ch. Artru Buff Baron

Ch. Artru Emeraude
Ch. Artru Jan-Myr Camelot
Ch. Artru Jan-Myr Entertainer
Ch. Artru Jan-Myr Music Man
Ch. Artru Jan-Myr Nature Boy
Ch. Artru Jan-Myr Pal Joey
Ch. Artru Jan-Myr Rocky
Ch. Artru Jan-Myr Solo
Ch. Artru La Toka's Cutlass

Ch. Artru Skyjack
Ch. Audrey's Sunrise
Ch. Dorobin Dance Band
Ch. Evdons Copper King
Ch. Feinlyne Flintstone
Ch. Golden Acre's Wild Honey
Ch. Greenelm Garnet Baron
Ch. Jan-Myr Artru April Love
Ch. Jan-Myr Artru My Fair Lady
Ch. Jan-Myr Artru True Love
Ch. Just Call Me A Bundle of Joy
Ch. Just Call Me Gingerbread Boy, CD
Ch. Just Call Me Hey There Pal Joey
Ch. Kapewood Prince Matchebelli
Ch. Kapewood Royal Baron
Ch. Kapewood's Rowesbeau

Ch. Kaplar's Kolleen
Ch. Kaplar's Luck O'The Irish
Ch. Kaplar's St. Patrick
Ch. Kekko's Komadori
Ch. Kekko's Ronin
Ch. La Toka's Tiara
Ch. Lorli's Sasa
Ch. Mi'Way Baron My Way
Ch. Mi'Way's Maximilian
Ch. Mi'Way Song of My Way
Ch. Mi'Way Travelling My Way
Ch. Mi'Way Wild Honey
Ch. Palm Hill's Cookie Monster
Ch. Shenanigans Of A Hooligan, CD
Ch. Upsan Downs Elegance

Ch. Forjay's Winterwood

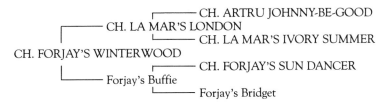

```
                          ┌──────── CH. ARTRU JOHNNY-BE-GOOD
          ┌──── CH. LA MAR'S LONDON
          │               └──────── CH. LA MAR'S IVORY SUMMER
CH. FORJAY'S WINTERWOOD
          │               ┌──────── CH. FORJAY'S SUN DANCER
          └──── Forjay's Buffie
                          └──────── Forjay's Bridget
```

Whelped: August 2, 1971
Breeder: Edward and Anne Johnston
Owner: Don Johnston

The sire of 47 Champions

Ch. B J's Girl Pollyann Go-Tee
Ch. Chidals London Mist
Ch. Cottonwood's Congressman
Ch. Cottonwood's Cotillion
Ch. Darling Winter Wonderland
Ch. Estell's Am-A-Devil
Ch. Forjay's Michael
Ch. Glenmere Greta
Ch. Judi-Jers Boy Wood
Ch. Judi-Jers Winter Black Touch
Ch. Judi-Jers Winter Day
Ch. Judi-Jers Winter Junebug
Ch. Judi-Jers Winter's Promise
Ch. Kane Venture Verve
Ch. Kokad's Winter Hunt
Ch. Mojo's Smart Alex
Ch. Peppygae Roxanne of Tibbett
Ch. Ramblewood Winter Dream
Ch. Russ' Amere Heart's Desire
Ch. Russ' Red Winter
Ch. Russ' Winter Beauty
Ch. Russ' Wood Crafter
Ch. Seesaus Cecil
Ch. Shadowridge Spring Fashion

Ch. Shady Creeks Storm of Winter
Ch. Sher-Ron's Wind Commander
Ch. Sher-Ron's Wind Song
Ch. Sher-Ron's Wind Storm
Ch. Sher-Ron's Wind Swept
Ch. Startrek's Winter Sun
Ch. Tibbett's Hot Winter
Ch. Timothy's Fly Robin Fly
Ch. Timothy's Hi-Lites
Ch. Timothy's Shady Lady II
Ch. Trishtello Tolouse-Lautrec
Ch. Tru-Will's Winter Holiday
Ch. Wibs Silver Touch
Ch. Wibs Winter Bear
Ch. Wibs Winter Blossom
Ch. Wibs Winter Classic
Ch. Wibs Winter Delight
Ch. Wibs Winter Dream
Ch. Wibs Winter Ice Follie
Ch. Wibs Winter Knight
Ch. Wibs Winter Snow Queen
Ch. Wibs Winter Stock
Ch. Wibs Winter Storm

Ch. Main-Dale's Mr. Success

```
                            ┌──── CH. BENWOOD ROCKAWAY
                ┌─── CH. MERRYHAVEN STRUTAWAY
                │           └──── Merryhaven Merrianne
CH. MAIN-DALE'S MR. SUCCESS
                │           ┌──── CH. HICKORY HILL HIGH JACK
                └─── CH. MAIN-DALE'S APRIL LOVE
                            └──── CH. MAIN-DALE'S WAMPETITE II
```

Whelped: September 10, 1959
Breeder/Owner: Dr. and Mrs. Carl Oldham

The sire of 46 Champions

Ch. Bardabra's Drummer Boy
Ch. Bardabra's Midnight Express
Ch. Camelot's Choirmaster
Ch. Camelot's Conserto
Ch. Carousel's Aldercliff
Ch. Colonial's Lively Lady
Ch. Condero Call Me Mr. Charlie
Ch. Dave's Dapper Dan
Ch. Denzil's Mister Successful
Ch. Dur-Bet's Certified Check
Ch. Dur-Bet's Sparkle 'N' Shine
Ch. Dur-Bet's Wheeler Dealer
Ch. Evdon's Ice Capers
Ch. Evdon's Prince Of Country View
Ch. Evdon's Sleet Storm
Ch. Flo-Bob's Success Story
Ch. Flo-Bob's Sweet And Lovely

Ch. Halfpenny Regent
Ch. Hickory Hill High Tradition
Ch. Hickory Hill High Treat
Ch. Hickory Hill High Tribute
Ch. Honey Hill Sun Dust
Ch. Korb's Sweet Lou-Ann
Ch. Leister's Dainty Cinderella
Ch. Main-Dale's Golden Touch
Ch. Main-Dale's Success Secret
Ch. Meri-Glad's Mr. Compact
Ch. Mijo's March Winds
Ch. Mijo's Martini
Ch. Mijo's Mint Julep
Ch. Mijo's Miss B Haven
Ch. Phi-Tau's Pattern
Ch. Pinefair Parson
Ch. Pinefair Password

Ch. R-Fun's Redoubtable
Ch. R-Fun's Remarkable
Ch. R-Fun's Risque
Ch. Rico's Travelin' Man
Ch. Shea's Leonardo
Ch. Shiloh Dell's Sho Kan

Ch. Shiloh Dell's Sonnet
Ch. Spring's Dark Knight
Ch. Trotter's Lil Dancer
Ch. Tucky-Ho Tonette
Ch. Tucky-Ho Touch 'N' Go
Ch. Valleydale Just Jane

Ch. Elderwood Bangaway

```
                              ┌───── CH. STOCKDALE RED ROCKET
              ┌───── CH. MYROY NIGHT ROCKET
              │               └───── CH. JOAQUIN RACHAEL
CH. ELDERWOOD BANGAWAY
              │               ┌───── CH. MYROY MASTERPIECE
              └───── CH. ELDER'S SO LOVELY
                              └───── Elder's Playgirl
```

Whelped: June 1950
Breeder: H. Stewart Elder
Owner: Mr. and Mrs. Robert J. Levy

The sire of 45 Champions

Ch. Abo's First Bit of Shakespeare
Ch. Allendale Mister Bang
Ch. Baliwick Banter
Ch. Benwood Rockaway

Ch. Bilpat's Flirt
Ch. Bilpat's Lady Luck
Ch. Carlano Cancan
Ch. Clarkdale Closing Quotation

Ch. Clarkdale Constant Comment
Ch. Clarkdale Copper Darlin
Ch. Debaway of Lazy Bend
Ch. DeKarlo's Dashaway
Ch. DeKarlo's Dreamboat
Ch. DeKarlo's Miss Demeanor
Ch. Double Star Linda Loma, CD
Ch. Gabrulee's Bangle Lee
Ch. Gayhurst Whizaway
Ch. Ginger Hill Mr. Bethcrest
Ch. Glenshaw's Greetings
Ch. Hickory Hill Heiress
Ch. Hickory Hill High Bang
Ch. Hopewood Bangle
Ch. Hopewood Bit O'Bilpat
Ch. Hopewood Knockout
Ch. Lazy Bend's Bea-Gay
Ch. Lazy Bend's Lookaway
Ch. Lazy Bend's Memory

Ch. Manorborn I Believe
Ch. Maribeau's Maid Thataway
Ch. Maribeau's Make-Away
Ch. Maribeau's Make-Way
Ch. Morrow's Miss Merry Gate
Ch. Morrow's Mr. Bang Up
Ch. Penthouse Classaway
Ch. Phi-Tau's Parade Master
Ch. Phi-Tau's Ring Master
Ch. Ricona Bang Up
Ch. Riteaway of Lazy Bend
Ch. Seehouse Dominic
Ch. Stanbara Cavalier
Ch. Stonehill Saturday Nighter
Ch. Stout's Whiz Bang
Ch. Veron Mark S
Ch. Viking Tullabang
Ch. Viking Wagaway

Top Producing Bitches

(Statistics complete through the February 1987 AKC *Gazette*)

1. Ch. Laurim's Star Performance . . . . R/W 20
2. Ch. Kaplar's Kolleen . . . . Buff 18
3. Ch. Kamps' Kountry Kiss . . . . R/W 17
4. Ch. Seenar's Seductress . . . . Black 15
5. Artru Delightful II . . . . Buff 14
5. Ch. Frandee's Susan . . . . B/W 14
5. Int. Ch. Honey Creek Vivacious . . . . R/W 14
6. Ch. Cobb's Kathleen . . . . Buff 13
7. Marquis Mistletoe . . . . R/W 12
8. Ch. Charmin Miss Carolyn . . . . R/W 11
8. Ch. Fi-Fo's Fiesta . . . . B/W 11
8. Can./Am. Ch. Hall-Way Fancy Free . . . . B/W 11
8. Ch. Hickory Hill High Night . . . . Black 11
8. Lanebrook's Dash O'Flash . . . . Black 11
8. Ch. Lanel's Rinky Dink's M and M . . . . Buff 11
8. Ch. Tallylyn My Liza Love . . . . Black 11
9. Ch. Bar-C-Kar's Peau Rouge . . . . Buff 10
9. Ch. Essanar Evening Song . . . . Black 10
9. Ch. Fancy Free Carmen . . . . R/W 10
9. Ch. Hickory Hill High Barbaree . . . . Black 10
9. Ch. Honey Creek Cricket . . . . R/W 10
9. Ch. Kaplars' Quicksilver . . . . Buff 10
9. Ch. Misty Mornin' Motif . . . . Black 10
9. Ch. Nor-Mar's Nice N' Neat . . . . B/W 10
9. Pounette Perrette . . . . R/W 10
9. Ch. Prime Time Crystal Pistol . . . . Buff 10
9. Ch. Sher-Ron's Windsong . . . . Buff 10

Ch. Laurim's Star Performance is the queen of all the top producers. Her total of 20 champions is remarkable in a Cocker Spaniel where big litters are not the rule. The Laurim Kennels of Dr. Jim and Marybeth Duncan have been turning out winners for many years.

The runner-up, Ch. Kaplar's Kolleen, is sired by one of the top-20 producers, Ch. Artru Red Baron. Her daughter, Ch. Kaplar's Quicksilver, also appears on the list. In turn, her son, Ch. Kaplar's Kassanova (by Ch. Artru Skyjack) has over 40 champions to his credit.

Another mother and daughter combination is the Sher-Ron combination of Ch. Tallylyn My Liza Love with 11 champions and her daughter, Ch. Sher-Ron's Wind Song with 10.

Ch. Honey Creek Vivacious with 14 champions is backed up by her dam, Ch. Honey Creek Cricket with 10 champions.

Ch. Lanel's M and M—the dam of 11 champions—is sired by Ch. Artru Skyjack and continues the Artru producing lines. M and M has been a great producer for the Rinky Dink's Kennel of the Petersens.

Pounette Perrette is the dam of 10 champions, among them Ch. Dreamridge Dinner Date. Dinner Date was a top winner and the dam of Ch. Dreamridge Dominoe, the sire of 109 champions.

Ch. Laurim's Star Performance

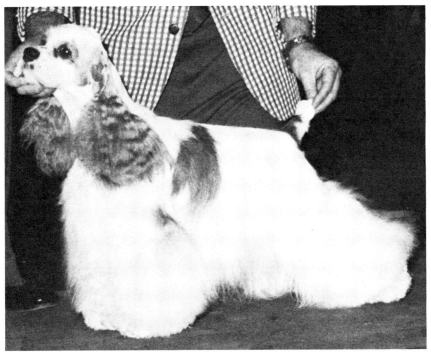

```
                           ┌────── CH. CAMBY'S CONTRIBUTION
              ┌────── CH. LAURIM'S COMMAND PERFORMANCE
              │            └────── CH. FI-FO'S LOVELY LAURIM
CH. LAURIM'S STAR PERFORMANCE
              │            ┌────── CH. BURSON'S BLARNEY
              └────── CH. LAURIM'S BIT OF BLARNEY
                           └────── CH. FI-FO'S LOVELY LAURIM
```

Whelped: April 2, 1973
Breeder: James and Laura Duncan & Mr. and Mrs. L. C. Kraeuchi
Owner: Dr. and Mrs. James R. Duncan

The dam of 20 champions:

Ch. Laurim's Classic Performance
Ch. Laurim's Flying Starlet
Ch. Laurim's Fox Star
Ch. Laurim's Happy To Perform
Ch. Laurim's Last Star
Ch. Laurim's Lick'em
Ch. Laurim's Powers Enchantress
Ch. Laurim's Shooting Star
Ch. Laurim's Starbright
Ch. Laurim's Stardust

Ch. Laurim's Starfire
Ch. Laurim's Starflight
Ch. Laurim's Star of Hi-D-Ho
Ch. Laurim's Star Point of Ditan
Ch. Laurim's Star Shine
Ch. Laurim's Super Performance
Ch. Laurim's Super Star
Ch. Laurim's Tell Star
Ch. Laurim's White Tail
Ch. Laurim's Wish Upon A Star

Ch. Kaplar's Kolleen

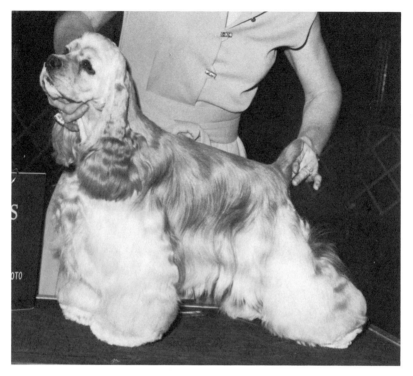

```
                                    ┌──────── CH. ARTRU JOHNNY-BE-GOOD
                    ┌──── CH. ARTRU RED BARON
                    │               └──────── Artru Katleen
CH. KAPLAR'S KOLLEEN
                    │               ┌──────── CH. ESSANAR'S EASTSIDE
                    └──── CH. KAPLAR'S CAMEO CAPER
                                    └──────── CH. SANDREX SARSAPARILLA
```

Whelped: March 17, 1976
Breeder/Owner: Laura and Harold B. Henson

The dam of 18 champions:

Ch. Kaplar's Flim-Flam Man	Ch. Kaplar's Kopper Key
Ch. Kaplar's Jackie Paper	Ch. Kaplar's Kreme Soda
Ch. Kaplar's Kahlua 'N Kreme	Ch. Kaplar's Kurtain Kall
Ch. Kaplar's Kard Shark	Ch. Kaplar's Lead On McDuff
Ch. Kaplar's Kassanova	Ch. Kaplar's Music Man
Ch. Kaplar's Katbird	Ch. Kaplar's Orange Krush
Ch. Kaplar's Kat Kall	Ch. Kaplar's Quicksilver
Ch. Kaplar's Kolt Forty-Five	Ch. Kaplar's Royal Klansman
Ch. Kaplar's Konspirator	Ch. Kaplar's Sends In The Klown

Ch. Kamps' Kountry Kiss

```
                                    ┌──── CH. REXPOINTE FLYING DUTCHMAN
                    ┌──── CH. REXPOINTE KOJAK
                    │               └──── Rexpointe Rachael
CH. KAMPS' KOUNTRY KISS
                    │               ┌──── CH. SANDY HILL SOLAR OF MYLISLEE
                    └──── CH. MIRWIN'S MERRY MISS
                                    └──── Azalea Hill's Christ-A-Belle
```

Whelped: December 6, 1976
Breeder/Owner: Harriet E. Kamps

The dam of 17 champions:

Ch. Kamps' Kall Me Klassy	Ch. Kamps' Kountry Road
Ch. Kamps' Kind-A-Nice	Ch. Kamps' Kountry Rose
Ch. Kamps' Kind A Special	Ch. Kamps' Kountry Smokehouse
Ch. Kamps' Kiss Me Kwik	Ch. Kamps' Kountry Time
Ch. Kamps' Koast To Koast	Ch. Kamps' Kredit Kard
Ch. Kamps' Kodiak Kountry Kid	Ch. Kamps' Krystal Pistol
Ch. Kamps' Kountry Dew	Ch. Kamps' Orange Krush
Ch. Kamps' Kountry Gentleman	Ch. Kamps' Sylvan Acres Sweet Shot
Ch. Kamps' Kountry Mist	

Ch. Seenar's Seductress

```
                              ┌─────── CH. HICKORKY HILL HIGH BRACKET
                ┌───────CH. RAM-BOW'S RAMBLER, C.D.X.
                │             └─────── Bejaks Lucky Heather, C.D.X.
CH. SEENAR'S SEDUCTRESS
                │             ┌─────── CH. PALMWOOD PROMENADER
                └─────── Palmwood Pantomine
                              └─────── CH. PALMWOOD PAMELA
```

Whelped: November 22, 1965
Breeder/Owner: Ramona and Carl M. Cantrell

The dam of 15 champions:

Ch. Seenar's Magician
Ch. Seenar's Mystic
Ch. Seenar's Seer
Ch. Seenar's Sinful
Ch. Seenar's Sorcerer
Ch. Seenar's Talk Talk
Ch. Seenar's Tamara
Ch. Seenar's Tana Liza, C.D.

Ch. Seenar's Tan Gent
Ch. Seenar's Tan Tasy
Ch. Seenar's Tan Temptress
Ch. Seenar's Tan Titian
Ch. Seenar's Tender Trap
Ch. Seenar's Tete-A-Tete
Ch. Seenar's Wizard

Artru Delightful II

```
                                  ┌────── CH. ARTRU JOHNNY-BE-GOOD
                    ┌────── CH. ARTRU SANDPIPER
                    │             └────── CH. BAR-C-KAR'S PEAU ROUGE
Artru Delightful II │
                    │             ┌────── CH. CA-DA'S PLUM BRANDY
                    └────── Request Plum Delight
                                  └────── Pen Del Burgundy Quest
```

Whelped: February 16, 1969
Breeder: Marie and Debra Kay Beauchamp
Owner: Kathleen M. Lane

The dam of 14 champions:

Ch. Artru Aquarius, C.D.
Ch. Artru Happiness Is Heather
Ch. Artru Jan-Myr's Mame
Ch. Artru La Toka Aviance
Ch. Artru La Toka Electron
Ch. Artru La Toka Masterpiece
Ch. Artru La Toka's Cutlass

Ch. Artru La Toka's Red Hot
Ch. Artru La Toka Terrific
Ch. Artru Snowbird
Ch. Artru Toyota
Ch. La Toka Artru Dulcimer
Ch. La Toka Moulin Rouge
Ch. La Toka's Tiara

Ch. Frandee's Susan

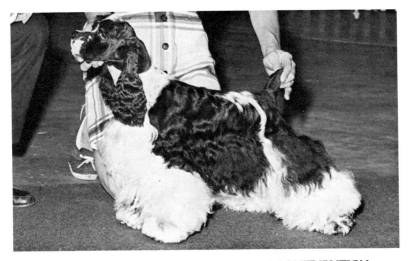

```
                                  ┌──── CH. CAMBY'S CONTRIBUTION
                   ┌──── Sonata's Holiday Caper
                   │              └──── CH. SONATA'S JUSTIN HOPE
CH. FRANDEE'S SUSAN
                   │              ┌──── CH. GIN-DI'S TRI BY JIMINY
                   └──── Mex./Am. CH. CORWIN'S DIAMOND LIL
                                  └──── CH. NOR-MAR'S NICE 'N' NEAT
```

Whelped: May 6, 1969
Breeder/Owner: Frank and Dee Dee Wood, Frandee Kennels

The dam of 14 champions:

Ch. Frandee's Bill Of Rights	Ch. Frandee's Flurry
Ch. Frandee's Cat's Meow	Ch. Frandee's Freedom
Ch. Frandee's Celebration	Ch. Frandee's Free N' Easy
Ch. Frandee's Dedication	Ch. Frandee's Gay Nineties
Ch. Frandee's Do Declare	Ch. Frandee's Miss Independence
Ch. Frandee's Farout	Ch. Frandee's Red White N' Blue
Ch. Frandee's Fireworks	Ch. Frandee's Tycoon

Int. Ch. Honey Creek Vivacious

```
                              ┌──── CH. BOBB'S SHOWMASTER
                 ┌──── Int. CH. SOGO SHOWOFF
                 │            └──── Sogo Suzette
Int. CH. HONEY CREEK VIVACIOUS
                 │            ┌──── CH. YOUNG'S LADDIE BOY
                 └──── CH. HONEY CREEK CRICKET
                              └──── CH. HONEY CREEK SUE
```

Whelped: November 1947
Breeder/Owner: Beatrice W. Wegusen

The dam of 14 champions:

Ch. Honey Creek Hallmark	Ch. Honey Creek Heller
Ch. Honey Creek Halo	Ch. Honey Creek Hero
Ch. Honey Creek Hankie	Ch. Honey Creek Hollander
Ch. Honey Creek Havana	Ch. Honey Creek Homework
Ch. Honey Creek Headline	Ch. Honey Creek Hosana
Ch. Honey Creek Heir Apparent	Ch. Honey Creek Hoyden
Ch. Honey Creek Heirloom	Ch. Honey Creek Hush

Ch. Cobb's Kathleen

```
                              ┌──────── Cobb's Red Jacket
               ┌───── CH. COBB'S RED COAT
               │              └──────── Cobb's Valentine Lace
CH. COBB'S KATHLEEN
               │              ┌──────── CH. BEAU'S FIRE BALL
               └───── CH. COBB'S KATYDID
                              └──────── Cobb's Hearts N' Flowers
```

Whelped: September 24, 1974
Breeder/Owner: Carolyn S. Cobb

The dam of 13 champions:

Ch. Cobb's Allison	Ch. Cobb's Jesse James
Ch. Cobb's Angelo Dan	Ch. Cobb's Keepsake
Ch. Cobb's Billy Jack	Ch. Cobb's Mountain Hi-C
Ch. Cobb's Chance For Waltann's	Ch. Cobb's Pale Moon
Ch. Cobb's Charlene	Ch. Cobb's Red Blazer
Ch. Cobb's Cherokee Fire	Ch. Cobb's String Of Hearts
Ch. Cobb's Country Breeze	

Marquis Mistletoe

```
                               ┌──────── CH. CAMBY'S CONTRIBUTION
                  ┌─────── Sonata's Holiday Caper
                  │            └──────── CH. SONATA'S JUSTIN HOPE
Marquis Mistletoe
                  │            ┌──────── CH. REXPOINTE SNOW JOB
                  └─────── CH. FEINLYNE FRIEZEE
                               └──────── CH. WOODSTOCK'S MAXI FEINLYNE
```

Whelped: June 8, 1977
Breeder/Owner: Karen Marquez

The dam of 12 champions:

Ch. Danzata's Daydream
Ch. Marquis Chantilly Lace
Ch. Marquis Dirty Dennis
Ch. Marquis Front Page
Ch. Marquis Hot To Trot
Ch. Marquis Muther Trucker

Ch. Marquis Next Move
Ch. Marquis Oh La La
Ch. Marquis Peter Pucker
Ch. Marquis Satin Doll
Ch. Marquis Step To My-Ida-Ho
Ch. Marquis Tri Jet

Ch. Charmin Miss Carolyn

```
                        ┌──────CH. REXPOINTE FLYING DUTCHMAN
          ┌────── CH. REXPOINTE KOJAK
          │             └────── Rexpointe Rachael
CH. CHARMIN MISS CAROLYN
          │             ┌────── CH. WINSOME WAY'S BLUE CHIP
          └────── CH. MARIBEAU'S MISS CHARMIN
                        └────── CH. RANITA'S MY LITTLE SUZI
```

Whelped: January 25, 1976
Breeder/Owner: Edna B. Peirce

The dam of 11 champions:

Ch. Charmin Call Me Luv
Ch. Charmin Cassandra
Ch. Charmin Celebrity
Ch. Charmin Chantilly Lace
Ch. Charmin Charade
Ch. Charmin Charcoal Patches

Ch. Charmin Collector's Item
Ch. Charmin Command Performance
Ch. Charmin Constant Comment
Ch. Charmin Crown Jewel
Ch. Charmin Happy Birthday

Ch. Fi-Fo's Fiesta

```
                                        ┌───── CH. SCIOTO BLUFF'S SINBAD
                        ┌──── CH. BALIWICK BAGHDAD
                        │               └───── Clarkdale Country Cathy
CH. FI-FO'S FIESTA
                        │               ┌───── CH. SCIOTO BLUFF'S SINBAD
                        └──── CH. FI-FO'S MADAM SPOOK
                                        └───── Fi-Fo's Untouchable
```

Whelped: November 29, 1966
Breeder: Marty L. Reed
Owner: Mrs. Eunice C. Reed

The dam of 11 champions:

Ch. Fi-Fo's Fanfares
Ch. Fi-Fo's Fantasy
Ch. Fi-Fo's Femme Fatale
Ch. Fi-Fo's Fidelity
Ch. Fi-Fo's Flashback
Ch. Fi-Fo's Folklore

Ch. Fi-Fo's Frivolous Tri
Ch. Fi-Fo's He Fullhouse
Ch. Mar La's Fi-Fo Mona Lisa
Ch. Mar La's Fi-Fo Tri-Fastic
Ch. Pett's Fi-Fo's Frolic

Can./Am. Ch. Hall-Way Fancy Free

```
                             ┌────── CH. REXPOINTE'S CAPTAIN HOLIDAY
                 ┌── Rexpointe Frostee Dutchman
                 │           └──CH. MARIBEAU'S MY LIL' DUTCH TREAT
Can./Am. CH. HALL-WAY FANCY FREE
                 │           ┌────── Norbill's High And Mighty
                 └──── CH. HALL-WAY HALLELU
                             └────── CH. HALL-WAY HEDY
```

Whelped: June 11, 1961
Breeder: Mr. and Mrs. Jim Hall
Owner: Mr. and Mrs. Thomas Duncan

The dam of 11 champions:

Ch. Ballinger's Sunday Angel	**Ch. Flintcrest Foster Fenwick**
Ch. Flintcrest Call Girl	**Ch. Flintcrest My Pleasure**
Ch. Flintcrest Farah	**Ch. Hall-Way Hoopla**
Ch. Flintcrest First Lady, C.D.	**Ch. Orient's Loving Pleasure**
Ch. Flintcrest First Nighter	**Ch. RMS Flintcrest Franchised**
Ch. Flintcrest Foreign Affair	

Ch. Hickory Hill High Night

```
                                    ┌──── CH. SUGARBROOK COUNTERPOINT
                    ┌──── CH. TAYLOR'S DARK NIGHT
                    │               └──── Sugarbrook Fancy
CH. HICKORY HILL HIGH NIGHT
                    │               ┌──── CH. STOCKDALE TOWN TALK
                    └──── CH. HICKORY HILL HIGH BARBAREE
                                    └──── CH. HICKORY HILL HIGH BID
```

Whelped: October 13, 1957
Breeder/Owner: Kay Mauchel

The dam of 11 champions:

Ch. Hickory Hill High Echelon	Ch. Hickory Hill High Tax
Ch. Hickory Hill High Handicap	Ch. Hickory Hill High Tradition
Ch. Hickory Hill High Jollity	Ch. Hickory Hill High Treat
Ch. Hickory Hill High Key	Ch. Hickory Hill High Treble
Ch. Hickory Hill High Note	Ch. Hickory Hill High Tribute
Ch. Hickory Hill High Tariff	

Lanebrook's Dash O' Flash

```
                                        ┌────── CH. DE KARLOS DASHAWAY
                        ┌────── CH. VALLI-LO'S FLASH-A'WAY
                        │               └────── Chuck O'Luck's Cassandra
Lanebrook's Dash O' Flash
                        │               ┌────── CH. CLARKDALE CAPITAL STOCK
                        └────── Meri-Glad's Miniature
                                        └────── CH. MERI-GLAD'S MAGNIFICENCE
```

Whelped: March 1966
Breeder/Owner: Capt. and Mrs. Stanley Chapman

The dam of 11 champions:

Ch. Lanebrook's Beau Bait	Ch. Lanebrook's Lancer
Ch. Lanebrook's Bondsman	Ch. Lanebrook's Lucky Buck
Ch. Lanebrook's Dividend	Ch. Lanebrook's Marksman
Ch. Lanebrook's Don Quixote	Ch. Lanebrook's Me Too
Ch. Lanebrook's Forrester	Ch. Lanebrook's Mr. Holden
Ch. Lanebrook's Gayla	

Ch. Lanel's Rinky Dink's M And M

```
                      ┌─────── CH. ARTRU RED BARON
          ┌─── CH. ARTRU SKYJACK
          │           └─────── CH. ARTRU TRINKET
CH. LANEL'S RINKY DINK'S M AND M
          │           ┌─────── CH. BRICES' BRASS BUGLE
          └─── CH. RINKY DINKS LANEL'S CINNAMON
                      └─────── Rinky Dink's Bonifide Bonus
```

Whelped: October 1975
Breeder/Owner: Roland E. Lavallee, Jr. and Bruce A. Nelson

The dam of 11 champions:

Ch. Rinky Dink's Bit Of Action
Ch. Rinky Dink's Candy Cane II
Ch. Rinky Dink's Copper Top
Ch. Rinky Dink's Flashy Ash Of J-Don
Ch. Rinky Dink's Happy Medium
Ch. Rinky Dink's Melissa

Ch. Rinky Dink's New Dawn Addition
Ch. Rinky Dink's Plantation Rhett
Ch. Rinky Dink's Rockefeller
Ch. Rinky Dink's Swingtime
Ch. Rinky Dink's Top Of The Mark

Ch. Tallylyn My Liza Love

```
                                    ┌────── CH. ARTRU JOHNNY-BE-GOOD
                    ┌───── CH. LA MAR'S LONDON
                    │                └────── CH. LA MAR'S IVORY SUMMER
CH. TALLYLYN MY LIZA LOVE
                    │                ┌────── Main Dales Blue Chip
                    └───── Shiloh Dells Sheba
                                     └────── CH. SHILOH DELLS SASHAY
```

Whelped: 3/21/72
Breeder: Barbara Bush
Owner: John & Carolanne Garlick and Constance S. Boldt

The dam of 11 champions:

Ch. Sher-Ron's After Dark	Ch. Sher-Ron's Tradewind
Ch. Sher-Ron's Bad News Bear	Ch. Sher-Ron's Wind Song
Ch. Sher-Ron's Ebony Elegance	Ch. Sher-Ron's Wind Storm
Ch. Sher-Ron's Lil' Liza Jane, C.D.	Ch. Sher-Ron's Wind Swept
Ch. Sher-Ron's Show Time	Ch. Sher-Ron's Wing Commander
Ch. Sher-Ron's Spit Fire	

Ch. Bar-C-Kar's Peau Rouge

```
                                    ┌─────── CH. ARTRU HOT ROD
                    ┌────── Can./Am. CH. CHARMA'S MR. O'HARRIGAN
                    │               └─────── CH. BRIDEY MURPHY II
CH. BAR-C-KAR'S PEAU ROUGE
                    │               ┌─────── CH. ARTRU SIR UPNOR
                    └────── Artru Bar-C-Kar
                                    └─────── Caroline's Sweet N' Lovely
```

Whelped: June 1961
Breeder/Owner: Mrs. Corinne E. Karcher

The dam of 10 champions:

Ch. Artru Red Gauntlet	Ch. Bar-C-Kar's Mr. Toy Town
Ch. Artru Sandpiper	Ch. Bar-C-Kar's Red Sherrie
Ch. Bar-C-Kar's Jeanne Soit Bonne	Ch. Bar-C-Kar's Sweet Kream
Ch. Bar-C-Kar's Mr. Chips	Ch. Bar-C-Kar's Tampa Lea
Ch. Bar-C-Kar's Mr. Sandman	Ch. Countryview's Count Bar-C-Kar

Ch. Essanar Evening Song

```
                              ┌─────── CH. MIJO'S MARTINI
                   ┌───── CH. WISTFUL WEARS MY HEART II
                   │          └─────── CH. MIJO'S MISS B HAVEN
CH. ESSANAR EVENING SONG
                   │          ┌─────── CH. HAR-DEE'S HELL BENDER II
                   └───── CH. HAR-DEE'S HEARTBEAT
                              └─────── CH. HAR-DEE'S FANCY DOLL
```

Whelped: April 18, 1967
Breeder: Hansi Rowland and Mildred Seger
Owner: Mr. and Mrs. James E. Pfrommer

The dam of 10 champions:

Ch. Sandrex Show Biz
Ch. Sandrex Soliloquy
Ch. Sandrex Songbird
Ch. Sandrex Southwind
Ch. Sandrex Susprucious

Ch. Sandrex Sweet Adversity
Ch. Sandrex Sweet Caroline
Ch. Sandrex Sweet Prince
Ch. Sandrex Sweet Someone
Ch. Sandrex Sweet Temperment

Ch. Fancy-Free Carmen

```
                                    ┌────── CH. SCIOTO BLUFF'S SINBAD
                        ┌────── CH. STONEWALK SHARPSHOOTER
                        │           └────── CH. NORBILL'S HEAVENLY
CH. FANCY-FREE CARMEN
                        │           ┌────── CH. GRYMESBY DAN SLAM
                        └────── Danzata Dotted Frock
                                    └────── CH. GRYMESBY FASHION FROCK
```

Whelped: March 1964
Breeder: Mr. and Mrs. Keith D. Oswald
Owner: George B. Coskey

The dam of 10 champions:

Ch. Sonata's Choir Boy	Ch. Sonata's Justin Time
Ch. Sonata's Heather On The Hill	Ch. Sonata's Justin Trouble
Ch. Sonata's Justin Hope	Ch. Sonata's Robert Morgan
Ch. Sonata's Justin Luck	Ch. Sonata's Snow Man
Ch. Sonata's Justin Rhythm	Ch. Sonata's Sound Of Music

Ch. Hickory Hill High Barbaree

```
                                  ┌─────── CH. ARGYLL'S ARCHER
                    ┌─── CH. STOCKDALE TOWN TALK
                    │             └─────── Audacious Lady
CH. HICKORY HILL HIGH BARBAREE
                    │             ┌─────── Dungarvan D. Day
                    └─── CH. HICKORY HILL HIGH BID
                                  └─────── Hickory Hill High Heels
```

Whelped: December 1947
Breeder/Owner: Mrs. Robert Mauchel

The dam of 10 champions:

Ch. Hickory Hill Heiress
Ch. Hickory Hill High Bang
Ch. Hickory Hill High Hickory
Ch. Hickory Hill High Ho Silver
Ch. Hickory Hill High Night

Ch. Hickory Hill High Pockets
Ch. Hickory Hill High Salute
Ch. Hickory Hill High Success
Ch. Hickory Hill Hullabaloo
Ch. Hickory Hill Jet Bomber

Ch. Honey Creek Cricket

```
                                    ┌──────── CH. EASDALE'S WINSOME LADDIE
                  ┌──────── CH. YOUNG'S LADDIE BOY
                  │                 └──────── Mistwood Evening Song
CH. HONEY CREEK CRICKET
                  │                 ┌──────── CH. BOBB'S SHOW MASTER
                  └──────── CH. HONEY CREEK SUE
                                    └──────── Honey Creek Flicka
```

Whelped: April 1945
Breeder/Owner: Beatrice W. Wegusen

The dam of 10 champions:

Ch. Honey Creek Cricket's Sogo
Ch. Honey Creek Exchecker
Ch. Honey Creek Harmonette
Ch. Honey Creek Heartsong
Ch. Honey Creek Hobby

Ch. Honey Creek Pamela Of Patlar
Ch. Honey Creek Prince of Patlar
Ch. Honey Creek Romancer
Ch. Honey Creek Trice Over
Ch. Honey Creek Vivacious

Ch. Kaplar's Quicksilver

```
                                    ┌──────── CH. ARTRU RED BARON
                     ┌────── CH. ARTRU SKYJACK
                     │              └──────── CH. ARTRU TRINKET
CH. KAPLAR'S QUICKSILVER
                     │              ┌──────── CH. ARTRU RED BARON
                     └────── CH. KAPLAR KOLLEEN
                                    └──────── CH. KAPLAR'S CAMEO CAPER
```

Whelped: November 10, 1978
Breeder/Owner: Laura and Harold Henson

The dam of 10 champions:

Ch. Kaplar's Dream Girl
Ch. Kaplar's Kalendar Girl
Ch. Kaplar's Kaptain Blood
Ch. Kaplar's Klaim To Fame
Ch. Kaplar's Koast N' Along

Ch. Kaplar's Komes A Kourtin'
Ch. Kaplar's Koppersmith
Ch. Kaplar's Kraftmaster
Ch. Kaplar's Kwik-Action
Ch. Kaplar's Kwik-Step

Ch. Misty Mornin' Motif

```
                                  ┌──────── CH. SUGARBROOK COUNTERPOINT
                    ┌──────── CH. HICKORY HILL HIGH CATCH
                    │             └──────── Hickory Hill Holly
CH. MISTY MORNIN' MOTIF
                    │             ┌──────── CH. SUGARBROOK COUNTERPOINT
                    └──────── Hickory Hill High Pitch
                                  └──────── Hickory Hill Holly
```

Whelped: November 1958
Breeder: Charles Milwain and William T. Nix
Owner: Mary B. Shannon

The dam of 10 champions:

Ch. Plantation Bit O'Shannon	**Ch. Shannondale Showcase**
Ch. Shannondale Chantilly	**Ch. Shannondale Skylark**
Ch. Shannondale Shamrock	**Ch. Shannondale Sugar N' Spice**
Ch. Shannondale Shillelagh	**Ch. Shannondale Suzanne**
Ch. Shannondale Shindig	**Ch. Shannondale's Sweet Lorraine**

Ch. Nor-Mar's Nice N' Neat

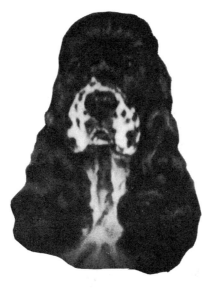

```
                                    ┌──────── CH. MARIBEAU'S MID SUMMER ECLIPSE
                      ┌──────── CH. MERIKAY'S TRI-SOX
                      │              └──────── Merikay's Mischief Miss
CH. NOR-MAR'S NICE N' NEAT
                      │              ┌──────── Barcliff's Best Bet For Nor-Mar
                      └──────── CH. NOR-MAR'S NETTIE OF MERETTY
                                     └──────── Gail's Miss Topsy
```

Whelped: November 23, 1961
Breeder: Norman and Mari Doty
Owner: Helen Rice

The dam of 10 champions:

Ch. Corwin's Calico
Ch. Corwin's Clean Sweep
Ch. Corwin's Colormatic
Ch. Corwin's Con-T-Rite
Ch. Corwin's Davy Crockett

Ch. Corwin's Diamond Lil'
Ch. Corwin's Hellzapoppin
Ch. Corwin's Mr. Comrob
Ch. Corwin's My Cheri
Ch. Corwin's Streak-O-Lightnin

Pounette Perrette

```
                                    ┌────── CH. HALL-WAY HOOT MON
                  ┌────── CH. SCIOTO BLUFF'S SINBAD
                  │                 └────── CH. SCIOTO BLUFF'S JUDY
Pounette Perrette │
                  │                 ┌────── CH. DAU-HAN'S DAN MORGAN
                  └────── CH. POUNETTE FANCY DANCER
                                    └────── Artru Pounette
```

Whelped: February 11, 1964
Breeder: Edward B. and Paule-Adree Alber
Owner: T. F. O'Neal

The dam of 10 champions:

Ch. Bard's Bonfire
Ch. Dreamridge Dainty Dish
Ch. Dreamridge Deck Hand
Ch. Dreamridge Demetrius
Ch. Dreamridge Demon Rum

Ch. Dreamridge Dinner Date
Ch. Dreamridge Drambuie
Ch. Dreamridge Dr. Pepper
Ch. Dreamridge Drum Major
Ch. Dreamridge Paean Panda

Ch. Prime Time Crystal Pistol

TATHAM PHOTO

```
                              ┌──── CH. LA MAR'S LONDON
                  ┌──── CH. SHIRMITCH STYLE
                  │           └──── CH. LORLI'S SASA
CH. PRIME TIME CRYSTAL PISTOL
                  │           ┌──── CH. MI'WAY BRASS BUTTON
                  └──── CH. PRIME-TIME PISTOL PACKIN' MAMA
                              └──── Donn Carm's Running Dear
```

Whelped: May 5, 1981
Breeder/Owner: Barbara G. Barham

The dam of 10 champions:

Ch. Grisard Annie Get Your Gun	Ch. Grisard Olympic Touch O Class
Ch. Grisard Gymnastic Gold	Ch. Grisard Persistance
Ch. Grisard Ice Crystal	Ch. Grisard Pistol Packin' Poppa
Ch. Grisard Little Coquette	Ch. Grisard Silver Crystal Dust
Ch. Grisard Olympic Gold Juliann	Ch. Grisard Silver Pistol Pete

Ch. Sher-Ron's Wind Song

```
                                    ┌──────── CH. LA MAR'S LONDON
                      ┌─────── CH. FORJAY'S WINTERWOOD
                      │             └──────── Forjay's Buffie
CH. SHER-RON'S WIND SONG
                      │             ┌──────── CH. LA MAR'S LONDON
                      └─────── CH. TALLYLYN MY LIZA LOVE
                                    └──────── Shiloh Dells Sheba
```

Whelped: May 6, 1976
Breeder/Owner: John H. and Carolanne Garlick and Constance S. Boldt

The dam of 10 champions:

Ch. Sher-Ron's Exhibitionist
Ch. Sher-Ron's Made To Order
Ch. Sher-Ron's Marksman
Ch. Sher-Ron's Master Charge
Ch. Sher-Ron's Matchmaker

Ch. Sher-Ron's Matinee Star
Ch. Sher-Ron's Paint N' Powder
Ch. Sher-Ron's Prime Minister
Ch. Sher-Ron's Tameron Elegante
Ch. Sher-Ron's Vatican Pac-Man

SECTION IX
Life in the Dog Show World

- *How the Dog Show Game Works*
- *Climbing the Ladder of Success*
- *Specialty Clubs*

CHAPTER 1

How The Dog Show Game Works

The backbone of the the dog show is the individual, the all-breed and specialty dog clubs. By joining a dog club you begin to learn the ins and outs of raising and showing dogs. Boy, is there a lot of information waiting for you out there! Getting that information can sometimes be difficult. By reading this book you have shown you are interested enough to get going on your own.

Most dog clubs have educational meetings where you can learn interesting facts about the sport. The best entry point is a specialty club, that is, a club dealing with a single breed. For instance, The American Spaniel Club is the "parent club" for Cocker Spaniels. If you are not a member, find the club nearest to you and inquire about joining.

Specialty clubs are the best place to learn about your breed. Their major goal is to educate their membership and to hold American Kennel Club (AKC) licensed shows. Specialty clubs are under the overall "jurisdiction" of their (parent) national club. However, in order to hold a dog show, they must be given approval by the AKC and hold the show under AKC rules. The club picks their own judges from a list of AKC-licensed judges.

It's apparent that the AKC is a pretty important organization, so let's talk about it before we go on to describing dog shows themselves.

The AKC is a private organization, not a government entity as is the case in many countries. The club is run by delegates who are elected by their local clubs. The local clubs in turn, are member clubs of the AKC. The delegates elect a Board of Directors from their own ranks. The Board is entrusted with formulating policy and direction for the club. The Board hires the President and he acts as its Chief Executive Officer. The AKC is over a 20 million dollar corporation and is located at 51 Madison Ave, New York, New York 10010. It is chartered in that state. The AKC only rarely puts on shows of its own. The major functions of AKC are:

- Registration of pure bred dogs
- Publication of a stud register
- Keeping and publishing statistics through the AKC *Gazette*, its monthly publication

- Recognizing new dog clubs as show giving entities under AKC development rules
- Education of the public through publications, seminars, and audio/visual media
- Sponsorship of research into major medical/physical problems of dogs
- Sanctioning of dates and places for dog clubs to hold their shows
- Licensing of judges to officiate at AKC licensed events
- Providing oversight of the shows themselves through AKC field representatives
- U.S. representative to international bodies interested in promoting the sport of pure bred dogs

Now, let's tackle the concept of dog shows themselves. Naturally, enough of you would like to participate. In order to do this you must have a purebred dog. By "purebred," it is meant that your dog must be eligible for registration by AKC. You will recall when you bought your puppy you were given registration papers. If you have not filled them out yet, do so now. Until your dog is registered with the AKC and gets an individual registration number, you can't show him. Once you have that magic piece of paper in your hands you can enter dog shows to your heart's delight. Of course, each entry fee will cost you a sum of money. The going rate today is about $16.00.

OK, now we get into it. Your local specialty club is going to hold a show and they are encouraging you to enter. So, nothing ventured, nothing gained. The show chairman makes sure you get an entry form and even waits around for you to fill it out. You need to put down your dog's registered name and number, his birthdate, his parents' names, who were the breeders (it's all on the registration form) and your name as owner. That's it—except for the check in the proper amount. Oh yes, you must select the class he will be in. Now what do we mean by class? Dog shows, like most sporting events, have various classifications— some by age and others by the amount of winning the dog has done. Let's take a look at the various classes offered and find out who is eligible for them.

The classes include:

- Puppy .... Over 6 months & under 9 months
- Puppy .... Over 9 months & under 12 months
- Novice .... Has not yet won a blue ribbon in adult classes, three first prizes in the Novice class, or one or more championship points prior to close of entry.
- Bred by Exhibitor .... Exhibited by the Breeder of Record (you must have bred and currently own the dog to show in this class)
- American Bred .... Must have been bred in America

- Open Class . . . . Open to all, including puppies
- Best of Breed . . . . AKC Champions only in this class

In certain specialty shows, there may be a class for 12–18 month old puppies.

Once entered, you need to make sure your dog is ready to be shown. If you have not learned to trim your dog, now is not the time to start practicing! Either take him back to the breeder or to a professional trimmer, one who knows about your breed. Observe them carefully; it's a good idea to learn to trim your own dog. Otherwise, it gets expensive. Consult the chapter, "As A Show Dog," to get a good idea what trimming is all about. That same chapter has very useful directions on training your dog for the show ring.

The dog show itself is a novel experience for the uninitiated. Sights and sounds like you've never seen or heard before. It's a good idea to latch onto a more experienced exhibitor to go with you the first time. Find your ring and be sure you carefully observe the time schedule, which you received from the show superintendent the week preceding the show. If you were lucky, there were even directions on how to get to the show site.

Since the dog show world still seems to cling to its male chauvinistic ways, dogs are shown first, followed by bitches. The procedure is to start off with the youngest age puppy classes and work their way through all the classes for males. (The classes are just like those listed above.) Once the judge has selected a winner for each of the classes, he brings back all the class winners to be compared against each other and the breed standard. Yes, there is a specific blueprint laid down by each breed's parent club and accepted by the American Kennel Club as to what each breed should look like. (Refer to the chapter on the standard for more in-depth information.) The judge's purpose in comparing all his male winners is to select the one closest to the standard to award AKC points toward his championship. The number of points for each breed is determined by the number competing on that day, in that geographic location. Look in front of a show catalog and you will find a schedule of points. It's different for each breed and each area of the country. It depends on the popularity of the breed and how many dogs were shown in this area last year. It's an intricate formula; all worked out by the statisticians of AKC.

To become a champion, your dog needs to earn 15 championship points, including two major wins. The major wins must be earned under two different judges and your dog cannot finish his championship without winning under a minimum of three different judges. A major win consists of 3, 4, or 5 points. The more dogs competing, the greater number of points awarded. Five is the maximum at any one show, no matter how many dogs are defeated.

After all the males have been shown, the judge repeats the same procedure when judging the bitches. After he has selected his point-winning bitch, the winners dog and the winners bitch come into the ring with the champions competing in the Best of Breed ("Specials") class to compete for Best of Breed or Best of Variety.

In Cocker Spaniels, there are three Varieties: There is the Black Variety (which includes blacks and black and tans competing); the ASCOB Variety (which means Any Solid Color Other than Black to include buffs, chocolates, and chocolate and tans). The third Variety is the Parti-Color, (which include red and whites, black and whites, and tri-colors— which are black and whites with the tan markings of the black and tan added), and roans (which are fairly rare in American Cocker Spaniels). Sidle over to the English Cocker ring if you want to see a good roan pattern.

Since this an all-breed show and all 130 AKC-approved breeds can be shown, there is no Best of Breed Cocker award given. The judge selects only a Best of Variety, a Best of Winners (that means either the dog or bitch is selected as the best of the winners of the day), and a Best of Opposite Sex to Best of Variety. That means that if a male Champion won Best of Variety, then the judge would pick a bitch to be the best of her sex. It can happen the other way around, too. The judge, if he sees fit, does not have to pick a champion for these top awards. The Winners Dog and Winners Bitch can be selected to be Best of Variety and/or Best of Opposite Sex. Each of the variety winners go on to compete in the sporting group against the 23 other breed winners that make up its group. Before this gets too complicated, please refer to Figure IX-1 which shows the classes and the winning progression at an all-breed dog show. In a way, it's like a basketball tournament. The seven groups make up the brackets and they move along until there are only seven finalists left. Then the judge makes the ultimate award of Best in Show. One last point, if the Best of Winners dog or bitch had earned fewer points by winning its portion of the competition than the animal it defeated, it will gain the greater number of points; *i.e,* the Winners Bitch won two points but the Winners Dog won five. By going Best of Winners, the bitch would pick up the three additional points awarded the dog and gain a major. The dog would still have his five points so the net effect would be that both took home five-point major wins.

All-breed shows are the most prevalent in this country. But, there is another type of show that is designed specifically for a single breed. It's called a Specialty Show. Any breed club that is recognized and licensed by the AKC may hold one. As a result there are hundreds of these shows held every year. The difference between a specialty show and an all-breed show is that the three variety winners compete directly for the

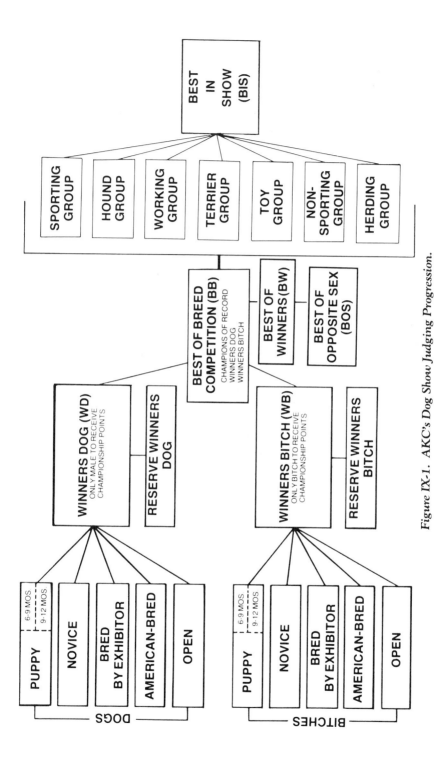

Figure IX-1. AKC's Dog Show Judging Progression.

coveted Best of Breed award. There is also a Best of Opposite Sex award. These are considered very important wins. AKC championship points are also awarded at these shows.

A third type of show—and one that seems to be the kind of event for novice and expert alike—is the Sanctioned Match. Again, most of these are held under AKC sanction but no championship points are awarded. It's a practice ground. New owners can show their own dogs and make all the first-timer mistakes without penalty or embarrassment. Experienced breeders use it as a training ground for their newest show prospects. The judges are usually professional handlers or breeders who want to qualify to become regular judges. It's fun and a great learning experience. There are both all-breed and specialty sanctioned matches. Check with your local dog club for information on these events.

On several occasions, reference has been made to "the judge" who selects the winning dogs. These ladies and gentlemen are duly licensed by the American Kennel Club. They are usually persons who have been successful breeders or professional handlers of many years' standing. They have filled out arduous questionnaires about their involvement in dogs, taken tests on the breeds they wish to judge, and have been interviewed by an AKC Field Representative. Once they have passed these "hurdles," their names are published in the *American Kennel Gazette*, the monthly magazine of the AKC. Persons having knowledge of these candidates may write to the AKC either for, or against, them. The final step is a review and analysis by an AKC panel. Using prescribed guidelines, they grant a candidate one or more breeds. The candidate must go through similar subsequent applications in order to judge additional breeds.

Once granted his or her initial set of breeds, the fledgling judge must judge all of these breeds on five occasions to be eligible to apply for others. During this period, the judge is known as a "provisional judge." Their actions are carefully watched by an AKC Field Representative and a report is given on their ring procedure and general knowledge. Even after being granted status as a regular judge, all judges are periodically evaluated and a report submitted to the judge and to AKC.

At this point, I must warn you about a terribly infectious disease you could pick up by attending your first dog show. It's called the "BUG" and people who catch it can become dog show bugs for the rest of their lives. Their friends think they are off their rocker since they suddenly start talking about "bitches" and "points" and other stuff that makes no sense to normal people. Dog show bugs often give up golf and on weekends can be found out in the sun in the middle of a ring howling about what a great win they just pulled off. Have pity on them, but beware—it could happen to YOU!

To learn more about the breed, I suggest you subscribe to one of the

Cocker Spaniel Magazines. They are:

The American Cocker Magazine
Michael Allen, Editor
14531 Jefferson
Midway City, California 92655
$25 per year

The Cocker Spaniel Leader
Shirley Estel, Editor
9700 Jersey Mill Road, N.W.
Pataskala, Ohio 43062
$20 per year

CHAPTER *2*

Climbing The Ladder of Success

When people seek the services of a doctor or a lawyer, they usually look for one with a good professional reputation and avoid the "quacks" and "shysters." When shopping for major purchases, "brand names" and "quality" are sought in preference to the unknown and untried.

Then why, *oh why*, does the novice breeder select an often unproved, or less than adequate, breeder as their "mentor"? It is so often a case of the blind leading the blind!

This is not universal by any means. There are many novices who have had the good fortune of enjoying the association of respected, successful breeders. From them, the novice receives a valuable education about many aspects of breeding and showing dogs as well as the basic rules of sportsmanship. Oftentimes, this association comes about purely by chance. Very seldom is it sought.

Most experienced and successful breeders neither need, nor want, the "coat-tail crowd"—those that look to him for every assurance, opinion, and then reflect his exact thoughts back to him. Through experience, it is not difficult for this breeder to discern fairly easily those worthy of his time and efforts. Novices are *NOT* expected to know it all—and those who act as though they do are quickly given the cold shoulder. Novices *ARE* expected to ask questions and shouldn't feel their questions will be regarded as silly or insignificant.

Perhaps it is from the "fear" that the big-name breeder will not want to bother with him, that makes the novice seek out "second best." Or, more than likely, an association with a lesser breeder is sought because in the eyes of the novice *ANY* accomplishment looms large beside his own insignificant or fumbling beginnings. To the novice, the word "champion" is truly the magic word—this, before he develops the ability to discern that there are champions and *THERE ARE CHAMPIONS!*

There are many breeders, both successful and near successful, who are more than happy to lend a helping hand. They have usually reached their own pinnacle of success due to another's assistance along the way. However, whereas successful breeders desire to help those deemed worthy, many not-so-successful breeders encourage the association of one and all. In fact, the more the merrier! To gather a group of "disciples" around gives many less-than-successful breeders a prop for their sagging egos. It's not uncommon to find these breeders with their own personal retinue accompanying them everywhere, hanging onto their every word and taking all they have to say as the gospel truth. They are seen at dog shows clustered around the breeder's crates listening only to him. They pay no attention to the other dogs, rarely watch the judging (where they might actually *learn* something!), and have eyes only for the dogs belonging to their "friend."

The disciples end up with very little true knowledge of the breed which they originally sought. Actually, they have been "used" rather than helped. They are often kept within the fold by being made to feel obligated as a result of "free" stud services, "gifts" of dogs and "deals." If they would only look around them and see the light, they would realize that "free" stud services are rarely offered on GOOD dogs; dogs are not "given away" that possess a monetary value and for which there is a demand, and "deals" rarely work out to everyone's satisfaction.

Many of these people have long ago lost sight of their original goals and have become enmeshed in all sorts of dog activities that lead them nowhere. These are the ones who throw in the towel and become yet another "five-year statistic." *(Author's Note: The average person lasts only this long in the dog game.)* Very few go on to become successful breeders on their own, for that requires independent thought and they have not been conditioned to do this.

It should not be too difficult to establish criteria of some sort to distinguish between those breeders capable of assisting the novice and those who use the novice to further their own interests. First off, what constitutes success? What assurance can the novice obtain that his would-be "mentor" has something to offer? Is it because he has bred a champion? Realize, please, that many a champion is the result of luck in breeding or persistence in showing. Maybe he has bred several champions. Then ask, what kind of champions? Did they finish quickly in good competition or were they dragged through to their titles winning against even more inferior competition? Also, ask how others regard these champions. Do other well-known breeders desire their offspring or breed to them or does their "popularity" result from the novice and pet trade? Is this person known only in their own locale or known throughout the state and country as well?

Answers to these questions—honest answers, that is—should provide the beginning breeder with some insight as to where they should look for assistance. Then, there is the matter of integrity. Does this breeder constantly knock dogs belonging to others? Does he start, or perpetuate rumors based on heresay or inconclusive evidence? Does he, when selling his stock, "guarantee" that eight-week old puppies will finish their championships? Does he imply that his stud dogs will sire top quality—regardless of the bitches bred to them? Does he profess expert knowledge of bloodlines with which he has had no experience? If the answer to most of these questions is "yes," look elswhere for your guidance. If you chose this kind of person as a role model, your chances for success are slim and none.

To become completely dependent upon another for your success in dogs will—in the long run—not serve you well. To be a good breeder, you must be able to think independently and, when ready, begin to make your own decisions—to buy that puppy, to line breed correctly, to keep that *one great puppy*. Learn all you can from your competent mentor and then go out and apply that knowledge on your own. Of course, you will make mistakes, who doesn't? Remember, you can learn as much from failure as you can from success. Go over the dogs who are winning, find out why. Ask questions when you don't understand something. Have an inquiring mind. And, by all means, watch the judging and learn by observing where the judge puts his hands, what he comes back to when he goes over a dog a second time. Many judges "signal" the ringside what they are looking for.

Now you will find some top breeders who are leery of helping a novice. That is because they have no doubt had some bad experiences. They have run into the know-it-alls, the stubborn ones who will do it their way only, and the troublemakers. Unfortunately, there are always novices out there who—in order to make a quantum leap to stardom—set out to accomplish something that has never been done before. Maybe an experienced breeder with a good knowledge of genetics may hazard such a venture, but the rank novice is headed for disaster. And when he crashes on the rocks he blames all but himself.

Let us say you have been fortunate enough to get yourself a good mentor and have learned your lessons well. You set out on your own and Dame Fortune has smiled upon you. All is wonderful, you are a winner and you bask in the reflected glory of your winning dogs. Great, except something is not quite right! You have the uncomfortable feeling that all your winning is not going over too well with your fellow exhibitors. Where did you go wrong? After all, isn't the idea of this whole thing to be a winner? Let's look into that part of the game a bit more.

Much emphasis has been placed on the importance of being a good loser, but little or nothing is said about the difficulty of being a good winner. To be a good loser is not difficult; in fact, it happens frequently to most of us. But acting appropriately as a winner, is something else indeed.

At any show, whether it is a specialty or an all-breed show, there can only be a few winners. Should one exhibitor's entries account for more than one win, the leftover pickings become even smaller. This means only a small number of people go home perfectly happy from a dog show. The vast majority console themselves that there will be another day or, at least, the judge did a conscientious job and gave them a fair shake.

Let's face it, we would rather win than lose on any given day. In the dog game, we have learned that a top dog probably will win three out of five times and be close when he loses. The average competitor will probably finish in 15-20 shows, winning perhaps six times. So you see, losing is the norm. However, we go into each show with the expectation of winning and, as a result, we get disgruntled when we don't. Turn to the person standing next to you and remark about the poor job of judging that old Nicholas Applebee is doing today and chances are you will get full agreement. What's so strange about that? However, point out that old Nicholas is really on the ball today and is picking the top ones and you will most likely get a baleful stare, unless you happen to be standing next to one of the day's few winners.

You learn that it's hard to be a winner by any standard. Everyone's goal is to be a winner and get to the top. But, for many, that winning spirit can get us into trouble with our peers and reaching the summit can become a hollow victory. Your dog has won, you're thrilled, elated, on Cloud Nine and you want to shout about it from the rooftops and let the world know about your accomplishments. But you don't, because— let's face it—YOU are happy but most of the other exhibitors are not! So you adopt the reserve of the English and smile inwardly. To have your dog's wins greeted by indifference or snide remarks takes the wind out of your sails and much that should be joyous becomes just the opposite. After coming up against the ''wet dish rag'' form of enthusiasm, you keep your happiness to yourself to be taken out later and savored privately. While it will have to suffice, winning's not what it *should* be like. The losers of the day, on the other hand, are walking around muttering under their collective breath's that they ''were robbed,'' or ''the judge was stupid,''or both. Perhaps some day there could be a cartoon that poses the question ''Guess who the losers at the dog show are?'' Not too long ago, a top-winning special went up for Best of Breed and one of the losers came over to the handler and said ''Nice win. Too bad he didn't deserve it.'' Comments like this cannot help to make a winner's day!

As you can see, being a winner is not easy—no matter how desirable this position looks from afar. To come up with winning dogs, year after year, places many breeders in the position of being a prime target for all the unsuccessful, jealous and petty breeders still striving for success. Because of some quirk of human nature, it seems that people feel the need to elevate their own kennel's status—not necessarily by breeding better dogs—but by downplaying those belonging to others. Everyone, at one time or another, has been guilty of this to some degree. However, the driven ones give little heed to the feelings of others and strive to demean other's accomplishments at every turn. Perhaps this is their way of lessening the threat to their own aspirations.

This type of behavior is not soley confined to those engaged in dog activities. It is evidenced even more clearly in the business world by price-cutting, false advertising, and disparaging your competition. It's frowned upon by the Better Business Bureau. In dogdom, we have no BBB, only virtually "unenforceable" club codes of ethics.

By now, you must recognize that a healthy competitive spirit and a thick skin are prerequisites to success in the dog game. Obviously, when competitive spirit meets competitive spirit, some sparks are going to fly. Think of it as two terriers being sparred against each other in center ring. It's a good show but when it's over, it's over!

In order for any one breeder in an area to attain success, others must—by necessity—lose along the way. This cannot be helped, for it takes many losers to make a winner. Those on the threshold of success might do well to remember that the time will come when they must come face-to-face with some of these same losers—as they lose their grip on the top rung and slide downward. No matter how good we are as breeders, there comes a time when not every success is topped with yet another success and we lose our momentum and backslide a bit.

Very few, if any, have the good fortune of having their cake and eating it too. That is to say, few breeders can continually enjoy success without ruffling some feathers of their losing breeder acquaintances. Some people just can't take the slings and arrows that come their way as the winner. They have thin skins and suffer grievously. What to do? Some breeders just up and quit. To them, it's just not worth it. Maybe they feel they have achieved what they set out to do and don't want to settle for second best. Many learn to compromise. That is, they can share the winner's mantle with others without feeling they are a "failure." These are the ones who survive. Their accomplishments and abilities are recognized but they no longer hold a monopoly on success. As a result they have a degree of popularity with their fellow breeders and have gotten out of the crossfire allowing them to enjoy their hobby.

These "old timers" no longer have to prove themselves at every outing. The "comers," on the other hand, strive and claw their way at every step. These are the ones who "work" the judge and demean the competition. This aggressiveness is what makes them tick and can lead to "success." But at what cost? Many of you have run across such people in the dog show game. The desire for recognition is one thing, but you can carry the craving for success too far and alienate everyone around you.

Once you have climbed that mountain and become "top dog," you may well find out that it's very lonely on top of that peak. There just isn't much room at the top; the kind of personality that's driven you there doesn't allow for sharing the top perch. This fact is usually not recognized by those hell-bent on getting there. It can only be truly understood by those who have experienced this heady sort of success with all of its accompanying drawbacks.

It doesn't have to be like this. In fact, in many instances it's not. However, there are too many cases where this is the norm in the dog game. They'll all love you when you're a "point maker." In fact, your dogs may not be bad and—with a little help and some good luck—might do some real winning. On the other hand, just as soon as you do start that *real* winning . . . well, after reading this chapter, it should be all too familiar.

CHAPTER 3

Specialty Clubs

The American Spaniel Club carries out many of its functions through local Cocker Spaniel Clubs that work for the betterment of the breed. In general, the purpose of the local clubs are in support of the major objectives set forth in the Certificate of Incorporation of the Parent Club. They are:

A. To encourage the promotion, breeding, protection and exhibition of American Cocker Spaniels and to do all possible to bring their natural qualities to perfection.

B. To urge members to accept the standard of the breed as approved by the American Kennel Club as the only standard by which Cocker Spaniels will be judged.

C. To do all in its power to protect and advance the interests of the breed and to encourage sportsmanlike conduct and competition at dog shows and obedience trials.

D. To conduct either under its own auspices or to encourage the conduct under the auspices of member clubs, sanctioned matches, specialty shows, field trials and obedience trials under the rules of the American Kennel Club.

E. And though not expressly stated in the ASC document, to provide the opportunity for educational programs on a variety of subjects to further the aims of the clubs and the breed.

The specialty club differs from the all-breed club in that its focus is on one breed alone. Its entire efforts should go into promoting the breed and educating its members about the dog and its attributes. Specialty clubs should be formed with the primary idea of promoting the breed in the geographical area in which they are located. Happily these motivating reasons generally dominate and the majority of clubs remain active and prosper throughout the years. The fact that a certain proportion of the clubs which were formed many years ago are now inactive or disbanded should be a cause for concern. There should only be one reason for a club to cease to function—the advanced age of its membership and its inability to attract bright and eager newcomers to its ranks. But probably the greatest reason for the falling away from the active participation in the "dog game" by any club is the lack of interest on the part of the membership.

When a club is first started, the initial enthusiasm that conceived the club will often carry it for a year or two without the necessity of any real constructive program of membership activities. Such zeal abates in the passing years and unless refreshed continually, will die down so that the club becomes nothing but a name. This is especially true of the smaller clubs initiated soley for the purpose of holding an annual AKC licensed dog show.

It is not necessary to go into detail regarding the paramount importance of licensed dog shows. The facts concerning their necessity are self-evident. But licensed dog shows are by no means the only important phase of canine activities. Any club that "puts on" a licensed AKC dog show is extremely altruistic and generous. Altruistic, because members of the show-giving club devote their time and energy to making the show a success with no reward for themselves; generous because they contribute financially for trophies and cash awards, and seldom win anything back for themselves. Usually everybody concerned benefits in one way or another, as a result of a licensed AKC show, *except* the members of the show-giving club.

One of the greatest stimulants to breeders is the AKC sanctioned match. At these, as much or as little of the pomp of a licensed show can be invested, as the club desires. The informality of a sanction match engenders more good feelings, more sheer fun and considerably greater enjoyment than is usually possible with the formality of a licensed show. A sanction match provides an inexpensive training ground with show-like atmosphere for novice owners and novice dogs; it furnishes a "try-out" opportunity for the young stock of experienced owners.

Because a sanction match can be held more inexpensively than a licensed show, the entry fee can be correspondingly lower, encouraging the new and untried dogs and owners to get a start in the show ring. As sanction matches are run primarily for the benefit of the match-giving club's members, they are a "continuing" activity to help maintain members' interest. Thus, they help keep the club alive and popular. Futhermore, sanction matches in general furnish an informal means of training newer faces of the club's managing personnel in the *modus operendi* of show-giving and the operation of licensed shows. New officials and new committees have to be taught administrative and show procedure just as a puppy needs to have "ring training" and manners instilled into it. Sanction matches do this.

Any specialty club which numbers twenty or more active members of different families on its membership roster could advantageously put on several successful sanction matches a year. Experience has shown that such sanction matches practically carry themselves financially. Also, where entries are not restricted to club members, one, two or more new members can usually be enrolled at each match.

It would be most helpful to those clubs not now having a sanction match program if the board of directors of these clubs would seriously consider these matters. First, there should be appointed a sanction match committee consisting of members willing to work!

This sanction match committee should select the type of match the club wishes to hold. Plan A matches are practically similar to a licensed show. They require the issuance of a premium list and a catalog. Plan B sanction matches are much more informal. No premium list or catalog is required. Entries may be taken at the match. There is no AKC fee for this type of match. Classes may be offered at the club's discretion. However, clearance from AKC is required. A third, and most popular type, is the "fun" match. This is not regulated by AKC and the club may set its own ground rules. All sorts of extra classes can be included.

After selecting the type of sanction match to hold, the committee should then decide whether the entries are to be open to all owners or restricted to the membership. It is also advisable at this time to plan on how many matches to hold that year and seek clear dates. A judge should be selected and invited; the AKC should be contacted and asked for the proper forms to be filled out by the club and returned to them for approval.

When AKC approval is received, notices should be sent out to all known breeders in the area. Local radio and TV stations should also be notified as many of them do community service announcements of this type. The local press should be contacted. If possible a picture of the Best in Match winner and the other awards should be given to the local press. Ribbons and rosettes with the proper inscriptions should be ordered in plenty of time for the match. Arm bands and posters pointing the way to the show can be obtained from many dog food companies.

Now the day of the match has arrived and the judging has begun. Usually the club will offer classes for puppies and adult dogs. Most of the time a club will restrict the entry to non-point winners. Many times, puppy classes as young as two months of age are offered. Judging can follow a regular variety format with a best puppy and adult from each variety. Finally a Best Puppy and Best Adult are picked. Most clubs do not have them compete for an ultimate Best in Match.

Just about every club holds at least one regular show a year. Most are successful. But the tough decisions that lead up to a show often cause internal problems, especially the selection of judges and who will run the club. The business of promoting, budgeting, housing, locating, selecting judges, selecting dates, establishing a prize list, choosing a show secretary and superintendent, securing entries, creating a gate, etc., is a business which must be understood and worked at if a club is to get the results they desire.

No specialty club is functioning in the best interests of quality dogs and their owners when it operates at a loss. A specialty club just can't do the things it should do to put on a top-flight show if it operates with a previous deficit and a fear of future deficits. And the farther a club falls from putting on a first-class show the greater the danger of financial loss and the harder it becomes to set things back on a right course.

A good club should be able to put on shows of sufficient quality that they should operate at a profit two out of every three shows. My own club, Mission Valley Cocker Spaniel Club, is a highly successful show-giving club. One of the ways they accomplish this is by having a policy on geographically selecting judges. Generally, in a three-year period, the club will select a judge from within the state of California, one from west of the Mississippi and in the third year a judge from a greater distance. This allows for coverage as well as controlling the amount the club will have to pay for a judge. Tying in with a top all-breed club on the following day, at the same show site, makes for a very favorable show and economic climate. Additionally, Mission Valley has an excellent working arrangement with the Santa Clara Valley Kennel Club and can recommend the Cocker judge on the following day. By presenting a double-balanced judging slate, Mission Valley has averaged close to 200 enteries per show.

A successful specialty club must attract the best quality dogs in their geographical area, and occasionally, by virtue of its judging slate and prize list, attract some of the top dogs from other points of the compass. It is this quality of dog which interests the new breeder. They can come to the show and actually see the dogs that have been widely written about and have won top awards. This is how they can visualize the breed and set standards for their own future breeding programs.

In order to have a degree of commonality, the American Kennel Club has promulgated a set of by-laws which it recommends each local club use. The local club's by-laws must be approved by the AKC and also be submitted to the American Spaniel Club, as the parent club. Each local club has an affiliation with the parent club. Each local club elects its own officers and holds its point shows under the auspices of the AKC. Before holding a show, the club must get permission from both AKC and ASC as to its judging slate. AKC alone approves dates and sites. The club must function under those regulations in a forceful, respectful manner developing a policy of good sportsmanship toward old and new fanciers. To do this effectively the club must give consideration to the:

1. Fraternal or social side of fancier's interests;
2. Informative aspects;
3. Complete and detailed reporting of the club's finances and events.

The informative aspects are of the greatest concern. If a specialty club does not inform its membership about the nuances of breeding and showing dogs they will soon lose their membership and become nothing more than a debating society. Because of the fierce competitive nature of the sport, new exhibitors who do not have early success tend to leave the dog game. They give many reasons: the judges are crooked; you can't beat the handlers; the clubs pick judges who are biased toward other exhibitors; etc, etc. But, if a club had done its job properly, most of these people would have a better perspective of the dog game, be informed about what it takes to achieve success in the game, and have an educational program that prepares them for the various phases of being a breeder and exhibitor. Unfortunately, most clubs do not carry out that function to the best extent possible.

Here is a recommended series of topics that could be used in planning a club's educational program:

- Sportsmanship
- Basics of Canine Genetics
- Breeding for Color
- The Stud Dog—Care and Breeding
- The Brood Bitch—Care and Whelping
- Campaigning Your Dog
- Evaluating Movement
- Judging Purebred Dogs
- Advertising Your Dog
- Grooming the Cocker Spaniel
- Choosing the Best Puppies
- Raising a Litter
- Parasites and Their Debilitating Effects
- The Role of the Professional Handler
- Interpreting a Pedigree Properly
- The Cocker as a Field Dog
- The Cocker in the Obedience Ring
- Diseases that Affect Dogs
- Cocker Eye Problems
- The Dollars and Cents Aspect of a Kennel
- Animal Nutrition

There are, of course, many other topics that would make excellent programs. The AKC and many dog food companies also have material available.

Training groups should be formed with other local clubs to hold classes for obedience, field trial and show ring training. Each club meeting should be viewed as an opportunity for club members to get acquainted with each other. Simple social activities should follow each meeting. New members should be encouraged to serve on committees.

A specialty club should encourage its members to exhibit not only at their own show but in nearby shows as well, so that a return entry may be expected and received.

A specialty club should maintain a question and suggestion box at each meeting and invite members to ask questions or suggest topics for future programs or to complain about an area of concern.

A Cocker Spaniel specialty club is usually what its members want and make it. Each member must realize they are the ones who elected the officers of the club and, therefore, it is wise to accept the results and attempt to contribute to the success of the club. It's very important to elect the right people to office or a large monkey wrench can be put in each breeder's machinery. It's important to attend meetings and help create interest. It's vital to contribute time and effort; to exhibit at the shows; to help secure trophies and pledges to the trophy fund; act with sportsmanlike behavior; be prepared to sell the breed to the public; in fact, to do all the things one expects others—and especially the club's officers—to do and to see to it that others do likewise. Be interested, contribute interest, get things done by doing your share; if there is cause for criticism, give it graciously and after exhaustive reflection. After all, YOU ARE THE SPECIALTY CLUB.

Cocker Spaniel Specialty Clubs in the United States
ZONE I

Capital City Cocker Club—Linda Johnson, Secretary
3400 Slade Court, Falls Church, Virginia 22042

Capital District Cocker Spaniel Club—Helen Pierce, Secretary
6 White Birch Court, Schenectady, New York 12306

Cocker Spaniel Breeders Club of New England—Claire S. Ayer, Secretary
P.O. Box 974, Belcher St., Essex, MA. 01929

Cocker Spaniel Club of Long Island—Joanne K. Schaal, Secretary
4 Collector Lane, Levittown, New York 11756

Cocker Spaniel Club of New Jersey—Ellen R. Passage, Secretary
35 Academy Road, Hohokus, New Jersey 07423

Cocker Spaniel Club of Rhode Island—Hazel O'Rourke, Secretary
16 Henry Street, Cranston Rhode Island 02905

Conn-Westchester Cocker Spaniel Club—Kathy Kayler, Secretary
RD2, Box 501B, Mahopac, New York 10541

Keystone Cocker Spaniel Club—Deborah Gunkle, Secretary
Pine Creek, Chalfont, Pennsylvania 18914

Maryland Cocker Spaniel Club—Marrion Bell, Secretary
1666 Yakona Road, Baltimore, Maryland 21204

Meadowbrook Cocker Spaniel Club—Catherine Fennelly, Secretary
20 Ridgewood Terrace, North Haven, Connecticut 06474

Niagara Cocker Spaniel Club—Helen Thomson, Secretary
7896 Fletcher Road, Akron, New York 14001

Pioneer Valley Cocker Spaniel Club—Carol Stewart, Secretary
Reeds Bridge Road, Conway, Massachusetts 01341

Southern New Jersey Cocker Spaniel Club—Joan Adams, Secretary
832 Columbus Street, Burlington, New Jersey 08016

Upstate Cocker Spaniel Club—Steven J. Caruso, Secretary
8270 Carnation Drive, Baldwinsville, New York 13027

ZONE II

Carolina Cocker Spaniel Club—Jeanne Smith, Secretary
644 Rock Creek Road, Chapel Hill, North Carolina 27514

Cocker Spaniel Club of Chattanooga—Gail McLeod, Secretary
402 Stoneway Lane, Chattanooga, Tennessee 37421

Cocker Spaniel Club of Kentucky—Mary Jo Sims, Secretary
181 Meadow Hill Drive, Bowling Green, Kentucky 42101

Cocker Spaniel Club of Memphis—Gale Gordon, Secretary
3555 Philwood Avenue, Memphis, Tennessee 38122

Cocker Spaniel Club of Southeast Florida—Sherie Janzer, Secretary
631 North 65th Avenue, Hollywood, Florida 33024

Cocker Spaniel Specialty Club of Georgia—Sandra Fields, Secretary
4503 Richard Road, Conley, Georgia 30027

South Atlantic Cocker Spaniel Club—Mrs. M. Picciuolo, Secretary
4502 Ortega Farms Circle, Jacksonville, Florida 32210

Suncoast Cocker Spaniel Club—Sandra St. John, Secretary
1681 Sherbrook Road, Clearwater, Florida 33546

ZONE III

Cocker Spaniel Club of Central Ohio—Glenn W. Price, Secretary
2390 Marcia Drive, Columbus, Ohio 43211

Cocker Spaniel Club of the Middle West—Kris Painter, Secretary
811 Oceola Drive, Algonquin, Illinois 60102

Cocker Spaniel Club of Northern Ohio—Kenneth Miller, Secretary
6247 Richmond Road, Solon, Ohio 44139

Cocker Spaniel Club of Northwest Indiana—Judy Marchand, Secretary
Route 2, Box 200Z, Delphi, Indiana 46923

Detroit Cocker Spaniel Club—Lois Fry, Secretary
P.O. Box 241, Lake Orion, Michigan 48035

Fanciers Cocker Spaniel Club of Southern Wisconsin
Joanne Thorpe, Secretary
13115-7½ Mile Road, Caledonia, Wisconsin 53108

Greater Peoria Cocker Spaniel Club—Donna Helmick, Secretary
1614 North Conn Road, Hanna City, Illinois 61536

Hiawatha Cocker Spaniel Club—Barbara Blum, Secretary
4072–120th Avenue, NW, Coon Rapids, Minnesota 55433

Mid-Michigan Cocker Spaniel Club—Bob McGrath, Secretary
707 East Loomis, Ludington, Michigan 49431

Ohio Valley Cocker Spaniel Club—Wilma Parker, Secretary
9 Pinehurst Court, Fairfield, Ohio 45014

Omaha, Council Bluffs Cocker Spaniel Club—Carol Halstead, Secretary
12967 Lairmore Avenue, Omaha, Nebraska 68164

Salamonie Cocker Spaniel Club—Nadine Meyers, Secretary
1910 East DuPont Road, Fort Wayne, Indiana 46825

Skyline Cocker Spaniel Club—Mrs. P. Gaynor, Secretary
3114 North 77th Avenue, Elmwood Park, Illinois 60635

Tall Corn Cocker Spaniel Club—Julia Kissell, Secretary
5829 Southwest 74th Street, Des Moines, Iowa 50321

ZONE IV

Bay Cities Cocker Spaniel Club—Mary Cushman, Secretary
P.O. Box 11, Alamo, California 94507

Cocker Spaniel Club of Arizona—Joy Ryan, Secretary
1002 East Glenn Drive, Phoenix, Arizona 85020

Cocker Spaniel Club of Hawaii—Geri Cadiz, Secretary
40A Kai One Plaza, Kailua, Hawaii 96734

Cocker Spaniel Club of Las Vegas—Jay Woodward, Secretary
69 Logan Street, Las Vegas, Nevada 89110

Cocker Spaniel Club of Orange County—Marleta McFarlane, Secretary
6543 Indian Trail Way, Fallbrook, California 92028

Cocker Spaniel Club of San Diego—Gayle Bologna, Secretary
1514 Taft, Lemon Grove, California 92045

Cocker Spaniel Club of Southern California—Ralf Reveley, Secretary
7811 Shady Spring Drive, Burbank, California 91504

Fort Vancouver Cocker Spaniel Club—Sandra Smith, Secretary
P.O. Box 1342, Vancouver, Washington 98666

Greater Denver Area Cocker Spaniel Club—Suzette Compton, Secretary
4834 East Costilla Avenue, Littleton, Colorado 80122

Great Salt Lake Cocker Spaniel Club—Debbie Williams, Secretary
110 South 400 East, Brigham City, Utah 84302

Mission Valley Cocker Spaniel Club—Annette Zuck, Secretary
6083 Randell Court, San Jose, California 95123

San Gabriel Valley Cocker Fanciers—Virginia Gilleland, Secretary
4110 Alamo Street, Riverside, California 92501

San Joaquin Valley Cocker Club—Karen Martin, Secretary
2486 Bliss, Clovis, California 93612

Southern Idaho Cocker Fanciers, Shirley Gore, Secretary
2855 Manchester, Boise, Idaho 83704

Washington State Cocker Spaniel Club—Nancy Hurja, Secretary
15544 - 11th Northeast, Seattle, Washington 98155

West Coast Cocker Spaniel Club—Linda Ciaravino, Secretary
3468 Tupelo Street, Chino, California 91710

ZONE V

Cocker Spaniel Club of Austin—Leann Cobb, Secretary
506 East Clayton, Cuero, Texas 77954

Cocker Spaniel Club of Central Oklahoma—Deborah Powell, Secretary
Route 4, Box 160, Tuttle, Oklahoma 73089

Cocker Spaniel Club of Eastern Missouri—Tracy Hefley, Secretary
6105 Erie Station Road, Belleville, Illinois 62208

Cocker Spaniel Club of Greater New Orleans—Jean Uhlich, Secretary
1101 North Woodlawn, Metairie, Louisiana 70001

Cocker Spaniel Club of Southern Texas—Tom Maahs, Secretary
P.O. Box 1130, Porter, Texas 77365

Cocker Spaniel Club of Tulsa—Richard Shackelford, Secretary
6719 South Troost Avenue, Tulsa, Oklahoma 74136

Cocker Spaniel Specialty Club of Dallas—Monty Barbar, Secretary
3508 Crescent, Dallas, Texas 75205

Heart of America Cocker Spaniel Club—Mary Worley, Secretary
7326 Mackey, Overland, Kansas 66204

Lone Star Cocker Spaniel Club—Carol Napper, Secretary
6048 Rickee Drive, Fort Worth, Texas 76148

Ch. Glenarden's Real McCoy—shown by Mike Pitts and bred and owned by Dottie McCoy, "Mac" distinguished himself in 1986 by having won more Best of Breeds than any other Cocker Spaniel shown during that year.

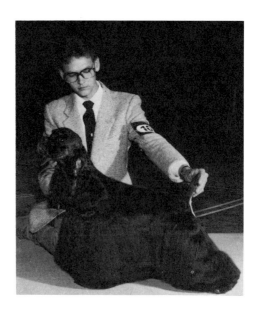

SECTION X
The Breed in Other Lands

- *Australia*
- *Denmark*
- *Great Britain*
- *Finland, Norway & Sweden*
- *France*
- *New Zealand*
- *Switzerland*

Since my last book, *Breeding Better Cocker Spaniels* was published in 1977, our breed has become very popular all around the world. Many of the breeders and clubs in these countries belong to the American Spaniel Club and follow activities in this country by subscribing to the breed magazines. In short, they know more about us than we know about them.

The object of this section is to better acquaint you with how the breed is doing elsewhere; to inform ourselves about how we can ship and receive dogs from countries with quarantine restrictions; and to familiarize ourselves with how their shows are run and how championships are obtained. Most importantly, it is an opportunity to become familiar with the breeders and dogs that play a significant role in that country's "dog world."

I have had the privilege of judging in each country or area represented and have found the breed to be in good hands. The breeders in these countries are dedicated to the improvement of the breed. Many of them have come over to observe our national specialties. The dogs in most of these lands are on a par with ours. That is, indeed, a compliment.

CHAPTER 1

Australia

Compiled by
Lorna Dougal & Dawn MacDonald Tuckerman

How A Dog Becomes An Australian Bench Show Champion

The championship award in Australia is based upon the Challenge Certificate. This is a certificate issued, at the discretion of the judge, to the best of each sex at Championship shows.

1. Challenge Certificates carry points allotted on the following basis:
    A basic 5 points, plus 1 point for each exhibit of the same sex competing in all ordinary classes (Baby Puppy classes excepted) at a Championship show. Maximum points for a Challenge Certificate are 25.
2. Best Exhibit in Group carries points allotted on the following basis:
    A basic 5 points plus 1 point for every exhibit (Baby Puppy Classes excepted) competing in all ordinary breed classes within the group. Maximum points for Best Exhibit in Group are 25.
3. Best in Show Award carries points allotted on the following basis:
    A basic 5 points plus 1 point for every exhibit (Baby Puppy Classes excepted) competing in ordinary classes at the show. Maximum points for Best Exhibit in Show are 25.
4. The points allotted under 1, 2 and 3 above are cumulative to the extent of 25 points only, i.e., no exhibit can receive more than 25 points at any one Championship Show.
5. Upon a dog attaining a minimum of 100 points (comprised of at least four Challenge Certificates under four different judges) the owner is entitled—upon application to and confirmation by the State Kennel Control Council—to be issued a Champion Certificate.

Facts and figures relative to the American Cocker Registrations in Australia:

*   There were 208 American Cockers registered in 1983.
*   There are 125 Breeds with German Shepherds being the #1 Breed with 312,332 registrations.

Quarantine Regulations

Australia does have a quarantine for imported dogs and cats.

Depending upon the country of origin, whether or not the imported animal has been a resident since birth of the exported country, or whether or not the animal is quarantined in a reciprocal quarantined area (i.e., Great Britain, Ireland, Hawaii or New Zealand), depends upon how long the Australian quarantine period will be. The quarantine period can range from two months minimum (from United Kingdom and the Republic of Ireland) to four months (Hawaii), to nine months maximum (United States).

For complete information, contact:

Commonwealth
Department of Health—Quarantine Division
P.O. Box 100
Woden, A.C.T. 2606
Telephone: 062-89 1555
Telegrams: 'Health'
Telex: AA 62149

The first known show-quality American Cocker Spaniel to arrive in Australia was Chandharas Trail Blazer (imp. U.K.), a black and white dog. He was exhibited at the Melbourne Royal Show in 1969, in the ownership of Mrs. P. Collins, but it is believed he never sired a litter.

Aust. Ch. Midnight Snow From Fortfenton (imp. U.K.), also a black and white dog, arrived in 1970. He appears in the pedigrees of a number of parti-colors in Victoria. He was exhibited by Messrs. L.G. Paelchen and L. Dally and was exhibited at the Sydney Royal Show in 1971.

The first bitch to arrive was Aust. Ch. Sundust Thomasina (imp. U.K.), a black imported by Messrs. John Edwards and Phillip Warburton from Mrs. Yvonne Knapper. Thomasina arrived in whelp to Sundust Artru Sunblaze (imp. U.S.A.), on February 17, 1972. Her puppies were the first litter of American puppies to be born in Australia and consisted of a buff bitch, a buff dog and two black dogs. All attained their titles, three in Australia and one in New Zealand. Thomasina went Runner-Up Best in Show at her first show in Australia. She was closely followed by four bitches, Aust. Ch. Gayvons Sweet Lover (imp. U.K.), black, Maplehursts Sugar and Spice (imp. U.K.), red and white, Cholsey's Sago Lily (imp.U.K.), red and white, and Aust. Ch. Lochranza Charmaine (imp. U.K.), black.

Sugar and Spice produced two litters, in quick succession, by Midnight Snow. Also at this time, both Thomasina and Sweet Lover were bred; Thomasina to the first black dog to be imported Aust. Ch. Cholsey's Ambassador and Sweet Lover to the buff dog from Thomasina's litter, Ch. Marsden Moonshine—who was to become the breed's first Best in Show winner in Australia.

Ambassador arrived in 1973, and although solid black, was also useful to the parti lines as his grandfather was Orient's It's A Pleasure. He was followed by three red and whites, namely Aust. Ch. Mittina Tiger's Tail (dog), Aust. Ch. Mittina Wednesdays Child of Idleacres (bitch) and Aust. Ch. Ardquin It's A Pleasure of Idleacres (bitch), to found the Idleacres kennel of Mr. and Mrs. Harry Begg.

Late in 1973, Aust. Ch. Sundust Percussion, a black bitch, came from England to Marsden kennels and, in 1974, eight more imports arrived from the United Kingdom. A host of dogs arrived in the 1970's and 1980's.

Of these imports quite a number have had an impact on the breeding lines in Australia today—mainly solid colour breeding. The most dominating dogs, through 1983, appear to be Ch. Sundust Picotee, Ch. Lochranza Stormalong, Ch. Sundust Personal Service and Ch. Eldwythe Exacto, while the bitches include Ch. Sundust Thomasina, Ch. Gayvons Sweet Lover, Ch. Sundust Percussion, Ch. Hirontower Elvire Madigan and Sundust Black Mystery.

The late 1970's saw the start of the importations direct from the U.S.A. There were two black dogs, Aust. Ch. Mistcliff Travlin To Erintoi and Am./Mex./Aust. Ch. Sebastian Rico's Affair, both of which are Best in Show winners and have sired Best in Show winners. In the early 1980's the first American bred bitches arrived, all to New South Wales, Aust. Ch. Rinky Dink's Seacliff Sara (black), Seacliff N Erintois Velvet (black) and Bobwin's Serenity at Marechal (black and tan).

The breed has been further bolstered by a large number of imports from New Zealand, both dogs and bitches. Two of these bitches have produced the Best in Show winners of the first three American Cocker Spaniel Club Championship Shows. (Authors Note: There are now two American Cocker clubs in Australia—the original one in New South Wales and the American Cocker Spaniel Club of Victoria.) They are Aust. Ch. Shandau Wotacharmer, bred by Mrs. Elsie Rennie, and Aust. Ch. Marsden Mahogany, bred by Mrs. Jean Gillies. Aust. Ch. Maragown Moon Rocket and Aust. Ch. Maragown Mr. Bill Cody, both bred by Mrs. Gillies, have also had an influence on the breed.

Four important imports to New Zealand have visted our country and left their mark: N.Z./Aust. Ch. Freeborne Snow Goose (imp. U.K.), buff bitch; N.Z./Aust. Ch. Sundust Mauritis of Maragown (imp U.K.), red dog; N.Z./Aust. Ch. Bullen Double Mint (imp. U.K.), red and white dog; and Am./Eng./Sh./N.Z. & Aust. Ch. Bobwin's Bangaway of Memoir (imp. U.S.A.).

NEW SOUTH WALES

With Sydney as its capitol, New South Wales is the largest population center in Australia. Sydney has a population of some three million persons.

Prominent Breeders:

"Telde"—Mrs. Julie Lawson

Julie came to American Cockers from having bred Dalmatians and Dachshunds. She obtained her first American Cocker, a combination of Pinefair and Artru breeding, in 1976 from New Zealand. She became Aust. Ch. Shandau Wotacharmer. Shortly thereafter, she obtained a silver-buff bitch who became Aust. Ch. Marsden Silver Dew. She was sired by Aust. Ch. Sundust Personal Service ex Aust. Ch. Sundust Thomasina. Julie liked the breeding so much that she purchased the sire, Personal Service. These three formed the foundation for Telde. Personal Service bred to Wotacharmer produced Aust. Ch. Telde Spring Bouquet —winner of the Challenge at the 1980 Sydney Royal. A repeat breeding produced Aust. Ch. Telde Spring Melody, a black and tan bitch who won Best in Show at the second Championship show of the American Cocker Club in 1980 under Winnie Vick. She was also Best in Show at the third club show.

Aust. Ch. Telde Once Upon A Time was the main stud dog at Telde and produced well.

A year to remember at Telde was 1985, when a lovely black and tan bitch, Aust. Ch. Telde Annies Song went Best Opposite Sex to Best in Show at both Cocker Specialties within a few months of each other under American judges Dr. Alvin Grossman and Mrs. Anita Roberts.

Aust. Ch. Telde Once Upon A Time

Aust. Ch. Telde Annies Song

"Erintoi"—John and Leona Sheppard

Leona Sheppard comes by her Cocker interest naturally as her mother, Mrs. Marie Howitt, imported Ch. Gayvons Sweet Lover, a foundation bitch of the breed. John and Leona's Erintoi kennel name is one to be reckoned with. To improve their bloodlines, they decided it would be necessary to import from the U.S.A. Fortunately, they acquired Aust. Ch. Mistcliff Travlin to Erintoi (Johnnie) and he has been most successful as a producer.

Their Aust. Ch. Rinky Dink's Seacliff's Sara won a Best in Show shortly after coming out of her nine month quarantine. She repeated this win at the sixth Championship show of the American Cocker Spaniel Club with her son, Erintoi Tis Lawrence, winning the dog C.C. from the puppy class. Lawrence easily went on to complete his title.

Their Ch. Erintoi Tis London, has proved to be a popular stud. London's litter sister, Ch. Erintoi Tisa Witch won the bitch C.C. at the American Cocker show in 1984. John has also handled the American champion bitch which belonged to Mrs. Bonnie Compas, Tri-L N' Bards Frosty Kiss, to her Australian Championshipin 1984.

John has had the good fortune to judge in both England and America, thus, the opportunity to see the best each country has available.

"Lynae"—Mrs. Babs Schou and Mrs. Joan Jones

They imported Ch. Eldwythe Exacto from England and at the same time Mrs. Schou acquired Ch. Eldwythe Estelora, a Best in Show winner. Exacto has figured prominently in their breeding. Mrs. Schou strongly favors parti-colors and, a few years ago, finished a black and white New Zealand import Ch. Lynmaken Lively Gambler.

"Valjanane"—Ken and Val Griffin

Ken and Val founded their kennel with two litter sisters, one of whom—Ch. Dantrine Alaskan Rose—won the bitch C.C. at the first A.C.S.C. Championship Show. They imported Best in Show winner Ch. Maragown Mr. Bill Cody from New Zealand to breed to their bitches thus, establishing their buff line. Mr. Bill Cody was the Reserve C.C. dog at the third A.C.S.C. Championship Show.

Their most successful brood bitch was Ch. Valjanane Calamity Jane who won Reserve C.C. at the seventh specialty show of the A.C.S.C. In the middle 1980's, they imported a red dog from the U.S., Pipershill Representative, who is by Ch. Cottonwood's Congressman. Among the foremost buff breeders down under, the Valjanane prefix is seen on ever more increasing winners in the show ring.

"Laramis"—Bronwynne Goyen

While Laramis is a small kennel with only an occasional litter, they are seen in the show ring consistently. Bronwynne owned and exhibited Ch. Erintoi Tisa Witch who won the bitch C.C. at the seventh specialty show of the A.C.S.C in 1984. She also exhibited a black and tan dog, Aust. Ch. Laramis Andrew Jackson with great success having won a number of Best in Show awards.

"Gassbar"—Walter and Helga Gassner

They have won consistently with their Aust. Ch. Gassbar Hot Lips who won the bitch Reserve C.C. at the fifth specialty show of the A.C.S.C., in 1982. They also campaigned a black dog, Aust. Ch. Millcreek Story Teller with much success.

"Erjuness"—Ernie and Judy Ness

Ernie and Judy have been involved with the breed for a number of years and did well with Erjuness Smokin Gun, a black dog sired by Aust. Ch. Keep Your Kool. This dog was owned in partnership with Les Bradney and Tom Tancred who were active early in the breed's history in Australia.

Tony and Sue Ikin

Their Ch. Alrobs Play It Again Sam, a multiple Best in Show winner, won Best in Show at the seventh specialty show of the A.C.S.C. and also was Best in Show at the Victoria Specialty under Dr. Alvin Grossman. Years earlier, they successfully campaigned the first black and tan dog bred in Australia, Ch. Kazah Montana.

"Yandilla"—Margaret Lane

Margaret had achieved success with the New Zealand import Aust. Ch. Maragown Mighty Eaglet and had been a fairly consistent exhibitor until business commitments forced her to curtail her activities.

"Marechal"—Edwina and Roslyn Thomas
and Erica Thomas Howe

Marechal has always been very much a family affair. They started in 1973, with Ch. Marsden Make Believe, a Best in Show winner. "Lincoln" was very shortly joined by the bitches Ch. Sundust Percussion (imp. U.K.) and Sundust Black Mystery (imp. U.S.A.).

Percussion bred to Am./N.Z. Ch. Sundust Maurits of Maragown produced three top puppies—all buff. Ch. Marechal Driftwood became a multi Royal C.C., Best of Breed and Best in Show winner, Ch. Marechal Sandalwood, CD and N.Z. Ch. Marechal Windsong who was BOB at the N.Z. National.

They also bred Ch. Marechal Lovem n Leavem who won Best in Show at the first American Cocker Championship show in Australia. After a string of successes in the whelping box and in the show ring, Marechal imported, from the U.S.A., Ch. Bobwin's Serenity at Marechal to further their breeding program. She has made her mark as a producer.

Their fondest memories are of the Winnie Vick show in 1980 (which was held at Edwina's home), and the preparations leading up to it.

Erica is now married to an American and we have had the opportunity of seeing her in America and watching her judge over here as well.

VICTORIA

Victoria, with Melbourne as its capitol, lies south of Sydney. It has its own American Cocker Club. The population in Melbourne is some two million people.

Prominent Breeders

"Zivv Kennels"—Jeanette Lees

The first American Cocker in the Zivv kennels was Ch. Kingston Kinda Kinky, a red and white dog by Ch. Mittina Tiger's Tail (imp. U.K.) ex Cholseys Sago Lily (imp. U.K.). He was purchased in 1976 and, in the next two years, became well known in the Best in Show

American Cocker Spaniel Club of Victoria Championship Show, March 9, 1985. Judge: Dr. Alvin Grossman. Best in Show—Aust. Ch. Alrobs Play It Again Sam (T. & S. Ikin); Best Opposite Sex to Best in Show—Aust. Ch. Telde Annies Song.

lineups due to his many Group wins. Kingston did a great deal to pro-mote the Breed in those early days and was the *only* American Cocker to qualify for the 1977 K.C.C. Guineas Final at the Royal Melbourne Show.

In 1977, a black dog—Am./Mex./Aust. Ch. Sebastion Ricos Affair —was purchased from America. This dog was the first U.S. bred dog, and the first American champion imported to Australia. He finished his Australian championship easily with three Best in Group awards included in his point tally. He is also a Best in Show winner. He is the sire of Australian, English and New Zealand champions.

Also in 1977, Jeanette purchased the black bitch Jus-Us Cleopatra. Cleopatra is a daughter of BeGay's Daffy D Hershey sired by Am./Can. Ch. Wynden's Fat Albert. Albert is a litter brother to Ch. Tabaka's Tidbit O' Wynden. Cleo was bred in the U.S. to Ch. Argyle Coco Caravelle before being exported to England. While in English quaran-tine, she whelped a litter containing three chocolates. These were the first chocolates in the British Isles and two of them—a dog, Hardrock Cafe and a bitch, Mona L. Hershey—were sent on to Zivv. To date, they are the only chocolates imported to Australia.

Mona became the foundation bitch for producing this color. After several litters, Jeanette seemed to find the formula for quality chocolates.

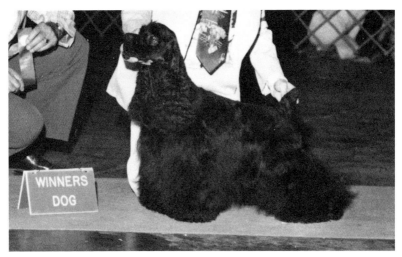

Am./Mex./Aust. Ch. Sebastian Rico's Affair (imp. U.S.A.)

To accomplish this, she combined the best available of Bobwin, Windy Hill, Jus Us, Artru, BeGay and Windridge lines.

Over the years Jeanette has been involved with the breed, her first priority was the promotion of these lovely dogs in the show rings of the four states and A.C.T of Australia.

"Kingston"—Alan Wassilieff

Alan bred his first litter, in 1974, by his two U.K. imports, Ch. Cholseys Ambassador ex Cholseys Sago Lily. Ambassador was a black dog while Lily was a red and white. Alan did a lot for the breed in the early days with his flair for handling and, as a result, did a great deal of winning. This helped to show the breed to the Australian judges in a good light. He did especially well with Ch. Sharonde Currant Affair, a black bitch who was bred in Canberra.

Alan also showed Ch. Marechal Momento, a black and tan, in partnership with Marechal Kennels who bred him. He also did very well with Ch. Marechal Driftwood, a red.

Marechal Madabout You was campaigned to her title and then sold to Ray Ellis and Dick Fahey to become the foundation bitch of their Madabout Kennels.

Lorna Dougall, the former editor of the *American Independent*, purchased her foundation bitch from Kingston from a breeding of Ch. Marechal Driftwood ex Chosley's Sago Lily. Alan has now retired from the dog show world.

"Macron"—Miss D. Cameron

A top U.K. import, Lochranza Charmaine, became the foundation bitch for Macron. When bred to Ch. Sundust Personal Service, she produced Hi Boots Chase, a buff male who was campaigned to his title and became the stud dog at Macron. Miss Cameron returned to her first love, the breeding of poodles.

"Wongan"—David and Stephanie Rickard

Wongan's fortunes began to soar with the acquisition of a black Eng./Aust. Ch. Hirontower Elvire Madigan (imp. U.K.). She was a well up-to-size bitch with incredible substance, superb movement and showmanship which she passed on to her offspring.

When David and Stephanie purchased her from Mr. and Mrs. Begg of Sydney, she was already an Australian champion and from her first litter had produced a champion. The Rickard's repeated that breeding to Ch. Lochranza Stormalong and five champions resulted. They include: Ch. Wongan Superstar (multi Best in Show winner), Ch. Wongan Supernova (multi Group winner), Ch. Wongan Starshine (multi Group winner), Ch. Wongan Stargazer (multi Group winner), and Ch. Wongan Wintersun.

Her second litter bred to Ch. Maragown Moon Rocket (imp. N.Z.) saw four puppies survive and one campaigned to his championship— Ch. Wongan Sandstorm.

Eng./Aust. Ch. Hirontower Elvire Madigan (imp. U.K.)

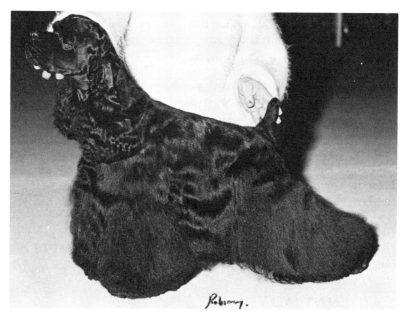

N.Z./Aust. Ch. Wongan Proper Posiedon

When bred to Ch. Marechal Momento, she produced Aust./N.Z. Ch. Wongan Proper Posiedon who was the top dog Victoria all breeds in 1982 and 1983, Ch. Wongan Apropos Apollo (Group winner), Ch. Wongan Always Athena (multi Best in Show winner), and Ch. Wongan Directly Diana (a multi Best in Show winner).

Elvire Madigan's last litter was to her son "Posiedon," and the Rickards retained the Best-in-Show-winning bitch, Ch. Wongan Rhapsody.

"Superstar" is the sire of Best in Show winners for Merriyank Kennels. "Stargazer" mated to Moon Rocket produced five champions for Amarour. When bred to Am./Eng./Aust./N.Z. Ch. Bobwin's Bangaway of Memoir, she produced Ch. Amarour Casino Royale and Ch. Amarour Ima Knockout, with several others pointed.

"Wintersun," when mated to Ch. Marechal Momento, produced Ch. Wongan Soul Singer and Ch. Wongan Satanic song. Soul Singer, mated to Moon Rocket, produced Ch. Wongan Moon Witch who, when mated to Stargazer, produced the Skudder's top winning Ch. Penita Rebecca Riots.

"Sandstorm" has sired Ch. Madabout High Command with many others pointed and probably finished at this writing.

"Directly Diana" was mated to N.Z/Aust. Ch. Sundust Maurits of Maragown and produced the Best In Show winning bitch, Ch. Wongan Ebony Evidence. But the star of the team has been Posiedon ("Sam").

Not only an incredible show dog but a sire of sound, typical puppies with his mother's attitude. Lightly used, he has sired Best in Show winner Ch. Idylewins It And A Bit for Max Winch (out of his "Superstar" daughter), N.Z./Aust. Ch. Quaymont Carbon Copy and Best in Show winner Ch. Alrobs Play It Again Sam.

Whelped in January of 1979, Posiedon began his Group winning at nine months of age. His Championship Best In Show winning at 14 months was launched at the first Victorian Specialty. He also won the next three in a row.

Sent to New Zealand for 1984, he quickly gained his title, returning home in time for the Melbourne Royal where, after winning the C.C. and Best of Breed, he was officially retired.

The American Cocker Spaniel Club of Victoria has honored him with a sash recognizing him as a "fine ambassador of the breed." (*Author's Note: When we stayed with the Rickards after the Victoria Specialty, Sam was my constant companion and buddy.*)

SOUTH AUSTRALIA

South Australia, with Adelaide as its capitol, lies south of Melbourne. Adelaide has a population of approximately one million people.

The earliest records of the breed in South Australia start in 1970, when one was entered, but not shown, at the Adelaide Royal show. This was an open dog, Midnight Snow from Fort Fenton—an import from the U.K. The first American Cocker to be actually exhibited was Chandaras Trail Blazer, exhibited at the Adelaide Royal in 1972. This dog was of all American breeding.

In 1976, the first two American Cockers attained their Championships in South Australia. They were Mrs. D. McCall's, Idleacres The Duchess and Ms's. C. Haas and C. Deverson's Marsden Mr. Success. While both of these dogs were owned by S.A. exhibitors, they were bred in N.S.W.

The first two litters were registered in S.A. in 1977.

In 1979, there was an upsurge of Americans with the import of N.Z. Ch. Maragown Milk N Honey, Erintoi Golden Rocket, Erintoi Tan Tribute and Zivv Afair Flirt. The total number of American Cockers shown by South Australians that year was 10. From that point on the numbers began to increase. In 1983, 23 Americans were entered in the Adelaide Royal. Through 1984, only three American Cockers from S.A. had obtained their titles; Guileann Starbuck, Guileann Dark Moment and Skyhawke Timely Tribute.

The breed is still numerically quite small but is on the upswing. The principal exhibitors are June Maudlen with her Julen prefix (formerly

Guileann), and Max Winch of Idylewins. Max has judged in the States and sets a dog down beautifully.

Prominent Breeders

"Julen"—June and Geoff Maudlen

Having bred Irish Setters for seven years, June decided to purchase another breed in the Gundog group. She chose the American Cocker. Her first two were a buff dog, Wyungare Aim To Fame and a buff bitch, Wyungare Adventuress. The dog won numerous group placings and a Best in Show as well as obtaining his title. The bitch was not campaigned. A year and a half later a buff puppy dog was purchased as a result of a trip to the Maragown Kennels of Jean Gillies in New Zealand. He was to be co-owned with Beverly Grant of Ankara Irish Setters. He became Ch. Maragown Moon's A Balloon and was South Australia's top Gundog puppy in 1981. In 1982, he gained the top spot among all Gundogs in South Australia. During his career he amassed over 20 Best in Groups and 4 Best in Shows. He was awarded Reserve Best in Show under Dr. Grossman at the 1985 Victoria Specialty.

Ch. Maragown Moon's A Balloon (N.Z.)

A bitch was purchased to be specially bred to him. She was Maragown Maid for a Moon, who went on to gain her title. Their litter produced Guileann Starbuck, a buff dog who obtained his title and was trained for field work by Geoff, who is a Field Trial Judge. The buff bitch, Guileann Starmaker, was well on her way to the title when this was written in 1984. A red bitch, N.Z. Ch. Maragown Melting Moment, was leased for showing and later purchased. Her first mating to Ch. Maragown Mark My Word produced the black bitch, Guileann Dark Moment, who obtained her title and—in the process—won many group and Best in Show awards. As the Guileann prefix was originally for Irish Setters (being a Gaelic word meaning ''The Noble Whelp''), and somewhat difficult to pronounce, a more suitable prefix was required for the Cockers. Julen was selected and registered in 1984.

Ch. Maragown Melting Moment's second litter was sired by Ch. Wongan Proper Poseiden. Two of the four puppies from this breeding completed their championships. They were Julen Candy Coloured and Julen Black Candy.

Most recently Julen has imported from the U.S.A., Am./Aust. Ch. I Just Be Invincible who is already a Best in Show Winner and Runner-up Best Exhibit, Battle of Champions 1987. Vince was obtained for his background and linebreeding to the Julen bitches.

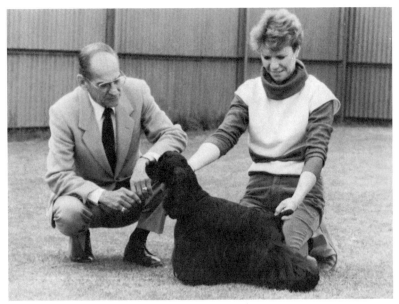

Ch. Guileann Dark Moment

Am./Aust. Ch. I Just B. Invincible

Idylewins—Max Winch.

Max has been involved with dogs over a long period of time. He has handled a number of breeds and is often seen judging around the globe. He campaigned a lovely black bitch, Ch. Idylewins It And A Bit to many important wins and is currently campaigning Ch. Idylewins Mac Brat to impressive records.

The kennel at Idylewins is shared with his partner, David Roche, who exhibits Afghans among other breeds. The kennel is the dream of anyone in dogs. It has all the amenities and then some. David's home, where they live, is like walking into the world's greatest antique collection. *(Author's Note: Doris and I had Tea there one afternoon after I had delivered a lecture in Adelaide. It was a visit to be treasured.)*

WESTERN AUSTRALIA

The American Cocker has only become a part of the Gundog scene in Western Australia since 1975. Trevor Anthony brought Idleacres Miss Louise into the state from N.S.W. at that time. Western Australia is far from the Coastal areas where Sydney, Melbourne and Adelaide are located. In fact, some 3,000 miles separates Perth, the largest city of the region, from Canberra, the capitol of the nation on the opposite coast. Perth is probably best known for the location of the Americas Cup defense in 1987.

There are three pioneer breeders in this area which is sparsley populated. They are the Krisvor Kennels, the Merewether Kennels and the Merrykane Kennels. (*Author's Note: Australia has a total population of 14 million in a land which is about the same size as the United States.*)

Prominent Breeders

"Krisvor"—Trevor Anthony

Miss Louise was the first American Cocker in Western Australia. She was a very showy, black bitch and did much to stimulate interest in the breed. She won many awards along the way to her Australian title.

Louise had two litters—the first to a buff dog, Idleacres Melody Man, who was out of the famous Ch. Hirontower Elvire Madigan by Ch. Lochranza Stormalong. This litter was whelped in 1977. From this breeding came Ch. Krisvor Amethyst who lives in Tasmania. (*Author's Note: Tasmania is an Island off the coast near Adelaide and is an intregal part of Australia.*)

Her second litter was to Am. Ch. Sebastian Rico's Affair (imp. U.S.). Whelping complications caused the loss of all except one puppy.

"Merewether"—Tony and Lesley Gibbs

The Gibbs purchased the litter sister of Louise at a year of age from N.S.W. and she became the foundation for their kennel. A black, she became Ch. Idleacres Martha. She had been winning in N.S.W. and had obtained half her championship points before coming to Western Australia. She was a lovely type of bitch but did not sparkle in the ring.

Her first litter was by the newly imported Aust. Ch. Hirontower Crown Destiny (imp. U.K.) and produced three black and tans and three blacks. From this breeding came the black and tan bitch, Ch. Merewether Rags To Riches who was sold to Sandy Walker. This bitch went on to win the coveted award of Best in Show at the 1979 Perth Royal Show and remains the only American Cocker (circa 1984) to win a Best in Show at a Royal anywhere in Australia.

Ch. Merewether Rag Doll, a black littermate of Rags To Riches, was retained by the kennel.

Martha's second litter was by Aust. Ch. Maragown Moon Rocket, a buff dog. From this mating came four blacks including the lovely Merewether Sweet Polly.

Rag Doll was mated to Ch. Maragown Moon Rocket in 1980. This mating produced the very showy, winning bitch, Ch. Merewether Just a Love. She was retired from the show ring, in 1984, after a star-spangled career.

"Merrykane"—Ian McLean and Barry Newmansparkes

In 1977, these two gentlemen formed the Merrykane kennel and brought to West Australia a very sound and showy black dog, Ch. Hirontower Crown Destiny (imp. U.K.) who was 12 months old at the time. Shortly thereafter, he was followed by the young black and tan bitch, Hirontower Eleanor Rigby. She was bred to Crown Destiny on three occasions. The first litter produced the black dog Ch. Merrykane Mean Machine, who went to Sandy Walker of Zekiah kennels, and a black and tan dog Ch. Merrykane Manov War, who went to the Midasand kennel in Tasmania.

The second breeding produced the top-winning black dog Ch. Merrykane Moondyne Joe, who was campaigned extensively by his owner, Paul Wilkes. Prior to his retirement, at the age of four years, he earned well over 1,000 challenge points and many Best in Shows.

Other up and coming kennels in the state are Staryanks of Paul and Debbie Wilkes, Zekiah Kennels of Sandy Walker, and Amcrest of Michelle Mattesmen.

QUEENSLAND

Queensland lies north of New South Wales and has Brisbane as its principal city. The famous Great Barrier Reef is within its confines. Cocker activity in this area is somewhat sparse.

Prominent Breeders

"Millcreek"—Mr. and Mrs. Duncan McGregor

The McGregors first became interested in American Cockers in early 1976, after having successfully bred Chihauhuas for several years under the Anahuac prefix. Duncan contacted Harry Begg and purchased a black puppy bitch, followed shortly by the black puppy dog, Idleacres Music Man—who was sired by Ch. Lochranza Stormalong ex the famous Eng./Sh. Ch. Hirontower Elvire Madigan. At the same time, the black import bitch Noslien Clarissa of Idleacres was purchased for breeding.

Music Man and his sister Madrigal both gained their titles. Music

Man won four Best in Show awards. Clarissa, when bred to him, produced three champions. Most notable was Anahuac Cracklin Rosie, who was a consistent C.C. winner.

In early 1978, they acquired from Yvonne Knapper of Sundust fame in the U.K., Sundust Maestro, a young buff dog. His show career started in 1979. At his second show, the Sydney Royal, he won the puppy class and at his third, as a junior, he was Best in Show. In April 1980, at the N.S.W. American Cocker Specialty, Mrs. Winnie Vick awarded him the C.C. and Runner-up in Show. He did quite well overall as a show dog.

The need for a compatible bitch to breed to him was quickly realized and another inquiry to Yvonne Knapper resulted in their obtaining Sundust Cricket of Jantu, who had recently whelped a litter by a litter brother of Maestro. "Sheba" was accompanied by a buff puppy bitch, Sundust Gemma. They were introduced to the show ring, in 1980, and later on that year, both were bred to Maestro. Sheba produced Ch. Anahuac Sweet Serenade, a buff bitch, and a black bitch was sent on to Janice and Ian Haygarth. Gemma produced a very nice buff bitch, Ch. Anahuac Forget Me Not.

The McGregors changed their kennel prefix to Millcreek. Their latest import, Smokey, Ch. Keep Your Kool was imported as an outcross for the Millcreek bitches. He is an all American-bred Ch. Bobwin's Sir Ashley son. Smokey enjoyed a very good show career with numerous top awards.

TASMANIA

Tasmania lies off the sountern coast of Australia.

The first American Cocker in Tasmania was the red and white bitch, Ch. Mittina Wednesday's Child of Idleacres, bought by Mrs. Ruth Chandler from the Begg's of N.S.W who had imported her from England. This was in 1976.

The early pioneers of the breed were Mrs. Ruth Chandler and Mr. and Mrs. Ian Haygarth.

The second American Cocker into Tasmania was the black and white bitch, Ch. Nobhill Hootnanny purchased by the Haygarths from Mrs. Betty Kingdom of Canberra.

Both bitches were bred and parti puppies began to appear in the ring followed by some solids including a buff male owned by the Haygarths purchased from Maragown Kennels of New Zealand, and another buff dog owned by Mr. and Mrs. A. Jones, purchased from Marsden Kennels of N.S.W.

The early winning dogs were Aust. Ch Nobhill Hootnanny, a Best in Show winner at all-breed shows. The next big winner was Aust. Ch.

Maragown Make Mine Music, a multiple Best in Show winner and Gundog Group winner. Aust. Ch. Marsden Light Myfire owned by Mr. and Mrs. A. Jones gained his title and did well at the shows. The next big winner was a tri-colored dog, Aust. Ch. Raylyndon Razzmatazz, a multiple Best in Show winner and Gundog Group winner, owned by the Haygarths. Then came the black bitch, Aust. Ch. Ooswen Tar Button also owned by the Haygarths. This bitch was a Royal Hobart Show challenge and Best of Breed winner.

The next top dog was the red and white dog, Aust. Ch. Raylyndon Jetsetter, also owned by the Haygarths. This dog set a great pace for others to follow by winning six all-breed Best in Shows in N.S.W and Queensland before arriving in Tasmania. Terry and Jean Skudder bought a black male, Aust. Ch. Amarsour Casino Royale and he also proved to be a winner of Best in Show and numerous "In Show" awards. The Skudders also leased two black bitches from Victoria, Aust. Ch. Wongan Directly Diana and Aust. Ch. Wongan Rhaposdy. Both of these bitches were multi "In Show" award winners.

Current breeders leading the way in Tasmania include: Mr. and Mrs. J.P. Skudder, Mr. and Mrs. I.P. Haygarth, Mr. and Mrs. R.J. Chandler. Current top exhibitors are: Mr. and Mrs. A. Jones, Mr. and Mrs. Skudder, Mrs. N.J. Percey and Mr. and Mrs. Haygarth.

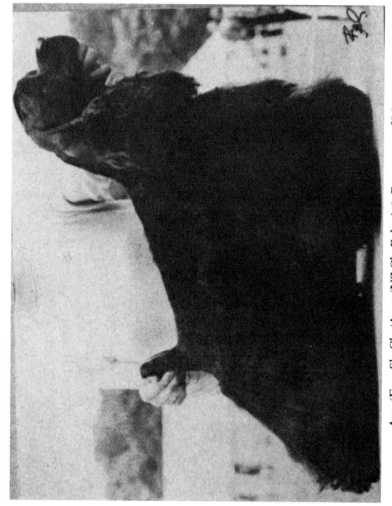

Am./Eng. Sh. Ch./Aust./NZ Ch. Bobwin's Bangaway of Memoir.

CHAPTER 2

Denmark

by Bent Westphall & Lottie Wissing

The first American Cocker Spaniel came to Denmark in 1964. It was a black dog imported from Sweden, however, he never influenced the breeding in Denmark. Then the Saxdalen kennels brought a beautiful golden bitch—Miss Globetrotter—to the country from Keljeager's in Canada. She had a considerable impact on the breeding of Cocker Spaniels in Denmark.

Upon completion of a short and glorious show career, Miss Globetrotter was bred to Ch. Stonehedge Mark-Ye-Well in Sweden, and delivered the first litter of American Cocker Spaniels born in Denmark. Out of the seven puppies, four finished their championship in Denmark, and one in Germany.

A male from the litter was aquired by the Kildeholm kennels, where he became their main stud dog. Kildeholm had imported two bitches—Queen from Sweden and Sandra Philandra De La Baia from Portugal—and bred largely and successfully until the late seventies. It should be mentioned that Int. Ch. Kildeholm's Funny Face was exported to France/USA and Int. Ch. Kildeholm's Golden Mirra-Melica went to the Philippines.

A new import from Canada—Keljeager's Buff Stuff—sired Miss Globetrotter's next litter. Additionally, he became an International, Danish, and Norwegian champion, and was the only American Cocker in Denmark, up to that time, who had won a Best in Show, this was at an all-breed show in 1970.

Out of the litter sired by Buff Stuff, came Saxdalen's Silver Snowflake who was acquired by the Two-Be kennels, and together with a Swedish bitch—Snorrehus Housekeeper (out of Merry-Wag's Happy Day and Ch. Windy Hill's Tis'-To-An-Fro) became the foundation of the breed in the Two-Be kennels. Snowflake also has a Best in Show victory, won over 450 dogs of many different breeds in 1972.

A couple of Snowflake's sons had their impact on the breed in this country: Ch. Two-Be's Silver Snowstorm, American Cocker of the Year in 1974, and Ch. Two-Be's Boys Mustapha, Male American Cocker of the Year in 1982, and still producing at the Tissoe kennels. Tissoe kennels additionally imported Jo-Bea's Sir Gallant Lad, in 1985.

Today, with the beginnings of the breed in our country at a reasonable distance, it must be admitted that the Canadian dogs, and especially their descendants, were handsome and successful on the show-side, but that their health left something to be desired. Only a few of the first two–three generations lived longer than seven–nine years, the reasons for early deaths naturally varied, but cerebral hemorrhages, liver and renal failures have been predominant.

In the beginning of the seventies, the Gyldenlund kennels imported a bitch in whelp from the United States. She was ordered by mail and when she arrived here, it turned out that she could literally not close her mouth, due to the bad state of her bite. Out of the seven puppies she delivered, only one had a correct bite. He started producing, which naturally resulted in plenty of bite defects in his descendants. Unfortunately, many breeders are still fighting that problem today.

While discussing health problems, we have also seen some cataracts but only sporadically, and though we have no established registry, it does not seem to present a problem to the serious breeders.

Another established kennel which should be mentioned is the Sankie kennels, whose breeding stock is essentially based on Dutch imports. Contrary to the Canadian imports, nearly all of these Dutch imports have lived to an old age.

In 1977, U.S. Ch. Artru Jan-Myr Nature Boy was imported by a private owner. A couple of years later, he was purchased by the Falstria kennels. He became an outstanding stud dog, having a major impact on the improvement of the toplines on many of the Danish Cockers.

Over the last two to three years the breed has been influenced by a lot of fresh blood through imports from Sweden, Finland and the Netherlands—mostly descendants of American specimens. The last imports are from the United States: Two bitches and one male from the Windy Hill kennels.

However, in spite of the relatively large number of imports over the last years, it has become clear that it has almost constantly been the male-side that has been reinforced, the female stock is more or less of the same "old" (and not too good) material. It is certainly about time that we get some good new "lasses."

Ever since the breed came to Denmark, its popularity has been steadily increasing. With a stud book registration of 332 puppies in 1980, the breed entered the All-Breed Top-Twenty List as #19, the two following years as #20 with, respectively, 402 and 397 registered puppies.

This popularity has unfortunately attracted cunning fortune hunters to mass-produce dogs that have very poor construction and, least of all, look like American Cockers. This is presumably an activity that is well-known in the United States, too.

Until 1979, the American Cocker belonged to the Spaniel Club. On May 15, 1979, the American Cocker Spaniel Club of Denmark was established—commonly referred to as the American Club. The American Club arranges five–six shows per year, in different parts of the country, and so does the Danish Kennel Club for all breeds.

In addition, we have the possibility of participating in shows in the rest of Europe—apart from the Sweden, Norway, and Finland—whose borders are closed for dogs due to the risk of rabies. The United Kingdom should also be mentioned in this respect. They even have six months of quarantine, while the three Nordic countries mentioned have four months. In Denmark, there is no quarantine obligation.

The judging system for the Danish shows is substantially different from the American system. The first entry into the ring is the puppies aged from 6-9 months, both sexes. The judge finds the best puppy of the breed of the day. Afterwards the male champions enter, they are followed by the male youngsters (9-15 months), then open class males (15 months–7 years), and finally the male veterans over 7 years of age. The procedure is repeated for the females.

The judging in the ring is, in principle, the same as in the U.S., but in addition, the judge dictates a judgment of every single dog to the ring secretary who types it down simultaneously, and a copy is given to the individual handler. This is called The Judgment by Quality, and a 1st-, 2nd-, or 3rd-quality prize—or a disqualifying 0 for the reasons listed in the breed standard—is given. Only the 1st prizes remain in the ring and participate in a competition judgment where the judge finds a 1st, 2nd, 3rd and 4th winner. 1st, 2nd and 3rd *prizes* are marked by red, blue and yellow ribbons respectively, and 1st, 2nd, 3rd and 4th *winners* are marked by red, blue, yellow and green ribbons.

In the youngsters class, the judge can award those of the placed dogs that he believes deserves it, an "Extremely Promising," marked by a narrow purple ribbon. This gives the right to compete on equal terms with the 1st prize dogs in the open class. The final 1st winner in open class is usually awarded the "Judge Certificate," marked by a red and white striped ribbon—but this is not compulsory. If the judge does not find the quality of the winning dogs to be high enough, he can omit this award. In case he does award the "Judge Certificate," he can also award, to as many of the participating dogs as he wants to, a "Of Certificate Quality," marked by a wide purple ribbon which gives admittance to the final competition—"Best in Breed." The best dogs in the champion and veteran classes are mostly also awarded the purple "Of Certificate Quality" ribbon and participate equally in the "Best in Breed." The winner automatically participates in the competition "Best in Group" in the all-breed shows. In Europe, we have eight groups and the winners of these compete for the award "Best in Show".

In international shows, a CACIB is awarded to the best male and the best female in the Best in Breed class. When four CACIB's are obtained in three different countries and by three different judges, the dog becomes International Champion. To become a Danish Champion, three "Judge Certificates" given by three different judges are required; the last certificate must be awarded after entering in open class (over 15 months). With only one certificate given per sex/per show, and 10–12 shows arranged per year, it is only possible to produce 3–4 champions per sex/per year in our breed.

CHAPTER 3

Great Britain

by Yvonne Knapper & Sheila Zabawa

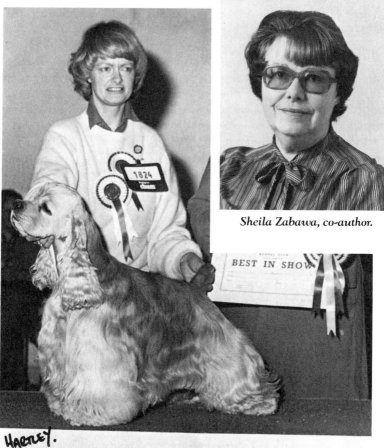

Sheila Zabawa, co-author.

Yvonne Knapper, co-author, shown with Sh. Ch./Am. Ch. Kaplar's Kwik-Step to Sundust—Top Gundog, 1984.

In 1964, a young Dutch girl took a plane to England to become the head kennelmaid at a British kennel and also to perfect her English. This young lady, Yvonne Knapper, first fell in love with the American Cocker Spaniel while training in Holland at the famous Cockerbox Kennel of English and American Cockers. These sporting dogs—with an outgoing nature and glamorous appearance—appealed to her, particulary as she was already an expert in trimming and grooming. It was not long before she had two American Cockers of her own, a dog and a bitch, both of which were CACIB winners in Europe. While working in England, Yvonne missed her own dogs so much that she decided to import them from Holland. By this time she had also realized that her previously acquired idea—that British breeders might not take kindly to a new breed—was false.

During 1965, Yvonne's bitch, Merryborne Just a Belle van der Cockerbox, in whelp to a son of Am. Ch. Pinetop's Fancy Parade, arrived in England with her dog, Myrica's Little Bit Naughty who was by a Parade son, to commence their statutory six months quarantine. They were the first American Cocker Spaniel show dogs in Great Britain and the start of Yvonne Knapper's Sundust Kennel.

Just a Belle was a very pretty bitch and had a super head but she was not linebred and never reproduced herself. The fact that there were no outstanding males in Britain, at that time, did not help the breeding plans. However, these ambassadors of the breed attracted a great deal of interest particularly from famous kennels such as Lochranza, Noslien, Mittina, Ardquin, Ballantrae, Montravia, Huntglen, Chandara, Tarina and Hardacre to mention but a few. Noslien, Ballantrae and Ardquin are still actively breeding today, and stock from the Mittina and Lochranza kennels is behind many current winners. Other famous prefixes associated with the breed from its early days here, and still active, are the Boduf, Bullen and Rengil names. The Eldwythes, bred by Dick Wylde (who now lives in Australia but judges here occasionally), made their special mark upon the breed by producing the only two full British Champions to date—Ch. Eldwythe Enchanto and Ch. Eldwythe Timothy's Black Tiffany. Gundogs in this country may achieve the title of "Show Champion" in beauty competition and the title of "Field Trial Champion" if they qualify in the field. It is only if they acquire both qualifications that the Kennel Club grants them the title of "Champion." For this reason American Champions which have also gained the necessary show ring awards here are referred to as "American Champion and Show Champion."

Many breeders were attracted to the glamorous new arrivals on the British show scene, and most of the original fanciers still have a soft spot in their hearts for them, but as their other breeds were not gundogs it became too complicated for them to exhibit dogs in different groups particularly as our Championship Shows have become spread over more and more days. This will, no doubt, seem strange to people living in countries so much larger than ours, and where distances are enormous. However, almost all American Cockers in this country are owner handled and only on one or two occasions has a professional handler been employed to exhibit one of our breed. Most exhibitors attend shows on a day-trip basis returning on a subsequent day only if they win the Gundog Group and become eligible to compete for Best in Show. The latter feat has been achieved only once at an all-breed show: Am. Ch./Sh. Ch. Dreamridge Delegate won Best in Show at Birmingham City Championship Show, and also won the Gundog Group at Crufts in 1972, the only American Cocker Spaniel to win the group at our most prestigious show. The black and white Delegate—a full brother to Am. Ch. Dreamridge Domino—was owned by Andrew Caine of the Ballantrae kennel. Though no longer with us, this great dog is still a force behind the Parti-Color breeding here. Andrew Caine also imported Am. Ch./Sh. Ch. Dreamridge Dan-Dee. Mike Bottomley and Bryan Morrison are the owners of Am. Ch./Sh. Ch. Sendos Pepper 'N' Salt of Boduf, Am. Ch./Sh. Ch. Smarti Parti Triple Pleasure of Boduf and also of the bitch, Am. Ch./Sh. Ch. Orient's Choice Pleasure of Boduf. These Parti-Colors form the nucleus of Parti breeding here to date as well as having been great winners in their own right.

Sh. Ch. Afterglow Sultan Of Swing. Photo by David Dalton.

The ASCOBs

In the buffs, a color which so many fancy for its various shades and eye-catching appeal, the influence of Aztec Mission Accomplished, a son of Am. Ch. Artru Sandpiper—owned originally by author Hilary Harmer and later by Joyce Grant of the Saldawn prefix—is still evident in the breed as is that of Sundust Artru Sunblaze and the red dog Golden Acres Grin And Bear It, a Sandpiper grandson. Artru La Toka of Mittina is another important buff dog in the breed; being one of several influential American Cockers imported by Mrs. A.M. Jones, MBE.

Sundust Artru Sunblaze

The black and tan color combination has several staunch devotees in Britain. In this color, Am. Ch. Lochranza Evdon's Escort, owned by Miss Joan MacMillan, and the multiple Challenge Certificate winner Am. Ch./Sh. Ch. Windy Hill 'N' Durbet's 'Tis Patti of Sundust are remarkable, as also is the younger bitch, Sh. Ch. Durbet's Binkidine Fanfare, who arrived here at the age of three months accompanied by her little brother, the black Sh. Ch. Durbet's Binkidine Damn Yankee; Fanfare, owned by Alice Martin, and Yankee, owned by Betty and Bernie Stoner, consolidated the success of the Binkidine kennel. Another black and tan of note is Mrs. and Miss Penny Iremonger's Sh. Ch. Durbet's Meg O' My Heart at Moonmist. Several years ago, the imported Can. Ch. Musblaik's Morganne's Light My Fire, a lightly marked black and tan, figured in several breeding programs. He was imported by Mr. and Mrs. Dave Taylor.

Sh. Ch./Am. Ch. Windy Hill 'N' Dur-Bet 'Tis Patti of Sundust. *Photo by Sally Anne Thompson.*

Sh. Ch. Sundust Glamour Boots. *Photo Courtesy of* Dog World.

An attempt has been made to establish the chocolate color here, and though many people have displayed an interest in chocolates, the only dog to acheive his title is Sh. Ch. Begay's Matti Brown at Kittimat. This dog was imported as a youngster by Hurst and Hughlock. Three other chocolate American Champions have been imported, Am. Ch. Jus Us Chocolate Kisses owned by Mrs. Jacky Tappenden, Am. Ch. Jus Us Buster Brown owned by Mrs. Linda Bishop, and Mrs. Lillian Whitely imported the chocolate male, Am. Ch. Pineshadow's Coco Bear, who won two Challenge Certificates. Chocolate Kisses made a few telling appearances in the show ring but her duties have been mainly in the nursery.

Buster Brown, the sire of Chocolate Kisses, has been offered at stud but did not—as far as is known—make any show ring appearances here. One or two others carrying the chocolate gene, including Am. Ch. Jus Us Commander Kane, have been imported from the U.S.A., and there have also been some chocolate/white and chocolate tri-colors in evidence but the chocolate color generally has yet to become thoroughly established here.

Blacks

Among the earlier influences on the black American Cockers, without doubt the strongest color in Great Britain, were Am. Ch. Cholseys Orient's Secret Pleasure, imported by Mrs. Herbert and later owned by Mrs. A.M. Jones, Am. Ch./Sh. Ch. Sundust Bleuaire's Repercussion, owned by Yvonne Knapper, Sh. Ch. Windy Hills Tis Travelling Man at Kelsmere, owned by David and Margaret Bett, Sh. Ch. Sundust Thanks Dur-Bet, bred and owned by Yvonne Knapper, and Am. Ch. Durbet's Dillinger of Teilwood, imported by Leslie and Alison Henson; Dillinger was the first arrival here from Elizabeth Durland's Durbet kennel. Penny Iremonger's Moonmist prefix is also to the fore in black breeding, particularly the females of which the latest is her young Sh. Ch. Moonmist Remembrance. The influence of such great dogs as Am./Can. Ch. Durbet's Knight to Remember and Am. Ch. Durbet's Pick the Tiger are obvious in our stock today. Another dog which has exerted a strong influence on black breeding is Am. Ch. Windy Hill's 'Tis Demi's Demon through his sons—the above mentioned Travelling Man and Sh. Ch. Bobwins Sundust What the Hell; the latter was imported from Winnie Vick by Yvonne Knapper who has, to date, imported eighteen American Cockers.

Problems

In breeds such as the American Cocker Spaniel, still numerically small in Great Britain despite its obvious attraction, breeders are hampered by the restricted gene pool both in color breeding and in the

Sh. Ch./Am. Ch. Sundust Bleuaire's Repercussion,
owned by Yvonne Knapper. Photo by Anne Cumbers.

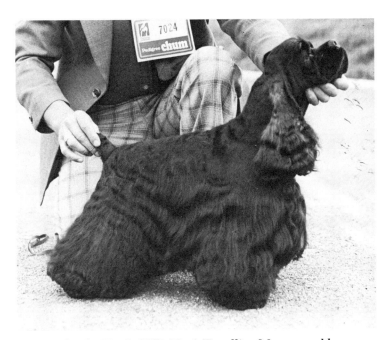

Sh. Ch. Windy Hill's Tis A Travelling Man, owned by
Mr. and Mrs. David Bett. Photo by Garwood.

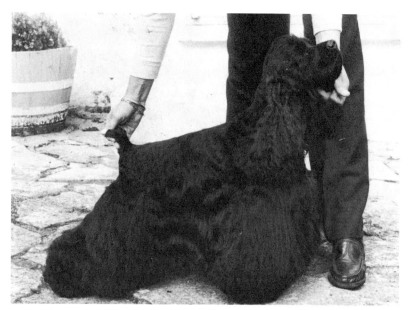

Sh. Ch. Sundust Thanks Dur-Bet, bred and owned by Yvonne Knapper.

Sh. Ch. Sundust Thanks Dur-Bet shown one month after winning the CC at Crufts 1979. *Photo by* Dog World.

elimination of hereditary problems. However, those who truly love the American Cocker never give up. During the comparatively early days of the breed in Great Britain, the initial problem of hereditary cataract was encountered although it was not understood at that stage what the mode of inheritance might be. Setbacks, when they occur, are seen as challenges by some people and many who fell in love with the breed on its arrival here, and still love it, found they had to fight a devastating battle against eye problems. This proved too much for some fanciers who chose to leave the breed; others struggled on. With the help and advice available through the British Veterinary Association/Kennel Club Schemes for the Control of Hereditary Diseases some progress has been made—and ours is noted as being one of the breeds making the best use of the official schemes. Unfortunately, not all breeders co-operate fully in using the examination schemes though a great many have done so. Today all newcomers to the breed who approach reputable breeders are made aware that eye problems still exist and that stock should be purchased with great care. We realize that we have no completely clear lines and that regular examination of breeding stock is the only way in which we can reduce the incidence of hereditary cataract.

Another difficulty which many of the earlier fanciers faced was the management of the full Cocker coat and the specialized trimming necessary to present the breed in tip-top condition. Presentation has improved vastly over the years, and even today's newcomers make a very good job of the necessary care. It should be added that our climate presents us with definite hazards in this respect—being, for the large part of the year, wet. It is interesting to note that among the leading exhibitors there is a definite preference for hand stripping back coats rather than scissor thinning and that several judges are known to prefer this method of show ring presentation. However, there are many adherents of the scissors technique as well.

Show Regulations

In Great Britain, American Cockers of all colors compete together and there are no specials classes. Thus, all newcomers must compete against crowned champions whether the coveted title was gained here or in any country with which the Kennel Club has reciprocal agreements. There are Champion Stakes classes scheduled at many of our Championship Shows; these are open to all breeds and American Cockers usually give a good account of themselves when entered in such classes.

It is only at Championship Shows that the Kennel Club's Challenge Certificates for the best dog and best bitch are offered; the dog and the bitch challenging each other for Best of Breed. Many of these are very large events with exhibits numbering well over 10,000 and some exhibitors choose to attend only this type of show; others also enter the smaller shows, Open Shows, Limited Shows or the less well attended licensed shows where competition is not so demanding. The latter types of show are usually local events, whereas, the Championship Shows always attract a country-wide entry with our senior Breed Club Championship Show drawing the highest entry of all. At other Championship Shows the American Cocker entry may fluctuate between 60 and 100 dogs. What determines the size of an entry is often a mystery but Scottish exhibitors are not so likely to attend shows in the southern coastal region which may indicate the peripheral venues are less popular for reasons of inaccessibility. Sometimes we have a run of shows within a very short period of time; this, too, tends to spread the entry somewhat thinly when it occurs.

Challenge Certificates for our breed are now available at virtually every general Championship Show, the exception being in Belfast. There are five Gundog Group Championship Shows and two Breed Club Championship Shows making a total of thirty-two shows at which Challenge Certificates may be won.

At Championship Shows there are always separate classes for dogs and bitches and each sex may have a Minor Puppy Class (6–9 months), and there is always a Puppy Class (6–12 months) and a Junior Class (6–18 months). These and the Veteran Classes are at all shows, (with the exception of Crufts at which certain special conditions are made), the only classes to which an entry is determined by age rather than a statutory number of wins in certain grades of exhibition. There may be a Novice Class at a Championship Show, and possibly some others should the number of exhibits increase, but there will certainly be a Post Graduate, Limit and Open Class as these together with the age classes qualify a dog for entry at Crufts—provided the dog wins a first prize! The Crufts qualifier was originally introduced in an attempt to limit the entry to this, the Kennel Club's own show. What it succeeded in doing was to make eligibility to enter so desirable that entries at all other Championship Shows increased and "qualified for Crufts" is what everyone wants their Cockers to be! Thus, Cruft's entry is still around the 10,000 mark and rising every year.

The fact that we have no separate classes for champions, and that a champion competes with all others for the Challenge Certificate on the day inevitably leads to some dogs winning a considerable number of CC's. To be granted a Show Champion's title, a dog must win three Challenge Certificates under three different judges. At each show there is also a Reserve Challenge Certificate for each best of sex. Should the CC winner be disqualified for any reason, the top award would then go to the Reserve CC winner on that particular day, but no amount of Reserve CC's in themselves count for anything toward the title otherwise. From this, it can be seen that an outstanding dog may appear to block the path of others on their way to the top. From the opposite point of view a Show Champion may be beaten by an up-and-coming dog; at each show that risk has to be faced. It is often argued that we should adopt the American system of scheduling special classes for champions but the general opinion is that to do so would lower the overall standard and produce "cheap" champions. In the numerically small breeds, it could well do so, though exhibitors in gundog breeds which regularly attract entries of over 400 dogs at one show may be less inclined to agree.

Another point to consider is that all judges at Championship Shows are reminded by the Kennel Club that if, in the opinion of the judge, there is no exhibit worthy of the title of Champion, or Show Champion in our case, the Challenge Certificate should be witheld. This happens occasionally, but not as far as can be recalled has this disappointment occurred in our own breed.

There have been between 400–500 American Cockers registered each year but that may not be an accurate reading of the number of Cockers being bred here. When the Kennel Club amended the regulations concerning the registration of puppies, the registration fee was raised by 500% and a "litter recording" scheme was introduced, under which, a breeder may either record the whole litter at a minimum fee or register some, or all, of the puppies at the higher cost. Before this amendment was introduced it was customary for breeders to register all of their puppies. The situation is now reversed and breeders tend to register only the pups they wish to keep themselves or those who are going to show homes. Others may be sold either without papers or with the recording form which allows the purchaser to register the puppy, but without the breeder's official affix. Pet purchasers often forget to register the puppy, or would rather not pay out more money; hence the apparent fall in the number of puppies bred. Show entries seem to remain at approximately the same level and breed classes are as well supported as ever.

Judges

At shows, our breed may be judged by a breed specialist, a gundog specialist or an all-rounder who officiates in many breeds in the gundog and also other groups. Though the majority of our judges are British, American Cocker classes here have been judged by people of many nationalities, including some specialists from the U.S.A. The senior breed club, the American Cocker Spaniel Club of Great Britain, makes a point of inviting an overseas judge to officiate at the annual Championship Show held in September. Judges who are invited to judge at any Championship Show have to be approved by the Kennel Club. Judges are not licensed; the Kennel Club's approval is for each individual show at championship level. Judges at open and other shows do not need Kennel Club approval.

There is no official training scheme for judges though many breed clubs sponsor teach-ins and seminars to help future judges—and refresh the memories of some others. There is a privately organized Judging Diploma course which some aspiring American Cocker judges have completed, as well as people interested in many other breeds, and although this does not have Kennel Club approval, the course is efficiently organized and the graduates consider it to be extremely beneficial. However, as far as appointments are concerned, it is a matter of waiting to be invited. The more experience which can be gained at any type of show licensed by the Kennel Club, the better for the aspiring Championship Show judge. Before being considered for approval to judge at the higher level and entrusted with the awarding of the Kennel Club's Challenge Certificates, the judge will be required to furnish an accurate judging *curriculum vitae*. Exhibitors and breeders whose only interest is the American Cocker Spaniel—a numerically small breed here, as we have said—may find it difficult to build up sufficient judging experience at the smaller shows to be approved to judge at championship level. Unfortunately, several breed specialists who were invited to judge at Championship Shows in 1983 and 1984, were not approved by the Kennel Club.

Each breed club (all breeds not just our own), compiles a Judges List but there are no hard and fast rules concerning how this task should be completed. Certain regulations apply, of course, but no definite directions because individual clubs may have different needs. Thus, some breed societies may call for nominations for their Judges List, others may not. The committee of some clubs may compile the list which may, or may not, be presented to the members for approval; other clubs may decide their list by postal ballot of all members. There is no need for a person's name to appear on any breed club list in order for him, or her, to be approved by the Kennel Club to judge at Championship Shows. It is the individual person's own experience which counts. When a judge is invited to award Challenge Certificates for the first time, the Kennel Club writes to the breed clubs requesting their opinions concerning the proposed judge's suitability. In some cases, the breed club may have no information about the judge concerned; in others the Kennel Club Judges Sub-Committee may overrule the breed club's opinions. In breeds which have several clubs, there may be a Breed Council Judges List which is a combination of the lists of all societies concerned; the American Cocker Spaniel breed has three breed clubs but no Breed Council, therefore, there is no composite Judges List at this time.

Winners

Many American Cockers in Great Britain have brought show ring success to their owners by winning at the highest levels and amassing a considerable number of Challenge Certificates. Bearing in mind that three CC's awarded by three different judges is the requirement for the title of Show Champion, the following records speak for themselves.

The highest number of Challenge Certificates won by an American Cocker here to date is 27. This figure was reached by the black bitch, Sh. Ch. Kiewa Its Chic, bred by Beryl Bennett and owned and campaigned by Frank Kane. Chic is a Gundog Group winner and also a Champion Stakes winner. Sired by Sh. Ch. Sundust Man of Action ex Sh. Ch. Kiewa Its Purdy, she is a granddaughter of Am. Ch./Sh. Ch. Windy Hill 'n' Durbet's 'Tis Patti of Sundust (winner of 16 CC's) and Sh. Ch. Sundust Thanks Durbet (winner of 13 CC's).

The male record holder, as of this writing, is Bottomley and Morrison's red and white Sh. Ch. Boduf Orient Express with 19 CC's to his credit. He was sired by Am. Ch./Sh. Ch. Sendos Pepper 'N' Salt of Boduf ex Am. Ch./Sh. Ch. Orient's Choice Pleasure of Boduf.

The first American Cocker to achieve a Show Champion's title in England was the black dog Sh. Ch. Lochranza Newsflash, a son of the buff Sundust Artru Sunblaze. The first British-bred bitch to gain her title was Sh. Ch. Mittina Kiss Me Too of Spawood. She was sired by the black Am. Ch. Orient's Secret Pleasure; a son of Orient's It's a Pleasure. Secret Pleasure was a dog with a beautiful head and very worthy of a British title but, after winning two CC's, he apparently decided that further showing was of no interest to him. Kiss Me Too was bred by Mrs. A.M. Jones, MBE and owned by Mrs. Marjorie Gunning-Turner.

The first of many American Cockers to win a Gundog Group was the black and tan Am. Ch. Lochranza Evdon's Escort; he was always handled for his owner, Joan MacMillan, by John Gillespie of the Lochranza kennel.

Progress

Although we have many good British-bred dogs, we are still dependent on top-quality imports from the U.S.A. to complement our breeding programs. During the last two years, American breeders have made a terrific impact on our show scene by winning the Top-Breeders Competition sponsored by the weekly paper *Our Dogs* and the manufacturer's "Pedigree Petfoods." This competition aims to discover and recognize the breeders in each breed who are producing Challenge Certificate winning stock.

In 1983, the top breeder was Mrs. Elizabeth Durland whose exports to our shores, Sh. Ch. Durbet's Meg O' My Heart at Moonmist, owned by Penny Iremonger, and Sh. Ch. Durbet's Binkidine Damn Yankee, owned by Bernie and Betty Stoner, together earned enough points from their Challenge Certificate wins to put Betty Durland in the lead.

In 1984, the leading breeders were Mr. and Mrs. K. Henson who exported Am. Ch./Sh. Ch. Kaplars Kwik Step to Sundust to Yvonne Knapper who campaigned this buff extroverted dog with great success. For the second year running, the top breeders in American Cockers in Great Britain were Americans! To add the icing to the cake, "Freddie" won Best in Show at the National Gundog Championship Show in November '84.

Yvonne Knapper with Sh. Ch./Am. Ch. Kaplars Kwikstep To Sundust receiving one of "Freddie's" trophies at Crufts 1985. Freddie's breeders, Mr. and Mrs. Henson (Kaplar's), became the leading American Cocker Spaniel breeders in the U.K. in 1984 and Freddie also won the award for the leading Gundog of the Year.

Yvonne and Freddie are shown with a representative of Pedigree Petfood, Ltd. and the assistant editor of Dog World *who jointly sponsored one of the above competitions.*

Quarantine

All dogs which are imported into the British Isles spend a statutory six months in quarantine. Basically, this means that once they are crated at their point of departure they are not released until they have been cleared through British customs and delivered by a licensed carrier into the safe confines of the quarantine kennel.

We have some excellent quarantine establishments which care so well for the dogs that exhibitors can take them straight from the kennels into the show ring and win! However, leaving the home kennel, the long journey, and the stress of quarantine restrictions affects some dogs very badly though others bounce through their six months detention in fine spirits.

Breeders considering exporting stock to Great Britain should ask themselves if their dogs are sufficiently outgoing by nature and steady in temperament to weather the strain of quarantine. This is even more important when the export is a bitch in whelp. Adult dogs which are coming to join our stud force should be proven sires before they leave the home kennel. That may sound a superfluous statement; it is included because disappointments have occurred in the past, and not only in our breed. Some very expensive pets have been acquired in this manner!

Breed Clubs

The senior breed club, The American Cocker Spaniel Club of Great Britain, was founded in June, 1967. This club drew up the British standard of the breed which is based on the American standard and has guided the breed safely through many of its difficulties. Not the least of these was the threat of the Kennel Club, in 1972, to transfer the American Cocker to the Utility Group. Many prominent people in the world of dogs supported the club in its efforts to have the breed retained in the Gundog Group; fortunately, the combined efforts were successful.

When the problems of hereditary cataract manifested themselves, the Great Britain club was instrumental in having the breed admitted to the British Veterinary Association/Kennel Club Schemes for the Control of Hereditary Diseases. Today, in conjunction with the youngest of the breed clubs, the Home Counties American Cocker Club, the Great Britain club publishes twice yearly the *Eye Compendium*. The Compendium is a record of the results of eye examinations carried out during the preceding six months by veterinarians with an ophthalmological qualification. Entries in the *Eye Compendium* are made on a voluntary basis, failures as well as successes being recorded. Copies are distributed free of charge to club members. Already the *Eye Compendium* is building into a most useful reference work.

The A.C.S.C. of Great Britain and the Northern Counties A.C.S.C. are both Championship Show societies holding one Championship and two Open Shows each year; these shows are open to all American Cocker exhibitors. The third club, the previously mentioned Home Counties American Cocker Club, has not yet achieved Championship Show status (1985) and holds a Members' Limited Show and two Open Shows a year. The smallest of the breed clubs, this society was the first to make arrangements for Eye Clinics to be held at club shows and the two longer-established societies subsequently followed suit. Although the three breed clubs are completely separate from one another, and in many ways serve different parts of the country, they appear to be in agreement over major issues which concern the breed as a whole.

Details of breed societies may be obtained from The Kennel Club, 1 Clarges Street, Piccadilly, London W1Y 8AB, England.

CHAPTER 4

Finland, Norway & Sweden

by Gun Granbom

The first Cockers came to Sweden in 1950. Mrs. Mary Aron brought a black male, Sir Gary of Stockholm, sired by Salaun's Stockdale and out of Lady Cherie of San Diego, from Mr. Arthur F. Hamby of the United States. Miss Barbo Neumuller purchased Penny Champagne sired by Breezeway Gold Strike ex Breezeway Sweetheart, from Mrs. Ruth Ravetti. A few years later, Mrs. Marta Bendz bought her first cocker from the States. It was a white and yellow male, Rye Pioneer, sired by Cian's Creme Glace ex Misty Black Scanties.

Those ladies were the early pioneers, but their efforts did not leave any lasting traces. It wasn't until almost 20 years later that the breed became well known and popular to the Scandinavian dog fancy.

These very first cockers were shown, but they did not get their titles. Here in Scandinavia, we don't have professional handlers, so almost every dog is breeder/owner handled. Our show system is a bit different from America. To become a champion in Scandinavia the dog needs three CC's, from two different judges, and one of the CC's has to be won from the open class, over 15 months of age. To get the National Championship in Sweden and Finland the dog has to pass a field trial, and that is not easy! We don't have the Show Champion title over here yet.

There are two kind of shows in Scandinavia: Nationals (where you can get CC's) and Internationals (where you can get CC's and CACIB's). When a dog has three CC's, it is no longer allowed to compete for the CC, so at an International show, the dog can—with a bit of luck—get the CACIB instead. The CACIB is an International CC and the dog needs four of them to get the International Championship. The CACIB has to be won in three countries, under three different judges. The dog has to be 15 months before he can compete for the first one and one year has to pass between the first and the fourth, before the dog gets the title.

Since the dogs don't compete by colors, there are only two CC's and two CACIB's awarded—one for best male and one for best female.

I'm going to use some abbreviations in Champion titles later on, and here is what they mean:

Sw. Ch. = Swedish Champion—with field trial and three CC's
SF Ch. = Finnish Champion—with field trial and three CC's
N. Ch. = Norwegian Champion—three CC's in Norway
Scand. Ch. = Scandinavian Champion—Champion in Sweden, Norway and Finland with field trial
Int. Ch. = International Champion

When I got my first Cocker in 1973, the registered number of Cocker Spaniels was 272; ten years later, in 1983, there were 599 registered. So, the breed is growing rapidly, which means that we need to get new dogs all the time. Mainly the purchases are made from the U.S.A. That means quarantine!

We have three quarantine kennels in Sweden—one in southern Sweden and two near Stockholm. Before a dog leaves the U.S.A. for it's new home in Scandinavia, it has to have a health certificate not older than ten days, a blood test for leptospirosis (a disease we don't have in Scandinavia). If the dog has been inoculated for leptospirosis three months has to have passed before we can bring the dog here. We don't have rabies either, so the dog has to have been inoculated for rabies. Thirty days has to have passed before the dog is allowed to cross our border. Inoculations for distemper, hepatitis and parvo are always given in quarantine.

When all this is settled, and the dog has arrived in Scandinavia, it has to spend four months in the quarantine kennels, and another two months in house quarantine. This is a very expensive business: the average quarantine bill is 9.000 Sw. Kr. ($5,607). So, when we buy dogs, we want good ones!

I'm going to present some breeders in Sweden to you. These are people that have spent a lot of time and money and didn't throw in the sponge when things got tough. We had a lot of difficulties when we began!

"Alheim's Kennel"—Mrs. Leila Axelsson bought her first Cocker in 1969, a buff bitch named Saxdalens Gold Opportunity (by Danish Ch. Stonehedge Mark-Ye-Well ex Saxdalen's Lady Corinne) from Mrs. Palmer's Keljjeagers Kennel in Denmark. In 1970, Mrs. Axelsson bought a buff male from the same kennel, Saxdalen's Buff Rocket, and a red male, Int. N. Ch. Cobb's Red Jacket (by Am. Ch. Artru Red Baron ex Bleauaries Hearts Desire) from Mrs. Carolyn Cobb of the U.S.A. "Timothy" was a Best in Show winner and sired champion offspring. These were the foundation dogs at Alheim's. Later, in 1977, Mrs. Axelsson imported a red bitch, Cobb's Rosemelon (by Am. Ch. Cobb's Red Coat ex Am. Ch. Cobb's Katydid). She was bred to Am. Ch. Scioto Bluff's Stockholder and this litter produced 1982's top-winning black dog, Alheim's Peter Pan—a dog with several Best in Shows and Group placements.

Int. N. Ch. Cobb's Red Jacket, owned by Leila Axelsson.

1982's top-winning Scandinavian Cocker—Alheims Peter Pan, breeder/owner Leila Axelsson.

"Beringen's Kennel"—Mrs. Elsie and Miss Lena Johansson became Cocker fanciers in the early 70's. Their first import, in 1974, was Am./Int./N. Ch. Artru Sundance Pacemaker (by Am. Ch. Artru Skyjack ex Andra Artru Sundance). "Packer" had a tremendous show career. At the age of five, he was Sweden's top-winning dog, all breeds and in 1983, at 10½ years, he was Best Veteran in Show at the big International Stockholm Show.

Packer is not only a Best in Show winner but has proven to be an outstanding sire with a number of champion offspring.

After the success with Packer, Beringen Kennel purchased Am./N. Ch. Artru La Toka's Red Hot (by Am. Ch. Jan Myr's Ready Teddy ex Artru Delightful II). "Sizzle" is also the sire of several noted offspring, among them Finland's top-winning dog in 1981 SF./N. Ch. Mistyway Sausey Red Tiger (his dam is a Cobb's Red Jacket daughter). He came out of retirement to go Best in Show under Dr. Grossman in 1983. Later, a buff bitch Int. N. Ch. Artru La Toka Jennifer was obtained (by Am. Ch. Artru Getaway ex Jan Myr's La Toka's Cherish). They also obtained N. Ch. Shardeloe's Sprite (by Am. Ch. Heyday Headhunter ex Shardeloe's Heavensent) and she became the dam of several champions.

In 1980, Am. Ch. Harrison's Shoe Shine Boy (by Am. Ch. Rinky

Dink's Sir Lancelot ex Pineshadows Picturesque—a litter brother to Peeping Tom, a top American winner) came to live at Beringen's. Among his champion offspring was Norway's top winning Cocker for 1982—N. Ch. Sibeja's Chanthal.

The kennel's latest import is Am./Int./N. Ch. Mica's Baron of Brooklands (by Am. Ch. Artru Buff Baron ex Am. Ch. Ashley's Miss Muffet). "Charlie" arrived in early 1983, and had a flying show start. He has many Best in Show wins and has sired many promising youngsters. He ended his first year in the ring as Sweden's top Sporting Dog.

Int./Am./N. Ch. Artru Sundance Pacemaker, owned by Elsie and Madeleine Johansson—shown at 10½ years of age. "Packer" was the topwinning dog (all-breeds) in Sweden in 1978 with 14 Best in Shows.

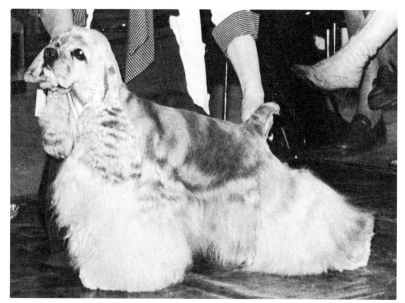

Am./N. Ch. Artru La Toka's Red Hot, owned by Elsie and Madeleine Johansson.

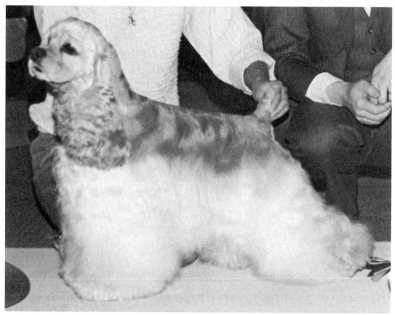

Beringens James Gold, Best in Show at the American Cocker Spaniel Club Specialty in Stockholm, 1984. Bred and owned by Elsie and Madeleine Johansson.

Int./Am./N. Ch. Harrison's Shoe Shine Boy, owned by Elsie and Madeleine Johansson.

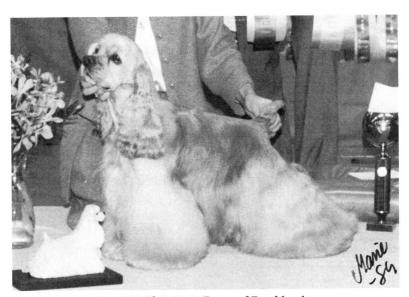

Am./N. Ch. Mica's Baron of Brooklands.

"Bluesette's Kennel"—Mrs. Gun Granbom started her kennel in 1973, with a black and white Cocker Spaniel as a wedding gift. She became N. Ch. Bluesette and was a Rexpointe Dream Date granddaughter. In 1977, Mrs. Granbom purchased a black and white bitch, N. Ch. Panderosa's Handmade (by Dreamridge Director II ex Panderosa's Amalie) from Miss Bjorg Larsen of Norway. "Emma" became the foundation bitch for Bluesette. She was mated to N. Ch. Marquis Fiddler On The Roof. This litter produced champions and CC winners. Among them was Int./Scand. Ch. Bluesette's Freckly N' Blue, a black and white bitch who was the top-winning Parti-Color in 1983, and N. Ch. Bluesette's Blue Fighter who was the #2 winning Cocker in Norway in 1982—owner-handled by Miss Larsen.

In 1983, Bluesette's acquired Soho's Tickertape Parade (by Am./ Int./Belg./Luxemb. Ch. Laurim's White Tale ex Am. Ch. Kamps' Kurtain Kall). He was obtained from Mr. Dan van Maris of Holland. "Perry" went on to an outstanding show career, easily completing his championship. *(Author's Note: While staying at Bluesette's, Perry made me his project and gradually we learned to communicate in Swedish.)*

Bluesette Kennel is mostly known for its Part-Colors but we had a few ASCOB litters. The top-winning buff from these breedings was Int./N. Ch. Bluesette's Captain Blue. In 1980, he was reserve top-winning dog all breeds, only two years after his famous father, Packer, won the top-winning award. "Chivas'" dam is a Sizzle daughter and he was owned and expertly handled by Lena Johansson of Beringen's.

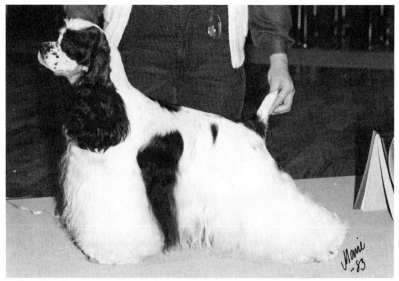

Int. N. Ch. Bluesette's Freckly 'N Blue, breeder/owner Gun Granbom.

Soho's Tickertape Parade, owned by Gun Granbom and bred by Dan van Maris of Holland.

Int. N. Ch. Bluesette's Captain Blue was Reserve Top-Winning Dog all-breeds in 1980. "Shiwas" was bred by Gun Granbom and is owned by Madeleine and Elsie Johansson.

"**Capri's Kennel**"—Mr. Bengt and Mrs. Irene Andersson started their kennel at the end of the 60's decade. Their foundation bitch, Kildeholm's Goldie Locks (by Danish Ch. Stonehedge Mark-Ye-Well ex Queen), was imported from Denmark. Through her, the kennel started with very good stock and produced several winning dogs.

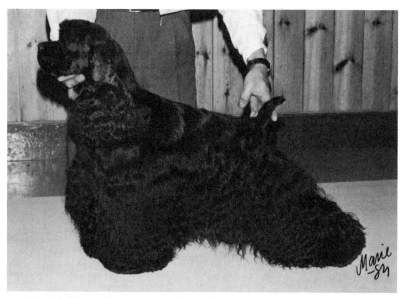

Capri's Huggy Bear, bred and owned by Bengt and Irene Andersson.

"**Cornerstone Kennel**"—Mrs. Gerd Nilsson-Cullin's Cocker kennel was launched in the middle of the 70's. One of the first dogs at the kennel was N. Ch. Mash, a buff Ch. Cobb's Red Jacket son. In early 1983, Mrs. Cullin got her buff bitch, Am. Ch. Cajun's Cobb L. Stone (Am. Ch. Ashley's Golden Rule ex Am. Ch. Cobb's String of Hearts) out of quarantine. She was purchased from Mrs. Betty Orgeron. "C.C." was bred to Mica's Baron of Brooklands and among the promising youngsters in this litter was Cornerstone's B. Bestman, a Best in Group winner at 10 months of age. He is owned by Miss Gunilla Wallenstrand.

"**Ekhorst's Kennel**"—Mr. Wilhelm Dufwa had a top-winning Cocker in 1974, Int./N. Ch. Ekhorst Am Apache Raider, a N. Ch. Merry Wag's Happy Day grandson. "Nixon" ended 1974 as Reserve top-winning dog all breeds in Scandinavia and is still in every Ekhorst pedigree. At the end of the 70's, Mr. Dufwa bought a black male, Am./Mex. Ch. Butch's Irresistable Imp (by Am. Ch. Rinky Dink's Sir Lancelot ex Corwell's Cricket). "Van" has also proven his producing ability. One of his best

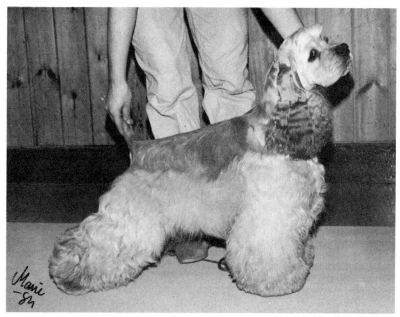

Cornerstones B. Bestman, bred by Gerd Nilsson-Cullin and owned by Gunilla Wallenstrand.

Am./N. Ch. Butch's Irresistable Imp, owned by Wilhelm Dufwa.

offspring is N. Ch. Cavatina's Goldisocks and is also owned by Miss Gunilla Wallenstrand.

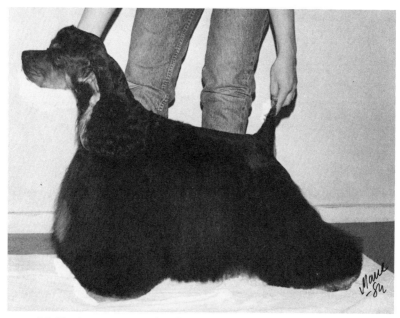

N. Ch. Cavatina's Goldisocks, owned by Gunilla Wallenstrand.

Monica Bergenstam-Hansson imported her first Cocker from the United States in 1975. It was the black and white male, N. Ch. Ga-Bark's Bombay's Souvenir (by Am. Ch. Uhlwin Unavailable ex Am. Ch. Ga-Bark's Barode). He and Brigadoon Indian Moccasin composed the foundation stock for Mrs. Bergenstam. A few years later new imports followed including N. Ch. Marquis Skip N' Go Naked (by Am. Ch. Frandee's Declaration ex Am. Ch. Windsong's Sonata), Frandee's Fancy Francy and Marquis Rebecca. "Rebecca" has produced several champion offspring. One of them was 1981's most winning Cocker, a black and white—N. Ch. Masterpiece.

"Pennylane's Rambler Kennel"—Mrs. Inga Enstad has been active in the breed since the late 60's. She originally imported two bitches from the Three Crown's kennel in Wisconsin, U.S.A. "Tequila" (by Am. Ch. Three Crown's Tomahawk ex Three Crown's Tomboy) and Int./N. Ch. Three Crown's Tea Wagon (by Am. Ch. Valli Lo's Viceroy ex Three Crown's Certainly Magic). A buff male followed a few years later. He was N. Ch. Merrywag's Happy Day (by Am. Ch. Merrywag's

N. Ch. Masterpiece, bred and owned by Monika Bergenstam-Hansson—1981's top-winning Cocker.

Mind Changer ex Sham-O-Jet's Dutch Miss). He proved to be a good stud dog and among his champion offspring is a buff bitch, Sw./SF. Ch. Chico's Ginny Buff Lady, the foundation bitch at Paradore's Kennel.

"Paradore's Kennel"—Miss Irene Abrahamsson has bred many winning dogs. Among them was Int./Scan. Ch. Paradore's Jasmine Buff Yankee (by Am./Int./N. Ch. Artru Sundance Pacemaker ex Paradore's Belizza). Another very good bitch from this kennel is Int./Scan. Ch. Paradore's Nadja (by Am./N. Ch. Artru La Toka's Red Hot ex Jasmine).

"Sibeja's Kennel"—The two bitches mentioned above also gave Mrs. Siv Lundgren a very good start for her Sibeja's kennel. Mrs. Lundgren is one of the pioneers in field training. She has spent many hours out in the field, training her dogs with very good results; four Swedish Champions. She is the breeder of Norway's top-winning dog of 1982, N. Ch. Sibeja's Chanthal.

"Snorrehus Kennels"—In 1968, Mrs. Karen Schmidt imported a buff bitch—Danish Ch. Windy Hill's Tis To An Fro (by Am. Ch. Kahola's Keybitzer ex Stonehedge Tis Me O' Windy Hill) and a buff male, N.

Int./Scan. Ch. Paradore's Jasmine Buff Yankee, bred and owned by Irene Abrahamsson.

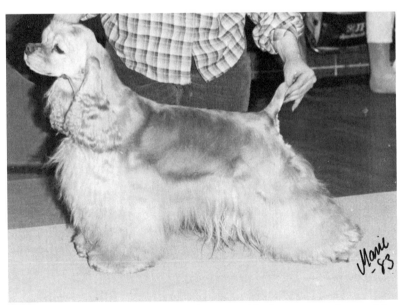

Int. N. Ch. Paradore's Nadja, bred by Irene Abrahamsson and owned by Siv Lundgren.

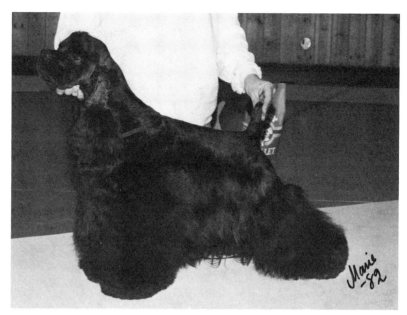

N. Ch. Sibeja's Chanthal, Norway's top-winning Cocker in 1982, bred by Siv Lundgren and owned by Bjorg Larsen.

Ch. Memoir's Snow Secret (by Am. Ch. Juniper's Just Snowed ex Dorobin Dimity). In the early 70's, a black and white bitch called N. Ch. Rexpointe Dream Date (by Am. Ch. Rexpointe Frostee Dutchman ex Dreamridge Double Date) arrived. She became the dam of champions and the foundation of Mrs. Schmidt's Parti-Color breeding.

Miss Susanne Soderberg has been in Cockers since the beginning of 1970. Her first American imports were in 1981 when a black and white male, N. Ch. Marquis Fiddler On The Roof (by Am. Ch. Rexpointe Shazam ex Am. Ch. Marquis Ms. Marie) arrived. Additionally, a black and white bitch Marquis Born to Queen (by Am. Ch. Checkerboard Ric-Rac ex Am. Ch. Feinlyne Friezee) was imported. "Fiddler" has been a remarkable stud dog with numerous champion offspring who have Best in Show and Group awards. One of them is the black and white dog, Bestseller. *(Author's Note: I judged in Finland in 1983, Fiddler was leased there and was distinctively stamping his get.)* The latest Soderberg acquistion is Frandee's Max Factor (by Am. Ch. Marquis Commander Cody ex Am. Ch. Frandee's Flurry).

"Tidlosa Kennels"—Miss Ulla Engstrom has been active in the breed for a few years. She is known for her beautiful black dogs. Her foundation stock was imported from the U.S.A.—first, a black male, Am. Ch.

N. Ch. Marquis Fiddler On The Roof, owned by Susanne Soderberg—a top sire in Scandinavia.

Best Seller, a son of "Fiddler On The Roof." Bred by Susanne Soderberg and owned by Marie Borresen.

Three Crown's Tru Grit (by N. Ch. Merry Wag's Happy Day ex Three Crown's Tomboy); then a black bitch, Windy Hill's Girl Scout Cookie (by Am. Ch. Windy Hill's Eagle Scout ex Am. Ch. Windy Hill's Tis Demi-Tasse). These imports produced very well and resulted in many champion offspring.

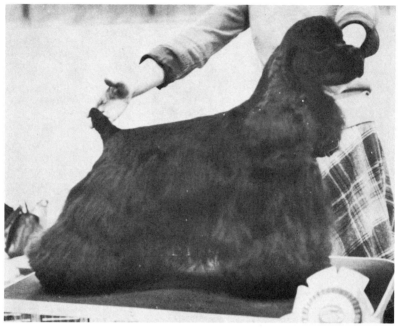

Int. N. Ch. Tidlosa Tammy—a Best in Show winner. Bred and owned by Ulla Engstrom.

"Urazzo's Kennels"—Mrs. Gunilla Norden purchased her first Cocker, in 1973, and he became N. Ch. Chico's Urazzo Charming Prince (by Am. Ch. Cobb's Red Jacket ex Rambler's Good Luck). Later that year, Mrs. Norden had the good fortune to be offered a bitch named N. Ch. Carlen's Chantilly (by Am. Ch. La Mar's London ex Carlen's Classique). "Candy" was an outstanding producing bitch—she had champions and CC winners in every litter. In a breeding to "Packer," there were two Int. and Scan. Champions—Urazzo's Delight Rosie and Urazzo's Dominant Boy. In 1976, Mrs. Norden imported a black male, Am. Ch. Scioto Bluff's Stockholder (by Am. Ch. Breeze Hill Sail Along ex Am. Ch. Scioto Bluff's Blueberry). "Hackie" was also a good producer, siring many champions—among them was the noted Alheim's Peter Pan. Mrs. Norden's latest import, Am. Ch. Piner's Mickey Gilley is to be handled by the American-trained Elisabeth Osth.

N. Ch. Carlen's Cantilly—a top producer owned by Gunilla Norden.

Int. N. Ch. Urazzo's Dominant Boy, bred by Gunilla

Am. Ch. Scioto Bluff's Stockholder, sire of N. Ch. Alheim's Peter Pan. Imported and owned by Gunilla Norden.

"Pennylane's Kennel"—Miss June Hallerberg was the first to embrace the brown color. She imported N. Ch. Windridge Chocolate Showman (by Windridge Chocolate Classic ex Windridge Chocolate Bonbon) in 1976. She also purchased a black male, Am. Ch. Sandrex Sentinel (by Am. Ch. Lurola's Lookout ex Am. Ch. Essanar Evening Song).

About the Breed in Neighboring Countries

Cocker Spaniels first reached Norway in the middle 60's. A red and white bitch, Rexpointe Rockette (in whelp to Am. Ch. Rexpointe Dutchmaster) was imported by Mr. Hans D. Neve. This breeding resulted in three champions.

In the early 70's, Mr. and Mrs. Ultveit-Moe, whose kennel name is "Wishbone," became interested in the breed. They imported Am. Ch. Bobwin's Did You Ever, Am. Ch. Bobwin's I'm Tops, Am. Ch. Bobwin's Black Bart, Int./N. Ch. Mar-Jac's Liberty of Wishbone and Am. Ch. Bobwin's Temptor of Wishbone. This resulted in numerous champion offspring for Wishbone and dramatically increased interest in the breed.

Miss Bjorg Larsen had 1973's top-winning Cocker in Norway, a black and white, Int./N. Ch. Panderosa's Honky Tonky (by Mublaiks's Sea Holly ex Ashgate Miss B'haven). Later, she imported a red and white male, Am./Can./N. Ch. Scioto Bluff's Noso Way'n, a son of the legendary Am. Ch. Scioto Bluff's Sinbad. "NoNo" was a very successful show dog as well as an outstanding stud dog.

The Mitella's kennel of Mrs. Brit Olufsen started with a black and white bitch, Panderosa's Crazy Daisy—a litter sister to Ch. Panderosa's Honky Tonky. A few years later, Mrs. Olufsen imported a red and white male, Am. Ch. Keamborne Kash N' Karry and a black and white male, Dreamridge Director II. Both became the sires of champion offspring.

In Finland, the pioneer was Mrs. Anja Pumala of Leavenworth kennels. She introduced the breed to the fancy in the late 1960's. Her best known champions were a buff bitch, Int. Ch. Nor-Mar's Notesome and a black dog, Mittina Love Me A Little.

Miss Annaliisa Heikkinen of Mistyway Kennel had a top-winning Cocker in 1981. He was Int./SF./N. Ch. Mistyway Saucy Red Tiger (by Am./N. Ch. Artru La Toka's Red Hot ex Mistyway Saucy Model, a Cobb's Red Jacket daughter). Many champions have come from this kennel.

Another top-winning Cocker in Finland is a red male, Am./N. Ch. Artru Jan-Myr Pal Joey (by Am. Ch. Artru Red Baron ex Am. Ch. Artru Jan-Myr's Mame). He is owned by Liisa and Tiina Helander of Bittersweet Kennel and was the top-winning Cocker in both 1978 and 1979.

Another pioneer in our eastern neighbor country of Finland is Mrs. Marja Hoffren, founder of von Mein-Heim. Mrs. Hoffren's imports are Am. Ch. Dreamridge Domineer, Am. Ch. Dreamridge Daybreak and Dreamridge Double Bet—dogs with winning offspring in both Finland and Sweden.

Other active and successful breeders are Pirkko Koskinen of Pebblestone Kennels, Hannu Palonen former president of the American Cocker Club and his wife Sirpa (Quartermaster Kennels), De Brightdale Kennels, Tiina Helender of Bittersweet Kennels, Jaana Nikkanen of Heart-Breaker Kennels and Maaret Mast of Melankolian kennels.

CHAPTER 5

France

by Claire Lauriot

Claire Lauriot with two five-month old De la Boudrague puppies.

In France, in order to achieve a French title of Champion of Beauty, an American Cocker must first achieve:

1. The CAC at *the* championship show for that year, for each sex, one CAC by color (one black, one buff, one parti-color—which includes chocolates and B/T's) or the CAC at the Specialty Championship Show. There is only one show of each type held each year.
2. One CAC in a CACIB (International) Show.
3. Two CACs in CAC shows.

If a dog wins two CAC's at championship shows, the Reserve winner of the last CAC obtained also gets the CAC. All wins for the CAC must be won under three different judges. Regardless of the number of entries there is a period of at least three years before the title is conferred. One year before—no CAC can be won by a dog under 12 months—and two years afterward.

For a dog to become an International Champion of Beauty he must win CACIB's in three countries under three different judges. The number of entries do not count, only the judges opinion that the dog is deserving of the award.

Up to now, the American Cocker could not get the full Champion title because it was not allowed to do field work. Only since 1985, have they been able to compete in field trials. There is hope that a number will participate but there is fear that they won't because of having to take care of the coat for the show ring. Cockers certainly can work in the field if they are trained properly.

To import a dog into France the only inoculation required is for rabies. The dog must have had two inoculations more than 15 days and less than one month after the first shot. Puppies of over three months may receive the inoculations.

For dogs sent to France to participate in dog shows only (three dogs or more), the breeder or owner must secure a letter from the show secretary to show to customs officials.

There is no quarantine period in France.

Participants of a dog show in the south of France.

The Pioneers—1957–1970

In 1957, two Cockers were registered in the *LOF* (French breeding book), where all puppies born in France and imported dogs are recorded. These two were owned by Colonel and Mrs. Shiras Blair, important American breeders. They were later transferred to Mr. Bedel. However, there is no record of these two dogs ever producing offspring.

In February of 1958, the first two American Cockers were imported to France by Mrs. Firminhac who had been breeding English Cockers under the De La Haulte Fortelle prefix. For several years, she had been looking for a brace of Cockers after having seen pictures of the breed in the *American Cocker Review* magazine. After an exchange of correspondence with Mrs. Robert Biggs, she obtained her brace: Bigg's My Silver Prince and Bigg's Promise. Prince was by Ch. Bigg's Snow Flurry ex Bigg's Silver Shine, a Bigg's Cover Charge and Rise and Shine granddaughter. Promise, a black bitch, was sired by Ch. Bigg's Eager Beaver ex Bigg's Platinum Doll (a granddaughter of Ch. Carolina Cotton Picker). She became both a French and International champion.

The first litter from these pillars of the French Cocker strain was whelped in September of 1959. In this litter there was a buff bitch named Ivory Pimpernel De La Haulte Fortelle. Many of today's French dogs have "Ivory" in their background.

Bigg's Mister Peppys, a silver dog, was imported in 1961. He was a son of Bigg's Blizzard and a grandson of Ch. Bigg's Snow Flurry and his dam was Bigg's Silver Light, a granddaughter of Ch. Carmor's Rise and Shine. Peppys also became a French and International champion.

Ch. Pinefair Parson, a black dog, was already a champion when he arrived in this country in 1965. Bred to Ivory Pimpernell they produced the first B/T born in France, the spectacular dog who became Ch. Panache De La Haulte Fortelle. In the same litter was Ch. Paprika, a black dog owned by Mrs. De Montmollin. This dog produced a very nice litter in Germany for the Von Der Birke kennel which included Ch. Phyllis, a black bitch who was purchased by Mrs. Guerville-Sevin. Ch. Pinefair Parson was by Ch. Main-Dale's Mr. Success ex Ch. Hickory Hill High Note. Parson went on to become both a French and an International champion.

Bigg's Snow Frolic, a silver bitch by Ch. Bigg's Snow Flurry ex Man Fo's Silver Halo, was imported in 1964. Bred to Mister Peppys she produced Ch. Quelle Belle Pompadour De La Haulte Fortelle ("Frolic") a silver bitch who became a French and International champion.

Bigg's Gay Cavalier, a buff dog born in August of 1968, did not carry the B/T factor so he produced only black and buff offspring. He was a popular stud and many of today's dogs trace their pedigrees back to him. He was a great producing dog and threw his beautiful head with good expression. This head can be seen in all his decendants. He also passed on good substance and a good flat coat that was easy to maintain. His nickname was "Sweet."

"Sweet" was the sire of eight champions, four of whom were International champions. Out of Ch. Phyllis De La Haulte Fortelle he produced Ch. Ayodia Black Tulip bred and owned by Mrs. Guerville-Sevin. Out of Ch. Quelle Belle Pompadour De La Haulte Fortelle came Ch. Une Jolie Praline and her brother, Usia Pacato De La Haulte Fortelle who were well-known under their call names of "Seigbeur" and "Praline." They did much to help publicize the breed. Out of the same dam

Ch. Usia Pacata De La Haulte Fortelle (L) and Ch. Une Jolie Praline De La Haute Fortelle (R). Breeder/owner Mrs. Firminhac.

came Ch. Palmyre and Impertinente Promise—both from the De La Haulte Fortelle kennel. Bred to Pavia De La Haulte Fortelle, he produced Ch. Insoumise Philomene De La Haulte Fortelle and owned by Mrs. Firminhac. Out of Rose Pompon De La Haulte Fortelle he produced Ch. Jobe Plumpy, a black dog owned by Mrs. Terrasse. From Riante Passerose De La Haulte Fortrelle he produced Ch. Irreel Phalene De La Haulte Fortrelle, a buff dog known as "Pussy." Unfortunately, many of "Sweet's" offspring did not become champions only because it was the time when France had only one champion per year by color and sex; but several have had nice show careers and have produced well.

In 1968, Mrs. Pashaus acquired Ravishing of Merrily, a black bitch by Ch. Pinefair Parson ex Look Me Over Van De Cockerbox. In 1969, she imported Ch. Fi Fo's Focus, a tri-color bitch by Ch. Be Gay's Tan

Man ex Fi Fo's Feminique who was linebred to Sinbad. She became the first French parti-color champion.

Mrs. Firminhac was almost alone in breeding American Cockers for the first 10 years—waiting for the breed to gain acceptance and recognition. It wasn't until the 70's, that Cockers in any number and multicolors began to make their appearance. During the 70's, the buff color overshadowed the others in popularity.

Two tri-color puppies bred by Mrs. Pashaus of de la Pasaudiere kennels.

The 1970 to 1980's Period

In 1969, the emergence of Mrs. Kapferer was seen with her Cockers representing various bloodlines and colors. She showed Ch. Phi-Tau's Sugarfoot, a B/T from the U.S.A.; Ch. Special Command V.D. Cockerbox a buff, from Holland; Aztec Wonder in the Skies, a buff bitch from England; Appleblossom V.D. Cockerbox, another buff bitch from Holland; Just Plain War Bonnet, a tri-color dog from the U.S.A.; and Just Plain Moon Shadow, a B/W bitch also from the U.S.A.

When bred to Special Command, Appleblossom produced Ch. Sleeping Beauty Philandra De La Baia, a buff bitch. She became the dam

Ch. Pryority's Passport (L); Ch. Phi Tau's Sugarfoot (C); Ch. Kildeholm's Funny Face (R)—owned by Mrs. Kapferer.

of several bitches who, in turn, became the foundation for new breeding kennels. Among them were Mrs. Berdoue's Des Monts Du Lys kennel; Mrs. Martinez's Bois De La Sagne kennel; the De La Vallee De Toscana kennels of Mr. Saliou; and the De L'Idee De Chali kennels of Miss Barat. All kennels are continuing to breed at this time.

In 1970, Mrs. Rufer and Mrs. Newton imported Nirvana Farm Laird Folly, a R/W bitch from Canada. She was by Ch. Be Gay's Tan Man ex Al-Cyn-Don's Whoopee, a Ch. Be Gay's Razzma Tazz daughter.

In 1971–72, Mrs. Kapferer imported Ch. Kildeholm's Funny Face, a B/T bitch from Denmark. Her sire, Ch. Just Plain War Bonnet came from tri-color lines and her dam Sandra Philandra De La Baia from a B/T line. Then she imported probably the best-known American dog, Ch. Pryority Passport, a spectacular B/T. The get from these two became well established in French pedigrees. They produced such influential dogs as: Ch. Vangogh, Vesuvia, Lollypop, Lot of Fun, Lisboa Antica, and Valase Philandra De La Baia. Valase, even today, has great-great grandchildren competing in the ring.

In 1971, Mrs. Rufer acquired Ch. Twinhaven's Kelly The Kid, a very well-marked tri-color dog and he did some very fine producing for the

Merrily kennel with imported bitches like Jem's Twinkle Mary of Nirvana and Nirvana Farm's Can Can Girl. Bred to Nirvana Farm's Laird Folly, he produced two well-known R/W's in one litter: Vega My Treasure and Venus My First Love of Merrily.

Venus My First Love of Merrily (L); Vega My Treasure of Merrily (R)—breeder/owner Mrs. Rufer.

In 1972, there began arriving in France a different appearing type of dog. They were light silver in color and appeared to have more coat and were also more up on leg. Sanstar Continental Trooper was among the first; he was imported by Mrs. Bergier for her Valambreuse kennel. Bred to Urgent! Send Powder Puff De La Haulte Fortelle (a litter sister of Praline and Seigneur), they produced very light silver: Isis Belle Deesse and Indy Mon Beau Prince Iaka owned by Valambreuse kennels. They also produced blacks and buffs including Insolente Peronelle which went to the Des Petuzous kennel of Mrs. Rispe.

As 1973 was beginning, Mrs. Goudinoux, who owned Torella Philandra De La Baia (a Sugarfoot daughter and granddaughter of Panache ex Appleblossom), bred her to Passport. This breeding produced Gamin De Calla Rossa, a B/T who—when bred to a red bitch imported by Mrs. Goudinoux (Isis Numis, an Ch. Ardee Impact daughter)—produced Ch. Tessa De Calla Rossa, an outstanding black bitch who was often a Best in Group and Best in Show winner.

In 1973, Mrs. Pashaus imported the first tri-colored bitch and, when bred three times to Kelly The Kid, they produced 13 tri-colored off-spring and 5 R/W's. The best known of the group was Ch. Isoline De La Pasaudiere, a tri-color owned by Mrs. Pashus.

In 1974, the first chocolate was brought to France when Ch. Chocolate Baron arrived. Then in 1976, Ch. Be Gay's Phillip's Hershey was imported by Merrily kennels. Merrily kennels also secured Windridge Jonquil, a red bitch with the chocolate factor. This color has not had any real success in France as yet.

Harlanhaven's Hemmingway was brought to France, in 1974, by Mrs. Firminhac. He was a silver buff of a very different type than had been seen before. He soon became the reigning fashion. His best known winning offspring are: Ch. Magic Pschit Lemon Malin Pluto, Ch. Mimipinson Mr. De Pourceaugnac, and Ch. Mousseuse Parisis—all owned by De La Haulte Fortelle kennels. For other kennels, such as that of Mrs. Marcellot, he produced Ch. Minochka De La Grande Steppe, a lovely black bitch whose dam was Ayodia Black Tulip. He produced numerous other offspring, however, most were not shown and the line seems to have come to an end.

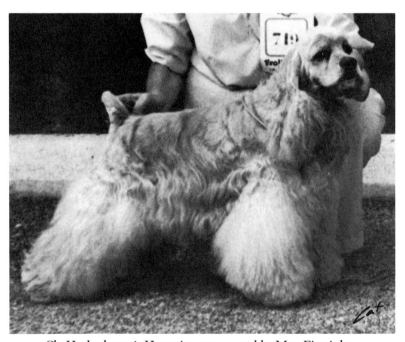

Ch. Harlanhaven's Hemmingway, owned by Mrs. Firminhac.

In 1974, Mrs. Doumenge's de La Marjoliere kennel, produced dogs in various colors. The best known were: Jazz and Jolie Coeur De La Marjoliere.

Mrs. Trey of Du Sapin De L'Artigaoux kennels produced some nice R/W's by Ch. Moody's Hi Point Super Star.

Also in 1974, Mrs. Gillot imported I Fancy You V.N. Stockpaardje, a buff bitch from Pett's Golden Eagle lines from the Netherlands. Her first litter was by Ch. Bigg's Gay Cavalier and produced a nice buff dog, Lilas Des Donzeaux who was owned by Mrs. Bouquet's De Charen Cone kennels. He produced very homogenous looking puppies.

In 1976, Mr. Cugnet imported a red dog, Ch. Windy Hill's Fancy Ruler, when he was a puppy. Mr. Cugnet, in turn, sold him to Mrs. Martinez as co-owner.

In 1978, the D'hervault kennel, who owned the bitch Myosotis De Charen Cone, bred her to Irreel Phalene De La Haulte Fortelle. This combination produced all buff offspring including: Ch. MG O'Beau Ble D'or, O'Beau Sable Blond and Ch. O'Une Boucle Blonde D'Hervault— all of whom seem to have good producing ability.

In 1981, at the De La Boudrague kennel of Miss Lauriot, a litter was whelped which she had been planning for many years. It produced dogs with the conformation she desired. On the male side was the breeding of Ch. Bigg's Gay Cavalier and Ch. Pryority Passport and on the dam's side Ch. Funny Face Riante Passerose De La Haulte Fortelle and I Fancy You V Mijn Stockkpaardje—all good producers. This litter is six generations from Ch. Biggs's Promise and contains the best of the bloodlines developed by Mrs. Firminhac in the 1960's and later by Mrs. Kapferer in the 1970's. This breeding is a litter brother-sister combination. The best two offspring were Shoot De La Boudrague, owned by Mrs. Tansorier and Sunny De La Boudrague owned by Miss Lauriot. Another line is beginning with O'Une Boucle Blonde who produced for me a promising litter, in 1983, of a black dog, two black bitches and two buff bitches by Ch. Windy Hill Royal Puddin owned and imported to Monaco by Mrs. Dell Campo Bacardi.

It seems that approximately every ten years we must import new bloodlines if we want to improve and progress. French breeders must give a great deal of thanks to American breeders who have, for the past thirty years, sent us top-quality dogs to maintain our stud stock. We hope our breeding parallels what you are doing in America.

The vast majority of French breeders are not professionals. For the majority, it's a passion, not a livelihood. Exhibitors come from all walks of life. Personally, I am a photographer. In 1970, I started in the dog world as a dog photographer with no experience in the dog game. My interest in American Cockers began when I first saw them at the shows.

The French fancier grooms and shows his own dogs. That's one

Ch. Windy Hill's Royal Puddin imported to Monaco by Mrs. Bacardi.

reason the French shows are not as organized as American shows. There are very few people who can be called "professional handlers." The French make the hobby a family one and all come out to enjoy the show. Win or lose, they show their own dogs.

My most unforgettable moment was when Dr. Grossman judged the French championship show (The Paris International). It was the first time Cocker fanciers would be judged by an American judge. Exhibitors that I knew well and who were often undisciplined, were doing their best to have the best-trained dog. No one was speaking while waiting to be judged in the ring—not like other times. What a thrill when the judge gave me "First." I couldn't believe it. My legs went all rubbery! French people have great emotions and that's probably why they handle their own dogs—they want the emotion of winning themselves, not for a handler.

In France, the breeding is less numerous than in other countries. If we have more than ten dogs we have to pay a high tax. We tend to keep our old dogs and that limits the number of young ones. The bad economic situation has also made many breeders reduce their stock.

CHAPTER 6

New Zealand

by Jean R. Gillies

The first American Cockers to be imported into this country arrived, late in 1972, from the United Kingdom, although there have been reports of several of the breed making an appearance at an earlier date—coming in as pets with Americans living here for a period of time.

I, myself, imported the first dogs into New Zealand. After some 20 years of involvement with English Cocker Spaniels, I fell in love with the Americans when I first saw them on a visit to the United Kingdom in 1970. At that time, there were not many in evidence in the U.K. and I was not able to acquire anything for myself. However, I visited England once again in 1972, and I saw a very lovely little silver bitch puppy who was a consistent winner in the puppy classes at that time. After much persuasion, I was able to buy her from an owner who was very reluctant to see her go so far away—the other side of the world! This bitch, Freeborne Snow Goose, arrived in New Zealand, in October of 1972. Just

Aust./N.Z. Ch. Freeborne Show Goose, foundation bitch of the breed in New Zealand—shown at 9 years of age.

before her arrival, I was able to get a black male puppy—Marsden Man Friday, whose dam had been imported into Australia in whelp to the United States import, Sundust Artru Sunblaze. This dog was the first of the breed to be registered with the New Zealand Kennel Club, the date being September 19, 1972.

Freeborne Snow Goose won both her New Zealand and Australian championship titles and is classified as the foundation bitch of the breed here in New Zealand, and through her progeny also contributed much to the breed in Australia. In a somewhat limited breeding career, she produced 15 champion sons and daughters, no less than 6 of whom have won the coveted award of Best in Show at all-breed championship shows on both sides of the Tasman.

From 1973 to 1975, six more dogs were imported from England and it is interesting to note that all were solid colours, the owners being Mr. and Mrs. W. Morris of Christchurch, Mrs. Elsie Rennie of Auckland and myself. The years 1975 through 1978 saw a spate of Australian imports, also the arrival of the first two American-bred dogs. These were actually whelped in England from dams imported in whelp. The two were Aus./N.Z. Ch. Sundust Maurits of Maragown and N.Z. Ch. Sundust Serena of Maragown, both being by the noted sire Am. Ch. Durbets Knight To Remember.

The first parti-color to arrive was N.Z. Ch. Idleacres of the Marquee, a R/W imported, from Mr. Harry Begg of Sydney, by Miss Heather Burns. This fellow was by a B/W and a tri-color. He arrived in 1977.

A total of 21 dogs came into the country from Australia and England up to the end of 1978 and since then many more have been imported. By this time, quite a pool of bloodlines was being built up—the majority being complete outcrosses to each other. As a result, dogs of varying types and quality were seen in the show rings, and indeed this still applies today.

A notable arrival on our scene was the first direct American import, the black dog, Am./Eng./Sh. Ch./Aust./N.Z. Ch. Bobwin's Bangaway of Memoir, acquired from Mrs. Winnie Vick and bred by Mrs. Anita Roberts. Already a top winner and a producer of champions in his homeland, this dog would be the most significant import to this country at the time. He won his English title while doing the required residence period there—no mean feat—and followed this by a brief, but spectacular show career, in New Zealand. He is a producer of sound, typical stock and still has a strong influence on breed type here and in Australia.

More parti-colors were brought in by Mrs. I. Turner of Christchurch, the majority from the Boduf kennels in England. The most important of these would be Eng./Sh. Ch./Aust./N.Z. Ch. Boduf Pleasure Tri. More recently, Mrs. Turner imported a R/W male, Kemkerry

Am./Eng./Sh. Ch./Aust./N.Z. Ch. Bobwin's Bangaway of Memoir.

Eng./Sh. Ch./Aust./N.Z. Ch. Boduf Pleasure Tri.

Prince Charmin, who carries strong Rexpointe lines in his pedigree. Heather Burns, mentioned before, has also brought in quite a number of dogs from England, mostly based on the Bullen lines, with Dreamridge background.

The only other dogs of note to come in, until more recently, were several from the well-known English kennel of David and Maragret Bett with Windy-Hill background.

The most recent imports have come from the Bobwin kennels of Winnie Vick, imported by myself. The first, N.Z. Ch. Bobwin's Sir Tanley of Maragown, a B/T full brother to the late Am. Ch. Bobwin's To Heck With Sir, and son of the great producer, Am. Ch. Bobwin's Sir Ashley. This glamorous young dog had a brilliant show career, winning several all-breed Best in Show awards. He has, as yet, been used sparingly at stud and his stock are only now beginning to make their presence felt in the show ring.

The latest two imports, as of this writing, are a heavily-coated male sired by Ch. Bobwin's Sir Buffington, and a red bitch also by Sir Buffington ex Bobwin's New Dimensions, dam of the famous Am. Ch. Bobwin's Go Go Girl.

There have been several more recent imports from Australia carrying the Rinky Dink and Streamside lines.

N.Z. Ch. Bobwin's Sir Tanley of Maragown, multiple all-breed Best in Show winner.

The fate of the Americans in the show ring have been rather mixed. As with all new breeds, judges tend to be a little wary of taking them through to group and best in show awards. And when this does happen, it is not always the best of the breed that do win! This is no reflection on our judges who have had little opportunity, as yet, of seeing many dogs of correct type. Over the last few years, the numbers of Americans being exhibited has increased greatly, at least in quantity, and as our judges have the chance of examining more of the breed, we hope they gain a better understanding of the American Cocker.

In spite of this somewhat chequered start, increasing numbers of our breed are taking top awards. To my knowledge, at least seven (circa 1985) have won the award of Best in Show at all-breed Championship Shows—a very good record.

From the 2 dogs registered with the Kennel Club in 1972, a mere 11 years later, in 1983, a total of 69 were listed, and 24 litters bred in the year January 1 through December 31, 1983.

Under the Regulations of the New Zealand Kennel Club, any breed recognized by The Kennel Club (England) is recognized here. This means that, regardless of numbers, Challenge Certificates are awarded for each sex. Points are not awarded but a dog must win eight Challenges to become a champion, one of which must be won over the age of 12 months. Many of our shows have small numbers of the breed entered and, indeed, it is possible for a dog to win a Championship title without ever having competed against another dog of its breed. However, this does not happen very often. But it does mean that dogs of rather poor quality can win their titles very easily. In New Zealand, champions enter in the regular classes which does counter the ease with which Challenges are won.

Dogs can be imported into New Zealand from Australia and England with no quarantine restrictions—other than they be confined to secure premises for 30 days after arrival. From the United States or Europe, the process is more complicated. Dogs must first go to England (now Hawaii has been added) where they go through a six-month quarantine period followed by a three-month residence. Then they come in as if direct from England.

American Cockers are not divided into color varieties at shows; all colors compete together. Blacks and buffs are the most numerous and have been the most successful in the show ring. Parti-colors have, unfortunately up to the present time, not been of the same quality as the solids. In a country as remote from the rest of the world as New Zealand, and with enormous expense involved in importing a dog, we depend very much on the honesty and interest of breeders in Australia and England. It is very sad to have to say that many of the dogs imported into this country are of no better than pet quality, leaving many disappointed importers.

It has been fifteen years since I got my first American Cocker. It has been exciting and rewarding to be able to import over the years, and to see the breed slowly coming up to the standard we would hope to see. I have been fortunate in judging the breed in many parts of the world, and, I am sure, that given a few more years of development, the best of our dogs here in New Zealand could compare favorably with those anywhere in the world.

7

Switzerland

by Laurent Pichard

The first American Cockers arrived in Switzerland in 1974. They came from England, imported by Laurent Pichard. The first one was a black and tan daughter of Ch. Musblaiks Morganne's Light My Fire, named Musblaiks Coquena; the second was a black daughter of Ch. Durbet's Dillinger of Teilwood, also imported by Laurent Pichard. Both were born in May 1974. The black bitch was called Kimtec I'm Romarin.

The first litter of American Cockers in Switzerland was by Lots of Fun Philandra De La Baia (Ch. Priority's Passport ex Ch. Kildelhomes Funny Face) out of Musblaik's Coquena. The affix was De La Vigie.

The first American Cocker from Switzerland to do some winning in the European rings was a silver dog, born in France in 1977. He was a true silver with black skin, named International and French Ch. Notre Petit Prince De La Sylve Noire. He was bred by Paul Cugnet (France) and was a combination of the Sanstar, La-Mar and Bigg's bloodlines. This dog belongs to La Vigie kennels.

Then I bought two bitches while in the United States. The first one became one of the top-winning bitches in Europe with 26 CACIBs. She was bred by Karen and Garry Bernstein of California, was born in April 1979, and is by Ch. Memoirs Billy Hilder out of Karga's Rugger Hugger. She is the Best in Show winner, Swiss, France, International, European, Youth world and Luxembourg Champion Karga's Pina Colada, a buff with outstanding movement. She was the first bitch to become a Swiss champion.

I then showed a bitch, born on September 14, 1979, also a buff, sired by Ch. Ashley's Golden Rule ex Oceanflight's Fannie Flag, bred by Sharon Gibson. She became an International and French Champion, winning the CACIB of Paris in 1982. Bred to Ch. Windyhill's Fancy Ruler (also a Ch. Ashley's Golden Rule's son) gave birth to Ch. Vive La Vie De La Vigie, another buff bitch. This bitch also became an International and French Champion.

Next, I bought a black dog who was already an American Champion. He was born March 21, 1981 and is by Ch. Stormhaven's Sagitarius out of Sam-O-Jet's Tinker of Al-Lee. He is still one of the top-winning dogs in Europe—perhaps the most titled Cocker Spaniel—being an American, French, Swiss, German, International Champion. In 1984, he won the very famous title of Best In Show at the Championnat de France. He is Best In Show Champion Kuhn's Sagitarius Too, bred by a very nice lady from Kansas, Judy Kuhn.

Ch. Kuhn's Sagitarius Too. *Photo by Claire Lauriot.*

At the same time, I have been showing a golden red dog that I bought in the States when he was still a puppy. He grew up to be a very nice dog, being Best In Show International and French Champion Alorah's Associate. Both dogs have been very much used at stud. Louie (the black) has sired over 100 puppies, with several doing very well at the shows, Dallas (the red) has sired over 130 puppies all over Europe.

Dallas' top winning litter was out of Ch. Vive La Vie De La Vigie. Puppies in that litter include Ch. Private Collection De La Vigie, who has been shown with success in the States by Jeff Wright, and Prelude Endiable De La Vigie who is about to finish his championship, owned by a French breeder Mme. Fabienne Catalaa.

I am indebted to Mrs. Alice Schnabel, of Alorah's Cockers. I can never thank her enough for her kindness, encouragement and advice. She built, for me. a super breeding foundation—selling to me between 1982–1984, a black and tan dog that very quickly became Champion Alorah's Right Garde (Ch. Alorah's Engarde ex Alorah's Lancette), and then a black bitch who just needs time to finish her championship, as she already has all the necessary points. She is Alorah's Bug En. I also imported her buff sister, Alorah's Flying Lady Bug. They are both from Alorah's En And En out of American Ch. Alorah's Bugg Off. My last import was a black and tan bitch from Ch. Alorah's En Garde out of Ch. Alorah's Bugg Off, who should arrive in Europe very soon.

Speaking of my own breeding now, I plan to combine the Windy Hill's and Alorah's lines, to form my own bloodline.

I bred Best in Show Ch. Karga's Pina Colada to American Ch. Windy Hill's Lone Eagle. I kept a black bitch who is International, French and Swiss Champion Ebouissante Angelina De La Vigie. Her sister, Ch. Extravagante Melusine De La Vigie, was sold to Germany to Monika Volkmar.

Ch. Eblouissante Angelina De La Vigie. Photo by Claire Lauriot.

I also bred Ch. Oceanflight's Flair to Best in Show Ch. Alorah's Associate. Out of that breeding I kept a very light buff bitch, Romance

Ch. Alorah's Associate. *Photo by Claire Lauriot.*

Inedite De La Vigie. She is doing very well at the shows.

I sold a silver dog in Hungary to Mrs. E. Kun, and he recently won, over 2,000 dogs, the title of Best In Show, Budapest 1984. He is Champion Don Juan De La Vigie and is a son of Ch. Notre Petit Prince De La Sylve Noire.

In Switzerland, without any doubt, the most famous kennels who have sent dogs are: Alorah, Windy Hill, Artru and Kuhn's lines. We are bereft of any publications, as mostly they are slanted toward English Cockers. Most of the American Cockers' fans in Switzerland are reading the *American Cocker Magazine*.

In Switzerland, there are certain restrictions on breeding. Before being allowed to breed, you have to show your dog or bitch at a dog show, and he/she must obtain at least the mention "Very Good." If he/she doesn't win this award, the puppies won't have any pedigrees. You can't keep more than eight puppies in a litter, and you can't breed more than three litters during two calendar years.

The breed was able to improve very fast in Switzerland, as we have been able to purchase very good dogs from the United States. As the country is very small, with very few breeders, most of them follow some very good breeding rules, with very close line-breeding. We have a high level of quality in blacks, black and tans and in all shades of buff, but we have poor quality in parti-colors. It would be a great asset to the breed if a Swiss breeder could obtain some nice parti-colors from America.

Most of the American Cockers are living in the French-speaking part of Switzerland and they are not very well-known in the German-speaking part of the country. Last year, at the International Dog Show at Lausanne, there were 47 American Cockers and 23 English Cockers entered. At the Bern Dog Show, there were only 8 American Cockers entered as opposed to 34 English Cockers.

Other Swiss Cocker Fanciers

Although I am probably the most heavily involved in the sport of breeding and showing American Cocker Spaniels in Switzerland, I would be remiss to not mention other fanciers whose contributions to the breed help provide the foundation for top-quality Cocker Spaniels in Europe. Some of these people include:

- *H. Kleeman* (Germany), breeder/owner of Swiss Champion Eddy Numis, a buff dog.
- *Wil De Vries* (Netherlands) and *Ursula Mayer* (Germany), breeder and owner, respectively, of Swiss Champion Ginger Snap Van Het Zwanekroost, a red and white dog.
- *Mr. Alain Mercier* of Saint-Barthelemy.
- *Mme. Anne-Marie Favre* of Favre, Villeneuve. Proprietress of D'Arvel Kennels.
- *Mme. Rita Choulat* of Boll. Proprietress of Jestaful Kennels.
- *Mr. and Mme. Raymond Delporte* of France with Waggy Tail Kennels.
- *Mr. and Mme. Jean Lorente* of Rousset, France of du Chateau de l'Arc Cocker Spaniels.
- *Mme. Ernone Kun* of Budapest, Hungary.
- *Mme. Fabienne Catalaa* of Champlay/Joigny, France.
- *Mr. Christian Perinel* of Verdun, France.

During 1980 there were 78 puppies whelped and three imports brought into Switzerland. In 1981, there were 37 puppies whelped and nine imports brought in. In 1982, there were 70 puppies whelped and 16 imports brought in. In 1983, 108 puppies were whelped and 19 imports brought into the country. The future is looking brighter and brighter for our lovely breed in both Switzerland and in Europe.

SECTION XI
Appendices

- Appendix A
  Guidelines for Breeding and Purchasing Cocker Spaniels

- Appendix B
  American Spaniel Club Working Certificate Tests— Rules and Regulations

- Appendix C
  American Spaniel Club Working Test Certificate Judging Guidelines

- Appendix D
  Working Dog Titles

- Appendix E
  List of Dual Champion (Bench & Field) American Cocker Spaniels

Appendix A
Guidelines for Breeding and Purchasing Cocker Spaniels
(Released by the American Spaniel Club
Hereditary and Congenital Defects Committee, and approved by the
Board of Directors of the American Spaniel Club, Inc.)

Many Cocker breeders are justifiably concerned about the problems posed by certain hereditary defects to the future of the breed. Their requests for information on how best to handle these problems in their breeding programs prompted the preparation of these guidelines. While these and future recommendations will concentrate on such problems as cataracts, progressive retinal atrophy (PRA), hip dysplasia and the Factor X blood-clotting defect, there is no intention of de-emphasizing the importance of breed type and basic soundness. However, there is no reason why there should be any ultimate incompatability. We can, in fact, improve type and soundness while also reducing the incidence of debilitating and life threatening hereditary defects. It is hoped that these guidelines will prove of value to those who really care about the Cocker and are sincerely dedicated to its future.

There is much concern and disagreement over the precise way in which the various genetic defects are inherited. Factor X deficiency and PRA appear to have a simple type of inheritance, and hopefully can be eliminated from the breed. Even in these cases, however, individual variation in response to the causative gene, as well as environmental influences can sometimes confuse the situation. In contrast, cataracts and hip dysplasia have a more complicated inheritance and are also affected by non-hereditary factors. This has led some breeders to ignore or downplay the importance of these defects. Some are purportedly waiting for the specific mode of inheritance to be determined before they attempt to select seriously against these defects. Unfortunately, we may never be able to determine the precise genetic basis for cataracts or hip dysplasia; although this doesn't mean we shouldn't try. On the positive side, we do know two important things about these traits; namely, *that they are inherited* and that *their incidence can be reduced by selective breeding!* In other words, the heritable contribution to the expression of these traits is large enough to yield to practical selection procedures. We may never completely eliminate cataracts or hip dysplasia, *but we can reduce them to a very low incidence.* This should be a realistic and obtainable goal.

The key to successfully avoiding heritable defects lies in one's ability to select the right dogs from the "lower risk" bloodlines. Selection is based on our prediction of an animal's chances of developing a defect or passing one on to its descendants. The accuracy of any prediction depends on the amount of reliable information on which it is based. The more we know about the bloodlines behind an individual, its immediate ancestors, relatives and offspring, the greater the confidence we can have in our prediction. In this respect, the ASC Health Registry will be an invaluable aid by providing this kind of information.

More specific guidelines and suggestions for the breeding and purchasing of Cockers will be presented for each of the four aforementioned heritable defects and for Hemophilla A and Von Willebrand's disease. Because of its high incidence, the first defect to be considered is heritable cataracts.

Inheritable Cataracts

As mentioned previously, the way in which cataracts are inherited is not known at this time. Speculation as to whether a major recessive or dominant gene causes a heritable form of cataracts is academic, because in reality we cannot consistently demonstrate a simple type of inheritance. Among the many genetic explanations should also be included the possibility that there may be more than one genetic form of cataract. In addition, it is a medical fact that not all cataracts are genetic. In general, the non-genetic types produce characteristic lesions and can be designated as non-hereditary by qualified canine opthalmologists. It is also possible that some unknown environmental effect may serve to trigger the development of our genetic type or types. However, even if this is the case, we still have to face the fact that some lines react with a different incidence of cataracts than do others. In any event, regardless of our present inability to determine the actual mode of inheritance, we can still reduce the incidence by careful selection within relatively low-incidence lines.

It is difficult to obtain accurate information on the cataract incidence in different genetic lines. Pedigree studies leave little doubt, however, that considerable difference does exist, with some lines showing most adults eventually developing cataracts. In these cases, it would be best for the breeders involved to abandon completely these lines. At the other end of the scale are those lines that produce only an occasional cataract unless outcrossed into high-incidence lines. Note that at this time, it is impossible to say that any line exists that is 100% clear of heritable cataract. The significant thing from the practical breeding standpoint, however, is the tremendous difference in the incidence among lines.

Eye Examinations. Proper eye examinations should be made by qualified veterinary ophthalmologists who have appropriate equipment (such as a slit lamp or bioscope) and experience to give an accurate diagnosis. The ASC Health Registry at the present time accepts for listing only examination results made by members of the American College of Veterinary Ophthalmologists (ACVO). One of their members is usually present at specific eye clinics that are set up on a regular basis now in most sections of the United States.

There are a number of reasons why it is necessary to have one's dogs slit lamp tested (SLT) by a qualified veterinarian. First, the examination often provides a valuable early diagnosis of developing cataracts, thus reducing the impact of that animal as a sire or dam by removing it sooner from the breeding population. The lag time between a SLT diagnosis of cataracts and the stage where they become visible to the naked eye may be as much as two years or longer. A second advantage of an accurate SLT examination is to find out whether or not a cataract is of the heritable type. However, remember that in case of doubt it is better to be on the safe side and consider the lesion to be genetic. Finally, if an animal is found to be free of cataracts as of the date he is tested, this information is of value to other breeders. Most will want medical verification of this fact, which you will have to show them and/or list your dogs in the ASC Health Registry.

Testing Procedures. All of your breeding stock should be tested for cataracts at least once a year. Ideally, all active stud dogs and all breeding stock six years of age or less should be tested twice a year. It is also very important to continue to test older animals to eliminate the possibility of the late expression of hereditary cataracts. For example, individuals from some lines rarely develop cataracts until they are 5 to 7 years old. Although there is no proven age after which the hereditary type would no longer develop, dogs still free of cataracts at 10 years of age might be allowed to forego subsequent tests. Where possible, litter mates of breeding stock sold as pets should also be slit lamp tested at approximately 2, 5 and 8 years of age. This procedure will provide valuable information for evaluating the cataract potential of the parents and litter mates, as well as providing an estimate of the overall incidence within specific lines. To accomplish this, some breeders send out questionnaires with a number of health-related questions, including questions on blindness and its causes when known. This approach will provide valuable additional information for your breeding program.

Breed or Purchase Only SLT Clear Animals. Do not purchase or use for breeding any animal who has not been tested and reported clear during the previous year by an ACVO veterinarian. Owners of stud dogs, breeding bitches or who have puppies for sale should not be offended when asked to see copies of official SLT results *for animals not listed in the Health Registry!*

Evaluating the Individual Animal. The most important decision finally filters down to selecting the individual dog, whether planning a breeding or purchase. Unless the individual is a young puppy then its own SLT record is important, becoming more so as the age of the animal increases. Less importance should be put on test results at 1 year than at 5 or 6 years of age. Major emphasis should be placed on the parents' and grandparents' SLT results and age, while also considering any other information on other relatives including progeny (when available). Remember that the SLT should have been made within the past year unless the animal is over 10 years of age or has died, then the age and status should be clarified.

Breeding Recommendations! Unfortunately, there are no set proven rules to use for predicting the results of a specific mating; however, some safe, scientifically-sound recommendations are presented below:

1. Never breed an individual who has cataracts regardless of its age or the stage of development of the eye lesions.
2. Do not use for breeding a son or daughter of an animal who has developed cataracts.
3. Full-brothers and sisters or grandchildren of an afflicted animal should be considered "suspect." Such an animal from a "low incidence line" with clear parents and grandparents is less of a risk than one from a family where several cataracts have occurred. If used, wait until the individual is at least 3 years of age and tests clear and then breed only to clear, older individuals from a low-risk line.
4. The progeny of "suspect individuals" (as in #3 above) should also be used for breeding with care, again mating them as suggested above. The careless use of these animals while young, could prove to be disastrous to a breeding program. If no further problems appear among their progeny over a period of time, then the "suspect" designation could be removed from these animals.
5. If there is evidence that a dog is producing more than a rare offspring with cataracts when bred to "low incidence lines," then it should no longer be used for breeding.
6. Participate in, and use, the Health Registry. Over a period of time this will help to identify the low incidence lines that are so badly needed for future breeding programs.

Your Responsibilities as a Breeder. Every breeder of Cocker Spaniels should feel a responsibility for the future of the breed that she or he has chosen to use for their own enjoyment. One of the obvious goals is to improve their stock's performance in conformation, obedience or field endeavors. Too often there is little or no attention paid to eliminating hereditary defects. As breeders, we owe it to the Cocker to make a serious effort to reduce the incidence of hereditary cataracts.

One of the important contributions we can all make is to communicate honestly with one another. If one of your animals develops cataracts, notify all purchasers of offspring that might be used for breeding, or in case of a stud, the owners of bitches that have been bred to him. In doing so you provide other breeders with the information they must have for their breeding programs. In this way, you are making a major contribution towards the future of the breed.

Finally, some may feel that the recommendations presented here are too restricting and severe. However, the incidence of cataracts has reached such proportions in Cockers that the situation can only be improved by strict adherence to proven genetic principles of selection. By following these principles, increasing honest communications between ourselves, and endeavoring to educate and guide new breeders as they come along, we can reduce the incidence of cataracts to a point whereby it no longer threatens the future of the Cocker Spaniel. (*Author's Note: Because of firm adherence to these principles, by 1988, the numbers of affected animals have been significantly reduced.*)

Hemophilia A and Von Willebrand's Disease

Disorders of the blood coagulation factor VIII complex are responsible for two distinct inherited diseases in many breeds of dogs. This plasma protein complex is comprised of *two* proteins, the factor VIII-coagulant or clotting protein (VIII:C) and the von Willebrand's factor protein (VWF). The first disease, Hemophilia A, results from significantly reduced factor VIII:C activity. The second disease, Von Willebrand's disease (VWD), is caused by reduced levels of VWF activity.

Hemophilia A, the same disorder as occurs in humans, is a relatively rare X-chromosomal linked genetic defect that is expressed in males and carried by females. VWD, on the other hand, is much more common than hemophilia and is inherited in American Cocker Spaniels as an autosomal incompletely dominant trait with variable penetrance or expression. Thus, both sexes can have the disease (bleeders) and both sexes can carry VWD without showing signs of bleeding. Pups that inherit a double-dose of the gene from two carriers do not survive (born dead or die in the first week of life), because homozygosity for the trait is lethal. Survivors that inherit the gene from one parent are heterozygous and can be either mildly- to moderately-severly affected or carriers that show no symptoms. The lower their level of VWF, the more severe the bleeding tendency is likely to be expressed.

Screening for Hemophilia A is performed by measuring factor VIII:C levels. Normal levels are 50–200%. Affected males usually have less than 5% factor VIII:C whereas, carrier females have levels around 50% (35–65%).

VWD is diagnosed by measuring VWF levels immunologically as factor VIII-related antigen (factor VIIIR:Ag). Normal dogs have levels between 60–172%. Levels between 50–59% are considered to be borderline normal/possible carrier range, and levels below 50% are abnormal.

Commencing with the 13th ASC Annal Health Registry, VWF levels (reported as factor VIIIR:Ag) will be included.

Breeding Recommendations

von Willebrand's Disease. Animals affected with or acquiring the VWD gene have levels of factor VIIIR:Ag less than 50%. Animals clinically affected with VWD *should not be used for breeding*. Carriers of VWD, having no symptoms of excessive bleeding, can be bred if they offer desirable features to the breed and provided they are mated to animals tested normal for the VWD gene. The puppies from such matings should be screened for the gene at any time after 10-12 weeks of age. The prevalence of VWD can readily be reduced to minimum levels with proper selective breeding practices.

Factor VIIIR:Ag	Level	Breeding Advice
Normal Range	60–172%	Can be bred
Borderline Normal/ Possible Carrier Range	50–59%	Can be bred to VWD normal dogs and pups should be checked
Carrier Range	50%	Breed only to VWD normal dogs and pups should be checked
Affected Range	Below 50%	Do NOT breed

Hemophilia A. This disease is a very severe bleeding disorder that is usually incompatible with survival in dogs except under very specialized housing conditions. It is usually not advisable to keep affected hemophiliacs as pets (too much risk and harm). Most testing for this disease is restricted to relatives of known afflicted families. If you suspect that your stock may have this problem, we suggest you contact: Dr. W. Jean Dodds, Veterinary Hematology Laboratory, Wadsworth Center for Labs/Research, New York State Department of Health, Empire State Plaza, Albany, New York 12201.

Dogs affected with, or carrying the gene for, Hemophilia A should NOT be used in a breeding program. Normal testing females from a known hemophiliac family should be bred only in specific cases and—in this event—all of the pups must be checked for the hemophiliac gene before sale or use as breeding stock. This is because hemophilia carrier detection by blood testing has an accuracy rate of about 90% and misclassification either way (carrier vs. normal) can occur. By contrast, normal testing males from hemophiliac families are perfectly safe to breed for they *cannot* transmit the gene (because their X-chromosome is normal at the hemophilia locus).

Factor X Deficiency

Factor X deficiency is a relatively rare, inherited blood coagulation factor disorder which causes severe bleeding. Factor X is one of the plasma proteins central to the process of clot formation, and hence reduction of Factor X produces weak clots and bleeding. Individuals born with very low levels of Factor X (less than 5%) from two carrier parents do not survive (*i.e.*, homozygosity for the trait is lethal). Survivors that inherit the gene from one parent are heterozygotes and are either mildly- to moderately-severly affected or occasionally can be carriers that do not show any symptoms of a bleeding tendency. Factor X deficiency is an autosomol incompletely dominant trait in dogs and was, at one time, prevalent in American Cocker Spaniels. This prevalence has been reduced over the past two decades as a result of diligent blood testing of their breeding stock by American Spaniel Club members. Today, however, testing has become less common so that current prevalence of the Factor X is not known.

Normal levels of Factor X are 80% or higher. Dogs testing 90% or better are considered to be high-normal. Dogs testing between 70–90% Factor X are low-normal/possible carriers, and levels below 70% are abnormal.

Breeding Recommendations

Factor X	Level	Breeding Advice
Normal Range	80–175%	Can be bred
Low-Normal/ Possible Carrier Range	70–89%	Breed only to Factor X-normal dogs and check the pups
Affected Range	70%	Do NOT breed
Carrier Range	70%	Do NOT breed

There are presently a number of laboratories besides Dr. Dodd's group that perform both VWD and Factor X testing. If the tests are obtained by one of these laboratories and the results are sent to Dr. Dodds for evaluation, she will issue test certificates (if she believes the tests were performed properly) and will indicate on the certificate which laboratory performed the assay.

A packet of in-depth material on Factor VIII and Factor X is available from the American Spaniel Club, Inc. If you are interested in receiving this material, please send a stamped, self-addressed envelope to:

Judith Wright
A.S.C. Health Registrar
2600 Ellsworth Road
Bladwinsville, New York 13027

Appendix B

American Spaniel Club, Inc.—Founded 1881

Working Certificate Tests—Rules and Regulations

Revised & Approved January 6, 1984

Philosophy

The ASC Working Certificate Test Program is designed:

1. To encourage Cockers and other flushing spaniels to achieve a high level of hunting skills;
2. To encourage a broad base of support for field work with many owners training their spaniels to a companion hunting level, measured by attaining working dog or working dog excellent titles;
3. To encourage the breeding of versatile, as well as beautiful, spaniels that are at home in the field as they are in the conformation or obedience rings or as a home companion;
4. To encourage the rare breeds of spaniels to take their place as capable hunters for their owners as well as in competition with other flushing spaniels;
5. To strive to reach member field trial status by 1990, thus re-establishing the field trial championship for Cockers and other flushing spaniels under ASC jurisdiction.

Procedures

Offering Working Tests

A working test may be offered by a flushing spaniel club or by a group of flushing spaniel owners. Permission to hold a test must be obtained from the chairman of the ASC Field Trial/Test Committee and notification must be sent to the appropriate breed club secretary if breeds not under ASC jurisdiction will be participating in the test. The test chairman must state the date and site of the test and name(s) of proposed judge(s). The judge(s) must be thoroughly familiar with the work of spaniels in the field. First preference should be given to persons who have been approved to judge a spaniel field trial. The judges' qualifications should be briefly listed on the test application. Breeds for which notification must be sent to the parent club secretaries include English Cocker Spaniels, English Springer Spaniels, Welsh Springer Spaniels and Clumber Spaniels. Dogs under ASC jurisdiction may participate in working tests offered by any of the above specialty or parent breed clubs and may receive working titles if the judging score sheets are sent to the ASC Field Trial/Test Chairman. Exhibitors should notify the ASC Field Chairman of the test date, site and judges before the test if at all possible. ASC test forms should be used whenever possible. If a test is given by a group not directly associated with a parent breed club, the Field Trial/Test Chairman may grant working titles after determining the quality of the judging and test procedures.

Entry Forms, Judging Forms, Certificates (*i.e.*, Paperwork)

Information on dogs to be tested should be entered on special working test entry/judging forms supplied upon request by the ASC Field Trial/Test Chairman.

On *any* entry/judging form used, all information requested on the dog, owner, handler and test chairman must be completed or title will not be conferred. The top two copies of the entry/judging form should be sent to the ASC Field Trial/Test Chairman immediately after the test. The original will be forwarded to the ASC Secretary, the first copy (yellow) will be kept on file by the ASC Chairman. The exhibitor shall keep the second (pink) copy; the judge or the chairman of the event may keep the last (golden) copy. The test chairman is reponsible for sending the correct copies of the form to the designated parties. For breeds other than those currently under ASC jurisdiction, the test chairman shall send the top two copies to the appropriate parent club secretary or to the ASC Field Trial/Test Chairman. The exhibitor should keep the last two copies. The ASC Secretary and Field Trial/Test Chairman shall keep permanent records of every dog that qualifies for a Working Dog (WD) or Working Dog Excellent (WDX) title. Records must be given to the next chairman and secretary holding office. The ASC Secretary shall complete and mail WD and WDX certificates to the owners of dogs that pass working tests. Only one WD and one WDX certificate is allowed for each dog.

How Titles Are Earned

Working tests are *not* competitive events. There should be no ranking or placing of dogs.

THREE flushing spaniels must run to constitute a valid test.

A dog must receive satisfactory ratings in all categories to receive a Working Dog certificate.

A dog must receive excellent ratings in all categories to receive a Working Dog Excellent certificate.

The judge or judges shall determine what title a dog receives provided the decision follows ASC guidelines.

A dog that damages a bird shall not receive either certificate. A hardmouthed spaniel is an unacceptable hunting companion or field event competitor.

WD/WDX Rules

Site Specifications

There should be suitable cover, such as stubble, brush, grass, etc., high enough to hide the birds used in the test. The area must be far enough away from houses, businesses, etc. so that birds can be shot.

Birds

Each dog should work at least two or three live birds. More may be used, if circumstances require it, to give the judges enough information on the dog's capabilities. Pigeons or other game birds may be used and should be planted a minimum of 60 to 80 feet ahead of the dog or the starting line, and apart from each other.

Gun Safety: When Birds Are Not To Be Shot—Set Up Retrieves

The established safe gunning rules must be followed. If a bird flies over the gallery or where any person might be in the line of flight, it should not be shot. Another bird should be put down for the dog. As many birds as are necessary may be put down to give the dog a chance to flush a bird and complete a retrieve. If a dog has demonstrated sufficiently that it can find and flush birds, but the birds can't be shot, a bird may be released by hand and shot to allow the dog to make a retrieve.

Stewards

At least one steward should be appointed to keep spectators, other handlers and dogs in a close group behind the judges or in an assigned place. This is to prevent interference with the work of the dog being tested, to give the gunners a chance to shoot, and to ensure safety.

State Hunting Requirements: Insurance

Permission to hold a working test that involves shooting birds, especially game birds, should be obtained from the state hunting department if required. A working test could fall in the safe category as a field trial under state hunting laws. Contact the appropriate state authority or the ASC Field Trial/Test chairman or insurance chairman.

Water Test Procedure

For the water test, a dead bird is thrown into the water from shore or from a boat, at a distance great enough to cause a dog to swim to make the retrieve. As the bird is thrown, a shot is fired. The distance of the retrieve isn't as important as making sure the dog has to prove it can swim and retrieve in water.

Land Test Requirements

In the land test, a flushing spaniel:
1. Should sit or stay behind or beside the handler at the starting line,

unleashed, until the judge instructs the handler to proceed. The handler then sends the dog and walks behind it, directing the dog on the course. Dogs are run singly, not braced.

2. Should show fairly reasonable, not necessarily immediate, response to whistle and/or command, and reasonable quartering of ground. The dog should not be completely out of control, although leniency and time should be given the handler to collect the dog.

3. Should not be required to be steady or sit on flush or shot.

4. Should demonstrate sufficient hunting ability to find and put up game in a workmanlike manner, without undue urging, and should show no evidence of pottering.

5. Should retrieve birds to hand or within reasonable distance so that the handler can take or pick up the bird without chasing the dog. Handler may direct the dog to the fall if the dog has not marked it. However, a dog should be expected to mark an open, direct fall and deliver to hand to earn a WDX.

6. Should not deliver a damaged bird—one that is chewed or crushed, as the reason for using dogs in hunting is to have game "suitable for the table." Damage caused by gunshot does not apply.

Water Test Requirements

A dog must pass a water test to earn a WD or WDX. In the water test the dog:

1. Should not be required to sit or stay on line unleashed. The dog may be held on leash until the handler is directed by the judge to send the dog.

2. Should retrieve to hand or within reasonable distance so the handler can take or pick up the bird without wading into the water or chasing the dog on land.

3. Should willingly enter the water on its own.

4. Should prove its ability to swim.

Additional Recognition

Members of the American Spaniel Club may earn a merit plaque or plate for one WD and WDX per dog by sending a copy of the dog's AKC registration papers and a copy of the Working Certificate to the current Merit Plaque Chairman, providing the owner meets all other merit award criteria.

Appendix C
American Spaniel Club
Working Test Certificate Judging Guidelines

Steady on Line

The dog does an unleashed sit—stay beside the handler for 30 seconds—after which it is released by the handler upon the judge's order to proceed. The judge shall state when the time starts and stops.

FAILED — The dog leaves the line before being released. Or the dog whines or barks excessively while on the line.

SATISFACTORY — The dog is given one extra command to sit or stay after the judge has started timing.

EXCELLENT — The dog sits and stays quietly the entire 30 seconds.

Quarters Efficiently

FAILED — The dog refuses to leave the handler's side. Or the dog only works 10 to 15 feet away and shows a poor quartering pattern. Or the dog is completely out of control. Or the dog shows excessive signs of pottering. Or the dog consistently works out of gun range, over 35 yards from the handler.

SATISFACTORY — The dog shows a reasonable quartering pattern and responds fairly well to commands.

EXCELLENT — The dog covers ground with enthusiasm and shows a good use of the wind, a good quartering pattern and responds well to commands.

Finds and Flushes Birds

FAILED — The dog blinks (actively avoids) the birds. Or the dog has trouble locating birds. Or the dog needs excessive encouragement to flush the birds.

SATISFACTORY — The dog finds and flushes the birds.

EXCELLENT — The dog exhibits a bold flush and an excellent nose.

DOGS ARE NOT REQUIRED
TO BE STEADY TO FLUSH OR SHOT

Marks Downed Birds

FAILED — The dog ignores the flushed bird and makes no attempt to mark the fall. Or the dog shows little interest in marking the fall.

SATISFACTORY — The dog runs in the general direction of the fall and eventually finds the bird. Or the dog is handled to the fall.

EXCELLENT — On an open and direct fall the dog runs directly to the bird. Or the dog does a good job marking a difficult fall.

Retrieves on Land

FAILED — The dog refuses to pick up the bird. Or the dog requires excessive commands or encouragement before it will pick up the bird. Or the dog picks up the bird and runs off with it and is chased by the handler. Or the dog drops the bird several times and must be coached in to the handler. Or the dog shows signs of being hard mouthed, delivering a chewed or crushed bird. (The bird must be fit for the table.)

SATISFACTORY — The dog promptly brings the bird within 3 feet of the handler.

EXCELLENT — The dog promptly delivers the bird to hand, sitting to deliver (in front of the handler or beside the handler) without undo urging.

Retrieves from Water

FAILED — The dog refuses to enter the water. Or the dog unwillingly enters the water. Or if the dog enters the water is "rescued" due to a lack of swimming ability. Or the dog leaves the water without attempting to retrieve the bird. Or the dog leaves the bird in the water after starting to retrieve it. Or the dog needs rocks thrown at the bird to help him locate it.

SATISFACTORY — The dog enters the water without undue urging and brings the bird out of the water to within 3 feet of the handler.

EXCELLENT — The dog willingly enters the water and retrieves the bird to hand.

Appendix D
Working Dog Titles

*Indicates dog earned same title previously
†Indicates dog holds WDX

Name of Dog	Date of Title	Owner
Ch. Glenmurray's Tam O'Shanter		
V-L's King of Clubs	7/28/78	Naomi R. Kibler
Ch. Frandee's Fireworks, CD	7/24/78	Jeff Wood
Jus-Us Pegasus	7/24/78	Mike & Suzie Williams
Ch. Don's Dartanun, CD	7/24/78	Don Ploke
Ch. Sharay's Sherbert Delight, CD	7/24/78	Sharon Landry
Merribark's Golden Belle	7/24/78	Dennis Blake
Lor-Jon's Hot Chocolate	7/24/78	John & Laura Ulrich
Merribark's Moonshadow	7/24/78	John & Laura Ulrich
Ch. Frandee's Fly Me	7/17/79	Ronald & Rebecca Thomson
Sher-Ron's Aristocrat	7/13/80	Ronnie Garlick
Dandy's Sir Michael	9/18/81	Lee Knapp
Ginger Kansas Summer Sunglow	5/9/82	Kenna Griffin
Sunglow's Magnolia Blossom	7/18/82	Kenna Griffin
Brown Sugar's Black Pepper, CD	7/18/82	John & Deborah Lindsey
Destiny's Diesel Dynamo	7/18/82	Patrick Bradley
*Ginger Kansas Summer Sunglow, UD	7/18/82	Kenna Griffin
Ch. Doggone Phil Silver	7/16/83	John & Julie Wolfe
Jo-Bea's Spring Fantasy	7/16/83	Katherine L. Bartee
Lancer's Chardonnay	7/16/83	Pam Cullum
Twelve Oaks Stargazer, CD	7/16/83	Marjorie & Larry White and Gloria Maxon
Doggone Comin' Up Roses	11/20/83	John & Julie Wolfe and David McBroom
Lady Victory Bell Deacon	11/20/83	Charlene Wooldridge
†Lady Melissa D'La Swanson	10/29/83	Al & Pat Swanson
Tabaka's Tan Lizzie, CD/TD	10/29/83	Ruth Tabaka and Debra Stephenson
Deidree Shannon Dodge, CD	6/23/84	Debra Dodge
Penny Creek Hot Stuff	6/23/84	Kelly Ferris and Darlene Mattson
*†Dandy's Sir Michael	7/21/84	Lee Knapp
Lickety Split's Wyckersham	7/21/84	Lee Knapp
*†Lady Melissa D'La Swanson	8/11/84	Al & Pat Swanson
*†Dandy's Sir Michael	9/8/84	Lee Knapp
*Risen's Bo	9/8/84	Julie Morrill
Deidree Shannon Dodge, CD	9/8/84	Debra & David Dodge
Ask Mee For The Sport Of It	1987	Kathleen MacCochran
Magic Makers TJ Madison	1987	Trish A. Jackson

Working Dog Excellent Titles

Indicates dog earned same title previously
†*Indicates dog holds WDX*

Name of Dog	Date of Title	Owner
Be Gay's Little Caesar	10/16/77	Paula & Marie Pietrucha
Ch. Artru Brandy Alexander, CD	5/28/78	Barbara Gorse
Pett's Captain Jack	5/28/78	Patricia A. Gale
Doggone Liberty Belle	7/24/78	John & Julie Wolfe
Sterling Silver Beau	7/24/78	Dennis Blake
Scott Fitzgerald	9/20/78	Tim & Phyliss Chantos
†VL King of Clubs, UDT	5/27/79	Naomi R. Kibler
†Jus-Us Pegasus	7/17/79	Suzie & Mike Williams
Sweet Sandy V		
Lady Melissa D'La Swanson	4/4/80	Al & Pat Swanson
†Ch. Sharay's Sherbert Delight, CD	5/30/80	Sharon Landry
Jo-Kay Mar-Jac Charly Chan	5/30/80	Joe, Kay & Robert Fielding
†Ch. Don's Dartanon, CD	5/3/80	Don Ploke
Marquis Ain't Misbehavin'	5/10/80	Kerry Lyons
Sharay's Delight of Myluv	5/10/80	Jeanne & Bob Boyd
Smarti Parti Rellim's Topaz, CDX	7/13/80	Debra Miller
Ch. Frandee's Fly Me		
*†Lady Melissa D'La Swanson	9/19/81	Al & Pat Swanson
Karavan's Poison Ivy	5/9/82	Gaile Gordon
Sugar Bear's Gay Galahad, CD/TD	7/18/82	John & Deborah Lindsey
Wyndsong's Special Kountry	7/18/82	Krystal Sue Dean
†Dandy's Sir Michael	7/16/83	Lee Knapp
Happy Go Tico	7/16/83	Lisa Binckes
*†Lady Melissa D'La Swanson	7/16/83	Al & Pat Swanson
*†Lady Melissa D'La Swanson	9/24/83	Al & Pat Swanson
†Lancer's Chardonnay	11/6/83	Pam Cullum
†Ch. Doggone Phil Silver	11/20/83	John & Julie Wolfe
Ebony Magic	11/20/83	Bill & Odet Kassey
†Ch. Jo-Bea's Spring Fantasy	11/20/83	Kathy Bartee
Charlie's Ebony Angel, UD	5/12/84	Heather Bartelme
Diamond's Jacobus Jonker, CD	5/12/84	Sherry Creighton
Fairfield Golden Girl	5/20/84	Dorine Odebralski
*†Lady Melissa D'La Swanson	7/21/84	Al & Pat Swanson
†Lady Rebecca D'La Swanson	8/11/84	Al & Pat Swanson
*†Dandy's Sir Michael	8/11/84	Lee Knapp
*†Lady Melissa D'La Swanson	9/8/84	Al & Pat Swanson
Marshwalker's Lady Bandit	10/13/84	Diane & Karl Aschenbrenner

Appendix E

List of Dual Champion (Bench & Field) American Cocker Spaniels

Name / Whelping Date

Don Pablo From Jourdains	— 1936
Live Oak Spring Storm	— 1936
Miller's Esquire, CDX	— 1938
My Own High Time	— 1929
Rowcliffe Hillbilly	— 1928

List of American Cocker Spaniel Field Trial Champions

Arbury Squib — 1937
Argonaut Dubonnet
Blue Waters Magnificent — 1929
Brown's Sunny Boy — 1937
Bunny *(unregistered)*
Camino Boy — 1944
Chequamegon Laddie — 1941
Cinar's Chuck — 1938
Cinar's Dash — 1939
Cinar's Ring — 1938
Cinar's Soot — 1937
Cinar's Spot of Earlsmoor — 1936
Craigden Consolation — 1928
Esquire's Dan — 1948
Hammer's Commodore — 1937
High Time Elcova — 1932
High Time Feller — 1937
Hollbrook Don — 1942

Horsford Delight 'Em — 1926
Magic of Lodgeleigh
Jimmy *(unregistered)*
Latch-Up George — 1935
Miller's Esquire — 1938
My Own High Time II — 1934
Nuggetts *(unregistered)*
Prince Chicot — 1937
Ravine-Top Freckles — 1936
Rex of Winsor — 1940
Rivington Bean — 1937
Roanfeather Argonaut — 1939
Robinhurst Hewer — 1933
Rowcliffe Bangaway — 1935
Rowcliffe Black Fury — 1935
Rowcliffe Blue Streak — 1933
Stipe's Cricket — 1934
Berol's Piccolo Pete — 1948

SECTION XII
Bibliography & Index

- *Bibliography*
- *Index*

Bibliography

Periodicals

Allen, Michael (ed.), *American Cocker Magazine,* numerous articles from several issues.

Ardnt, T.K., "Breeders Forum." *Akita World,* December 1985.

Asseltyne, Claire, "Form Follows Function," *The Great Dane Reporter,* May–June, July–Aug., Sept.–Oct. 1980.

Bierman, Ann, "Feeding Your Puppy," *The Golden Retriever Review,* March 1987.

Brown, Russell V., "Nutrition and Feeding of the Basenji," *The Basenji,* Feb. 1987.

Burnham, Patricia Gail, "Breeding, Litter Size and Gender," *American Cocker Review,* 1981.

Donnely, Mary, "Caesarian Section . . . The Home Care," *Min Pin Monthly,* March 1987.

Furumoto, Howard H., "Frozen and Extended Semen," *The ILIO,* Hawaii's Dog News, Oct. & Nov. 1986.

Grossman, Alvin, "The Basis of Heredity," *American Kennel Club Gazette,* April 1980.

Grossman, Alvin, "Color Inheritance," *The American Cocker Review,* March, April, May and June 1974.

Grossman, Alvin, "Faults and Double Faults," *The American Cocker Review,* March 1980.

Grossman, Marge, "Evolution of the Cocker Head," *The American Cocker Review,* June 1961.

Grossman, Marge, "To the Victors," *The American Cocker Review,* August 1966.

Hane, Curtis B., "Training Your Dog, A Consumers Guide," *The Great Dane Reporter,* March–April 1987.

Mohrman, R.K., "Supplementation—May Be Hazardous To Your Pet's Health," *The Great Dane Reporter,* March–April 1980.

Schaeffer, Ruth C., "The View From Here, A Breeder's Report On Collecting Frozen Sperm," *American Kennel Club Gazette,* November 1982.

Wittels, Bruce R., "Nutrition of Newly Born and Growing Individuals," *The Great Dane Reporter,* Jan./Feb. 1985.

Books

Benjamin, Carol L., *Mother Knows Best, The Natural Way to Train Your Dog.* New York: Howell Book House, 253 pgs., 1987.

Burnham, Patricia G., *Play Training Your Dog.* New York: St. Martin's Press, 1980.

Burns, Marsh A. & Fraser, Margaret N., *The Genetics of the Dog.* Farnham Royal Eng.: Commonwealth Agricultural Bureau, 1952.

Collins, Donald R., D.V.M., *The Collins Guide to Dog Nutrition.* New York: Howell Book House, Inc., 1973.

Connett, Eugene V., *American Sporting Dogs.* D. Van Nostrand Co., Inc.

Craig, Ralph, *Elementary Spaniel Field Training.* New York: American Spaniel Club, 21 pgs, 1947.

Evans, Job M., *The Evans Guide For Counseling Dog Owners.* New York: Howell Book House, Inc., 1985.

Fox, Michael W., *Understanding Your Dog*. New York: Coward, McCann & Geoghegan, 1972.

Gaines Dog Research Center, *Training The Hunting Dog*. General Foods Corporation, 15 pgs, 1973.

Greer, Frances, Editor, *A Century of Spaniels; Vols. I & II*. Amherst, Massachusetts: American Spaniel Club, 1980.

Holst, Phyllis A., *Canine Reproduction—A Breeder's Guide*. Loveland, Colorado: Alpine Publications, 1985.

Hutt, Fredrick B., *Genetics For Dog Breeders*. San Francisco: W.H. Freeman & Co., 245 pgs, 1979.

Little, C.C., *The Inheritance of Coat Color In Dogs*. New York: Howell Book House, Inc., 194 pgs, 1973.

McAuliffe, Sharon & McAuliffe, Kathleen, *Life for Sale*. New York: Coward, McCann & Geoghegan, 243 pgs, 1981.

Moffit, Ella B., *The Cocker Spaniel: Companion, Shooting Dog and Show Dog*. New York: Orange Judd Publishing Company, 335 pgs, 1949.

Sabella, Frank & Kalstone, Shirlee, *The Art of Handling Show Dogs*. Hollywood: B & E Publications, 140 pgs, 1980.

Smith, Anthony, *The Human Pedigree*. Philadelphia: J.B. Lippincott Company, 308 pgs, 1975.

Tayton, Mark (revised and updated by Silk, Sheila T.), *Successful Kennel Management, Fourth Edition*. Taylors, South Carolina: Beech Tree Publishing Company, 248 pgs, 1984.

Whitney, Leon F., D.V.M., *How to Breed Dogs*. New York: Orange Judd Company, 1947.

Whitney, Leon F., D.V.M., *This is the Cocker Spaniel*. New York, Orange Judd Company, 1947.

Winge, Dr. Ojvind, *Inheritance in Dogs*. Comstock Publishing Company, Ithaca, New York: 1950.

Wolters, Richard A., *Game Dog*. New York: E.P. Dutton & Company, 201 pgs, 1983.

Wolters, Richard A., *Gun Dog*. New York: E.P. Dutton & Company, 150 pgs., 1961.

Index

Index ☐ 9